House Keywords and More . . .

Michael Munkasey

Second Edition, 2017

Copyright 2017 by Michael Munkasey
All rights reserved.

No part of this publication may be reproduced or transmitted in any form or by any means, electronic or mechanical, including photocopy, fax, recording, or in any information storage or retrieval system, without permission in writing from the publisher. Reviewers who wish to quote brief passages in connection with a review written for inclusion in a magazine, newspaper, or broadcast need not request such permission.

ISBN: 978-0-86690-668-5

Munkasey, Michael P., 1938 -
    House Keywords, and more ... / by Michael Munkasey
    1. Astrology   2. Keywords   3. Horary Astrology
    4. Electional Astrology   5. Mundane Astrology

Published by:
American Federation of Astrologers
6553 S. Rural Road
Tempe, AZ 85283
www.astrologers.com

The author may be contacted by writing him at the publisher's address above. There is no guarantee that letters to the author will be answered, but they will be forwarded. Please enclose a stamped, self-addressed envelope or $1.00 US to cover postal expenses for the reply.

A special word of thank you to the many others who over the years have stood by and contributed ideas and suggestions and encouragement for this work.

Michael Munkasey
California, USA
June, 2017

Preface

How this Book Began

Capturing and recording keywords is a never-ending task. Ideas and words just keep popping out of the air and into the text. Eventually you reach a point where you yell "Enough!," stop, and declare the work finished. But, it is never really finished—and inwardly you accept that. Words keep cropping up, worming their way in, spreading themselves like lures before the author and compiler. Language is an interesting field of endeavor.

This book grew out of personal frustrations: frustration with not having a large enough vocabulary; frustration with not being able to differentiate between subtle shades of word meanings; frustration with not knowing life well enough that words could be placed with their appropriate astrological symbolism; frustration with not being able to differentiate among astrological planetary symbolism, sign symbolism, or house symbolism; frustration from finding so much incorrect or otherwise just inaccurate astrological information; frustration with the format and layout of similar works; etc. Much time and hard work went into addressing such frustrations.

The book was great fun to compile. The way it just grew, and formed, and shaped, and changed, and grew again was a fascinating and happy experience. I lost count of the number of times I thought enough words had been included. In every book or article read, every conversation, every new idea I was exposed to, etc., prime words, ideas, or entries kept appearing.

Words were the ultimate deciding factor though. Growth was finally halted around 14,000 words. When reviewing the manuscript one friend said: "Too many words!," while another said: "Not enough words." I knew then this was the time to stop the compilation.

The house description written accounts were added after the word compilation was completed. These write-ups were intended to complement the word lists by giving each house a different perspective and insight.

Bold-faced words in the opening House chapters show important House concepts. Any particular word placement or assignment can be argued ad infinitum. The choices made when assigning the words represent a studied judgment. I understand if your opinions differ. Such is the stuff of life.

This book is something to be used, cherished, expanded, personalized, etc. Look for words or ideas in here. If you can't find the word you seek then look for a synonym. If you can't find that then try a root idea (like: food, housing, clothing, etc.), until you do make an association. Have fun running your mind through this book and its ideas. Good hunting and good exploring.

Foreword

Some Words to the Spiritual Apprentice

You might be asking yourself "Why do you need a book like this?" or, "How could you possibly use a book like this?" Answers to questions like these are complex. Think of this as an introductory phrase book for a language about the qualities of time and space. Think of this as a book similar to one that you would buy to learn some French, Japanese, Arabic, Pashto, or Turkoman phrases.

Books have the power to open you to new ideas. Books have the power to expand your daily vistas. Books have power, and when used, books can confer power. This is a book that can help you gain understanding and insight into certain parts of everyday living.

This book is about a way of thinking that can help you organize the activities and things of everyday life. This book helps explain a small part of astrology. Astrology can help you understand something about time and space. In school you are taught history, grammar, math, science, social studies, etc. But only life teaches you that there are good times and bad times for doing certain activities, or that you can be in a good space or a bad space. Schooling doesn't teach you how to recognize such times or spaces. This book can help you understand something about this part of life. This book is a learner's manual on these subtle divisions of astrological space and time. Astrology offers handy categories, i.e., Houses, for placing and viewing the things of life.

How can this book do this? This is a book about ideas. At once this book opens you to ideas both in English and in astrology. This book can help teach you how to translate the everyday objects of your life into the symbols that astrologers use. Is learning this of any use to you?

That, of course, is a more difficult question to answer, and it certainly depends on your personal circumstances. This book can't help you if it sits unused in a room, on a shelf, in a closet, or packed away. It can't help you if you don't work with it. It can't help you if you are not interested in astrology. It can't help you if you think that astrology is nonsense, or the work of evil or incarnate spirits. Thoughts like those have nothing to do with this book.

This book is, simply, a book. It is a book about some studied and collected ideas on certain areas of astrology. If you feel that starting with these ideas can help you understand life better, why you feel the way you do, or why you meet people who act like they do, then maybe this book can help answer some questions. No book can really answer such questions, but maybe this book can help you look at and identify the inner feelings, urges or pushes which lead you across one day of life after another. Life always raises questions. It is up to you to provide the answers. And today's correct answers are not necessarily tomorrow's correct answers either.

The hardest part of starting to study a new subject is learning what questions to ask. It is not so difficult to blatantly flaunt your ignorance before others. Sometimes you just want to be accepted and loved. Sometimes you want to learn all of these new ideas immediately. There are no shortcuts in life.

Impatience is not easily cured, and instant knowledge is available primarily for foolish or superficial people. A seeker is a person who asks questions about life. If you ask questions like 'what is life about?' or 'how can you cope more effectively with the world's demands?,' then this book is essential for you. This book doesn't give answers, but it does provide many keys that can help you find answers.

Considering yourself an astrological novice does a disservice to you. You are the world's best expert on a very important subject: you. It is with you that any study of life should start. The hardest people to interest in astrology are those who are not interested in themselves. Complacent people who are satisfied with life's lot, people who shun inquiring within, people who quote pat answers for life's complexities, or people who have few interests in exiting their daily rut, are people who benefit little from new answers.

An aspirant is someone who questions life or its rules, or asks questions about issues which lie beyond the obvious rituals of living. For these people, there are no stupid questions. There are only inquiries that can open doors. Their questions help shed light on life's little mysteries.

Tolerance of self breeds satisfaction. Questions about the life's processes beget searches. Inner restlessness about the superficiality of life's existence spawns searches for meaning. Probing into personal motives gives rise to questions about godhood. Thirsting for spiritual satisfaction calls forth difficult choices about instant pleasure vs. longer-term satisfaction. Life doesn't provide answers, you do. But without help, without study, or without inquiry and work, questions cannot be answered.

This book contains many keys to help you translate the stuff of everyday life into universal symbols. No more and no less is promised. If this promise tweaks your inner self, then this book begs you to buy, use, and work with it. Where you stand with life's social status, or where you are in your study of astrology has nothing to do with satisfying a restless curiosity. Satisfying those needs is your responsibility. Maybe you can begin that here.

Michael

Contents

Preface	iii
Foreword	v
Chapter 1, Astrology and Keywords	1
The seven parts of astrology; astrological symbol sets; learning about houses	
Chapter 2, Keyword Theory	9
How to use keywords; astrological grammar; translating between astrology and English	
Chapter 3, Words Abounding . . .	15
Where keywords come from; how to use this book	
Chapter 4, Quadrants and Hemispheres	23
The role of quadrants and hemispheres	
Chapter 5, How to Choose a House System	31
Some ideas about how to select a house system	
The Individual Houses	45
First House	47
Second House	59
Third House	69
Fourth House	87
Fifth House	103
Sixth House	115
Seventh House	131
Eighth House	143
Ninth House	157
Tenth House	171
Eleventh House	183
Twelfth House	193
Keywords in Alphabetic Order	205
Alphabetical Index by House Category	311
Appendix A, A Description of the Various House Systems	361
Appendix B, Mathematical Formulae for House Systems	369
Appendix C, Quadrant, Hemisphere, Angular, Succedent, and Cadent Keywords	381
Appendix D, References	397

Chapter 1

Astrology and Keywords

Introduction

This is a book about the houses of astrology. But it is also more than just a book about houses. This is a book about keywords for the houses. But it is more than a book about keywords. This is both a reference book and a textbook on the astrological houses, their meanings, and keywords or ideas associated with the houses. But this book also includes ideas about the astrological quadrants and hemispheres, how to choose a house system, and the mathematical formulations for many described house systems (you can probably impress your friends by showing them these even if you personally don't relate to math).

This book contains many ideas. It began as a book about house keywords, but other information about the theory and usage of houses politely asked to be included, and was accepted, expanded, and worked into the text. Read the text to learn about houses. Use the keyword sections and references to expand your knowledge about the meaning of the houses, and use the parts on the quadrants and hemispheres to expand your knowledge about astrology. This book is like three books in one. Use it, and don't forget that there are always parts of this work that beg you to explore.

Keywords are the words or ideas you use in your astrological thinking and communicating. Keywords are the bridge between everyday language and astrological symbols. Keywords are crucial for astrological work. Learning the meanings behind astrological symbols is a never-ending pursuit and requires a good grasp of powerful keywords. Astrological symbols are ancient, yet filled with profound substance. They convey a deep and subtle heritage.

Through habit you use personalized keywords daily to define and explain yourself. This book can help you translate astrological house meanings into popular words and ideas. This book can also help you tie many common English words and expressions to the astrological houses. Houses, the topic of this book, lend important shades of meaning to astrological interpretations.

Few tasks are more difficult for an astrologer than blending meaningful keywords with the current chart symbols and patterns. The astrological *chart*, often miscalled the "horoscope," is a symbolic diagram of the heavenly bodies. The chart is an astrologer's primary working tool. Technically, a "horoscope" is the marker of the First House, now often associated with the Ascendant, but a horoscope can be more than just the Ascendant. It is any marker that is used to denote the cusp of the First House. The chart is the diagram used by astrologers. Figure 1 on the next page shows an astrological chart.

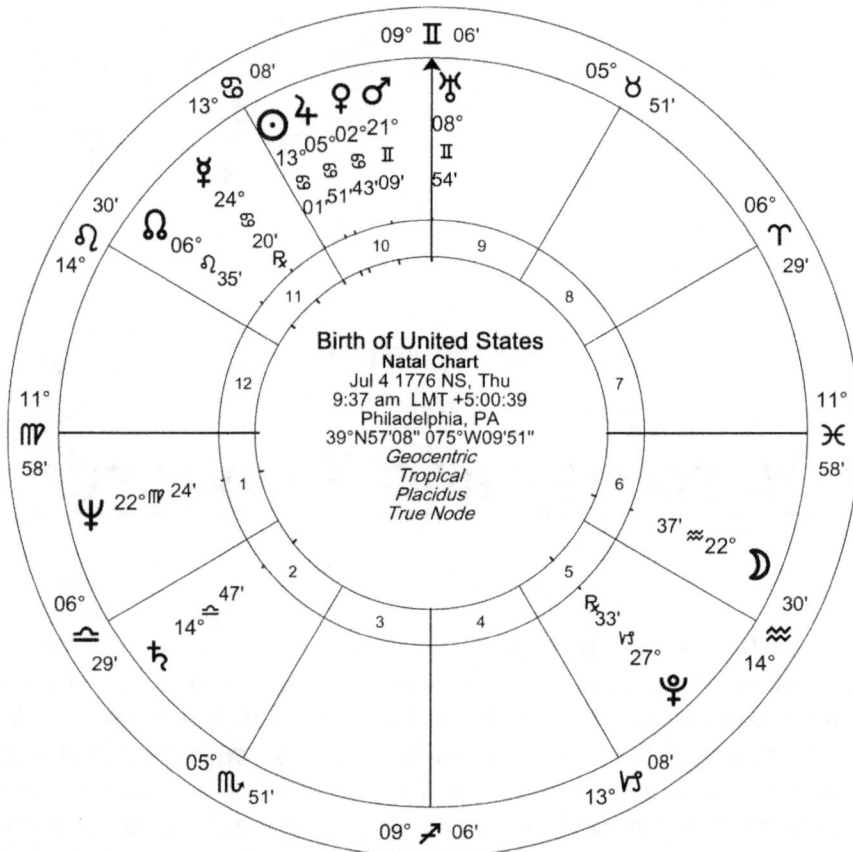

Astrologers look for patterns among the symbols in a chart. While the patterns in a chart may seem random to a casual observer, astrologers interpret the order behind their complexity. Learning to read and use these symbolic patterns requires learning both their rules and keywords. To see the order which lies behind a chart you should learn that there are simple and direct ways of translating astrological patterns into daily working thoughts and expressions. An astrologer's job is to learn to read such universal patterns and symbols and to translate them into meaningful everyday language.

A chart is used by astrologers to show universal information in a compact way. The first part of learning to read charts is understanding that astrology uses seven distinct, yet related, symbol sets to create the patterns within a chart.

The seven astrological symbol sets are named *planets, signs, houses, aspects or harmonics, the personal sensitive points, fixed stars, and long precessional cycles*. These symbol sets help make up a chart's patterns.

Once you learn what a chart looks like and how to draw or erect one, then your next step is to learn the names and symbols of the parts within each symbol set. Next you should learn how these sets are interrelated and communicate meaningful information among each other. Then through practice you should learn to translate these symbol sets into a common and everyday language. This is done by learning good keywords (or ideas) and then linking these into your daily expressions.

But recognize that just because the various parts of astrology can share information, this does not necessarily mean that each exclusively rules or owns that information. Houses have their distinct core meanings, signs have their core meanings, planets have their core meanings, etc. This book is about the keywords, meanings, and theory of the astrological houses, quadrants, hemispheres. Ideas on the philosophy of house systems are also presented.

The Astrological Symbol Sets

Astrology begins with planets. Planets are the most important symbols used in chart interpretation. Astrologers popularly use ten planets. Listed in their traditional astrological order, the names of the *planets* are Sun, Moon, Mercury, Venus, Mars, Jupiter, Saturn, Uranus, Neptune, and Pluto. Astrologers refer to the Sun and the Moon as planets although astronomers do not.

Planets have been known since our earliest times and a person with normal vision may be able to see Mercury, Venus, Mars, Jupiter, or Saturn on a clear night. Uranus, Neptune, and Pluto are not visible directly by eye and were discovered using telescopes and other means around the years 1783, 1848, and 1930.

Astrologers define a planet as a heavenly body which psychologically mirrors defined activities, circumstances, qualities, or situations. Many planetary-type bodies exist in space but only the major planets listed above are given an astrological *rulership* or connection with the other parts of astrology.

The planets are the major 'gods' or 'goddesses' of our ancestors and their mythological affinity and portrayals are told in ancient stories. As used in this book, the word *body* can mean a planet(s), personal sensitive point(s), the Moon's or a planet's node(s), star(s), asteroid(s), etc.

The planets are ordered according to the hierarchy given in the following table. The planets each have unique two, three, or four letter and symbolic abbreviations and these are (reading down the left hand column and then down the right hand column for the correct planetary ordering):

Sun	SUN, or SU	Su	Jupiter	JUP, JU	Ju
Moon	MOON, MO	Mo	Saturn	SAT, SA	Sa
Mercury	MER, ME	Me	Uranus	URA, UR	Ur
Venus	VEN, VE	Ve	Neptune	NEP, NE	Ne
Mars	MARS, MA	Ma	Pluto	PLU, PL	Pl

The *signs of the zodiac*, or signs, are equal divisions of space along the ecliptic in a narrow band of sky referred to as the zodiac. The zodiac is a narrow band of the sky close to the path of the Sun in its yearly travel. The signs of the zodiac are different from the constellations in the sky, although unfortunately some constellations and signs share identical names. It is chiefly within the zodiac's boundaries that the planets travel (Pluto wanders out at times). Reading down the left column first and then into the right columns for the correct order, the signs of the zodiac, their letter and symbol abbreviations, and their offset in degrees from their Aries starting point are:

Aries	ARI, or AR	Ar	000	Libra	LIB, LI	Li	180
Taurus	TAU, TA	Ta	030	Scorpio	SCO, SC	Sc	210
Gemini	GEM, GE	Ge	060	Sagittarius	SAG, SG	Sg	240
Cancer	CAN, CA	Ca	090	Capricorn	CAP, CP	Cp	270
Leo	LEO, LE	Le	120	Aquarius	AQU, AQ	Aq	300
Virgo	VIR, VI	Vi	150	Pisces	PSC, PS	Ps	330

Popularly, the signs each have one or two planetary rulers, or one ancient and one modern planet. The planetary rulers of a sign have a strong affinity for that sign, and astrological characteristics between the planet and sign are passed back and forth between the planets and their signs. This rulership association allows astrologers to draw planet and sign analogies. All rulership associations are astrologically important. The planets in the following table are purposely placed in two distinct columns. Some signs are shown with one planetary ruler and some with two. Notice that Mars has an affinity with both Aries and Scorpio, and Venus has an affinity with both Taurus and Libra, etc.

Ancient and modern planetary rulerships are:

Sign	Yang	Yin	Sign	Yang	Yin
	Rulers			*Rulers*	
Aries	Ma	Pl	Libra		Ve
Taurus	Ve		Scorpio	Pl	Ma
Gemini	Me		Sagittarius	Ju	
Cancer	Mo		Capricorn	Sa	
Leo	Su		Aquarius	Sa	Ur
Virgo		Me	Pisces	Ju	Ne

The planets each have dual sign rulership affinities and lend either a yang or a yin flavor to their signs. This yang or yin division by *each* planet is astrologically important. It is mirrored in the unfinished columns above. The ordering of the planets in the columns above (down to up, or, up to down) shouts loud hints about completing the order of this matrix. Analogies between signs and planets can help with astrological interpretation.

Houses symbolically represent the qualities and division of space in a chart. Astrologers over centuries have proposed different ways to divide space and show spatial divisions in a chart. A very popular method of house division is called Placidus and is named after a professor of mathematics who lived in the 17th century. The Placidian house system was printed by a British publishing house in the early 1800s and for over one hundred years was the only table of houses available to astrologers. Thus it gained in popularity and usage due to its exclusive availability, and is now, by far, the most requested house system today according to people who run computer based public astrological chart services. Chapter Five presents some ideas on why you may want to choose one system of house division over another.

In astrological literature over twenty house systems have been described Appendices A and B describe many known house systems. All house systems have a unique role in astrology depending on the circumstances of their use. Houses are formed in one of three ways using the ecliptic, equatorial, and horizon astronomical planes in space. Regardless of the house system chosen the individual houses are traditionally referred to by a number and are called houses one through twelve.

Houses have a direct one-for-one relation with the signs of the zodiac, and through them with their ruling planets. The first house relates to the zodiacal sign of Aries (yang Mars and yin Pluto), the second house to the sign of Taurus (yang Venus and yin Psyche—I use a planetary body which is ***not*** the asteroid with the same name), the third house to Gemini (yang Mercury and yin Vulcan. I use the Ebertin's identified planet Transpluto, which I call Vulcan, whose positions are given in their ephemeris), and so forth through the twelfth house which relates to Pisces (yang Jupiter and yin Neptune).

Aspects or harmonics can provide a rich and varied insight into all situations. *Aspects or harmonics* are the angles in space between planets or the personal sensitive points. The planets and personal sensitive points when taken together are often just called points. The difference between the term aspect and the term harmonic is that aspects are called by names (e.g., conjunction, opposition, trine, quintile, sesqui-quadrate) while harmonics refer to the same angular separation but call them by their equivalent numbers (one, two, three, five, eight). The numbers are easier to pronounce, but aspect names are more traditionally used. Modern preference is to use the word harmonics, but each term—aspect, harmonic, or angle—refers to the same angular separation of planets or points in space.

The following relationship equates the planets with the harmonics. The following table is read down the left column first for harmonic numbers one through six and then down the right column for harmonics seven through twelve.

Aspect	Angle	Harmonic	Planet	Aspect	Angle	Harmonic	Planet
Conjunction	0°	1	Su	Septile	51° 26'	7	
Opposition	180°	2	Mo	Semi-Square	45°	8	Ma
Trine	120°	3	Ju	Novile	40°	9	Ne
Square	90°	4	Sa	Decile	36°	10	Me
Quintile	72°	5	Me	Undecile	32°44'	11	Ur
Sextile	60°	6	Ve	Semi-Sextile	30°	12	Pl

The angles shown above are found by dividing the 360° in a circle by the number of the harmonic, where conjunction is one, opposition is two, trine is three, etc., as shown. The seventh and eleventh harmonics have a fractional or non-integer angle. People familiar with music theory will recognize much harmony (harmonics!) within this table. Multiplying these basic angles repeats the harmonic. That is, three times the decile, or 3 times 36°, gives 108°. Thus, two planets separated by 108° of zodiacal longitude exchange energy at a decile or Mercury vibration. Such integer multiplication gives many important angles beyond those just listed in the table above. Such repeats or multiples of the basic harmonic are called *repetitions*. The repetitions carry the same astrological theme as the basic harmonic. The number of the repetition does not seem to be important (i.e., a separation at a decile angle or three times the decile still carries a decile meaning, etc.).

Other special combinations of angles, like the sesqui-quadrate (at 135°), and the quincunx or inconjunct (at 150°) also exist in traditional astrology. The sesqui-quadrate is a special case of the 45° aspect or the eighth harmonic, which relates to Mars. The harmonics listed above are formed by whole or integer numbers but the quincunx is a unique aspect that is formed by the division of a fractional (non-integer or real) number into 360°. Harmonics with real numbers are also valid. Harmonic theories are exciting and show very powerful ways of finding astrological significance. Other harmonics beyond those mentioned or discussed here may also determine planetary or point activation. Exciting possibilities are offered by the squares or cubes of the basic integers, by the midpoints of the planets equated to harmonics, etc.

The personal sensitive points and harmonics remain the most unexplored area of astrology. Seven *personal sensitive points* (PSPs) are recognized and the Node of the Moon can be considered as an eighth personal sensitive point. The personal sensitive points are called by the name shown in the left column in the table which follows and their opposing paired point in the right hand column is always understood to be opposite in the heavens from the named point.

The personal sensitive points exist as two opposite placements in the zodiac. They depict intersections of psychologically important reference points in space and represent the qualities of time. The personal sensitive points provide symbolic references for sunrise, noon, sunset, and midnight. Their locations are defined by combining the Earth's position in our Solar System, a place on Earth, the day of a month and year, and the time of that day in an astronomical way. The names of the personal sensitive points, their abbreviations and their equivalent paired point are:

Primary Name	(abbrev.)	Paired Name	(abbrev.)
Ascendant	(ASC, AS, A)	Descendant	(DSC)
Midheaven	(MC, M)	Lower Heaven	(IC)
Equatorial Ascendant	(EQA, EQ)	Equatorial Descendant	(EQD)
Vertex	(VTX, VT)	Anti-Vertex	(AVX)
Co-Ascendant	(CAS, CA)	Co-Descendant	(CDS)
Polar Ascendant	(PAS, PA)	Polar Descendant	(PDS) and,
The Aries Point	(ARI, AR, Ar)	The Libra Point	(LIB, Li)

The Node of the Moon can be logically included with these personal sensitive points and its name, symbolic abbreviation and its opposing point is:

North Node   (NN, NNod)   South Node   (SN, SNod)

Although the personal sensitive points always exist as opposing pairs that lie across the chart, only one side is popularly used as the point's name. The side most commonly referred to is listed in the left-most column in the table above. When using the personal sensitive points it is important to remember that they exist as a pair of locations lying across the zodiac, and do not occupy single positions in a chart like the planets. Figure 2 (see page 24) shows how the important astronomical circles lie in space and how some of the personal sensitive points are formed by the intersections of these circles.

Learning About Houses

Interpreting a chart requires the development of complex astrological skills. Interpreting a chart involves translating the astrological symbol sets into an everyday language that you or your astrological client can understand. The chart presents much information. It is easy to get lost between what the individual symbols represent and how to extract information from the overall chart diagram. It is easy to state the astrological symbols in a chart without giving meaningful insight about their placement and interaction.

Typical questions asked when a person first sees a chart seem simple, yet are profound. How does Jupiter influence this chart? How does the eighth house affect this chart? What does Jupiter in the eighth house mean? How does Jupiter connect to the other planets and points in this chart? Answering questions like these require experience, some deep thought, and reflection. To help gain this insight you need good astrological keywords.

This book lists keywords associated with the astrological houses. Houses operate on two distinct levels. On one level houses represent reality. This can be common objects of life, the types of people you experience, places, etc. Objects are the common things you touch and see as you go through life books, tables, chairs, floors, walls, our home spaces, etc. The people types you encounter involve all of the labels you attach to people because of their profession, their dress, habits, or mannerisms, such as executive, thief, laborer, politician, weirdo, rancher, lawyer, etc. The twelve astrological houses symbolize and divide these obvious things of life.

These categories help you place the people and objects of daily living into a symbolic perspective that begins your trip of astrological understanding. House categories at this level are particularly important when answering questions (Horary Astrology), choosing appropriate times to begin activities (Electional Astrology), or working with governmental, political or business events (Mundane Astrology). Seventeen separate house categories are described in this book and others could be created.

On a second level houses represent inner psychological attitudes and feelings. Natal Astrology and Compatibility Astrology (Synastry) use houses this way. Natal Astrology uses a chart for helping a person understand inner drives and yearnings. Natal Astrology helps bring answers about who you are, why your life is important, what you should be learning or doing, etc.

Astrological houses can provide important psychological insight into these patterns of life. When reading a natal chart an astrologer may start by reading the patterns of the planets in the houses. Charts showing some houses empty and other houses containing one or more planets quickly bring a focus to areas of life where meaningful exchanges can occur. By combining keywords for the planets along with keywords using the other parts of astrology, important chart themes can be described. Discovering these themes by combining appropriate keywords defines astrological chart interpretation. It also takes a lot of practice to do this consistently.

Compatibility between people (synastry) is an emotionally complex subject. It involves judging the potential interaction between people, e.g., man and woman, parent and child, boss and employee, person and pet, friend and friend, siblings, etc. The astrological comparison goes beyond the interpretation of one chart, because now the inter-action of one person's planets, signs, personal sensitive points, etc., in the chart of the other person is examined and delineated. This requires a level of chart delineation experience beyond the simpler natal interpretations. Also, people in relationships may live at different psychological levels of awareness about life—and this too complicates the process of explaining the interpersonal synastry.

Because houses have a dual role—representing both the deeper psychological symbolism and the common things of life—they hold perhaps the greatest single storehouse for astrological keywords. Houses have the richest keyword treasury and their depth is mostly untapped within other astrological works. Thoroughly learning houses can enrich your overall astrological knowledge. This book was written to help you learn more about house symbolism. Hopefully this book can help bring some new insight into astrological keywords that the houses represent.

Some astrologers choose not to use houses, claiming that houses are not well defined in either their derivation or interpretation. Other astrologers use planets different from the traditional ones listed earlier. Experience has shown that the standard ancient symbols provide a wealth of adequate information, and that the modern usage of asteroids, comets, hypothetical planets, etc., amplify the basic information already provided by the basic patterns in a chart. Both students and practitioners are encouraged to learn the traditional astrological basics thoroughly and practice them daily. May this book be of much use to you in this regard.

Chapter 2

Keyword Theory

How to Use Keywords

Keywords are the stuff of life. Without a good grasp of at least some basic astrological keywords you cannot correctly and clearly interpret the astrological symbols or patterns in a chart. Simple and fundamental rules for using keywords have been developed. Evolving these rules was not easy. They took years to develop and clarify, but can now be explained in minutes. Such is the plight of a pioneering researcher. Good astrological keywords do not appear magically. They are the result of years of searching and sifting through many different sources.

Astrology is a language like English is a language. Both have their form of vocabulary and syntax. English vocabulary has nouns, adjectives, adverbs, verbs, pronouns, prepositions, etc., as its parts of speech. Any good dictionary shows you the part of speech for each word listed. The vocabulary of astrology is the seven symbol sets shown earlier for the planets, houses, signs, etc. Study those tables again in Chapter One if the symbol sets are not yet completely familiar to you.

In English we use phrases, sentences, paragraphs, chapters, etc., to string parts of speech together to convey information. In our speech and writing we string our thoughts together with grammatical rules that govern the creation of phrases, sentences, etc.

English has many grammatical forms. Here is one example: "Nice day!," Jack says. The phrase "Nice day!" conveys the meaning of Jack's idea, and the words "Jack says" completes the formal sentence structure by adding the subject and verb of the sentence. The phrase Jack used, "Nice day!" contains an adjective and a noun. The combination of adjective and noun in English is the simplest basic expression for conveying information. For additional information on English grammar and syntax you should check with an appropriate reference.

Astrological grammar is used to combine the astrological vocabulary of the seven symbol sets into meaningful statements. The grammar of astrology is much simpler than the grammar used when speaking or writing. There are only seven rules of astrological grammar—or, there are only seven grammatical combinations within any chart. That is, any chart pattern can be broken down into these seven fundamental parts regardless of how complex any chart pattern seems to be.

Astrology has seven grammatical forms used for conveying information. One is planets in signs. The astrological symbols "Sun Lib" convey an idea similar to the "Nice day!" idea which Jack expressed in his sentence above. Since we always understand that the universe speaks to us through astrology, the equivalent of "Jack says" is not a required form within the astrological grammar.

Astrological Grammar

The seven grammatical parts of astrology are:
- Planets in signs
- Planets in houses
- Personal sensitive points in signs
- Personal sensitive points in Houses
- Signs on house cusps
- Midpoints
- Planets in aspect

Every astrological combination in a chart can be broken down into these seven parts. For instance, the astrological statement Sat Vir 12th Cnj Asc Vir Opp Mar Psc 6th (which is read Saturn in Virgo in the twelfth house conjunct the Ascendant in Virgo, all in opposition to Mars in Pisces in the sixth house) is a very complex expression. The translation of those written astrological symbols into everyday language could occupy the whole chapter of a book. Yet even as complex as that astrological statement is it can be broken down into its respective parts:
- Saturn in Virgo
- Saturn in the 12th house
- Saturn conjunct the Ascendant
- Ascendant in Virgo
- Mars in Pisces
- Mars in the 6th house
- Mars opposition Saturn
- Mars opposition the Ascendant

Once this breakdown into component parts is done each part can be interpreted separately. *Then these partial interpretations should be combined into a whole and coherent thought to present the overall astrological theme.*

Translating Astrology in English using Keywords

English uses nouns, adjective, adverbs, verbs, etc., to convey information. Astrology uses planets in signs, planets in houses, etc., to convey information. To learn how to interpret astrology effectively we must learn how to move easily between the parts of astrological grammar and the parts of English grammar.

The simplest form of any English language statement has an adjective and a noun combination to convey information. "Nice day," "large book," and "funny line" are English adjective and noun combinations. "Moo Leo," "Jup 5th," and "MC Gem" are astrological combinations. To translate between astrology and English, or between English and astrology we need to correlate the nouns, adjectives, etc., of language with astrological planets and signs, planets in houses, etc. This is not so difficult to do.

Planets can be represented by either nouns or adjectives. Signs can be represented by either nouns or adjectives. The personal sensitive points can be represented by either nouns or adjectives. Therefore to interpret a basic astrological statement like "Jup Cap" we can string adjectives for Jupiter and nouns for Capricorn together, or we can choose adjectives for Capricorn and nouns for Jupiter (our choice) and get meaningful English phrases. Five practice words appear in each category below for combining keywords:

Jupiter Adjectives	Capricorn Nouns
additional	procedures
generous	seriousness
accepts	respect
sufficient	correctness
increases	ambition

Combining, at random, any one word from the left column with any one word from the right column we can get adjective and noun phrases which can be used to describe some sides of Jupiter in Capricorn. Here are some examples:
- generous ambition
- sufficient respect
- an increase in procedures
- additional correctness
- increasing seriousness
- accepting ambition

In general the adjectives of column one were combined with the nouns of column two to give meaning to Jupiter in Capricorn. The word "frase" has been coined to describe these phrase-like combinations. The individual frases are not meant to be particularly meaningful by themselves, but when a group of frases are taken together they begin to form a picture of the shades of meaning behind "Jupiter in Capricorn."

Linking words required by good English usage (prepositions, conjunctions, pronouns, articles, etc.) can always be added to the word combinations because English requires these for grammatical sense but astrology has no equivalent for these linking words. In the same way the gerund of the verb form on some of the words in the list was used to convey information (e.g., increasing seriousness).

Astrological grammar is simpler than English language grammar. Astrology has fewer and different parts of speech. Concessions to the rules of English grammar for readability do not alter the important basic concept that English adjective and noun words can be combined to bring everyday meaning to astrological patterns.

Astrology and English Equivalents

The seven grammatical parts of astrology listed earlier can now have their English language parts of speech assigned. The seven parts are:
- Planets in signs
- Planets in houses
- Personal sensitive points in signs
- Personal sensitive points in houses
- Signs on house cusps
- Midpoints, and,
- Planets in aspect

Planets in signs can be represented by adjective and noun combinations. Horary and Electional Astrology tell us that houses represent the "things" of our everyday lives, like cars, purses, money, irons, toasters, chairs, etc. But "things" are always nouns in English. Since planets can be represented by either nouns or adjectives, then planets in houses can be represented with adjective and noun combinations also.

The personal sensitive points behave just like the planets. They too can be represented by either adjectives or noun words. For all practical purposes the personal sensitive points and the planets can be considered together as one part when discussing astrological grammar. The personal sensitive points in signs and the personal sensitive points in houses can also be represented by adjective and noun combinations in English. Here is an example of how to do this from the breakdown listed before:

Ascendant Adjectives	Virgo Nouns
sensory	services
mental	compliance
personal	precision
perceives	neatness
reacts to	efficiency

Combining these adjectives and nouns we get Ascendant in Virgo frases:
- mental compliance
- a perception of efficiency
- reactions to (create) neatness
- precise sensory (observations)

Some of these frase combinations were deliberately altered to show the flexibility of expression allowed by this method of translation between astrology and English. The English language has many ways of allowing you to express the same idea while using different words. This adaptability is one reason why it has evolved into a language used world-wide. "Reacts to neatness" is an acceptable frase, but a slight language alteration to the frase "reactions to (create) neatness" is still an acceptable translation.

Six of the seven grammatical parts of astrology are represented by adjective and noun combinations. Signs on house cusps are represented by adjective and noun combinations. So are midpoints. Since planets can be represented by either adjectives or nouns, then adjective planet to noun planet combinations are acceptable ways of creating meaning for midpoint combinations.

Deciphering the linguistics behind the seventh part of astrology, planets in aspect, requires more creative thinking. In an aspect, a planet, or one of the personal sensitive points, lies at a significant angle (the aspect) to another planet or point. For planets in aspect, the initiating planet makes an astrological connection that is carried at some aspect or harmonic wavelength to the receiving planet. Thus there are three parts to an aspect: an initiating or modifying element, a transmitting principle, and a receiving object. By the rules of English grammar and traditional usage nouns receive actions, verbs convey actions, and adverbs modify verbs. Therefore, planets in aspect can be represented by adverb, verb, and noun combinations.

Planets can take either a noun or adjective form. When used in aspect combinations planets can also be used as adverbs. Aspects (or harmonics) use verbs as their parts of expression. Knowing this the entire English dictionary can now be divided by the parts of speech indicated therein for each word! If a dictionary word is a verb it takes on an astrological aspect or harmonic expression. If the word is an adverb it represents a planet. If the word is an adjective then it can represent either a planet, personal sensitive point, or a sign.

If the word is a noun, then see if it is a noun thing or a noun attribute. If it is a noun thing the word rightly belongs to the houses of astrology. If it is a noun attribute the word may be related either to planets, signs, the personal sensitive points, or sometimes houses. Such attribute words can be shared among the astrological modalities. This completes the dictionary's word apportionment! This is a book primarily about English language words used as nouns and their placement as keywords in the astrological houses.

House, Sign and Planet Keyword Sharing

Houses share keywords and ideas with both signs and planets through their correlation with the signs of the zodiac, and also the planets ruling these signs. This idea of keyword sharing is well known yet little is written about this process. The rules for keyword sharing are straight-forward.

For example, Mars rules Aries, and Aries has an affiliation with the first house (this analogy continues with the Venus and Taurus affinity for the second house, etc., through all twelve houses—the specific correspondences were shown in earlier tables). Mars traditionally rules action and activity and, well, martial things. Webster's Ninth New Collegiate Dictionary defines martial as "of, relating to, or suited for war or a warrior; ... experienced in or inclined to war (see: war-like)." Mars was the ancient god of war. War involves activity, action, and movement, and Mars astrologically rules such ideas. Through its affinity with Aries, and Aries with the first house, keywords like action, activity, movement, etc., are assigned to the first house.

Carrying this analogy further, keywords about the implements of war-like actions, armaments, munitions, etc., acquire a first house association. This leads to words with similar concepts like knives, sharp edges, etc., which acquire a first house rulership. However, the first house also is traditionally related to the person being inquired about. Therefore words like you, your intentions, the self, etc., are also placed in the first house. In a similar fashion words for all houses can be assigned.

Houses represent the tangible things of life. Tangible, touchable or real things are nouns. Words like money, purses, knives, daughters, aircraft, etc., are nouns. Houses also represent abstract noun trait ideas, like communication, self-worth, marriage, debt, solemnity, etc. Mercury rules communication and shares this idea with the third house. Thus noun words that indicate less tangible ideas, like communication, home life, pride, sharing, ethics, etc., can also share house affiliations. It may be difficult to separate out which words should be assigned to the planets or signs and which specific words should be assigned to the houses. Therefore, as many practical, everyday noun words as possible were included in this book on the assumption that a clever reader could always associate some of the less tangible ideas with other astrological modalities like planets and signs.

Chapter 3

Words Abounding . . .

Where Do Keywords Come From?

Astrology has a rich heritage that has been persisted over many centuries of practice. Most astrological writing does not translate this legacy well into modern languages. This book attempts to combine the traditional astrological heritage with the thousands of words that have become our modern language idiom. The words given here were mainly accumulated by copying words from dictionaries and thesauruses by their shade of meaning into this book.

Lists of words in other astrological texts were not used as a primary source for this text. Much effort was spent to ensure that this work remained original yet did not significantly differ from traditional astrological sources. Some words are listed in their singular form and some in their plural form. Either form is acceptable, depending on usage.

The strength of this book lies in the richness and diversity of its words. It has many (but not all) of the ideas and concepts mankind has incorporated into 20th century thinking. One weakness of this book is that it is difficult to cross check ideas to ensure consistency of expression. Some ideas that are close in meaning may be assigned to different houses when they should be in the same house. Every effort has been made to cross check words, ensure consistency and remove duplications.

This book is a collection of nouns for the astrological houses organized into eighteen commonplace categories. Future books are planned to give keywords for the planets, signs, the personal sensitive points, etc. This book began because it was needed. Earlier keyword books were both difficult to use and missed much of the psychological richness that astrologers associated with houses. House Keywords and more ... attempts to correct this lack.

History

Collecting keywords began because of my dissatisfaction with the amount and arrangement of astrological keywords found in earlier astrological works. Astrologers talked at one set of keyword depth but wrote at another. In the beginning my collected keywords were divided into astrological categories. First words were hand written and then manually typed. By 1982 the typed keyword list had grown to over 3000 words. It was fun to create. Using it was both fun and informative.

It sat unchanged until about 1989 because having been typed on a manual typewriter there was no easy way to sort that list of words into alphabetical order. By the 1980s personal computer technology had advanced and the manually typed word list could be electronically scanned, entered into a data base and sorted. Thus, for the first time, a comprehensive look at the original word list in any order desired could be made. Further, a word processor interface could be used to add new words, and correct or change prior entries.

After the original list was sorted and entered, errors and duplicate entries were discovered and corrected. Then other new words began to appear. Words were grabbed from newspaper articles, magazine articles, discussions, conversations, advertisements, etc. Anywhere words were used, new ideas worked their way into this list. Many friends encouraged the publication of the word list. The original list was added to, improved and updated. Much care was used in the words selected and used in this list.

Generic ideas, such as "fruit" were included, but specific ideas like types of fruit: bananas, apples, peaches, pears, plums, etc., were not included. Generic ideas like electric appliances were included, but specific ideas like irons, toasters, etc., were not included. Excluding lists of specific items provided better overall readability. Also tree or plant species, flower types, city names, etc., were purposely not included. Many good words were found by reading sequential entry after entry from dictionaries and thesauruses. This book is the end result.

Keywords and Rulerships

It is one thing to collect words, it is quite another to assign astrological rulerships or categories to these words. There are two ways to assign an astrological category to a word. The easiest is to find a word with a similar meaning and then associate the new word into the same category. The second is to use derived houses.

As an example of the first method, use the traditional fourth house astrological rulership of land. Modern word associations for land, such as "back yard" or "living space" can thus be assigned by inference to the fourth house. This same line of thinking can be applied to planets and signs when looking for house associations. As an example, Saturn traditionally rules stoppages; therefore a word like "stoppers" (as used in a sink drain) has a Saturn connotation, and because it is a thing of life is assigned to the tenth house. The tenth house, as was noted in Chapter 1, is ruled by Saturn. The word "plug," which is a synonym for "stopper," also has a tenth house rulership assigned. Remember that an astrological rulership denotes an affinity with, not possession of, the idea or word.

Rulership is a tricky concept. Astrologers spend a lot of time trying to find the proper rulership of an idea or trait. Finding the correct rulership is important because once that key is found it opens the chart to interpretation. Using an incorrect rulership can waste a lot of time. Correct rulership assignment of astrological ideas gives an astrologer the key to unlocking a chart.

That is one reason why this book is an important astrological tool. Without some guidance as to where to begin with an idea, a thought, a phrase, a concept, a pattern—much time can be lost. This book provides a wealth of ideas to help astrologers at all levels find the key between words and their astrological correlations.

Derived Houses

Another way to assign words to houses is called "turning the houses," or "derived houses." The practice of derivative houses is commonly used in Horary or Electional Astrology. It blends house ideas by combining two or more house meanings. For example, the second house traditionally rules money and the fourth house rules land. Thus, money you receive from land or land holdings is denoted by the second house from the fourth house, which is the fifth house.

An easy way to calculate the derived house is to add the two original house numbers and then subtract one from the result. For this example, 4 + 2 - 1 = 5, or the fifth house. You subtract one because the original house, in this case the fourth house, is always the first house of itself. When calculating a derived house of a derived house remember to subtract one for each level of deriving.

Example: the money your maternal aunt earns from her land uses the 6th (maternal aunt), 4th (land), and 2nd (money from) houses, minus 2 for the level of deriving a house of a house of a house. The math looks like 6 + 4 + 2 - 2 = 12 (the twelfth house). One variation occurs when the addition results in a number greater than twelve (for traditionally there are only twelve houses).

Distant travel is ruled by the ninth house and partners are ruled by the seventh house. Therefore, distant travel by one's partner would be ruled by the, 9 + 7 - 1 = 15th house, which, subtracting 12 for the number overage, is the third house. Using derived houses can open new astrological insight. Many word concepts assigned in this book were formulated using the derived house concept.

The first house symbolizes the theme itself, the second house the use of that theme, the third house communication within or about that theme, the fourth house the origin of the theme, etc. Taking a concrete example for how ideas can evolve by turning the houses, we can examine the concept of "military" which has a sixth house traditional rulership.

The result or use of military could lead to war, which is a seventh house concept. It can also lead to peace if military is used defensively, and peace is also a seventh house concept. Continuing is a derived house fashion, military communications would be ruled by the eighth house (6 + 3 – 1 = 8); military bases (the home of the military) the ninth house; pride in the military by the tenth house; military strategy by the eleventh house; enemies of the military by the twelfth house; military destruction by the first house; military overseas bases by the second house; military reputation by the third house; military legislation by the fourth house; and scandals within the military by the fifth house.

Other concepts are formed in the same way. You can use houses of houses of houses. For example rulership of money spent on your sister's pet dog's illness would be calculated by third house for sister—plus—second house for money spent—plus—sixth house for pet dog —plus—sixth house again for illness. Thus, 3 + 2 + 6 + 6 - 3 = 14th house, which, after subtracting twelve, becomes the second house. The second house rules the money spent on the illness of your sister's pet.

Another important way of assigning words to houses is by planetary or other rulership association. Chapter 1 gives lists of planets, signs, etc., and their traditional planetary rulerships. Thus, Mars rules Aries and Scorpio, Venus rules Taurus and Libra, etc. Aries is traditionally associated with the first house and an Aries keyword is "aggressive actions." Thus the psychological noun keyword "aggression" can be associated with the first house through its relationship to Aries. This type of thinking, analysis, and development was applied to thousands of words in this book. If you are interested in becoming a better astrologer then you should cultivate keyword association skills like this.

House keywords are relatively easy to assign given a bit of practice with words in general. Midpoint word rulers are more difficult to assign because midpoint word mixtures involve combining words from two sources into a single concept. Normally, for planets, signs, houses, etc., single word concepts suffice, unless you are combining concepts by turning the houses as discussed previously. Midpoints are always combinations of at least two ideas. Sorting midpoint ideas always involves a double action, one for each word in the description. Another book, *Midpoints: Unleashing the Power of the Planets*, interprets astrological midpoint concepts from astrology into English.

This Book's Role

This book is intended to be used as both a reference work and a learning tool. It was intended to be an invaluable reference for teachers, students, researchers and casual practitioners of astrology. This is a book that asks to be used, not kept hidden away. When properly used this book can help you learn more about the practice of astrology.

This book provides many keywords for the astrological houses. Keywords for planets, signs, aspects, etc., may be addressed in other books. This book is divided into three major parts: the house section list, the category related list, and the alphabetical list. The house portion of the book contains the house keywords by category preceded by a short write-up on each house. The alphabetical section contains the keywords in a computer sorted alphabetical order. The category related list allows you to reference all keywords within their category, except the "things" topic. To reference the house things in alphabetical order please use the alphabetical listing. If you have trouble locating a word try the alphabetical list. If it is still not in the alphabetical list then try a synonym for the word.

Reading the house write-up at the front of each house can help you gain insight into more important psychological meanings of a house. Words there in bold face type show some key ideas of the house. The keyword section is useful as a Horary or Electional tool but can also serve as a learning guide for all areas of astrology. The house write-up serves as an introduction to some of the concepts that a house exhibits. It is best to both read the write-up and also examine the particular section of the house keywords that currently interest you (e.g., psychological associations, places, occupations or person types, etc.) It is the combination of all of the book's resources taken together which may help you develop your own working concept of the house and its meaning to you. The idea of using all of the book's resources taken together is important. Use them to help you understand houses better.

After the initial house write-up the keywords included are divided into eighteen categories for each house. The categories for each astrological house in the order they are presented in this book are:

- Horary or Electional Ideas—the Key Ideas
- Things
- Psychological Qualities
- Occupations or Person Types
- Places associated with a House or Home
- Family Members or Close Relations
- Mundane Ideas
- Parts of Our Body or Body Functions
- Afflictions or Diseases
- Colors
- Gems or Minerals
- Animals
- Mythical Figures or Constellation Names
- Parts of an Organization
- Industry Categories
- Parts of an Automobile
- Parts of a House
- Parts of a Ship

The ideas presented within the categories listed above should be self-explanatory. "Parts of Our Body or Body Functions" lists things like fingers, arms, legs, toes, breathing, etc. "Psychological Qualities" should be read with the connotation of "need for," or, "sense of," where appropriate. "Parts of a Ship" lists bow, stern, wheel, navigational lights, etc. "Family Members or Relations" lists family members like father, mother, brother, sister, uncle, aunt, etc. Sometimes a word is listed in more than one category. This helps include similar ideas within different categories. Other words may seem to apply in different categories but may be listed in only one category. A word is usually listed in more than one category if that word both strengthens the category and helps you follow the keyword ideas better. The animals included were correlated with both the Chinese and traditional western astrological assignments.

The following categories: "Parts of Our Body or Body Functions," "Afflictions or Diseases," "Occupations or Person Types," "Places," "Colors," and "Gems or Minerals" can be associated with either astrological signs or houses. They were included in this house listing because they are noun things. But, using these ideas with their appropriate sign or planet equivalent is acceptable. The keywords in this book, and especially the keywords in the psychological, body, or affliction sections, are not medical recommendations, nor are they meant to be a substitute for sound medical advice or tests. They are astrological rulership notations only. For medical or psychological advice of any kind please consult a competent and authorized practitioner.

The words and ideas found in the "Horary or Electional Ideas" section provide both traditional and modern keywords. The "Things," "Psychological Qualities," "Occupations or Person Types," "Places," and "Family Members or Relations" categories also derive from traditional sources, but were augmented by reading a dictionary and/or thesaurus through and including those words that seemed appropriate. Most other categories are not defined well in traditional astrological sources and represent new work. Mundane words are traditionally associated with Business, Political, or Historical usages.

The "Gems and Minerals" section derived from formal notes taken from classes with certified gemologists. They were augmented by college courses in crystals and the crystalline structures of metals and gems. After many other abortive attempts to classify gem and mineral groups, their crystalline structures and color variations were used. From this work, assignment into the twelve working categories was done. This work is based on the author's original insight.

The "Occupations or Person Types" category is to be used with care. House strength in a natal chart does not necessarily imply that you are locked into an occupational selection for only that house. The occupation you choose has little to do with the rulership of any house over an occupation. It has a LOT to do with the overall talents you have and how you wish to exercise those talents. If you have a talent for working alone, have physical strength, etc., then you could just as easily apply yourself to being a wild animal trainer as being a day laborer. Both occupations require these talents. There is a great difference in the social connotations, the specific skills required, the working circumstances, etc., between these occupations however.

The occupation you choose in life should be based on your preferences, talents, schooling, intentions, opportunities presented, and overall life skills—not on the rulership or planetary placements of any one house or sign in your natal chart. There is a big difference between the rulership of an occupation and the choosing of an occupation. Rulership categories for occupations are included for reference purposes—not for choosing occupations for self or clients. By knowing an occupation's rulership a skilled astrologer is better able to correlate that occupation with the chart(s) being studied. Employers hire the entire person for a job, not just a person's house rulerships.

The "Industry Categories" section was mostly derived from the headings in the Yellow Pages" section of the telephone book.

The "Mythical Figures or Constellation Names" category was created because the idea of myth is very important in our human heritage and an astrological reference list was needed. This section lists the names of the constellations in the sky, mythical Gods or Goddesses, etc. It was easy to include such ideas under the houses with the understanding that these things or people might also be associated with astrological signs, harmonics or planets. Primarily Greek and Roman gods, goddesses or mythical figures were included. Persons or ideas from other religions and cultures may be included later. Much work remains to be done to develop this category, but this list provides a start. The house assignments were based solely on the author's study and perceptions of this subject.

Using this Book

The entries in this book are designed to be easy to follow, almost self-explanatory. However some explanation of how to read or use the entries is needed. If another word is shown in parenthesis behind the lead word then take the meaning of the lead word to follow in this direction. A few examples from the book might help you see how to read and use the entries. Practice helps you gain familiarity with any new tool.

bow	since the category is "ship" then this is the bow of the ship
bow (weapon)	as in bow and arrows
bow	as in "a hair ribbon"—see also accessory or cloth
bow	as in "bow-wow" was not included; see "loud things" for the noise, or see "dogs" for the animal
bow, to take a (e.g., on a stage)	see also praise, adulation, etc.
box seats (theater)	the word "theater" helps place the idea
brushes (in general)	e.g., hand brushes; hair brushes, dust brushes, etc.
causes, attachment to	should be read as "attachment to causes"

The question of where to place the ideas denoted by mother and father raises disagreement among astrologers. Some astrologers feel that mother belongs to the fourth house and father to the tenth house; while other astrologers feel that mother belongs to the tenth house and father to the fourth house. Some astrologers separate these ideas into "the nurturing parent" (assigned to the fourth house) and "the disciplining parent" (assigned to the tenth house). This complicates things further because in some families the nurturing parent and disciplining parent may be the same person.

This book associates the idea of mother with the fourth house, and father with the tenth house. These houses were selected because of the Moon's (i.e., mother image) association with the fourth house and Saturn's (father image) association with the tenth house. If you need different house placements then please adjust the relevant words for all mother and father ideas. To do this reverse this book's house location for not only mother and father, but also each associated idea, such as "mother's kin" (i.e., for a house reversal swap the sides of the chart for each house, the twelfth house becomes the sixth house, the first house the seventh house, etc.)

The sort order for the words used is a computer standard sort order. That is, special characters (like periods, parenthesis, etc.) sort first, then numbers, then capital letters and then lower case letters. Spaces between words are counted in the sort order, so words like "backhoe" and "back hoe" would sort the word "backup" between them. Sometimes the plural of a word will appear last in the sort order. Sometimes the plural of a noun may come after an intervening different noun than its singular version.

One example is the word "spy" which alphabetically sorts considerably after its plural "spies." Some of the entries are in a singular form and some are in a plural form. Whatever form seemed best for the entry was used, but wherever possible the singular form was used. In general either the singular or the plural form of an entry may be used. Please check for both the singular and the plural of each word before ending your search. Any duplicated word entries within the same category are unplanned, but some words and ideas are duplicated across the categories for easier reference.

The alphabetical category lists all keywords in this book. Entries are followed by a code and a number showing which category and house rules that entry. Typical entries look like:

exposure (lay bare)	Th05
exposure (vista)	Th09
expressions of emotion	Ps05

extra Oc	05
eyes Bd	01

These entries have two parts: the word or phrase entry and the code entry. The word entry describes the intended keyword idea. A key is printed at the bottom of each right hand page, and at the front of the alphabetical section: Th = thing; Ps = psychological quality; etc. In the above list you can find "expressions of emotion" in the fifth house in its "psychological qualities" category. You can find "eyes" under the first house's "body" category, etc. The word "extra" is taken in an occupation or person type sense and refers to someone performing as an extra in, say, a movie. You can see that there are two ideas for the word "exposure" included: exposure in the sense of vista is a ninth house concept, while exposure in the sense of laying bare has a fifth house affinity.

This book has both an instructional side and a fun side. The instructional side is used when scanning and reading the book's word lists. You can learn much about the meanings of the houses in various departments of life by doing this. The word lists contains words that should both educate you and expand your knowledge of the houses in general. Look through the alphabetical section and see the rich diversity of words and how subtle shades of word meaning can change the house rulerships of those words quite quickly. One example is "shortening (abbreviating)" associated with the third house, or "shortening (fat)" which is associated with the twelfth house.

Fun comes from the games you can invent using this book. When in a class or a group you could read three words from a house entry (usually in the order presented in the book— ut the sequential order of the words read is not important—also you can skip around in a house's word list) from one of the book's lists and then ask the others which house was associated with those words. For instance "impressions of others, indecision, and inequitable things" are three words associated with the seventh house. Going through such word groupings helps you can gain better insight into the individual house meanings. The discussions that ensue from games like this can be very educational. This is a great game to break up the tedium within any astrological classroom setting.

What should you do if you can't find the word or concept you are looking for within the house you reference? First, reference the alphabetical list in this book to see if your word is in the book. Often words are assigned into a house that may at first seem wrong to your thinking. Much thought was given to the placement of each individual word in this book. The house placements suggested in this book are not random or contrived—nor were they copied from existing sources. Indeed, copying them from existing sources would have resulted in the chaos of having multiple rulerships for the same idea, and this was one pitfall that was deliberately avoided. If you don't find your word in the alphabetical list, then try a synonym of your word to see if that is listed in the alphabetical list. If you still can't find your word(s) then try some ideas or concepts that have similar meanings. Then try combinations of words or word ideas that have similar meanings. If you still can't find your word then write it into your copy of the book.

Words were assigned to houses in this book only after considerable thought for each placement. Years of astrological testing with clients, discussions with other astrologers, reading other astrological material, etc., have been used to create the word placements used in this book. The testing of these word placements with other professional astrologers has shown that there is very little controversy about most house word assignments. You personally may differ with the placement of a word, and therefore space is provided for you to write in your comments, notes or ideas.

Use this word list in your everyday astrological work. Make notes about the words which you use but cannot find in this book. The words in this book are nowhere near as important as the final learning process you go through to improve yourself as a person.

Chapter 4

Quadrants and Hemispheres

Overview

A yet to be fully explained cosmic mechanism ties the position of the planets in space and time with events on Earth. Such a "mirroring" does exist. We do not understand how this works, but it does. David Wilcock in his works describes a "Source Field" that interconnects all things, and there is good evidence for this. (See: *The Source Field Investigations*, David Wilcock, 2011, ISBN:978-0-525-95204-6). Such interconnection among all things is not generally recognized by society or science. We are still learning.

It is important to notice and recognize quadrant and hemisphere emphasis in an astrological chart. The astrological quadrants (a four way division of the astrological chart) and hemispheres (a two way left-right, or up-down, division) help place planet energies into a four and a two fold set. These four quadrant divisions represent: inception, growth, attainment, and adaptation. The two left-right hemisphere divisions represent personal (me) vs. other people (you) emphasis. The up-down hemisphere division represents an outer world vs. an inner personal world emphasis. Often one or more of these quadrant or hemisphere areas in a chart can be emphasized by the placement of the planets.

Quadrants are divided by the sensitive points, e.g., the Ascendant (ASC), MC, etc. An astrological chart pictures this spatial division for a particular time and place. Such a chart is erected to show how the planets are oriented in space and time. Once drawn it is available for reading or interpreting. The process of reading or interpreting an astrological chart is called delineation.

A very important part of chart delineation is determining the individual phases of each planetary cycle which the person, business, or event is experiencing. The chart can show a Mars phase (a two year cycle—all cycle times given are approximated to the nearest year of cycle length), a Jupiter phase (twelve years), a Saturn phase (twenty-nine years), a progressed Moon cycle (twenty-nine years), a Nodal cycle (nineteen years), Solar Arc cycles (every twenty-two and a half years), etc.

It is helpful during delineation to see where each of the bodies (planets, personal sensitive points, etc.) lie in their phase of development. The astrological quadrants and hemispheres naturally divide these important planetary cycles into meaningful sectors. The quadrants and hemispheres are marked by the personal sensitive points and thus are sensitive to the time of day for which the chart is erected. People born only a few moments apart on the same day can be at different phases in their transiting or progressed cycles. Important times in these cycles occur when the bodies cross the quadrant delimiters. These times of life should be noted and studied.

The traditional method of using a four-fold division of time and space is used here. Astrological quadrants exist for every chart erected regardless of whether or not they are used. This chapter introduces some important concepts about these quadrants and their possibilities. Use the quadrants and hemispheres for marking the phases of development within life for the charts being studied. You should find this practice to be worth the time invested. How each person experiences these cycles of life is a very important astrological concept. Unfortunately, this topic is often lightly treated elsewhere

Quadrants

There are four traditional astrological parts to life's daily cycle. These are marked by midnight, sunrise, noon, and sunset. These four markers are so basic to the psychological division of our daily lives that they often pass unnoticed. Yet they serve to divide and order the regimen of our days and the events and circumstances of our lives in ways beyond normal cognitive sensing.

Traditionally, midnight is the division of one day from the next; sunrise is the start of our working day; noon is our meal or rest break; and sunset is the traditional end of the working day. These same four psychological markers divide the chart into the astrological quadrants and hemispheres.

Charts include seven important astronomical circles that derive from three astronomical planes in space. Together these are used with the planets and signs to construct the chart's framing. Regardless of whether you draw a chart by hand or use a computer to print it out, the act of creating a chart incorporates these circles and planes into a symbolic diagram. The three planes (listed alphabetically) are the:

- ecliptic
- equator
- horizon

The names of the seven circles (listed alphabetically) are the:

- co-equator

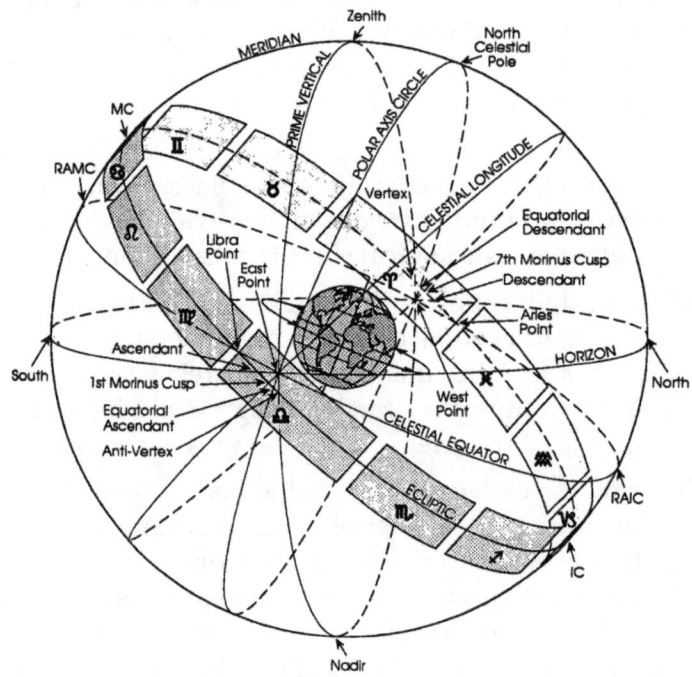

Figure 2

- Earth's equator
- ecliptic
- horizon
- meridian
- polar axis circle
- prime vertical

Coordinate Planes

Astrological tradition creates a chart's quadrants by using the horizon and the meridian circles. Using the prime vertical and equatorial circles should also prove to be important, but research on this is lacking. Use of the co-equator and polar axis circle is almost nonexistent. Certainly there is room here for much future investigation and development. The traditional chart is divided by the horizon into an upper and lower hemisphere, each of which contains two quadrants. The meridian similarly divides a chart in an eastern or left part and a western or right part, each of which also contains two quadrants. The superimposition of the horizon and meridian divisions gives the quadrant system most popularly used.

Quadrant Numbering Systems

Quadrants are numbered counterclockwise because the planets move in that direction. The figure below depicts this quadrant unfolding.

```
                        MC
    THIRD Quadrant          SECOND Quadrant
    ATTAINMENT              DEVELOPMENT
    ─────────────────────────────────────────
      ASC                       DSC
    FOURTH Quadrant         FIRST Quadrant
    ADAPTATION              INCEPTION
                        IC
```

The daily movement of the zodiacal degrees across the chart angles proceeds with a clockwise motion. The planets move in a counter-clockwise direction. The two movements work across each other. Thus, where to start a quadrant numbering system?

There are different ideas on how to number astrological quadrants. One method in use starts at the Ascendant and goes counterclockwise where quadrant one holds houses one through three. This approach to numbering quadrants derives from the numbering scheme aligned with the house numbers.

The disadvantage to starting quadrant numbering from the Ascendant, or the sunrise point, is that it does not follow the day start and end point (midnight). If you want to follow natural daily rhythms it is better to start from the midnight point of the chart (IC), which both traditionally and through keywords portrays beginnings.

The IC starting point for quadrant numbering offers a better and more natural approach. The advantage is that it starts with the traditional astrological point of "beginnings" and also it ends its cycle with the traditional point of "endings" (both points are at the IC). *The numbering scheme starting with the midnight point is advocated and described further in this book.*

There is another advantage to starting a quadrant numbering scheme with the fourth house cusp and placing the fourth, fifth and sixth houses in the first quadrant. The traditional keywords assigned to the houses follow better with this method. This approach also more logically follows the unfolding of human experience within life's cyclical events.

Further, the transits, solar arcs, and progressions of the major planets through the quadrants can be naturally followed and interpreted. Examining the development of a thought, project, idea, etc., through a complete chart cycle of the quadrants can help you see how the houses themselves lend their traditional flavors to the inception, development, attainment, and adaptation phases of this natural quadrant division and numbering scheme.

Quadrant and Hemisphere Definition

Cyclical events in life have a beginning or starting point as well as an ending point. These 'starts and ends' should occur from the same point in order to maintain continuity. Traditional astrology assigns the key concept of starts and ends to the IC, or the cusp of the fourth house. The quadrants then describe a natural scheme of growth and evolution in one's consciousness, education, social skills, or work abilities.

Often the working of these cycles pass completely unnoticed on our conscious level. The cycles and the developments they promote often proceed completely beyond our daily involvements with satisfying the demands of living. It is usually, and then only in retrospect, that we are able to realize that a cycle has begun, developed, unfolded and passed. Whether consciously noticed or not, the process continues and affects all phases of our life's progress.

In the beginning one's schemes are started and work is done to define and structure tasks. This occurs during the first quadrant of astrological cycle, and draws from the fourth, fifth, and sixth house energies. The fourth house is your roots, your beginnings and your base of operations. The fifth house represents creativity and the fun you can have in exploring life. The sixth house represents the personal dedication that you choose to put into your projects. Thus this combination of energies placed in the first quadrant serves as an excellent set of energies for fueling a cycle's inception phase.

The Ascendant-Descendant line separates the sixth and seventh houses and the first and second quadrants. The second quadrant expresses the ideas behind development through the seventh, eighth, and ninth houses. This quadrant continues the growth begun in the first quadrant by focusing your needs on gaining support from others for the activities already started. Working with and through others helps expand any individual efforts. Seeking others out, gathering support, and expanding the scope of events is directly related to the seventh, eighth, and ninth house concepts. When the second quadrant cycle is completed, the development phase should have reached the peak of its evolution and projection into the external world.

The second quadrant involves promoting interest in your ideas and activities, finding financing and support for your interests, and then setting your purpose forward for others to examine. The second quadrant phase draws upon the seventh, eighth, and ninth house energies. The seventh house describes partnership arrangements and criticism. It represents those with whom you choose to ally with for your schemes. The seventh house also represents those who choose to oppose you or interfere with your work. The eighth house represents the resources other people can bring to help you, and how you allow others to interfere with or modify your inner creations. The eighth house also represents any lessening of scope, as well as restructuring of ideas that you should accommodate. The ninth house represents the many variations that can arise from the path set for yourself, as well as your ability to sell your idea to others. The ninth house embodies the core of your idea and how well it may be received by others.

The third quadrant contains the tenth, eleventh, and twelfth houses. It marks the start of the halfway point through the quadrant cycle. The momentum built through the first half of your cycle reaches its apex and is now ready for further testing. At this apex of progress you may receive some reward or recognition for your efforts so far. The third and the fourth quadrants help you capitalize on the fruits of your previous labors. If your efforts have been poorly defined or prepared so far, then this half of the cycle may be trying. If you have prepared well and worked your ideas and schemes through, then the last half of this cycle can bring you many rewards—both tangible and intangible.

The tenth house helps you concentrate on building your career and reputation based on activities started during the previous two quadrant phases. Through the tenth house you confront the question of how to use the power associated with what you are developing, while in the eleventh house you gather others or organizations to comment on and then maintain your schemes. In the twelfth house you have returned to you what you have given to others through the earlier parts of this cycle. The twelfth house offers you an opportunity to make some restitution or changes in your thinking or approaches (i.e., your direction can still be adjusted and/or changed if such is warranted).

During the third quadrant phase the concepts put forth earlier bear fruition and your reputation is called into focus. You gather whatever support from others is needed to promote your schemes and maintain them. Then you await feedback from this society, be it good or bad, on whether or not your scheme is worthy. These developments correspond to the traditional keyword meanings of the tenth, eleventh, and twelfth houses. The tenth house represents your reputation and honors received. The eleventh house is the societal support you receive or can muster. The twelfth house is either the compassion you show to others, or the compassion you receive from others. The twelfth house is also where you must face any self-undoing energies which you have set in motion during the cycle.

The fourth quadrant's influence calls on you to reflect inwardly on what you have done and determine whether or not you have accomplished your inner goals. This final phase of inward application and thinking (or rethinking) of the approaches and the dissemination of your schemes shows how you have absorbed the lessons of your cycle of activity. This is the final phase of the overall cycle and is necessary for the reflection and inner absorption of the lessons learned during the cycle's operation. During the fourth quadrant phase you must stand alone, apart from others, to determine for yourself the worthiness (or lack of it) of previous efforts.

The fourth quadrant helps you reflect on what has been done, and to grow or not grow from this on a personal level. Here too you have the opportunity financially to benefit (or lose) from the cycle. The fourth quadrant, through the third house, also gives you the final say about the experience of the entire cycle and what may or may not be published or disseminated to others before the next cycle begins. The fourth quadrant, then, is an introspective or quiet quadrant where you are left alone to face your own creation. This too is in keeping with the meanings of the houses of this quadrant although not in such a direct and obvious way as in the other quadrants. In some recent astrological works the inner reflection possibilities of the first, second, and third houses have been neglected.

It may help you when delineating a natal chart to note how the planets are arranged in the quadrants. A person with a strong second quadrant planetary emphasis will have personality thrusts quite different from a person with a strong fourth quadrant planetary emphasis, etc. While noticing this arrangement within the quadrants is not the answer to all personal motivations it can help in understanding why some people are driven by the actions of others while others are driven only by their own inner callings.

Astrologically the zodiacal sign of Aries is associated with the first house, and the keyword relationship of Aries with initiating and pioneering efforts shifts these meanings to the first house too. The first house is usually associated with keyword ideas like the self, you or your nature. Tradition places the beginning and ending of cyclical activities with the fourth house. Realize that the first house with its Aries association does not carry the implication that efforts are also started with Aries. "Beginnings" and "endings" have traditionally been associated with the fourth house cusp or IC, and an over-emphasis of the zodiacal sign keywords with the house keywords may have caused a shift for the beginning of cycles to the Ascendant.

Astrological tradition tells us that there is a relationship between signs and houses, but there is not necessarily an interchange of keywords between signs and houses. Each has its own keyword role. Performing a keyword interchange between signs and houses has somehow shifted the sense of starting from the fourth house where it was traditionally assigned, to the first house where it does not fit.

The key ideas of "beginning" and "ending" have traditionally been associated with the IC. It is time to set an errant course straight and to return the beginning and the ending of the quadrant cycles to where they rightfully belong. This can be rectified by clearer and more direct thinking on the nature of cycles, quadrants and the role of the houses in general. In our overall phases of life what we go through on a daily basis is shown by the activities through the astrological quadrants.

Use of the quadrants can also be helpful when assessing the transits of the slower moving planets through the astrological chart. Jupiter, for example, takes about twelve years to complete one cycle, and as Jupiter goes through its transit of the natal chart it activates the potential of each quadrant.

Angular, Succedent and Cadent

The houses in each quadrant lend other shades of meaning to life beside their quadrant and hemisphere significance. Each house is assigned either an angular, succedent, or cadent label. This label helps further refine the individual qualities of the house. Starting at the chart angle initiating each quadrant and moving counter-clockwise there lie three houses, generically labeled angular, succedent, and cadent.

As the first house in the quadrant the angular house urges you to heed what transpires while this quadrant's energies are activated. Angular houses initiate the quadrant's role. Angularity as a key concept involves personal growth, development, or growing toward the quadrant's central influences (see Figure 3). The angular house sets the motivation and style for how the quadrant is to function during the cycle.

The succedent house helps consolidate and form what the angular house initiates for this quadrant. The succedent house helps to build, shape and add stability or firmness to ongoing efforts. The succedent house helps solidify the actions initiated by the angular house. It helps shape how the idea or action can proceed and form. The succedent house emphasis is one of utilization, or finding the means or purpose for the action or process. Through the succedent house you consolidate the material or psychological resources needed. It helps bring purpose and equilibrium to what has been started. One purpose of the succedent house is to bring a definite aim and direction to fulfill the roles of the quadrant.

The cadent house emphasizes the evaluation, understanding, completion and testing of any processes started and solidified through the previous two quadrant houses. The cadent house ensures that what is being created has the shape and direction of what is needed for the following quadrant. If your scheme or development is still unprepared, then there is a cadent house mechanism that allows for the testing and alteration of plans. Sometimes this testing and alteration can be psychologically or materially painful. You have an obligation to self to become aware of the transpiring cycles. The cadent house ensures that you face and heed the messages generated by the passages of bodies through the quadrant.

If you do not read the signals generated by the cadent house, or if you do not modify your cyclical processes in accordance with what is being directed through the cadent house, then the cadent house allows for the disintegration of the ongoing process and its collapse, with the subsequent turmoil of withdrawal that accompanies this change. This may come as a psychic, mental, or physical shock as this happens. The depth of this shock may be in direct relationship to your awareness of what is happening. Your awareness of the relative merit or non-merit of your current cyclical activities and how these affect self and others is confronted through the cadent house.

Overall the cadent house function is to harmonize your efforts with what is needed to fulfill the quadrant's directions. If you are following your cycle's phases well, then the cycle can continue and the next quadrant entered without change. If there are modifications to be made, then the cadent house may initiate situations that show this need for modification. If the energies are heeded and appropriate changes made, then the changes can be absorbed. If not, there may be difficulties or trauma that may occur until the appropriate corrections are made. Please refer to Appendix C which shows keywords for the angular, succedent, and cadent qualities.

Hemispheres

In addition to the quadrants the personal sensitive points divide the chart into two distinct sets of hemispheres. The first hemisphere set is called left or eastern, and its pair is the right or western. The second set is called lower or northern, and its pair is the upper or southern hemisphere. Charts cast for localities north of the Earth's equator show the southern compass direction at the top of the chart and the northern compass direction at the bottom of the chart. For charts cast south of the Earth's equator (in Chile, South Africa, Australia, etc.) the compass directions are reversed. This is done so that a proper perspective on the Sun's travels can be kept, but this in no way changes the hemisphere meanings or symbolism. These are the symbolic directions where you would face the Sun at noon in these areas.

The hemispheres function along with the quadrants during the cycles of planetary passage. They do not alter the quadrant functions, but they do enhance them. The hemispheres super-impose themselves upon the activities of the quadrants and the quadrant development cycle. The hemispheric energies come before the quadrant energy push. The quadrants work with and through the hemispheres for their expression.

Regardless of where on Earth the chart is cast, there will be a lower and an upper hemisphere in the chart. The upper hemisphere symbolically represents daylight-oriented interests, while the lower hemisphere depicts nighttime concerns. Despite which compass direction is applied to this directional notation, the hemisphere keywords given in Appendix C apply. The upper hemisphere symbolizes activities that are out in the open, before others. The bottom half of the chart symbolically represents activities that are performed in private or closed circumstances. The difference in the influences of these hemispheres is dramatic. One represents activities that are exposed to the scrutiny of others, while the other represents endeavors that take place internally and privately.

The left or eastern hemisphere holds the tenth, eleventh, twelfth, first, second, and third houses. It symbolizes activities that help you to develop yourself as a person. There is an emphasis on free will expression in this hemisphere. Matters about personal involvement become daily issues. The left hemisphere directs your focus on inner development and personal individuality. Personal aggressiveness becomes an important matter. There is a heightened sense of "me." Matters of self's desires, or matters concerning self, come into focus. The left hemisphere spurs you to develop powers of observation. Inner calls for rethinking your actions or to look carefully at the consequences of your actions and effect on others become highlighted. This is where your self-interests and self-development become accented. There is more personal latitude for decision and action here than when the western or right hemisphere is activated.

The right or western hemisphere brings an increasing complexity to life. Others place demands on your time and resources. Compared to the left hemisphere, when the right hemisphere is active, there is less personal control over daily events or circumstances. Events occur which are dictated more by what others want than what you desire. You find yourself reacting to situations set up by others. The sense of personal control and freedom the left hemisphere provided diminishes. In the right hemisphere others create situations that involve you in their destiny or reasons for being. You find you must learn to work with and through situations that others initiate. The right hemisphere raises topics where you face issues about cooperation. There is a need to control your responses to the experiences noted or encountered to gain more control over or responsibility for your actions. The right hemisphere brings increased socialization needs into your life.

The lower or northern hemisphere is concerned with the development of self as a person. In this hemisphere things of personal interest are emphasized There is a strong push toward inner development and self-realization. It emphasizes the process of self-unfolding, or seeing your relationships with others as a means for developing self. There is also an emphasis on the continuing development of skills learned earlier in life. Common sense in dealing with the different phases of life is emphasized, as is the need for personal privacy. There is a push to live your life so that your own needs for protection and security are met first before the needs of others. The lower hemisphere may prompt you to withdraw from the mainstream of life's worldly flow and to be more inwardly focused in your interpersonal and living involvements. A call to look and live within self prevails here. It may also direct you to become more dependent upon a stronger personality.

The upper or southern hemisphere pushes you to develop inter-personal psychological qualities that you need for living among others, rather than in an inner world. Here the emphasis is not on retreat and anonymity, but on popularity and exposure. There is a desire towards externalizing self and learning how to become more public. When this hemisphere is emphasized your interpersonal goals need to be better defined. Plans for including others in your life become important. What you do is carefully scrutinized by others. There is little room for musing or mulling over theoretical possibilities. From this hemisphere comes a need for increasing self-confidence and building self-esteem through actions that others can see and evaluate. There is a push to gain recognition or prominence, or to place yourself in an open and visible position. The drive for achieving power and recognition is enhanced. The upper hemisphere urges you to express yourself more openly and directly.

Viewpoint

There is nothing good or bad about the various facets of astrology. There is no more or no less merit in one quadrant or hemisphere than another. Each shows a facet of human development. The fact that one side shows a Yin type of development and its opposite a Yang type of development does not make either one of them any better or any worse than the other. Each represents a part of existence. Each has its role to play in life. Remember this when making judgments about the placement of planets in the chart. The chart is neutral. It does not judge. It simply is. It simply provides for all facets of exposure and development within the human mechanism. Only those interpreting a chart place judgments on the meanings extracted using astrology.

Chapter 5

Choosing a House System

Overview

Houses are one of the seven distinct parts of astrology. The other parts are planets, signs, personal sensitive points, harmonics or aspects, fixed stars and long-term cycles. Some Uranian or Cosmobiology practitioners feel that houses have not been sufficiently defined, and thus state they need not be used. Houses exist and whether or not anyone uses them is their choice. To imply, however, that houses are unimportant is wrong. Houses have a definite role in astrology. The information they give is necessary and serves to round out and shape the other astrological energies. It is folly to consider practicing Horary or Electional astrology without considering the prominent and enriching role that houses lend to those disciplines.

Houses add structure and framework to the energies that come from the planets and signs. Houses provide a basis to anchor the energies available through the cosmos. The chart's houses depict areas of space that define various categories of life and how these may manifest. Houses set a practical basis for considering the many different material things that enter and are a part of life. Houses allow us to see such diverse things as land, books, foreign interests, commercial banks, children, dietary habits, brothers and sisters, taxes, etc. Houses help place or locate the different things of life that are so important to us. We all have the things of existence in our lives. Houses serve as the delineating vehicles for showing where these things belong in the chart. Houses receive and mold the other cosmic energies giving them meaning within the things of our personal world.

The purpose of any house system is to divide the sky into sectors or wedges of space. House systems were devised to mirror the concepts of day and night divisions into a chart. Since daylight and nighttime differ by month, season, and location on Earth, then projected houses can be of different sizes depending on the chart's originating criteria. It is this mirroring of the number of daylight and the number of nighttime hours that houses symbolically represent.

Since the length of day or night is locally oriented to a place on Earth, the question of how to erect a chart for a position on the Moon, Mars, a space station, in deep space, etc., (where there are only artificial horizons and artificial day and night hours) should be addressed. But, how to include house and personal point systems for events that occur off the Earth (like on an orbiting space station, another planet, etc.) is deliberately left unanswered for now. There are some good answers, of course, but they lie beyond the scope of this book.

Houses allow us to include sectors of space in a chart. These are divided into daylight and night divisions, usually by the personal sensitive points. In ancient times the length of an hour was determined by the amount of time between sunrise and sunset at a particular location. Six (or twelve) daylight hours and six (or twelve) nighttime hours were allowed. The number and length of the minutes in each such "hour" varied by culture and according to time of year and place on Earth, however. These "hours" divided sectors of the sky into divisions of time. House systems continue this tradition of dividing the day and night portions of a chart into sectors of space.

The process and refinement of calculating houses has changed since antiquity. Many things caused this change. For one, the quality of keeping time has become more standardized (timekeeping systems began to substantially improve during the 17th and 18th centuries) and mathematics has advanced to allow us to calculate circular motions in space more directly.

Concerning the perception of time in our daily lives, in the years before and around A.D. 400 most people were happy to know the season of the year. By the 900s people wanted to know which month of the year they were in. By the 1500s people wanted to know the week, by the 1700s the day, by 1850s the minute, etc. Today we measure time in billionths of a fraction of a second and better. In a millennia and a half or so we have moved from gross time comprehension to super accurate time usage. During this process events have speeded up and inner psychological space has become more crowded.

Because houses lend such importance to astrology it is important to understand something about how to choose a house system to fit your particular needs. Not all house systems fit all needs. Any house system may be appropriate for one task but not another. House systems can be selected by how they provide their particular services. Houses represent space in a chart. There are many different ways to present and divide space—and there are many different ideas on house division. Let us begin to explore the concepts behind house division.

House Division

The space around an event described in a chart is divided into four quadrants, as described in the last chapter. The Ascendant and Midheaven personal sensitive points define these quadrant boundaries. These quadrants do not necessarily contain the same amount of space however. Due to the angle of the Sun at the particular place on Earth being charted there may be more space for the Sun to move between sunrise and noon on one day of the year, or there may be more space for the Sun to move between noon and sunset at another time of the year, etc. The tilt of the Earth against the Sun also influences this spatial division. It is the unevenness of daylight or night space that gives houses their unequally sized shapes. It is this unevenness of space between the quadrant divisions that various house systems seek to emulate. Even when the houses and space appear to be balanced, this is an exception rather than the rule.

There are three categories of house division: direct, projection, and intersection. Direct house systems ignore any attempt to emulate unevenness in space division, while projection and intersection systems create mathematically complicated ways of trying to represent the unevenness of space within the divisions of our days (sunrise to noon, sunset to midnight, etc.).

Direct house systems do not tie their house cusps to the astrological quadrants as completely as the projection and intersection systems do. Some projection house systems are mathematically simplified versions of other projection house systems. Before computers could be used to do house calculations any mathematically simplified methods had some merit. Today, with computers available to instantly calculate any house system desired, the space dividing house systems can provide additional insight.

Within each of these categories different houses systems like Placidian, Regiomontanus, Campanus, Koch, and Equal House, are placed. There are at least twenty-four house division systems defined in astrological literature. Some are identical except in name. A few of these are popularly used, but most are quite obscure. Here is a breakdown of their names. Definitions of the house systems can be found in Appendices A and B.

The direct house systems are named:

Natural Hours	Equal	MC	Moon
Natural Graduation	Earth	Whole Sign	
Porphyry	Solar		
	Sun		

The projection house systems are named:

Alcibitius Declination	Alcibitius Semi-Arc	Arcturan
Campanus	Classical	Horizontal
Meridian	Morinus	Octopos
Placidian	Radiant	Regiomontanus
Topocentric	Zariel	

The intersection house system is named:

Koch

The chart embraces within it the ecliptic, the equatorial, and the horizon astronomical planes. The outer circular edge of a chart is the ecliptic, and it is onto the ecliptic that astrologers wish to project these other planes of information. Each plane is further divided into meaningful parts by circles that help them define up and down, east and west, etc. The names of some of these circles are prime vertical, meridian, horizon, celestial equator, etc.

When drawing these circles in an astronomical diagram there will be places where they meet called poles. These poles are similar in function to the Earth's north or south poles. From these axes other circles can be drawn to help project cuts of space onto the astronomical planes. Some names of these projection circles are house, longitude, etc. See Appendices A and B for further information on this subject. See also the Coordinate Planes diagram.

Direct house systems cut the ecliptic circle directly without the use of an intervening astronomical circle to project a house cusp onto the ecliptic. Projection and intersection house systems use an intervening circle to project or intersect their cuts. Direct house systems produce rather evenly spaced houses. Direct house systems like Porphyry, Natural Graduation, and Natural Hours try to imitate the effect of projection systems without complicated mathematics.

Direct house systems provide divisions of space but not any proportionally sized sectors of space. Projecting space onto a place on the Earth's surface can be a complicated matter. To do this you need to project a circle at an odd angle on top of another circle. The particular odd angle chosen depends on the inclination of the Earth to the Sun, the time of day, day of the year, and location on Earth. Such projection distorts the roundness of either one circle or the other when these circles are then drawn on a flat piece of paper. Projection techniques use the mathematics of spherical trigonometry.

Direct house systems ignore any such projection and its possible distorting effects in favor of a more simplified mathematical approach. Direct house systems require little complicated mathematics. They can often be found without a calculator or pencil and paper. This is one part of their appeal. Another part of their appeal lies in using them in locations where the Sun never sets or rises. Without a sunrise and a sunset to divide the day, the quadrant system disappears and the mathematics for certain projection systems may fail. Direct house systems avoid this failure.

Projection house systems cut another circle (like the celestial equator, prime vertical, etc.,) into equal parts, and then project these divisions onto the ecliptic through another circle (like house circles, longitude circles, etc.). Projection house systems thus introduce a distortion, and by doing so calculation of their house cusps becomes mathematically complicated. Projection systems make sense where these quadrant divisions are well defined. Such definition occurs in the middle latitudes of Earth, where the bulk of humanity lives.

This projection can produce houses that are sometimes quite big or quite small. Any projection of circles in space onto the surface of the Earth will produce some distortion to the roundness of the circle being projected. For circles like the ecliptic the amount of distortion shown depends on time of day, place on Earth, etc., for which they are drawn. It is unusual to find equally spaced houses when using a projection house system. However any projection system more closely mirrors the amount of space included in a section of the sky than direct house systems do. The intersection system uses a set of lines in space that intersect the ecliptic for their cut. The Koch system is neither strictly a projection system nor a direct system. It merits its own category.

One advantage of using direct house systems is that they are easy to calculate. They often require little or no mathematical manipulation of circles or planes in space. Projection systems, however, require the use of spherical trigonometry for cusp calculation. Projection and intersection systems, in their defense, do mirror more precisely the movement of the ecliptic around the Earth. They are more difficult to calculate but provide a clearer representation of cosmic motion around a given location on Earth

More western astrologers use the Placidian House system than any other house system. The Placidian House system is a powerful house system for doing natal astrological work. For other uses of astrology other house systems may be more appropriate. This chapter addresses some reasons for choosing one house system over another for a particular practice or look at a set of circumstances. To do this the theoretical construct of the different great circles of astronomy and the implications they carry should be addressed. Once you understand houses, you may come to appreciate why some house systems are better than others for your circumstances.

Astrology is an elastic practice. Techniques which one person finds useful another may not. There is enough overlap of cosmic information so that you can choose your own comfortable techniques. There are different ideas about how to practice astrology. Some astrological techniques are more thorough than others. Some are simpler. You can choose any level of astrological sophistication you desire. However, traditional astrological methods return more information more accurately. The same is not true for house systems, however. Choosing a house system with more complicated mathematics does not necessarily provide more or better information than one that uses simpler mathematics.

Any house system you select should always:

1. Provide cusps for the accurate timing of events, and,

2. Divide space to properly place bodies into their correct spatial divisions.

If the house system you are using for a particular purpose does not do this, then it is not fulfilling its primary objectives. It matters little that the house system is used by others, is a popular system, is an unpopular system or fails in certain areas of the world. If it gives correct results use it. If it does not give correct results, then try another system for dividing space.

There is a wide-range of house options available, and there should be a system of dividing space that can satisfy your needs given that the basic chart data is correct. If the chart does not accurately represent the person or event (it is usually the chart time which is off by a few minutes or hours) then the time of the chart needs to be rectified. Rectification is a process that adjusts the time of a birth to events in a life. The rules of rectification lie beyond this discussion.

The ecliptic, horizon, celestial equator, meridian, prime vertical, and polar axis circles are all used to create the various house systems. Here are some advantages and disadvantages of the three systems of house division.

System

Advantages	Disadvantages

Projection

Advantages	Disadvantages
Cuts true "wedges" of space to represent houses	Can astronomically fail in certain areas of the world
Ties the great circle framework into the chart	Difficult to mathematically compute cusps
Contains the most popularly used house systems	Difficult to find any astronomical reasoning for some of the house systems described
Presents usable cuspal arrangements	

Direct

Advantages	Disadvantages
Seldom fails astronomically	Does not tie the other great circles into the chart
Was used by ancient astrologers	
Is very easy to compute mathematically	Does not always cut true "wedges" of space for houses

Intersection

The arguments for or against using the Koch house system are similar to the ideas presented in the projection section above.

Some astrologers believe that the Koch system creates the best house system. Other astrologers feel the Koch cusps are less helpful for natal or psychological usage than other systems. There is a "cult" of Koch house system users who claim that the method was resurrected from ancient times. This claim for ancient use is not clearly substantiated. The Koch house system is very difficult to either clearly explain or to reproduce in an astronomical diagram. The Koch system may be very good for circumstances involving the direct interaction of a person with events around them.

Some Esoteric Implications of the Great Circles

The pros and cons of the different systems of house division do not answer the often asked question of which house system to choose for a given astrological application. To make this choice intelligently take a deeper look at the different house system theories and study the esoteric implications of the great circles they use. This is best done by first understanding the astronomical, and from that the derived esoteric role, for each circle. Examining the six basic house division circles used is a good starting point toward this understanding. These circles are called the ecliptic, celestial equator, horizon, prime vertical, meridian, and polar axis circle.

The Ecliptic

The ecliptic is the most astrologically important of the astronomical circles. The ecliptic directly places the planetary and sign energies into the chart. The motion of the Earth and Sun in space define the ecliptic. The Sun psychologically represents both the ideas of center (or central) and ego or self. Thus, these terms can be associated with the esoteric idea of what the ecliptic represents. Due to the symbology of the Earth's yearly revolution around the Sun the idea of completeness can be added to the ecliptic's esoteric keywords. The ecliptic is the first of the closed astronomical circles. A completed circle has no beginning or end. It simply is. A circle's existence is defined by the fact that it is, and not by a definite beginning or end point.

The cardinal point of Aries is the chosen starting point for the ecliptic because it can be defined and measured accurately. The Aries Point helps to locate the other cardinal points: Cancer, Libra, and Capricorn. The signs of the zodiac are measured along the ecliptic circle. Actual planetary, sensitive point and stellar positions can also be moved to the ecliptic regardless of whether or not the body is located on the ecliptic. All house cusps in all systems of house measurement are measured to the ecliptic. All harmonics are measured along the ecliptic. If nothing else the ecliptic represents wholeness and stability. It is the origin for all of what is produced with astrology. The ecliptic often becomes the sole reference point for all heavenly information represented in a chart.

Astrology relies on the ecliptic for the definition of all human expressions and experiences. The ecliptic shows what you can learn and encounter in life. It is the only one of the great circles that is not dependent upon any of the other circles. It is the most important of the great circles. The ecliptic plane is defined by the Sun, the Earth, and the direction of the Earth's motion. Incorporating the qualities of these bodies and movement the ecliptic represents the most important universal esoteric features.

The ecliptic brings the other planetary positions into the Earth's sphere of existence. Without the ecliptic's role other planetary energies could not be brought into the perspective of their relationship with either the Earth or Sun. The ecliptic serves as a foundation for including other bodies. Because this plane of reference exists the energies of the other bodies is symbolically brought into our Earthly existence. Only the Moon does not require the ecliptic to transmit its planetary energy. The Moon uses the plane defined by its interaction with the Earth (called the Moon's nodal plane—shown by the Moon's nodal axis) as its vehicle of energy expression. For the chart to remain consistent, however, the Moon is placed using its ecliptic reference. Thus, the ecliptic carries and transmits all symbolic and astrological energies.

The ecliptic also defines the placement of the signs of the zodiac. Without something like the ecliptic the signs could not be represented in a chart. The zodiacal signs add color and flavor to the individual planetary energies. The signs also feed energy into the ecliptic. The ecliptic allows us to place a cosmic energy distribution around our location in a chart. The ecliptic both originates and facilitates. The ecliptic's dual role elevates it in importance above the other astronomical circles. The ecliptic is the most important astrological circle.

The Celestial Equator

The celestial equator provides a measure for the orientation of the Earth in space against the ecliptic. The celestial equator is the extension of the Earth's equator infinitely into space. It is this orientation that allows us on Earth to tie into the celestial energies that are available to us through the ecliptic. The tilt of the celestial equator vis-a-vis the ecliptic defines the important angle of obliquity. It is the value of this angle of obliquity that has much to do with the notion of how much celestial energy is received by the two hemispheres of the Earth in their summers and winters. The greater the angle of tilt (or obliquity) the greater the disparity in the amount of celestial energy received between summer and winter. As the angle of obliquity decreases the temperature tends to remain more constant all over the Earth, and the light variation among the seasons begins to diminish.

It is through the rotation of the celestial equator that we measure our days. As the Earth turns on its axis, once each day it returns to an orientation with the same point in the sky. This sky point measures our daily celestial movement. The celestial equator delimits our individual daily progress towards the goal of solar integration, or the involvement of self with life. The ecliptic measures our yearly progress in this direction. Since the day is the most primary of the different biological cycles the celestial equator represents the concept of daily reinforcement.

It is this reinforcement of the daily cycle that serves to remind all living things where their source and origins are replenished. This cycle subconsciously reminds us that it is to the cosmos we must eventually return. It is not possible to see or measure progress without understanding the vehicle that measures our progress. The celestial equator serves as this universal reference. Hence, any idea or concept in our lives that employs the concept of either daily or repetition should be associated with the celestial equator.

It is through the celestial equator that we are able to tie the Earth to the Sun, and hence the ecliptic. The celestial equator serves as our local or daily esoteric exposure mechanism to the solar and planetary energies. The celestial equator takes the activities that we go through daily on Earth and apportions them to the ecliptic according to a seasonal scheme. The celestial equator serves as our delimiter for measuring this daily and seasonal progress or lack of it. The celestial equator is a daily reminder of how any point on Earth returns to the same solar or sidereal Sun angle after one rotation. The celestial equator ties the global view of our life to the cosmos. It is Earth's daily rotational effort that gives us the 24-hour exposure we receive to the different energies of the cosmos.

On any part of the Earth we are only exposed to about one-half of the Sun's rays at any one moment. Since the Earth rotates, this rotational effect eventually exposes us to all of the cosmic energies within any 24-hour period. The celestial equator serves as our esoteric filter for insuring that we get an even distribution of these energies over any one 24-hour period. The celestial equator serves to give us an exposure of a different nature during our diurnal cycle. The celestial equator is also our representation for the midpoint of one year's worth of solar declination. As such the celestial equator serves as our delimiter for the different seasonal changes that we have on Earth.

The celestial equator serves as our link between the Earth itself and the cosmic interactions of the signs and the planets. It is like a middleman or broker in business, insuring that the cosmic distribution system remains fair, and that none of us miss exposure to the full energy effects of each place or location in the universe. The celestial equator insures that the planets, signs, stars, etc., have a means for the even distribution of their cosmic energies to the people who live here on Earth.

The celestial equator performs two functions. It:
- Measures our exposure to any deviations in the universal energy shifts caused by seasonal or cyclical changes in the declination cycles. As such it is the primary cosmic reminder of such seasonal or cyclical changes, and,
- Expresses the Earth's daily rotational cycle, which ensures that we get a daily exposure to all heavenly locations

The celestial equator functions as an intermediary between the outer parts of the solar system, the galactic system and beyond, and the Earth itself. It is the primary gateway through which the other cosmic energies we use enter or exit. As such it is the most important circle for intercepting those energies and ensuring they become a part of our lives.

The Polar Axis Circle

The Earth's polar axis circle divides the celestial equator into two even hemispheres. The polar axis circle passes through the celestial equator (which are 90 degrees or 1/4th of the way from the Aries or Libra Points) and the north and south poles of the celestial sphere (which are the projections of the Earth's poles into infinity). The highlight of the polar axis circle is these two polar points, one in the north and one in the south. Physically, it is through these two points that the majority of the cosmic particles come pouring into the Earth.

These points are very close to the magnetic poles of the Earth that form the shield or guide through which the particles of the solar wind come into the surface of the Earth. The magnetic shield of the Earth forms close to the poles of the Earth and in the polar regions there is a type of magnetic "weakness" which allows the cosmic particles from the Sun and elsewhere to enter within the Earth's protective shield. The northern (or southern) lights or aurora borealis or australis demonstrate this.

The polar axis circle serves as the representation for both the intake and the exhaust of all type of solar or other cosmic particles that enter the Earth's region in space. The polar axis circle also serves as the representative of both the magnetic and ozone Earth shields. These shields contain a deliberate weakness. The psychological symbology of this weakness may correlate with the concept of aging, forecasting or etheric planes. The polar axis circle represents the basic point from which all measurements can be taken, because they serve as definite and definable points on the Earth.

It has been reckoned that the architects of the Great Pyramid used the Earth's polar axis as the basis for their primary unit of measure: the cubit. Scientists have speculated that the basic unit of measurement used in the English world, the foot and the inch, derive from the distance from the Earth's north pole to its center along the Earth's axis—the foot being one-five-hundred millionth of the measurement of that distance. The metric system uses a similar fraction of the distance along the Earth's equator as its basis of measure.

Like the celestial equator, the polar axis circle reminds us of the Earth's diurnal or daily rotation and the exposure that gives us to the heavenly domains. The polar axis circle gives us a true north and south orientation and serves as one reference point for directions from Earth to space. It also gives a reference point for our local space directions. The Great Pyramid is aligned with the Earth's polar axis circle very accurately. Our road maps are aligned to the polar axis circle very accurately. The basis for land measurement on the Earth's surface accurately uses the polar axis circle.

Coupled with the celestial equator the polar axis circle defines one of the three planes used to orient the Earth and the planets in space. The polar axis circle is the other part of the celestial equator that serves to give the celestial system of coordinates form and definition within its projective plane of influence. The two great circles work together, one with the other, to define how the Earth is oriented into space. The celestial equator orients the Earth to the Sun, and the Earth's polar axis represents where we anchor our terrestrial measurements. It is the origin and the ending of our basic system of Earth measurement and reference. It may also be symbolic of whatever cosmic or etheric interference we allow into our lives.

The Horizon

The horizon is a very personal circle and it is esoterically associated with the "here and now" of your environment and perceptions. The horizon separates your world into an up and a down, that which is in the sky and that which is below the Earth. It is also tied into a particular place on Earth at a particular time. Its perspective is easily moved and altered.

The horizon that one person has is not the same horizon for another person. Whereas the celestial equator, the polar axis circle, and the ecliptic each tie the Earth and cosmos together, the horizon, meridian, and the prime vertical tie your immediate circumstances on Earth to the cosmos. The horizon orients where a person is on Earth to events in space. It is the most personal astrological great circle. It directly relates what you see, and defines your immediate perspective to the heavens.

The horizon is what you see when you look where the Earth and sky meet in the distance. The horizon requires and gives perspective. Astronomically four different horizons are used, but the visible horizon can easily substitute in your mind for the celestial horizon that is actually used in house mathematics. As you move from location to location your perspective shifts and you alter your horizon.

Imagine several people sitting in the same room. Each of them has their own horizon perspective. The horizon from one person's orientation is not exactly the same horizon or orientation that another person has, even if they are standing next to each other. The horizon is a very personal circle. It is the circle that psychologically ties our location and perspective of space to the planets and energies of the cosmos.

Esoterically the horizon symbolizes what you are doing in the here and now. It is your immediate and direct perspective on how you are relating to the events around you. It represents how and where you mentally interface to this immediate environment. It is through the horizon that you are able to gain a perspective on how to view your world. The horizon is locally oriented. The horizon gives its orientation because the Earth's gravity keeps your feet oriented towards the Earth's center. Since you walk with your feet on the ground you are given some perspective about our environment through your horizon. The horizon in turn separates your piece of Earth from the heavens.

Your horizon always exists at some particular angular relationship to the celestial equator. This is important to understand. This angular relationship is shown by terrestrial latitude. If you are standing at 40° North, then your horizon relationship to the celestial equator is different from the horizon relationship a person has at 35° North, or 20° South, or whatever. Each person's relationship on Earth to the celestial equator is also governed by their terrestrial longitude.

Two people at the same terrestrial longitude may have different horizons, as each may be at a different latitude. The celestial equator in turn relates each individual horizon to the ecliptic, and the ecliptic in turn relates your horizon to the planets. Each piece has its own function and purpose—and each works and interacts with the others.

A chart for a place not on this Earth would have to create the horizon concept in order to include the personal sensitive points. There are many ways for doing this, some of them quite arbitrary. The concept of houses and personal sensitive points for a chart done off of the Earth is an issue which astrology may have to face in the near future.

The Prime Vertical and Meridian

The prime vertical and the meridian work along with the horizon in giving us a left and right definition to where we are and what we see in our Earthly environment. The prime vertical and the meridian are always ninety degrees from each other. They represent different perspectives in their lines of division. The prime vertical divides the celestial sphere perpendicular to the horizon, dividing the horizon into a northern and southern part. The meridian divides the celestial sphere and the horizon into eastern and western halves. The prime vertical and the meridian are used for synchronizing the Earth's rotation with the horizon. They serve as the two primary measuring circles for determining how the horizon is oriented to the celestial equator and polar axis circle at any moment.

The prime vertical and the meridian go through the zenith and the nadir points of the celestial sphere. The zenith and nadir are the highest and the lowest points of the heavens, as seen from an observer's viewpoint. The zenith is the heavenly point directly over your head, and the nadir is the heavenly point directly under your feet. The zenith and nadir change as an observer moves around on the surface of the Earth. For two observers standing in close proximity to each other, even within the same room, each has their own zenith and nadir points, each has their own horizon circle, and each has their own prime vertical and meridian. The prime vertical, the meridian, and the horizon only exist when there are circumstances that use them. Then the occasion or event itself defines its horizon, prime vertical, and meridian.

The prime vertical and the meridian bring consistency to the coordinate systems used for defining Earthly location. The prime vertical or the meridian helps you find a celestial correspondence that has personal meaning. Neither the prime vertical nor the meridian takes the heavens or planets into consideration. They deal strictly with the person or the event occurring on the surface of the Earth. The prime vertical and meridian define the orientation of that event, as seen through the horizon system, to the heavens. Thus the prime vertical and the meridian work not through a heavenly hierarchy or scheme, but through a personal and local scheme. The prime vertical and the meridian serve to give the local space of any event Earthly consistency.

The prime vertical and the meridian work together to define a concept of time and time passage in the Earthly plane. They symbolically represent here and now to us. The prime vertical conveys a sense of "rising" and "setting." The meridian gives us consistency in time measurement. Thus the meridian represents consistency, while the prime vertical represents opportunity—yet each works together with the horizon in defining the event framework between our local orientation and what is occurring in the heavens. The prime vertical and the meridian drape like a tent over the horizon, and give the flatness of the horizon some depth and character. Like a tent these circles serve to define the framework of our awareness and perceptual systems, assuring that the events we go through incorporate the energies of the cosmos.

Considerations

Each projection house system is some combination of the different great circles. If you understand the esoteric implications of the different great circles you are better prepared to determine which of these circles, or which combination of these circles, are the ones that you would want to use for your house system of choice. Astrology confronts you with choices, and the choice of which house system to use at any particular time can be confusing.

If, however, you understand the nature of the event you want to astrologically portray and if you understand the esoteric implications of the great circles available to build a house system, then you can choose which house system would best fit your circumstances and needs. The rules when selecting a house system are to think, apply knowledge, and choose. Here are some examples of how to make your house system choices.

If you desire to incorporate the immediacy of events around you (going to a race track and timing when a race starts demands immediacy), then choose a house system which has the horizon and meridian prominent in its calculations, like the Koch, Campanus, Horizontal, or Arcturan systems. If you desire a house system with an esoteric or cosmic primary view, then choose a house system like the Equal, Porphyry, or Solar systems that primarily use an ecliptic point of view. If you desire a house system that incorporates a worldly view along with cosmic insight, then choose a house system that incorporates the celestial equator and the ecliptic interacting, like the Placidus, Regiomontanus, or Topocentric systems. If you desire a house system with a strong emphasis on timing, then choose a house system like the Meridian or Zariel.

Suppose you wish to do a general chart interpretation for a client and desire a general usage house system that would show that person's place in the world and their general relationship with the cosmos. With these criteria chosen the sense of "world" and "cosmos" are decided—yet a sense of the personal must be maintained, too. These criteria imply using a house system that has the celestial equator prominent as well as the ecliptic, and certainly the horizon or ascendant projected through this. The Placidian, Regiomontanus, and Topocentric house systems meet these demands. If these are your requirements then you should consider using either the Placidian, Regiomontanus, or Topocentric house systems for this astrological chart.

Another set of circumstances might require a chart reading for the start of a horse race at a particular racetrack. The criteria now would be more immediate and local—certainly the horizon, meridian, and prime vertical should be prominent in the house system used. With these criteria then, the Horizontal, Koch, Zariel, Campanus, Alcibitius, or Arcturan systems should be considered for usage.

The house system used should fit the circumstances. There is no easy answer to which house system to use at any particular time. The choice, as always, lies with the practitioner. It is through the understanding of what makes up the choices of the different house systems though that your intelligence shows through. There is no guarantee that what works for one set of circumstances may always work for another set of circumstances.

Realize that often it is only the intermediate house cusps that are altered between one house system and another. Study and understand the circumstances of the life situation that is to be astrologically portrayed, and determine which of the great circles best fit these circumstances. Then choose that house system that best fits that combination of great circles. Appendix A goes into greater detail on how house systems are constructed and which circles they use prominently. Appendix B gives mathematical formulae for deriving these house systems.

Within this set of thinking ecliptic-based house systems show the general energy of the cosmos well, but do little to relate this flow of energy to the horizon. Celestial equator-based systems relate the general influences in the world to the cosmos better, but do little to take into account the influences of what is occurring in the here and now of our daily existence. The horizon-based systems cannot relate the general influences in the world as well as a celestial equator-based system can. The choices remain up to the astrological practitioner. Through knowledge of how houses are formulated an astrologer can be better prepared to use their interpretive art.

Big and Little Houses—Empty Houses—Intercepted Houses

When the house system of choice is a projection or intersection system, there may be certain times during the day when somewhat bigger or smaller houses may be projected. Depending on terrestrial latitude and time of the year, there can be times of the day when some houses will be extraordinarily large, and there can be times when some houses are very small. An average house size is thirty degrees. House size in projection systems depends on latitude, season, and time of day. Sometimes houses as smaller than 13 degrees occur and sometimes houses larger than 45 degrees, or almost one and one-half again as big as they should be, occur.

What do these big and little houses mean? Obviously house size has no relevance unless a house system is chosen that can generate different sized houses. Direct house systems do not create much house size diversity, but projection and intersection house systems do. The size of a house seems to have something to do with the importance of that house to the chart. A house smaller than about 24 degrees seems to diminish the priorities of that house. A house of 36 degrees or larger seems to assign a more important role. An extraordinary house size seems to convey meaning. If you are using a projection house system while interpreting a chart look at the house sizes. This may help you begin to understand where some of the more important and personal astrological priorities lie.

Houses that are empty—those which have no planetary occupants—are just as important, if not even more so, than those that have planets occupying them. Visualize the chart as emitting a stream of energy from its center. This stream of energy spouts forth equally in all directions through the twelve houses of the chart. It is available for use by the person or event depicted by the chart. The source of this energy is the cosmos itself. The flow of energy through the houses is either smooth or turbulent depending on the planets placed in the twelve house paths. Like the waters from a stream that flows through the countryside, this energy flows through the chart. If the flow of a river or stream encounters rocks, then the water shows a turbulent surface. If the flow of a river or stream is over a smooth bottom, however, then the surface of the flowing water remains calm.

In life, activities that show action or turbulence tend to grab and occupy our attention. Similarly, the flow of energy from the source of the chart shows either turbulence or smoothness depending on the location of planets in the houses. If a house has planets in it the planets may act as rocks in a stream and create some turbulence. The flow of energy in that house is disturbed and may subconsciously gain our attention. If the house has no planets in it then the flow is smoother and undisturbed. We notice the turbulence of life more than we do those areas where activity is calmer. Disturbance draws attention.

Similarly, those houses that have planets in them may occupy more of our attention in life than houses with no planets. All houses are a part of our existence, but it is those houses having planets that may consume most of our attention. That does not imply that empty houses go unused, but that we tend to live or spend time and/or personal energy concentrating where life's tumult grabs our attention. Empty houses have their role and may occupy our time too, but not as much as houses which show a greater planetary activity. Remember that transits and progressions of planets through a house, even a natally empty house, will alter a house's occupancy rate.

One important use of the empty houses is *projection* (in a psychological sense). People are able to project planetary qualities across the chart into an empty house (or sign). For example, if one has their Sun in the fourth house, and the tenth house is an empty house, then their behavior at times may mirror that of a Sun in the tenth house person. This projective mechanism is not well studied, but it has been observed often enough to realize that it is a real and persistent phenomena. Not every person projects their cosmic energies. It is difficult to predict beforehand if someone may perform psychological projection. Be aware that it can happen and allow for it in chart interpretation practices. Boredom with life's situations seems to stimulate this projection process.

Houses may contain intercepted signs. *Intercepted signs* are signs of the zodiac which are completely contained within a house and do not occupy a house cusp. This primarily occurs when using a projection house system. For a sign to be intercepted the house has to be greater than 30 degrees in size, which means that it may already be somewhat increased in importance. When a sign is intercepted there is no cusp through which the sign's energies can exit. The energies of the sign are locked within that house. They lack an outlet or direction. Intercepted signs may provide unfocused energy.

The person who has an intercepted sign may have difficulty using this sign's energy in a consistent way. Without a channel to guide it the sign energy may tend to eddy and curl. The energy of the sign may come out in an unusual manner. If there is a planet (or planets) in the sign, then the planetary energies may also be difficult to focus within the person's life.

The advantage to this is that the person is able to study this locked-in energy at their unconscious leisure and thus gain a better understanding of the potentials that this energy offers. The disadvantage of an intercepted sign is that it causes an additional restlessness, and this restlessness is often difficult to cope with psychologically. It is easy to correct this problem, if in fact this is a problem. Move! Change your location to a place different from your birthplace. Move to a location where you can erect a "new" chart and the sign is no longer intercepted. Then the energy patterns can be released.

Hemispheric Emphasis and Planetary Patterns

The overall patterns the planets form in the whole chart have been described by Marc Edmund Jones, Dane Rudhyar, Charles Jayne, and others. The patterns formed by the planets within the different hemispheres and quadrants of the chart are important but incompletely researched. These patterns can show the primary emphasis and thrust of our lives through the categories that are represented For instance, a large number of planets (four or more in a house is a stellium) in the developmental quadrant may show that a person should not spend much time in introspection; a stellium in the introspection quadrant may show that this person works best alone, etc. If there are groupings of planets in a chart under study, then these groupings may tend to go left or right, or up or down. Appendix C of this book lists keyword associations for the astrological quadrants and hemispheres.

The Cycles of Life

One of the more important reasons you should study astrology is to gain an understanding of the different life cycles you experience. Astrology includes learning about these cycles, their symbology and importance. Each planet has its own cycle of movement through the chart. Each has its own rhythm. One of the better-studied cycles is the 29-year Saturn cycle that depicts responsibility and steadiness as it transits the chart quadrants; another is the twelve-year Jupiter cycle. The two-year

Mars cycle is less well studied, as is the yearly Sun cycle, or the monthly Moon cycle. Be aware that the chart is a symbolic diagram and shows you which category of life these cycles are activating. As, say, Uranus transits the inception quadrant you may be urged to look quite differently on life than when Uranus is transiting the adaptation quadrant.

Each cycle of life operates with an up or down pattern. This movement is neither good nor bad, but shows the interplay of the yin and yang sides of astrology. This up and down can be thought of like a sine wave. The sine wave is a periodic function that goes through its cycles in an up and a down fashion, showing completeness only when it has gone through its total cycle. There is an emphasis on rhythm and completion.

In a similar manner the cycles of life that the planets put us through may take us through the up and down cycles of life. This is neither good nor bad, but is simply a manifestation of the different parts of our existence. How would we be able to understand and appreciate the highs of life if we were not able to compare them with the lows? It is this interplay of the ups and the downs, the highs and the lows, the yin and the yang, which gives us the contrasting energies that power astrology and our lives. People have the freedom to pull either yin or yang energy from the planets whenever they choose to do so, and regardless of where they are in their planetary cycles.

Astrology is the study of cyclical energy flows in their every facet. The path and duration of our energy flow is presented symbolically through the chart. Like dreams (which contain personal symbols), it is through the study of astrological cycles that we can place our experiences into perspective. This book introduces you to some of the underlying but not too often explained facets of astrology. Through study of this work you should:

- Realize that houses are important and have an astrological role
- Learn more about house keywords and meanings
- Determine which house system to use and when
- Better understand the hemispheres and quadrants
- Gain a better overall understanding of astrology in general

This book is written to help you understand houses. This book is intended to be both a reference work and a working textbook. Read parts of this book for information, and use parts of this book as a reference.

Studies consistently show that planets placed near or about the different personal sensitive points in a chart are powerfully placed. Chart services can draw the rising and setting lines for your planets on a local or world map. These maps can quickly pinpoint where planets are conjunct the angles (i.e., the personal sensitive points) of a chart, and thus where you can find the individual planetary power point locations.

Much research and work remains to be done with the personal sensitive points, as well as with the quadrants, hemispheres, and houses. This book only begins to emphasize the importance that lies here. This book primarily serves as a bridge between keywords and astrological practice. Good word-smithing to you.

Houses of the Fourth Quadrant

Poetry for the Houses of the Fourth Quadrant

First House

    First off be with me when
    Myself to you does send
    Loud calls for all to see
    The more substantial me.

Second House

    Beyond comfort, value or money
    Inner worth is prized by many
    Through Heaven's gate try getting inside
    Having neglected your spiritual side.

Third House

    Twists of the cosmic eternals
    New ways of finding external
    Wisdom not learned from schools
    But streetwise tricks and rules.

An Overview of the First House

An Angular House of the Fourth Quadrant
Placed in the Left and Lower Hemispheres

The First House focuses on developing **personality**, **individua**lity, and **character**. It represents you! The First House helps you develop the self which you allow others to see, that part of you which faces the world, and the approach you take when confronting life's challenges. Through the First House you meet that part of yourself concerned with forming, presenting, and maintaining your **identity**. The First House describes how you may establish and present the most visible parts of you. If you have no planets in the First House does this mean you have no **personality**? No planets here mean that evolving a personality is not as important as developing another house's qualities. The First House helps mold your **attitudes toward self**, personality, or your **needs for recognition**. A person with an empty First House has just as many personal needs for self identification as a person with Neptune in the First House, who has just as many **selfhood needs as a person** with many planets in the First House, etc. Individual differences in First House emphasis show the inner importance placed on developing and maintaining day to day individuality.

Planets in a house add extra importance to that house by just being there. No planets in a house mean that no extra accent of that house's themes are sought. However, the sign on the house cusp, the planetary ruler(s) of that sign, aspects to the planetary ruler(s), and the natural planetary ruler(s) of the house still influence the development of that house's qualities. A person with only the planet Neptune in the First House may find that they have an unsure **image of who they are** as a person, or how they should demand personal recognition from others. A person with many planets in the First House may find that issues of defining who self is, how self is named or addressed, and the personal priorities which they ask of others, may dominate much of life's procedures.

The First House represents **your identity**, how you maintain your identity, how you project this identity, and how you shape and define self's identity. The First House symbolizes the enjoyment you get from taking **personal risks** while moving through life. These risks may involve an emphasis on personal appearance or grooming, motorcycle riding, assaults on another's territory or person, the use of daring colors while painting, etc. The form of **expression** is not as important as the emphasis of the **personal statement** which the activity chosen makes about your needs. Your definition, shape, and personal emphasis on the development of your persona starts with the First House.

The First House describes your approach to the various **personal style nuances** which you use to define self. Here you find your **mannerisms** astrologically depicted. How differently someone may approach life if they have Venus as a single planet in the First House, as opposed to a person who has their Mars conjunct Saturn in the First House. The person with Venus in the First House may find that life can be quite pleasant and relaxed while the person with the Mars conjunct Saturn in the First House may find that little is gained from life without constant struggle and battle against all. One person will define self by taking a relaxed approach to living while the other will view self as one who must constantly fight to carve their niche in life.

The First House focuses on your needs for **self-discovery** or **self-identification**. The risks taken with life, the emphasis placed on how self can be projected before others, or the personal noise you are willing to make about how others should notice your selfhood is shown here. There are many ways to project self into life. The work of **projecting and defining the person** who resides in your body is shown through the First House. Identifying what self is and how to work with this self is also a part of the First House.

The projection of self is only one part of First House functions. Another important part is the freedom allowed for **expressions of individuality**. It is through the First House that you begin to learn how to vary the expressions of what other people see as you. It is through the First House that you begin to experiment with the various **shades of expression** which you allow for yourself and then test how these begin to mold and define self to others. Such testing, definition, and redefinition may occupy an entire lifetime.

The development, nurturing, or abandoning of **habits, nuances, styles, appearance**, etc., are reflected by the First House. The First House represents the **style of personality** you define and develop for facing others and the world. We all come with various ideas on how to face life, and it is through the First House that we shape and mold these innate abilities into the **persona** we wish to present. The First House helps us define our unique characterizations. Developing and honing our unique **individual identity** is a constant lifelong pursuit.

First House keywords are filled with words of a Martian nature. Words like **guns, armor, male things, action, arousal, exploits, insertion, noise, might, your name** and its variations, etc. fill the keyword list for the First House. **Barren areas, empty places, wastelands**, and especially **the forefront of anything** dominate the First House word lists. Because of its connections with both Mars and Aries, the First House represents initial impressions both given and received. Therefore, words of this nature rightly belong to the First House, like the **front** bumper of a car, the **entryway** of a home, the start of individual events, the home team, etc. **Your overall health** is also shown here.

All houses are important in their own way. None is better or worse than another. None is more or less important than another. However, by its very nature the First House demands attention from all that you do in life before the other houses should be considered. "**Me first**" really sums up the First House.

Horary or Electional Ideas

- accidents, the likelihood of actions upon one's life
- activities in one's own interest
- anger
- appearance
- body, one's
- danger (peril)
- dangerous activities
- desolate places
- difficulty
- first person, the (grammatical)
- health (in general)
- here
- identity
- life's circumstances
- my things or rights
- myself
- new venture
- personal interests
- personal involvements
- plaintiff, the
- present, the
- present circumstances
- querent (questioner)
- self, the
- today
- us
- we
- you, yourself

Things

- absent unrelated person
- acceleration
- accent (emphasis)
- access (admittance)
- access (entryway)
- accessibility
- accident (chance)
- accidents, liability to
- acid
- act (deed)
- act (process of doing)
- action (effort)
- action (movement)
- activation
- activity (movement)
- activity (undertaking)
- address (location)
- admittance (entry)
- affair (event)
- affirmation
- aggravation
- aggression (assault)
- air (character)
- alarm (warning)
- amazement
- ammunition
- anatomy
- anger
- animal spirits
- animosity
- annoyance
- anonymous letter
- anterior thing
- antidote
- anvil
- approach (mannerism)
- architecture
- armaments
- arms (ordnance)
- arousal (wakening)
- arrivals
- arson
- artillery
- aspect (look)
- assault (striking)
- assertion (claim)
- astonishment (amazement)
- attempt (try)
- attendance (presence)
- attention (heed)
- attitude (posture)
- attribute
- audacity
- audio-visual displays
- availability
- awakening (arousal)
- axe
- bad taste, in
- badge
- barrenness
- battery (striking)
- battle
- bayonet
- beat (strike)
- beating
- bedlam
- belligerence
- big bang theory
- bill (bird's)
- bite (animal)
- bite (insect)
- bloodshed
- blow (a striking)
- blow-out (at a wellhead)
- blow-out (big win)
- body of a vehicle
- boldness
- bolt (crossbow's)
- bolt (mad dash)
- bomb (explosive)
- bomber (aircraft)
- bonnet
- boo-boo (hurt)
- boom (noise)
- bother (annoyance)
- bothersome thing
- bout (fight)
- bravery
- brawl
- breach (violation)

Things Continued
break (rupture)
breakage
breaking in (interruption)
bug (bother)
bug (insect)
bugle
bullet
burning
butchery
butting in
buzzing sounds
callous actions
callous words
cannon
career change
cast (appearance)
catastrophe
catch-22 situation
cauterization
certainty (free of doubt)
challenge
chance (accident)
chance (risk)
chance (try)
chase
chivalry (gallantry)
circumstances (in general)
circumstances beyond control
circumstantial developments
claim (charge)
claim (maintain)
clairvoyance
clamor
clash
cleaver
close call
club (weapon)
coarseness
combat
combativeness
coming (arrival)
commencement
commitments, unwilling to make
competitive posture, a
conflagration
confronting (anything)
constructive force
contour (outline)
conviction (strong belief)
counteragent
courage
crank (handle)
creative visualization
creature
cross (shows anger)
crudeness
cruelty
curse (profanity)
dagger
danger (peril)
dare (provocation)
daring (boldness)
dawn (inception)
dawn (sunrise)
daybreak
deal (transaction)
death of a pet
debut
deed (feat)
demand (command)
desire for action
desolation
dial
dictate (order)
diction
differences (disputes)
difficulty (laboriousness)
difficulty (trouble)
din (noise)
discharge (detonation)
discomfort (ache)
discord (musical)
discovery, the process of
dismay (alarm)
distemper
distinctiveness
distraction (madness)
disturbances
disturbances, origins of
double-time speed
draft (military)
dress (appearance)
drive (advance)
drought (aridity)
drums
dryness
duel
dynamite
eagerness
east, the direction of
edge (blade)
effect (operation)
effort (exertion)
effrontery
ejection
ember (spark)
emergency
emphasis
emptiness
enclosure (insert)
end of career matters
end of tenth house parent
enemies, overcoming
energy (personal)
enterprise (drive)
entry (approach)
entry (way in)
episode (event)
event (happening)
excitability
excitement
execution (accomplishes)
exertion
exploit (feat)
explosion (detonation)
explosion (outburst)
explosives
expression (look)
expression (style)
expressions, facial

expulsion
face (visage)
face, what you
feat
feature (attribute)
feature (visage)
feel, sense of
fetching
fight
fighter (airplane)
find (discovery)
fire (flames)
firearm
firecracker
fireworks
first aid
fist fighting
flame(s)
flesh (physical nature)
flood control
food spill
foolhardiness
force (wrest)
form (shape)
forward motion
foundation (founding)
frame (physique)
fray (quarrel)
fresh (new) thing
freshman (grade)
gauntlet (challenge)
gavel
gaze
gesture (indication)
glance
glimpse
go (attempt)
graphology
greetings
grenade
grit (guts)
group acting as an entity
gun
gunpowder

gunshot
guts (audacity)
hail (shout)
hairbreadth
hallmark (distinguishing trait)
halter (rope)
handgun
handshake (greeting)
handwriting
happening (occurrence)
hardening
haste
hat
hatchet
hazard (danger)
head (in front)
head (source)
high stakes
hit (blow)
hit (contact)
hollowness
home team
horary astrology
horn (antler)
horrible thoughts
hot things
how others see you
identification
identity crisis
impact
impetus
impression (effect)
impression (imprint)
impression (mark)
impressions made on others
imprint (mark)
impudence
impulse (sudden action)
impulse (urge)
impulsiveness
inauguration
incendiary material
incident (event)
incineration

indication (marker)
indication (signal)
indicator
indoctrination
infectious substances
inferno
inflow
influx
infringement
ingratitude
initiating (starting)
initiation of projects
initiative
inoculation
insertion
insult
intentions
interruption
introduction
intrusion
iron (eliminates wrinkles)
irritant
irritation
jack-knife
jumping
key (for lock)
kicking
knife
knocking
label (brand name)
label (descriptive phrase)
label (for commercial recordings)
label (name)
label (tag)
lance
launching
lead (front position)
leash
length of life
life
lighter (cigarette)
lightning
line (mark)

listening
live steam
locale (position)
location (whereabouts)
location, changing
logo
loud things
lunge (rush)
madness (anger)
male things
manipulation (usage)
mar (scratch)
march (hike)
margin (narrowness)
mark (sign)
marker
martial arts
masculinity
match (light)
matrix (die)
matter (predicament)
medium (environment)
meeting (encounter)
meeting (introduction)
might (power)
milestone (epoch)
missile (projectile)
missile (rocket)
mockery
mold (shape)
motion (movement)
mouthpiece (on an instrument)
move (movement)
movement (activity)
movement (motion)
mug (face)
munitions
muzzle (face)
muzzle of a gun
name(s)
narrowness
nastiness
new projects
new venture

nick (cut)
nitroglycerine
noise
nomenclature
notice (attention)
notification
now
nuisance (bother)
oath (cursing)
object (anything perceived)
obnoxiousness
occasion (occurrence)
occurrence
offense (attack)
one-sidedness
onrush
onset (beginning)
opener
opening (initiation)
operation (action)
opportunity (self created)
ordnance
origin (birth)
outbreak (burst)
outburst
outcry
outline (contour)
outline (shape)
outside chance
outsides (exterior)
overture (introduction)
overture (proposal)
paddle (oar)
paddle (used for hitting)
pain, causing
pass (toss)
penetration
perforation
personal appearance
personal space
pest (destructive plant)
phenomena (incident)
physiognomy
pinch (squeeze)

pistol
poker (metal rod)
position (place)
position (situation)
postmark
potency
powder (explosive)
power (strength)
predicament
present, the
pressure (urgency)
pressure vessel
production (introduction)
projectile
propellant
propulsion
provocation (cause)
pugnacity
puncture (hole)
pursuit (chasing)
quivering (trembling)
race (running)
racket (noise)
racket (paddle)
rap (knock)
rash action
rashness
rattle (clatter)
razor
razzing
reaction (response)
readiness
reading thoughts
reality
reception (greeting)
recklessness
report (detonation)
response (action)
reverberation
rifle
rip
rising
risk (peril)
road grader

roaring
roll (drumbeat)
roll of thunder
rough spot
rough-housing
roughness (quality)
rowdiness
rule (guide)
running
rupture (break)
saber
salute (firecracker)
salute (greeting)
saw (tool)
scalpel
scene
scientific equipment
scientific work
scissors
scorching
scraper
scraping
scratch
scratching
scream
screw (propeller)
scythe
seal (mark)
shaking (quivering)
shape (form)
sharp objects
sharpness
shears
ship at sea
shooting(s)
shouting
show and tell
shut-out (big win)
sight
sign in
sign on
significance (meaning)
siren
situation (location)

situation (plight)
situation (status)
skewer
sleepwalking
slicing (cutting)
sliver
smash (collision)
snag (jagged tear)
snap (abrupt closing)
snap (as in football)
snare (difficulty)
snoring
sound
spark
spatula
spear
speed
splatter
spoor (track)
sports, competitive
spring season, the
springboard
spur (cowboy's)
spurt of activity, a
squeak (sound)
squeegee
squeeze (handclasp)
stab (attempt)
stab (lunge)
stamp (characteristic)
stamping (pounding)
stamping (tramping)
starting
starts
state of a ship at sea
steel
stimulant (energizer)
stimulus (activator)
strife
stroke (blow)
style (mannerism)
subliminal perceptions
surface (outer face)
surge

sword
symbol (mark)
tag (marker)
tag (name)
taking chances
tang (strong taste)
tank (military)
tasks involving risk
taunt (jeer)
tear (rip)
tears of pain
teasing (taunting)
telephone number
temper (anger)
temper (disposition)
tenor (meaning)
tension (stretching)
theme (motif)
thermodynamics
things you begin
thoughtlessness
threshold (beginning)
threshold (point of action)
thrill (excitement)
throw (toss)
thrust (assault)
thrust (shove)
thrust (stab)
thunder
ticket (tag)
tickling
tidings
title (name)
TNT
topic (theme)
torpedo
toss (cast)
trace (sign)
track (mark)
trademark
trail (track)
travel of children
travesty (mockery)
tread (footfall)

trembling (shaking)
trim (cutting)
try (endeavor)
try (trial)
try out (attempt)
tug (pull at)
turn (chance)
turn (deed)
turn (shock)
turn on (arousal)
undertaking (endeavor)
undertaking a task (doing it)
unruliness
urge (drive)
vacancy (emptiness)
vacancy (opening)

valor
vanguard
velocity
veneer (facing)
view (look)
view (vision)
vigilance (alertness)
vigor (energy)
violence
visible event
vital issue
vividness
vociferousness
void (emptiness)
volatility
volume (loudness)

voraciousness
walking
warning (alarm)
waterfall
wave (rush)
wave (salutation)
waving motion
weapon
weed
whine
wild thing
window (for re-entry)
work with sharp instruments
zest

Psychological Qualities

abruptness
alertness
allocated space
appearance
assertion of self
assertive attitude
attention, focus of
attention span
attitude (disposition)
awareness of surroundings
badness
character
characteristics
completeness, a lack of
condition, physical
confronting (anything)
confronting obstacles
consciousness
demeanor
discovering of self
disposition
emergence
emptiness, feelings of
fights going asleep
fortitude
frame of mind (attitude)

free will
freedom of action
gait (manner of walking)
general well-being
habits, personal
harshness
health
identification
identity
idiosyncrasy (peculiarity)
image you give out, the
impatience
impression one makes
including self
individuality
insistence
intentions
interests
liberty
life
manifestation (indication)
mannerisms
me, sense of
meanness
myself
one (you)

ornery disposition, an
outlook
outward show
participating
particularity
personal affairs
personal interests
personal outlook
personal prowess
personality
perspective on one's life
physical you, the
plight, current
pose (mannerism)
posture (attitude)
presence, one's
pressure (distress)
pronunciation
propensity
public affairs, your
rancor
recrimination
representation of self
rights, one's
roughness of character
self, the

self-assertion	self-preservation	tone (attitude)
self-confidence	spirit, your	traits
self-discovery	state (frame of mind)	urgency
self-hood	state of mind	viability
self-image	stimulation	well being, your overall
self-improvement	tastes, personal	yourself
self-involvement	temperament	

Occupations or Person Types

aggressor	graphologist	pathfinder
ambulance driver	haberdasher	perpetrator
armament manufacturer	handwriting expert	person, a
artillery man	harbinger	pest (nuisance)
barber	instigator	pioneer
barrister	interloper	pitcher
bomber	intruder	plaintiff, the
bully	iron worker	play maker
butcher	landlord	querent (questioner)
claimant	loud person	racer
defender	males	receptionist
director	men	steel worker
doorman	men, ages 25 to 35	stuntperson
fighter	newcomer	uncultured person
fire eater	order giver	warrior
gladiator	participant	women from the past

Places

abandoned place	barren place	lobby
ammunition depot	butcher shop	location, your
ante-chamber	desert (wasteland)	millinery
anterior place	desolate places	public place, a
arid land	dry wash	surroundings
armory	front line	vacant property
arsenal	gangway	wasteland
barbershop	gate (entryway)	where you spend your time
barren ground	incinerator	

Family Members or Relations

child, fifth	grandmother (maternal)	self, the
family patriarch(s)	great grandchildren	you
grandfather (maternal)	niece or nephew by marriage	

Mundane Ideas

attitudes of the people	civil violence	country, the
buyer (in an exchange)	corporate position	department of defense

Mundane Ideas Continued
disappointing earnings
domestic considerations
domestic interests
home front, the
identity, the country's
interior affairs

living conditions in general
methods of business
nation, the
nation's capitol
nation's constitution
national lifestyles
neighborhood politics

population
regime, the
republic, the
short selling
state, the
tax records

Parts of Our Body

adrenal gland
arteries
blushing
body, one's
chewing
chin
complexion
decapitation
eye color
eyes
face
flesh (tissue)
forehead

hair on head
head
health (in general)
hearing
lips
mouth
muscle system
muscles (in general)
muscular system (in general)
nail (finger)
pallor
physical body
physical constitution

physique
pimple
pore
posture (bearing)
reflexes
retina
scalp
seeing, sense of
shivering
sinus
skull

Afflictions or Diseases

abrasion (scrape)
ache
acid body condition
acne
ague
baldness
blindness
blister
bruise
bullet wound
burn
callous
complexion problems
concussion
cut
deafness
disfiguring illness
dizziness

encephalitis
exhaustion, heat
facial injuries
fever(s)
gunshot wounds
hair lip
head injury
headache
heat exhaustion
heat rash
hemorrhage
high blood pressure
infection
injury (self-inflicted)
insect bite
laceration
lisp
male disorders

measles
mouth ulcerations
neuralgia
pain, having
physical abnormality
puncture wound
rash
rupture
scald
scalp infection
scar
scrape
sharp ache
sore
stab wound
vertigo
wind burn
wound

Colors

carmine
fiery red

infrared
red

Gems or Minerals

corundum	metals (in general)	spinel
iron	ruby	
magnesium	sapphire	

Animals

animal (creature)	boar	grizzly bear
anteater	chimpanzee	polar bear
ape	cock	ram
badger	critter	rooster
bear	gnat	

Mythical Figures or Constellation Names

Ares (the warrior)	Hercules (warrior)	Ursa Major (great bear)
Argus (the adventurers)	Mars	Ursa Minor (smaller bear
Aries	Toucana (toucan)	

Parts of an Organization

board of directors	lobby	organization's image, the
company, the	location	receptionist
executive board	organization, the	scientific staff

Industry Categories

abrasives	ammunition Manufacture	firearms & Ammunition
alarm systems	bodyguards	

Health and Fitness

security services	steel (integrated)	transportation (ambulances)
steel (general)	training (health and fitness)	

Parts of an Automobile

body	front bumper	starter system
body ding	front grill	throttle
door	horn	
driver's seat	ignition system	

Parts of a House

design (shape)	entryway	reception room
door	foyer	stoop
doorway	front door	threshold (gate)
entrance	lobby	vestibule

Parts of a Ship

armament(s)	bridge	fire control (for guns) gear
bow	conn	fire power

fo'c'sl   magazine (armament storage)   starboard side
fore deck   pilot house
gangway   propeller

An Overview of the Second House

A Succedent House of the Fourth Quadrant
Placed in the Left and Lower Hemispheres

Through the Second House you become concerned with the **value** of what you receive, seek, or earn in life. Value has many subtle shades of meaning, all expressed through the astrological nuances of the Second House. The **benefit** you get from the **material things** you receive or accumulate, the **value of money earned**, the way to **keep** and **increase** (or decrease) this money while it is in your possession, the value to you of **money as a medium of exchange**, the value placed on **the personal role of finances**, etc., are all Second House issues.

The Second House represents the value you place on your **personal and psychological worth**. It is difficult to accumulate things and be happy with possessions if you find no happiness with your inner or personal worth. The personal **comforts** you allow yourself from the **finances** and **possessions** you seek or acquire are Second House concerns. It is one thing to receive **compensation** for services and it is quite another to be **satisfied** with the place and lot in life which these allow. Shown here are both the value received for effort expended and the **personal value** placed on the services rendered or given to others.

The Second House invites you to examine the balance between **your needs for materiality and your needs for spirituality**. Materiality involves the ability to take ideas or values, make them workable for others, and receive compensation for efforts done. How you let **attachment to material things** affect your daily life and yet not impede **your spiritual progress** is a Second House concern. You must be able to balance your wants for material things with the inner happiness you get from having these things. The Second House serves to increase your awareness about having material possessions and the **medium of exchange** needed to get these possessions, i.e., money for effort expended. It also urges you to realize the enhanced **personal worth** you can receive for **inner happiness gained from spiritual progress**. Neither compensation nor material things are bad -- but giving up spiritual progress to obtain material things is short sighted.

The Second House serves to either **increase or decrease spiritual involvement** in the material world. Some persons are so rooted to spiritual thoughts and values that they are oblivious to the simple acts of living together within society. The Second House shows these persons how to **bring spiritual ideas into a more harmonious adjustment with daily needs**. Others are so rooted in the material world that they are unable to recognize that they too are spiritual beings and must eventually return to their spiritual roots. The Second House invites them to achieve a balance between the extremes of spirituality and materiality. Unbalancing these extremes may bring circumstances which call for them to readjust their lifestyle.

The Second House helps increase your awareness about the importance of **financial clout**. But, financial influence in the material world does not buy spiritual leverage in an afterlife. Therefore, the Second House encourages you to take a look at your material growth and to place your ideas in balance with your feelings about your need for **spiritual growth**. You can gauge your progress in each category: the self-esteem you build through the works you produce and efforts you undertake to become a balanced person. If you can measure some growth in your personal happiness while maintaining material growth, then you might have met an important Second House challenge.

Basic internal feelings about the **ownership**, **borrowing**, and **lending of personal possessions** are also shown here. Ideas about the ownership or possession of material things, **attitudes about property** which others have, your **identity through the goods or things** which you crave or own, and how you inwardly feel about the **accumulation and use of these things** are all matters of the Second House. The Second House helps you build on your sense of **material discretion**.

The care which you give your possessions, the **care** which you show other people's possessions, and the care which others show your possessions are shown through Second House activity.

The Second House also represents your ability to **relax** and **take comfort** in the material world. **Relaxation** is an important concept in life. Rushing from one event to another is the realm of the First House. The Second House asks that you take stock of what you want, where you are going, and what you will do to relax and enjoy yourself after your arrival. The Second House represents the inner value you place on material things, but it also concerns itself with your desires to use your material means to increase your **comfort**. It is one thing to acquire financial or material possessions, but it is quite another to feel comfortable with them. Without some balance between materiality and spirituality you may not be able to fully enjoy the richness of this house.

The Second House reflects **benefits received for services offered**. Some people receive money or status through birthright, some through hard work, but all try to earn it somehow. The Second House represents your attitudes toward acquiring and using material resources. It represents your **recognition of materiality**, and the balance you seek to satisfy the pull between materiality and spirituality. The Second House asks that you explore the benefits found from gaining **financial insight** while guarding your innate spirituality.

Traditionally the Second House rules **money** and **finances**. The Second House invites you to closely and personally examine the **richness of self-developed appreciation**, the benefits of taking a rest during the hectic pace of life, and the enjoyment of the finer things in life such as **good music, a comfortable easy chair**, or **an expensive home**.

Horary or Electional Ideas

advantage	future, the	personal possessions
benefit, things of	gems	relaxation
ease	gratitude	salary
evaluation (valuing)	income	size
expenses	investments, nonspeculative	slowing down
finances	livelihood	survival
financial affairs, handling of	monetary gain	them
financial investing	money	tomorrow
financial loss	money matters	
financial matters	negotiable assets	

Things

ability to handle funds	assessment (appraisal)	bulk (size)
accession (appeasement)	asset (benefit)	bunk (bed)
accessory (adornment)	asset (property)	burden (encumbrance)
account (financial)	asset, liquid or monetary	burnt items
acknowledgment (gratitude)	asset, negotiable	cake
actuality	avarice	calm
adornment (jewelry)	awkwardness	cameo (broach)
adornment, articles of	ballad	candy
adultery, prolonged	band (musical)	capital
advance (pre-payment)	bank account	carbohydrates
advantage (benefit)	bank deposit	card suit: diamonds
advantage (edge)	bank note	career, money from
affinity (partiality)	banking	career of children
affluence	bargain (deal)	carpet
affordability	bed	cash
air (tune)	bedding	cash box
album (recording)	belongings (goods)	cash register
allotment	benefit, things of	chattel
allowance (salary)	benevolence (kindliness)	check (financial draft)
amount (quantity)	billfold	check book
aplomb (composure)	biology	checking account
appeal (charm)	blinders	chimes
appeasement	blossom	clairaudience
appliance (prosthesis)	bolster (pillow)	clothes as possessions
appreciation (gratitude)	bonus	coins
approbation (praise)	boost (praise)	cologne
appropriation (allocation)	borrowing	comfort (ease)
approval (acceptance)	bow (in hair)	compliment
approval (regard)	bracelet	condiments
aroma	branch of a tree	congratulations

Things Continued
content (form)
content (gist)
content (volume)
context, things taken in
cork
cosmetic surgery
cosmetics
cost of an item
courtesy
covetousness
cradle
cuff link
currency
cushion (pillow)
cut (a piece)
death of someone inquired about
decorations
decorative objects
defuse (calm)
degree of involvement
delicacy
denomination (value)
deodorant
deposit (down payment)
dessert
dimension (size)
dirt (soil)
dollars
dormancy
dough (money)
draft (payment)
dream diary
dream interpretation
drift (snow)
drifting (in water)
droop (sag)
durability
earnings
earrings
earth, the
ease (comfort)
ease (composure)

ease (relaxation)
easy chair
effects (property)
eggs
endearment
enormity (size)
enrichment
envy (jealousy)
equanimity (calmness)
equity (assets)
estimate (evaluation)
evaluation (assessment)
evaluation (valuing)
existence (actuality)
expenditure
expense account
expenses
extent (size)
fare (price)
fecundity
femininity
fertility
fertilization
fertilizer
finances
financial assistance
financial condition, one's
financial incentive
financial matters
financial transaction
fine living
fiscal matters
flavoring
flowers
flush (rich)
fondness (liking)
fragrance
frieze (decoration)
fruitfulness
fullness
furniture
furniture, heavy
gains through science
garland

gauge (evaluation)
gems
gentility
gentleness
gifts you give
girth
gist
glucose
gluttony
goods (possessions)
grant (allotment)
grass
gratitude
hairdo
hammock
handbag
hang (droop)
harmonica
harp
having
heavy object
herbs (in general)
hi-fi
homeopathy
honey
hood (blinder)
horticulture
hotel stay at a distance
humming sounds
idleness
ignorance (illiteracy)
ignorance (unfamiliarity)
illiteracy
immaturity
immediate future
impregnation
inaction
incense
income
income, ability to add to
income, efforts to increase
income, source of
indolence
indulgence

inertia
inflammability
inflexibility
innocence
insulator, electrical
intrinsic value
investing
investment(s)
investments, nonspeculative
items for practical comfort
jewelry (in general)
jewelry as wealth
keyboard (music)
kindness
large tree
lay (rest position)
layout (expense)
laziness
leaf (foliage)
lending
lichen
lingerie
liquidity (financial)
listlessness
litter (bed)
livelihood Income)
locket
log (tree)
lullaby
lumber
luxurious things
luxury (comfort)
luxury (wealth)
lyrics (words)
magnitude (size)
make-up
march (tune)
market value
material (possession)
material (raw stuff)
material possessions
material resources
materialism
materialization

mattress
meaning (substance)
means (funds)
megalomania
melody
merit (substance)
mild things
mirror (vanity object)
moderation
momentum
money
money matters
money others owe to you
money supply, personal
monitor (sensor)
movable possessions
murmur (soft sound)
music
musical instrument
nap
necklace
nectar
new place of residence
nightgown
nitrogen
node (on musical string)
note (currency)
object of value
odor
ointment
one of a kind item
opulence (riches)
orchestra
order (calm)
organ (musical instrument)
ornament
ornamentation
outlay (expenditure)
ownership
pacification
packaging
packing (stuffing)
pad (bed)
padding (cushioning)

paraphernalia (furnishings)
pastry
payment
payment received
pecuniary affairs
perfume
personal belongings
personal finances
personal property
personal things
personal wealth
pertinacity
phonograph
phonograph record
piano
picket (stake)
pillow
pin (brooch)
plant (flora)
plant (organic)
plant life
pocketbook
portable possession
possession
possession, movable
postage
postage stamp
potential action
precious possession
preciousness (value)
price
price tag
proceeds (profit)
profit (compensation)
profit (gain)
promissory note
property (non-real estate)
property, movable
prosthesis (artificial appendage)
purse (pocketbook)
quantity (amount)
quantum (amount)
quilt

Things Continued
rare wood
receipt (profit)
recompense
reek (smell)
reel (dance)
refreshments
refund
relaxant
release from tension
relief (easement)
rent (fee)
report card
repose
resin
resonance
resources (funds)
rest (relax)
rest (remain motionless)
rest (sleep)
return (election result)
return (profit from investment
revenue
rhapsody
riches
ring (jewelry)
roll (coast)
rouge
royalty (commission)
sachet
safe (strongbox)
safe deposit box
sag
salary
salary received
sap
sapling
savings
scale (musical)
scarf
score (musical)
seaplane
seasoning
seat (chair)

secret, sibling's
securities (bonds, etc.)
seed
serenade
serenity
significant thing
silk
sitting
size
sleep
sleeping posture
slide (coast)
slip (undergarment)
slowing down
slowness
slumber
smile
smooth things
smoothness
smothering (inundate)
snooze
sofa
soft item
softly curved object
softness
soil preparation
solid
solidity
sonata
song
soul music
speaker (hi-fi)
spice
spore
sprig
sprout
stake (involvement)
stake (post)
stereo equipment
stereo music
stick
stillness
stipend
stock (inventory)

stoutness
strength
stroke (caress)
stumbling
stupor
subculture
subsidy
subsistence
subsistence levels
substance (essence)
substance (matter)
substance (merit)
substance (possessions)
substance (solidity)
sugar
supplemental income
support (upkeep)
surety
sustenance (economic)
swallowing
sweetness (taste)
sweets
symphony
syrup
tag (bill)
take (proceeds)
tangible assets
tea dance
tedium
temperance (moderation)
tenacity
texture
thickening
things of beauty
thud (dull sound)
thump (thud)
tie (necktie)
timber
timbre
tip (gratuity)
tiredness
tomorrow
tone (musical)
touch (texture)

tranquility	value (expensive)	wealth
travelers check	vanity (make-up case)	wealth, father's
treasure	vegetation	wealth, having
tree	velvet	weight (bulk)
tune	vine	whistle
tuning fork	vineyard	whistling
unfamiliarity	viscosity	whittling
upholstery	voice (tenor, baritone, etc.)	wickerwork
use (convenience)	volley (salvo)	winnings
use (worth)	volume (quantity)	wood (in general)
useful things	volume (size)	wood pile
utility (convenience)	wages	worldly possessions
valuable	wallet	worth, current
valuable thing	waltz	writer's block
valuation	wave (curl)	yield (rate of return)

Psychological Qualities

adequacy	overindulgence	significance
aesthetic sense	ownership, attitude about	speech, the quality of
complacency	personal importance	stubbornness (unbending)
completeness	personal values	survival, need for
considerateness	physical comfort	sustained efforts
contentment (satisfaction)	placidity	sweetness (kindness)
desirability	pleasing others	temerity
earning power	politeness	tenderness
endurance	poverty, the fear of	thoughtfulness
entanglement	recover ability to	utility
financial needs	relaxation	utilizing
goodness	satisfaction	value (merit)
gratitude	satisfaction, receiving	valuing
languor	self-esteem sense of	worth, self
materiality	self-indulgence	worthiness
money, attitude toward	self-worth	
obstinacy	sensuous enjoyment	

Occupations or Person Types

assayer	composer	epicure
assessor	confectioner	evaluator
bank teller	connoisseur	faith healer
banker	cosmetician	financial advisor
bard	dancer	financier
biologist	dealer in ornaments	florist
cashier	decorator	flower grower
clothing designer	digger	furniture maker

Occupations or Person Types Continued

glutton
gourmet
immature person
investment banker
lady
lass
lender
loafer
lyricist
maiden
make-up artist
money lender
money maker
muscular persons
musician
orchard worker
perfumer
piano tuner
retired person
singer
song writer
spendthrift
survivalist
teller, bank
voice trainer
women, young
woodworker
young people (age 20 to 30)

Places

apiary
bank (depository)
beehive
botanical garden
concession stand
credit union
dance hall
farmland
florist shop
flower garden
forest
grove (thicket)
hedgerow
hothouse
jungle
orchard
park (preserve)
place where money is kept
rain forest
thicket
treasury, the
vault (safe)
virgin land
waiting room
where money is kept
woodland

Family Members or Relations

step-sibling (father's side)

Mundane Ideas

assets of the people
banking house
banking system, the
bond (security)
business finances
capitalism
cash flow
costs
credit (allowance)
credit union
currency
earning capacity
finances, competitor's
financial institution
long term appreciation
mint (makes money)
money market
negotiable assets
poll, result of
price stability
public investment
revenue
securities
treasure
treasury, the
venture capital
wages
wealth

Parts of Our Body

adenoids
appendage, artificial
artificial limb
blood cholesterol
bone marrow
cheeks
dimples
ears
larynx
limb, artificial
natural beauty
neck
nose
nosebleed
palate
pharynx
plasma (blood parts)
sensations
sense perceptions
senses
smell: sense of
taste
throat
thymus gland

tonsils
touch: sense of
veins

venous blood
vocal cords
voice organs

windpipe

Afflictions or Diseases

arteriosclerosis
bad breath
calcium balance
clumsiness

goiter
hearing problem
mumps
scrofula

sore throat
throat infection
tonsillitis

Colors

azure
blue

greenish blue
red-orange

sea blue
sea green

Gems or Minerals

azurite
chrysocholla
copper

dioptase
gypsum
malachite

olivine
peridot
precious stone

Animals

bee
bull
helpful biological insect

mule
ox
rabbit

sloth

Mythical Figures or Constellation Names

Cadmos (musician)
Faunus
Gaia

Leto (gentleness)
Lyra (lyre)
Orpheus (musician & poet)

Pan
Taurus (bull)

Parts of an Organization

benefits for employees
cashier's office

credit union
treasurers office

treasury, the

Industry Categories

acoustical materials
banks (commercial)
banks (money center)
contractors (landscape)
currency exchanges
financial (miscellaneous)
financial services

florists
forest products
forestry services
gardening services
heavy duty trucks
jewelry (appraisal)
landscaping services

money management services
Musicians/Orchestras
Savings and Loan
Thrift Institutions
Yard Design and Maintenance

Parts of an Automobile

padding on the dashboard
seats, the

upholstery, the
value retention

Houses of the Fourth Quadrant

Parts of a House

basic raw materials	construction methods	furniture
bedroom	decorations	garden, flower
boudoir	furnishings	shrubbery

Parts of a Ship

bunk	hoist

An Overview of the Third House

A Cadent House of the Fourth Quadrant

Placed in the Left and Lower Hemispheres

The **Third House** shows your **inner cleverness** at examining and using the various **angles** that life presents. These angles can offer the personal latitude, space, or adjustments which you may come to feel are your right. Angles involve not only points of view but also focus and perspective. **Playing the angles** is a common term which denotes living life close to the edge, or getting more from your lot than others. A basic concept behind the Third House is discovering that there are **few limits** to what you should accept in life.

The Third House traditionally represents **short journeys, transportation, brothers and sisters**, and **early education**. But, short journeys to where? Brothers and sisters in what context? Early education is only the start of continuing education—or the learning that life has many different faces. Should we ever stop learning about that? Should we ever stop investigating the different **possibilities** or angles of life which we can **twist or turn** to our advantage? Not if we pay attention to the way we wish to use our Third House energies.

Life can be difficult. Consider the lot of a brooding bird, nesting from four to nine eggs. When the first hatchling appears and demands food, the parents feed and nurture the youngster's demands. The youngster learns and grows from its insistence. As its siblings hatch over the coming hours or days the first born enjoys the advantage of the early special care and feeding. Its strength increases as it **learns** to **communicate** its demands. Should food become short or the parents fail in their caring, then the oldest and strongest have the best chance to survive the crisis. Cruel as this may seem it is raw nature in action. Simple and basic as this story is, it illustrates the Third House in action. When considering survival who should be placed first: me or **siblings** or **visitors**?

Humankind generally takes a kinder view of life than starving creatures. Through our educational systems in America we are taught to treat all beings equally. However, issues between **brothers and sisters** will still arise. It is from our **siblings**, if any, that we receive our first social lessons, our first lessons about sharing, our first lessons about the place of "me." The process of **early education** begins, well, early. Often the Third House is confused with formal education, but many people (or animals) have no such luxury. The Third House requests that we **learn, try, repeat, relearn**, and then **travel to learn** again. Those born without siblings learn from others who represent the concept of sibling to them. The Third House influence doesn't stop on technicalities.

Astrologers have expended much energy trying to explain the differences between Third House **"short" journeys** and Ninth House "long" journeys. Let the Third House represent what we each learn from our daily encounters with life, and let the Ninth House represent the formal schooling or education for which we obtain official recognition. In America, such formal recognition is not generally given until the first graduation exercise occurs at the end of high school. Other countries have similar systems of reward, but again, usually not until more basic skills have been acquired. In America today basic "reading, writing and 'rithmatic" represent **expected skills**, and it is these expected skills, whatever form they may take for the culture or circumstance involved, that are ruled by the Third House.

The Third House represents **communication** in all forms. Think about the analogy of the nested hatchlings. Not the loudest, but the one which communicated most effectively receives the first food. In modern society effective communication has different shades of meaning Hatchlings don't care about writing **term papers** or doing **homework** for **learning lessons**, but school children do. A well placed truth can receive more attention than thousands of babbled **words**. The needs and **communications** as expressed by the Third House can and do vary from situation to situation. The Third House urges **adaptability** within all present situations. But current situations are meant to change. **Devious twists and turns** can appear through the Third House.

There is a **mental** side to the Third House due to its association with the zodiacal sign of Gemini and the yang side of Mercury, its ruling planet. It takes much **mental adaptability** to examine the various **twists of fate** which can be created for your needs. Again, referring to the nested hatchlings, you can realize that it is not just the volume of noise which gets the first food, but the **cleverness** with which the noise gains the provider's attention. Similarly, the Third House tells us that it is not what you write or speak but the appropriateness of those communications which will make you remembered, cherished, or fed.

Beyond **journeys, transportation, siblings,** or **education,** the Third House represents your capacities for **adapting**. It also represents your capacity for **duplicating**. Adaptation involves the use of mental powers to make the most of current situations. It is through your **mental adaptability** that you are able to meet and face all which life demands. Duplicating is the "angle" which allows you to recognize that no work presented needs to be completely original.

The Third House also calls for a use of **cleverness**, and this ties to similar concepts like **thinking, reasoning,** etc. which are also Third House related. Other keywords indicate the use of **wit, repartee,** things having to do with the **distribution of goods** (like **transportation, vehicles,** etc.), **distribution systems** (anything from **down spouts** to **trucking routes**), alibis (which are another form of angle), and **weather**. The word lists are quite long and varied—but isn't **variety** just one of the many concepts the Third House portrays?

Horary or Electional Ideas

adaptability	information related questions	short distance travel
angles	inquisitiveness	short trips
by-laws	learning	sibling
car	letters (mail)	similarity
circumventing	memory	travel, alone
cleverness	mental efforts	visiting
communication(s)	message	visitors
distribution	neighbor	visits
education	neighborhood	writing(s)
explanation	point of view	
focus	schooling	

Things

abbreviations	amorphousness	auto trip
absurdity (nonsense)	androgyny	autobiography
accent (speech)	android	autograph
accession (joining)	anecdote	automobile
acclimatization	angle (bend)	avenue (roadway)
account (reason)	angle (new twist)	avenue (way)
account (report)	angle (point of view)	babble
accustomization	animation	back up (copy)
acerbity	annotation	background taken for granted, a
act (pretense)	announcement	bait
acumen	answer (reply)	band (rubber)
acute angles	antics	bargaining
ad-lib	application (request)	barter
adaptability	approach (access)	basic education
adaptation	approach (draw closer)	bauble (trinket)
address (speech)	arbitrary actions	beeper
adult education classes	archetype (model)	bend (curve)
advertisement, written copy	argument (reasoning)	bias (diagonal)
affectation (pretense)	arteries (roadways)	bicycle
affinity (similarity)	article (news)	blow (move air)
agility (suppleness)	articulation	bluff (ruse)
agreement (written)	artifice	book
air (atmosphere)	aspect (point)	book learning
air current	association (connection)	brain matter
alias	associative memory	breath of air, a
alibi	atmosphere, the earth's	breeze
allocation (distribution)	attentiveness	bridge (connection)
allusion (reference)	authorship	bridge (structure)
alphabet	auto (automobile)	brochure

Things Continued
browsing
buckle
bus (vehicle)
bus stop
buying
cab (taxi)
cable (notice)
cajolery
camper (vehicle)
cant (singsong)
car
caricature
cart
cartoon
caster
catalyst
change (swapping)
change (variation)
channel (communications)
channel (way)
cheating
chicanery
childishness
children of friends
circular
circulation
circumlocution
circumventing
claim (call for)
class (school)
clause (part of a sentence)
claws
clipping (news item)
close kin
close relative
coach (vehicle)
comings and goings
commentary
communication
communication (in general)
communications equipment
communique
commuting
compass
complexity, increasing
complications
con game
conduit
connection (coupling)
connection (relation)
context
context (setting)
context, things taken out of
continental drift
contortions
contract, act of signing
contract, written
conversation
conveyance
conveying information
convolution (twists)
cooking, chemistry of
copy (reproduction)
copy (story)
corners
correction fluid
correspondence (communication)
costume
costuming
counterfeit item
coupon
cover-up
criteria (example)
crowbar
curiosity
curious objects or events
curvature
daily comings and goings
dealings (transactions)
dealings with neighbors
dealings with siblings
debate
deceit
deception (fraud)
deception (trick)
declaration (notice)
declaration (statement)
decongestant
decoy
decree (proclamation)
deed (written)
deflection
delivery (handing over)
departing
description (portrayal)
description (variety)
desks
detour
deviation (wandering)
device (plot)
diagonal
dialect
dialogue
diary
dictation
diffusion (wordiness)
dig (cutting remark)
digression
direction (line of movement)
direction (line of thought)
direction (way)
direction indicator
disbursement (allocation)
disciplined thinking
discourse
discussion
disguise
dispatch (message)
distortion
distribution (dissemination)
distribution systems
divergence
diversification
diversion (deflection)
diversity (variety)
document
dodge (sidestep)
doll (figurine)
dope (tip)
double (counterpart)

doubles
down-spout
draft of air
drawing (sketch)
drift (implication)
drive (outing)
drivel (rambling)
driving
duality
duet
dump truck
duo
duplicate
duplicity
early education
echo
edict
editing
education
education (lower)
education, elementary
educational advancement
effigy
elastic
elasticity
elementary education
elevator
elongation
emulation
enunciation
envelope
epic (saga)
epigram (witty saying)
epistle
epitome (representation)
escalator
escapade
escape (diversion)
essay
euphemism
evasive action
examination (test)
example (model)
exchange (bartering)

exchange (interchange)
excursion
explanation (accounting)
explanation (description)
express mail
expression (wording)
expressions, verbal
facsimile
faculty (wit)
fake
false appearances
falsehood
falseness
falsity
familiarity (accustomization)
fan (blower)
farce (mockery)
faucet
favor (resemblance)
fax
feint (bluff)
ferry (boat)
fidgeting
figure of speech
fin (appendage)
flexibility
focus (perspective)
folder (brochure)
folly
foolishness
forgery
forum (a radio program)
fraud
freehand drawings
freight
frivolity
gambit
gargling
gas(es)
gasket
gathering of facts
gauntlet (glove)
gesture (movement)
gibe (taunt)

give (flexibility)
glibness
gloss (explanation)
gloves
gossip
grace (suppleness)
grip (holding place)
groove (furrow)
guest (visitor)
guide (instructions)
gust of wind
gutter (bowling)
gyp (scam)
gyrations
hack (taxi)
haggling
halftone (image)
hand-bill
handbook
handout (circular)
hang (gist)
hard back book
hearsay (rumor)
heuristics
hieroglyph
hinge
hit (request)
hocus-pocus
homonym
hose (watering tool)
icebreaker (comment)
idea (hint)
idea (mind picture)
idiom
illness of mother
illustration
image (replica)
image (representation)
imitation
imitation (mimicry)
impersonation
impertinence
impiety
implication

Things Continued
impromptu action
inarticulateness
income supplement
inexperience
inference
information
inhalation
inquiry
inquisitiveness
insert
instruction books
intellectual activity
interviews
jargon
jeers
jerky motions
jests
jewelry (costume)
jingle (rhyme)
jingle (telephone call)
joint (linkage)
joint ventures
joke
journal
journalism
journey, partner's
journeys, short
juggling
juncture (joining)
juvenile delinquency
kaleidoscope
keenness
kink (twist)
lane (bowling)
lane (ocean or air route)
lane (strip of road)
language
lap (course)
lap (one turn)
leaf (page)
learning (in general)
lease document
lengthening

letters (mail)
letters of the alphabet
license (document)
lie
likeness
limerick
limousine
limpness
line (in a play)
line (note)
line (transit route)
linkage (connection)
literary ability
literary work
literature
local matters
local travel
locality
lock (at a canal)
locomotion
log (diary)
looseness
lore
lower education
lure (bait)
lying
machination (scheme)
magazine (periodical)
magazine article
magic (mentalism)
magic (slight of hand)
mail
mail box
mandate (decree)
maneuver
manicure
manifold (piping)
manual (book)
manuscript
market price
mass transit
matter (textual material)
maze
meandering

meaning (implication)
media
member (appendage)
memorandum
memorization
memory jog
mental interests
mental pursuits
mentality
mention of something, the
message
meteorology
microphone
mimicry
mind (in general)
mischief
misconception
misdirection
misinformation
misnomer
misrepresentation
mnemonic
mobility
model (replica)
mold (ilk)
mold (the form itself)
momentary thought
monitor (TV type)
monograph
monologue
motion (gesture)
motorcycle
move (change of location)
movement (restlessness)
movement, facilitating
multi-media presentations
mumbling
muttering
namesake
narration
nervous energy
news
newspapers
nip (sharp comment)

node (orbital)
nonsense (foolery)
notation
note (memo)
notekeeping
notice (information)
noticing
notion (idea)
novel (book)
nugget (wisdom)
obliqueness (slyness)
observation
odd-shaped thing
one-liner
operator (math)
oration (address)
oratory
organ (publication)
orientation (familiarization)
outline (profile)
outline (silhouette)
overtone (hint)
oxidation
oxygen
package (parcel)
packet (mail)
pad (writing)
pairs
pamphlet
pantograph
pantomime
paper (document)
paper (stationery)
papers, one's
parchment
parley (discussion)
parody (imitation)
parrot (mimic)
path
pattern (form)
pattern (idea)
pen (writing instrument)
pencil
perception

periodical
personification
petty thievery
phone call
picture (representation)
pilfering
pipe (conduit)
plagiarism
poaching
poetical phrasing
point (item)
point of view
pointer
poster
presentation, informal
pretense (trick)
printer (computer)
printing
private study
proclamation
profile (outline)
projection (geometrical)
promenade (dance step)
proportion (ratio)
prose
prototype
publications, ephemeral
pulp novel
pun
qualifier (modifier)
quantifier (modifier)
query
question
questionnaire
quickness
quiz
quotation
radio
radio as communication
railroad
range (variety)
ray (protuberance)
reading
reason (thinking)

recall (remember)
recall (retrieve information)
receiver (electrical)
receiving news
recital (discourse)
recitation
recognition (met before)
recognition (noticing)
record (account)
recording medium
recounting
redundancy
reference (in relation to)
reference (source)
reference, indirect
referral
refrain (in music or poem)
rehearsal
reiteration
relation (kin)
relocating
remarks
remembering
remembrance (memory)
reminder
rendition
repartee
repeating
repetition
replacement (substitute)
replay
replica
replication (answer)
replication (copy)
reply
report (account)
reprint
reproduction (copying)
request (application)
rerun
resemblance
respects (greetings)
respiration
response (reply)

Things Continued

restatement
retelling
retort
review (journal)
rhetoric
rhyme
ribaldry
riddle
ridicule
river barge
roll (scroll)
roller skates
routine movement or travel
rubber
rumor
ruse
sales transaction
sample (specimen)
sarcasm
satire
scheme
schooling
script (cursive writing)
script (manuscript)
scroll (for writing)
seam (joint)
section (specimen)
semantics
semaphore
sentence (grammar)
sequel
sequence (episode)
serial
sexual harassment
shadow (imitation)
shaft (handle)
shelving (for books)
shift (dodge)
shift in location, a
shipment
shoplifting
short changing
short trips

shortcut
shortening (abbreviating)
shorthand
shortness (lack of height)
shoulders (of road)
shrewdness
sidestepping
sign (message)
sign language
signage
signal
signature
signing of papers
silhouette
similarity
simulation
simulator
sketch
skew (slant)
ski tow
skill (cunning)
slack (looseness)
slang
slant (diagonal)
sled
sleeve
sleigh
slide (chute)
slight of hand
slip (boat ramp)
slip (sideways movement)
slip of the tongue
slyness
small talk
smallness
smirk
snarl (knot)
sneer
social call
solution (explanation)
sound (drift)
speaking
specimen (sample)
speech (lecture)

speech (talking)
spigot
spoken communication
spoof
spout
sprawl
spur (branch off)
spur (projection)
squelch
stammering
stamp (postage)
statement
stealing
steering (navigation)
stencil
stop (visit)
stop, transit
strangulation
street car
stretch (elasticity)
stroke (in writing)
stroll
studies
studiousness
stunt (trick)
subscription to periodicals
substitute (replacement)
subterfuge (trick)
subway
suffocation
suitcase
superficiality
suppleness
surveillance
swapping
swindle
switchboard
synonym
tablet (writing paper)
tale (falsehood)
talk
talking
talking book
talons

tangent (digression)
tangent (trigonometric)
tap (faucet)
tape recorder
tasks involving travel
taxicab
team (pair)
tear sheet
teeth, false
telecopier (facsimile)
telegram
telegraph
telephone
telephone call
teletype
television, educational
term (word)
terminal, computer
testimony (statement)
text (text material)
textbook
theme (essay)
thesis (paper)
thin clear objects
things dependent on something
things with sharp angles
thirst for water
thought (idea)
thoughts
tic (twitch)
ticket (admission)
tie (bond)
tilt (slant)
tip (slant)
tongue (dialect)
topic (text)
touch (contact)
touch (deftness)
toupee
tourists, native
tow (pulling)
track (course)
track (rail)

tract (pamphlet)
trade (retail)
trade, local
trade-off
trading (barter)
traffic (dealings)
traffic (local)
traffic (movement)
traffic signal
trailer
train, railway
transaction
transcription
transfer (a move)
transfer (iron-on design)
transfer (ticket)
transferred, being
transit
translation
transmitting
transport
transportation
transportation equipment
trap (ruse)
travel
travel, local
travel, nearby
travel, short distance
travel plans
traveler, known to you
trespassing
trestle
trial (practice)
triangle
trick (clever act)
trick (joke)
trick (ruse)
trip, short journey
trip along (skip)
trips nearby
trips quick or short
triviality
trolley
trotting

trough (channel)
truck
trudging
tube
tuition
turn (bend)
turn (curve)
turn (stroll)
twins
twist (approach)
twist (curl)
twist (tangle)
twitching
typeface
typewriter
u-haul
unwanted delivery
update
van (vehicle)
vane
variation (difference)
vehicle (means)
vehicle (transportation)
vent (disclosure)
ventilation
ventriloquism
verbosity
verge (edge)
vernacular
verse (rhyme)
viaduct
vicissitude (mutability)
videotape
viewpoint
visit (call)
visiting
vocabulary
vocalization
voice (speech)
wagon
watch (look)
watch (surveillance)
water tap
wave (gesture)

Houses of the Fourth Quadrant

Things Continued
weather
weather along the coast
well head
wheedling
wheel
wheel and deal
wheelbarrow
whisper
wind
wind sock
windings
wisecracks
wit
wittiness
word
work requiring wit or knowledge
writing skills
writing(s)
written document
xerox copy
youth
zephyr
zigzag

Psychological Qualities

adaptability
changing one's mind
cheating
cleverness
communication
complicating matters
concrete mind, the
copying (mimicking)
craft (artifice)
craftiness
cunning
curiosity
cynicism
deceiving sense of
delinquency
deviousness
dexterity
duality
educational attitudes
elocution
eloquence
finesse (wile)
guile
imitative behavior
improvisation
intelligence (intellect)
leaning (bent)
learning ability
linguistic ability
maneuverability
memory
memory problems
mental activity
mental adaptation
mental attitudes
mental efforts
naiveté
nervous habits
nervous twitches
nervousness
observing powers
perceiving
perceiving ability for
polygamy
presence of mind
pretension
reasoning ability
recalling
replying
restlessness
sanity
self-expression
sharpness (alertness)
shifting positions
shyness
sibling rivalry
spastic effort
studying
talking
thinking
transacting
trickery
versatility
wile

Occupations or Person Types

acrobats
ad writer
adolescents
amateur
announcer
ass (fool)
auctioneer
author
auto dealer
barker
book binder
book seller
bookworm
boy
brethren
bridge builder
bridge worker
brokerage
bus driver
busybody
buyer
canary (talker)
canvasser
cartoonist
cheater
chiseler
classmate

clown	imp	operator (of a fraud)
columnist	impersonator	orator
commentator	impostor	palmist
commuter	information analyst	passenger
con artist	information clerk	pattern maker
con man	information specialist	pickpocket
concierge	intellectual	pitchman
conductor (vehicle)	interviewer	playwright
coordinator	jester	postal employee
correspondent	joker	press (reporters)
counterfeiter	journalist	printer
courier	juggler	punk (novice)
cynic	juvenile	punster
damsel	lad	pupil
deadbeat	letter carrier	pygmy (dwarf)
dealer (negotiator)	liar	questioner
debater	librarian	railroad worker
deceiver	linguist	rascal
delivery personnel	lookout	reader
dispatcher	magician (stage)	receiver (fence)
distributor	mail carrier	reporter
dolt (idiot)	manicurist	respiratory therapist
dope (dummy)	market maker	rover
driver	media personnel	schemer
dummy	men, young	school child
dunce	messenger	schoolmate
dupe	middleman	scribe
dwarf	midget	shoplifter
expediter	mime	shyster
fellow traveler	mimic	signatory
ferryman	minor	speaker
fool (jester)	moocher	spectator
franchiser	mouthpiece (spokesperson)	speech pathologist
girl	mover	spokesperson
gnome	narrator	sprite
gossiper	neighbor	square (unsophisticated)
gyp (swindler)	neophyte	stationer
hack (writer)	neurologist	stenographer
half-wit	news commentator	stool pigeon
harlequin	news personnel	student (observer)
huckster	newspaper worker	student (pupil)
hustler	novelist	swindler
idiot	observer	talker
illustrator	onlooker	tattletale

Occupations or Person Types

taxi driver	truant	weather forecaster
teamster	truck driver	wheeler-dealer
teenager	trucker	witness
thin person	typist	writer
thinker	tyro (beginner)	young, the
those who brings news	uninvited guest	young children
transcriber	urchin	young people (under age of 20)
transferee	ventriloquist	youth
transportation worker	viewer	
	visitor	

Places

aisle	information booth	print shop
alley	interchange (junction)	reading room
alleyway	junction (linkup)	road
aqueduct	junior high school	school
book shelf	labyrinth	school, elementary
book store	lane (narrow way)	school, secondary
borough	library	school room
canal	local neighborhood	sidewalk
crosswalk	median strip	stairs
curve (bend)	middle school	station (transit stop)
depot	near neighborhood	stationers
dike (ditch)	neighborhood	street
exchange (e.g. money)	neighboring environment	telegraph office
expressway	news rooms	thoroughfare
fish farm	observatory	ticket counter
freeway	parking lot	trail
halls (corridors)	pass	vicinity
hallway	post office	where books are kept
highway	prep school	

Family Members or Relations

adopted sibling	friends of one's children	relative
brother	godmother	sibling
brother or sister	kin	sister
brother or sister #1	kinfolk	younger brother
close blood relative	near relatives	

Mundane Ideas

bridge	commercialism	general trade
business forms	communication systems	internal distributions systems
commerce	communications satellite	journeys, short
commercial trade	form, business	market statistics

mayoral appointees
money, paper based
neighbor
neighboring country
newspapers
object of state importance
paper money
post office

postal system
price fixing
price quotation
primary education facilities
public, attitudes of the
public school system
road
school

signing a contract
sorrow, public
telephone system
trade within borders
transportation hub
transportation systems
travel within the country
weather

Parts of Our Body

appendage (subordinate body part)
armpits
arms (limbs)
autonomic nervous system
brain
breathing
bronchi
bronchial tubes
circulatory system (lungs)
co-ordination
coordination
dentures

extremity (appendage)
finger
finger nail
fingerprint
forearms
hands
limb
lungs
mental faculties
nerves
nervous system, the
palm of hand

puberty
pupil (eye)
regurgitation
respiratory system, the
ribs
shoulders
skin blemish
thoracic region of chest
thumb
tongue
umbilical cord
wrist

Afflictions or Diseases

arm fractures or breaks
asphyxiation
asthma
brain injury
breathing problems
bronchial infection
bronchitis
cough
dehydration
delirium tremens

epilepsy
fit
hand fractures or breaks
heart irregularities
learning disability
lung problems
nervous disorders
neuritis in arms or shoulders
pleurisy
pneumonia

respiratory problems
scurvy
sneeze
sore eyes
speech defect
speech problem
st. vitus dance
stuttering
tongue disease
tuberculosis

Colors

international orange
orange

pink
rose

Gems or Minerals

almandine
andradite
carbuncle
grossular

mercury
mica
pyrope
rhodolite

spessartine
uvarovite

Houses of the Fourth Quadrant

Animals

chameleon	hare	parrot
coyote	monkey	raven
crow	octopus	weasel
fox	orangutan	

Mythical Figures or Constellation Names

Antinous	Eridanus (river)	Mnomosyne (memory)
Auriga (the charioteer)	Gemini (twins)	Pleiades, the
Castor and Pollux	Hermes (the swift traveler)	Prometheus (thinker, humanist)
Chamaeleon	Kastor and Polydeukes	Rheia
Corvus (crow)	Lepus (hare)	Thamus (steersman)
Delphinus (dolphin)	Mercury	Vulpecula (fox)

Parts of an Organization

community relations office	messenger	telephone system
dispatchers dept.	motor pool	transportation dept.
driver's rooms	parking area	
mail room	relocation office	

Industry Categories

air cargo	natural gas (Pipeline)	transportation dispatching
auto and truck	natural gas fistribution	transportation equipment
broadcast media	newspapers	trucking
cable manufacturers	paper products	typesetting
coal (distribution)	pipeline companies	videoconferencing
contractors (drainage)	printing	water fistribution
electrical power distribution	railroads	weather forecasting
electronic games	specialty printing	
mobile communications	taxicabs	

Parts of an Automobile

connecting parts	fuel pump	tie rod
distributor	hoses	turn signal
engine fan	linkage	ventilation system
fan	manifold	wheel rim
fan belt	radio	
fender	steering system	

Parts of a House

chimney	gutter (roof)	telephone
corridors	halls (corridors)	
driest part of the house	hallway	
ductwork	stairway	
flue	steps	

Parts of a Ship

annunciator	helm	radio room
auxiliary steerage	ladder	rudder
combat information center	observation deck	ship's log
communication lines	passageway	signal deck
communication quarters	quarterdeck	signal equipment
compass	radio equipment	wheel

Houses of the First Quadrant

Poetry for the Houses of this Quadrant

Fourth House
    Home and family, hold them close,
    Moods abound, most morose,
    Inside of you, most protected
    Lie inner places, not all accepted.

Fifth House
    Seek love and romance, play games robust,
    Find inner happiness, not sex untrussed,
    Develop your self, inner satisfaction is good,
    But gamble not with parenthood.

Sixth House
    Service is expected, habitual working,
    A willing attitude, without any smirking,
    Keep the body clean, small pets unconfined,
    Take care of your health, discipline your mind.

An Overview of the Fourth House

An Angular House of the First Quadrant
Placed in the Right and Lower Hemispheres

The Fourth House reflects whatever **home, family,** or **tradition** means for you. This especially includes **early and later life experiences** with these ideas. The Fourth House is psychologically powerful because it shows the depth and core of **emotional attitudes** about any matters you use to build **basic personality foundations.** The Fourth House also depicts the **beginning and ending of all matters,** and for that reason the start and end of many important life's cycles begin here. The Fourth House shows the style in which you choose to **roost** or **live.** It represents **your basic inner nature, personal matters, fixed possessions** such as **houses** or **land,** concerns about **privacy,** attitudes toward **family,** and anything involving your **instinctive emotional motivations.**

The Fourth House represents your basic **emotional roots** and **origins.** These are generally defined by the **nurturing parent** or **caretaker,** usually the **mother.** The Fourth House represents the **care and devotion** this mother gives, how this care and devotion is received, and the strings attached to these qualities. Your **initial adjustment to life** in this world is shown by the Fourth House. This adjustment involves any combination of **heredity traits, family support, loving care, ethnic traditions,** etc., which you receive or are denied. The Fourth House calls for the eventual fusion of these **subjective building blocks** to create the self.

The Fourth House involves learning self-sufficiency, or the way you create an individual personality outside of direct **family influence.** Your early encounters with a mothering figure eventually begin a process of separation from family to become an individual who can then start his or her own family. **Developing self-sufficiency** requires that you gain some perspective on what you must do to become self-sufficient. Becoming self-sufficient is a necessary task of living. It is just the beginning of a long journey. Realizing that you must eventually break away from your family and **define your own life** is a constant Fourth House process. Completing this process by early middle life prepares you for meeting later life obligations. Failure to complete it may lock you into difficult **emotional patterns of dependency.**

The Fourth House mirrors the **psychological makeup** of your life, especially concepts about **your personal space** and how you guard your **privacy** or **personal matters.** It is through the Fourth House that you first begin to integrate your **inner personality** and the self you wish to build. Taking distinct pieces and building a self is shown through the Fourth House. The Fourth House shows what inner resources the material world allows, and how these can be allowed to mold and form the emotional resources of your emerging self. The Fourth House shows how you can achieve greater inner personal strength, develop more as a person, and increase **your overall emotional growth.**

The Fourth House represents a **basic** and **fundamental** side of your nature. It is that part of your nature which you work through to initiate life processes and other important life experiences. See the discussion on the astrological quadrants in Chapter 4 for further elaboration on this theme. The Fourth House represents how your quest for completion or recognition in life begins. Central to the Fourth House are the **resources** which you accumulate to help in this effort. Using the Fourth House you can build a **psychological base** to create a **personality foundation** for a worldly expression of your life.

Accumulation involves the amassing of material resources to help you get through life. The Fourth House represents the type of home you choose to live in, and how you care for this **home, its importance** to you, **its nature, style, usages**, etc. The way you **accumulate and store your household goods** within the home is also shown through the Fourth House. But, the Fourth House represents more than just your **physical home**. It also shows the **space** you set aside about you and the importance you attach to this **personal space**. The Fourth House shows how you nurture this space, and the thought and effort you may put into protecting its privacy. This space may extend through your home, your **property**, your **work area**, or wherever you feel a need for it.

The Fourth House represents things of the past: **history, culture, tradition, folklore**, etc. It is through the Fourth House that these are bought forth from the depths of your being and into your life. The Fourth House is the basis you use for projecting the thoughts of your prior experiences into your current world. Things which you hold **sentimental**, such as your fondest **memories**, have a Fourth House representation. There is also a call to the middle way, the **ordinary**, or the **commonplace** through the Fourth House. Here you can find the expectations which **the average person** has about you or your services.

Merchandising and **sale transactions** are also shown here. This involves the efforts you are willing to endure to have **goods sold or traded**. Part of merchandising is the creation of the **goods for sale**. **Agricultural products** especially have their sources shown through the Fourth House. The Fourth House can show **the abundance of goods available**, their quality and condition, and the intrinsic worth these goods may have in the **market place**.

The Fourth House shows what kinds of things you hold emotionally close. Your **attachment to objects** and what value these objects have is also shown here. Your means of **attachment and holding**, your means of **acquisition**, your means of **accumulation**, and your means of protecting what is yours, are all shown here. The Fourth House represents **the hold you have on your possessions**, or vice versa, and what you may do to **protect these possessions**.

Horary or Electional Ideas

accumulation	ground, the	ordinary, the
basics, the	home	outcome of anything, the
change of location, a	house	personal matters
decisions	land	privacy
end of the matter, the	living space	property related items
environment, the	mankind (in general)	real estate
family	mislaid item	routine activities
family affairs	missing item	ship
fixed possessions	mother	wealth, accumulating

Things

absorption (soak up)	atom	bonding with another
accommodation (room)	attachment (fastening)	bore (hole)
accumulation	audience (spectators)	bore (hollow part)
acquisition (acquiring)	average (mean)	bottle
acreage	average (normal)	bottom (of anything)
addition (math)	average (par)	bowl
adhesion (sticks to)	back log	box (container)
adhesives	bag (container)	breakfast
adjournment	band (cinch)	breeding
affairs of later life	banner	brick
agricultural products	barge	brine
agriculture	barn	bulk purchase
album (photo)	base of operations	bunting (flag)
alternation	basic security	burial
ancestry	basics, the	buried treasure
anchor	beat (rhythm)	burying motions
andiron	becoming	butter
anniversary	beginning of life	cable (wire rope)
anthology	beginnings	cadence
antique	beneath the ground	candle
antiquity	beverage	capriciousness
anything hidden in the ground	bias (tendency)	capture devices
apartment (residence)	bibliography	capturing
aperture (opening)	bindings	career of partner
appetite for food	biological rhythms	catch (fish)
application (adhesion)	birthday	caulking material
arc (crescent)	birthright	cavity
area (expanse)	bleat	cemetery plot
area (region)	boarding house	centripetal force
armor (protection)	boat	chaff
article (object)	bolt (fastener)	chair
assignment (post)	bond (cord)	change (fluctuation)

Things Continued
change in fortune
change of location, a
channel (stream)
cheese
chinaware
circumference
cladding
claim (right)
clamp
clan
clasp
clearance (space)
cleat
cleavage
cliche
climax (end point)
clinch
clip (fastener)
coating (outer layer)
cocoon
coffee
cola
cold water
collection
collector's items
comfort (basic food or shelter)
commemoration
commodity (possession)
commodity made into goods
common people, the
commonplace things
complement (a rounding out)
complement (ship's personnel)
complement (the entirety)
completion (ending)
concealed treasure
concealment
conception (beginning)
consuming
container (for liquids)
container (storage)
contents (thing contained)
convention (accepted practice)

conventional things
cooking
cord (line)
cornerstone
counter-clockwise motion
court, criminal ruling
court, ruling from a
coverings (in general)
craft (water craft)
crafts (goods)
crazes (popular)
crescent symbol
crest
crevasse
crevice
crops
crowd
crumb
crust
cultivation
culture
cup
cushion (leeway)
custody (care)
customary things
customs (habits)
cycle
damage from earthquakes
damage from natural disasters
dampness
dark (nightfall)
darkness
dead of night
deal (portion)
decision (conclusion)
decision (verdict)
decisions of a court of law
defense
definition (gives form to)
deluge
dent (depression)
deposit (pile)
depression (pit)
detachment (disconnection)

dew
dinner
disposition (tendency)
domestic affairs
domestic chores
domesticity
dominion (empire)
doodad
doom (verdict)
dormitory
dot (speck)
downpour
drink (beverage)
drip (trickle)
drop (drip)
drop (trace)
drowning
dump (shack)
early home life
early life
earth's surface, the
eating
eclipse (darkening)
ecology
electroplating
emblem
embodiment
embrace
empire
enclosure (fencing)
end (finish)
end (outcome)
end of a cycle
end of anything, the
end of life period
end of long-term affairs
end of the matter, the
enrollment (registration)
entomology
envelopment
essentials (the basics)
estates (land, real estate)
everyday items
everything

eye, left of male
eye, right of female
eyeglasses
fad
family
family, conditions of the
family affairs
family group
family tree, the
farm implement
farming
fashion (habit)
fastener
faults in the earth
fear (phobia)
feeding
feeling of security
female concerns
female things
fence (enclosure)
filament
file (collection)
final outcome of any question
final preparations
final resort
finality
financial abundance
financial acquisition
finish (completion)
fixed possessions
fixture (familiar sight)
flag
flashback
flask
flat taste
flatness (level surface)
flesh (mankind)
flood
flood damage
flow (stream)
fluctuation
fluids
fluorescence
fortifications

fortune (wealth)
fountain
fragile item
frame (mounting)
franchise (exclusive market)
frequency (iteration)
friend's health
fruit
fundamental particles (physics)
fundamentals (essentials)
furrow
fuse
garden (fertile area)
gardening
gas can
gene
genealogy
general public
generality
generalization
generation
genetics
germs
girdle (corset)
glasses, drinking
glue
good-byes
goods (merchandise)
gouge (nick)
gourd
grain (small particle)
grappling hook
grasp (embrace)
grasp (scope or reach)
grate (covering)
grave, one's
grip (grasp)
groove (habit)
ground, the
growing
gutter (roadway)
habit (practice)
habitation
half (portion)

hallmark (mark of origin)
hand hold
handful (small number)
handle (hold)
handling (usage)
hard hat
harness
head (climax)
health of friends
heap (accumulation)
heirloom
helmet
hemisphere
heraldry
herd
herding
hereditary traits
heredity
heritage
hidden (lost) thing
hidden treasure, regained
hiding place of thieves
hit (bite)
hitch (fasten)
hoarding
hold (grasp)
holding (property)
holding (ruling of a court)
hole (golf)
hole (opening)
home
home environment
home life
hood (covering)
hood (crest)
house
house for sale
house you plan to buy
houseboat
housing
hull (husk)
humanity (the masses)
humid air
humidity

Things Continued
hunger
husk
hyperactivity
hypersensitivity
ideology
illness of friend
immersion (wetness)
immobility
impression (feeling)
inauspicious portent
inbreeding
incapacity
incarnations
incidental (minor item)
including (containing)
inconsistency
inconstancy
increment (variation)
indentation
indentation (notch)
indispensability
indivisibility
infinitesimal things
ingredient
inherent things
inheritance by descent
inhibiting factors
inner things
insignia
insignificance
installment
internal, that which is
inundation
investments, land
involuntary actions
iridescence
irrationality
irrigation
island
items
jacket (apparel)
jelly
judge's decision in a lawsuit

judgment (finding)
judicial decision
juice
juicy things
keepsake
kernel
kettle
keystone
knot
lamp
land
lap (little waves)
lap (panel)
lap (take in food)
last illness
latch
latent things
later life
latitude (room)
lattice (framework)
lawsuit, result of
lead (leash)
lease
leasing
leeway (room)
leftovers
lens
life support system
lighter (boat)
line (cord)
line (lineage)
line (wrinkle)
lineage
lining
liquids (in general)
lock (security device)
lodging
loss (misplacing)
lost article
lost item
lost possession
lot (land)
lower, things which are
lowliness

lump (a piece of)
lunch
luncheon
majority (the masses)
man (humankind)
manacle (shackle)
margin (leeway)
masses, the
masses of people
material (constituents)
matrix (embedding material)
matrix (starter base)
matter (material)
meal
mean (average)
meat
mediocrity
melon
memoir
memorabilia
merchandise
mezzanine (theater)
micro-organism
microbe
microcosm
microscope
midnight
milk
minimum
minor (unimportant)
minutiae
miscellany
mislaid item
mislaying things
misplaced item
missing item
mission (assignment)
mittens
moisture
money, recovery of lost
morass
morsel (nibble)
moss
mote (speck)

motherhood	opinion (feeling)	pod (container)
mount (frame)	opposition (planetary)	popular item
move (as in chess)	option (claim)	portfolio
movies, home	oral tradition	possession, fixed
moving (relocating)	organism (living thing)	possession, sibling's
mug (cup)	orifice (opening)	pots and pans
multitudes	origin (ancestry)	pouch
mummy	origin (source)	precipitation
natural touches	oscillate	prerequisite
nature of land purchased	outcome of the matter, final	presence, takes a major
nautical things	outer covering	present residence
necessity of life	oval	preservation
nest	overalls	private thing
net (mesh)	oversight (care)	product
netting (protection)	pad (ink stamp)	property (land)
new beginning	padlock	property, personal
nibble	pail	property matters
niche in life	paleontology	prophylactic
night	pan	protection
nip (small portion)	parabola	protectionism
nipple (artificial teat)	parameter (element)	protective wrapper
node (mass of substance)	parasol	proton
nodule	parcel (lot)	publicity received
norm (average)	parcel (small piece)	puff (whiff)
north, the direction of	parentage (lineage)	pulling (drags along)
nostalgia	parish (congregation)	purchase (buying)
nostalgic item	particle	quicksand
notch	past life	race (nationality)
nourishment	paste	raft
novelty (fad)	pendulum	rage (mania)
numismatics	pennant	rain
nut meats (in general)	people (in general)	raincoat
object taken for granted	period (ending)	ration
occult, study of	phase (stage)	rationale
occult religion	phase of the tide	real estate transaction
occupancy	phosphorescence	real property
occupy (take up space)	pile (heap)	receptacle (container)
occupy time, things which	pinch (small amount)	reception (acquiring)
odds and ends	pit (dimple)	recess (cavity)
office holdings	pizza	recipe
old age	planting	recollection (remembering)
opening (hole)	plate (for eating)	recovered wealth
opening (vacancy)	plow	reel, fishing
ophthalmology	pockmark	reflection (memory)

Things Continued

reflection (return of image)
reflex (inborn response)
relativity
relic
remains
remembrance (memento)
repast
responsiveness
restraint (shackle)
result (outcome)
result of a lawsuit
retention
return (recurrence)
rhythm
ripeness
river
rivet
rocking chair
romantic tragedy
room (margin)
room (space)
root (basic element)
root (of plant)
root (origin)
rope
routine (everyday things)
routine activities
rule (custom)
ruling (final decision)
safety
safety cushion
sandwich
saturation (permeation)
saving (activity of)
scab
scenery (landscape)
schooner
science fiction
score (nick)
scrapbook
screen (for hiding)
screw (fastener)
sea, the

seam (furrow)
seasons, the
seaweed
section (installment)
sector (zone)
security (defense)
security (free from danger)
security blanket
sensitization
sentence (verdict)
sentiment (opinion)
shackles
shawl
sheath (covering)
sheath (knife case)
shield
shimmy (vibration)
ship
shipping
shower (rain)
silverware
slat
small boat
snack
snare (trap)
snugness (fits closely)
soda
sophomore (grade)
space (roominess)
space (seating)
spaciousness
spare (reserve)
speck
spectacles (eyeglasses)
speculation (losses from)
spending
splice (knot)
spool
spray (water droplets)
spread (food)
spread, bed
spur (climbing tool)
squall
staff (flagpole)

stamp (seal)
staple
start of a cycle
stereotype (preconception)
stickiness
stitch (all of something)
stitch (shred)
stock (cattle)
stock pile
stoneware
stool (chair)
stored wealth
storms, the effect of
string (cord)
strip (piece)
stuff (material)
stuffing
sub sandwich
sub-soil
subconscious mind
submarine
submerging
succession (series)
sudden acts of God
sunglasses
supplies (goods available)
support (brace)
surf
surface (covering)
sustaining
swing (to and fro)
symbol (emblem)
synchronicity
syncopation
tad (a little bit)
tallness
tank (storage)
tank, fish
target (objective)
tasteless humor
tea
tearjerker
temporary plans
territory

tether
thing (object)
things lost or stolen
things that engulf
thriving conditions
throb
tidal force
tide
tie (rope)
tieback
ties of consanguinity
tightness
tillage of the earth
timing (synchronicity)
tiny object (miniature)
token (money substitute)
token (symbol)
tongs
topical items
torrent
total (sum)
totem
touch (trace)
trade (wholesale)
tradition (custom)
tradition (legend)
transient activities
trap (snare)
treasure, buried or hidden
treatment (handling)
tribe (related strain of animals)
trifle (morsel)

trivia
trivial matter
truss (band)
tub
tuck (gather)
turn (shift)
tweezers
twine
type (specimen)
typical things
umbrella
uncertainty (hesitancy)
under the earth, anything
underclothes
undercurrent (riptide)
undergarment
undertone (sense)
underwater object
undulation
unimportant matter
unit (part)
unrecognized potential
urge for security
urn
usage (practice)
usage (treatment)
usual, the
vapor (moisture)
variable
vegetable
vent (opening)
verdict (judgment)

vessel (container)
vessel (ship)
vestige (trace)
vial
vibration (periodic oscillation)
vicissitude (chance)
vision (sight)
vogue (fashion)
voices, hearing
wall (defense)
walling in
wares
water
wave (pulsation)
wave (swell of water)
weld
well (hole)
wetness
wire
wobble
womb
women's articles
women's clothes
work with liquids
worth, future
wrappings
yearbook
yeast
zipper
zone (region)

Psychological Qualities

addiction (dependency)
arbitrariness
backwardness
base, your basis or start
caring
childhood environment
claustrophobia
concealment, need for
conditioned response
cope, ability to

core identity
culture, attitude towards
defenses
defensive qualities
dependence (reliance on others)
dependency (addiction)
dependency (needs for help)
disorientation
eating habits

emotional isolation
emotional needs
emotional pain
emotional security
essential nature
fear(s), inner
feelings
fickleness
foundation
functioning, inner ways of

Psychological Qualities Continued

futility
greed (selfishness)
harboring (holding in)
home, quality of
homespun virtues
human nature
identifying with
inability to fee complete
inborn trait
inclusion (containment)
individualization
inferiority complex
inhibitions
insecurity
instability
instinctive behavior
instincts
introversion
keeping
life principles
life-style
life-style approach
life-style orientation
maintaining
mood
mothering
nationalism
needs (in general)
negative views
nesting instincts
nurturing
ordinary, the
passivity
patriotism
patterning
personal life
personal matters
phobia
privacy
private life
private matters
problem, personal
proclivity
producing
protection
protective instincts
protective urges
qualms
reasons, underlying
receptivity
reflectiveness
reliance
response to situations
retaining
secret fear
security
security needs
self-integration
sensitivities, one's
sensitivity to others
sentiment (feeling)
separation anxiety
shift in attitudes, a
shift of values, a
sleeping posture
subconscious attitudes
susceptibility
sympathy
tendency (inner inclinations)
uncertainty (doubt)
undercurrent (mood)
uniformity
urgings
vein (mood)
vulnerability
wealth, need for
whim

Occupations or Person Types

agrarian
agricultural worker
angler
archivist
baker
botanist
builder
camper (occupies land)
catcher
caterer
civilian
client (patron)
clinger
coal miner
collector
conservator
consumer
cook
crop grower
crusty people
custodian
dairy farmer
dairy worker
dealer in liquids
deep sea diver
democrat
denizen
diner
farm hand
farmer
females
fisherman
founder
gardener
genealogist
generalist
grave digger
hardware dealer
historian
home maker
hotel worker
illegal alien
inhabitant
introvert
keeper (custodian)

landowner	peasant	shipper
life guard	pilot, ship	shipping clerk
lost person	plebeian	shopkeeper
lunatic	plumber	shopper
manufacturer	populace, the	silversmith
mariner	powder (particulates)	storekeeper
merchandiser	predecessor	those beneath the surface
merchant	produce dealer	those residing in your house
microbiologist	producer	those who work with liquids
miser	property owner	tool (pawn)
mortals	protector	union member
mother	purchaser	vendor
naturalist	purchasing agent	vice-president
nature, mother	rancher	warder
night worker	resident	wholesaler
oceanographer	sailor	women
patriot	seaman	

Places

abode	cellar	expanse
anchorage	cistern	falls (waterfall)
aquarium	city	farm
archive	claim (mining)	fatherland
atoll	community (locale)	field (meadow)
back stage	concession (franchise)	final resting place
bank (river)	continent (land mass)	flat (apartment)
barn	corral	fort
basement	cove	fortress
bath house	cul-de-sac	forum (marketplace)
bay	cultural center	forum (public meeting place)
bayou	dairy	garden
beach	damp place	green (common area)
birthplace	den (shelter)	ground, irregular
bog	department store	habitat
booth (shelter)	diggings (excavations)	hamlet
booth (stand)	ditch	harbor (port)
brook (stream)	dock (wharf)	harem
bunkhouse	domain (estate)	hole (cave)
burial place	domicile	home
burrow	dwellings	home port
camp	eatery	home range
campground	emporium	home room
castle	environs (local vicinity)	home stretch
catacomb	estate	homestead

Houses of the Fiirst Quadrant

Places Continued
homestretch
hometown
hotel
house you live in or own
hut
kingdom
lagoon
lair
lake
landed property
lay (lair)
levee
living space
lodge
low spot
lowlands
mall
manger
mansion
market
marsh
meadow
moat
moor
motel
mount (embankment)
museum
natural settings
new surroundings
oasis
ocean
ocean depths
open country
open farmland
outlet (shopping place)
packing house
pasture
pen (animal)
pen (corral)

pier
place near water or plumbing
place of residence
place of rest or abode
place one currently occupies
plains
pond
pool of water
port (home)
post (station)
prairie
produce market
quagmire
rampart
ranch
range (pasture)
rapids
realm
rear (back part) of anyplace
rental property
rental resided in, the
reservation
reservoir
residence
resting place, your final
river
room (cubicle)
rooming house
roost
ruins
sandy place
seaport
seashore
seat (residence)
section (area)
shack
shelter
shoe store
shop
shopping mall

shore (land)
shore (seacoast)
site
slip (berth)
soggy ground
sound (body of water)
spa
spot (location)
spread (ranch)
spring (water)
square, town
stall (retail place)
stand (retail outlet)
station (post)
steerage
stockade
store (retail)
stream
stronghold (fort)
structure (building)
suburb
sump
swamp
tank farm
tenement
terrain (ground)
tongue of land
town
tunnel
undersea places
valley
village
waterfront area
watery place
well
wharf
where living things grow
where you reside
yard

Family Members or Relations

ancestors
cousin, paternal
family, member of immediate

folks
forefather
mother

parent-in-law

Mundane Ideas

agricultural interests
agriculture
body of water
bounty from the land
citizenship
city
civilian population
civilization
clientele
coastline, the nation's
commodity (economic factor)
commodity (product)
community affairs
community's weather history
consumable commodities
consumer needs
consumerism
consumption of goods
crop raising
crops
cultural life
debt expansion
democracies
department of personnel
durable goods
electorate, the
environment, the
family

food production (growing)
free market
geography of the country
goods, demand for
historical perspective
history
hotel
housing
inhabitant
interior, department of
land
landed interests
leader of the opposition
lower house of government
lower legislative house
mandate (territory)
marketplace, the
mercantilism
merchandising
middle class, the
municipality
national security, concerns of
natural resources
oceans bordering the nation
office of an agent
office of the partner
ordinary business
political party in opposition

political party not in power
political party out of power
price war
procurement interests
procurement policy
procurement practices
profit from a publication
protectionist concerns
public, the (in general)
public opinion
raw material
real estate
relations with family
relations with parents
resource (natural wealth)
river
seaport
succession rights
supplies for consumption
tribal customs
tribal groups
tribe (social group)
uniformity
urban development
voters in an election
water supply

Parts of Our Body

alimentary canal
body fluids
body rhythms (biorhythms)
breasts
chest
chest region
digestion
digestive juices
digestive system
ductless gland
ducts, tear
emotions

endocrine system
esophagus
eyesight, quality of
fertility cycle
fluid flows
fluid retention
glands
glandular system (in general)
hormones
immune system
lymphatic system
mammary glands

menses
menstruation
nipple
organ
periodic condition
perspiration
physical condition
pulse
salivary glands
stomach
tear drop
tear ducts

Parts of Our Body Cotninued
thorax
tissues of the body
tumor
uterus
vision
womb

Afflictions or Diseases

acid/alkaline balance	edema	lunacy
allergy	emotional problems	mania
appetite abnormality	eyesight problems	myopia
astigmatism	halitosis	nausea
atherosclerosis	heart afflictions	nearsightedness
cancer causing attitude	heart disease	stomach ache
cancerous growth	heart problems	stomach cramp
caries, dental	homesickness	ulcers, stomach
crusty growth	hurt feelings	vomiting
dropsy	indigestion	

Colors

aqua	silvery gray	turquoise
pearl	silvery-blue	white-gray
silver	silvery-green	yellow-green

Gems or Minerals

amazonite	microcline	sand (common)
chalk	moonstone	sanidine
coral	orthoclase	shell
feldspar	pearl	silver
ivory	pewter	silverplate
laboradorite	platinum	

Animals

armadillo	lobster	shrimp
barnacle	mammal	slug
clam	marsupial	snail
cow	mascot	sponge
crab	omnivore	swine
crustacean	opossum	teddy bear
great cattle	oyster	tortoise
hen	pig	turtle
hog	pigeon	
livestock	shellfish	

Mythical Figures or Constellation Names

Artemis	Chaos	Erebos
Cancer (crab)	Crateris (cup)	Hera (the loyal friend)
Carina (keel of ship Argo)	Diana	Juno

Milky Way, the
Niobe
Persephone

Pontos (sea)
Reticulum (net)
Scutum (shield)

Selene (moon)

Parts of an Organization

customers
middle management

parts underground
personnel, the

purchasing
real estate

Industry Categories

agriculture (growing)
capital goods
catalog services
communication equipment
    manufactuers
containers (paper)
flower growers
food retailers
food wholesalers
general merchandise chains

grocery
hospital management
housing
insurance (property/casualty)
manufactured housing
marine contractors
maritime
merchandising (small business)
packaging & container

real estate investment
restaurant
retail (department stores)
retail (drugstore)
retail (food chain)
retail (special lines)
retail stores
security system providers
water utility

Parts of an Automobile

fuel lines
interior roominess
passenger seat

seat belt
seating room
undercoating

water hose
water pump

Parts of a House

addition
back yard
basement
cellar
counter space
family room
floor (story)
foundation
garden, vegetable

hot water heater
informal dining area
insulation
lawn
lower floors
outbuilding
parts underground
plumbing
storm door

storm window
sump pump
support (pillar)
tap water
threshold (sill)
water pipes
water tank
yard, the

Parts of a Ship

anchor
captain's cabin
crew's quarters
fender
fresh water supply

hawser
icebreaker (vessel)
instability
passenger quarters
registry

shore line (hawser)
stateroom
wardroom
water tank

An Overview of the Fifth House

A Succedent House of the First Quadrant
Placed in the Right and Lower Hemispheres

Giving or receiving **love** or **romantic feelings** is an important part of the Fifth House. Some feel the Fifth House reveals all kinds of love, but love is a complex and psychologically diverse emotion. The Fifth House rules **romantic love**, the Eighth House sexual love, the Eleventh House brotherly love, etc. Giving or finding love can occupy much time and effort. Pursuing romantic love is a Fifth House topic which can occupy an entire lifetime. **Romance** involves the fabrication (i.e., creation) of a mood, a setting, a frame of mind which takes self away from daily cares into more pleasurable areas. Learning to take self above the trials of life to a realm where **pleasure** replaces pain is a Fifth House activity. The Fifth House does not ask you to abandon life's battles, but to elevate them to internal levels where you can **find inner satisfaction** and **pleasure** from meeting and conquering them.

You may face both pleasant or unpleasant things in life. The Fifth House traditionally rules many pleasant categories of life, but it still may not be an easy house to master. **Mastery of self** and self's goals is a central Fifth House theme. To attain mastery, you must thoroughly understand what you need to master. You must learn all about yourself before you can achieve **self-mastery**. You must learn to use your talents and also how to capitalize on your capabilities. Other people may have a greater awareness of who you are than you do. But, other people's ideas about how you should develop or what you should do in life may not match your feelings. **Mastery** of self comes with maturity. Mastery of your problems involves sorting and prioritizing demands of life. These are Tenth House and Sixth House issues. Through the Sun as primary ruler, the Fifth House's influence spreads into other houses. Fifth House issues go to the very core and depth of your personality. As the second house of the Fourth House, the Fifth House shows how you mold the **inner self's yearnings** into issues which define you. **Developing self's abilities** and **creativity** starts here.

The **children** (either your biological children or those assigned to your care as a teacher, a guardian, etc.) you produce or influence become a major part of your external Fifth House projections. These children, their **rearing**, their **molding**, their **teaching**, the care given them, the **values imparted** to them, etc. are central Fifth House issues. The care and the time you take to teach children values may be returned to you through Fifth House astrological patterns. Your legacy lives on through **the values and lessons you give** to others. Interests in becoming a proficient **teacher** are also a Fifth House concern.

The Fifth House represents many forms of **entertainment**, like **theater, sports, gambling, stock market investing**, etc. **Games** and other forms of **play** can also become a part of daily work and career. Through the Fifth House you are asked to create **entertainment** from routine tasks. You may find that you are happiest when you **enjoy tasks** while doing them. The Fifth House can teach you that much **contentment** and **satisfaction** can come from your internal attitudes about life. **Happiness** may generate prosperity. When success surrounds you, people and opportunities seek you out. **Luck, prizes, winnings**, etc. are tied to the Fifth House. If you can **master self** through your Fifth House, then the **lucky breaks** and **prizes** of life can come to you. Be careful not to let the **games** you create with life control you, but instead work to find an **inner joy** from your tasks. **Being true to your self** can bring much **inner happiness**.

Interest in the **theater** or **dramatics** is a part of the Fifth House's scope. The Fifth House rules **how you emotionally relate** to things which you feel are important. The Fifth House prompts you to project **contrived emotionalism** (i.e., **theatrics**) into life's activities. The Fifth House asks you to bare the core or central you to the world. This can include developing your **sense of humor**, or an ability to **laugh** at or with life. The Fifth House contains many keywords which involve **the expression of emotion**, like **dynamics, celebrations, applause, affection, matters of the heart, performances, spontaneity, humor**, etc. A strong Fifth House may not make you a successful **actor or actress**, but it can heighten your interest in the **emotional expression** of your creations. Emotional expression is not solely derived from the Fifth House activity, but **mastery** of lessons here may better help you **express your feelings**.

The Fifth House shows what kind of activities bring you **pleasure** and **joy**. Through the Fifth House you can learn to find **enjoyment** or **satisfaction** from the routine tasks of life. You can **gain satisfaction** from whatever you must face in life,- no matter how unpleasant it may seem at first. The Fifth House helps you find **inner joy** beyond any suffering you may feel as life's events demand your attention and resources. The Fifth House helps you transport yourself from the depths of emotional despair to the heights of any **fulfillment** as you encounter life's experiences. The Fifth House can help you find **spontaneity** and **fun** in life no matter how routine activities force you to do unwanted things.

Another important Fifth House issue is **popularity**,- your popularity. Popularity involves being able to relate to others in meaningful ways. You can not demand popularity or **success**. Popularity includes appearing before others in ways which identify your uniqueness. The Fifth House reflects inner attitudes toward acquiring **fame**. If you encourage idolization you may mirror a lack of inner esteem. If you demand **hero worship** you may find rejection of other creative efforts. The best way to work with the Fifth House is to seek **inner happiness** by cheerfully bearing with the tasks or tribulations of life. **Popularity** or **fame** may then follow. Learn to live with what you receive, but learn to live your life in ways which you find personally satisfying. **Satisfaction** from doing ordinary tasks is important. **Creating play from work** is necessary too. Have fun enjoying the tasks, obligations, or pleasures which life sends your way.

Horary or Electional Ideas

ability	exhibit	potential ability
aptitude	gambling	praise
capability	games of chance	pregnancy
children	hobby	recreation
core (essence of anything)	love	risk, taking on a
creative ability	luck	romance
diversion (pastime)	pleasure	speculation (gambling)
entertainment	popularity	vacation

Things

ability (capability)	ball (round)	capacity (ability)
acclamation (ovation)	ball game	card game
acorn	banquet	card suit: hearts
act (play part)	bathing suit	cards (game)
acting	beacon	caress
addition (extra)	beloved pet	carving
adoption	bet	cast (people)
adulation (praise)	betting	catch (a person)
advance (overture)	billiards	cause (motive)
affair (celebration)	bingo	celebration
affair (relationship)	birth	celebrations as festivities
affairs of the heart	birth rate	center of anything, the
affection (attachment)	blaze (fire)	centerpiece
ammunition of a besieged town	bliss	chance (luck)
amorousness	boasting	chandelier
amusement(s)	boisterousness	charisma
ante, the (as in poker)	booby prize	childbirth
anything created by you	bow, to take a	children's affairs
applause	brainchild	cinema as entertainment
ardor (feeling)	brawn	circle
art (creativity)	break (luck)	circular symbol
artistic work	brocade	clapping (applause)
artistry	bulge	clean up, a (large win)
athletic contests	bulk (greater part)	clothes as vanity
athletics	bullfight	coasting (without power)
attention (wooing)	bump	cocktail party
audience (audition)	bungee jumping	coincidence (luck)
audition	burlesque	colorful objects
aura	cable TV	combustion
avocation (recreation)	calisthenics	comedy
baby	cameo (small role)	comics, the
baby shower	camping (tenting)	commodity trading

Things Continued
conception of children
concert
conjunction (planetary)
convulsions (fits of laughter)
core (central part)
corny joke
coronation
corpulence
courtliness
courtship
creation (origination)
creative hobby
creative work
cremation
crown (royalty)
crucible
crux (core)
daily exercise
dance
dating
daylight
daytime
dealings with a loved one
dealings with children
dealings with young people
death of a parent
death of career
dejection
deliberations of a jury
delight
demonstration (display)
dice
dining out
dinner engagement
disc (or disk)
display (exhibition)
dissipation
distension (swelling)
distraction (diversion)
diversion (pastime)
dominion (rule)
drama (play)
draw (attraction)
dream (joy)
driver's test
dynamics
earthquake damage
easel
eating out
education (junior high)
educational pursuits
effervescence (liveliness)
egoism
egotism
elation
electrolyte
electromagnet
elegance
embellishment
embryo
emotions, pleasurable
enabling
encore
encouragement
endowment (talent)
energy (resource)
energy potential
engines (in general)
enjoyment
entertainment (diversion)
enthusiasm
enzyme
establishment (forming)
estate of mother
exaltation
exaltation (praise)
exercise (practice)
exercise (training)
exercise, athletic
exercise, recreational
exhibit (display)
exhibition
exhibitionism
exhilaration
exorbitance
expansion (swelling)
exposition
exposure (lay bare)
exposure, sought after
expression (emotional tone)
exterior surface
extra (addition)
extra things
extravagance (waste)
exuberance
eye, left of female
eye, right of male
face (confidence)
faculty (capability)
fanfare
farce (comedy)
farce (horseplay)
favorable, that which is
favorite activity
feast (banquet)
feast (holiday)
feature (highlight)
felicity (happiness)
festival
festivity
fete (party)
field day (opportunity)
film (movie)
financial speculation
finish (luster)
fire, the act of lighting a
fire screen (grate)
fireball
firing a kiln, the act of
flamboyance
flash of inspiration
flash of light
flashlight
fling (love affair)
flirtation
flourish
focal point
focus, a central
focus of things
fondling
food, chemistry of

force (energy)
force (significance)
formation (founding)
formation, the act of
fortuity
fortune (destiny)
fruition
full spectrum lighting
fun
furlough
furnace
gaiety
gain (winnings)
gambling
gambling equipment
games
games of chance
garden furniture
garnish
gaudiness
gender of the fetus
generosity
genesis
geniality
germination
gestation
getting high
giddiness (frivolity)
gift (talent)
giggles
gilt
giving love
gladness
glamour
gleam (inkling)
gleam (ray)
glee
glimmer
glitter (luster)
glorification
glory (splendor)
glory (worship)
gloss (finish)
glow

go (ambition)
golf
good fortune
good life, the
good luck
graft (shoot)
grandeur
grandiosity
grate (fireplace)
gusto
halo (aurora)
halo (magnificence)
happy hour
heart condition, present
heat (passion)
heat (warmth)
highlights
hit upon (happen on)
hobby
hoe down
holiday (vacation)
honor (unearned)
honorable mention
horsepower
hospital records
hot tub
hugs and kisses
humor
hydroelectric power
hydrogen
idol (hero)
illness of aunts or uncles
illumination (lighting)
imagination
imaginative ability
inbound direction
incandescence
income from real estate
increment (addition)
incubator
infancy
infatuation
instillation (imparting)
instruction

invention
investments, speculative
irradiation
jamboree
jewelry as adornment or vanity
jewels
joust
joviality
joy
jubilation
jury, deliberations of
keeping an inn
kiln
kiss
kite
labor (giving birth)
lap (overlap)
laughter
lavish things
leave (vacation)
lectern (platform)
legitimacy of children
leisure activities
leverage (advantage)
levity
liaison (affair)
libido
light (illumination)
light bulb
light ray
lighting (natural)
limelight
literary creative output
litter (newborn)
locomotive
loop (circle)
loose living
lottery
love (fondness)
love (romance)
love, questions of
love affair
luck
lucky break

Things Continued

luminosity
lump (knot)
luster
luxuries (excesses)
magnificence
majesty (splendor)
marquee (tent)
marvel (wonder)
masterpiece
matinee
medal (decoration)
melodrama
merit, things without
merriment
middle (center)
midst
mirth
miscarriage
mixer (dance)
money of a parent
mother's money
motif (theme)
motion picture
motion picture industry
motivation
motor
movies
mural
musical
narcissism
night on the town
nightfall
nucleus (of atom)
nudity
object of affection
obstetrics
odds (chances)
offshoot (sprout)
offspring (ideas)
one-night stand
one-upmanship
opportunity (happenstance)
optimism

orgy
ornate style
ostentation
outgrowth (shoot)
outing
ovation (tribute)
oven
pageant
pageantry
parade (circus like)
parade (vaunting)
parent, death of
part (lines in a play)
party (recreational)
party supplies
pass (overture)
pastime
pathos
percentages (odds)
performance (acting)
personal creativity
phenomena (wonder of life)
picnic
picture (movie)
plasma (charged particles)
platform (rostrum)
plaudit
play (recreation)
play (theatrical)
playing (having fun)
playing cards
pleasant time
pleasure, things of
poker (card game)
polish (shininess)
pollution control device
pomp
poorly paid occupation
positiveness
power (energy)
practice (rehearsal)
prana
prize
prize fight

procession
procreation
production (show)
program (curriculum)
program (performance)
projection (juts out)
projector (movie)
promenade (ceremonial march)
promenade (leisurely walk)
promiscuity
protein
protuberance
proxy fight
public teaching
puff (swelling)
purse (prize)
quality
radial symmetry
radiance
radiation
radiator (source of heat)
radio as entertainment
raffle
range (domain)
rattle (toy)
ray (line of light)
ray (radiance)
reassurance
recess (playtime)
recreation
recreational sex
regalia
relish (pleasure)
reproduction (procreation)
resource (leisure time)
resourcefulness
resplendence
rider (addition)
risk (speculation)
risky ventures
rock concert
rodeo
roller coaster
rostrum (podium)

roulette
roulette wheel
round object
routine (skit)
routine, an entertainer's
rule (dominion)
rule (reign)
rulership
sailing (recreational)
scenery (backdrop)
scenery (vista)
scepter
school functions
searchlight
seat (center)
sensationalism
series (progression)
sexual activity
shirt
shorts (clothing)
show business
sitcom
skates (ice, roller, etc.)
skirt
skit (performance)
skydiving
slice (graft)
smelter
snag (protuberance)
sob story
solar collector
solar panel
somersault
souvenir
spare (extra) item
spark of life
spectacle (event)
spectacular things
speculation (gambling)
splendor
spontaneity
sport (recreation)
sporting event
sports, non-professional

sports, recreational
sports, spontaneous
spotlight
spread (commodity purchase)
squeeze (hug)
staged efforts
stake (wager)
stamina
state of a woman with child
status symbol
steam
stock (ownership)
stock option
stock trading
stove
strayed animals
stretching exercises
stroke (of luck)
summer
sun
sun bathing
sundial
sunshine
supremacy
sureness
surfing
swelling (knot)
swimming
swing (on a play ground)
syzygy
tablet (plaque)
talent (musical, artistic, etc.)
tassel
teaching
telemarketing
television
television, for entertainment
temperature
test-drive
testimonial
theater
theatrics
things dependent on chance
things that are noticed

throne
tingle (flutter)
tinsel (decoration)
title (crown)
toast (commemoration)
torch
tournament
toy
tragedy (theatrics)
transplant
treadmill
treat (that which pleases)
tribute (honor)
trifle (trinket)
trim (embellishment)
trinket
trophy
tryst
tuft (as of hair)
twinkle
vacation
verve (liveliness)
vestment
view (vista)
vim (vigor)
virility
vitality
vitamin
wager
warmth
wedding of a friend
win
wonder (a marvel)
wood stove
work out
work with fire
worship (praise)
yacht
yard work
yoga exercises

Psychological Qualities

affection, warmth of	gratefulness	praise
aptitude	happiness	preciousness (likability)
arrogance	humor	pride
assurance (confidence)	imposing one's will	prosperity
bootstraps (self-reliance)	instructing, ability for	prowess (bravery)
bragging	invincibility	relaxing activities
bravado	learning, the process of	role playing
capability (innate skill)	leisure	romance
capacity (skill)	likability	romance without commitment
captivation	macho display	romantic feelings
central focus	matters of the heart	romantic love
cheer	merry making	seeking of admiration
compensation	morale	self, pride in
competence (ability)	mother love	self-centeredness
conceit	motivation	self-importance
confidence (self-assurance)	motives	self-interest (things done in)
conviviality	notability	self-possession
creative talents	noticed, being	sense of humor
creativity	omnipotence	sexual pleasure
credit reputation	oomph (vitality)	splendidness
deriving enjoyment	originality	spontaneity
domination	ostentatious behavior	superiority
dramatics, flair for	passion (emotion)	superiority complex
ego	passion (love)	talent
emotional expression	performing, ability for	tragedy, playing out
essence (basic quality)	personal liberty	vanity (pride)
expression of emotion	personhood	veneer (facade)
expressions of emotion	pet as surrogate child	vigor (enthusiasm)
expressiveness	playing, fondness for	warmth
flair	pleasurable pursuit	will
flattery	pleasure	willfulness
focus, your	popularity	willpower
frolic	positive view	winning
fulfillment	potential	
generosity	power, one's personal	

Occupations or Person Types

actor	boxer	children
actress	boy friend	comedian
amusement park worker	bug (hobbyist)	comic
artist	carny	commodity dealer
athlete	cheerleader	coward

dandy
darling (sweetheart)
dealer (cards)
educational profession
educator
entertainer
enthusiast
entrepreneur
exhibitor
exposer
extra
extrovert
film actor
food chemist
girl friend
goldsmith
goof-off
government representative
heart specialist
hero
heroine
impresario (promoter)
infants
knight
love (beloved)
lover
master of ceremonies
men, ages 35 to 45
midwife
movie maker
muse (guiding spirit)
nightclub performer
nudist
obstetrician
optimist
park ranger
patron of the arts
performer
phenomena (remarkable person)
philanderer
player
principal
profiteer
projectionist
quack doctor
queen
rich people
ruler
school master
school teacher
showoff
speculator
stockbroker
stockholder
sweetheart
teacher
theatrical agent
theatrical worker
those in artistic careers
those who cater to pleasure
those who entertain
those with wealth or influence
trifler

Places

amphitheater
amusement park
arcade
arena
arena of action in a contest
auditorium
breeding place
cabaret
casino
cinema
circus
coliseum
commodity exchange
commodity market
concert hall
court of a king
crematory
drive-in
exchange (brokerage)
exciting places
exclusive club
fun house
gambling casino
golf course
grandstand
great mansions or estates
gymnasium
hang out
hangout
haunt
hub (main place)
lateral side, the
lounge
middle, the
movie house
node (center or hub)
outside (out-of-doors)
oven
palace
park (recreational area)
parks and preserves (gardens)
patio
place for pleasure
place of amusement
place of entertainment
place of fun
playground
playhouse
pool room
resort, pleasure
resort area
rink
saloon
showboat
solarium
sport arena
stadium
stage, the
steam bath
stock exchange

Places Continued

stock market
studio

swimming hole
swimming pool
theater

track, race
vacation resort
warmest part of the house

Family Members or Relations

adopted child
brother or sister #2
child, biological

child, first
daughter
descendant

famous relative
offspring (children)
son

Mundane Ideas

birth rate
business obligation
celebrity, national
community resources
educational matters
folk culture
gain from speculation
gambling
high society

imperialism
loss from speculation
market leverage
music, national
national glory
national pastimes
options market
popularity of state
recreation area

risks, national
sound currency
speculation (venture)
speculation, market
stock certificate
stock markets
teacher
theater
world's fair

Parts of Our Body

back (in general)
belly
blood circulatory system
chakra
circulatory system (blood)
gross motor control
heart (in general)

heart sac
metabolism
palpitations of heart
pericardium
pregnancy
repair processes
shoulder blades

sides of the body
solar plexus
spine (in general)
swelling
trunk (torso)
vertebrae (in general)
waist

Afflictions or Diseases

abortion, spontaneous
aneurysm
angina
bloating
blood disease
convulsions (spasms)
cyst

enlarged heart
fainting spell
heartburn
hematoma
hernia
inflammation
myocardial infarct

prickly heat
spinal problem
subluxation
sun stroke
sunburn
weakness

Colors

bright-yellow
gold
golden colors
honey color

orange-brown
rich colors
sandy color
sienna

yellow
yellow-orange

Gems or Minerals

amber	gold	topaz
brass	sunstone	

Animals

hatchling	maggot (larva)	seal
larvae	otter	tiger
lion	peacock	
lizard	pheasant	

Mythical Figures or Constellation Names

Admetos (exaggerated promises)	crown)	Leo (lion)
Apollo (the healer)	Cupid	Leo Minor (little lion)
Apollon	Dionysos (the escapist)	Liber
Apus (bird of paradise)	Eros	Narcissus
Baccus	Fornax (furnace)	Pavo (peacock)
Corona Australis (southern. crown)	Helios (sun)	Perseus (the hero)
Corona Borealis (northern	Hyperion	Theseus (hero)
	Lacerta (lizard)	Titans

Parts of an Organization

chief executive's office	office directors	stockholder
customer satisfaction	quality of products	stockholder relations
energy costs	share holders	

Industry Categories

cable TV	gold/silver Mining	professional sports
commodity services	golf course maintenance	recreation
driver's instruction	Investment (banking)	solar panel installation
electrical switches	investment (brokerage)	securities brokerage
energy	leisure time	sports
entertainment	lighting equipment	teaching
event management	motivational trainers	toys
gambling	nuclear power generation	training (educational)
gaming	power generation	training (sports)

Parts of an Automobile

body bolt	engine mount	piston
chassis	engines (in general)	ride
combustion chamber	headlights	
engine block	motor, the	

Parts of a House

back porch	ballroom	child's room

Parts of a House Continued
deck
den
fireplace
furnace
game room
gazebo
hearth, the
heating system, the

lighting
living room
main hall
nursery
ornate decoration
patio
patio door
play area
playroom

porch
recreation room
skylight
stove
studio
sun room
swimming pool
television room
veranda

Parts of a Ship

boiler
engine
engine room
heating plant

keel
lighting
power plant
recreation area

sail
swimming pool

An Overview of the Sixth House

A Cadent House of the First Quadrant
Placed in the Right and Lower Hemispheres

Cadent houses help spur an evolution of inner personal qualities which ultimately benefit society. Attributes like **productivity, attitude toward work, services willingly given, duty assumed or assigned**, and **hygiene** (in all forms) are such Sixth House traits. The Sixth House is also associated with **illness, diet, healing, nutrition, food preparation, food served, clothing, tools, analysis, coping with stress**, and **domestic pets**. The Sixth House has an affinity with the zodiacal sign of Virgo and the yin side of the planet Mercury.

The Sixth House imparts an inner restlessness about attitudes or positions taken toward **work, assignments, duties, chores**, etc. Perhaps you feel that your contributions are never quite psychologically acceptable. This could raise **personal insecurities**, and if nurtured may affect your **health**. Your **nervous system** may over react to private fears of inadequacy or rejection. Nurturing or encouraging, or addressing and stopping such insecurities, is a Sixth House lesson. **Feeling insecure** and **working harder to gain recognition or acceptance** in life is a positive process. Feeling insecure and letting this vulnerability ruin your health through worry is a less positive Sixth House theme. One need not follow from the other. The Sixth House does not cause **illness**. It does not mirror illness. Illness is an internal issue which may arise from **misplaced stress** or worry about issues such as **fear of rejection, constant worry, general insecurity**, etc. Such results may then be shown through the Sixth House.

The Sixth House reflects your **work attitudes**, not the actual work you do. It does not show your choice of career; it shows your **feelings about employment**. Your career choice should be based upon your general educational and employment skills, not just any Sixth House astrological emphasis. You probably have several **skills** which others may find employable. These skills are shown throughout the horoscope, not just in the Sixth House. When using astrology to help you with career choices consider your entire potential, not what one element offers. Prospective employers want to hire the entire person and all their capabilities, not just their Sixth House.

Taking personal responsibility for your **work output** is an important Sixth House trait. The Sixth House prompts for an improvement of self through **applied discipline**. Improving your self-image by taking **responsibility for your efforts** is a Sixth House activity. If what you produce does not meet another's expectations, then maybe the expectations were too high. Maybe you did not produce well enough. Maybe you could not meet your own expectations. It is how you handle both your **internally generated rejection** and the possible rejection from others which is mirrored by the Sixth House. The Sixth House does not criticize you, it leaves that to your own inclinations.

The Sixth House encourages development of qualities like **devotion to tasks, dedication, loyalty, faithfulness, allegiance**, etc. Through the Sixth House you are asked to constantly reexamine your internal commitment to people, tasks, etc. Sometimes you are forced to make internal compromises about this **commitment**, and sometimes these compromises may cause **psychological or physical stress**. Unconsciously this **stress** can build and may appear as various forms of illness. The illness may become real or it may be imagined. This is a typical Sixth House process. To use the Sixth House positively, recognize that stress can accumulate if it is not addressed or relieved. Alleviate that which causes stress by refusing to nurture **stress building attitudes**. Turn a Sixth House potential illness into a **healing process**.

The **efficient functioning** of your body, your being, or your organism is a Sixth House matter. The Sixth House prompts you to examine your life, your lifestyle, the personal satisfaction you get from your work, living, etc. This process of examination and reexamination is a never ending one. You are called to look at the **efficiency of your output**, your **work methods**, your **loyalty**, every aspect of your working or interdependent relationships with others, including the efficient functioning of your body. Whenever there are blockages or stoppages, known or unknown, the Sixth House has a way of bringing these to your attention. This may cause some stress or illness in those cases when Sixth House matters are not correctly addressed.

People who are dependent on you, like **employees, co-workers, servants, domestics**, etc. are shown through your Sixth House. These **dependents** offer loyalty and dedication and in return they expect fair treatment and appreciation of their efforts. They also expect **discipline** when they are out of line or when they do not perform to expectations.

Diet, food, and **dietary interests** also fall under the Sixth House. The diet which is best for you is that diet which most efficiently uses your body type. Some people prefer to eat light foods, some demand heavy foods. Some like to fast while others would not miss a meal. Another person's **diet** or **fare of food** is not necessarily your diet or fare. It is your responsibility to find and follow a **dietary regimen** which suits you best. There is more to choosing diet than astrology. Consider also heredity, environment, lifestyle, religious preferences, glandular inclinations (e.g., pituitary body type, thyroid type, pancreas type), etc. The way you choose and practice diet and **body cleansing** is shown by your Sixth House. Expect to meet **feedback from your body** when it is unhappy with the way it is either being treated or ignored.

The Sixth House covers many important areas of life. Learn to reexamine your life from **diet** to **work** to **dedication** by learning about your Sixth House.

Horary or Electional Ideas

assistance	facts	sickness
bureaucracy	food preparation	small animals
clothing	healing	stress
colds (illness)	hygiene	technique
criticism	illness	tenant
dedication	nutrition	training
dependents (subordinates)	people one works with	work
diet	pet	working conditions
duty	productivity	
employees	service	

Things

absorption (assimilation)	assignment (homework)	bracket (parenthesis)
abuse (criticism)	assimilation	bread
accuracy (exactness)	assistance (help)	briefcase
action (operation)	associate (co-worker)	broom
actions that affect health	associating (classifying)	brush (in general)
acupuncture	astringent	bulk storage
agenda	athletic supporter	bunting (for baby)
ailment (disorder)	atlas	bureaucracy
altimeter	attachment (extender)	cabinets (furniture)
amount (sum)	attendance (roll)	cache
analysis (reasoning)	attire (dress)	calculation
animal husbandry	axiom	calculator
antibiotic	backpack	cam
antiseptic	bandage	canister
apparatus	barometer	canning food
apparel	basic necessities	cap (hat)
appliance (tool)	baton	capacitance (electrical)
application (put to use)	beasts of burden	capacity (for storing)
apprenticeship	beat (assignment)	car repair
aptness (effectiveness)	bed linen	care of pets
armada	being of service	casting (molding)
armed forces, the	bird call (summons)	catalog
armed services	birds as pets	categorization
armies	bit (piece)	category
army, the	black magic	celibacy
arrangement (grouping)	blanket	census
array (display)	bodily well being	cereals
art (technique)	bolt (cloth)	chart
article (item)	bookcase	chasteness
artistic output	bracket (classify)	chisel

Houses of the Fiirst Quadrant

Things Continued
chore
class (grouping)
classic work
classifying
clean, things which are
clean air regulations
cleaning
cleaning item
cleanliness
cleanser
climate (distinct from weather)
climate (in general)
cloth
clothes, formal dress
clothing (in general)
coat (outerwear)
comb
compliance
component
computer media
computer programming
computer storage
computer
computing equipment
concordance
confetti
conscientiousness
conservation
contribution (work)
cottage industry
count (tally)
court procedures
craftsmanship
crew
criteria (standard)
crocheting
crusade (military)
cubicle (work place)
cure
curing (healing)
curing (smoking)
custom work
daily duties

data (facts)
day (work day)
day care
death of a friend
decency (decorum)
dedication (commitment)
defect (flaw)
deference (obedience)
degree (measure)
dehydrating food
delineation
detailing
details
devices, labor saving
diagram
diameter
dictionary
diet
dietary habits
dietetics
digest (summary)
direction (guideline)
direction (instruction)
dirty things
disbelief (doubt)
discipline (regimen)
discipline (training)
discrimination (separation)
dish (food)
dish (plate)
dish (portion)
disinfectant
disorder (ailment)
distinction (differentiation)
distress
distressing condition
division (branch)
division (math)
division (separation)
doctoring
domain (field of work)
domestic pets
dossier (record)
doubt (uncertainty)

dough (bread)
down (feathers)
draft (outline)
draperies
drawers (underclothing)
dress (clothing)
dressing table
drill (exercise)
driving test
drudgery
dry goods
dust
duties, daily
duty (obligation)
duty (responsibility)
echelon (formation)
efficiency
efficient routines
element (piece)
emergency supplies
employees, treatment of
employment
employment matters
engagement (employment)
enrollment (enlistment)
ensemble (outfit)
enterprise (undertaking)
entry (record)
ephemeris
equipment
errand (mission)
evening
everyday duties
evidence (fact)
exactness (precision)
exam, physical
examination (analysis)
example (specimen)
excerpt
execution (performance)
explicitness (precision)
fabric (material)
fabrication (making)
facet (aspect)

facet (cut)
facility (ease)
factors
facts
faculty (knack)
faculty (staff)
fare (range of food)
fault (defect)
feed (cater)
feed (devour)
feed (nourishment)
feet (measurement)
figures (numbers)
file (row)
file (storage)
file cabinet
fixture (device)
flatiron
flatware
fleet, naval
flour
fodder
folder (storage envelope)
follow through
food
food industry
food preparation
food preservation
food products
food service
food storage
forage
fork (eating utensil)
formation (arrangement)
formula
fragment (piece)
freehand work
freeze dried food
funk (depression)
game preserve
garb
garment
gauge (meter)
gear (cog)

gear (material)
genre (grouping)
glossary
goods on a shelf
gown
grace (skill)
grain (seed)
grammar
graph
green eyeshade
grip (suitcase)
group (classification)
guest (boarder)
guidelines
guise (attire)
habit (dress)
halter (clothing)
hammer
hamper (basket)
handicraft work
handicrafts
handiwork
handkerchief
hanger (clothes)
hard work
hardware
harvest
hay
healing
healing measures
health (problems with illness)
health food
health improvement
health maintenance
hierarchy (ranking)
histogram
hit list
hitch (enlistment)
home, mobile
home of a neighbor
home of a sibling
homespun goods
homework (piecework for pay)
homework (school assignment)

household chores
housework
hygiene
hygienic practices
illness (in general)
illness, acute
imperfection (flaw)
implement
income property
index
industriousness
infantry
inspections
installation (to set for use)
instrument, gauge
instrument, medical
instrument, tool
instrumentation (devices)
intricate work
involuntary labor
ironing board
itemizing
itinerary
job opportunities
job sought if you have no job
job you work at
jobbing
journey- father's
keyboard (input device)
keyword
kneeling
knitting
kosher inspections
labor (duties)
labor (effort expended)
labor (work)
labor force, the
labor intensive task
labor organization
laboratory apparatus
laborious effort
lap (clothing)
lather
laundry

Things Continued

lawn mower
layer (stratum)
layout (arrangement)
legibility
length (measurement)
lever (pry tool)
line (policy)
linen (household)
liniment (ointment)
list (roll)
list making
listing
load (capacity)
logic
loom
lopsided objects
luggage
magazine rack
magic (ceremonial)
making (producing)
mallet
manifest (list)
manufacturing
map
mark (grade)
massage
material (apparatus)
material (cloth)
material (repertoire)
mathematics
matrix (math form)
mechanism (internal works)
medication
medicinal herb
medicine
men's clothes
mending (healing)
mending (patching)
menu
metallurgy
meter
method (technique)
methodical task

military regimen
miniature thing
model building
nail (tool)
napkin
naturopathy
necessary service
necktie
needlework
negligee
nicety (small detail)
numbers (in general)
nutrition
obligingness
optimization
orbit
orchestration (arrangement)
order (arrangement)
order of magnitude
orders of the day
organized labor
ornithology
outfit (ensemble)
output
overcoat
overhaul
overstrain
pack (bundle)
pajamas
panel (piece)
parade (procession)
parameter (rule)
parcel (package)
part (piece)
part (share)
particulars (details)
partition
patch (fix)
percentage (part of)
performance (exercise)
performance review
personal computer
personal effort(s)
personality test

perusal
phase (facet)
physical examination
physical therapy
picket (sentinel)
piece
place setting (utensils)
plan (map)
plan (scheme)
pliers
plume (feather)
ply (layer)
pocket
policing
portion
post (marker)
posting an entry
pottery
poultice
powder (medicinal)
practice (drill)
precision
preparation (training)
prescription
preserved food
preventive medicine
problems of others
product information
production (making)
professional sports
   management
proficiency
program (description)
program (list of instructions)
program (schedule)
project
proportion (quota)
provision (supply)
prudery
pump
punctuation mark
puppet (marionette)
puppet (pawn)
purity

quantity (sum)
rank (ordering)
rating
ratio
receipt (voucher)
reckoning (counting)
record keeping
redoing
redone work
regiment
regimentation
register (ledger)
registered mail
registration
remedy (cure)
remodeling
repair work
repairing
repairs
repertoire
repertory
replenishment (restocking)
reserve (stockpile)
resource (support)
respect (detail)
retrofitting
review (ceremonial inspection)
review (critique)
ribbon
rigor
robe
roll (food)
roll (roster)
roster
routine (computer program)
rule (measure)
ruler (measure)
salve
sanitation
satchel
scenario (outline)
schedule (agenda)
schedule (timetable)
schematic

scientific societies
screening processes
scrub brush
seam (layer)
section (branch)
segment (piece)
selection
senior (grade)
separation (division)
sequence (succession)
service
service, military
service freely given
service rendered or received
service to others
serving
serving platter
servitude
sewing
sextant
shampoo
share (portion)
shift (of work)
shortcoming (fault)
sickness
sickness, its quality or causes
siphon
situation (job)
skepticism
skill (craft)
skill (prowess)
sleep, inability to
slip (pillowcase)
smoking (food preserving)
snip (fragment)
soap
sorting
specialization
specialty
specification
spell
split (division)
spoon
squadron

staff (crew)
state (ritual)
statistics
stitch (suture)
storage
stored crops or grains
stored products
storing away
strain
strata
stratification
straw
stress
stretcher
string (procession)
stub (receipt)
stuff (gear)
style (type)
subject matter
submission
submissiveness
subordinate role
subservience
suit (of clothes)
sunset
surgical supplies
survey (a map)
survey (a poll)
sustenance (food)
swab (mop)
symptom
syndrome
system (method)
systematic thinking
table (dining)
table (list)
tablet (medicinal)
tabulation
tack (approach)
tack (nail)
tackle (equipment)
tactic (maneuver)
tactic (scheme)
tally

Houses of the Fiirst Quadrant

Things Continued

task (chore)
technical ability
technicality
technique (procedure)
technique (skill)
technology
tediousness
telephone directory
template
tenant (boarder)
test (exam)
testimony (evidence)
tete-a-tete
textiles
therapy
thermometer
thimble
thoroughness
threshing
through-put
tincture (medicinal)
togs
toil
toilet articles
tonic (restorative)
tool (implement)
tool (means)
top (lid)
tow (tugboat)
towel
train (retinue)
train (succession)
training

trajectory
trappings (dress)
treadle
treatise
treatment (medical)
trial run
triangulation
tribe (taxonomic classification)
trick (knack)
trigonometry
troops, military
trousers
trunk (luggage)
tugboat
tunic
twilight
type (class)
unclean, the
under-rating
underwear
unit (quantity)
urge to adapt to others
use (utility)
utensil
utility (usefulness)
vacuum cleaner
validity (factual grounds)
valise
vanity (dressing table)
vein (strata)
verification
vice (fault)
vinyl tile
virginity

virus
viscera
voluntary service
volunteer labor
voucher
wardrobe
wash, the
washcloth
washing
watercourse
weakening
weather instruments
wedding picture
weights and measures
wheat
white magic
witchcraft
woodworking
wool
work
work force
work gang
work performance review
work room
work schedule
work with heavy tools
workmanship
worry
wrench (tool)
written test
yardstick
year
zip code

Psychological Qualities

accuracy
anxiety
bashfulness
busyness
chastity
cleanliness
compliance
correction, need for giving

craft (skill)
craft (trade)
criticism
dedication
defect of character
depression
despair (hopelessness)
despondency

devotion (dedication)
devotion to a task
dietary concerns
diffidence (reserve)
disciplined living or work
discouragement
discriminating sense
duty

efficiency
employers, attitude towards
excellence, working for
fault-finding
fear (anxiety)
gathering information
guilt
health attitudes
helpless feelings
hopelessness
humility
hygienic practices
inadequacy, feelings of
inferiority, feelings of
intolerance of others
maladjustment
malaise
mathematical ability
meekness

melancholy
mental instability
modesty
modify, ability to
nagging
negativity
nervous aggravation
nervous breakdowns
nervous tension
obedience
over-tiredness
perfection, meeting
personal inadequacies
pessimism
physical discomfort
practical efforts
precision
prowess (skill)
psychological problem

repair efforts
scruples (anxiety)
selectivity
service
storing food
stress
submission
subordination
suffering, bearing
technique (style)
timidity
transference
volunteering
weakness (in general)
work, willingness to
work habits
worry
worthlessness

Occupations or Person Types

accountant
adjutant
aide (assistant)
airline host/hostess
angel (backer)
apprentice
artisan
assistant
attendant
auditor
bailiff
blacksmith
boarder
bookkeeper
bus boy
butler
cabinet maker
cadet
caretaker
carpenter
chiropractor
civil servant
civil service worker

cleaner
clerk
clock repairer
clothier
co-worker
computer analyst
computer operator
computer programmer
contractor
copy editor
craftsman
critic
customer engineer
data processor
day laborer
deed recorder
dental hygienist
dental technician
dependents (subordinates)
deputy
dictator
dietician
doctor

doer
domestic
domestic (servant)
draftsman
dressmaker
drudge
druggist
dry cleaner
electronic technician
emergency worker
employees
fellow employee
file clerk
food preparer
food server
forest ranger
forester
governess
government worker
grocer
harvester
healer
health official

Occupations or Person Types Continued

hired hand
hireling
house servant
household help
husbandry
hygienist
hypochondriac
inferior
information processor
innkeeper
inspector
intern
janitor
laborer
lodger
longshoreman
maid
marshal
massager
mathematician
mechanical engineer
media analyst
mental health worker
mercenary
metal craftsman
metal worker
meter reader
migrant farm laborer
military (person in)
nurse
operator (worker)
optician
optometrist
orderly
packer
patient
patrolman
pessimist
pharmacist
physician
police (in general)
poll taker
porter
poultry farmer
proofreader
public health official
public servant
ranger
record keeper
recorder
registrar
renter
repair person
repairer
retainer
sanitation worker
seamstress
second (helper)
secretary
sentry
serf
servant
service repairman
sexual deviant
shepherd
shrew
skeptic
slave
smith
socially inferior person
soldier
specialist
statistician
steward
subordinate
surveyor
systems analyst
tailor
taxidermist
technician
television technician
tenant
textile worker
therapist
those in the armed forces
those who deal with clothing
those who tend the sick
tradesman
trainer
underling
understudy
usher
valet
veterinarian, small animals
virgin
volunteer
waiter
waitress
watchman
welder
witch
workers
workers at routine jobs
workers in all trades
wrangler
yeoman
zoo worker

Places

bakery
barracks
bath, public
bathroom
blacksmith shop
boot camp
cafe
cafeteria
cannery
clean room
clinic
closet
compartment
depository
diner
dining room
dispensary
doctor's office
drug store
dry cleaners
dry dock

employment agency
food markets
forge
garage
garage workshop
grain elevator
granary
grocery stores
haystack
hold (storage place)
inn
kennel
kitchen

labor area
laundry
laundry room
lawyer's office
mobile home
office where one works
paddock
pharmacy
pigsty
place where food is kept
record storage place
repository
restaurant

sick room
silo
smoke house
station house
storehouse
storehouse for dairy products
storeroom
terrace
tier (row)
warehouse
where food is disbursed
work area
workshop

Family Members or Relations

aunt, maternal
father's kin

uncle, maternal
uncles on the mother's side

Mundane Ideas

air force
animals
army, the
bureaucracy, the
civil service
civil workers
coast guard, the
construction equipment
corporation law
domestic employees
eating establishment
economic outlook
employees
granary
healing
hiring of employees
inventory

labor force, the
labor union
laboring class
manufacturing
military forces
military service
military stores
mortality tables
national health policies
navy
people who give service(s)
personnel, the
police
price of a house for sale
price of land
public ceremony
public health

public works
sanitary practices
servants of the country
storage facility
store's inventory
strike (labor)
strikes, inception of
technical indicator
trade patterns
trades, the
unions, trade
water distribution system
working classes
working conditions
working environment

Parts of Our Body

abdomen
belching
bile
body, care of the
bowels

diaphragm
flatus
food assimilation
gall bladder
hiccups

intestinal gas
intestine
nerve sheath
peptic ulcer
small intestine

Houses of the Fiirst Quadrant

Afflictions or Diseases

appendicitis	disease (in general)	malady
bowel disturbance	dysentery	malnutrition
bowel obstruction	flatulence	mental illness
colds	frigidity	nervous illnesses
colic	hay fever	peritonitis
colitis	hypoglycemia	stress
complaint (malady)	infirmity	tension (stress)
dietary problems	intestinal problems	

Colors

beige	cream	light brown
brown	earth tones	subdued colors
camouflage	lemon	

Gems or Minerals

bronze	forging	magnetite
casting	jade	nephrite
chrome	jadite	potassium
chromite	jet	

Animals

animals, small domesticated	fowl	poultry
bat	goose	quadruped
birds (in general)	hamster	sheep
buck	heron	small animals
cat	hound	squirrel
chicken	lynx	turkey
deer	mount (steed)	wild fowl
dog	owl	
duck	pet (small)	

Mythical Figures or Constellation Names

Athena (the counselor)	Grus (crane)	Ophiuchus (serpent holder)
Caelum (chisel)	Hephaistos (the wage earner)	Sextans (sextant)
Canes Minor (small dog)	Hestia (Vesta, the homemaker)	Vesta (the homemaker)
Ceres	Microscopium (microscope)	Virgo (virgin)
Circinus (compass)	Minerva	Vulcan
Demeter (the caregiver)	Octans (instrument)	

Parts of an Organization

agency (bureau)	customer service	section (branch)
branch (division)	data processing	technical staff
cafeteria, the	department (division)	utility shop
clinic, the	information services	

Industry Categories

accounting services
aerospace/defense
agriculture (harvesting)
alloy treating
animal handlers
animal husbandry services
apparel (designers)
apparel (manufacturers)
automobile repair
blacksmithing
carpet manufacturers
cleaning services
clerical services
computer systems
contractors (defense)
contractors (military)
dental services
dry cleaners
electronic Instrumentation

electronics (defense)
equipment repair
eye care (supplies)
eye care (treatment)
fire prevention services
food processing
hardware and tools
health care (diversified)
healthcare HMOs
home appliances
hotel/motel services
household appliances
household products
housewares
industrial equipment manufacters
industrial Services
instrumentation
Janitorial Services

Jewelry (Manufacture)
Jewelry (Repair)
Light Machining
Machine Tools
Medical (Supervisory Care)
Medical Services
Metal Casting Services
Metal Fabricating
Office Equipment & Supplies
Parking Lot Equipment
Precision Instrument
Records Management
Retail (Apparel)
Semiconductor Equipment
Shoe Repair
Specialized Services
Textiles
Veterinarians (Small Animal)
Welding

Parts of an Automobile

emission control system
fuel or oil filter
glove compartment
instrumentation

jack, the
piston ring
preventive maintenance
repairs made

rust prevention
spare tire
valve lifter

Parts of a House

alcove (recess)
bathroom
bathtub
closet
counter top
cupboard
dining room
dishwasher
food preparation area
food storage areas
garage

hamper, laundry
hobby room
kitchen
kitchen appliance
laundry
main bathroom
medicine cabinet
out buildings (utility)
pantry
refrigerator
scullery

sewing room
shelving (for storage)
shower
shower stall
sick room
sink
storeroom
utility closet
workshop

Parts of a Ship

cargo hold
chain locker
chart house

chart table
cofferdam
commissary

dispensary
dry dock work
galley

Parts of a Ship Continued
aundry
mate

mess
mess deck
sick bay

store (retail outlet)

Houses of the Second Quadrant

Poetry for the Houses of this Quadrant

Seventh House

    Working with others is your choice,
    Acting jointly, as with one voice,
    Calling loudly for the world to see,
    Joint efforts done between you and me.

Eighth House

    Control and exchange versus trust,
    Complex questions — thoughts of lust,
    Learn respect for deaths far side
    Or reincarnate with gain denied.

Ninth House

    Go beyond all, expand your mind,
    Live life fully, there's worlds to find,
    Make it legal, but don't get caught
    Publishing opinion lacking deep thought.

An Overview of the Seventh House

An Angular House of the Second Quadrant
Placed in the Right and Upper Hemispheres

The Seventh House involves seeking out and winning the **cooperation** of others (i.e., **partners**) for your purposes, and the **participation, interaction, opposition,** or **arguments** you receive in return **Shaping and honing efforts** to convince others that your ideas or efforts are worthy starts with the Seventh House. It is difficult to convince others that your ideas are worthy if you do not sincerely believe in them. **Burden sharing** or **mutual helping** ideas dominate Seventh House keywords. **Sharing** as used here means **convincing others** that your views should also be their views. **Competition** starts when another person airs different views from yours. Bouncing around among **cooperation, compromise,** and **competition**: welcome the Seventh House.

Cooperation involves the pursuit of goals in common with others. Cooperation invites **comparison** between differing methods or ideas. Compromise between **opposing views** and subsequent **agreement** is a Seventh House matter. The Seventh House reflects inner attitudes about ideas like **compromise, harmony, agreement,** etc. When these attitudes are expressed with **anger, uncertainty, abruptness, superiority of purpose,** etc., then similar emotions may be returned to you. The Seventh House does not guarantee that you will see **fairness** from others returned for your efforts. Rather it promises that others may **return to you** only what they feel you deserve.

Compromise implies that some middle ground exists around which **opposing views** can be **reconciled**. Keywords like **equality, mutuality, counterpart, clarification,** and **alternatives** are found in the Seventh House. Compromise and reconciling different views involves creating increased **harmony** between parties—especially those who feel that they have the same views or ideas. Emotionally strong opinions are often expressed when setting ideas forth. Different people may express different ways of **working toward** something. Bringing **agreement** to differing views where only a **common purpose** exists is a central Seventh House issue. The learning of this lesson lies not in whether you **compromise** but in how you work on achieving **agreement**.

Obstruction, blockage, or **withdrawal** are negative counterparts to **agreement**. The Seventh House calls for parties to work around their **obstacles** and find **compromise**. The Seventh House calls for working through the **interference** which arises between parties. The Seventh House calls for working through **disagreement** and finding **mutual satisfaction**. Turning **dilemma** into **harmony** is preferred to turning **partnership** into **warfare**. How any particular outcome is reached is primarily controlled by the person who best understands how to work with their Seventh House functions.

Behavior and **manners** are Seventh House topics. Intentionally **blocking** someone's efforts, throwing an emotional **tantrum**, correcting a child's behavior, trying to impress another with your character, or breaching an unknown rule of **etiquette**—these each call for you to face Seventh House topics. Your recovery from either failure or stupidity in **social situations** may be done by increasing your Seventh House awareness. A **social mistake** does not mean public failure. Despite such blunders you may still win agreement if you can effectively soothe the emotions of the allegedly injured parties. Learning **inter-personal skills**, overcoming **social faults**, and progressing with **understanding others** are called for with Seventh House insight. Gaining **harmony** and **agreement** is one key to getting successful **interaction between people**. The way you act can influence **how others either help you** or fight you.

The Seventh House represents **relationships**, **partnerships**, and **togetherness**. It especially represents a formal or legal **marriage** partnership. Marriage involves a social, legal, or religious **teaming**. The purpose of a religious marriage is to create a family atmosphere for the raising of children. It demands you produce surroundings where each **partner's** values can be imparted to offspring. The purpose of a marriage in business is to create **cooperation** while increasing market share. The purpose of a marriage between political entities is to create **a union of ideas**. **Matrimony** implies that a legal or religious sanction has been given to a **union**. But, the Seventh House is only concerned with how the **union** is created and worked, not its legal status.

Social involvements imply a loose arrangement among peoples for mutual protection or expansion. The **growth of society** usually benefits some people more than others. While **equality** may be stated as a reason for urging greater **union** or **cooperation** between groups, **inequality** of social groups may really be intended. Effecting union or agreement does not imply that **unbiased goals** are being sought. **Fairness** is an attribute which we must be constantly strive for to offset **potential conflict**. Open **conflict, disagreement, clashes**, or **disapproval** are just as much a part of the Seventh House as **peace** and **harmony**. Which result succeeds depends on the overall will of the participants.

The Seventh House offers you **social choices**. It reflects your attitudes about **working with others as equals**. It shows the room you demand for **social maneuvering**, and the **bias** you have toward **tolerating the views of others**, even when these dominate your leanings. An important lesson of the Seventh House is learning that yours is not the only **credible view**. Another important lesson is learning to live **peacefully** with the **opinions** of others without **compromising** your own interests or feelings. The Seventh House calls for **equality** and **fairness**, but it never promises these **virtues**. The Seventh House asks that you examine the imperfections found within your present **social circumstances**.

Horary or Electional Ideas

agreement	disagreement	open enemy
arbitration	disapproval	opponent
competition, the	disputes	other persons
compromise	divorce	partners
contracts	harmony	partnership arrangement
contractual agreement	joint arrangements	public enemy
cooperation	lawsuit (open dispute)	relationships
denial (refusal)	marriage	there
deportment	marriage partner	those with whom you consult
dilemma	mate, one's	

Things

abduction	antipathy	banishment
abnormal behavior	antithesis (opposition)	bar (stripe)
accommodation (compromise)	antithesis (reverse)	beautification
accords	apathy	beauty (in general)
accusation	apology	beauty contest
acknowledgment (admission)	apparentness (open to view)	being centered
acrimony	appointment (engagement)	betrayal
adjustment (settling up)	appraisal (evaluation)	bias (prejudice)
admission (permission)	appreciation (understanding)	bid (invitation)
admonishment (chiding)	approval (permission)	bigamy
admonition (reprimand)	arbitration	bilateral symmetry
aesthetics	argument (quarrel)	bitchiness
affront (insult)	armistice	bond (attractive force)
agent of justice	artifact	bond (binding agreement)
aggression (hostility)	arts, the fine arts	bottleneck (impasse)
agreement (harmony)	aspersion (slur)	bout (session)
agreement (understanding)	assault (threat)	bout (skirmish)
allegation (assertion)	assent (agreement)	braiding
alliance (agreement)	assistance (collaboration)	break-in (theft)
alliance (partnership)	associating (social)	breathing exercise
allied effort	association (relationship)	burglary
altercation (dispute)	attention (courtesy)	camps - opposing
alternatives	authorization	capitulation
ambiguity (vagueness)	autumn	censure (reprimand)
ambivalence	aversion (dislike)	ceramic figurine
amends (apology)	awareness (realization)	ceramic tile
anklet	backbiting	ceramics
anonymous gift	balance (scale)	charge (accusation)
antagonism	ball (dance)	chivalry (politeness)
anti-spasmodic	ballet	clarification

Houses of the Second Quadrant

Things Continued
clarity
class (style)
clause (stipulation)
cohabitation prompted by love
coincidence (at the same time)
collusion
color harmony
colors (in general)
committed relationships
communion (togetherness)
comparisons
compatibility
compensation
   (counterbalancing)
competition (contests)
competition (rivalry)
compromise
concession (yielding)
condemnation (disapproval)
conflict
conformance (agreement)
conformity (obedience)
congruity
conjugation (coupling)
consensus
consent
contact with another
contact with equals
contempt
contention (rivalry)
contest
contested affair
contract (legally binding)
contract - marriage
contractual agreement
contradiction
contrast
controversy
cooperation (agreement)
cooperation (participation)
copyright
correlation
correspondence (agreement)

count (allegation)
counterpart
coupling (joining)
court, disputes in
covenant
creative writing
credentials (authorization)
criminal at large
criminal on trial
date (appointment)
deadlock
dealings with partner
decorum
defamation (slander)
defection
definition (clarification)
denial (refusal)
denunciation
deposition
diatribe
differences (contrasts)
differing opinions
dilemma
diplomacy
disagreement
disapproval
disclaimer
discord (disagreement)
discrepancy (variance)
discrimination (bias)
disdain (scorn)
disfavor (disapproval)
disgrace (disfavor)
disgust
dish (good looking person)
dislike (distaste)
disloyalty
disobedience
disorder (disturbance)
disputes (quarrels)
disqualification
disregard
dissension
dissent (discord)

disservice (injustice)
dissolution of a partnership
distribution (arrangement)
divorce(s)
draw (deadlock)
drop in position - a
education (high school)
elitism
eloping
embargo
embezzlement
embroidering
embroidery
encounter (battle)
end of fourth house parent
endorsement
enemies, known
enemies, open
engagement (appointment)
engagement (betrothal)
engraving
enmity
equal relationships
equality
equation
equator
equilibrium
equity (fairness)
equivocation
esthetics
estrangement
etiquette
event (contest)
exasperation (irritation)
exchange (verbal)
expelled party
extra luggage
fabrication (falsehood)
faction (discord)
fairness
faithlessness
fall (season)
false teeth
familiarity (impropriety)

fancy (liking)
fashion (apparel)
fatigue
faux pas
favor (approval)
favor (good turn)
feature article
feud (dispute)
fib
figures (shapes)
figurine
fine art
finery
formal notice
formal notification
formal occasion
formality
formals
foul (infringement)
foul (penalty)
function (social)
fury
gale (storm)
geometry
give and take relationships
glare (disapproving look)
glare (reflection)
glass (clear)
glass, colored or stained
glass eye
good taste
gravitation
gravity (attraction)
grievance (injustice)
gynecology
gyroscope
half-truth
handshake (agreement rite)
happenstance
heated gases
hitch (marriage)
hold up (robbery)
honeymoon
horizontal direction

hot air
house you plan to move to
hue
illumination (clarification)
image (reflection)
immediate outcome of events
impartiality
impasse
impoliteness
imposition
impressions from others
improper action
impropriety (incorrect action)
inanity (emptiness)
inclemency (stormy)
including (involving)
inconsiderateness
indefiniteness
ineligibility
inequality
inequitable things
inequity
iniquity
injunction
injustice
instrument, legal
instrument, musical
insubordination
insurgence
insurrection
interference
intermarriage
intermediate things
interpersonal relationships
invitation
involvement (take part in)
jealousy
joblessness
joint actions
joint activity
joint undertakings
junior (grade)
known adversaries
labor trouble

lace
lacquer
landscape (picture)
lap (polish)
larceny
lassitude
lattice (geometrical pattern)
lawlessness
lawsuit
laxity
layoff
lease agreement
leave (consent)
legal contract
legal dispute
level (tool)
levelness
libel
liberty (familiarity)
lighting fixtures (decorative)
liking (affinity)
linen (fine)
loitering
manners
marital concerns
marital love
marriage
match (contest)
match (counterpart)
match (prospective partner)
matrimony
matter (affair)
matters regarding strangers
meddling
mediation
meetings - small gatherings
melee
mindfulness
mirror (reflection)
misbehavior
misconduct
misdemeanor
mixed signals
modulation (tempering)

Things Continued
money from renter or tenant
motion (proposal)
musical harmony
mutiny
negotiation
neutering
neutrality
neutralization
neutralizing
neutron
nicety (refinement)
no obligation offer
objection
offering (gift)
offset (displacement)
onus (burden of proof)
opacity
open warfare
opportunity (through others)
opposing view
opposites
option (alternative)
orientation (sense of direction)
ostracism
other, the
other side in an issue, the
outcome of contentions
outcome of opposition (enmity)
outcome of pleas
outlet (opening)
overmatched confrontation
pad (on animal's foot)
paint
par (evenness)
parallelogram
parity (equivalence)
participation (joining in)
participation (joint action)
participation (sharing)
party (social)
passage (opening)
pastel
peace

pet (favored one)
pick (choice)
pigment
pin-up photo
plaster
plea
pleading (legal)
poetry
poise
polar opposites
polarity
porcelain
pose (airs)
pose (posture)
power of attorney
preconception
prejudice
pressure (force against force)
pretext
proportion (balance)
proposal (invitation)
proposed place to remove to
prospective marriage
protocol
proxy
pull (attraction)
quarrel
quibbling
rage (anger)
rainbow
rally (competitive try)
randomness
rank (pay class)
rank (relative position)
rank (social class)
rap (blame)
rebuff
rebuke
rebuttal
receivership
receptacle (receiver)
reception (party)
reciprocal agreement
reciprocal arrangement

recital (concert)
reconciliation
redecorating the home
refinement
reflector
refusal
rejection (denial)
relationships
representation
reprimand
reproach (blame)
repulsion
requirement (condition)
resistance (opposition)
resonance (orbital)
right-of-way
rivalry
robbery
satin
scale (weighing)
schism
scolding
scorn
scroll (ornamental)
sculpture
sedition
selfishness
separation, undergoing
separation in marriage
session (meeting)
shadow (partial darkness)
shiftlessness
side trips on vacation
sit-in
skirmish
snare (capture)
snobbery
snootiness
snub
social functions, formal
social graces
social transformation
sonnet
space, the use of

spectrum	tapestries	unfaithfulness
split (divergence)	tardiness	union of two people
split (rift)	team (sports team)	unison, things done in
splitting up	team play	unwilling conformity
sports car	teamwork	uprising (rebellion)
squabble	thank you	valentine
square (evenness)	theft	variance
stability (equilibrium)	thievery	variation (discrepancy)
stabilization	tie score	varnish
stalemate	ties of conjugality	vase
standstill (deadlock)	ties of legality	victor in battle
static (interference)	tiff	visiting team
statue	tile	wall hanging
stipulation	tilt (contest)	wallpaper
stolen article	tilt (dispute)	war
storm	tincture (dye)	weariness
storm (incoming), forming	tirade	wedding
stripe (pattern)	toleration	wedding announcement
style (fashion)	tone (color)	wedding of a child
stylish clothes	transgression	west, the direction of
substitute (alternative)	trial, legal	white things
sudden death	triteness	wig
symmetry	tuxedo	willful oversight
tablecloth	ultimatum	window
taking	unanimity	yoke
tangle (dispute)	understanding (agreement)	
tantalize, things which	unemployment insurance	

Psychological Qualities

agility (grace)	deportment	inappropriate behavior
alienation	dishonesty	including others
attachment (caring)	effeminacy	indecision
attraction (appeal)	emotional instability	involvement (connecting with)
balance	equality	irresponsibility
behavior	equivalence	lethargy
characteristics, another's	finesse (tact)	marriage, feelings about
charm	form	middle position
civil behavior	getting even	mutual actions
civil disobedience	graciousness	neutral stand
color, sense of	harmony	non-participation
competition, sense of	hate (disgust)	non-violence, principle of
compromise	hospitality	obtrusiveness (interfering)
conduct in public	hostility	oneness
cooperation	image of another, one's	openness

Psychological Qualities Continued

outlet (means of expression)
outrage
peer pressure
people awareness
perjury
poise
polish, social
posture (attitude), another's
procrastination
projection
public you face, the
rationalizing
receiving love
refinement
rejection, fear of
relating (connecting)
relationships
role (expected behavior)
romance with commitment
rudeness
self-projection(s)
selfishness
sensibility
shadow nature
shallowness (lack of depth)
slander
sociability
social sense
social skills
social urges
sophistication
stability (personal)
tact
teamwork
thankfulness
tolerance
unity (co-operation)
using others
vacillation
war of nerves
whining
wholeness
willingness
wrath

Occupations or Person Types

accessory (accomplice)
adversary
agent
ally
appraiser
arbiter
arbitrator
architect
art dealer
assailant
bandit
banished person
beautician
bedfellow (ally)
belly dancer
bitch
bride
bridegroom
burglar
business partner
challenger in a contest
collaborator
competitor(s)
confederate (ally)
contestant
contract negotiator
courtier
crook
culprit
date (escort)
debutante
defendant
designate
designer
dilettante
dishonest person
elite (select), the
embezzler
emissary
engraver
envoy (representative)
escaped convict
escort
favorite (front runner)
favorite one
fiance, fiancee
foe
friend, close
fugitive
gentleman
graphic artist
groom (in a wedding)
guilty party
gynecologist
hairdresser
hoodlum
host
hostage
hostess
interior decorator
intermediary
landscaper
lapidarian
lawbreaker
lawsuit, defendant in
lawyer in a court action, your
lazybones
matchmaker
mediator
missing person
model
moderator
negotiator
notary
ombudsman
open enemy
opponent
opposition (rival)

other party in a contest
other people (in general)
outlaw
outlawed person
painter (artist)
painter (house)
partners
peacemaker
person inquired about
person stealing
personal representatives
potter
prospect (client)
push-over

quesited, one being asked about
recipient
referee
representative (business)
rival
robber
rogue
runaway
sculptor
social equal
socializer
sparring partner
sponsor
surrogate

suspect
teammate
thief
those met in public
those with whom you consult
those you borrow money from
thug
trans-sexual
transvestite
umpire
undesignated other person
villain
weaver
workers in stone

Places

arbitration office
back (behind you)
ball room
battlefield
boutique
bridal chamber
galleries, art

location, another's
middle position
orchestra (theater)
partner's room
pavilion
place of removal
place with clean air

place you are moving to
posterior
relocation, place of
salon
where partner spends time

Family Members or Relations

anyone unrelated by blood
brother or sister #3
child, second
grandfather (paternal)
grandmother (paternal)

grandparent (in general)
husband
male relations
mate, one's
nephew

niece
spouse
spouse #1
wife

Mundane Ideas

ally
business associate
business partnerships
censorship
civil unrest
collaboration
competitive marketplace
competitor(s)
confederation (alliance)
contract negotiation
contractual relationship
cooperative arrangements

dealings with the public
department of state
disputes
enemies, known
enemies, open
establishment (rulers), the
fair exchange
foreign policy, a nation's
internal opposition
international disputes
international relations
loss of public office

marriage policies
messengers of the state
negotiation
opposite party
pact (treaty)
partnership
party to a contract
people, those who oppose the
position in society
public enemy
quarrel with another
redistribution of wealth

Houses of the Second Quadrant

Mundane Ideas Continued
relating to other countries
relations with other countries
relations with the public
seller (in an exchange)
settlement of disputes
trade embargo
treaty
truce
war
warfare
warlike situation

Parts of Our Body

alignment
back, lower half
back, small of the
bladder
buttocks
haunches
kidney
loins
lower back
lumbar region
navel
ovaries
pancreas
sex organs, internal
small of the back
urethral structures
urinary system
urinary tract

Afflictions or Diseases

albumin in urine
alkaline condition
anemia
bladder disorder
bladder problem
cramps in toes
debility, in general
diabetes
female disorders
gall stone
hepatitis
jaundice
kidney disease
kidney stone
kidney weakness
lower back pain
menstrual problems
uremia
urinary tract problems

Colors

bright green
clear
colorless (clear)
green
lime
opaque color
white

Gems or Minerals

alabaster
aquamarine
beryl
emerald
goshenite
heliodor
limestone
marble
morganite
stone sculpture
tanzanite

Animals

butterfly
koala bear
lamb
panda bear
raccoon
swan
unicorn

Mythical Figures or Constellation Names
Aphrodite (the lover)
Cepheus
Columba (dove)
Cygnus (swan)
Eris (discord)
Flamingo

Libra (scales)
Monoceros (unicorn)
Norma (level)
Pictor (painter's easel)
Psyche
Sculptor (sculptor)
Venus

Parts of an Organization

competitor(s)
operations department
owner's cooperation
partners

Industry Categories

aircraft manufacturing	cosmetics	retail building supply
arbitration services	decorators	space planning
art galleries/dealers	designers	store designers
artists	furniture/home furnishings	store display equipment
beauty supplies/equipment	graphic designers	talent agencies
claims adjusters	hair care services	telecommunications (foreign)
contractors (siding)	household furnishings	telecommunications (long dist)
contractors (tile/stucco)	modeling agencies	toiletries/cosmetics
copper	recreational vehicles	vending machine retailers

Parts of an Automobile

alignment	styling, the	window
shock absorbers	suspension system	windshield
spring	torsion bar	windshield wiper

Parts of a House

art, works of	drawing room	picture window
art studio	dressing room(s)	rug
curtains (drapery)	landscaping	window
decor	parlor	

Parts of a Ship

fantail	port side	stability
poop deck	salon	stern

An Overview of the Eighth House

A Succedent House of the Second Quadrant

Placed in the Right and Upper Hemispheres

The Eighth House asks us to understand some deep motivations within our psyches, like needs for **controlling another's feelings** through demands on their material or psychological resources, the value to you of **mutually sharing in another's emotions or trust**, variations in personal demands designed to **gain subconscious control**, and personal needs for **being and sharing with another. Deep**: in a single word the mystery of the Eighth House can be heard. Between that compound sentence and that short word the Eighth House symbolism covers many complex human needs and personal interactions.

Central questions like **the exchange of innermost feelings** vs. **support offered**, or **respect demanded** vs. **value offered**, etc., lie at the core of Eighth House meanings. If you want **sex** your Eighth House partner can give it. If you want **control** your Eighth House partner can **yield**. If you want—whatever, you can get it! But, only for **the right price**—and this may be an emotional or monetary price far beyond **expectations. Ob-ligation** incurred for **support given** becomes an important focus. The Eighth House asks whether you can demand and receive **respect** from another—even if you **promise** to pay for that respect with money, **promises, pledges**, etc. Can the offer of some **present or future compensation** control another's **loyalty**? This is an Eighth House **question**.

The Eighth House covers **exchanges** like where an offer of an **emotional gift** is made, and the receiver is then presented with the dilemma of accepting that offer and **paying some emotional or monetary price** for the **exchange**, or **rejecting** the offer and perhaps incurring **wrath** for the **refusal** of a good-faith gift. **Sex** is an exchange. **Reciprocation**: Is what you gave me equal to what I gave you? Is what you offer to me equal to what I offer to you? **Interchange**: can I share and willingly offer you my inner self without having to worry if you will waste my gift? **Retaliation**: if you waste (in my thinking) what I gave you then what price shall I extract from you for this spoilage? **Compensation**: if I extend you love and support, will you grant me a legacy? **Swapping**: if I pay you money for a service will I receive what I expect for this exchange? **Giving**: if I share my talents with you will you appreciate me more for having freely given them?

Complex questions all. No easy answers here. The Eighth house does not offer easy answers. It does not even point the way to find any answers, much less easy ones. It only offers human situations which create **questions** and then more questions How they are answered, their ramifications, their continuance, their resolution, etc.,— these are yours to determine. One person may offer love in exchange for **sex**, while another may offer sex in exchange for love. Whether this is an **equal exchange** or not does not concern the Eighth House. The Eighth house only raises the question of whether you feel this exchange is equal or not. The **resolution** of whether equality was reached is for you to resolve.

Any **removal** of emotions, goods, people, **garbage**, etc., is an Eighth House matter. Even to the removal of self from the body at **death**. Does the Eighth House show death? Does it show the time of death? Does it show an impending death. No, not necessarily, but it may under some circumstances be activated for such matters. However, it is into **removal** very strongly. The Eighth House rules removal and its subtleties like **eradication, disconnection, uprooting, amputating, transferring, deposing,** and **subtraction**. One idea behind removal is **transformation**. This may be a **psychological exchange** with the subsequent release of a part of self which needed releasing, or it may be the **destruction** of another's property through direct action like **carnage**, or an indirect action like **contamination**. Add into this any idea which **lowers** the value of an object, and you will be in an Eighth House realm. **Warnings** given for displeasure felt, like the buzzing of a rattlesnake's rattles, is an Eighth House subject.

Removal of the self from the body in any form presents a **mystery**, and good mysteries are tied to the Eighth House. The mystery of what happens through **death**, the **process of death**, the questions raised by the concept of **afterlife, re-incarnation, soul travel**, etc., all have an Eighth House rulership. How can a person split their mind and gain access to **a non-physical realm of information**? How can a person remove themselves from their body while another soul takes over and gives discourses or teachings? What is involved in the process of **creating a soul**? Where do souls come from? Where do they go at death? How can you accept the concept of soul on faith alone? These are the types of mysteries which the Eighth House presents. It also give a means for their **resolution** (i.e., providing some easily stated answers), but not their explanation (i.e., how can this be done). A person can use their Eighth House to allegedly give information from a disincarnate spirit, but they can not necessarily explain clearly how they do this. Do it—don't worry about the reason or cause. This is the Eighth House, look for understanding in the Ninth House.

The Eighth House concerns itself with any process of **distillation, extraction, removal** (again—that Eighth House word!), **investigation, probing,** or **analysis**. Getting to the **depth**, the **innards**, **the core of anything** is an Eighth House concern. Simple answers are not good enough; good answers only raise more questions; enlightened answers require deeper thinking and that is an Eighth House trip. Oh, the Eighth house is frustrating because it doesn't provide answers, it only provides further material which then raises additional **questions**. However, without the Eighth House prodding us to **look deeper within self**, at life, or at various **mysterious realms**, just imagine how boring life would be. We need the Eighth House to confront us with the very things which we are unwilling or **unable to face** in life. How can it do this to us!?!

Horary or Electional Ideas

cause of death	inheritance	psychic matters
conquest	injuries, the likelihood of	reforming activities
control	insurance matters	removal
credit	intensification	restitution
death	investigation	retirement
depletion	jointly held property	sex
descent	legacy	sexuality
diminishing	loan	shared things or values
disaster	lowering	sharing
dowry	money of others	sin
elimination	mysteries	surgery
evacuation	non-personal resources	synthesis
exhaustion	obsession	taxes
expelling	occult matters	transformation
favor (gift)	partner's money	trust
fidelity	permission	will (legal document)
gifts	probing	

Things

abdication (vacates)	analysis (examination)	auction
abolishing	animal magnetism	audit, tax or financial
abolition (ending)	annexation	autopsy
abomination	annihilation	auxiliary item
abridgment	annuity	avalanche
abstract	aphrodisiac	back-handed compliment
abuse (misuse)	apparition	bacteria
accidental death	appetite, sexual	bail bond
adherence (complies with)	appreciation (growth)	bankruptcy
adjustment (tuning)	appropriation (taking)	barbarity
admonishment (warning)	archeology	being consumed by ...
adulteration	argument (summary)	belittling
afterlife	arrears (overdue debts)	bequest
airplane crash	ascendancy (domination)	bid (offer)
alchemy	assessment (taxes)	bill (invoice)
alimony	assistance (financial support)	biodegradation
allegiance (loyalty)	assumption (appropriation)	bioengineering
allowance (discount)	atheism	biomedicine
alteration (modification)	atomic energy	bird call (device)
amendment (revision)	atomic weapon	birth control
amputation	atrocity (outrage)	birth control devices
analysis (breakdown)	attention (concentration)	bleach
analysis (evaluation)	attenuation (weaken)	bomb (nuclear)

Things Continued
boon (favor)
boot (dismissal)
bootlegged item
booty
bounty (reward)
breaking up
brooding
brush off
brutality
budget statement
business, nobody's
by-product
cadaver
calamity
cannibalism
cap (for closing off)
card suit: spades
carnage
carrion
casket
cast (pall)
castigation
cataclysm
catafalque
cause of death
caution (warning)
cessation
chain of events
change (conversion)
change order
changeover
charge (debit)
charge (obligation)
charge card
chasm
check (inspection)
cleaning out
clear-cutting
clearance (removal)
clearance sale
clearing away
cliff-hanger
clipping (cutting short)

clipping (extraction)
clue
coercion
coffin
commission (board)
commission (fee)
commitment
compelling forces
compendium (abstract)
compensation (payment)
completion (termination)
compression (compacting)
compression (squeezing)
compulsive acts
compulsive sex
condemnation (punishment)
condensation
confiscation
conjugal rights
conquest
conscription
constriction (shrinking)
constriction (tightening)
consuming thoughts
contaminant
contamination
contract (an order to kill)
contraction (shrinkage)
contraction (tightening)
contribution- a forced
corpse
correction (change)
corroboration
corruption
count (reckoning)
crackdown
credit
crisis (turning point)
cropping (clipping)
crucifixion
curse (denunciation)
curtains (the end)
customs (tolls)
cyclone

damage (cost)
damage (harm)
damages (compensation)
deadening agent
death
death, kind of
death, physical and spiritual
debacle
debasement
debit
debt (obligation)
decadence
decay
decomposition
decontamination
deduction
deep motives
defacing activities
default
deficits
deflation
deflowering
deformation (change for worse)
degeneration
degradation (disgrace)
deletion
demise
demolition
demonstration (sign)
demotion
depletion
depravity
depreciation
depression (economic)
depth (deeper)
depth psychology
derailment
derision
descent
desecration
destroying
destruction
destructive forces
detection (discovering)

deterioration
detraction
detriment
devastation
diagnosis
dilapidation
dilution
dimension (depth)
diminishing
diminishing returns
dirge
disability benefits
disappearance (vanishing)
disaster (catastrophe)
disasters, natural
discharge (drainage)
disconnection
discount (deduction)
disembodied entity
disgrace (shame)
disintegration
dislocation
dislodging (ouster)
dismemberment
dismissal (discharge)
displacement
displeasure
disposal
disposition (control)
disposition (final settlement)
distillate
distillation
distilling unit (water)
divestiture
donation (gift)
doom (end of all)
doom (ruin)
dowry
drain (conduit)
drain (draw off)
drainage
drama (suspense)
drop (decline)
drop (dismiss)

dwindle away
dying
eclipse (diminishing)
effluence
egress (exit)
elimination (rejection)
elimination (removal)
encroachment
end (death)
ending (finish)
endowment (legacy)
enema
enforcement
enormity (villainy)
epitaph
eradication
eraser
erasure
erotica
eruption (volcanic)
escrow
essence (concentration)
estate of partner
eternity (immortality)
eulogy
evacuation (emptying)
evacuation (removal)
evaporation
evil (sin)
execution (slaying)
exemption (deduction)
exhaust system
exhaustion
exit (way out)
exorcism
expel (drive out)
expelling (dismissing)
expiation
expiration
exploitation
expropriation
extermination
extinction
extinguishing

extortion
extract (essence)
extraction
extreme (limit)
extremity (end)
failure (bankruptcy)
faith in others, having
faithfulness
fall (decline)
familiarity (intimacy)
famine
fatalism
fatality
fateful loss
favor
favor (gift)
fear (fright)
feces
fee
ferocity
fetish (charm)
fetish (obsession)
filter (absorber)
filtration
finances of spouse or partner
financial condition, partner's
financial dependence
financial obligation
financial settlement
finder's fee
fine
fire walking
firing (from job)
firing squad
fission
fitting (for alteration)
flash freezing
flush (discard)
forces inclining to dissolution
forcing
foreboding
foreclosure
forfeiture
fortune, changes in

Things Continued
fracture (separation)
freemasonry
freezer
freezing things
frenzy
fright
frost
funeral
gain due to death
garbage
garbage disposal
genital love
germicides
ghost (spirit)
gift (legacy)
gift (present)
gifts you receive
giving
glacier
goblin
graft (corruption)
grand losses
grant (bequest)
gratification
gratuity
grease (bribe)
grudge
guarantee (pledge)
guarantee (warranty)
gulf (chasm)
gully (ditch)
hail (frozen rain)
halter (noose)
harassment
harm (injury)
harm (wickedness)
havoc
hazards from natural phenomena
healing crisis
health insurance
herbicide
heresy

hidden talents
hideousness
hissing sounds
hock (debt)
holocaust
honoraria
horror
hot water
humiliation
hunger after
hypnotism
ice
ice berg
ice flow
ignominy (humiliation)
illegal acts
immersion (study)
immoral things
immorality
impenetrable
imperviousness
impotence
impurity
inappropriate things
incision
income, tax return on
income from others
income taxes
incongruity
incursion (assault)
incursion (invasion)
indecency
indignation
indiscretion
inexplicable things
infidelity
inheritance
inheritance from others
inherited money
inhumanity
injection
injury (harm)
inquest
inquisition(s)

insatiability
insincerity
insolvency
installment buying
installment plan buying
instrument, torture
instrumentation (means)
insurance
insurance for fire or damage
insurance policy
insurance settlement
intensity
intercourse
intimate, that which is
invasion
inversion (reversal)
investigation
investigative activities
invoice
involvement (entail)
IOU
irony
IUD
joint finances
joint financing
joint savings
junk
junk bond
justification
killing
kundalini
lack of air circulation
lapse (decline)
lapse (discontinuance)
laser
last will and testament
laxative
lay (sexual act)
lead (clue)
leak (loss)
legacies from others
legacy
less of anything
lewdness

liability (financial)
license (permission)
licentiousness
lien
life after death
life insurance
liquidation (settlement)
literary output
loan
loan company
loathsome things
longing (craving)
loot (plunder)
loss (destruction)
loss (forfeiture)
loss due to death
love (passion)
lowering, as in value
loyalty
lust
lust after
lustful love
lynching
magic (occult)
magnetism (magnetic force)
maiming
make-over
malevolence
malice
manslaughter
market research
massacre
medical discovery
menace
mending (revising)
metamorphosis
mid-afternoon
mindless destruction
misdeed
missing link
mistreatment
misunderstanding
misuse
mob (mafia)

mob fury
mobilization
modification
molestation
molting
money belonging to others
money by marriage
money for retirement
money of a deceased person
money of others
money you owe to others
morbid things
morbidity
mortality
mortgage
muck (sewage)
murder
murder victim(s)
mutation
mutilation
mystery (puzzle)
nightmare
non-personal resources
noose
nothingness
nuclear physics
nuclear weapon
obituary
obligation (pledge)
obliteration
oblivion
obscene thing
obscenity
occult, the
occult experience
occult matters
occupations involving
    unreality
offense (outrage)
offensive (unpleasant) thing
omen
onslaught (attack)
operation (surgical)
oppression

outline (synopsis)
painkiller
pandemonium
panic
paradox
partner's possessions
partnership finances
passage (death)
password
pathology
peat
penalty
pension
peril
perishing
permit
persecution
pest (plague)
pestilence
phallic symbol
plague
pledge (promise to pay)
plume of smoke
plunder
plundering
poison
poisonous bite
pollution
pornography
portent
postmortem
powder (light snow)
precariousness
prediction
premium
premonition
presage
present (gift)
pressure (compression)
prey (hunted game)
preying upon
probate
probe
problem

Houses of the Second Quadrant

Things Continued
profanity
promise
proof
propagation (reproduction)
property in escrow
property jointly held
property tax
prosecution
prostitution
psychiatric treatment
psychic ability
psychic experience
psychic phenomena
psychism
psychoanalysis
psychotherapy
pull (extract)
puncture (deflation)
purge
purification
puzzle
quality of land or houses
quality of real estate
quandary
quarry (hunted prey)
quintessence
raise (in salary)
rampage
rancid item
ransom
rape
rate
rattle of death
ravaging (destroying)
re-examination
reaction (change)
rebate (abatement)
rebirth (reincarnation)
rebirthing
rebound (recoil)
rebound (recovery)
recall (call to return)
recall (revoke)

recognizance
recombination
recouping
recovery (restoration)
recovery of debts
rectification (adjusting)
recuperation
recycling
redress (reparation)
reduction (diminishing)
reforms
refrigeration
regeneration
regulation (control)
reimbursement
reincarnation
reinforcement (assistance)
reinforcement (fresh addition)
reinforcement (reward)
rejuvenation
relay (control device)
relentlessness
reluctance
remake
removing (extracting)
removing the excess
remuneration
rendering
renewal
renewed or restored thing
renovation
rent (tear)
reorganization
reparation
repayment
repeal
repellent
repercussion
replacement (restoration)
repossession
reprisal
request (demand)
resale
research

research project
researching new methods
resentment
reservation (guarantee)
reshape
resilience
resolution (persistence)
restoration
resurgence
resurrection
resuscitation
retainer (fee)
retaliation
retirement
retraction
retrieval
retrospection
returns (restitution)
revenge
reversal
reverses
reverting
review (re-examine)
revision (change)
revival
revocation
revulsion
rheostat
ridding
riot
rot
rubble
sabotage
sadism
sado-masochism
salary owed
salvage
savagery
scare
scarecrow
science
scrap (junk)
scrutiny
scum

seance
search (investigation)
search (scrutiny)
search warrant
secret belief
secret dealings
security (pledge)
seduction
seizure (taking)
separateness
separateness (being apart)
separation (breaking apart)
settlement (finality)
severance
sewage
sexual affairs
sexuality
shade (ghost)
shambles (wreckage)
shared assets
shared expenses
shift (displacement)
shipwreck
shovel
shrinkage (shortening)
shroud
siege
sign (hint)
sin
singularity
sins of commission
sins of omission
slack (shortfall)
slag
slime
sludge
smear (slander)
smothering (suffocation)
smut
snow
sorcery
soundproofing
sovereignty (control)
spade (shovel)

spill
spirit (ghost)
spiritualism
spoilage
spoils
stagnant air conditions
stagnation
staleness
stampede
stamping out (eliminating)
stench
sterilization (birth control)
sterilization (germ killing)
stimulus (incentive)
stool (excrement)
subscription (pledge)
substantiation
subtraction (math)
succession (assumption)
succumb
superstitions
suppression
surcharge
surgery
surtax
suspense
suttee
synopsis
taboo (ban)
taint (smear)
tainted thing
talisman (charm)
tantrum
tar
tariff
tarot cards
tattoo
tax audit
taxes
telepathy
tempest
terms (stipulations)
terror
testament

therapeutic activity
thermostat
thesaurus
thirst (desire)
threat (intimidation)
threat (menace)
throes (upheaval)
thwarting
ticket (summons)
title search
title to property
toasted bread
toilet (flush)
tombstone
tornado
torture
toxic waste
tragedy, disaster
tragedy, experiencing a
transfiguration
transfusion
transition
transmigration
transmutation
transposition
trash
trashcan
trespass (on a right)
tribunal
tribute (payment)
trim (condition)
trump card (final resource)
trust funds
trustfulness
tumult
tyranny
ugliness
unadaptable thing
underground, the
underhandedness
underneath, what is
unearthing
unequal relationships
unfair thing

Houses of the Second Quadrant

Things Continued
unhinging
unknown, that which is
unreasonableness
unseating
unseemly thing
unsuccessful attempt
unthinkable act
upheaval
uprooting
urge (craving)
urine
usury
vacuum (emptiness)
vehemence

venom
vent (exhaust)
vice (corruption)
viciousness
violation (breach)
violent crime
virulence
vitalization
voodoo
vow (promise)
vulgarity
waiver
wake (backwash)
wake (vigil)
wariness (caution)

warning (sign)
warrant (permit)
warranty
waste basket
wasting away
wealth, mother's
whip
wickedness
will (legacy)
wind shear
with-holding (anything)
withdrawal (monetary)
wreckage
wrinkle (twist)
zero

Psychological Qualities

abuse
alteration (internal)
amorality
analysis, self
compulsions
concentration (mental focus)
confirmation (substantiation)
control, need for
conversion (transformation)
cravings
death, attitude towards
deprivation
depth of feelings
disappointment (let down)
domination (supremacy)
elimination
faith, giving up on
fall (corruption)
fidelity
fixation
gratification
harassment
hate (detest)
immorality
intense emotions
intensification
intensifying, needs for
intimacy
likes or dislikes

lowering
loyalty, showing
magnetism (attraction)
making love
maliciousness
modify, one's ability to
need for another
obligation, meeting an
obsession
occult ability
particular (fastidious)
passage, rights of
permission (consent)
possessiveness
probing
promise made
psychic feeling
rally (summon or muster up)
reciprocity
repression (control)
resentment, harboring
resignation (acceptance)
respect, demanding
restitution
retribution
ridding
ruin, desires to
satisfaction, seeking
seizing

self-analysis
self-judgment
self-transformation
sensuality
setting fires
sex appeal
sexual energy
sexual merging
sexual passion
sexual power
sexual release
sexuality
sharing
slip (decline)
spiritual pain
spiritual rebirth
spoiling
stealthiness
striking (hitting)
support, given or received
synthesis
transformation
treachery
trust
turning point
vengeance
vexation
vindictiveness
wasting, needs for

Occupations or Person Types

adjuster (claims)	funeral director	pensioner
analyst	gangster	persecutor
analytical scientist	garbage collector	phantom (ghost)
anti-christ	grouch	private investigator
archaeologist	guard	prostitute
atheist	harlot	psychiatrist
baby sitter	heathen (barbarian)	psychic
bad (evil) person	heir	psychological counselor
bail bondsman	heir apparent	psychologist
beneficiary	heretic	racketeer
bigot	hussy	raider
bill collector	hypnotist	rapist
biochemist	infidel	reformer
bounty hunter	insurance adjuster	regulator
brute	insurance agent	reorganizer
budget manager	insurance broker	researcher
cad	insurance worker	ruffian
cannibal	insurer	sadist
cemetery worker	invader	satan
censor	investigator	savage
concubine	junk collector	scientist
coroner	lab technician	seal (navy unit)
credit manager	madam (of brothel)	security guard
creditor	magician (occultist)	sex object
criminologist	malicious person	sheriff
dead, the	marauder	sorcerer
debtor	medical technician	special forces (army unit)
demon	medium	spook
destroyer	miner	surgeon
detective	mistress	tax collector
devil, the	molester	tax consultant
disciplinarian	monitor (proctor)	terrorist
distiller	mortician	those in confidential position
diver	murderer	those who waste
donor	nihilist	tyrant
embalmer	occultist	undertaker
enforcer	pagan	union leader
estate lawyer	pall bearer	usurer
excavator	paramour	vampire
executioner	pathologist	vandal
fiend	pawnbroker	victim of a murder
fortune teller	payee	vocational counselor

Houses of the Second Quadrant

Places

abyss (deep pit)	graveyard	ravine
after world	grotto	refinery
archaeological dig	hades	research organization
brothel	hell	rest room
cave	junk yard	seance room
cavern	lab	sepulcher
cemetery	laboratory	sewer
cesspool	landfill	slaughter house
deep, the	lavatory	slough
disposal area	lending institution	tar pit
distillery	mausoleum	toilet
dump (disposal area)	mine	tomb
dunghill	morgue	torture chamber
excavation	mortuary	trench
frozen place	outhouse	trust company
funeral parlor	pawnshop	turnaround
gallows	pit (hole)	underground places
garbage dump	public toilet	underside
gift shop	purgatory	underworld, the
gorge	quarry	volcano

Family Members or Relations

step-sibling (mother's side)

Mundane Ideas

benefit package	insurance company	profit from a move
budget	insurance practices	profit from a partnership
casualty (disaster)	interest rates	prostitution
charge account	internal revenue service, the	public money
collection agency	lending agency	rackets, the
community property	liability	restructuring a corporation
containment (prevention policy)	loss (financial)	retirement fund
credit, national	mine (pit)	sales tax
credit standing	mine (tunnel)	secession
crisis, economic	mob rule	settlement, financial
customs	monetary partnerships	shared resources
cutthroat competition	monetary standards	social security
debt	monopoly	social security benefits
deficits	mortality rates	socialized medicine
epidemic	mortgage companies	state funeral
escrow account	national cemetery	taxation
estate (assets of)	national debt, the	taxes
insurance	national policy	totalitarian regimes
insurance, unemployment	natural wealth of country	will of the people
	pollution	workman's compensation

Parts of Our Body

anus	homeliness	scrotum
bowel movement	interior part of the belly	seat (buttocks)
climax (sexual)	lap, one's	secretions
clitoris	leak (urinating)	semen
colon	masturbation	sex
defecation	orgasm	sex, orgasmic
ejaculation	part (organ)	sex organs, external
elimination system, the	pelvis	sexual intercourse
excretion	penis	sexual organs
excretory system	phlegm	sperm
external sex organs	place near genitals	sweat glands
fecal matter	private parts	testicle
flanks	prostate gland	urination
genitals	pus	vagina
groin area	rectum	vulva
hair transplants	recuperative powers	

Afflictions or Diseases

abortion, surgical	epidemic	pollution, afflictions from
abscess	frostbite	seizure (attack)
AIDS	heart palpitations	sexual disease
blood clot	hemorrhoids	sting
boil	hysteria	toxemia
carbuncle	injuries (in general)	toxic condition
castration	leukemia	venereal disease
cramps	paranoia	wasting diseases
diarrhea	piles	worms in the body
disease, sexually transmitted	poison accumulation	

Colors

crimson	Gems or Minerals	jacinth
dark black	alexandrite	jargoon
dark brown	arsenic	sulphur
dark red	borax	uranium
magenta	chrysoberyl	zircon
maroon	hyacinth	

Animals

buzzard	ferret	mosquito
destructive biological insects	fleas	mouse
dragon	hawk	pest (destructive insect)
drone (parasite)	insect	predator
eagle	lice	rat

Houses of the Second Quadrant

Animals Continued

reptile	skunk	vulture
rodent	snake	wasp
scavenger	spider	weevil
scorpion	stinging insect	wolverine
serpent	tapeworm	worm
	vermin	

Mythical Figures or Constellation Names

Aquilla (eagle)	Griffin	Plouton
Canes Venatici (hunting dogs)	Hades	Pluto
Chiron	Hydra (water snake)	Satyr
Dis Pater	Hydrus (little water snake)	Scorpius (scorpion)
Draco (dragon)	Lupus (wolf)	Serpens (serpent)
Gorgons (monsters)	Phoenix (phoenix)	

Parts of an Organization

budget office	loan department	retirement plan
credit department	research and development	security force
debt management	rest room	waste management

Industry Categories

auto parts (after market)	garbage disposal	notaries
auto parts (oem)	healthcare information	oil drilling
auto parts (replacement)	home inspection	personal loans
bank holding companies	home remodeling	research services
bankruptcy services	insurance (diversified)	rust proofing
building demolition	insurance (life)	salvage brokers
cemetery management	medical examiners	scrap metal dealers
coal (mining)	medical products	toxicology services
contractors (remodel)	medical supplies	vacuum producing equipment
contractors (sewer)	metals and mining	vital records storage
credit agents	mortgage brokers	waste management
drain cleaning	multi-line insurance	

Parts of an Automobile

dents and scratches	exhaust port	voltage regulator
exhaust	muffler	
exhaust pipe	radiator	

Parts of a House

clogged drain	septic system	toilet
compost pile	settling	water closet
exhaust vent	sewer drain	

Parts of a Ship

bilges	sanitary systems

An Overview of the Ninth House

A Cadent House of the Second Quadrant

Placed in the Right and Upper Hemispheres

The Ninth House urges you to seek out and unearth new experiences in life. It encourages you to experiment with life by going beyond your present boundaries. Discover and then explore new worlds which lie beyond your present thinking or knowledge. Learn about new feelings or vistas. Dare to travel to foreign areas and see how other people live. Challenge yourself to live for some time among unfamiliar customs or with different ways of thinking. Discover the values which lay behind other cultures. Hear their stories. Gain some insight into their theologies. Dust off your wanderlust and pack its suitcase. Expand, travel, experience, learn, meet, encounter, appreciate, or compare what the universe offers to what you presently know. Broaden yourself. Dare yourself to expand your present mental concepts. Discover the Ninth House.

Expanding your mind to learn new things can be done through education, travel, or just by simply experiencing common events as new directions. The Ninth House rules learning in a formal sense, as at a college, but it also rules the experiences you gain from living life and learning from its many variations. The Ninth House challenges you to take advantage of a universe of opportunity. It presents you with an abstract version of life—not concrete examples. It urges you to explore the variations of nature which may lie behind the various legends or myths which comprise mankind's collective unconscious memories. You are asked to seek out different viewpoints by your Ninth House. You are presented with a vast array of choices, alternatives, options, etc. Explore ideas or worlds!

Expanding your consciousness is directly tied to creating a definition of deity for your lifestyle and individual purposes. Deity may be a complex and emotionally loaded word to you personally, but it remains an important Ninth House concept. Deity can represent an omnipotent and powerful male-oriented God who oversees all aspects of life. Deity may mean a basis for natural knowledge which permeates existence. Deity may mean only a few or maybe a whole related series of images who represent elfin-like spirits, animals, plant life, trees, rocks, etc. From the concept of the "Great Spirit" referred to by the American Indians, to the multiple images of Hindu divinities, to the inner enlightenment sought by meditators, the concept of deity certainly is diverse.

Seeking inner unfolding may or may not have anything to do with the image of god to you. The concept of what your god is may simply be ignored or denied, may be complex, may be based entirely on Biblical concepts, may be explained as "science," or whatever. God concepts can explain many things which are otherwise difficult to define. It may be easier to blame a deity for events beyond your control than face responsibility for the consequences of your actions. Suppose your child causes a terrible incident where several people die, and you are legally called to account as the responsible guardian. You may psychologically feel that "god" caused this to happen to you. You may feel this is your child's responsibility. You may feel that the civil authorities are unjustly persecuting you. The temper of this event presents a strong Ninth House exposure. Your ability to handle this may depend on your **moral courage**.

The Ninth House rules such moral courage, and also **abstract principles**, **fate**, **karma**, **worship**, **religious pursuits**, **belief structures**, **benedictions**, **penances**, **inner unfolding**, **meditation**, etc. Whether you resolve complex god caused dilemmas by seeking **absolution** (a Roman Catholic reaction), **meditating** for an answer (a new age reaction), seeking psychological help for self or another (a scientific answer), or whatever, Ninth House influences continue. **Deity** or **god concepts** may not seem important to you when you are hungry or looking for financial support, but how you treat, define, and use god concepts in life may be extremely important in defining your **personal ethics, philosophy, truths, basic understanding** about how life works, etc. There is no one correct answer to solving life's mysteries. The Ninth House doesn't say that any one **philosophy** is better than another, but it does ask that you create a **philosophical basis** for defining your lifestyle. **Philosophy, advice,** and **opinion** are Ninth House words.

Through the Ninth House you can become involved with **the acquisition of knowledge**. Knowledge can come in many different forms, such as knowledge gained from **travel**, knowledge gained from the **study of ancient cultures**, knowledge gained from **participating in sports**, etc. The **pursuit of knowledge** in a formal way is ruled by the Ninth House—especially where there is an official recognition of this deed, like the award of a **diploma**, conducting a **graduation ceremony**, the awarding of a **scholastic degree**, etc. The Third House rules learning about anything. It also rules the knowledge and wisdom you gain by trying to understand the consequences lying behind your experiences.

The Ninth House rules all aspects of the **law**, systems of **justice**, the **courts, judges,** etc. The rules and machinery of the **legal system** are Ninth House matters. This especially includes **ceremonies** of any type which **legalize** or officially **sanction** anything. This could include events like the **blessing** of a fishing fleet by a **religious person**, **a formal retirement parade** for a governmental official, **opening day ceremonies**, a woodland-type spring **ritual**, the setting of a **judicial precedent**, etc. Words or ideas like **legalization, judgment, cause, courtroom protocol, court briefs, plea bargaining, legal maneuvers, jury selection, sentencing, judicial decisions**, etc., belong to the Ninth House.

The molding of another's **opinion** is a Ninth House matter. An easy way to **shape thinking** is to formally **publish** a work which is backed up by some **educational or philosophical credibility**. Issuing a **legal decree** with the force of authority behind it is another way. The ease with which you **present ideas** and have them accepted by others demonstrates your mastery of the Ninth House.

Horary or Electional Ideas

- abstraction
- acceptance
- adventure
- advertising
- broadcasting
- deity
- expansion of consciousness
- experimentation
- exploration
- faith
- foreign travel
- higher education
- inner unfolding
- justice
- law
- lecture
- legal action
- long journey
- looking beyond
- marketing
- persuasiveness
- philosophy
- prophecy
- publications
- religion
- religious pursuits
- spiritual matters
- sportsmanship
- travel to unfamiliar places
- universality
- wisdom

Things

- absent related person
- abstract mind, the
- abstract thinking
- abstraction(s)
- abundance
- academia
- academic aims
- academic subjects
- acceptance (receiving)
- act (law)
- adage (proverb)
- addendum
- addition (extension)
- adjudication (judicial decision)
- adoration
- advanced educational degrees
- advanced learning
- adventure
- advertisement (notice)
- affidavit
- afternoon
- aim (marksmanship)
- aiming point
- allegory
- allowable, things which are
- altar
- altitude
- amperage
- amplification (expansion)
- amplifier
- analogy
- angel (heavenly being)
- anointment
- anticipation (expectation)
- antonym
- appendage (attachment)
- appendix (addition)
- arch (vault)
- arrow
- assumption (belief)
- athletic sports for show or gain
- attitude toward God
- augmentation
- auspices (portents)
- auspicious portents
- awe (reverence)
- awe (wonder)
- balloon
- baptism
- barb
- belief system(s)
- beliefs
- benedictions
- benefit (privilege)
- bias (slant)
- bible, the
- big game hunting
- billboard
- binoculars
- birds in flight
- blessing
- blessing in disguise
- blotch
- border
- bouncing (jumping)
- bounty (goodness)
- bow (weapon)
- bramble
- briars
- broadening
- buoyancy
- candor
- canon (regulation)
- cast (distance thrown)
- catechism
- cause (legal action)
- cellular growth
- censer (incense holder)
- centrifugal force
- ceremony
- ceremony to legalize matters
- christ consciousness
- church matters
- church service
- circumnavigation
- classified ad
- coaxing

Houses of the Second Quadrant

Things Continued
college education
comet
commencement ceremony
communication over distances
communion (religious)
compensation from insurance
competence (legal power)
compilation
compilation (all inclusive)
comprehension
concept
conceptual framework
conference (denomination)
conference (discussion)
conference (of groups)
conference call
confession (creed)
confession (religious beliefs)
confidence (trust in another)
consummation (realization)
contingency
conviction (opinion)
convocation
cornucopia
cosmology
court case
creative manipulation of ideas
credo
creed
crossing a border
cultural knowledge (wisdom)
curb (edge)
current wisdom
curriculum
dart
debauchery (excess)
decisions, arbitrary
deed of virtue
degree (scholastic)
deliberation
denomination (religious)
departure (digression)
departure (leaving)

dependent (contingent on)
destination
destiny
discernment
disclosure
disparity
disproportion
dissertation (treatise)
distant connections
distant contacts & interests
divination
divinity (holiness)
divinity (theology)
divorce proceedings (legal)
divulgence (disclosure)
doctrine (belief)
dogma
dome
dream consciousness
dreams (visions)
dreams as mental journeys
earnestness
edification (enlightenment)
education, higher
efforts to promote yourself
elaboration
eligibility (acceptance)
embarkation
emigration
encyclopedia
enervation
enhancement
enlargement
enlightenment
epilogue (addendum)
escalation
estimate (surmise)
estimation (judgment)
ethics (moral code)
exaggeration
excess
expansion (increasing)
expansion (spreading)
expansion of consciousness

expansiveness
expedition
experimentation
experiments
exploration
exposure (vista)
extension (addition)
extension (lengthening)
extenuating circumstances
extreme (excess)
fable
faith (belief)
far away people
far neighborhood
farewell
farm team
fate (karma)
fates, the
favoritism
fear (awe)
feeler (proposal)
financial trade (foreign)
fire engine
fishhook
flotation device
flow (outpouring)
flow (progression of material)
flying saucer
folklore
foray
forecast
forecasting
foreign things
foreign travel
foresight
foretaste (advanced indication)
franchise (right)
friend of a friend
fuel
fundraising
future plans
gain (increase)
gaining publicity
gap (disparity)

gasoline
genuineness
geomancy
geyser
global travelers
glut (oversupply)
glyph
god
going abroad
good (benefit)
gospel (biblical)
gospel (ultimate truth)
grace (holiness)
graduation
grease (lubricant)
guess (estimate)
guidance
handicap (odds)
hang glider
hanging
healing after an operation
heat exchanger
heaven (the sky)
higher education
higher studies
hiking
hint
holy object
home repair work
honesty
horse racing
house repair work
hunting
hydrocarbons
hymn
hymnal
hypodermics
hypothesis
idea (suggestion)
ideals
idol (icon)
idolatry
illness of father
image (idol)

immigration
immunity
inaccessibility
inaccuracy
incantation
incompatibility
incompleteness
incomprehensible, the
increase
incredibility
increment (enlargement)
indemnity for damage suffered
industry (zeal)
infallibility
infinite, the
infinity
inflation
informal notification
informality
initiation (rites)
inner development
innuendo
insight
insinuation
inspiration
intangible
intellectual pursuits
interjections
interpretations
intuition
itinerancy
job change
journeys, long
judgment (opinion)
judiciary, the
judiciousness
jurisprudence
jury
jury as an executive body
jury duty
jury in a court of law
justice
justice of the peace
juvenile court

kerosene
key (information)
key (solution hint)
kindling
kindred of the spouse
knowledge, accumulating
koan
kosher
largess
lava
law, the
law profession, the
learning, higher
leaving (departing)
lecture
legal, things which are
legal action
legal activities
legal advice
legal affairs
legal claim
legal practice
legal procedure or transaction
legal question
legalization
legalization, the process of
legalizing by ceremony or
  ritual
legend
legitimacy
levitation
liability to accidents
liberal attitude
liberal things
liberalization
lift (boost)
litany (prayer)
literature, profound
litigation
long journey
long-range plans
lot (fate)
lot (much)
love of freedom

Things Continued
lubricant
lubrication
macrocosm
magnanimity
magnification
making something legal
margin (edge)
mark (spot)
marksmanship
maximum, the
meditation
megaphone
metaphor
metaphysics
migration
ministry, the
mission (envoy)
moral philosophy
morality (ethics)
multiplication (math)
mystery (sacred rite)
myth (fantasy)
myth (legend)
mythology
natural gas
needle
next lifetime
nickname
notion (belief)
oath (solemn word)
obtuse angle
odyssey
offer (proposal)
oil (lubricant)
oil well
omission
opinion (belief)
opinion (conjecture)
optimum conditions
opulence (profusion)
ordainment
order (ministry)
order (religious rite)

ordinance (rule)
ordination
origins of disturbances
orthodox observance
orthodox religion
orthodox rite
outcome of illness
outflow
outlook (possibility)
outpouring
outside influence
overproduction
oversight (omission)
oversupply
palette
panorama
parable
parade (ceremonial)
paradigm (ideal)
parting
pass (permit)
passage (traveling)
passport
patronage
periphery
periscope
personal transformation
persons aged 45-60
persons of middle age
persuasion
persuasiveness
petroleum
philanthropy
philosophical society
philosophy
pilgrimage
pin (straight)
pledge (word of honor)
plot (story line)
plunge (dive)
plurality
point (tip)
pointed object
possibility

prayer (worship)
predicting the future
presentation, formal
presumption
privilege
professional sports
profligacy
profound study
profundity
profusion (plenty)
prognostication
promotion (selling)
prong
pronouncement
propaganda
propagation (travel)
prophecy
prophetic dream
prophetic vision
proposal (offer)
proposition
prospect (outlook)
prospect (view)
prospectus
proverb
provision (anticipation)
publications
publications, non-ephemeral
publicity
publishing
puff (exaggeration)
pulley
pungency
quantity (greatness)
quantum leap
quantum mechanics
quest
quest for knowledge
radiology
rapture
reconnaissance (scrutiny)
redistribution
reference (analogy)
religion

religious items
religious preferment
reminiscence
remoteness
revelation
reverence (awe)
righteousness
rite
ritual
rosary
sacrament
saddle
sagacity
sailing (departure)
sales
sales promotion
samadhi
saturation (fullness)
saying
scripture
sea voyage
search (hunt)
selling
separation (parting)
sermon (lecture)
sermon (preaching)
session (term)
short trips of partner
shower (rush of things)
sign off
significant vision
sky
slant (bias)
slip (lapse)
slipperiness
smear (stain)
solicitation
soul (spiritual self)
soul research
special offer
specialized education
speculation (hypothesis)
sphere
spike (briar)

spiritual emergence
spiritual matters
spiritual pursuits
spiritual sustenance
sports, organized
sports coat
sports team
spot (stain)
spread (expanse)
spring (leap)
stain
stand (position)
statute
story telling
stretch (expanse)
students in a university
studies, advanced
stupidity
subpoena
success in law
success in religion
success in science
successful ventures
sudden break
suggestion (advice)
suggestion (hint)
suit (law suit)
suitability
supernova
supplement (extension)
supply (market)
surgery, healing after
surplus
suspension (hanging)
synod
take (catch)
tale (hearsay)
tale (story)
tang (hint)
tasks involving adventure
telecommunication
teleconferencing
telekinesis
telemetry

telephoto lens
teleportation
teleprocessing
telescope
tenet
test (try)
text (sermon)
text (theme)
thaw (melting)
theology
theoretical research
theory (doctrine)
theory (idea)
thesis (conjecture)
things in the sky
thorn (sharp spine)
thrill (adventure)
throwing missile
tilt (bias)
tip (hint)
tip (pointed end)
title (legal right)
tour
tourists, foreign
trace (hint)
train (appendage)
transportation- distant
trapeze
travel by air
traveler, unknown
traveling light
treat (pick up the tab)
trial (law)
tribal consciousness
trine (planetary)
trip, long or distant journey
truism (obvious truth)
truth
understanding (knowledge)
undeserved reward
unfinished item
up, the direction of
useless things
validity (truthfulness)

Things Continued
vastness
vault (dome)
veneration
venture
veracity
verbiage
vespers
view (opinion)
visibility (clarity)
visibility (view)
vision (prophecy)
vista
visualization
voice (opinion)
voyage
wandering
wanderlust
waterfowl
wax
wholesomeness
widening
wider vision
wonder (speculation)
work with oil
world wide contacts
worship (reverence)
worship service
x-rays
yoga (discipline)
zeal
zone (destination)

Psychological Qualities

abstract thought processes
analogy
apprehension (comprehension)
assumption making processes
belief structures
broader views, adapting
candidness
church affiliation
conceptualization
conscience
contemplation
conversion (religious)
convincing, ability for
deity, attitude towards
development of the mind
ecstasy
ethical responsibility
ethics
expansion of consciousness
experiencing
fair play
faith
foreign things, role of
gathering experiences
grasp (comprehension)
guidance
hindsight
idealism
ideals
infallibility
infinite, the
inner unfolding
intuition
justice
knowledge, searches for
legal sense
looking beyond
marketing
meditative desire
mental speculation
misjudgment
morals
persuasive ability
philanthropy
philosophical thinking
philosophy
position (opinion)
profound mental interests
prophecy
publicity, personal
pursuit, philosophical
reality, search for
religious sense
religious views
relying on another
right and wrong (sense of)
righteousness
salesmanship
scruples (ethics)
seeing through anything
soul, feelings about
sound judgment
spiritual attunement
spiritual consciousness
spiritual feelings
spiritual needs
spiritual richness
spirituality
sportsmanship
staying informed
straight forward
superconscious mind
travel, desires for
truth
ultimate truths
unconscious activity
understanding
value (ideal)
wisdom
world view

Occupations or Person Types

academic
adventurer
advertiser
agnostic
alien
alumnus

ambassador
archer
attorney
barbarian
believer
benefactor
bishop
broadcaster
channel (medium)
churchman
clergy
college professor
counsel (lawyer)
deity
diplomat
distant people
divinity (a god)
editor
educated classes, the
emigrant
explorer
fanatic
fireman
forecaster
foreigner
franchisee
grocery clerk
groom (for animals)
guide (scout)
gypsy
holy person
horse trainer
hospital administrator
hunter
importer, exporter
interpreter
itinerant
Jesuit

jockey
judge
jurist
juror
jury member
lawyer
lay person
lecturer (academic)
lecturer (in general)
liberal
living saint
magistrate
marketer
marketing agent
marksman
metaphysician
minister (clergy)
missionary
monk
mythical character
nun
opinionated person
oracle
parson
patron
personal ambassador
philanthropist
philosopher
pilgrim
pious person
pope
preacher
presiding judge
priest
professor
projector (promoter)
promoter
prophet
prospector

publicity director
publisher
rabbi
rector
religious person
religious workers
sage
saint
sales person
scholar
scout
second (runner-up)
seer
seller
soothsayer
sportsman
stable owner
story teller
stranger
swami
theologian
those at a distance
those in a ceremony
those of a different race
those of a different rearing
tracker
transient
translator
trapper
travel agent
traveler
trial lawyer
tutor
wanderer
wise person
wizard
x-ray operator
yogi

Places

abbey
academy
across the border
advertising agency
annex

ashram
attic
back country
balcony
bar (law court)

cathedral
chapel
church
college
colony

Houses of the Second Quadrant

Places Continued

country, foreign
court of justice
court of law
courthouse
courtroom
distant place
distant shore
edge (border)
embassy
exotic land
fire department
foreign country
frontier
gap (opening)
gap (pass)
gasoline station
high court
highlands
horse track
institute of higher learning
institutions of higher learning
lecture hall
minaret
mission
monastery
mound
oil field
oil tank
other places
outskirts
overseas
paradise
parish (church district)
philanthropic institution
place high up
place of worship
port (non-home)
preserve, game
pulpit
race track
remote place
satellite (outpost)
service station
shrine
space (the heavens)
space, outer
stable
stall (animal den)
tabernacle
temple
threshold (end boundary)
tower
travel agency
unexplored area
university
upper levels
vantage point
wilderness

Family Members or Relations

affairs of in-laws
anyone who is a stranger
black sheep
brother or sister #4
brother-in-law
child, third
distant relative
father-in-law
godfather
grandchildren
mother-in-law
partner's relatives
relations of the quesited
sister-in-law
spouse #2
spouse's siblings

Mundane Ideas

advanced schooling
advertising
air rights
boom (economic)
borders of country
business dealings abroad
cable, overseas
ceremony
ceremony, official
church
code of ethics
colonial offices
confines (boundaries)
consulate
diplomat
diplomatic corps
educated classes, the
exports
folklore, national
foreign affairs
foreign associate
foreign commerce
foreign country
foreign items
foreign people
foreign relations
foreign trade
import-export business
imports
inflation
international trade
interstate commerce
journeys, long
judiciary, the
justice as practiced
law
legal agencies
manipulated economies
money laundering
philosophical institution
political propaganda
public faith

public relations
public trust
publications
relations with educators
religion, national
religious affairs

religious education
social change
sports, professional
supreme court, the
tourism
trade, international

travel, distant
travel, long distance
university
world assemblies like the U.N.
world trade

Parts of Our Body

adipose tissues
cellular development
hips
insulin

legs, upper part
liver
liver system (in general)
obesity

sciatic nerve
thighs

Afflictions or Diseases

apoplexy
disease caused by excess(es)
dislocated bones or joints
hip displacia

insomnia
liver problems
low blood pressure
migraine headache

osteoporosis
overweight condition
sciatica

Colors

checkered patterns
plaid

saffron
scarlet

spotted colors
spotted patterns

Gems or Minerals

agate
black opal
bloodstone
carnelian (cornelian)
cat's eye
chalcedony
chert

chrysoprase
fire opal
flint
jasper
niter
onyx
opal

palladium
sard
sardonyx
water opal
white opal

Animals

burrowing animals
horse
kangaroo

leopard
mongrel
porcupine

race horse

Mythical Figures or Constellation Names

Ara (altar)
Bootis (the herdsman)
Centaur
Coma Berenices (Berenice's hair)
Epimetheus (afterthought)
Equuleus (horse)

Faun
Indus (the indian)
Ixion (treachery)
Janus
Jason (adventurer)
Jupiter
Orion (the hunter)

Sagitta (arrow)
Sagittarius (archer)
Telescopium (telescope)
Themis (justice)
Triangulum (triangle)
Zeus (the ruler)

Parts of an Organization

advertising department	legal department	publications department
fire department	marketing	sales

Industry Categories

advertising	golf course design	radio/TV
automobile sales	immigration services	religious services
broadcasting	legal services	sightseeing services
charter services	lubricating services	tour brokers/agents
church (religious services)	naturalization services	travel agents
church (religious supplies)	oil exploration	travel services
foreign trade services	publishing	vending machine manufacturers

Parts of an Automobile

convertible top	fuel tank	sun roof
demonstrator	oil pan	universal joint

Parts of a House

attic	eaves (roof)	study
balcony	library	upper floors
ceilings	rafters	
day room	reading room	

Parts of a Ship

fire suppression system
fuel tank
library
radar

Houses of the Third Quadrant

Poetry for the Houses of this Quadrant

Tenth House

    Age and time build reputation,
    Authority comes when integration
    Of self with cosmos and all you see
    Add finishing touches just right for thee.

Eleventh House

    Hopes and wishes are no new craze,
    Meet your friends at clubs on days,
    Pushing thoughts in political ways
    While mixing in some friendly praise.

Twelfth House

    Self undoing, harbor not!
    Degrading thoughts are best forgot,
    Bondage, punishment, let them go!
    Self-development is your show.

An Overview of the Tenth House

An Angular House of the Third Quadrant
Placed in the Left and Upper Hemispheres

The Tenth House asks that you examine your **achievements, fulfillments, completions, recognitions, accomplishments, excellence**, or **realizations** in life. The Tenth House calls for setting **high standards of conduct**, and then meeting these. This includes **setting and meeting goals**. Often these goals are unconscious, unknown, or not well defined. Sometimes these goals are defined as **business or career objectives**. You probably have **ambitions** to improve yourself. This may include becoming more **mature, learning about life**, growing more **tolerant** about the needs or demands of others, etc. You may not even recognize that you have these as **goals in life**, but you should. As you gain experience you change your core self, that inner you. **Change, growth, tolerance, maturity**, these are Tenth House concepts. Through living you gain insight into self and others. You may become more tolerant of the demands of others. You may find others look to you for advice or wisdom. The Tenth House rules this type of **change, internal maturity, respect earned**, and **fulfillment**.

Through the Tenth House you are exposed to the possibility of **gaining credit** for your **achievements**. This does not necessarily always mean **rewards**. If your prior tasks included law-breaking then you may meet your reward (jail) here. If your tasks included using others unfairly, then your reward may be that others will treat you unjustly when your Tenth House is activated. If you have been working for years on improving self, society, or a product, then your Tenth House may bring some appropriate **fulfillment** or **recognition**. This may be continuing international recognition, or it may be only a one-time notice in a company newsletter. The Tenth House delivers only what you have worked for and deserve, nothing more or nothing less. It does not embellish. It does not glamorize. It only **returns in kind** what you have earned. Often it takes years for such **recognition** to accumulate. Thus, included in the Tenth House are ideas like **aging, time, seniority, continuity, the elderly**, etc. With the passage of **time, maturity** and **wisdom** may accumulate within you.

Reputation, standing, stature, or **esteem** are important Tenth House concepts. The Tenth House positions you so others can use or test your **wisdom** and maturity. Others can **look up to you** in ways you may not see. You may represent an **authority** or **father figure** to them. They may accept you as a **boss**. Gaining, using, and wielding **authority** over others is a Tenth House matter. The Tenth House does not give authority or **recognition**, but it is concerned with how you **use the authority** which others may grant you. It is also concerned with how you handle the **rewards** or **recognition** received from your prior activities. The **reputation** you build through your actions, intentions, and directives are measured by others through your Tenth House activities.

Business objectives, setting goals, administration, trying again and again despite failure are Tenth House matters. The Tenth House does not bring **success**. It does not guarantee **recognition**. It does ask you to act in socially and **morally correct** ways, however. If you start a business and fail, the Tenth House does not care. If you walk away from your **responsibili**-

ties and cause others harm, the Tenth House does not care. But, the Tenth House will **return to you**, in some way eventually, exactly what you have given to others. If your business fails, and you **accept responsibility**, pay the bills, and **work to overcome** the adverse publicity and reputation, then you will be **rewarded appropriately**. If your business fails and you blame others for the loss, steal from the assets of others, etc., then you will also be appropriately rewarded for that too. Eventually, either the planets or the Tenth House will return **your just rewards** to you.

The Tenth House is concerned with **the consequences of actions**. If you bring trouble or hard luck to others this may be returned to you through additional **blockages, bad luck, discomfort, limitations**, etc. The Tenth House is concerned with the **roadblocks** you meet in life and how you **work to overcome** these. Do you hit them head on and come away bruised? Do you tend to run around them? Do you push right through them? These are the techniques of life, and techniques are not a Tenth House concern. It is, however, concerned that you **meet life** in your own way, live through it, **grow and mature** as a person, and **earn your just rewards** for such prior actions.

If you feel you have a **meaningless role** in life, then the fault lies with you, not with your Tenth House or astrology. **Accomplishment** and **recognition** in life are given for work done, not work promised. Gaining meaning from life comes from **hard work** and **application of effort** on your part. Nothing ventured, nothing gained. Astrology will not find you a satisfying **career, job, employment**, or **feelings of fulfillment or recognition**. However, it may show you when the best time is for changing **employment**. It will not mail your **resumes**. It will not go through your **job interviews**. It does not guarantee **success**. It only highlights inner needs for you to address these matters in the best way you can.

If your best way is only a halfway effort then expect halfway results. If your best effort is to **procrastinate**, then expect that your rewards will probably be **delay**ed too. **Equal return for equal effort**, and not as measured on a task by task basis, is all that the Tenth House promises. It may take another lifetime for you to get your rewards, but they will come as you have prepared for them.

The Tenth House may show **delays**. It may ask that you **repeat your efforts** so that tasks become a part of you. Taking time to **age**, taking time to fully learn, taking time to **master tasks** is what the Tenth House asks. The Tenth House is not the Midheaven or MC. The cusp of the Tenth House may be the MC depending on which house system you choose. The houses represent keyword qualities like those shown in this book. The personal sensitive points give astrological points in space useful for timing events. They are quite different.

Horary or Electional Ideas

accomplishment	experience	prestige
achievement	father	profession
age	goals	public life
ambition	government	purpose
authority, persons in	importance	recognition, earning
boss, the	incompetence	reputation
business matters	integrity	resale value
business outcomes	matters depending on others	responsibility
business potentials	matters outside of the home	rewards
career	maturity	stall (delay)
conviction for a crime	objectives	success
dignity	organization	superiors
elevation	parents (in general)	time
evolution	perseverance	vocation
excellence	persistence	

Things

abeyance (postponement)	air pollution	autonomy
absence	alarm (apprehension)	award
accolade (reward)	ambition (goal)	axis
accomplishment (completion)	amplitude (extent)	aye
achievement (acquired skill)	ancient things	bad luck
achievement (realization)	annulment	ban (restraint)
acknowledgment (recognition)	answer (solution)	barrier
acme	apex, the	base of anything, the
acquisition (achievement)	appointment (designation)	belt (for pants)
action (feat)	area (scope)	betterment
active head of an enterprise	aristocracy	big business
administration	arm (offshoot)	bisexuality
admiration (regard)	arrangement (plan)	bitterness
adulthood	arrest (stoppage)	blankness
advancement (progress)	ascension (ascent)	blockade
advancement potential	ascent (advancement)	blockage
adversity	asphalt	blue ribbon panel
affair (personal business)	aspirations (objectives)	bones
affairs of parents	assurance (pledge)	boom (arm for hanging)
aftermath (consequence)	astronomy	boost (lift)
age (duration)	attainment	boredom
age (eon)	austerity	boulder
age (epoch)	authenticity	bounced check
age (seniority)	authority, document granting	boundary (edge)
agency (power)	authority, symbol of	box seat (theater)
aim (objective)	authority over, having	break a record

Things Continued

brevity
bringing to justice
building
building materials
burden (responsibility)
business
buttress
cactus
calcification
calendar
calendar of events
campaign
cancellation
cane (walking aid)
canopy
cap (ceiling)
carbon
career
career activities
caution (wariness)
cellular decay
cement
certificate
certification
chain (restraint)
cheap item
chill (coolness)
chronology
chronometer
circular motion
circumpolar motion
circumpolar object
clearance (authorization)
climbing
clock
clockwise motion
cold
coldness
collapse (buckling)
command
command, having
commandment
commendation

commission (in military)
compensator device or circuit
conciseness
concrete (fused stone and sand)
concrete structure
conformation (structure)
congestion (obstruction)
consequence (result)
consistency
constancy
constant
constraint
contact with superiors
continuity
controls (limitations)
conviction for a crime
cooling trends
correcting (fixing)
correctness
count down
creation (the universe)
credentials (qualifications)
cross shaped symbol
crystal
crystallization
culmination
curb (restraint)
curtailment
cut (absence)
date (era)
day (date)
day, a calendar
deadline
dealings with superiors
dearth (lack)
decision (decisiveness)
decline (downgrade)
deference (honor)
deficiency
delay(s)
demand put upon you
demonstration (proof)
density
dentistry

designation
determination (ruling)
deterrent
development (progress)
developments (new events)
diploma
direction (management)
discomfort (hardship)
discontinuation
dispensation (authorization)
disposition (organization)
distance (far)
distance (stand-offish)
distinction (excellence)
doldrums (gloom)
dope (preparation)
dotage
down, the direction of
downgrade
drawback (obstacle)
drill (tool)
drilling machine
driver's license
drop (descent)
drought (shortage)
dullness
duration (term)
earthquake
economy, the
economy of scale
edifice (building)
effect (influence)
effect (result)
efforts to get ahead
elderly, the
electron
elevation (height)
elevation (promotion)
eminence
Emmys
encumbrance
end (goal)
end (limit)
end of a marriage

Tenth House

endeavor (try)
enduring things
eon
epoch
era
eternity (forever)
event (milestone)
eventuality (result)
evolution (development)
excellence (quality)
exclusivity
experience (episode)
experience (knowledge)
expertise
extent (term)
external, that which is
fabric (framework)
face (reputation)
facility (building)
facing reality
fall (tumble)
fame
fangs
fasces
fasting
fault (responsibility)
feather
fence (barrier)
field (domain)
final result
fixing (correcting)
flywheel
forethought (planning)
forever
form (rules or procedures)
fossil
foundation (base)
framework (skeleton)
frozen food
frugality
fulcrum
fur
gap (interval)
garter

geology
gloom
glory (honor earned)
goal (objective)
goal (score)
good (virtue)
good will
grave (serious) matters
gravel
gravity (seriousness)
greatness
gross (total)
grounding
groundwork (preparation)
growth (progress)
growth (tumor)
halt (cessation)
handcuffs
hardness
hardship
head (first position)
head (upper end)
hearing aid
hearse
heaviness
height
hesitation
hide (animal skin)
hindering factors
hindrance
hit (winner)
hitch (knot)
hitch (stoppage)
hobble
hold (delay)
hold over (postponement)
honor (earned)
honor (privilege)
honor (respect given)
hook
how the marriage will end
ideal (objective)
immensity
immortality

impediment
important people
impossibility
improvement
incest
incline
inconvenience
indebtedness
indelibility
industry (business)
infamy
influence (sway)
influence, a dominating
influential person
insides (of anything)
insolubility
installation (induction)
instant of time, an
instructions (directions)
instructions, a set of
insufficiency
intellect (common sense)
intermission
interval
invalidation
irregularity (dishonesty)
job, one's
juncture (moment)
jurisdiction
labor (a cause of distress)
laborious matters
lack
landmark
lasting things
lateness
latitude (geographic)
lay (plan)
leather article
lecturing (correcting)
load (burden)
longitude (geographic)
march (progress)
mark (objective)
masonry

Things Continued
material (relevance)
means (method)
measurement
measuring device
medium (means)
membrane
memorial
merit (virtue)
meritorious work
method (purpose)
methodology
mid-day
millennia
mineral products
minute (moment)
moment of time
monochrome
monogamy
monotony
monument
moral (lesson)
moral credit
moratorium
mortar
mortification
mounting (climbing)
mounting (climbs on)
mud
mute (noncommittal)
mute (silent)
narrow-mindedness
necessity
negation
noon
note (importance)
notoriety
nozzle
nugget (ore)
obliqueness (slant)
obstacle
obstruction
occupation (career)
office (employment)

office (status)
old, that which is
old thing
ooze (mud)
operation (influence)
ordeal (trial)
order (command)
orderliness
organization
organizing ability
Oscars
outcome (consequence)
outgrowth (the result of)
package (complete assemblage)
parachute
parenthood
passing grade
patent
paternalism
pause
pavement
pebble
pedigree
period (interval)
permanent thing
perpetuation
perpetuity
persons of mature age
pick of the lot (best)
pillar (support)
pinnacle
pivot
plainness
plan (intention)
plan for the future
plant (industrial)
plaque (honor)
plug (stopper)
point (purpose)
position (job)
position of management
post (support)
posterity
posthumous work

postponement
power (authority)
pragmatism
precaution
precedence (importance)
precedence (priority)
precedent
preferment
preparation (precaution)
preparation efforts
press (apparatus)
prevention (forestalling)
prevention (stopping)
probation
procedure
process
profession
professional sports ownership
progress
prohibition (preventing)
promotion (advancement)
proposal (plan)
provision (requisite)
pull (influence)
punctuality
puritanism
pyramid
qualification (limit)
qualification (standard)
quiet
quota
ramrod
rarity (scarcity)
ratchet
ratification
rationing
realism
realization of ambition
rebate (diminish)
recapitulation
recognition (honor)
recommendation (reference)
record (background)
record (unbeaten mark)

rectangle
rectitude
reduction (consolidation)
regular, the
regularity
regulation (rule)
relevance (pertinence)
reliability
renown
requirement (necessity)
requisition (formal demand)
reserve (reticence)
resignation (quitting)
resolution (solving)
respect (regard)
respectability
responsibility (liability)
restriction (limitation)
restrictions (rules)
restrictive conditions
result (accomplishment)
result (consequence)
reticence
reverence (honor)
reward (appreciation)
reward (prize)
right (authority)
right angle
rigidity
rock
roll (tumble)
rotation
rotor
rule (regulation)
salt
salute (honor)
sameness
scaffold
scale-back
scantiness
scarcity
scope (extent)
sealant
second of time

sediment
seismology
seniority
seriousness
severity
sharpening stone
shingle (roofing)
shortage (deficit)
shortage (lack)
sick leave
significance (importance)
silence
silt (fine dirt)
silt (obstruction)
simplicity
simplification
skeleton
skid (support)
slant (slope)
sling
slip (drop)
slip (fall)
slope (incline)
smash (hit)
snag (delay)
snag (hazard)
social place or standing
social recognition
soil
solemnity
soliloquy
solution (resolution)
sourness
south, the direction of
space (interval)
sparseness
spin
splint
spot (difficulty)
spouse's real estate
spring (elastic body)
square (planetary)
square (rectangle)
stabilizing influence

staff (cane)
stall (delay)
stand (platform)
stand (support)
standardization
starch
starvation
station (social status)
stationary object
steadfastness
stiffness (formality)
stiffness (rigidity)
stone
stop (cessation)
stopper
straightness
stretch (duration)
stricture
stroke (tolling of chime)
structure (organization)
stumbling
success
summary
summation
summons
supervision
suspenders
suspension (stoppage)
syntax
system (organization)
taciturnity
tackle (lift equipment)
tectonics
tenure
term (span)
termination
terseness
test case
threadbare item
thrift (frugality)
thriftiness
throw (unseat)
time (duration)
time (experience)

Things Continued
time (tempo)
timeliness
title (rank)
toothbrush
toothpick
top (first place)
top billing
torsion
tower (mainstay)
tremors
tribal loyalty
trip (stumble)
tripod
triumph (success)
truss (beams)
truss (medical)
turn (spin)
turn off
turning, the act of
turntable
unavailability
universe, the
unnamed item
upper classes
upshot (consequence)
upward (that which is)
vertical direction
victory (triumph)
vigilance (caution)
vintage (era)
virtue (moral strength)
vocation
wait (delay)
waiting
watch (clock)
whirling motion
whirlpool
whirlwind
wilting
winter
wisdom gained
workload
worldly success, power to get
writ
zenith

Psychological Qualities

accomplishment (achievement)
achievement
ambition
authority, aura of
bossiness
cheapness
command of situation, in
common sense
consequences of one's actions
court, questions of law in
credibility
determination (tenacity)
dignity
diligence
embarrassment
esteem (regard)
executive acumen
experience(s), learned
function (purpose)
hesitancy
honor (honesty)
importance
incompetence
influence, extent of
integration
integrity
lack
male concerns
mastery
maturing, ability to
maturity
objectives
organization
orthodoxy
overcoming adversity
parents, feeling towards
paternal role
patience
peak experience
pensiveness
performance (attainment)
permanence
perseverance
persistence
place in society
planning ahead
prestige
principles
profession
professional ability
professional affairs
professional standing
professional work
professionalism
promptness
propriety
prudence
public, being out in the
public life
public recognition
public status
purpose
recognition received
relevance
reputation
responsibility, accepting
restraint (control)
self-development
self-fulfillment
self-restraint
sincerity
sobriety
stability of emotions
standing (status)
stature (social class)
status
stoicism
strictness
stubbornness (persistency)
suitable behavior

Occupations or Person Types

account executive	genius	people aged 60-70
administrator	gentry	person of rank
ambitious person	geologist	persons of old age
aristocrat	giant	persons with authority over you
astronomer	governor	
authority (specialist)	graduate	physicist
authority figure	great person	piker
bore	guardian (protector)	position (status)
boss, the	guru	powerful people
bricklayer	head (leader)	premier
chief executive	hermit	president
civil engineer	higher-ups	prime minister
clock maker	ideal (hero)	prodigy
coach	industrialist	professional
commander	killjoy	proprietor
commissioner	king	real estate agent
conductor (orchestra)	labor leader	realist
conqueror	land developer	realtor
conservative	leader	republican
crank	leather worker	ringleader
critical (necessary) worker	manager	rock climber
dentist	mason	rock hound
diamond cutter	master	role model
dignitary	mayor	royalty (nobility)
drag (spoilsport)	member of a wedding	seniors (older people)
driller	men from the past	serious people
duke	mentor	social climber
earl	mermaid	soil ecologist
economist	millionaire	soloist
elder	monarch	spinster
eminent people	monument maker	statesman
emperor, empress	mountain climber	superintendent
employer	mute	superior
engineer	nobility	superiors
executive	nobleman	taskmaster
executive, business	official	those in authority
executive head	old people	those in responsible positions
expert	older person	those publicly noticed
fair weather friend, a	organizer	tightwad
famous person	osteopath	valedictorian
foreman	overseer	veteran
general	patriarch	victor
		virtuoso

Houses of the Third Quadrant

Places

ancient dwelling	high places	rocky ground
base of anything, the	hill	roof garden
bluff	lighthouse	shade (cool place)
brick kiln	mesa	skyscraper
business suite	mountain range	steep ground
construction site	mountains	summit
crag	office (work place)	terminal
crown (apex)	office building	top (highest point)
derrick	office space	top of anything, the
dukedom	peak	vaulted place
heaven (paradise)	private club	where business is conducted
heights	range of mountains	
high office	ridge	

Family Members or Relations

cousin, maternal	female relations	maternal kin
father	guardian (legal custodian)	parent

Mundane Ideas

affairs of officials	executive work	people of high status
aristocracy, the	fundamental indicator	persons having power
boss, the	gaining an office	place of business
building	governing authority	platform (policy)
business	government, the	police as authority
business affairs	government agencies	policy
business standing	government officials	political party in power
business success	governmental authority	political success
business world	head of an organization	positions of power or authority
chairman of the board	head of government	power struggle
checks and balances (limits)	ideals, national	price market will bear
city officials	jobs	prime minister
commander-in-chief	law enforcement	prince or princess
community standing	leader	professional classes
conduct of business, the	management	public attention
construction	manufactured goods	recession
corporation	national affairs	relations with leaders
dam	national approval, need	reputation
dealings with government	national celebrities	right-wing movements
demand for goods or services	national reputation	ruling classes
department heads	office (work place)	social status
economy, the	officers in authority	standing before the world
employers	official business	style of government
establishment (business)	people in power	supreme authority

upper house of government
upper legislative house

war, the end of
whoever has authority

worldly position

Parts of Our Body

beard
body hair
bones
cartilage
elbow
frown
hair

hair on body
joint
knee
kneecap
ligament
nakedness
skeletal system

skin
skin condition
spleen
stature
teeth
tendons

Afflictions or Diseases

arthritis
atrophy
blood, loss of
blood impurities
bone bruise
bone disease
bone fracture
broken bone
cataract
chills
constipation
continence
dandruff

dull ache
eczema
gangrene
gout
impetigo
itches
joint problems
kink (cramp)
knee injury
leprosy
numbness
occlusions (blockages)
old age problems

rheumatism
rickets
ringworm, skin
scaly skin
senility
skin rash
skin ulcer
sprain
tooth decay
toothache
warts
water on the knee

Colors

black
dark blue
dark shades

dull color
gray
navy

slate gray

Gems or Minerals

antimony
clay
coal
diamond
ebony
granite
graphite

hiddenite
kunzite
lead
mineralogy
minerals
obsidian
ore

petrified wood
slate
spoumodine
stone (in general)
zinc

Animals

alligator
amphibian
crocodile

frog
giraffe
goat

ray (fish)
salamander
wolf

Houses of the Third Quadrant

Mythical Figures or Constellation Names

Camelopardus (giraffe)
Capricorn (sea goat)
Cassiopeia
Cronos
Crux (southern cross)
Horologium (water clock)
Kronos (saturn)
Medusa
Mensa (table mountain)
Saturn

Parts of an Organization

administrative services
chairman of the board
construction
engineering
management
planning
reputation

Industry Categories

aagriculture (equipment)
air purification
amusement equipment manufacturer
assembly and fabricating services
boat/ship construction
building designers
building materials
cement and aggregates
church (design/construction)
construction equipment
contractor's equipment
contractors (roofing)
eEnergy conservation
engineering and construction
environmental services
fireproofing services
gas products (compressed air)
jewelry (sales)
machinery (construction/mining)
naval architects
parking lot management
pollution Control
school construction
school equipment
surveyors

Parts of an Automobile

clutch
coolant
drive shaft
drive train
emergency brake
fuel economy
governor
transmission

Parts of a House

ceiling area
coldest part of house
floor (level base of room)
formal dining room
joist
office in the home
roof
structure (in general)
wall (partition)

Parts of a Ship

ballast
bulkhead
deck
hull
list
mast
railing
shaft alley
skin
spar (rib)
support members

An Overview of the Eleventh House

A Succedent House of the Third Quadrant

Placed in the Left and Upper Hemispheres

The Eleventh House asks that you define and resolve the many **choices** which you face in life. Choices mainly arise from **internal desires for change**. Your **hopes, wishes, aspirations, expectations, longings**, etc., about self, others, or circumstances, open many **different possibilities** for you. Urges to **improve the lot** of self or others, **motivation**s for seeking change, and **expectations** about creating your niche in the world begin with the Eleventh House. The Eleventh House is also concerned with your perception of and attitude about **humanity**. It is through this house that the possibilities of **having others do your bidding** arises. You can find that the world is not a lonely or isolated place. There are always people willing and ready to listen to your ideas. There are always others who can create what you want if you **prepare** them well enough. The Eleventh House is concerned with your attitudes about how others can best **serve your purposes** in effecting the **changes** in life which you desire.

A strong Eleventh House idea involves **joining with others for mutual purposes**. The role of **groups, assemblies, cliques, gangs, syndicates, clusters, organizations**, etc., in your life is shown through here. The Eleventh House helps you focus on your need for **togetherness**. It places your needs for **impersonal companionship** into a central place in your consciousness. It helps make you aware that people can serve roles different from comfort giving, loving, or sexual relationships. Your need for others in roles outside of a one-to-one companionship are shown through the Eleventh House. Here you are able to explore your needs for **affiliations**. Here you are able to explore the role of **groups** or **societies**. Here you are able to gain the benefits you need from the **clubs** or **groups** which bring **informal bonding relationships** into your life.

Impersonal friendliness is ruled by the Eleventh house. Relationships with **no emotional interchange** or interference belong here. **Camaraderie, brotherhood**, or the **banding together** for friendliness or such **mutual support** as this can bring belongs here. Often the desire for mutual support arises because of a **cabal** or **clique** which is interested in control over others. The group may decide to use subtle forms of **manipulation** or **control**. Ideas concerning the **tampering** of another's freedom or rights, **infringing** upon another's time or resources, using others for your (or the group's) purposes, etc. belong to the Eleventh House. The use, employment, handling, manipulation, operation, or deceptive **control of others for personal or group means** is an Eleventh House matter. Desires for greater **impersonal control** belong here.

Often **collaborations** form because people are attracted by a **cause, principle**, or **purpose**. **Shared convictions or beliefs** within a group formed for mutual benefit(s) belong to the Eleventh House. **Pleading for causes, seeking support for an idea**, or **pushing for an endorsement** from others belongs here. Sometimes it is necessary to gain another's attention through boycotts, protests, or public rejections. Such **mutually supported protests** are an Eleventh House matter. The **obstruction** of another's purposes and intentions, and **rejection** of their concerns starts here. Forms of **mutual discontent**, publicly expressed, can lead to **political changes**. Politics is an

Eleventh House word.

Any concerns involving the **legislative process, civic matters, balloting, elections, political awareness, vote gathering, consensus, caucus**, etc., belong in the Eleventh House. The **social movements which shape politics** begin through Eleventh House involvements. **Conditions, compromises, riders, amendments, home rule, shaping and effecting change** within the political or social system, inducements for effecting change, **politics** in the name of **forging new alliances**, etc., all belong here. The Eleventh House is concerned with **effecting change**. Not change for change's sake, but change because the old no longer works well and a new way of seeing current reality is needed. The **shaping and molding of public opinion** to effect such change also begins here.

The Eleventh House is concerned with anything **new**. **New trends, bohemianism, non-conformist activity, trends, futuristic programs, new age matters, modern ways of shaping old ideas**, etc., all belong here. **Oddities, eccentricity, queer ideas**, that which is **unconventional** or **unorthodox** start here. **Abnormalities** or **deviations** from established means are an Eleventh House matter. These often begin because of a **seething** or **churning** which starts an **internal restlessness**. Ideas and movements can become internally **mixed, agitated, stirred up, blended** with other forms, etc. This type of **amalgamation** is an Eleventh House matter. The **spreading** or dissemination of ideas and **networking with others** is an Eleventh House concern.

The Eleventh House rules any process which can help **shorten work efforts. Automation, machinery, labor saving devices, stored energy devices,** the **vibrations** caused by these devices, the pollution which results from these processes, etc., all begin here. **Large machinery, office automation, assembly lines, modern production methods, protective product packaging, hydraulic** or **electrical** or **electronic labor saving devices**, etc., can be found here. Here belong the **computers** which make our lives easier, the **earth moving equipment** which allows **large construction, manufacturing processes** which speed output, or, chemicals or **products which make life easier** and more efficient.

The Eleventh House may begin with **discontent**, either social or inner, and transform that into **shaping** a new way of adjusting to or living with life. Sometimes it is a **sudden revelation**, other times ideas come from slowly changing conditions, but it is through the Eleventh House that change is sought. **Change** need not be dramatic, and it need not revolutionize life, but as sure as the Eleventh House operates, such **change** will work its way through all of life.

Horary or Electional Ideas

abnormality	forthrightness	membership
advice	freedom	mixing
astrology	friction	new, the
causes	friendliness	objectivity
choices	friends	personal independence
club (organization)	group memory	political awareness
death in the family, a	groups	politics
desires	hopes	shaping the future
discontent	humanity, attitude toward	society (social group)
dispensing	impersonal reactions	strategy
dispersal	inclinations	suddenness
eccentricity	joining	trend
effecting change	legislation	wishes
exception	manipulation	
expectations	meeting others	

Things

aberration (abnormality)	altruism	backhoe
aberration (irregularity)	altruistic undertakings	baffle
abnormality (deformity)	amalgamation	ballot
abnormality (deviation)	amendment (constitutional)	battery
abrasion (wearing down)	anarchy	bizarre, the
accessory (accompaniment)	anomaly (deviation)	blending
accompaniment	anomaly (rarity)	blizzard
add-on	antenna	bohemianism
adjunct (rider)	appliance (work saver)	borrowed time
adultery, casual	apportionment	boycott
advice (intelligence)	aptitude test	break in a relationship
advice (recommendation)	aspirations (hopes)	breakthrough
advocacy	assemblage	brotherhood
aerial (antenna)	assembly (gathering)	brotherly love
aerodynamics	assignment (apportionment)	bus (electrical)
affiliation (association)	associate (friend)	cabal
agglomeration	associations (groups)	card suit: clubs
aggregate (composite)	assortment (variety)	casual ties with others
agitation	astral projection	caucus
air conditioning	astrological affairs	cause (principle)
air travel	astrology	celestial mechanics
aircraft	atomizer	celestial object
aircraft noise	automation	ceremony, group function
airline travel	avant-garde, the	change (revolution)
airplane	aviation	choice

Houses of the Third Quadrant

Things Continued

chorus
churn
circuitry
civics
clique
close friend
club (organization)
cluster (grouping)
coalescing
column (line)
combinations
combining
communal living
community (social group)
companionship
complaint (grievance)
complementary copy or gift
composite materials
composites
compressed gases
comradery
concentration (gathering)
condition (stipulation)
conductor (eletrical)
confederacy
conference (caucus)
conference (consultation)
conference (large meeting)
congealing (coagulating)
congestion (crowding)
conglomeration
congregation
congress
consolidation
consultation (meeting)
convection
convention (large meeting)
convergence (coming together)
cosmic awareness
cosmic intelligence
counsel (advice)
crease
criticism, friendly

crowding
crusade (rally)
cult
dearest wish
death in the family, a
defiance (rebelliousness)
deformity (abnormality)
delegation
demonstration (protest)
detachment (impartiality)
deviation (variation)
diffusion (spread)
dire straits
discarding
discontent
discretion
disinterest
dispensation (apportionment)
dispersal
dispersant
disruptions
dissatisfaction
dissatisfying experience
dissemination (spreading)
dreams (wishes)
dynamo, electrical
eccentric (mechanical device)
election (choice)
election (voting)
elective (option)
electric motor
electrical fuse
electrical linkage
electrical meter
electricity
electrocution
electrode
electronic circuit
electronic device
electronic linkage
embedded memory
emergency lighting
environmental pollution
erosion

estate of father
eviction
exception (exemption)
exception (leave out)
exception to the rule
exemption (exception)
expectation (anticipation)
extraordinary, the
faction (group)
familiarity (informality)
father's money
federation
feedback
fellowship
file (tool)
filibuster
filter (separator)
floating objects
flock (group)
flying
foible
fold
forcible control of people
formulation (mixture)
forum (assembly)
foster relationships
franchise (ballot)
fraternal group
fraternal organization
freebie
freedom
freedom, concept of
frequency (tone)
friction
friendliness
friendly help
friendship
fusion (uniting)
fusion, nuclear
futuristic programs
gadget
galaxy (stellar)
garbage can
gases, pressurized

Eleventh House

gathering (assembly)
gelatin
get-togethers with friends
give-away (donation)
go-carts
goad (stimulus)
grievance (complaint)
grinding
grinding machine
grindstone
gripe (grievance)
group (assemblage)
group, fraternal
group activities
group connections
group gatherings
group interests
group memory
grouping together
grumbling
ham radio
hankering (longing)
hearing (conference)
helicopter
helium
hologram
home repair at relatives
home rule
hopes
horoscope
hose (socks)
hosiery
humanitarian activities
humanitarian ideals
humanitarianism
hurricane
hydraulic machinery
hydraulics
illegitimacy
illness of pet
immodesty
inattention
incentive
including (embracing)

income from business or career
incomparability
independence
inducement
informal notices
ingenuity
innovation
integration (racial)
intelligence (news)
interactions
intolerance
irregularity (not conforming)
jet (airplane)
job sought if you have a job
journey, sibling's
journeys by air
junk food
jury as counseling body
kinship
ladder
large public meeting
league (alliance)
legislation
liberation
liberty (freedom)
light (low weight)
lighting (artificial)
lightning rod
likelihood
line (circuit)
line (queue)
lodge (fraternal)
love (friendliness)
machine (labor saving)
machinery
magnet
manipulation (adjustment)
manipulation (influence)
many (large number)
marital happiness
marriage of child
marriage vows
mass production
matchless (incomparable)

mechanical adjustments
mechanical advantage
mechanical linkages
medley (assortment)
meeting hall
meetings, large gatherings
membership in clubs
mid-morning
mill (grinder)
millstone
mingling
misfortune, unexpected
mistrust
mixer (churn)
mixes, mixing
mixture (combination)
mob (crowd)
modern, things which are
modern gadget
modernization
money from career
motorized equipment
movement (crusade)
muster (assembly)
navigation
network (interconnection)
networking
new, that which is
new age
new age gadget
new method
nomination
oddity (unusual)
offbeat thing
open secret
opera
option (freedom of choice)
order (society)
orgone
outbound direction
overturning
panel discussion
paralysis (incapacity)
parent's money

Houses of the Third Quadrant

Things Continued
party (surprise)
perverseness
perversity
petition
philia (love)
physical sciences, the
picketing
plane (aircraft)
planet (body)
platonic relationship
pleat (fold)
plumbing problem (leak)
pneumatics
potpourri
preparation (mixture)
prerogative
press (of crowd)
pressure (atmospheric)
pressure suit
product recall
property damage
prospect (hope)
protest
purchase (advantage)
quality, things without
quantum (form of energy)
quasar
queer idea
radical idea
radio broadcasting
rapport (comradery)
rebellion
recall (of a product)
recall (remove by vote)
recommendation (urging)
referendum
relay (teamwork)
reshuffle
resistance, electrical
reunion
revolt
revolution
ring (group)

robot
rocket
sandpaper
satellite (space)
scanner
scattering
science of astrology
scouring
search (probe)
seat (membership)
sect
segregation
service of repair person
sewing machine
shock, electrical
social affair
social consciousness
social contact
social functions, informal
social gathering
social group
social life
society (social group)
sociology
socks (stockings)
solution (mixture)
space exploration
space station
spacecraft
spaceship
spiral
splicing (combining)
spray gun
spreader
spur (goad)
staged burglary
stars, the
stirring things up
stockings
strange, the
strategy
subdividing
success in politics
suction

sudden event
sudden happening
supplement (rider)
support (back up)
support group
surprise
suspicion (hunch)
suspicion (mistrust)
suspicion (reservation)
switch (electrical)
symposium
syndicate
team (gang)
temperature change
term (standing)
throng (crowd)
ticket (ballot)
ties of friendship
ties with groups
traction (adhesive friction)
tractor
traffic laws
transformer (electrical)
trend
triplets
troop (band)
turbine
turbulence
twist (surprise)
unbonded relationship
uncommon, the
unconventional, the
unexpected, the
unexpected thing
unification (uniting)
uniform (special clothing)
union (combination)
union (togetherness)
unique, the
uniting
unity (togetherness)
unorthodox, the
unprecedented thing
unrest

unusual, the	veteran's group	water pollution
unusual method	veto (rejection)	wedge
uproar	vibration (quivering)	whetstone
upset	vicarious experience	windmill
upsetting condition	vindication (support)	wishes
upward mobility	voltage	wishful thinking
urge (wish)	vote (ballot)	women's liberation
valve	vote (election)	worthless things
variation (type)	want (desire)	wrinkle (crease)
variety (assortment)	want (need)	zodiac
variety (diversification)	washing machine	
version	water damage	

Psychological Qualities

acquaintance (friendship)	friendship	nonchalance
aloofness	groups, use of	objectivity
belonging	hopes	opening up
blahs, the	humanity, attitude towards	peculiarity
causes, attachment to	impersonal, sense of the	perversion
causes, use of	incentives received or given	platonic love
civic-mindedness	inclinations	politics
desire (craving)	independence	preference
desires	indifference	progressive thought
detachment, ability for	joining, willingness to	rebelliousness
discontent	judgment (discretion)	results orientation
eccentricity	leadership qualities	sexual perversion
effecting change	loyalty to causes	shaping attitudes
emotional depletion	manipulated, being	sharing feelings
emotional desires	manipulation	shock, psychological
expectations	marriage, happiness in	undermining
forthrightness	mental reservations	volition
freedom	misgivings	wants
friend, response of a	need (desire)	wishes
friendliness	new idea	yearnings

Occupations or Person Types

accompanist	airline personnel	backer
accomplice	alderman	buddy
acquaintance	anarchist	candidate
adherents	anti-hero	chancellor
advisor	apostle	city manager
advocate	astrologer	cohort (companion)
affiliate	auto manufacturer	colleague
agitator	aviator	companion

Occupations or Person Types Continued

comrade
confidante
consultant
counselor (advisor)
dealer in future trends
delegate
demonstrator (protester)
devil's advocate
disciple
dissident
eccentric
electrician
exponent (advocate)
fellow
fellow club member
finder
flier
follower
free-thinker
friends (supporters)
gad-fly
gods or goddesses

guide (advisor)
hard core (diehard)
hippie
hobo
hold out
humanitarian
inventor
legislator
liberator
lighting specialist
machinist
malcontent
manipulator
maverick
mechanic
member
member of a support group
navigator
new acquaintance
non-conformist
partisan
people aged 70-85
pervert
picket (protester)

pilot, airline
politician
progressive person
punk rocker
radical
rebel
renegade
representative (political)
senator
society people
sociologist
space explorer
supporter (advocate)
teetotaler
test pilot
those who act strange
trendsetter
uniformed worker
vegetarian
visionary
well wisher
yankee
zealot

Places

airport
capitol building
city hall
club (organization)
club room
conference room
convention hall
council
factory

fraternity
fuse box
hanger (aircraft)
inventor's workshop
meeting room
mill
mineral spring
place where people gather
queue

rally (meeting)
rendezvous
residence while abroad
society (club)
sorority
strip (airstrip)
town hall
vortex

Family Members or Relations

brother or sister #5
child, adopted
child, another's
child, fourth
child, step

daughter-in-law
foster child
friends
godchild
illegitimate children

son-in-law
spouse #3
step child

Mundane Ideas

advancement, economic
advisor

airport
board of directors

business assets
business income

business prosperity
chamber of commerce
city council
civic organization
coalition
collective bargaining
committee of a fraternal group
communism
conglomerate
constitution
consultant
corporate assets
council
electrical system
factory
friends of the nation
geopolitics
goals, national
governmental interference
heavy industry
house of parliament
house of representatives
international friendships

leadership
leadership, the country's
left-wing movement
legislation
legislative activity
legislative body
legislative house
legislative practice
lockout, management
machine (political)
money of the business
money supply, a business's
money supply, a country's
municipal government
new technology acceptance
ouster
overthrow
parliament
party (political)
person holding office
political atmosphere
political convention
political election

political force
political machine
political preferment
politics
profit from a business
profit from a corporation
public convention
public gathering
public office
public utility
radio or television acceptance
senate
social alliance
social forces
social organization
social ties
socialism
society (social group)
state legislature
town council
union, labor
voting
working capital

Parts of Our Body

ankle
blood (in general)
blood pressure
calves (of legs)
coagulation of blood

gases in the blood
hemoglobin
legs, lower part
legs from knees to ankles
physical control over body

shins
tremors in body
wrinkles

Afflictions or Diseases

lesion
odd skin disorder
paralysis (loss of function)

shin splints
sprained ankle
stroke

varicose veins
water imbalance

Colors

brilliant blue
electrical blue

indigo
medium blue

sky blue
ultramarine

Gems or Minerals

achroite
aluminum
bauxite
buergerite

dravite
elbaite
halides (salts)
indicolite

lapis lazuli
liddicoatite
rubellite
rutilated stones

schorl
siberite
tourmaline
turquoise
uvite

Animals

burrowing reptiles
camel
dolphin
hippopotamus
ostrich
reindeer
sea gull

Mythical Figures or Constellation Names

Antila (air pump)
Aquarius
Eurydice (the unattainable)
Pegasus (winged horse)
Pyxis (compass)
Typhoon
Uranos (sky)
Vela (sails of the Argo)
Volans (flying fish)

Parts of an Organization

conference room
consultant
electrical wiring
emergency lighting
meeting room
profit
profit sharing plan
relations with elected officials
social club
sprinkler system

Industry Categories

air transport
alternate energies
aluminum
auto leasing/rental
avionics
business consulting
business management
computers and peripherals
computer software/services
contractors (aerospace)
electrical equipment
electrical utility
electronics
engineers (consulting)
furniture rental
high tech
leasing/rental services
lobbying
machinery (electrical)
rental/leasing services
semiconductor manufacturers
telecommunication equipment
telecommunication services
telecommunications (domestic)
transportation leasing
truck leasing

Parts of an Automobile

air (in tires)
battery
carburetor
electrical system, the
electrical wiring
exhaust header
fuel injectors
generator
hydraulic system
interior lamps
mechanical linkages
power assist systems
valve

Parts of a House

electrical appliance
electrical wiring
formal living room
fuse box, the

Parts of a Ship

auxiliary power
emergency lighting
generator
navigation desk
navigational lights
piping
rigging
running lights
shaft
winch
windlass

An Overview of the Twelfth House

A Cadent House of the Third Quadrant

Placed in the Left and Upper Hemispheres

Unlike other houses which have some sharply defined but rather narrowly focused themes, the Twelfth House presents many themes. They represent parts of life or personality which can not be explained easily. Words like: **charity, selfless deeds, disadvantages, isolation, self-pity, confinement, atonement, personal limitations, inevitability, pleading, drugs, freeing, forgiveness, self-imposed limits**, etc., present strong images, but do not demand deep theme development. Contrast the many Twelfth House themes with the few First House issues. The variety and richness of the many subtle Twelfth House word forms shows through with an incredible **diffusion**.

Because of the variety of its themes the Twelfth House is not easy to understand. One way to master your Twelfth House is to consider each of its themes separately. Do not try to group or categorize these variations because by its very nature the Twelfth House does not want this. The Twelfth House asks that you learn about it by **indirectly absorbing** its meanings through a different side of your brain than that part which demands linear and thorough rigidity. **Picture** the Twelfth House themes, but do not try to strictly define them. **Feel the themes** as they call for attention, but do not try to analyze them. **Meditate** on the themes, but when explaining them to others ask that these people **absorb them in their own way**, not from your definitions. The Twelfth House deals with the **subjective, the inner**, the **changing part of inner definitions**, not the pre-defined, pre-canned, pop analysis given in two paragraphs or less.

What are these many themes? Should we start our Twelfth House paragraph definitions with ideas like **escape, confinement, bondage, remote consequences, aid, rehabilitation**, or, . . . , well the list is just too long. The words are in the adjacent word lists, start there! The problem with choosing just a representative set of Twelfth House ideas is that there are no few, simple typical themes which clearly show all Twelfth House meanings. There are many such complex ideas. Some of these ideas have whole scholarly books written about them. Read the books, yes, but better still, define these themes in your own way, for an inner and personal definition of the Twelfth House is requested.

You may wish to start with the many Twelfth House words which deal with the theme of **escape**. Escape from reality using **drugs**. Escape from people into **isolation**. Escape from scenes of **poverty** by impersonal works of **charity**. Escape from **hidden problems** by **avoiding the issues**. Escape from **disappointment** with your lot in life by **ignoring self-development**. Escape from **personal limitations** by hiding behind a **disability**. Escape from **sorrow** or **grief** by blaming others for conspiring against you. Escape by explaining that others caused your **sorrows**. The Twelfth House shows a diversity which lies beyond written, pictured, or explained definitions. Discover your own way to be alone within self by defining how you should learn your Twelfth House.

You may wish to start with some Twelfth House ideas which deal with **personal limitations**. This can mean setting up strong internal psychological barriers which are very artfully and craftily woven by unconscious parts of self. Better than any **chains**, better than any **prison**, the mental mindset you create can **limit** you to narrow definitions of life. They are uniquely yours. **Break through** them by using your Twelfth House astrological knowledge! Know that through the Twelfth House you have to face the **barriers** which you create for yourself. Break through your own barriers. Use your Ninth House vision to look beyond them. The Ninth House is the sister (or, brother) house of the Twelfth House. They work as an integrated pair because they each share Neptune and Jupiter as their planetary rulers. If you don't like the yin side of your Neptune energies then work through its yang side. If you don't like your yang Jupiter then work through its yin side, etc. It may take you a lifetime to **break old patterns** and weave new ones but realize that the future realities you can create for yourself hold either your **redemption** or further **confinement**.

Many Twelfth House themes deal with **confinement**, **serious illness** or **hospitalization**, **institutions** which continue practices which you may feel **bind** you, **conspiracies** by government or authority to hold you back, etc. Your rigidity of Twelfth House definition holds you back, not societal conspiracy. As an individual you are a part of society, yet you are beyond society too. Where does happiness start? Within self, or **doled out** by a seemingly impersonal society? If you thwart or break the rules of society you may be **punished**, perhaps even severely. But who made you break these rules? Did some God or Devil magically appear and point angrily at you, shouting for you to break society's rules, harm others, wreak destruction, cause misery, etc.? Is this how you see life? Or, did your thinking go astray? Did you start to weave a barrier around you which says that you are unliked, in a **disadvantaged** position, not able to **cope** as well as others, have a **handicap**, etc. This is the **deception** of the Twelfth House. This is how **personal limitations** begin. Break out of your **self-imposed personal limitations**. Recognize that just as easily as you create them you can **dissolve** them. Learn from the issues of the Twelfth House.

Examine the Twelfth House word lists in this book if you want to learn more about the Twelfth House. See the variety and richness of the words presented and study these Twelfth House themes. You may not like to face some of these issues, but that is another matter entirely. You will have to face them sometime in your life, and the sooner you make peace with these issues the sooner your Twelfth House will give you some peace. Unlike other houses the Twelfth House **does not demand** anything of you except that you define and face all Twelfth House issues in your own way.

Horary or Electional Ideas

atonement	hidden (secret) matters	personal ruin
charity	hidden side of life	psychological health
compassion	hospitalization	punishment
concern for others	illogical solutions	reaping (returning)
confidential matters	imprisonment	redemption
confusion	inevitability	rehabilitation
conspiracy	introspection	remote consequences
crime	isolation	reprieve
delusion	kidnapping	secret enemy
denial (disavowal)	large animals	secrets
disability	life threatening actions	self-denial
disadvantages	limitations, self-imposed	self-pity
disappointment	nebulousness	self-undoing
drugs	pardon	sorrow
escape	parole	unwanted things
exoneration	past of the matter, the	welfare
freeing	personal limitation(s)	

Things

abandonment	anesthesia	bad habit
abnegation	anesthetic	bafflement
absent-mindedness	animals, threatening	bail, get out on
abstinence (denial)	animals beyond control	bar (restriction)
acknowledge, refusal to	anonymity	begging
acquittal	anticlimax	behind the scenes
admission (confession)	appeal (plea)	belt (of whiskey)
afflictions, all manner of	apprehension (arrest)	benevolence (charity)
afterthought	apprehension (uneasiness)	bereavement
agony (suffering)	arrest (apprehension)	bias (error)
agony (trial)	artificial object	blackmail
aid (charity)	asceticism	blasphemy
aid (comfort)	assassination(s)	blemish (flaw)
aid (help)	astonishment (bewilderment)	blind spot
alcohol	astral entity	blot
allopathic medicine	atonement	blunder
alms	attrition (sorrow)	boat trip
aloneness	attrition (weakening)	bogus thing
ambulance	avocation (distraction)	bond (restraint)
ambush	avoidance (shunning)	bondage
amnesty	avowal (admission)	boner (mistake)
amphetamine	awe (fright)	boo-boo (mistake)
analgesic	backward motion	boomerang

Things Continued
boots (shoes)
botch (mess)
breaking free
brewing
bribery
bubble
bug (listening device)
bungled attempt, a
burning of debris
butt (leftover)
butt (of a joke)
caffeine
cage
camera
captivity
carelessness
cast (tinge)
cast-off
cattle, large
chaos (confusion)
charades
charitable act
charitable work
charity
chemical reactions
chemicals
chemistry (in general)
chronic illness
cigar
cigarette
clandestine affair
clandestine relationship
clandestine work
clearing (vindication)
clemency (mercy)
cloudiness
clouds
clutter
cocaine
comedown
comfort (cheering up)
comfort (solace)
concern for others

confession (disclosure)
confidence (secrecy)
confidential activities
confinement (limitation)
confinement (restraint)
confusing elements
confusion
contacts with hospitals
contacts with invalids
contribution (alms)
contrition
convalescence
correction (punishment)
corrosion
cosmic fair
covertness
cowardice
crack (failure)
crime
cross (burden)
crying
curse (burden)
daydreaming
death of a child
debris
decline (deterioration)
defeat
defraud
deliverance
delusion (misbelief)
deportation
derangement
desertion
desperation (need)
destitution
detention
devotion (fervor)
dirt (grime)
disability (disadvantage)
disability (handicap)
disadvantages
disagreeable duty
disappointing events
disarray (disorder)

disavowal
discarded item
discharge (release)
discoloration
discrediting (defaming)
dishonor
dismissal (release)
disorder (mess)
disowning (denial)
disowning (forsaking)
dispossession
disrespect
dissolution
dissolving
dole (welfare)
dope (drugs)
downfall (ruin)
drag one's feet
dread (fear)
dream or sleep patterns
dregs (residue)
drop (abandon)
drug addiction
drugs (in general)
drugs, illicit
drunkenness
dye (tint)
eavesdropping
electronic music
elixir (cure-all)
eluding
elusiveness
emancipation
enchantment
encription
end (leftover)
enemies (in general)
enemies, secret
enigma (puzzle)
enticement
entity, astral
error (mistake)
error in judgment
escape (avoidance)

escape (breakout)	fissure	hidden defect
escape (seepage)	flaw	hidden factors in experience
escape from bondage	flimsiness	hidden vices
escapism	flow (discharge)	hiding
ESP	foam	hoax
ethnic food	fog	hokum (evasion)
evasion (avoidance)	food stamps	hole (flaw)
excluded element	footwear	hole (in a fix)
exclusion (banning)	foreseeing the future	hospital care
excuse	forgetfulness	hospital stay
exile	foul-up	hospitalization
exit (withdrawal)	freak (monster)	house hunting
exodus	freedom, gaining of	house of detention
exotic food	fumigation	illegibility
expedience (help)	fungus	illness, chronic
expendable item	gaff	illness of partner
expose	galoshes	illogical solution
exposure, unsought	gambling, illicit	illusion
extrasensory perception	gauze	impairment
fading	gibberish	impractical idea
failing (shortcoming)	gimmick	imprisonment
failure (deterioration)	grace (mercy)	improbability
failure (disappointment)	grease (lard)	impunity
failure (failing)	grief (misery)	incarceration
failure (neglect)	grief, periods of	incognito
faint mark	grime (dirt)	incurable illness
fall (surrender)	grit (dirt)	inductance
fallacy (flaw)	hallucination	ineffectual actions
fallacy (misconception)	hallucinogen	ineptness
false pregnancy	hand off	inevitability
fantasy	hand-me-down	inferior things
fascination	handicap (defect)	infestation
fat(s)	handout (dole)	inscrutability
fault (error)	hang up	institutionalization
fear (foreboding)	hangover	intemperance
feebleness	haze (mist)	intoxicating substance
fermentation	help when in need	intoxication
fiasco (failure)	heroin	intrigue
fiction	hex	invisibility
fictitious things	hibernation	involuntary incarceration
film on a surface	hidden (secret) matters	involuntary labor ordered by law
filmy things	hidden (secret) problem	
filth (dirt)	hidden (secret) relationship	isolation
filthiness	hidden affair	jail

Houses of the Third Quadrant

Things Continued
jinx
joint (dope)
journey, mother's
journeys by water
jumbles
karma
kidnapping
lament
lapse (slight error)
large institution
large thing
leak (escape)
leniency
let down (discouragement)
lighting (indirect)
limit
limitation
limiting condition
liquor
litter (rubbish)
litter (trash)
loneliness
loose ends
loss (defeat)
loss (deprivation)
lost, being
malformation
malpractice (negligence)
martyrdom
mask (cover-up)
mask (false face)
masquerade
matters taken for granted
maya (illusion)
Medicaid
medicine, socialized
memory, loss of
mercy
mess (clutter)
mildew
miracle
mirage
miscalculation

misery
mishap
mist
mistake (blunder)
mix-up (mistake)
mold (fungus)
monster (deviant)
monstrosity
morning
mourning
movie film
murkiness
mushroom
mystery (unknown thing)
mystical things
mysticism
narcotic
nebulousness
negatives (photographic)
neglect
nicotine
nothing (obscurity)
nuisance (blight)
obscure thing
obsolescence
offering (sacrifice)
onus (stigma)
opiate
opium
ordeal (misery)
organism (institution)
organized crime
organized crime activities
out on bail
overshoes
overused things
panacea
pardon
parole
past, your
past mistake
past moment
pawned item
pedal

penance
penury
permeability
perplexity
personal ruin
photograph
photographic image
photography
pinch (discomfort)
pipe (smoker's)
pipe dream
plastic
plating
pleading (cry for help)
plot (conspiracy)
porousness
potion
prayer (plea)
predestination
private scandal
prohibited act
protective custody
pseudonym
psychedelia
psychedelic drug
psychic fair
psychometry
punishment
quarantine (isolation)
quitting
rag (cloth)
reason (excuse)
reckoning (settling accounts)
recognize, refusal to
rectification (setting right)
redemption
refraining (abstaining)
refuse (waste)
regression
regrets
relapse
release (freedom)
releasing
relief (respite)

relief (welfare)
relief work
remainder, the
remaindered items
remedy (relief)
remission
remnant
remote consequences
renunciation
repression (captivity)
reprieve
repudiation
rescue
residuals
residue
rest (remainder)
retardation
retreat (withdrawal)
retrogression
returning (coming back)
reverie (daydream)
rose colored glasses
rubbish
rust
sacrifice
sadness
sandals
scandal
screen (projection)
seclusion (solitude)
secrecy
secret
sedative
selfless deed
selfless giving
selfless service
service (involuntary)
service, hidden
shabbiness
shakeout
sham (hoax)
shape shifter
shoes
shortening (fat)

shrinkage (drawing back)
shunned objects / people
shut-out (excluded)
sieve
sigh
sinister actions
skeleton in the closet
skid (wheel substitute)
slavery
slide (photographic)
slip (evasion)
slipshod work
slouch (droop)
slump (lapse)
slump (slouch)
smoking (tobacco, etc.)
smothering (concealment)
smuggling
snap (weather change)
snapshot
sobbing
solace
solitaire
solitary things
solitude
soot
sorrows, secret
special effects
spot (disgrace)
spouse's health
stab (pang)
statement of purpose
stealth
stigma
story line
struggle
stub (end)
stuffiness
subtlety
subversion
suffering
suicide
suit (plea)
sunrise

support (boost)
surrender (give up)
synthetic material
tail (end)
tangle (confusion)
target (butt)
tarnish
tatters (rag)
tear gas
temptation (enticement)
thorn (bane)
throes (anguish)
through a glass darkly
throw-away item
time to be alone
tissue paper
tobacco
tongue of shoe
trance
translucency
transparency (film)
trial (trouble)
tribulation (bad luck)
tribulation (unhappiness)
trident
trip (err)
trip mechanism (release)
trouble (difficulty)
turbidity (unclear)
turmoil, inner or psychic
twist of fate, a
ulterior motive
unauthorized action
undercover work
undertow
undisclosed condition
undoing (reversal)
undoing (ruin)
uneasiness
unemployment
unexpected obstacle
unforeseen event
unfortunate activity
unfortunate circumstance

Things Continued
unhappiness
unhealthy condition
unidentifiable thing
unknown adversary
unluckiness
unreality
unruly mob
untimely event
unwanted thing
vagueness
veil
verdict (jury's finding)
vicarious things
vindication (exoneration)
wail
want (a lack of money)
waste (rubbish)
waste matter
welfare
whiskey
widowhood
wine
withdrawal into fantasy
woes
work behind the scenes
work commonly avoided
work done in solitude
work done quietly or alone
wreck
wrong way movement
yawn
yesterday
yield (give up)
yield (relinquish)

Psychological Qualities

abstaining (refraining)
anguish
being alone
character defects
charity, given
charity, received
collapse (breakdown)
coming unglued
compassion
confession (of guilt)
confusion
crime, involvement with
delusion, self
denial (disavowal)
disillusionment
drugs, dependence upon
duress
emotional blocks
escape
escape, ability to
forsaking
freeing
frustrations
hidden, sense of what is
hidden fear
illness, coping with
imposing limitations
institutions, attitudes toward
integrating, ability to
introspection
karmic responsibilities
laboring under an illusion
letting go
limitation, facing
misfortune
negligence
obscurity
passion (suffering)
passive resistance
personal limitation(s)
piety
poverty
private problems
psychic influence
punishment
reaping (finding)
reciprocal acts received
regret
release, wanting to effect
relinquish, ability to
relinquishing
remorse (regret)
renunciation, ability for
repentance
returning
reversion
sacrifice
secret, keeping a
secret enmity
secret sorrow
secret worry
secretiveness
self-defeating behavior
self-denial
self-destruction
self-destructive processes
self-injury
self-pity
self-sacrifice
self-undoing
self-wastage
shame
sloppiness
solitary pursuits
sorrow
sorrow- profound
sorrowful conditions
sublimation
subversion
surrendering
torment
travails
unburdening
unconscious mind
understanding (sympathy)
vanishing
victimization
withdrawal

Occupations or Person Types

addict	homeless, the	secret enemy
alcoholic	illusionist	sensitive people
ascetic	informer	shoe repairer
assassin	invalid	shoemaker
barmaid	jailer	shut-in
bartender	junk dealer	siren
beggar	kidnapper	sleazy person
bimbo	martyr	sneak
bootlegger	monster (demon)	social worker
brewer	moron	solitary person
castaway	mourner	spy
charity worker	needy, the	sucker
charlatan	nomad	those on welfare
chemist	non-entity	those under detention
clandestine associate	organ donor	those who work with alcohol
confidential agents	orphan	those who work with criminals
convict	outcast	traitor
criminal	parasite	tramp
cripple	pauper	undercover operator
degenerate	persons in misery	underdog
deportee	persons on relief	underworld character
derelict	photographer	undesirable person
disabled, the	pirate	unfortunate
displaced person	podiatrist	unscrupulous person
dreamer	poet	used car salesman
dregs (riff-raff)	poor, the	vagabond
drip (jerk)	prey (victim)	vagrant
drug dealer	prisoner	veterinarian, large animals
drunkard	private enemy	victim
dyer	property dealer	ward
exile	recluse	warden, game
fairy	refugee	welfare recipient
felon	reprobate	welfare worker
firebug	savior	widow, widower
foreign spies	scapegoat	wimp
forger	scrap dealer	
ghost writer	secret agent	

Places

ale house	brewery	charity
asylum	canteen (bar)	church yard
bar (tavern)	charitable institution	clip joint

Houses of the Third Quadrant

Places Continued

confessional	hospice	rescue mission
convent	hospital	rest home
correctional institution	infirmary	retreat
corrections, house of	institute	safe haven
dead end	institution (establishment)	sanatorium
den (retreat)	jail	sanctuary
dungeon	joint (tavern)	sanitarium
ghetto	loft	secluded place
ghost town	nursing home	seclusion (hiding place)
government building	penal colony	slum
harbor (haven)	penitentiary	stronghold (refuge)
haven	place hidden or out of sight	tannery
hidden places	prison	taproom
hiding place	reform school	tavern
home for the aged	refuge	zoo
	relief agency	

Family Members or Relations

aunt, paternal	paternal kin	step-parent
aunts from the father's side	paternal uncle	uncle, paternal
mother's kin	relative of a parent	uncles on the father's side

Mundane Ideas

asylum	occult society	secret service
charity, national	opposition, behind the scenes	secret society
communal possessions	opposition-underhanded or sneaky	self-undoing
concentration camp		serving mankind
confidential matters	prison	spending beyond means
conspiracy	prisoner-of-war	spy
enemies, secret	public institution	subversive
espionage	public sales	trade union
fall from power	public welfare	treason
hidden ills	punishment of crime	utility, public
hospital care, national	secret cabal	utility company
institutions, large public	secret enemy	welfare agency
money manipulation	secret organization	welfare systems
	secret police force	

Parts of Our Body

arches of feet	instep	toe
feet	mucous	

Afflictions or Diseases

afflictions	athlete's foot	chronic ailment
amnesia	bunion	chronic ill health

coma
consumption
corns
deformity (disfigurement)
foot diseases
frustrations, illness causing

glaucoma
insanity
lameness
mental strain
neurosis
pain

pain, chronic
physical handicap
psychosis
spasm
sprained/broken toe

Colors

lavender
mauve
purple

royal purple
ultra-violet
velvet

violet

Gems or Minerals

amethyst
asbestos
fluorescent mineral
imitation stone

quartz
quartzite
rock crystal
rose quartz

smoky quartz
synthetic stone
tiger's eye
YAG

Animals

animals, large or wild
animals in zoos
big game
birds, wild
condor
cougar
elephant

fish
hyena
large animals
marten
mink
panther
parasite

rhinoceros
walrus
whale
wild animal
wild dog
wildcat

Mythical Figures or Constellation Names

Allspy (Panope)
Andromeda
Canes Major (large dog)
Cetus (sea monster)
Cottos (many headed monster)
Cyclops
Dorado (goldfish)
Echo (the repeater)

Eos (dawn)
Hyades
Lynx (lynx)
Musca (fly)
Neptune
Nymph
Panope (Allspy)
Pisces (fishes)

Pisces Austrinis (southern fish)
Poseidon
Puppis (stern of the Argo)
Sasquatch
Sisyphos (betrayal)
Tthetis (shape changer)
Yeti

Parts of an Organization

allocation of assets
company benefits
company good will

medical/nurses station
parts hidden from view
quality control

welfare offices

Industry Categories

animal control
animal health services

bail bond services
beverage (alcoholic)

beverage (soft drink)
chemical (basic)

chemical (diversified)
chemical (specialty)
coal (processing)
conglomerate
containers (metal/plastic)
diversified company
drug abuse treatment
drugs
fish processing

fishing
home building
imaging/photography
insurance (health)
movie making
museum/museum services
natural gas (diversified)
oil field services/equipment
petroleum (integrated)

petroleum (producing)
pharmaceuticals
photography/imaging
shoe manufacturers
tire and rubber
tobacco
used car/truck dealers
veterinarians (large animal)
yacht brokers

Parts of an Automobile

body rust
flat tire

tire
trunk

Parts of a House

areas behind walls
door, rear or side

drainage of the land
fire escape

Parts of a Ship

auxiliary boat
launch
smoke stack

House Keywords in Alphabetical Order

Key	Subject area
Af	Afflictions, Diseases, Infirmities, etc.
An	Animals, Insects, Birds, Reptiles, Amphibians, etc.
Au	Parts of an Automobile
Bd	Parts of a Human Body, Body Functions, etc.
Co	Colors
Ge	Gems, Minerals, Metals, Crystals, etc.
Ho	Horary or Electional Ideas,- the Key Ideas of a House
Hs	Parts of a House, Home, Structure, etc.
In	Industries, Types of Businesses
Mn	Mundane Ideas (Political, Business, Historical, etc.)
My	Mythical Figures, Constellations, Ancient Gods, etc.
Oc	Occupations, Persons, Stereotypes, etc.
Or	Parts of a Business Organization
Pl	Places, Locations, etc.
Ps	Psychological Qualities
Re	Family Members, Close Relations, etc.
Sh	Parts of a Ship, Naval Vessel, Boat, etc.
Th	Things, Objects, Stuff, Curiosities, etc.

A

abandoned place	Pl 01	abundance	Th 09	account (reason)	Th 03
abandonment	Th 12	abuse	Ps 08	account (report)	Th 03
abbey	Pl 09	abuse (criticism)	Th 06	account executive	Oc 10
abbreviations	Th 03	abuse (misuse)	Th 08	accountant	Oc 06
abdication (vacates)	Th 08	abyss (deep pit)	Pl 08	accounting services	In 06
abdomen	Bd 06	academia	Th 09	accumulation	Ho 04
abduction	Th 07	academic	Oc 09	accumulation	Th 04
aberration (abnormality)	Th 11	academic aims	Th 09	accuracy	Ps 06
aberration (irregularity)	Th 11	academic subjects	Th 09	accuracy (exactness)	Th 06
abeyance (postponement)	Th 10	academy	Pl 09	accusation	Th 07
ability	Ho 05	acceleration	Th 01	accustomization	Th 03
ability (capability)	Th 05	accent (emphasis)	Th 01	acerbity	Th 03
ability to handle funds	Th 02	accent (speech)	Th 03	ache	Af 01
abnegation	Th 12	acceptance	Ho 09	achievement	Ho 10
abnormal behavior	Th 07	acceptance (receiving)	Th 09	achievement	Ps 10
abnormality	Ho 11	access (admittance)	Th 01	achievement (acquired skill)	Th 10
abnormality (deformity)	Th 11	access (entryway)	Th 01		
abnormality (deviation)	Th 11	accessibility	Th 01	achievement (realization)	Th 10
abode	Pl 04	accession (appeasement)	Th 02	achroite	Ge 11
abolishing	Th 08	accession (joining)	Th 03	acid	Th 01
abolition (ending)	Th 08	accessory (accompaniment)	Th 11	acid body condition	Af 01
abomination	Th 08			acid/alkaline balance	Af 04
abortion, spontaneous	Af 05	accessory (accomplice)	Oc 07	acknowledge, refusal to	Th 12
abortion, surgical	Af 08	accessory (adornment)	Th 02	acknowledgment (admission)	Th 07
abrasion (scrape)	Af 01	accident (chance)	Th 01		
abrasion (wearing down)	Th 11	accidental death	Th 08	acknowledgment (gratitude)	Th 02
abrasives	In 01	accidents, liability to	Th 01		
abridgment	Th 08	accidents, the likelihood of	Ho 01	acknowledgment (recognition)	Th 10
abruptness	Ps 01				
abscess	Af 08	acclamation (ovation)	Th 05	acme	Th 10
absence	Th 10	acclimatization	Th 03	acne	Af 01
absent related person	Th 09	accolade (reward)	Th 10	acorn	Th 05
absent unrelated person	Th 01	accommodation (compromise)	Th 07	acoustical materials	In 02
absent-mindedness	Th 12			acquaintance	Oc 11
absorption (assimilation)	Th 06	accommodation (room)	Th 04	acquaintance (friendship)	Ps 11
absorption (soak up)	Th 04	accompaniment	Th 11	acquisition (achievement)	Th 10
abstaining (refraining)	Ps 12	accompanist	Oc 11	acquisition (acquiring)	Th 04
abstinence (denial)	Th 12	accomplice	Oc 11	acquittal	Th 12
abstract	Th 08	accomplishment	Ho 10	acreage	Th 04
abstract mind, the	Th 09	accomplishment (achievement)	Ps 10	acrimony	Th 07
abstract thinking	Th 09			acrobats	Oc 03
abstract thought processes	Ps 09	accomplishment (completion)	Th 10	across the border	Pl 09
abstraction	Ho 09			act (deed)	Th 01
abstraction(s)	Th 09	accords	Th 07	act (law)	Th 09
absurdity (nonsense)	Th 03	account (financial)	Th 02	act (play part)	Th 05

act (pretense)	Th 03	adjunct (rider)	Th 11	advertisement, written copy	Th 03
act (process of doing)	Th 01	adjuster (claims)	Oc 08	advertiser	Oc 09
acting	Th 05	adjustment (settling up)	Th 07	advertising	In 09
action (effort)	Th 01	adjustment (tuning)	Th 08	advertising	Ho 09
action (feat)	Th 10	adjutant	Oc 06	advertising	Mn 09
action (movement)	Th 01	Admetos (exaggerated promises)	My 05	advertising agency	Pl 09
action (operation)	Th 06	administration	Th 10	advertising department	Or 09
actions that affect health	Th 06	administrative services	Or 10	advice	Ho 11
actions upon one's life	Ho 01	administrator	Oc 10	advice (intelligence)	Th 11
activation	Th 01	admiration (regard)	Th 10	advice (recommendation)	Th 11
active head of an enterprise	Th 10	admission (confession)	Th 12	advisor	Mn 11
activities in one's own interest	Ho 01	admission (permission)	Th 07	advisor	Oc 11
		admittance (entry)	Th 01	advocacy	Th 11
activity (movement)	Th 01	admonishment (chiding)	Th 07	advocate	Oc 11
activity (undertaking)	Th 01	admonishment (warning)	Th 08	aerial (antenna)	Th 11
actor	Oc 05	admonition (reprimand)	Th 07	aerodynamics	Th 11
actress	Oc 05	adolescents	Oc 03	aerospace/defense	In 06
actuality	Th 02	adopted child	Re 05	aesthetic sense	Ps 02
acumen	Th 03	adopted sibling	Re 03	aesthetics	Th 07
acupuncture	Th 06	adoption	Th 05	affair (celebration)	Th 05
acute angles	Th 03	adoration	Th 09	affair (event)	Th 01
ad writer	Oc 03	adornment (jewelry)	Th 02	affair (personal business)	Th 10
ad-lib	Th 03	adornment, articles of	Th 02	affair (relationship)	Th 05
adage (proverb)	Th 09	adrenal gland	Bd 01	affairs of in-laws	Re 09
adaptability	Ho 03	adulation (praise)	Th 05	affairs of later life	Th 04
adaptability	Ps 03	adult education classes	Th 03	affairs of officials	Mn 10
adaptability	Th 03	adulteration	Th 08	affairs of parents	Th 10
adaptation	Th 03	adultery, casual	Th 11	affairs of the heart	Th 05
add-on	Th 11	adultery, prolonged	Th 02	affectation (pretense)	Th 03
addendum	Th 09	adulthood	Th 10	affection (attachment)	Th 05
addict	Oc 12	advance (overture)	Th 05	affection, warmth of	Ps 05
addiction (dependency)	Ps 04	advance (pre-payment)	Th 02	affidavit	Th 09
addition	Hs 04	advanced educational degrees	Th 09	affiliate	Oc 11
addition (extension)	Th 09			affiliation (association)	Th 11
addition (extra)	Th 05	advanced learning	Th 09	affinity (partiality)	Th 02
addition (math)	Th 04	advanced schooling	Mn 09	affinity (similarity)	Th 03
address (location)	Th 01	advancement (progress)	Th 10	affirmation	Th 01
address (speech)	Th 03	advancement, economic	Mn 11	afflictions	Af 12
adenoids	Bd 02	advancement potential	Th 10	afflictions, all manner of	Th 12
adequacy	Ps 02	advantage	Ho 02	affluence	Th 02
adherence (complies with)	Th 08	advantage (benefit)	Th 02	affordability	Th 02
adherents	Oc 11	advantage (edge)	Th 02	affront (insult)	Th 07
adhesion (sticks to)	Th 04	adventure	Ho 09	after world	Pl 08
adhesives	Th 04	adventure	Th 09	afterlife	Th 08
adipose tissues	Bd 09	adventurer	Oc 09	aftermath (consequence)	Th 10
adjournment	Th 04	adversary	Oc 07	afternoon	Th 09
adjudication (judicial decision)	Th 09	adversity	Th 10	afterthought	Th 12
		advertisement (notice)	Th 09	agate	Ge 09

age	Ho 10	air (tune)	Th 02	alley	Pl 03
age (duration)	Th 10	air cargo	In 03	alleyway	Pl 03
age (eon)	Th 10	air conditioning	Th 11	alliance (agreement)	Th 07
age (epoch)	Th 10	air current	Th 03	alliance (partnership)	Th 07
age (seniority)	Th 10	air force	Mn 06	allied effort	Th 07
agency (bureau)	Or 06	air pollution	Th 10	alligator	An 10
agency (power)	Th 10	air purification	In 10	allocated space	Ps 01
agenda	Th 06	air rights	Mn 09	allocation (distribution)	Th 03
agent	Oc 07	air transport	In 11	allocation of assets	Or 12
agent of justice	Th 07	air travel	Th 11	allopathic medicine	Th 12
agglomeration	Th 11	aircraft	Th 11	allotment	Th 02
aggravation	Th 01	aircraft manufacturing	In 07	allowable, things that are	Th 09
aggregate (composite)	Th 11	aircraft noise	Th 11		
aggression (assault)	Th 01	airline host/hostess	Oc 06	allowance (discount)	Th 08
aggression (hostility)	Th 07	airline personnel	Oc 11	allowance (salary)	Th 02
aggressor	Oc 01	airline travel	Th 11	alloy treating	In 06
agility (grace)	Ps 07	airplane	Th 11	Allspy (Panope)	My 12
agility (suppleness)	Th 03	airplane crash	Th 08	allusion (reference)	Th 03
agitation	Th 11	airport	Mn 11	ally	Mn 07
agitator	Oc 11	airport	Pl 11	ally	Oc 07
agnostic	Oc 09	aisle	Pl 03	almandine	Ge 03
agony (suffering)	Th 12	alabaster	Ge 07	alms	Th 12
agony (trial)	Th 12	alarm (apprehension)	Th 10	aloofness	Ps 11
agrarian	Oc 04	alarm (warning)	Th 01	alphabet	Th 03
agreement	Ho 07	alarm systems	In 01	altar	Th 09
agreement (harmony)	Th 07	album (photo)	Th 04	alteration (internal)	Ps 08
agreement (understanding)	Th 07	album (recording)	Th 02	alteration (modification)	Th 08
agreement (written)	Th 03	albumin in urine	Af 07	altercation (dispute)	Th 07
agricultural interests	Mn 04	alchemy	Th 08	alternate energies	In 11
agricultural products	Th 04	alcohol	Th 12	alternation	Th 04
agricultural worker	Oc 04	alcoholic	Oc 12	alternatives	Th 07
agriculture	Mn 04	alcove (recess)	Hs 06	altimeter	Th 06
agriculture	Th 04	alderman	Oc 11	altitude	Th 09
agriculture (equipment)	In 10	ale house	Pl 12	altruism	Th 11
agriculture (growing)	In 04	alertness	Ps 01	altruistic undertakings	Th 11
agriculture (harvesting)	In 06	alexandrite	Ge 08	aluminum	Ge 11
ague	Af 01	alias	Th 03	alumnus	Oc 09
aid (charity)	Th 12	alibi	Th 03	amalgamation	Th 11
aid (comfort)	Th 12	alien	Oc 09	amateur	Oc 03
aid (help)	Th 12	alienation	Ps 07	amazement	Th 01
aide (assistant)	Oc 06	alignment	Au 07	amazonite	Ge 04
AIDS	Af 08	alignment	Bd 07	ambassador	Oc 09
ailment (disorder)	Th 06	alimentary canal	Bd 04	amber	Ge 05
aim (marksmanship)	Th 09	alimony	Th 08	ambiguity (vagueness)	Th 07
aim (objective)	Th 10	alkaline condition	Af 07	ambition	Ho 10
aiming point	Th 09	allegation (assertion)	Th 07	ambition	Ps 10
air (atmosphere)	Th 03	allegiance (loyalty)	Th 08	ambition (goal)	Th 10
air (character)	Th 01	allegory	Th 09	ambitious person	Oc 10
air (in tires)	Au 11	allergy	Af 04	ambivalence	Th 07

ambulance	Th 12	anchor	Th 04	annotation	Th 03
ambulance driver	Oc 01	anchorage	Pl 04	announcement	Th 03
ambush	Th 12	ancient dwelling	Pl 10	announcer	Oc 03
amendment (constitutional)	Th 11	ancient things	Th 10	annoyance	Th 01
		andiron	Th 04	annuity	Th 08
amendment (revision)	Th 08	andradite	Ge 03	annulment	Th 10
amends (apology)	Th 07	androgyny	Th 03	annunciator	Sh 03
amethyst	Ge 12	android	Th 03	anointment	Th 09
ammunition	Th 01	andromeda	My 12	anomaly (deviation)	Th 11
ammunition depot	Pl 01	anecdote	Th 03	anomaly (rarity)	Th 11
ammunition manufacture	In 01	anemia	Af 07	anonymity	Th 12
ammunition of a besieged town	Th 05	anesthesia	Th 12	anonymous gift	Th 07
		anesthetic	Th 12	anonymous letter	Th 01
amnesia	Af 12	aneurysm	Af 05	answer (reply)	Th 03
amnesty	Th 12	angel (backer)	Oc 06	answer (solution)	Th 10
amorality	Ps 08	angel (heavenly being)	Th 09	antagonism	Th 07
amorousness	Th 05	anger	Ho 01	ante, the (as in poker)	Th 05
amorphousness	Th 03	anger	Th 01	ante-chamber	Pl 01
amount (quantity)	Th 02	angina	Af 05	anteater	An 01
amount (sum)	Th 06	angle (bend)	Th 03	antenna	Th 11
amperage	Th 09	angle (new twist)	Th 03	anterior place	Pl 01
amphetamine	Th 12	angle (point of view)	Th 03	anterior thing	Th 01
amphibian	An 10	angler	Oc 04	anthology	Th 04
amphitheater	Pl 05	angles	Ho 03	anti-christ	Oc 08
amplification (expansion)	Th 09	anguish	Ps 12	anti-hero	Oc 11
amplifier	Th 09	animal (creature)	An 01	anti-spasmodic	Th 07
amplitude (extent)	Th 10	animal control	In 12	antibiotic	Th 06
amputation	Th 08	animal handlers	In 06	anticipation (expectation)	Th 09
amusement equipment manufacturer	In 10	animal health services	In 12	anticlimax	Th 12
		animal husbandry	Th 06	antics	Th 03
amusement park	Pl 05	animal husbandry services	In 06	antidote	Th 01
amusement park worker	Oc 05			antila (air pump)	My 11
amusement(s)	Th 05	animal magnetism	Th 08	antimony	Ge 10
analgesic	Th 12	animal spirits	Th 01	Antinous	My 03
analogy	Ps 09	animals	Mn 06	antipathy	Th 07
analogy	Th 09	animals, large or wild	An 12	antique	Th 04
analysis (breakdown)	Th 08	animals, small domesticated	An 06	antiquity	Th 04
analysis (evaluation)	Th 08			antiseptic	Th 06
analysis (examination)	Th 08	animals, threatening	Th 12	antithesis (opposition)	Th 07
analysis (reasoning)	Th 06	animals beyond control	Th 12	antithesis (reverse)	Th 07
analysis, self	Ps 08	animals in zoos	An 12	antonym	Th 09
analyst	Oc 08	animation	Th 03	anus	Bd 08
analytical scientist	Oc 08	animosity	Th 01	anvil	Th 01
anarchist	Oc 11	ankle	Bd 11	anxiety	Ps 06
anarchy	Th 11	anklet	Th 07	anyone unrelated by blood	Re 07
anatomy	Th 01	annex	Pl 09		
ancestors	Re 04	annexation	Th 08	anyone who is a stranger	Re 09
ancestry	Th 04	annihilation	Th 08	anything created by you	Th 05
anchor	Sh 04	anniversary	Th 04	anything hidden in	Th 04

the ground		appreciation (growth)	Th 08	archive	Pl 04
apartment (residence)	Th 04	appreciation (understanding)	Th 07	archivist	Oc 04
apathy	Th 07			ardor (feeling)	Th 05
ape	An 01	apprehension (arrest)	Th 12	area (expanse)	Th 04
aperture (opening)	Th 04	apprehension (comprehension)	Ps 09	area (region)	Th 04
apex, the	Th 10			area (scope)	Th 10
aphrodisiac	Th 08	apprehension (uneasiness)	Th 12	areas behind walls	Hs 12
Aphrodite (the lover)	My 07	apprentice	Oc 06	arena	Pl 05
apiary	Pl 02	apprenticeship	Th 06	arena of action in a contest	Pl 05
aplomb (composure)	Th 02	approach (access)	Th 03		
Apollo (the healer)	My 05	approach (draw closer)	Th 03	Ares (the warrior)	My 01
Apollon	My 05	approach (mannerism)	Th 01	argument (quarrel)	Th 07
apology	Th 07	approbation (praise)	Th 02	argument (reasoning)	Th 03
apoplexy	Af 09	appropriation (allocation)	Th 02	argument (summary)	Th 08
apostle	Oc 11	appropriation (taking)	Th 08	Argus (the adventurers)	My 01
apparatus	Th 06	approval (acceptance)	Th 02	arid land	Pl 01
apparel	Th 06	approval (permission)	Th 07	Aries	My 01
apparel (designers)	In 06	approval (regard)	Th 02	aristocracy	Th 10
apparel (manufacturers)	In 06	aptitude	Ho 05	aristocracy, the	Mn 10
apparentness (open to view)	Th 07	aptitude	Ps 05	aristocrat	Oc 10
		aptitude test	Th 11	arm (offshoot)	Th 10
apparition	Th 08	aptness (effectiveness)	Th 06	arm fractures or breaks	Af 03
appeal (charm)	Th 02	Apus (bird of paradise)	My 05	armada	Th 06
appeal (plea)	Th 12	aqua	Co 04	armadillo	An 04
appearance	Ho 01	aquamarine	Ge 07	armament manufacturer	Oc 01
appearance	Ps 01	aquarium	Pl 04	armament(s)	Sh 01
appeasement	Th 02	Aquarius	My 11	armaments	Th 01
appendage (attachment)	Th 09	aqueduct	Pl 03	armed forces, the	Th 06
appendage (subordinate body part)	Bd 03	Aquilla (eagle)	My 08	armed services	Th 06
		Ara (altar)	My 09	armies	Th 06
appendage, artificial	Bd 02	arbiter	Oc 07	armistice	Th 07
appendicitis	Af 06	arbitrariness	Ps 04	armor (protection)	Th 04
appendix (addition)	Th 09	arbitrary actions	Th 03	armory	Pl 01
appetite, sexual	Th 08	arbitration	Ho 07	armpits	Bd 03
appetite abnormality	Af 04	arbitration	Th 07	arms (limbs)	Bd 03
appetite for food	Th 04	arbitration office	Pl 07	arms (ordnance)	Th 01
applause	Th 05	arbitration services	In 07	army, the	Mn 06
appliance (prosthesis)	Th 02	arbitrator	Oc 07	army, the	Th 06
appliance (tool)	Th 06	arc (crescent)	Th 04	aroma	Th 02
appliance (work saver)	Th 11	arcade	Pl 05	arousal (wakening)	Th 01
application (adhesion)	Th 04	arch (vault)	Th 09	arrangement (grouping)	Th 06
application (put to use)	Th 06	archaeological dig	Pl 08	arrangement (plan)	Th 10
application (request)	Th 03	archaeologist	Oc 08	array (display)	Th 06
appointment (designation)	Th 10	archeology	Th 08	arrears (overdue debts)	Th 08
appointment (engagement)	Th 07	archer	Oc 09	arrest (apprehension)	Th 12
apportionment	Th 11	arches of feet	Bd 12	arrest (stoppage)	Th 10
appraisal (evaluation)	Th 07	archetype (model)	Th 03	arrivals	Th 01
appraiser	Oc 07	architect	Oc 07	arrogance	Ps 05
appreciation (gratitude)	Th 02	architecture	Th 01	arrow	Th 09

211

arsenal	Pl 01	assault (striking)	Th 01	(amazement)	
arsenic	Ge 08	assault (threat)	Th 07	astonishment	Th 12
arson	Th 01	assayer	Oc 02	(bewilderment)	
art (creativity)	Th 05	assemblage	Th 11	astral entity	Th 12
art (technique)	Th 06	assembly and fabricating	In 10	astral projection	Th 11
art, works of	Hs 07	services		astringent	Th 06
art dealer	Oc 07	assembly (gathering)	Th 11	astrologer	Oc 11
art galleries/dealers	In 07	assent (agreement)	Th 07	astrological affairs	Th 11
art studio	Hs 07	assertion (claim)	Th 01	astrology	Ho 11
Artemis	My 04	assertion of self	Ps 01	astrology	Th 11
arteries	Bd 01	assertive attitude	Ps 01	astronomer	Oc 10
arteries (roadways)	Th 03	assessment (appraisal)	Th 02	astronomy	Th 10
arteriosclerosis	Af 02	assessment (taxes)	Th 08	asylum	Mn 12
arthritis	Af 10	assessor	Oc 02	asylum	Pl 12
article (item)	Th 06	asset (benefit)	Th 02	atheism	Th 08
article (news)	Th 03	asset (property)	Th 02	atheist	Oc 08
article (object)	Th 04	asset, liquid or monetary	Th 02	Athena (the counselor)	My 06
articulation	Th 03	asset, negotiable	Th 02	atherosclerosis	Af 04
artifact	Th 07	assets of the people	Mn 02	athlete	Oc 05
artifice	Th 03	assignment	Th 11	athlete's foot	Af 12
artificial limb	Bd 02	(apportionment)		athletic contests	Th 05
artificial object	Th 12	assignment (homework)	Th 06	athletic sports for	Th 09
artillery	Th 01	assignment (post)	Th 04	show or gain	
artillery man	Oc 01	assimilation	Th 06	athletic supporter	Th 06
artisan	Oc 06	assistance	Ho 06	athletics	Th 05
artist	Oc 05	assistance (collaboration)	Th 07	atlas	Th 06
artistic output	Th 06	assistance (financial	Th 08	atmosphere, the earth's	Th 03
artistic work	Th 05	support)		atoll	Pl 04
artistry	Th 05	assistance (help)	Th 06	atom	Th 04
artists	In 07	assistant	Oc 06	atomic energy	Th 08
arts, the fine arts	Th 07	associate (co-worker)	Th 06	atomic weapon	Th 08
asbestos	Ge 12	associate (friend)	Th 11	atomizer	Th 11
ascendancy (domination)	Th 08	associating (classifying)	Th 06	atonement	Ho 12
ascension (ascent)	Th 10	associating (social)	Th 07	atonement	Th 12
ascent (advancement)	Th 10	association (connection)	Th 03	atrocity (outrage)	Th 08
ascetic	Oc 12	association (relationship)	Th 07	atrophy	Af 10
asceticism	Th 12	associations (groups)	Th 11	attachment (caring)	Ps 07
ashram	Pl 09	associative memory	Th 03	attachment (extender)	Th 06
aspect (look)	Th 01	assortment (variety)	Th 11	attachment (fastening)	Th 04
aspect (point)	Th 03	assumption	Th 08	attainment	Th 10
aspersion (slur)	Th 07	(appropriation)		attempt (try)	Th 01
asphalt	Th 10	assumption (belief)	Th 09	attendance (presence)	Th 01
asphyxiation	Af 03	assumption making	Ps 09	attendance (roll)	Th 06
aspirations (hopes)	Th 11	processes		attendant	Oc 06
aspirations (objectives)	Th 10	assurance (confidence)	Ps 05	attention (concentration)	Th 08
ass (fool)	Oc 03	assurance (pledge)	Th 10	attention (courtesy)	Th 07
assailant	Oc 07	asthma	Af 03	attention (heed)	Th 01
assassin	Oc 12	astigmatism	Af 04	attention (wooing)	Th 05
assassination(s)	Th 12	astonishment	Th 01	attention, focus of	Ps 01

attention span	Ps 01	authenticity	Th 10	auxiliary steerage	Sh 03
attentiveness	Th 03	author	Oc 03	availability	Th 01
attenuation (weaken)	Th 08	authority (specialist)	Oc 10	avalanche	Th 08
attic	Hs 09	authority, aura of	Ps 10	avant-garde, the	Th 11
attic	Pl 09	authority, document granting	Th 10	avarice	Th 02
attire (dress)	Th 06			avenue (roadway)	Th 03
attitude (disposition)	Ps 01	authority, persons in	Ho 10	avenue (way)	Th 03
attitude (posture)	Th 01	authority, symbol of	Th 10	average (mean)	Th 04
attitude toward God	Th 09	authority figure	Oc 10	average (normal)	Th 04
attitudes of the people	Mn 01	authority over, having	Th 10	average (par)	Th 04
attorney	Oc 09	authorization	Th 07	aversion (dislike)	Th 07
attraction (appeal)	Ps 07	authorship	Th 03	aviation	Th 11
attribute	Th 01	auto and truck	In 03	aviator	Oc 11
attrition (sorrow)	Th 12	auto (automobile)	Th 03	avionics	In 11
attrition (weakening)	Th 12	auto dealer	Oc 03	avocation (distraction)	Th 12
auction	Th 08	auto leasing/rental	In 11	avocation (recreation)	Th 05
auctioneer	Oc 03	auto manufacturer	Oc 11	avoidance (shunning)	Th 12
audacity	Th 01	auto parts (after-market)	In 08	avowal (admission)	Th 12
audience (audition)	Th 05	auto parts (OEM)	In 08	awakening (arousal)	Th 01
audience (spectators)	Th 04	auto parts (replacement)	In 08	award	Th 10
audio-visual displays	Th 01	auto trip	Th 03	awareness (realization)	Th 07
audit, tax or financial	Th 08	autobiography	Th 03	awareness of surroundings	Ps 01
audition	Th 05	autograph	Th 03		
auditor	Oc 06	automation	Th 11	awe (fright)	Th 12
auditorium	Pl 05	automobile	Th 03	awe (reverence)	Th 09
augmentation	Th 09	automobile repair	In 06	awe (wonder)	Th 09
aunt, maternal	Re 06	automobile sales	In 09	awkwardness	Th 02
aunt, paternal	Re 12	autonomic nervous system	Bd 03	axe	Th 01
aunts from the father's side	Re 12			axiom	Th 06
		autonomy	Th 10	axis	Th 10
aura	Th 05	autopsy	Th 08	aye	Th 10
Auriga (the charioteer)	My 03	autumn	Th 07	azure	Co 02
auspice (portent)	Th 09	auxiliary boat	Sh 12	azurite	Ge 02
auspicious portents	Th 09	auxiliary item	Th 08		
austerity	Th 10	auxiliary power	Sh 11		

B

babble	Th 03	back country	Pl 09	background taken for granted, a	Th 03
baby	Th 05	back log	Th 04		
baby shower	Th 05	back porch	Hs 05	backhoe	Th 11
baby sitter	Oc 08	back stage	Pl 04	backpack	Th 06
Baccus	My 05	back up (copy)	Th 03	backward motion	Th 12
back (behind you)	Pl 07	back yard	Hs 04	backwardness	Ps 04
back (in general)	Bd 05	back-handed compliment	Th 08	bacteria	Th 08
back, lower half	Bd 07	backbiting	Th 07	bad (evil) person	Oc 08
back, small of the	Bd 07	backer	Oc 11	bad breath	Af 02

213

bad habit	Th 12	banking house	Mn 02	bat	An 06
bad luck	Th 10	banking system, the	Mn 02	bath, public	Pl 06
bad taste, in	Th 01	bankruptcy	Th 08	bath house	Pl 04
badge	Th 01	bankruptcy services	In 08	bathing suit	Th 05
badger	An 01	banks (commercial)	In 02	bathroom	Hs 06
badness	Ps 01	banks (money centers)	In 02	bathroom	Pl 06
baffle	Th 11	banner	Th 04	bathtub	Hs 06
bafflement	Th 12	banquet	Th 05	baton	Th 06
bag (container)	Th 04	baptism	Th 09	battery	Au 11
bail, get out on	Th 12	bar (law court)	Pl 09	battery	Th 11
bail bond	Th 08	bar (restriction)	Th 12	battery (striking)	Th 01
bail bond services	In 12	bar (stripe)	Th 07	battle	Th 01
bail bondsman	Oc 08	bar (tavern)	Pl 12	battlefield	Pl 07
bailiff	Oc 06	barb	Th 09	bauble (trinket)	Th 03
bait	Th 03	barbarian	Oc 09	bauxite	Ge 11
baker	Oc 04	barbarity	Th 08	bay	Pl 04
bakery	Pl 06	barber	Oc 01	bayonet	Th 01
balance	Ps 07	barbershop	Pl 01	bayou	Pl 04
balance (scale)	Th 07	bard	Oc 02	beach	Pl 04
balcony	Hs 09	bargain (deal)	Th 02	beacon	Th 05
balcony	Pl 09	bargaining	Th 03	bear	An 01
baldness	Af 01	barge	Th 04	beard	Bd 10
ball (dance)	Th 07	barker	Oc 03	beasts of burden	Th 06
ball (round)	Th 05	barmaid	Oc 12	beat (assignment)	Th 06
ball game	Th 05	barn	Pl 04	beat (rhythm)	Th 04
ball room	Pl 07	barn	Th 04	beat (strike)	Th 01
ballad	Th 02	barnacle	An 04	beating	Th 01
ballast	Sh 10	barometer	Th 06	beautician	Oc 07
ballet	Th 07	barracks	Pl 06	beautification	Th 07
balloon	Th 09	barren ground	Pl 01	beauty (in general)	Th 07
ballot	Th 11	barren place	Pl 01	beauty contest	Th 07
ballroom	Hs 05	barrenness	Th 01	beauty supplies/ equipment	In 07
ban (restraint)	Th 10	barrier	Th 10		
band (cinch)	Th 04	barrister	Oc 01	becoming	Th 04
band (musical)	Th 02	bartender	Oc 12	bed	Th 02
band (rubber)	Th 03	barter	Th 03	bed linen	Th 06
bandage	Th 06	base, your basis or start	Ps 04	bedding	Th 02
bandit	Oc 07	base of anything, the	Pl 10	bedfellow (ally)	Oc 07
banished person	Oc 07	base of anything, the	Th 10	bedlam	Th 01
banishment	Th 07	base of operations	Th 04	bedroom	Hs 02
bank (depository)	Pl 02	basement	Hs 04	bee	An 02
bank (river)	Pl 04	basement	Pl 04	beehive	Pl 02
bank account	Th 02	bashfulness	Ps 06	beeper	Th 03
bank deposit	Th 02	basic education	Th 03	beggar	Oc 12
bank holding companies	In 08	basic necessities	Th 06	begging	Th 12
bank note	Th 02	basic raw materials	Hs 02	beginning of life	Th 04
bank teller	Oc 02	basic security	Th 04	beginnings	Th 04
banker	Oc 02	basics, the	Ho 04	behavior	Ps 07
banking	Th 02	basics, the	Th 04	behind the scenes	Th 12

Alpha Sort with Industries

beige	Co 06	bid (offer)	Th 08	bizarre, the	Th 11
being centered	Th 07	big bang theory	Th 01	black	Co 10
being consumed by ...	Th 08	big business	Th 10	black magic	Th 06
being of service	Th 06	big game	An 12	black opal	Ge 09
belching	Bd 06	big game hunting	Th 09	black sheep	Re 09
belief structures	Ps 09	bigamy	Th 07	blackmail	Th 12
belief system(s)	Th 09	bigot	Oc 08	blacksmith	Oc 06
beliefs	Th 09	bilateral symmetry	Th 07	blacksmith shop	Pl 06
believer	Oc 09	bile	Bd 06	blacksmithing	In 06
belittling	Th 08	bilges	Sh 08	bladder	Bd 07
belligerence	Th 01	bill (bird's)	Th 01	bladder disorder	Af 07
belly	Bd 05	bill (invoice)	Th 08	bladder problem	Af 07
belly dancer	Oc 07	bill collector	Oc 08	blahs, the	Ps 11
belonging	Ps 11	billboard	Th 09	blanket	Th 06
belongings (goods)	Th 02	billfold	Th 02	blankness	Th 10
beloved pet	Th 05	billiards	Th 05	blasphemy	Th 12
belt (for pants)	Th 10	bimbo	Oc 12	blaze (fire)	Th 05
belt (of whiskey)	Th 12	bindings	Th 04	bleach	Th 08
bend (curve)	Th 03	bingo	Th 05	bleat	Th 04
beneath the ground	Th 04	binoculars	Th 09	blemish (flaw)	Th 12
benedictions	Th 09	biochemist	Oc 08	blending	Th 11
benefactor	Oc 09	biodegradation	Th 08	blessing	Th 09
beneficiary	Oc 08	bioengineering	Th 08	blessing in disguise	Th 09
benefit (privilege)	Th 09	biological rhythms	Th 04	blind spot	Th 12
benefit, things of	Ho 02	biologist	Oc 02	blinders	Th 02
benefit, things of	Th 02	biology	Th 02	blindness	Af 01
benefit package	Mn 08	biomedicine	Th 08	bliss	Th 05
benefits for employees	Or 02	bird call (device)	Th 08	blister	Af 01
benevolence (charity)	Th 12	bird call (summons)	Th 06	blizzard	Th 11
benevolence (kindliness)	Th 02	birds (in general)	An 06	bloating	Af 05
bequest	Th 08	birds, wild	An 12	blockade	Th 10
bereavement	Th 12	birds as pets	Th 06	blockage	Th 10
beryl	Ge 07	birds in flight	Th 09	blood (in general)	Bd 11
bet	Th 05	birth	Th 05	blood, loss of	Af 10
betrayal	Th 07	birth control	Th 08	blood cholesterol	Bd 02
betterment	Th 10	birth control devices	Th 08	blood circulatory system	Bd 05
betting	Th 05	birth rate	Mn 05	blood clot	Af 08
beverage	Th 04	birth rate	Th 05	blood disease	Af 05
beverage (alcoholic)	In 12	birthday	Th 04	blood impurities	Af 10
beverage (soft drink)	In 12	birthplace	Pl 04	blood pressure	Bd 11
bias (diagonal)	Th 03	birthright	Th 04	bloodshed	Th 01
bias (error)	Th 12	bisexuality	Th 10	bloodstone	Ge 09
bias (prejudice)	Th 07	bishop	Oc 09	blossom	Th 02
bias (slant)	Th 09	bit (piece)	Th 06	blot	Th 12
bias (tendency)	Th 04	bitch	Oc 07	blotch	Th 09
bible, the	Th 09	bitchiness	Th 07	blow (a striking)	Th 01
bibliography	Th 04	bite (animal)	Th 01	blow (move air)	Th 03
bicycle	Th 03	bite (insect)	Th 01	blow-out (at a wellhead)	Th 01
bid (invitation)	Th 07	bitterness	Th 10	blow-out (big win)	Th 01

blue	Co 02	bond (cord)	Th 04	boredom	Th 10
blue ribbon panel	Th 10	bond (restraint)	Th 12	borough	Pl 03
bluff	Pl 10	bond (security)	Mn 02	borrowed time	Th 11
bluff (ruse)	Th 03	bondage	Th 12	borrowing	Th 02
blunder	Th 12	bonding with another	Th 04	boss, the	Ho 10
blushing	Bd 01	bone bruise	Af 10	boss, the	Mn 10
boar	An 01	bone disease	Af 10	boss, the	Oc 10
board of directors	Mn 11	bone fracture	Af 10	bossiness	Ps 10
board of directors	Or 01	bone marrow	Bd 02	botanical garden	Pl 02
boarder	Oc 06	boner (mistake)	Th 12	botanist	Oc 04
boarding house	Th 04	bones	Bd 10	botch (mess)	Th 12
boasting	Th 05	bones	Th 10	bother (annoyance)	Th 01
boat	Th 04	bonnet	Th 01	bothersome thing	Th 01
boat trip	Th 12	bonus	Th 02	bottle	Th 04
boat/ship construction	In 10	boo-boo (hurt)	Th 01	bottleneck (impasse)	Th 07
bodily well being	Th 06	boo-boo (mistake)	Th 12	bottom (of anything)	Th 04
body	Au 01	booby prize	Th 05	boudoir	Hs 02
body, care of the	Bd 06	book	Th 03	boulder	Th 10
body, one's	Bd 01	book binder	Oc 03	bounced check	Th 10
body, one's	Ho 01	book learning	Th 03	bouncing (jumping)	Th 09
body bolt	Au 05	book seller	Oc 03	boundary (edge)	Th 10
body ding	Au 01	book shelf	Pl 03	bounty (goodness)	Th 09
body fluids	Bd 04	book store	Pl 03	bounty (reward)	Th 08
body hair	Bd 10	bookcase	Th 06	bounty from the land	Mn 04
body of a vehicle	Th 01	bookkeeper	Oc 06	bounty hunter	Oc 08
body of water	Mn 04	bookworm	Oc 03	bout (fight)	Th 01
body rhythms (biorhythms)	Bd 04	boom (arm for hanging) boom (economic)	Th 10 Mn 09	bout (session) bout (skirmish)	Th 07 Th 07
body rust	Au 12	boom (noise)	Th 01	boutique	Pl 07
bodyguards	In 01	boomerang	Th 12	bow	Sh 01
bog	Pl 04	boon (favor)	Th 08	bow (in hair)	Th 02
bogus thing	Th 12	boost (lift)	Th 10	bow (weapon)	Th 09
bohemianism	Th 11	boost (praise)	Th 02	bow, to take a	Th 05
boil	Af 08	boot (dismissal)	Th 08	bowel disturbance	Af 06
boiler	Sh 05	boot camp	Pl 06	bowel movement	Bd 08
boisterousness	Th 05	booth (shelter)	Pl 04	bowel obstruction	Af 06
boldness	Th 01	booth (stand)	Pl 04	bowels	Bd 06
bolster (pillow)	Th 02	Bootis (the herdsman)	My 09	bowl	Th 04
bolt (cloth)	Th 06	bootlegged item	Th 08	box (container)	Th 04
bolt (crossbow's)	Th 01	bootlegger	Oc 12	box seat (theater)	Th 10
bolt (fastener)	Th 04	boots (shoes)	Th 12	boxer	Oc 05
bolt (mad dash)	Th 01	bootstraps (self-reliance)	Ps 05	boy	Oc 03
bomb (explosive)	Th 01	booty	Th 08	boy friend	Oc 05
bomb (nuclear)	Th 08	borax	Ge 08	boycott	Th 11
bomber	Oc 01	border	Th 09	bracelet	Th 02
bomber (aircraft)	Th 01	borders of country	Mn 09	bracket (classify)	Th 06
bond (attractive force)	Th 07	bore	Oc 10	bracket (parenthesis)	Th 06
bond (binding agreement)	Th 07	bore (hole) bore (hollow part)	Th 04 Th 04	bragging braiding	Ps 05 Th 07

brain	Bd 03	bridge (structure)	Th 03	budget	Mn 08
brain injury	Af 03	bridge builder	Oc 03	budget manager	Oc 08
brain matter	Th 03	bridge worker	Oc 03	budget office	Or 08
brainchild	Th 05	briefcase	Th 06	budget statement	Th 08
bramble	Th 09	bright green	Co 07	buergerite	Ge 11
branch (division)	Or 06	bright-yellow	Co 05	bug (bother)	Th 01
branch of a tree	Th 02	brilliant blue	Co 11	bug (hobbyist)	Oc 05
brass	Ge 05	brine	Th 04	bug (insect)	Th 01
bravado	Ps 05	bringing to justice	Th 10	bug (listening device)	Th 12
bravery	Th 01	Broadcast Media	In 03	bugle	Th 01
brawl	Th 01	broadcaster	Oc 09	builder	Oc 04
brawn	Th 05	broadcasting	In 09	building	Mn 10
breach (violation)	Th 01	broadcasting	Ho 09	building	Th 10
bread	Th 06	broadening	Th 09	building demolition	In 08
break (luck)	Th 05	broader views, adapting	Ps 09	building designers	In 10
break (rupture)	Th 01	brocade	Th 05	building materials	In 10
break a record	Th 10	brochure	Th 03	building materials	Th 10
break in a relationship	Th 11	broken bone	Af 10	bulge	Th 05
break-in (theft)	Th 07	brokerage	Oc 03	bulk (greater part)	Th 05
breakage	Th 01	bronchi	Bd 03	bulk (size)	Th 02
breakfast	Th 04	bronchial infection	Af 03	bulk purchase	Th 04
breaking free	Th 12	bronchial tubes	Bd 03	bulk storage	Th 06
breaking in (interruption)	Th 01	bronchitis	Af 03	bulkhead	Sh 10
breaking up	Th 08	bronze	Ge 06	bull	An 02
breakthrough	Th 11	brooding	Th 08	bullet	Th 01
breasts	Bd 04	brook (stream)	Pl 04	bullet wound	Af 01
breath of air, a	Th 03	broom	Th 06	bullfight	Th 05
breathing	Bd 03	brothel	Pl 08	bully	Oc 01
breathing exercise	Th 07	brother	Re 03	bump	Th 05
breathing problems	Af 03	brother or sister	Re 03	bungee jumping	Th 05
breeding	Th 04	brother or sister #1	Re 03	bungled attempt, a	Th 12
breeding place	Pl 05	brother or sister #2	Re 05	bunion	Af 12
breeze	Th 03	brother or sister #3	Re 07	bunk	Sh 02
brethren	Oc 03	brother or sister #4	Re 09	bunk (bed)	Th 02
brevity	Th 10	brother or sister #5	Re 11	bunkhouse	Pl 04
brewer	Oc 12	brother-in-law	Re 09	bunting (flag)	Th 04
brewery	Pl 12	brotherhood	Th 11	bunting (for baby)	Th 06
brewing	Th 12	brotherly love	Th 11	buoyancy	Th 09
briars	Th 09	brown	Co 06	burden (encumbrance)	Th 02
bribery	Th 12	browsing	Th 03	burden (responsibility)	Th 10
brick	Th 04	bruise	Af 01	bureaucracy	Ho 06
brick kiln	Pl 10	brush (in general)	Th 06	bureaucracy	Th 06
bricklayer	Oc 10	brush off	Th 08	bureaucracy, the	Mn 06
bridal chamber	Pl 07	brutality	Th 08	burglar	Oc 07
bride	Oc 07	brute	Oc 08	burglary	Th 07
bridegroom	Oc 07	bubble	Th 12	burial	Th 04
bridge	Mn 03	buck	An 06	burial place	Pl 04
bridge	Sh 01	buckle	Th 03	buried treasure	Th 04
bridge (connection)	Th 03	buddy	Oc 11	burlesque	Th 05

burn	Af 01	business consulting	In 11	butcher	Oc 01
burning	Th 01	business dealings abroad	Mn 09	butcher shop	Pl 01
burning of debris	Th 12	business finances	Mn 02	butchery	Th 01
burnt items	Th 02	business forms	Mn 03	butler	Oc 06
burrow	Pl 04	business income	Mn 11	butt (leftover)	Th 12
burrowing animals	An 09	business management	In 11	butt (of a joke)	Th 12
burrowing reptiles	An 11	business matters	Ho 10	butter	Th 04
burying motions	Th 04	business obligation	Mn 05	butterfly	An 07
bus (electrical)	Th 11	business outcomes	Ho 10	butting in	Th 01
bus (vehicle)	Th 03	business partner	Oc 07	buttocks	Bd 07
bus boy	Oc 06	business partnerships	Mn 07	buttress	Th 10
bus driver	Oc 03	business potentials	Ho 10	buyer	Oc 03
bus stop	Th 03	business prosperity	Mn 11	buyer (in an exchange)	Mn 01
business	Mn 10	business standing	Mn 10	buying	Th 03
business	Th 10	business success	Mn 10	buzzard	An 08
business, nobody's	Th 08	business suite	Pl 10	buzzing sounds	Th 01
business affairs	Mn 10	business world	Mn 10	by-laws	Ho 03
business assets	Mn 11	busybody	Oc 03	by-product	Th 08
business associate	Mn 07	busyness	Ps 06		

C

cab (taxi)	Th 03	cake	Th 02	camper (vehicle)	Th 03
cabal	Th 11	calamity	Th 08	campground	Pl 04
cabaret	Pl 05	calcification	Th 10	camping (tenting)	Th 05
cabinet maker	Oc 06	calcium balance	Af 02	camps, opposing	Th 07
cabinets (furniture)	Th 06	calculation	Th 06	canal	Pl 03
cable (notice)	Th 03	calculator	Th 06	canary (talker)	Oc 03
cable (wire rope)	Th 04	calendar	Th 10	cancellation	Th 10
cable, overseas	Mn 09	calendar of events	Th 10	Cancer (crab)	My 04
cable manufacturers	In 03	calisthenics	Th 05	cancer causing attitude	Af 04
cable TV	In 05	callous	Af 01	cancerous growth	Af 04
cable TV	Th 05	callous actions	Th 01	candidate	Oc 11
cache	Th 06	callous words	Th 01	candidness	Ps 09
cactus	Th 10	calm	My 02	candle	Th 04
cad	Oc 08	calm	Th 02	candor	Th 09
cadaver	Th 08	calves (of legs)	Bd 11	candy	Th 02
cadence	Th 04	cam	Th 06	cane (walking aid)	Th 10
cadet	Oc 06	camel	An 11	canes major (large dog)	My 12
cadmos (musician)	My 02	Camelopardus (giraffe)	My 10	canes minor (small dog)	My 06
caelum (chisel)	My 06	cameo (broach)	Th 02	canes venatici (hunting dogs)	My 08
cafe	Pl 06	cameo (small role)	Th 05		
cafeteria	Pl 06	camera	Th 12	canister	Th 06
cafeteria, the	Or 06	camouflage	Co 06	cannery	Pl 06
caffeine	Th 12	camp	Pl 04	cannibal	Oc 08
cage	Th 12	campaign	Th 10	cannibalism	Th 08
cajolery	Th 03	camper (occupies land)	Oc 04	canning food	Th 06

218   Alpha Sort with Industries

cannon	Th 01	carelessness	Th 12	catacomb	Pl 04
canon (regulation)	Th 09	caress	Th 05	catafalque	Th 08
canopy	Th 10	caretaker	Oc 06	catalog	Th 06
cant (singsong)	Th 03	cargo hold	Sh 06	catalog services	In 04
canteen (bar)	Pl 12	caricature	Th 03	catalyst	Th 03
canvasser	Oc 03	caries, dental	Af 04	cataract	Af 10
cap (ceiling)	Th 10	carina (keel of ship Argo)	My 04	catastrophe	Th 01
cap (for closing off)	Th 08	caring	Ps 04	catch (a person)	Th 05
cap (hat)	Th 06	carmine	Co 01	catch (fish)	Th 04
capability	Ho 05	carnage	Th 08	catch-22 situation	Th 01
capability (innate skill)	Ps 05	carnelian (cornelian)	Ge 09	catcher	Oc 04
capacitance (electrical)	Th 06	carny	Oc 05	catechism	Th 09
capacity (ability)	Th 05	carpenter	Oc 06	categorization	Th 06
capacity (for storing)	Th 06	carpet	Th 02	category	Th 06
capacity (skill)	Ps 05	carpet manufacturers	In 06	caterer	Oc 04
capital	Th 02	carrion	Th 08	cathedral	Pl 09
capital goods	In 04	cart	Th 03	cattle, large	Th 12
capitalism	Mn 02	cartilage	Bd 10	caucus	Th 11
capitol building	Pl 11	cartoon	Th 03	caulking material	Th 04
capitulation	Th 07	cartoonist	Oc 03	cause (legal action)	Th 09
capriciousness	Th 04	carving	Th 05	cause (motive)	Th 05
Capricorn (sea goat)	My 10	cash	Th 02	cause (principle)	Th 11
captain's cabin	Sh 04	cash box	Th 02	cause of death	Ho 08
captivation	Ps 05	cash flow	Mn 02	cause of death	Th 08
captivity	Th 12	cash register	Th 02	causes	Ho 11
capture devices	Th 04	cashier	Oc 02	causes, attachment to	Ps 11
capturing	Th 04	cashier's office	Or 02	causes, use of	Ps 11
car	Ho 03	casino	Pl 05	cauterization	Th 01
car	Th 03	casket	Th 08	caution (wariness)	Th 10
car repair	Th 06	Cassiopeia	My 10	caution (warning)	Th 08
carbohydrates	Th 02	cast (appearance)	Th 01	cave	Pl 08
carbon	Th 10	cast (distance thrown)	Th 09	cavern	Pl 08
carbuncle	Af 08	cast (pall)	Th 08	cavity	Th 04
carbuncle	Ge 03	cast (people)	Th 05	ceiling area	Hs 10
carburetor	Au 11	cast (tinge)	Th 12	ceilings	Hs 09
card game	Th 05	cast-off	Th 12	celebration	Th 05
card suit: clubs	Th 11	castaway	Oc 12	celebrations as festivities	Th 05
card suit: diamonds	Th 02	caster	Th 03	celebrity, national	Mn 05
card suit: hearts	Th 05	castigation	Th 08	celestial mechanics	Th 11
card suit: spades	Th 08	casting	Ge 06	celestial object	Th 11
cards (game)	Th 05	casting (molding)	Th 06	celibacy	Th 06
care of pets	Th 06	castle	Pl 04	cellar	Hs 04
career	Ho 10	Castor and Pollux	My 03	cellar	Pl 04
career	Th 10	castration	Af 08	cellular decay	Th 10
career, money from	Th 02	casual ties with others	Th 11	cellular development	Bd 09
career activities	Th 10	casualty (disaster)	Mn 08	cellular growth	Th 09
career change	Th 01	cat	An 06	cement	Th 10
career of children	Th 02	cat's eye	Ge 09	cement and aggregates	In 10
career of partner	Th 04	cataclysm	Th 08	cemetery	Pl 08

cemetery management	In 08	chance (luck)	Th 05	chasm	Th 08
cemetery plot	Th 04	chance (risk)	Th 01	chassis	Au 05
cemetery worker	Oc 08	chance (try)	Th 01	chasteness	Th 06
censer (incense holder)	Th 09	chancellor	Oc 11	chastity	Ps 06
censor	Oc 08	chandelier	Th 05	chattel	Th 02
censorship	Mn 07	change (conversion)	Th 08	cheap item	Th 10
censure (reprimand)	Th 07	change (fluctuation)	Th 04	cheapness	Ps 10
census	Th 06	change (revolution)	Th 11	cheater	Oc 03
Centaur	My 09	change (swapping)	Th 03	cheating	Ps 03
center of anything, the	Th 05	change (variation)	Th 03	cheating	Th 03
centerpiece	Th 05	change in fortune	Th 04	check (financial draft)	Th 02
central focus	Ps 05	change of location, a	Ho 04	check (inspection)	Th 08
centrifugal force	Th 09	change of location, a	Th 04	check book	Th 02
centripetal force	Th 04	changing one's mind	Ps 03	checkered patterns	Co 09
Cepheus	My 07	channel (communications)	Th 03	checking account	Th 02
ceramic figurine	Th 07	channel (medium)	Oc 09	checks and balances	Mn 1
ceramic tile	Th 07	channel (stream)	Th 04	(limits)	
ceramics	Th 07	channel (way)	Th 03	cheeks	Bd 02
cereals	Th 06	chaos	My 04	cheer	Ps 05
ceremony	Mn 09	chaos	Th 12	cheerleader	Oc 05
ceremony	Th 09	chapel	Pl 09	cheese	Th 04
ceremony, group function	Th 11	character	Ps 01	chemical (basic)	In 12
		character defects	Ps 12	chemical (diversified)	In 12
ceremony, official	Mn 09	characteristics	Ps 01	chemical (specialty)	In 12
ceremony to legalize matters	Th 09	characteristics, another's	Ps 07	chemical reactions	Th 12
		charades	Th 12	chemicals	Th 12
Ceres	My 06	charge (accusation)	Th 07	chemist	Oc 12
certainty (free of doubt)	Th 01	charge (debit)	Th 08	chemistry (in general)	Th 12
certificate	Th 10	charge (obligation)	Th 08	chert	Ge 09
certification	Th 10	charge account	Mn 08	chest	Bd 04
cessation	Th 08	charge card	Th 08	chest region	Bd 04
cesspool	Pl 08	charisma	Th 05	chewing	Bd 01
Cetus (sea monster)	My 12	charitable act	Th 12	chicanery	Th 03
chaff	Th 04	charitable institution	Pl 12	chicken	An 06
chain (restraint)	Th 10	charitable work	Th 12	chief executive	Oc 10
chain locker	Sh 06	charity	Ho 12	chief executive's office	Or 05
chain of events	Th 08	charity	Pl 12	child, adopted	Re 11
chair	Th 04	charity	Th 12	child, another's	Re 11
chairman of the board	Mn 10	charity, given	Ps 12	child, biological	Re 05
chairman of the board	Or 10	charity, national	Mn 12	child, fifth	Re 01
chakra	Bd 05	charity, received	Ps 12	child, first	Re 05
chalcedony	Ge 09	charity worker	Oc 12	child, fourth	Re 11
chalk	Ge 04	charlatan	Oc 12	child, second	Re 07
challenge	Th 01	charm	Ps 07	child, step	Re 11
challenger in a contest	Oc 07	chart	Th 06	child, third	Re 09
chamaeleon	My 03	chart house	Sh 06	child's room	Hs 05
chamber of commerce	Mn 11	chart table	Sh 06	childbirth	Th 05
chameleon	An 03	charter services	In 09	childhood environment	Ps 04
chance (accident)	Th 01	chase	Th 01	childishness	Th 03

children	Ho 05	circle	Th 05	claim (charge)	Th 01
children	Oc 05	circuitry	Th 11	claim (maintain)	Th 01
children of friends	Th 03	circular	Th 03	claim (mining)	Pl 04
children's affairs	Th 05	circular motion	Th 10	claim (right)	Th 04
chill (coolness)	Th 10	circular symbol	Th 05	claimant	Oc 01
chills	Af 10	circulation	Th 03	claims adjusters	In 07
chimes	Th 02	circulatory system (blood)	Bd 05	clairaudience	Th 02
chimney	Hs 03			clairvoyance	Th 01
chimpanzee	An 01	circulatory system (lungs)	Bd 03	clam	An 04
chin	Bd 01			clamor	Th 01
chinaware	Th 04	circumference	Th 04	clamp	Th 04
Chiron	My 08	circumlocution	Th 03	clan	Th 04
chiropractor	Oc 06	circumnavigation	Th 09	clandestine affair	Th 12
chisel	Th 06	circumpolar motion	Th 10	clandestine associate	Oc 12
chiseler	Oc 03	circumpolar object	Th 10	clandestine relationship	Th 12
chivalry (gallantry)	Th 01	circumstances (in general)	Th 01	clandestine work	Th 12
chivalry (politeness)	Th 07			clapping (applause)	Th 05
choice	Th 11	circumstances beyond control	Th 01	clarification	Th 07
choices	Ho 11			clarity	Th 07
chore	Th 06	circumstantial developments	Th 01	clash	Th 01
chorus	Th 11			clasp	Th 04
christ consciousness	Th 09	circumventing	Ho 03	class (grouping)	Th 06
chrome	Ge 06	circumventing	Th 03	class (school)	Th 03
chromite	Ge 06	circus	Pl 05	class (style)	Th 07
chronic ailment	Af 12	cistern	Pl 04	classic work	Th 06
chronic ill health	Af 12	citizenship	Mn 04	classified ad	Th 09
chronic illness	Th 12	city	Mn 04	classifying	Th 06
chronology	Th 10	city	Pl 04	classmate	Oc 03
chronometer	Th 10	city council	Mn 11	clause (part of a sentence)	Th 03
chrysoberyl	Ge 08	city hall	Pl 11	clause (stipulation)	Th 07
chrysocholla	Ge 02	city manager	Oc 11	claustrophobia	Ps 04
chrysoprase	Ge 09	city officials	Mn 10	claws	Th 03
church	Mn 09	civic organization	Mn 11	clay	Ge 10
church	Pl 09	civic-mindedness	Ps 11	clean, things which are	Th 06
church (design/construction)	In 10	civics	Th 11	clean air regulations	Th 06
		civil behavior	Ps 07	clean room	Pl 06
church (religious services)	In 09	civil disobedience	Ps 07	clean up, a (large win)	Th 05
church (religious supplies)	In 09	civil engineer	Oc 10	cleaner	Oc 06
church affiliation	Ps 09	civil servant	Oc 06	cleaning	Th 06
church matters	Th 09	civil service	Mn 06	cleaning item	Th 06
church service	Th 09	civil service worker	Oc 06	cleaning out	Th 08
church yard	Pl 12	civil unrest	Mn 07	Cleaning Services	In 06
churchman	Oc 09	civil violence	Mn 01	cleanliness	Ps 06
churn	Th 11	civil workers	Mn 06	cleanliness	Th 06
cigar	Th 12	civilian	Oc 04	cleanser	Th 06
cigarette	Th 12	civilian population	Mn 04	clear	Co 07
cinema	Pl 05	civilization	Mn 04	clear-cutting	Th 08
cinema as entertainment	Th 05	cladding	Th 04	clearance (authorization)	Th 10
circinus (compass)	My 06	claim (call for)	Th 03	clearance (removal)	Th 08

clearance (space)	Th 04	clothes as vanity	Th 05	coincidence (at the same time)	Th 07
clearance sale	Th 08	clothier	Oc 06	coincidence (luck)	Th 05
clearing (vindication)	Th 12	clothing	Ho 06	coins	Th 02
clearing away	Th 08	clothing (in general)	Th 06	cola	Th 04
cleat	Th 04	clothing designer	Oc 02	cold	Th 10
cleavage	Th 04	cloudiness	Th 12	cold water	Th 04
cleaver	Th 01	clouds	Th 12	coldest part of the house	Hs 10
clemency (mercy)	Th 12	clown	Oc 03	coldness	Th 10
clergy	Oc 09	club (organization)	Ho 11	colds	Af 06
clerical services	In 06	club (organization)	Pl 11	colds (illness)	Ho 06
clerk	Oc 06	club (organization)	Th 11	colic	Af 06
cleverness	Ho 03	club (weapon)	Th 01	coliseum	Pl 05
cleverness	Ps 03	club room	Pl 11	colitis	Af 06
cliche	Th 04	clue	Th 08	collaboration	Mn 07
client (patron)	Oc 04	clumsiness	Af 02	collaborator	Oc 07
clientele	Mn 04	cluster (grouping)	Th 11	collapse (breakdown)	Ps 12
cliff-hanger	Th 08	clutch	Au 10	collapse (buckling)	Th 10
climate (distinct from weather)	Th 06	clutter	Th 12	colleague	Oc 11
		co-ordination	Bd 03	collection	Th 04
climate (in general)	Th 06	co-worker	Oc 06	collection agency	Mn 08
climax (end point)	Th 04	coach	Oc 10	collective bargaining	Mn 11
climax (sexual)	Bd 08	coach (vehicle)	Th 03	collector	Oc 04
climbing	Th 10	coagulation of blood	Bd 11	collector's items	Th 04
clinch	Th 04	coal	Ge 10	college	Pl 09
clinger	Oc 04	coal (distribution)	In 03	college education	Th 09
clinic	Pl 06	coal (mining)	In 08	college professor	Oc 09
clinic, the	Or 06	coal (processing)	In 12	collusion	Th 07
clip (fastener)	Th 04	coal miner	Oc 04	cologne	Th 02
clip joint	Pl 12	coalescing	Th 11	colon	Bd 08
clipping (cutting short)	Th 08	coalition	Mn 11	colonial offices	Mn 09
clipping (extraction)	Th 08	coarseness	Th 01	colony	Pl 09
clipping (news item)	Th 03	coast guard, the	Mn 06	color, sense of	Ps 07
clique	Th 11	coasting (without power)	Th 05	color harmony	Th 07
clitoris	Bd 08	coastline, the nation's	Mn 04	colorful objects	Th 05
clock	Th 10	coat (outerwear)	Th 06	colorless (clear)	Co 07
clock maker	Oc 10	coating (outer layer)	Th 04	colors (in general)	Th 07
clock repairer	Oc 06	coaxing	Th 09	columba (dove)	My 07
clockwise motion	Th 10	cocaine	Th 12	column (line)	Th 11
clogged drain	Hs 08	cock	An 01	columnist	Oc 03
close blood relative	Re 03	cocktail party	Th 05	coma	Af 12
close call	Th 01	cocoon	Th 04	Coma Berenices (Berenice's hair)	My 09
close friend	Th 11	code of ethics	Mn 09		
close kin	Th 03	coercion	Th 08	comb	Th 06
close relative	Th 03	coffee	Th 04	combat	Th 01
closet	Hs 06	cofferdam	Sh 06	combat information center	Sh 03
closet	Pl 06	coffin	Th 08		
cloth	Th 06	cohabitation prompted by love	Th 07	combativeness	Th 01
clothes, formal dress	Th 06				
clothes as possessions	Th 02	cohort (companion)	Oc 11	combinations	Th 11

combining	Th 11	commodity exchange	Pl 05	comparisons	Th 07
combustion	Th 05	commodity made into goods	Th 04	compartment	Pl 06
combustion chamber	Au 05			compass	Sh 03
comedian	Oc 05	commodity market	Pl 05	compass	Th 03
comedown	Th 12	commodity services	In 05	compassion	Ho 12
comedy	Th 05	commodity trading	Th 05	compassion	Ps 12
comet	Th 09	common people, the	Th 04	compatibility	Th 07
comfort (basic food or shelter)	Th 04	common sense	Ps 10	compelling forces	Th 08
		commonplace things	Th 04	compendium (abstract)	Th 08
comfort (cheering up)	Th 12	communal living	Th 11	compensation	Ps 05
comfort (ease)	Th 02	communal possessions	Mn 12	compensation (counterbalancing)	Th 07
comfort (solace)	Th 12	communication	Ps 03		
comic	Oc 05	communication	Th 03	compensation (payment)	Th 08
comics, the	Th 05	communication (in general)	Th 03	compensation from insurance	Th 09
coming (arrival)	Th 01				
coming unglued	Ps 12	communication equipment manufacturers	In 04	compensator device or circuit	Th 10
comings and goings	Th 03				
command	Th 10	communication lines	Sh 03	competence (ability)	Ps 05
command, having	Th 10	communication over distances	Th 09	competence (legal power)	Th 09
command of situation, in	Ps 10			competition (contests)	Th 07
commander	Oc 10	communication quarters	Sh 03	competition (rivalry)	Th 07
commander-in-chief	Mn 10	communication systems	Mn 03	competition, sense of	Ps 07
commandment	Th 10	communication(s)	Ho 03	competition, the	Ho 07
commemoration	Th 04	communications equipment	Th 03	competitive marketplace	Mn 07
commencement	Th 01			competitive posture, a	Th 01
commencement ceremony	Th 09	communications satellite	Mn 03	competitor(s)	Mn 07
				competitor(s)	Oc 07
commendation	Th 10	communion (religious)	Th 09	competitor(s)	Or 07
commentary	Th 03	communion (togetherness)	Th 07	compilation	Th 09
commentator	Oc 03			compilation (all inclusive)	Th 09
commerce	Mn 03	communique	Th 03	complacency	Ps 02
commercial trade	Mn 03	communism	Mn 11	complaint (grievance)	Th 11
commercialism	Mn 03	community (locale)	Pl 04	complaint (malady)	Af 06
commissary	Sh 06	community (social group)	Th 11	complement (a rounding out)	Th 04
commission (board)	Th 08	community affairs	Mn 04		
commission (fee)	Th 08	community property	Mn 08	complement (ship's personnel)	Th 04
commission (in military)	Th 10	community relations office	Or 03		
commissioner	Oc 10			complement (the entirety)	Th 04
commitment	Th 08	community resources	Mn 05	complementary copy or gift	Th 11
commitments, unwilling to make	Th 01	community standing	Mn 10		
		community's weather history	Mn 04	completeness	Ps 02
committed relationships	Th 07		Mn 04	completeness, a lack of	Ps 01
committee of a fraternal group	Mn 11	commuter	Oc 03	completion (ending)	Th 04
		commuting	Th 03	completion (termination)	Th 08
commodity (economic factor)	Mn 04	companion	Oc 11	complexion	Bd 01
		companionship	Th 11	complexion problems	Af 01
commodity (possession)	Th 04	company, the	Or 01	complexity, increasing	Th 03
commodity (product)	Mn 04	company benefits	Or 12	compliance	Ps 06
commodity dealer	Oc 05	company good will	Or 12	compliance	Th 06

complicating matters	Ps 03	concern for others	Ho 12	confession (religious beliefs)	Th 09
complications	Th 03	concern for others	Th 12	confessional	Pl 12
compliment	Th 02	concert	Th 05	confetti	Th 06
component	Th 06	concert hall	Pl 05	confidante	Oc 11
composer	Oc 02	concession (franchise)	Pl 04	confidence (secrecy)	Th 12
composite materials	Th 11	concession (yielding)	Th 07	confidence (self-assurance)	Ps 05
composites	Th 11	concession stand	Pl 02		
compost pile	Hs 08	concierge	Oc 03	confidence (trust in another)	Th 09
comprehension	Th 09	conciseness	Th 10		
compressed gases	Th 11	concordance	Th 06	confidential activities	Th 12
compression (compacting)	Th 08	concrete (fused stone and sand)	Th 10	confidential agents	Oc 12
				confidential matters	Ho 12
compression (squeezing)	Th 08	concrete mind, the	Ps 03	confidential matters	Mn 12
compromise	Ho 07	concrete structure	Th 10	confinement (limitation)	Th 12
compromise	Ps 07	concubine	Oc 08	confinement (restraint)	Th 12
compromise	Th 07	concussion	Af 01	confines (boundaries)	Mn 09
compulsions	Ps 08	condemnation (disapproval)	Th 07	confirmation (substantiation)	Ps 08
compulsive acts	Th 08				
compulsive sex	Th 08	condemnation (punishment)	Th 08	confiscation	Th 08
computer	Th 06			conflagration	Th 01
computer and peripherals	In 11	condensation	Th 08	conflict	Th 07
computer analyst	Oc 06	condiments	Th 02	conformance (agreement)	Th 07
computer media	Th 06	condition (stipulation)	Th 11	conformation (structure)	Th 10
computer operator	Oc 06	condition, physical	Ps 01	conformity (obedience)	Th 07
computer programmer	Oc 06	conditioned response	Ps 04	confronting (anything)	Ps 01
computer programming	Th 06	condor	An 12	confronting (anything)	Th 01
computer software/services	In 11	conduct in public	Ps 07	confronting obstacles	Ps 01
		conduct of business, the	Mn 10	confusing elements	Th 12
computer storage	Th 06	conductor (orchestra)	Oc 10	confusion	Ho 12
computer systems	In 06	conductor (vehicle)	Oc 03	confusion	Ps 12
computing equipment	Th 06	conduit	Th 03	confusion	Th 12
comrade	Oc 11	confectioner	Oc 02	congealing (coagulating)	Th 11
comradery	Th 11	confederacy	Th 11	congestion (crowding)	Th 11
con artist	Oc 03	confederate (ally)	Oc 07	congestion (obstruction)	Th 10
con game	Th 03	confederation (alliance)	Mn 07	conglomerate	In 12
con man	Oc 03	conference (caucus)	Th 11	conglomerate	Mn 11
concealed treasure	Th 04	conference (consultation)	Th 11	conglomeration	Th 11
concealment	Th 04	conference (denomination)	Th 09	congratulations	Th 02
concealment, need for	Ps 04			congregation	Th 11
conceit	Ps 05	conference (discussion)	Th 09	congress	Th 11
concentration (gathering)	Th 11	conference (large meeting)	Th 11	congruity	Th 07
concentration (mental focus)	Ps 08			conjugal rights	Th 08
		conference (of groups)	Th 09	conjugation (coupling)	Th 07
concentration camp	Mn 12	conference call	Th 09	conjunction (planetary)	Th 05
concept	Th 09	conference room	Or 11	conn	Sh 01
conception (beginning)	Th 04	conference room	Pl 11	connecting parts	Au 03
conception of children	Th 05	confession (creed)	Th 09	connection (coupling)	Th 03
conceptual framework	Th 09	confession (disclosure)	Th 12	connection (relation)	Th 03
conceptualization	Ps 09	confession (of guilt)	Ps 12		

connoisseur	Oc 02	consumption of goods	Mn 04	contractors (defense)	In 06
conqueror	Oc 10	contact with another	Th 07	contractors (drainage)	In 03
conquest	Ho 08	contact with equals	Th 07	contractors (landscape)	In 02
conquest	Th 08	contact with superiors	Th 10	contractors (military)	In 06
conscience	Ps 09	contacts with hospitals	Th 12	contractors (remodel)	In 08
conscientiousness	Th 06	contacts with invalids	Th 12	contractors (roofing)	In 10
consciousness	Ps 01	container (for liquids)	Th 04	contractors (sewer)	In 08
conscription	Th 08	container (storage)	Th 04	contractors (siding)	In 07
consensus	Th 07	containers (metal/plastic)	In 12	contractors (tile/stucco)	In 07
consent	Th 07	containers (paper)	In 04	contracts	Ho 07
consequence (result)	Th 10	containment	Mn 08	contractual agreement	Ho 07
consequences of one's actions	Ps 10	prevention policy) contaminant	Th 08	contractual agreement contractual relationship	Th 07 Mn 07
conservation	Th 06	contamination	Th 08	contradiction	Th 07
conservative	Oc 10	contemplation	Ps 09	contrast	Th 07
conservator	Oc 04	contempt	Th 07	contribution (alms)	Th 12
considerateness	Ps 02	content (form)	Th 02	contribution (work)	Th 06
consistency	Th 10	content (gist)	Th 02	contribution- a forced	Th 08
consolidation	Th 11	content (volume)	Th 02	contrition	Th 12
conspiracy	Ho 12	contention (rivalry)	Th 07	control	Ho 08
conspiracy	Mn 12	contentment (satisfaction)	Ps 02	control, need for	Ps 08
constancy	Th 10	contents (thing contained)	Th 04	controls (limitations)	Th 10
constant	Th 10	contest	Th 07	controversy	Th 07
constipation	Af 10	contestant	Oc 07	convalescence	Th 12
constitution	Mn 11	contested affair	Th 07	convection	Th 11
constraint	Th 10	context	Th 03	convent	Pl 12
constriction (shrinking)	Th 08	context (setting)	Th 03	convention (accepted practice)	Th 04
constriction (tightening)	Th 08	context, things taken in	Th 02		
construction	Mn 10	context, things taken out of	Th 03	convention (large meeting)	Th 11
construction	Or 10				
construction equipment	In 10	continence	Af 10	convention hall	Pl 11
construction equipment	Mn 06	continent (land mass)	Pl 04	conventional things	Th 04
construction methods	Hs 02	continental drift	Th 03	convergence (coming together)	Th 11
construction site	Pl 10	contingency	Th 09		
constructive force	Th 01	continuity	Th 10	conversation	Th 03
consulate	Mn 09	contortions	Th 03	conversion (religious)	Ps 09
consultant	Mn 11	contour (outline)	Th 01	conversion (transformation)	Ps 08
consultant	Oc 11	contract (an order to kill)	Th 08		
consultant	Or 11	contract (legally binding)	Th 07	convertible top	Au 09
consultation (meeting)	Th 11	contract, act of signing	Th 03	conveyance	Th 03
consumable commodities	Mn 04	contract, marriage	Th 07	conveying information	Th 03
consumer	Oc 04	contract, written	Th 03	convict	Oc 12
consumer needs	Mn 04	contract negotiation	Mn 07	conviction (opinion)	Th 09
consumerism	Mn 04	contract negotiator	Oc 07	conviction (strong belief)	Th 01
consuming	Th 04	contraction (shrinkage)	Th 08	conviction for a crime	Ho 10
consuming thoughts	Th 08	contraction (tightening)	Th 08	conviction for a crime	Th 10
consummation (realization)	Th 09	contractor contractor's equipment	Oc 06 In 10	convincing, ability for conviviality	Ps 09 Ps 05
consumption	Af 12	contractors (aerospace)	In 11	convocation	Th 09

convolution (twists)	Th 03	corporation law	Mn 06	count (tally)	Th 06
convulsions (fits of laughter)	Th 05	corpse	Th 08	count down	Th 10
		corpulence	Th 05	counter space	Hs 04
convulsions (spasms)	Af 05	corral	Pl 04	counter top	Hs 06
cook	Oc 04	correcting (fixing)	Th 10	counter-clockwise motion	Th 04
cookies	Th 02	correction (change)	Th 08		
cooking	Th 04	correction (punishment)	Th 12	counteragent	Th 01
cooking, chemistry of	Th 03	correction, need for giving	Ps 06	counterfeit item	Th 03
coolant	Au 10			counterfeiter	Oc 03
cooling trends	Th 10	correction fluid	Th 03	counterpart	Th 07
cooperation	Ho 07	correctional institution	Pl 12	country, foreign	Pl 09
cooperation	Ps 07	corrections, house of	Pl 12	country, the	Mn 01
cooperation (agreement)	Th 07	correctness	Th 10	coupling (joining)	Th 07
		correlation	Th 07	coupon	Th 03
cooperation (participation)	Th 07	correspondence (agreement)	Th 07	courage	Th 01
				courier	Oc 03
cooperative arrangements	Mn 07	correspondence (communication)	Th 03	court, criminal ruling	Th 04
				court, disputes in	Th 07
coordination	Bd 03	correspondent	Oc 03	court, questions of law in	Ps 10
coordinator	Oc 03	corridors	Hs 03		
cope, ability to	Ps 04	corroboration	Th 08	court, ruling from a	Th 04
Copper	In 07	corrosion	Th 12	court case	Th 09
copper	Ge 02	corruption	Th 08	court of a king	Pl 05
copy (reproduction)	Th 03	corundum	Ge 01	court of justice	Pl 09
copy (story)	Th 03	corvus (crow)	My 03	court of law	Pl 09
copy editor	Oc 06	cosmetic surgery	Th 02	court procedures	Th 06
copying (mimicking)	Ps 03	cosmetician	Oc 02	courtesy	Th 02
copyright	Th 07	cosmetics	In 07	courthouse	Pl 09
coral	Ge 04	cosmetics	Th 02	courtier	Oc 07
cord (line)	Th 04	cosmic awareness	Th 11	courtliness	Th 05
core (central part)	Th 05	cosmic fair	Th 12	courtroom	Pl 09
core (essence of anything)	Ho 05	cosmic intelligence	Th 11	courtship	Th 05
		cosmology	Th 09	cousin, maternal	Re 10
core identity	Ps 04	cost of an item	Th 02	cousin, paternal	Re 04
cork	Th 02	costs	Mn 02	cove	Pl 04
corners	Th 03	costume	Th 03	covenant	Th 07
cornerstone	Th 04	costuming	Th 03	cover-up	Th 03
corns	Af 12	cottage industry	Th 06	coverings (in general)	Th 04
cornucopia	Th 09	Cottos (many headed monster)	My 12	covertness	Th 12
corny joke	Th 05			covetousness	Th 02
Corona Australis (southern. crown)	My 05	cougar	An 12	cow	An 04
		cough	Af 03	coward	Oc 05
Corona Borealis (northern crown)	My 05	council	Mn 11	cowardice	Th 12
		council	Pl 11	coyote	An 03
coronation	Th 05	counsel (advice)	Th 11	crab	An 04
coroner	Oc 08	counsel (lawyer)	Oc 09	crack (failure)	Th 12
corporate assets	Mn 11	counselor (advisor)	Oc 11	crackdown	Th 08
corporate position	Mn 01	count (allegation)	Th 07	cradle	Th 02
corporation	Mn 10	count (reckoning)	Th 08	craft (artifice)	Ps 03

craft (skill)	Ps 06	cremation	Th 05	crucifixion	Th 08
craft (trade)	Ps 06	crematory	Pl 05	crudeness	Th 01
craft (water craft)	Th 04	crescent symbol	Th 04	cruelty	Th 01
craftiness	Ps 03	crest	Th 04	crumb	Th 04
crafts (goods)	Th 04	crevasse	Th 04	crusade (military)	Th 06
craftsman	Oc 06	crevice	Th 04	crusade (rally)	Th 11
craftsmanship	Th 06	crew	Th 06	crust	Th 04
crag	Pl 10	crew's quarters	Sh 04	crustacean	An 04
cramps	Af 08	crime	Ho 12	crusty growth	Af 04
cramps in toes	Af 07	crime	Th 12	crusty people	Oc 04
crank	Oc 10	crime, involvement with	Ps 12	crux (core)	Th 05
crank (handle)	Th 01	criminal	Oc 12	Crux (southern cross)	My 10
crateris (cup)	My 04	criminal at large	Th 07	crying	Th 12
cravings	Ps 08	criminal on trial	Th 07	crystal	Th 10
crazes (popular)	Th 04	criminologist	Oc 08	crystallization	Th 10
cream	Co 06	crimson	Co 08	cubicle (work place)	Th 06
crease	Th 11	cripple	Oc 12	cuff link	Th 02
creation (origination)	Th 05	crisis (turning point)	Th 08	cul-de-sac	Pl 04
creation (the universe)	Th 10	crisis, economic	Mn 08	culmination	Th 10
creative ability	Ho 05	criteria (example)	Th 03	culprit	Oc 07
creative hobby	Th 05	criteria (standard)	Th 06	cult	Th 11
creative manipulation of ideas	Th 09	critic	Oc 06	cultivation	Th 04
		critical (necessary) worker	Oc 10	cultural center	Pl 04
creative talents	Ps 05			cultural knowledge (wisdom)	Th 09
creative visualization	Th 01	criticism	Ho 06		
creative work	Th 05	criticism	Ps 06	cultural life	Mn 04
creative writing	Th 07	criticism, friendly	Th 11	culture	Th 04
creativity	Ps 05	critter	An 01	culture, attitude towards	Ps 04
creature	Th 01	crocheting	Th 06	cunning	Ps 03
credentials (authorization)	Th 07	crocodile	An 10	cup	Th 04
		Cronos	My 10	cupboard	Hs 06
credentials (qualifications)	Th 10	crook	Oc 07	Cupid	My 05
		crop grower	Oc 04	curb (edge)	Th 09
credibility	Ps 10	crop raising	Mn 04	curb (restraint)	Th 10
credit	Ho 08	cropping (clipping)	Th 08	cure	Th 06
credit	Th 08	crops	Mn 04	curing (healing)	Th 06
credit (allowance)	Mn 02	crops	Th 04	curing (smoking)	Th 06
credit, national	Mn 08	cross (burden)	Th 12	curiosity	Ps 03
credit agents	In 08	cross (shows anger)	Th 01	curiosity	Th 03
credit department	Or 08	cross shaped symbol	Th 10	curious objects or events	Th 03
credit manager	Oc 08	crossing a border	Th 09	currency	Mn 02
credit reputation	Ps 05	crosswalk	Pl 03	currency	Th 02
credit standing	Mn 08	crow	An 03	currency exchanges	In 02
credit union	Mn 02	crowbar	Th 03	current wisdom	Th 09
credit union	Or 02	crowd	Th 04	curriculum	Th 09
credit union	Pl 02	crowding	Th 11	curse (burden)	Th 12
creditor	Oc 08	crown (apex)	Pl 10	curse (denunciation)	Th 08
credo	Th 09	crown (royalty)	Th 05	curse (profanity)	Th 01
creed	Th 09	crucible	Th 05	curtailment	Th 10

curtains (drapery)	Hs 07	customer engineer	Oc 06	cutthroat competition	Mn 08
curtains (the end)	Th 08	customer satisfaction	Or 05	cycle	Th 04
curvature	Th 03	customer service	Or 06	cyclone	Th 08
curve (bend)	Pl 03	customers	Or 04	Cyclops	My 12
cushion (leeway)	Th 04	customs	Mn 08	Cygnus (swan)	My 07
cushion (pillow)	Th 02	customs (habits)	Th 04	cynic	Oc 03
custodian	Oc 04	customs (tolls)	Th 08	cynicism	Ps 03
custody (care)	Th 04	cut	Af 01	cyst	Af 05
custom work	Th 06	cut (a piece)	Th 02		
customary things	Th 04	cut (absence)	Th 10		

D

dagger	Th 01	darkness	Th 04	dealer (cards)	Oc 05
daily comings and goings	Th 03	darling (sweetheart)	Oc 05	dealer (negotiator)	Oc 03
daily duties	Th 06	dart	Th 09	dealer in future trends	Oc 11
daily exercise	Th 05	data (facts)	Th 06	dealer in liquids	Oc 04
dairy	Pl 04	data processing	Or 06	dealer in ornaments	Oc 02
dairy farmer	Oc 04	data processor	Oc 06	dealings (transactions)	Th 03
dairy worker	Oc 04	date (appointment)	Th 07	dealings with a loved one	Th 05
dam	Mn 10	date (era)	Th 10	dealings with children	Th 05
damage (cost)	Th 08	date (escort)	Oc 07	dealings with government	Mn 10
damage (harm)	Th 08	dating	Th 05		
damage from earthquakes	Th 04	daughter	Re 05	dealings with neighbors	Th 03
		daughter-in-law	Re 11	dealings with partner	Th 07
damage from natural disasters	Th 04	dawn (inception)	Th 01	dealings with siblings	Th 03
		dawn (sunrise)	Th 01	dealings with superiors	Th 10
damages (compensation)	Th 08	day (date)	Th 10	dealings with the public	Mn 07
damp place	Pl 04	day (work day)	Th 06	dealings with young people	Th 05
dampness	Th 04	day, a calendar	Th 10		
damsel	Oc 03	day care	Th 06	dearest wish	Th 11
dance	Th 05	day laborer	Oc 06	dearth (lack)	Th 10
dance hall	Pl 02	day room	Hs 09	death	Ho 08
dancer	Oc 02	daybreak	Th 01	death	Th 08
dandruff	Af 10	daydreaming	Th 12	death, attitude towards	Ps 08
dandy	Oc 05	daylight	Th 05	death, kind of	Th 08
danger (peril)	Ho 01	daytime	Th 05	death, physical and spiritual	Th 08
danger (peril)	Th 01	dead, the	Oc 08		
dangerous activities	Ho 01	dead end	Pl 12	death in the family, a	Ho 11
dare (provocation)	Th 01	dead of night	Th 04	death in the family, a	Th 11
daring (boldness)	Th 01	deadbeat	Oc 03	death of a child	Th 12
dark (nightfall)	Th 04	deadening agent	Th 08	death of a friend	Th 06
dark black	Co 08	deadline	Th 10	death of a parent	Th 05
dark blue	Co 10	deadlock	Th 07	death of a pet	Th 01
dark brown	Co 08	deafness	Af 01	death of career	Th 05
dark red	Co 08	deal (portion)	Th 04	death of someone inquired about	Th 02
dark shades	Co 10	deal (transaction)	Th 01		

debacle	Th 08	dedication	Ps 06	deity	Ho 09
debasement	Th 08	dedication (commitment)	Th 06	deity	Oc 09
debate	Th 03	deduction	Th 08	deity, attitude towards	Ps 09
debater	Oc 03	deed (feat)	Th 01	dejection	Th 05
debauchery (excess)	Th 09	deed (written)	Th 03	delay(s)	Th 10
debility, in general	Af 07	deed of virtue	Th 09	delegate	Oc 11
debit	Th 08	deed recorder	Oc 06	delegation	Th 11
debris	Th 12	deep, the	Pl 08	deletion	Th 08
debt	Mn 08	deep motives	Th 08	deliberation	Th 09
debt (obligation)	Th 08	deep sea diver	Oc 04	deliberations of a jury	Th 05
debt expansion	Mn 04	deer	An 06	delicacy	Th 02
debt management	Or 08	defacing activities	Th 08	delight	Th 05
debtor	Oc 08	defamation (slander)	Th 07	delineation	Th 06
debut	Th 01	default	Th 08	delinquency	Ps 03
debutante	Oc 07	defeat	Th 12	delirium tremens	Af 03
decadence	Th 08	defecation	Bd 08	deliverance	Th 12
decapitation	Bd 01	defect (flaw)	Th 06	delivery (handing over)	Th 03
decay	Th 08	defect of character	Ps 06	delivery personnel	Oc 03
deceit	Th 03	defection	Th 07	Delphinus (dolphin)	My 03
deceiver	Oc 03	defendant	Oc 07	deluge	Th 04
deceiving sense of	Ps 03	defender	Oc 01	delusion	Ho 12
decency (decorum)	Th 06	defense	Th 04	delusion (misbelief)	Th 12
deception (fraud)	Th 03	defenses	Ps 04	delusion, self	Ps 12
deception (trick)	Th 03	defensive qualities	Ps 04	demand (command)	Th 01
decision (conclusion)	Th 04	deference (honor)	Th 10	demand for goods or services	Mn 10
decision (decisiveness)	Th 10	deference (obedience)	Th 06		
decision (verdict)	Th 04	defiance (rebelliousness)	Th 11	demand put upon you	Th 10
decisions	Ho 04	deficiency	Th 10	demeanor	Ps 01
decisions, arbitrary	Th 09	deficits	Mn 08	Demeter (the caregiver)	My 06
decisions of a court of law	Th 04	deficits	Th 08	demise	Th 08
deck	Hs 05	definition (clarification)	Th 07	democracies	Mn 04
deck	Sh 10	definition (gives form to)	Th 04	democrat	Oc 04
declaration (notice)	Th 03	deflation	Th 08	demolition	Th 08
declaration (statement)	Th 03	deflection	Th 03	demon	Oc 08
decline (deterioration)	Th 12	deflowering	Th 08	demonstration (display)	Th 05
decline (downgrade)	Th 10	deformation (change for worse)	Th 08	demonstration (proof)	Th 10
decomposition	Th 08			demonstration (protest)	Th 11
decongestant	Th 03	deformity (abnormality)	Th 11	demonstration (sign)	Th 08
decontamination	Th 08	deformity (disfigurement)	Af 12	demonstrator	Au 09
decor	Hs 07	defraud	Th 12	demonstrator (protester)	Oc 11
decorations	Hs 02	defuse (calm)	Th 02	demotion	Th 08
decorations	Th 02	degenerate	Oc 12	den	Hs 05
decorative objects	Th 02	degeneration	Th 08	den (retreat)	Pl 12
decorator	Oc 02	degradation (disgrace)	Th 08	den (shelter)	Pl 04
decorators	In 07	degree (measure)	Th 06	denial (disavowal)	Ho 12
decorum	Th 07	degree (scholastic)	Th 09	denial (disavowal)	Ps 12
decoy	Th 03	degree of involvement	Th 02	denial (refusal)	Ho 07
decree (proclamation)	Th 03	dehydrating food	Th 06	denial (refusal)	Th 07
dedication	Ho 06	dehydration	Af 03	denizen	Oc 04

denomination (religious)	Th 09	depth (deeper)	Th 08	detailing	Th 06
denomination (value)	Th 02	depth of feelings	Ps 08	details	Th 06
density	Th 10	depth psychology	Th 08	detection (discovering)	Th 08
dent (depression)	Th 04	deputy	Oc 06	detective	Oc 08
dental hygienist	Oc 06	derailment	Th 08	detention	Th 12
dental services	In 06	derangement	Th 12	deterioration	Th 08
dental technician	Oc 06	derelict	Oc 12	determination (ruling)	Th 10
dentist	Oc 10	derision	Th 08	determination (tenacity)	Ps 10
dentistry	Th 10	deriving enjoyment	Ps 05	deterrent	Th 10
dents and scratches	Au 08	derrick	Pl 10	detour	Th 03
dentures	Bd 03	descendant	Re 05	detraction	Th 08
denunciation	Th 07	descent	Ho 08	detriment	Th 08
deodorant	Th 02	descent	Th 08	devastation	Th 08
departing	Th 03	description (portrayal)	Th 03	development (progress)	Th 10
department (division)	Or 06	description (variety)	Th 03	development of the mind	Ps 09
department heads	Mn 10	desecration	Th 08		
department of defense	Mn 01	desert (wasteland)	Pl 01	developments (new events)	Th 10
department of personnel	Mn 04	desertion	Th 12		
department of state	Mn 07	design (shape)	Hs 01	deviation (variation)	Th 11
department store	Pl 04	designate	Oc 07	deviation (wandering)	Th 03
departure (digression)	Th 09	designation	Th 10	device (plot)	Th 03
departure (leaving)	Th 09	designer	Oc 07	devices, labor saving	Th 06
dependence (reliance on others)	Ps 04	designers	In 07	devil, the	Oc 08
		desirability	Ps 02	devil's advocate	Oc 11
dependency (addiction)	Ps 04	desire (craving)	Ps 11	deviousness	Ps 03
dependency (needs for help)	Ps 04	desire for action	Th 01	devotion (dedication)	Ps 06
		desires	Ho 11	devotion (fervor)	Th 12
dependent (contingent on)	Th 09	desires	Ps 11	devotion to a task	Ps 06
dependents (subordinates)	Ho 06	desks	Th 03	dew	Th 04
		desolate places	Ho 01	dexterity	Ps 03
dependents (subordinates)	Oc 06	desolate places	Pl 01	diabetes	Af 07
		desolation	Th 01	diagnosis	Th 08
depletion	Ho 08	despair (hopelessness)	Ps 06	diagonal	Th 03
depletion	Th 08	desperation (need)	Th 12	diagram	Th 06
deportation	Th 12	despondency	Ps 06	dial	Th 01
deportee	Oc 12	dessert	Th 02	dialect	Th 03
deportment	Ho 07	destination	Th 09	dialogue	Th 03
deportment	Ps 07	destiny	Th 09	diameter	Th 06
deposit (down payment)	Th 02	destitution	Th 12	diamond	Ge 10
deposit (pile)	Th 04	destroyer	Oc 08	diamond cutter	Oc 10
deposition	Th 07	destroying	Th 08	Diana	My 04
depository	Pl 06	destruction	Th 08	diaphragm	Bd 06
depot	Pl 03	destructive biological insects	An 08	diarrhea	Af 08
depravity	Th 08			diary	Th 03
depreciation	Th 08	destructive forces	Th 08	diatribe	Th 07
depression	Ps 06	detachment (disconnection)	Th 04	dice	Th 05
depression (economic)	Th 08			dictate (order)	Th 01
depression (pit)	Th 04	detachment (impartiality)	Th 11	dictation	Th 03
deprivation	Ps 08	detachment, ability for	Ps 11	dictator	Oc 06

diction	Th 01	dinner engagement	Th 05	disc (or disk)	Th 05
dictionary	Th 06	Dionysos (the escapist)	My 05	discarded item	Th 12
diet	Ho 06	dioptase	Ge 02	discarding	Th 11
diet	Th 06	diploma	Th 10	discernment	Th 09
dietary concerns	Ps 06	diplomacy	Th 07	discharge (detonation)	Th 01
dietary habits	Th 06	diplomat	Mn 09	discharge (drainage)	Th 08
dietary problems	Af 06	diplomat	Oc 09	discharge (release)	Th 12
dietetics	Th 06	diplomatic corps	Mn 09	disciple	Oc 11
dietician	Oc 06	dire straits	Th 11	disciplinarian	Oc 08
differences (contrasts)	Th 07	direction (guideline)	Th 06	discipline (regimen)	Th 06
differences (disputes)	Th 01	direction (instruction)	Th 06	discipline (training)	Th 06
differing opinions	Th 07	direction (line of movement)	Th 03	disciplined living or work	Ps 06
difficulty	Ho 01			disciplined thinking	Th 03
difficulty (laboriousness)	Th 01	direction (line of thought)	Th 03	disclaimer	Th 07
difficulty (trouble)	Th 01	direction (management)	Th 10	disclosure	Th 09
diffidence (reserve)	Ps 06	direction (way)	Th 03	discoloration	Th 12
diffusion (spread)	Th 11	direction indicator	Th 03	discomfort (ache)	Th 01
diffusion (wordiness)	Th 03	director	Oc 01	discomfort (hardship)	Th 10
dig (cutting remark)	Th 03	dirge	Th 08	disconnection	Th 08
digest (summary)	Th 06	dirt (grime)	Th 12	discontent	Ho 11
digestion	Bd 04	dirt (soil)	Th 02	discontent	Ps 11
digestive juices	Bd 04	dirty things	Th 06	discontent	Th 11
digestive system	Bd 04	Dis Pater	My 08	discontinuation	Th 10
digger	Oc 02	disability	Ho 12	discord (disagreement)	Th 07
diggings (excavations)	Pl 04	disability (disadvantage)	Th 12	discord (musical)	Th 01
dignitary	Oc 10	disability (handicap)	Th 12	discount (deduction)	Th 08
dignity	Ho 10	disability benefits	Th 08	discouragement	Ps 06
dignity	Ps 10	disabled, the	Oc 12	discourse	Th 03
digression	Th 03	disadvantages	Ho 12	discovering of self	Ps 01
dike (ditch)	Pl 03	disadvantages	Th 12	discovery, the process of	Th 01
dilapidation	Th 08	disagreeable duty	Th 12	discrediting (defaming)	Th 12
dilemma	Ho 07	disagreement	Ho 07	discrepancy (variance)	Th 07
dilemma	Th 07	disagreement	Th 07	discretion	Th 11
dilettante	Oc 07	disappearance (vanishing)	Th 08	discriminating sense	Ps 06
diligence	Ps 10			discrimination (bias)	Th 07
dilution	Th 08	disappointing earnings	Mn 01	discrimination (separation)	Th 06
dimension (depth)	Th 08	disappointing events	Th 12		
dimension (size)	Th 02	disappointment	Ho 12	discussion	Th 03
diminishing	Ho 08	disappointment (let down)	Ps 08	disdain (scorn)	Th 07
diminishing	Th 08			disease (in general)	Af 06
diminishing returns	Th 08	disapproval	Ho 07	disease, sexually transmitted	Af 08
dimples	Bd 02	disapproval	Th 07		
din (noise)	Th 01	disarray (disorder)	Th 12	disease caused by excess(es)	Af 09
diner	Oc 04	disaster	Ho 08		
diner	Pl 06	disaster (catastrophe)	Th 08	disembodied entity	Th 08
dining out	Th 05	disasters, natural	Th 08	disfavor (disapproval)	Th 07
dining room	Hs 06	disavowal	Th 12	disfiguring illness	Af 01
dining room	Pl 06	disbelief (doubt)	Th 06	disgrace (disfavor)	Th 07
dinner	Th 04	disbursement (allocation)	Th 03	disgrace (shame)	Th 08

231

disguise	Th 03	displeasure	Th 08	distinction	Th 06
disgust	Th 07	disposal	Th 08	(differentiation)	
dish (food)	Th 06	disposal area	Pl 08	distinction (excellence)	Th 10
dish (good looking person)	Th 07	disposition	Ps 01	distinctiveness	Th 01
		disposition (control)	Th 08	distortion	Th 03
dish (plate)	Th 06	disposition (final settlement)	Th 08	distraction (diversion)	Th 05
dish (portion)	Th 06			distraction (madness)	Th 01
dishonest person	Oc 07	disposition (organization)	Th 10	distress	Th 06
dishonesty	Ps 07			distressing condition	Th 06
dishonor	Th 12	disposition (tendency)	Th 04	distribution	Ho 03
dishwasher	Hs 06	dispossession	Th 12	distribution (arrangement)	Th 07
disillusionment	Ps 12	disproportion	Th 09		
disinfectant	Th 06	disputes	Ho 07	distribution (dissemination)	Th 03
disintegration	Th 08	disputes	Mn 07		
disinterest	Th 11	disputes (quarrels)	Th 07	distribution systems	Th 03
dislike (distaste)	Th 07	disqualification	Th 07	distributor	Au 03
dislocated bones or joints	Af 09	disregard	Th 07	distributor	Oc 03
		disrespect	Th 12	disturbances	Th 01
dislocation	Th 08	disruptions	Th 11	disturbances, origins of	Th 01
dislodging (ouster)	Th 08	dissatisfaction	Th 11	ditch	Pl 04
disloyalty	Th 07	dissatisfying experience	Th 11	diver	Oc 08
dismay (alarm)	Th 01	dissemination (spreading)	Th 11	divergence	Th 03
dismemberment	Th 08			diversification	Th 03
dismissal (discharge)	Th 08	dissension	Th 07	Diversified Company	In 12
dismissal (release)	Th 12	dissent (discord)	Th 07	diversion (deflection)	Th 03
disobedience	Th 07	dissertation (treatise)	Th 09	diversion (pastime)	Ho 05
disorder (ailment)	Th 06	disservice (injustice)	Th 07	diversion (pastime)	Th 05
disorder (disturbance)	Th 07	dissident	Oc 11	diversity (variety)	Th 03
disorder (mess)	Th 12	dissipation	Th 05	divestiture	Th 08
disorientation	Ps 04	dissolution	Th 12	divination	Th 09
disowning (denial)	Th 12	dissolution of a partnership	Th 07	divinity (a god)	Oc 09
disowning (forsaking)	Th 12			divinity (holiness)	Th 09
disparity	Th 09	dissolving	Th 12	divinity (theology)	Th 09
dispatch (message)	Th 03	distance (far)	Th 10	division (branch)	Th 06
dispatcher	Oc 03	distance (stand-offish)	Th 10	division (math)	Th 06
dispatchers dept.	Or 03	distant connections	Th 09	division (separation)	Th 06
dispensary	Pl 06	distant contacts and interests	Th 09	divorce	Ho 07
dispensary	Sh 06			divorce proceedings (legal)	Th 09
dispensation (apportionment)	Th 11	distant people	Oc 09		
		distant place	Pl 09	divorce(s)	Th 07
dispensation (authorization)	Th 10	distant relative	Re 09	divulgence (disclosure)	Th 09
		distant shore	Pl 09	dizziness	Af 01
dispensing	Ho 11	distemper	Th 01	dock (wharf)	Pl 04
dispersal	Ho 11	distension (swelling)	Th 05	doctor	Oc 06
dispersal	Th 11	distillate	Th 08	doctor's office	Pl 06
dispersant	Th 11	distillation	Th 08	doctoring	Th 06
displaced person	Oc 12	distiller	Oc 08	doctrine (belief)	Th 09
displacement	Th 08	distillery	Pl 08	document	Th 03
display (exhibition)	Th 05	distilling unit (water)	Th 08	dodge (sidestep)	Th 03

doer	Oc 06	doubles	Th 03	dregs (riff-raff)	Oc 12
dog	An 06	doubt (uncertainty)	Th 06	dress (appearance)	Th 01
dogma	Th 09	dough (bread)	Th 06	dress (clothing)	Th 06
doldrums (gloom)	Th 10	dough (money)	Th 02	dressing room(s)	Hs 07
dole (welfare)	Th 12	down (feathers)	Th 06	dressing table	Th 06
doll (figurine)	Th 03	down, the direction of	Th 10	dressmaker	Oc 06
dollars	Th 02	down-spout	Th 03	driest part of the house	Hs 03
dolphin	An 11	downfall (ruin)	Th 12	drift (implication)	Th 03
dolt (idiot)	Oc 03	downgrade	Th 10	drift (snow)	Th 02
domain (estate)	Pl 04	downpour	Th 04	drifting (in water)	Th 02
domain (field of work)	Th 06	dowry	Ho 08	drill (exercise)	Th 06
dome	Th 09	dowry	Th 08	drill (tool)	Th 10
domestic	Oc 06	Draco (dragon)	My 08	driller	Oc 10
domestic (servant)	Oc 06	draft (military)	Th 01	drilling machine	Th 10
domestic affairs	Th 04	draft (outline)	Th 06	drink (beverage)	Th 04
domestic chores	Th 04	draft (payment)	Th 02	drip (jerk)	Oc 12
domestic considerations	Mn 01	draft of air	Th 03	drip (trickle)	Th 04
domestic employees	Mn 06	draftsman	Oc 06	drive (advance)	Th 01
domestic interests	Mn 01	drag (spoilsport)	Oc 10	drive (outing)	Th 03
domestic pets	Th 06	drag one's feet	Th 12	drive shaft	Au 10
domesticity	Th 04	dragon	An 08	drive train	Au 10
domicile	Pl 04	drain (conduit)	Th 08	drive-in	Pl 05
domination	Ps 05	drain (draw off)	Th 08	drivel (rambling)	Th 03
domination (supremacy)	Ps 08	drain cleaning	In 08	driver	Oc 03
dominion (empire)	Th 04	drainage	Th 08	driver's instruction	In 05
dominion (rule)	Th 05	drainage of the land	Hs 12	driver's license	Th 10
donation (gift)	Th 08	drama (play)	Th 05	driver's rooms	Or 03
donor	Oc 08	drama (suspense)	Th 08	driver's seat	Au 01
doodad	Th 04	dramatics, flair for	Ps 05	driver's test	Th 05
doom (end of all)	Th 08	draperies	Th 06	driving	Th 03
doom (ruin)	Th 08	dravite	Ge 11	driving test	Th 06
doom (verdict)	Th 04	draw (attraction)	Th 05	drone (parasite)	An 08
door	Au 01	draw (deadlock)	Th 07	droop (sag)	Th 02
door	Hs 01	drawback (obstacle)	Th 10	drop (abandon)	Th 12
door, rear or side	Hs 12	drawers (underclothing)	Th 06	drop (decline)	Th 08
doorman	Oc 01	drawing (sketch)	Th 03	drop (descent)	Th 10
doorway	Hs 01	drawing room	Hs 07	drop (dismiss)	Th 08
dope (drugs)	Th 12	dread (fear)	Th 12	drop (drip)	Th 04
dope (dummy)	Oc 03	dream (joy)	Th 05	drop (trace)	Th 04
dope (preparation)	Th 10	dream consciousness	Th 09	drop in position, a	Th 07
dope (tip)	Th 03	dream diary	Th 02	dropsy	Af 04
Dorado (goldfish)	My 12	dream interpretation	Th 02	drought (aridity)	Th 01
dormancy	Th 02	dream or sleep patterns	Th 12	drought (shortage)	Th 10
dormitory	Th 04	dreamer	Oc 12	drowning	Th 04
dossier (record)	Th 06	dreams (visions)	Th 09	drudge	Oc 06
dot (speck)	Th 04	dreams (wishes)	Th 11	drudgery	Th 06
dotage	Th 10	dreams as mental journeys	Th 09	drug abuse treatment	In 12
double (counterpart)	Th 03			drug addiction	Th 12
double-time speed	Th 01	dregs (residue)	Th 12	drug dealer	Oc 12

drug store	Pl 06	ductless gland	Bd 04	durability	Th 02
druggist	Oc 06	ducts, tear	Bd 04	durable goods	Mn 04
drugs	In 12	ductwork	Hs 03	duration (term)	Th 10
drugs	Ho 12	duel	Th 01	duress	Ps 12
drugs (in general)	Th 12	duet	Th 03	dust	Th 06
drugs, dependence upon	Ps 12	duke	Oc 10	duties, daily	Th 06
drugs, illicit	Th 12	dukedom	Pl 10	duty	Ho 06
drums	Th 01	dull ache	Af 10	duty	Ps 06
drunkard	Oc 12	dull color	Co 10	duty (obligation)	Th 06
drunkenness	Th 12	dullness	Th 10	duty (responsibility)	Th 06
dry cleaner	Oc 06	dummy	Oc 03	dwarf	Oc 03
dry cleaners	In 06	dump (disposal area)	Pl 08	dwellings	Pl 04
dry cleaners	Pl 06	dump (shack)	Th 04	dwindle away	Th 08
dry dock	Pl 06	dump truck	Th 03	dye (tint)	Th 12
dry dock work	Sh 06	dunce	Oc 03	dyer	Oc 12
dry goods	Th 06	dungeon	Pl 12	dying	Th 08
dry wash	Pl 01	dunghill	Pl 08	dynamics	Th 05
dryness	Th 01	duo	Th 03	dynamite	Th 01
duality	Ps 03	dupe	Oc 03	dynamo, electrical	Th 11
duality	Th 03	duplicate	Th 03	dysentery	Af 06
duck	An 06	duplicity	Th 03		

E

eagerness	Th 01	easy chair	Th 02	economy, the	Th 10
eagle	An 08	eatery	Pl 04	economy of scale	Th 10
earl	Oc 10	eating	Th 04	ecstasy	Ps 09
early education	Th 03	eating establishment	Mn 06	eczema	Af 10
early home life	Th 04	eating habits	Ps 04	edema	Af 04
early life	Th 04	eating out	Th 05	edge (blade)	Th 01
earnestness	Th 09	eaves (roof)	Hs 09	edge (border)	Pl 09
earning capacity	Mn 02	eavesdropping	Th 12	edict	Th 03
earning power	Ps 02	ebony	Ge 10	edification (enlightenment)	Th 09
earnings	Th 02	eccentric	Oc 11		
earrings	Th 02	eccentric (mechanical device)	Th 11	edifice (building)	Th 10
ears	Bd 02			editing	Th 03
earth, the	Th 02	eccentricity	Ho 11	editor	Oc 09
earth tones	Co 06	eccentricity	Ps 11	educated classes, the	Mn 09
earth's surface, the	Th 04	echelon (formation)	Th 06	educated classes, the	Oc 09
earthquake	Th 10	echo	Th 03	education	Ho 03
earthquake damage	Th 05	echo (the repeater)	My 12	education	Th 03
ease	Ho 02	eclipse (darkening)	Th 04	education (high school)	Th 07
ease (comfort)	Th 02	eclipse (diminishing)	Th 08	education (junior high)	Th 05
ease (composure)	Th 02	ecology	Th 04	education (lower)	Th 03
ease (relaxation)	Th 02	economic outlook	Mn 06	education, elementary	Th 03
easel	Th 05	economist	Oc 10	education, higher	Th 09
east, the direction of	Th 01	economy, the	Mn 10	educational advancement	Th 03

educational attitudes	Ps 03	electrical power distribution	In 03	emancipation	Th 12
educational matters	Mn 05			embalmer	Oc 08
educational profession	Oc 05	electrical switches	In 05	embargo	Th 07
educational pursuits	Th 05	electrical system	Mn 11	embarkation	Th 09
educator	Oc 05	electrical system, the	Au 11	embarrassment	Ps 10
effect (influence)	Th 10	electrical utility	In 11	embassy	Pl 09
effect (operation)	Th 01	electrical wiring	Au 11	embedded memory	Th 11
effect (result)	Th 10	electrical wiring	Hs 11	embellishment	Th 05
effecting change	Ho 11	electrical wiring	Or 11	ember (spark)	Th 01
effecting change	Ps 11	electrician	Oc 11	embezzlement	Th 07
effects (property)	Th 02	electricity	Th 11	embezzler	Oc 07
effeminacy	Ps 07	electrocution	Th 11	emblem	Th 04
effervescence (liveliness)	Th 05	electrode	Th 11	embodiment	Th 04
efficiency	Ps 06	electrolyte	Th 05	embrace	Th 04
efficiency	Th 06	electromagnet	Th 05	embroidering	Th 07
efficient routines	Th 06	electron	Th 10	embroidery	Th 07
effigy	Th 03	electronic circuit	Th 11	embryo	Th 05
effluence	Th 08	electronic device	Th 11	emerald	Ge 07
effort (exertion)	Th 01	electronic games	In 03	emergence	Ps 01
efforts to get ahead	Th 10	electronic instrumentation	In 06	emergency	Th 01
efforts to promote yourself	Th 09	electronic linkage	Th 11	emergency brake	Au 10
		electronic music	Th 12	emergency lighting	Or 11
effrontery	Th 01	electronic technician	Oc 06	emergency lighting	Sh 11
eggs	Th 02	electronics	In 11	emergency lighting	Th 11
ego	Ps 05	electronics (defense)	In 06	emergency supplies	Th 06
egoism	Th 05	electroplating	Th 04	emergency worker	Oc 06
egotism	Th 05	elegance	Th 05	emigrant	Oc 09
egress (exit)	Th 08	element (piece)	Th 06	emigration	Th 09
ejaculation	Bd 08	elementary education	Th 03	eminence	Th 10
ejection	Th 01	elephant	An 12	eminent people	Oc 10
elaboration	Th 09	elevation	Ho 10	emissary	Oc 07
elastic	Th 03	elevation (height)	Th 10	emission control system	Au 06
elasticity	Th 03	elevation (promotion)	Th 10	Emmys	Th 10
elation	Th 05	elevator	Th 03	emotional blocks	Ps 12
elbaite	Ge 11	eligibility (acceptance)	Th 09	emotional depletion	Ps 11
elbow	Bd 10	elimination	Ho 08	emotional desires	Ps 11
elder	Oc 10	elimination	Ps 08	emotional expression	Ps 05
elderly, the	Th 10	elimination (rejection)	Th 08	emotional instability	Ps 07
election (choice)	Th 11	elimination (removal)	Th 08	emotional isolation	Ps 04
election (voting)	Th 11	elimination system, the	Bd 08	emotional needs	Ps 04
elective (option)	Th 11	elite (select), the	Oc 07	emotional pain	Ps 04
electorate, the	Mn 04	elitism	Th 07	emotional problems	Af 04
electric motor	Th 11	elixir (cure-all)	Th 12	emotional security	Ps 04
electrical appliance	Hs 11	elocution	Ps 03	emotions	Bd 04
electrical blue	Co 11	elongation	Th 03	emotions, pleasurable	Th 05
electrical equipment	In 11	eloping	Th 07	emperor, empress	Oc 10
electrical fuse	Th 11	eloquence	Ps 03	emphasis	Th 01
electrical linkage	Th 11	eluding	Th 12	empire	Th 04
electrical meter	Th 11	elusiveness	Th 12	employees	Ho 06

employees	Mn 06	endowment (legacy)	Th 08	enormity (villainy)	Th 08
employees	Oc 06	endowment (talent)	Th 05	enrichment	Th 02
employees, treatment of	Th 06	endurance	Ps 02	enrollment (enlistment)	Th 06
employer	Oc 10	enduring things	Th 10	enrollment (registration)	Th 04
employers	Mn 10	enema	Th 08	ensemble (outfit)	Th 06
employers, attitude towards	Ps 06	enemies (in general)	Th 12	entanglement	Ps 02
		enemies, known	Mn 07	enterprise (drive)	Th 01
employment	Th 06	enemies, known	Th 07	enterprise (undertaking)	Th 06
employment agency	Pl 06	enemies, open	Mn 07	entertainer	Oc 05
employment matters	Th 06	enemies, open	Th 07	entertainment	In 05
emporium	Pl 04	enemies, overcoming	Th 01	entertainment	Ho 05
emptiness	Th 01	enemies, secret	Mn 12	entertainment (diversion)	Th 05
emptiness, feelings of	Ps 01	enemies, secret	Th 12	enthusiasm	Th 05
emulation	Th 03	Energy	In 05	enthusiast	Oc 05
enabling	Th 05	energy (personal)	Th 01	enticement	Th 12
encephalitis	Af 01	energy (resource)	Th 05	entity, astral	Th 12
enchantment	Th 12	energy conservation	In 10	entomology	Th 04
enclosure (fencing)	Th 04	energy costs	Or 05	entrance	Hs 01
enclosure (insert)	Th 01	energy potential	Th 05	entrepreneur	Oc 05
encore	Th 05	enervation	Th 09	entry (approach)	Th 01
encounter (battle)	Th 07	enforcement	Th 08	entry (record)	Th 06
encouragement	Th 05	enforcer	Oc 08	entry (way in)	Th 01
encription	Th 12	engagement (appointment)	Th 07	entryway	Hs 01
encroachment	Th 08			enunciation	Th 03
encumbrance	Th 10	engagement (betrothal)	Th 07	envelope	Th 03
encyclopedia	Th 09	engagement (employment)	Th 06	envelopment	Th 04
end (death)	Th 08			environment, the	Ho 04
end (finish)	Th 04	engine	Sh 05	environment, the	Mn 04
end (goal)	Th 10	engine block	Au 05	environmental pollution	Th 11
end (leftover)	Th 12	engine fan	Au 03	environmental services	In 10
end (limit)	Th 10	engine mount	Au 05	environs (local vicinity)	Pl 04
end (outcome)	Th 04	engine room	Sh 05	envoy (representative)	Oc 07
end of a cycle	Th 04	engineer	Oc 10	envy (jealousy)	Th 02
end of a marriage	Th 10	engineering	Or 10	enzyme	Th 05
end of anything, the	Th 04	engineering and construction	In 10	eon	Th 10
end of career matters	Th 01			Eos (dawn)	My 12
end of fourth house parent	Th 07	engineers (consulting)	In 11	ephemeris	Th 06
		engines (in general)	Au 05	epic (saga)	Th 03
end of life period	Th 04	engines (in general)	Th 05	epicure	Oc 02
end of long-term affairs	Th 04	engraver	Oc 07	epidemic	Af 08
end of tenth house parent	Th 01	engraving enhancement	Th 07 Th 09	epidemic epigram (witty saying)	Mn 08 Th 03
end of the matter, the	Ho 04	enigma (puzzle)	Th 12	epilepsy	Af 03
end of the matter, the	Th 04	enjoyment	Th 05	epilogue (addendum)	Th 09
endearment	Th 02	enlarged heart	Af 05	epimetheus (afterthought)	My 09
endeavor (try)	Th 10	enlargement	Th 09		
ending (finish)	Th 08	enlightenment	Th 09	episode (event)	Th 01
endocrine system	Bd 04	enmity	Th 07	epistle	Th 03
endorsement	Th 07	enormity (size)	Th 02	epitaph	Th 08

epitome (representation)	Th 03	essay	Th 03	everyday duties	Th 06
epoch	Th 10	essence (basic quality)	Ps 05	everyday items	Th 04
equal relationships	Th 07	essence (concentration)	Th 08	everything	Th 04
equality	Ps 07	essential nature	Ps 04	eviction	Th 11
equality	Th 07	essentials (the basics)	Th 04	evidence (fact)	Th 06
equanimity (calmness)	Th 02	establishment (business)	Mn 10	evil (sin)	Th 08
equation	Th 07	establishment (forming)	Th 05	evolution	Ho 10
equator	Th 07	establishment (rulers), the	Mn 07	evolution (development)	Th 10
equilibrium	Th 07			exactness (precision)	Th 06
equipment	Th 06	estate	Pl 04	exaggeration	Th 09
equipment repair	In 06	estate (assets of)	Mn 08	exaltation	Th 05
equity (assets)	Th 02	estate lawyer	Oc 08	exaltation (praise)	Th 05
equity (fairness)	Th 07	estate of father	Th 11	exam, physical	Th 06
equivalence	Ps 07	estate of mother	Th 05	examination (analysis)	Th 06
equivocation	Th 07	estate of partner	Th 08	examination (test)	Th 03
equuleus (horse)	My 09	estates (land, real estate)	Th 04	example (model)	Th 03
era	Th 10	esteem (regard)	Ps 10	example (specimen)	Th 06
eradication	Th 08	esthetics	Th 07	exasperation (irritation)	Th 07
eraser	Th 08	estimate (evaluation)	Th 02	excavation	Pl 08
erasure	Th 08	estimate (surmise)	Th 09	excavator	Oc 08
erebos	My 04	estimation (judgment)	Th 09	excellence	Ho 10
eridanus (river)	My 03	estrangement	Th 07	excellence (quality)	Th 10
Eris (discord)	My 07	eternity (forever)	Th 10	excellence, working for	Ps 06
Eros	My 05	eternity (immortality)	Th 08	exception	Ho 11
erosion	Th 11	ethical responsibility	Ps 09	exception (exemption)	Th 11
erotica	Th 08	ethics	Ps 09	exception (leave out)	Th 11
errand (mission)	Th 06	ethics (moral code)	Th 09	exception to the rule	Th 11
error (mistake)	Th 12	ethnic food	Th 12	excerpt	Th 06
error in judgment	Th 12	etiquette	Th 07	excess	Th 09
eruption (volcanic)	Th 08	eulogy	Th 08	exchange (bartering)	Th 03
escalation	Th 09	euphemism	Th 03	exchange (brokerage)	Pl 05
escalator	Th 03	Eurydice (the unattainable)	My 11	exchange (e.g. money)	Pl 03
escapade	Th 03			exchange (interchange)	Th 03
escape	Ho 12	evacuation	Ho 08	exchange (verbal)	Th 07
escape	Ps 12	evacuation (emptying)	Th 08	excitability	Th 01
escape (avoidance)	Th 12	evacuation (removal)	Th 08	excitement	Th 01
escape (breakout)	Th 12	evaluation (assessment)	Th 02	exciting places	Pl 05
escape (diversion)	Th 03	evaluation (valuing)	Ho 02	excluded element	Th 12
escape (seepage)	Th 12	evaluation (valuing)	Th 02	exclusion (banning)	Th 12
escape, ability to	Ps 12	evaluator	Oc 02	exclusive club	Pl 05
escape from bondage	Th 12	evaporation	Th 08	exclusivity	Th 10
escaped convict	Oc 07	evasion (avoidance)	Th 12	excretion	Bd 08
escapism	Th 12	evasive action	Th 03	excretory system	Bd 08
escort	Oc 07	evening	Th 06	excursion	Th 03
escrow	Th 08	event (contest)	Th 07	excuse	Th 12
escrow account	Mn 08	event (happening)	Th 01	execution (accomplishes)	Th 01
esophagus	Bd 04	event (milestone)	Th 10	execution (performance)	Th 06
ESP	Th 12	event management	In 05	execution (slaying)	Th 08
espionage	Mn 12	eventuality (result)	Th 10	executioner	Oc 08

executive	Oc 10	expansiveness	Th 09	express mail	Th 03
executive, business	Oc 10	expectation (anticipation)	Th 11	expression (emotional tone)	Th 05
executive acumen	Ps 10	expectations	Ho 11		
executive board	Or 01	expectations	Ps 11	expression (look)	Th 01
executive head	Oc 10	expedience (help)	Th 12	expression (style)	Th 01
executive work	Mn 10	expediter	Oc 03	expression (wording)	Th 03
exemption (deduction)	Th 08	expedition	Th 09	expression of emotion	Ps 05
exemption (exception)	Th 11	expel (drive out)	Th 08	expressions, facial	Th 01
exercise (practice)	Th 05	expelled party	Th 07	expressions, verbal	Th 03
exercise (training)	Th 05	expelling	Ho 08	expressions of emotion	Ps 05
exercise, athletic	Th 05	expelling (dismissing)	Th 08	expressiveness	Ps 05
exercise, recreational	Th 05	expendable item	Th 12	expressway	Pl 03
exertion	Th 01	expenditure	Th 02	expropriation	Th 08
exhaust	Au 08	expense account	Th 02	expulsion	Th 01
exhaust header	Au 11	expenses	Ho 02	extension (addition)	Th 09
exhaust pipe	Au 08	expenses	Th 02	extension (lengthening)	Th 09
exhaust port	Au 08	experience	Ho 10	extent (size)	Th 02
exhaust system	Th 08	experience (episode)	Th 10	extent (term)	Th 10
exhaust vent	Hs 08	experience (knowledge)	Th 10	extenuating circumstances	Th 09
exhaustion	Ho 08	experience(s), learned	Ps 10		
exhaustion	Th 08	experiencing	Ps 09	exterior surface	Th 05
exhaustion, heat	Af 01	experimentation	Ho 09	extermination	Th 08
exhibit	Ho 05	experimentation	Th 09	external, that which is	Th 10
exhibit (display)	Th 05	experiments	Th 09	external sex organs	Bd 08
exhibition	Th 05	expert	Oc 10	extinction	Th 08
exhibitionism	Th 05	expertise	Th 10	extinguishing	Th 08
exhibitor	Oc 05	expiation	Th 08	extortion	Th 08
exhilaration	Th 05	expiration	Th 08	extra	Oc 05
exile	Oc 12	explanation	Ho 03	extra (addition)	Th 05
exile	Th 12	explanation (accounting)	Th 03	extra luggage	Th 07
existence (actuality)	Th 02	explanation (description)	Th 03	extra things	Th 05
exit (way out)	Th 08	explicitness (precision)	Th 06	extract (essence)	Th 08
exit (withdrawal)	Th 12	exploit (feat)	Th 01	extraction	Th 08
exodus	Th 12	exploitation	Th 08	extraordinary, the	Th 11
exoneration	Ho 12	exploration	Ho 09	extrasensory perception	Th 12
exorbitance	Th 05	exploration	Th 09	extravagance (waste)	Th 05
exorcism	Th 08	explorer	Oc 09	extreme (excess)	Th 09
exotic food	Th 12	explosion (detonation)	Th 01	extreme (limit)	Th 08
exotic land	Pl 09	explosion (outburst)	Th 01	extremity (appendage)	Bd 03
expanse	Pl 04	explosives	Th 01	extremity (end)	Th 08
expansion (increasing)	Th 09	exponent (advocate)	Oc 11	extrovert	Oc 05
expansion (spreading)	Th 09	exports	Mn 09	exuberance	Th 05
expansion (swelling)	Th 05	expose	Th 12	eye, left of female	Th 05
expansion of consciousness	Ho 09	exposer	Oc 05	eye, left of male	Th 04
		exposition	Th 05	eye, right of female	Th 04
expansion of consciousness	Ps 09	exposure (lay bare)	Th 05	eye, right of male	Th 05
		exposure (vista)	Th 09	eye care (supplies)	In 06
expansion of consciousness	Th 09	exposure, sought after	Th 05	eye care (treatment)	In 06
		exposure, unsought	Th 12	eye color	Bd 01

eyeglasses	Th 04	eyesight, quality of	Bd 04		
eyes	Bd 01	eyesight problems	Af 04		

F

fable	Th 09	fairy	Oc 12	family tree, the	Th 04
fabric (framework)	Th 10	faith	Ho 09	famine	Th 08
fabric (material)	Th 06	faith	Ps 09	famous person	Oc 10
fabrication (falsehood)	Th 07	faith (belief)	Th 09	famous relative	Re 05
fabrication (making)	Th 06	faith, giving up on	Ps 08	fan	Au 03
face	Bd 01	faith healer	Oc 02	fan (blower)	Th 03
face (confidence)	Th 05	faith in others, having	Th 08	fan belt	Au 03
face (reputation)	Th 10	faithfulness	Th 08	fanatic	Oc 09
face (visage)	Th 01	faithlessness	Th 07	fancy (liking)	Th 07
face, what you	Th 01	fake	Th 03	fanfare	Th 05
facet (aspect)	Th 06	fall (corruption)	Ps 08	fangs	Th 10
facet (cut)	Th 06	fall (decline)	Th 08	fantail	Sh 07
facial injuries	Af 01	fall (season)	Th 07	fantasy	Th 12
facility (building)	Th 10	fall (surrender)	Th 12	far away people	Th 09
facility (ease)	Th 06	fall (tumble)	Th 10	far neighborhood	Th 09
facing reality	Th 10	fall from power	Mn 12	farce (comedy)	Th 05
facsimile	Th 03	fallacy (flaw)	Th 12	farce (horseplay)	Th 05
faction (discord)	Th 07	fallacy (misconception)	Th 12	farce (mockery)	Th 03
faction (group)	Th 11	falls (waterfall)	Pl 04	fare (price)	Th 02
factors	Th 06	false appearances	Th 03	fare (range of food)	Th 06
factory	Mn 11	false pregnancy	Th 12	farewell	Th 09
factory	Pl 11	false teeth	Th 07	farm	Pl 04
facts	Ho 06	falsehood	Th 03	farm hand	Oc 04
facts	Th 06	falseness	Th 03	farm implement	Th 04
faculty (capability)	Th 05	falsity	Th 03	farm team	Th 09
faculty (knack)	Th 06	fame	Th 10	farmer	Oc 04
faculty (staff)	Th 06	familiarity	Th 03	farming	Th 04
faculty (wit)	Th 03	(accustomization)		farmland	Pl 02
fad	Th 04	familiarity (impropriety)	Th 07	fasces	Th 10
fading	Th 12	familiarity (informality)	Th 11	fascination	Th 12
failing (shortcoming)	Th 12	familiarity (intimacy)	Th 08	fashion (apparel)	Th 07
failure (bankruptcy)	Th 08	family	Ho 04	fashion (habit)	Th 04
failure (deterioration)	Th 12	family	Mn 04	fastener	Th 04
failure (disappointment)	Th 12	family	Th 04	fasting	Th 10
failure (failing)	Th 12	family, conditions of the	Th 04	fat(s)	Th 12
failure (neglect)	Th 12	family, member of	Re 04	fatalism	Th 08
faint mark	Th 12	immediate		fatality	Th 08
fainting spell	Af 05	family affairs	Ho 04	fate (karma)	Th 09
fair exchange	Mn 07	family affairs	Th 04	fateful loss	Th 08
fair play	Ps 09	family group	Th 04	fates, the	Th 09
fair weather friend, a	Oc 10	family patriarch(s)	Re 01	father	Ho 10
fairness	Th 07	family room	Hs 04	father	Re 10

father's kin	Re 06	feedback	Th 11	fictitious things	Th 12
father's money	Th 11	feeding	Th 04	fidelity	Ho 08
father-in-law	Re 09	feel, sense of	Th 01	fidelity	Ps 08
fatherland	Pl 04	feeler (proposal)	Th 09	fidgeting	Th 03
fatigue	Th 07	feeling of security	Th 04	field (domain)	Th 10
faucet	Th 03	feelings	Ps 04	field (meadow)	Pl 04
fault (defect)	Th 06	feet	Bd 12	field day (opportunity)	Th 05
fault (error)	Th 12	feet (measurement)	Th 06	fiend	Oc 08
fault (responsibility)	Th 10	feint (bluff)	Th 03	fiery red	Co 01
fault-finding	Ps 06	feldspar	Ge 04	fight	Th 01
faults in the earth	Th 04	felicity (happiness)	Th 05	fighter	Oc 01
Faun	My 09	fellow	Oc 11	fighter (airplane)	Th 01
Faunus	My 02	fellow club member	Oc 11	fights going asleep	Ps 01
faux pas	Th 07	fellow employee	Oc 06	figure of speech	Th 03
favor	Th 08	fellow traveler	Oc 03	figures (numbers)	Th 06
favor (approval)	Th 07	fellowship	Th 11	figures (shapes)	Th 07
favor (gift)	Ho 08	felon	Oc 12	figurine	Th 07
favor (gift)	Th 08	female concerns	Th 04	filament	Th 04
favor (good turn)	Th 07	female disorders	Af 07	file (collection)	Th 04
favor (resemblance)	Th 03	female relations	Re 10	file (row)	Th 06
favorable, that which is	Th 05	female things	Th 04	file (storage)	Th 06
favorite (front runner)	Oc 07	females	Oc 04	file (tool)	Th 11
favorite activity	Th 05	femininity	Th 02	file cabinet	Th 06
favorite one	Oc 07	fence (barrier)	Th 10	file clerk	Oc 06
favoritism	Th 09	fence (enclosure)	Th 04	filibuster	Th 11
fax	Th 03	fender	Au 03	film (movie)	Th 05
fear (anxiety)	Ps 06	fender	Sh 04	film actor	Oc 05
fear (awe)	Th 09	fermentation	Th 12	film on a surface	Th 12
fear (foreboding)	Th 12	ferocity	Th 08	filmy things	Th 12
fear (fright)	Th 08	ferret	An 08	filter (absorber)	Th 08
fear (phobia)	Th 04	ferry (boat)	Th 03	filter (separator)	Th 11
fear(s), inner	Ps 04	ferryman	Oc 03	filth (dirt)	Th 12
feast (banquet)	Th 05	fertility	Th 02	filthiness	Th 12
feast (holiday)	Th 05	fertility cycle	Bd 04	filtration	Th 08
feat	Th 01	fertilization	Th 02	fin (appendage)	Th 03
feather	Th 10	fertilizer	Th 02	final outcome of any question	Th 04
feature (attribute)	Th 01	festival	Th 05	final preparations	Th 04
feature (highlight)	Th 05	festivity	Th 05	final resort	Th 04
feature (visage)	Th 01	fetching	Th 01	final resting place	Pl 04
feature article	Th 07	fete (party)	Th 05	final result	Th 10
fecal matter	Bd 08	fetish (charm)	Th 08	finality	Th 04
feces	Th 08	fetish (obsession)	Th 08	finances	Ho 02
fecundity	Th 02	feud (dispute)	Th 07	finances	Th 02
federation	Th 11	fever(s)	Af 01	finances, competitor's	Mn 02
fee	Th 08	fiance, fiancee	Oc 07	finances of spouse or partner	Th 08
feebleness	Th 12	fiasco (failure)	Th 12		
feed (cater)	Th 06	fib	Th 07		
feed (devour)	Th 06	fickleness	Ps 04	financial (miscellaneous)	In 02
feed (nourishment)	Th 06	fiction	Th 12	financial abundance	Th 04

financial acquisition	Th 04	fire screen (grate)	Th 05	flat taste	Th 04
financial advisor	Oc 02	fire suppression system	Sh 09	flat tire	Au 12
financial affairs, handling of	Ho 02	fire walking	Th 08	flatiron	Th 06
		firearm	Th 01	flatness (level surface)	Th 04
financial assistance	Th 02	firearms and ammunition	In 01	flatterer	Oc 07
financial condition, one's	Th 02	fireball	Th 05	flattery	Ps 05
financial condition, partner's	Th 08	firebug	Oc 12	flatulence	Af 06
		firecracker	Th 01	flatus	Bd 06
financial dependence	Th 08	fireman	Oc 09	flatware	Th 06
financial incentive	Th 02	fireplace	Hs 05	flavoring	Th 02
financial institution	Mn 02	fireproofing services	In 10	flaw	Th 12
financial investing	Ho 02	fireworks	Th 01	fleas	An 08
financial loss	Ho 02	firing (from job)	Th 08	fleet, naval	Th 06
financial matters	Ho 02	firing a kiln, the act of	Th 05	flesh (mankind)	Th 04
financial matters	Th 02	firing squad	Th 08	flesh (physical nature)	Th 01
financial needs	Ps 02	first aid	Th 01	flesh (tissue)	Bd 01
financial obligation	Th 08	first person, the (grammatical)	Ho 01	flexibility	Th 03
Financial Services	In 02			flier	Oc 11
financial settlement	Th 08	fiscal matters	Th 02	flimsiness	Th 12
financial speculation	Th 05	fish	An 12	fling (love affair)	Th 05
financial trade (foreign)	Th 09	fish farm	Pl 03	flint	Ge 09
financial transaction	Th 02	fish processing	In 12	flirtation	Th 05
financier	Oc 02	fisherman	Oc 04	floating objects	Th 11
find (discovery)	Th 01	fishhook	Th 09	flock (group)	Th 11
finder	Oc 11	fishing	In 12	flood	Th 04
finder's fee	Th 08	fission	Th 08	flood control	Th 01
fine	Th 08	fissure	Th 12	flood damage	Th 04
fine art	Th 07	fist fighting	Th 01	floor (level base of room)	Hs 10
fine living	Th 02	fit	Af 03	floor (story)	Hs 04
finery	Th 07	fitting (for alteration)	Th 08	florist	Oc 02
finesse (tact)	Ps 07	fixation	Ps 08	florist shop	Pl 02
finesse (wile)	Ps 03	fixed possessions	Ho 04	Florists	In 02
finger	Bd 03	fixed possessions	Th 04	flotation device	Th 09
finger nail	Bd 03	fixing (correcting)	Th 10	flour	Th 06
fingerprint	Bd 03	fixture (device)	Th 06	flourish	Th 05
finish (completion)	Th 04	fixture (familiar sight)	Th 04	flow (discharge)	Th 12
finish (luster)	Th 05	flag	Th 04	flow (outpouring)	Th 09
fire (flames)	Th 01	flair	Ps 05	flow (progression of material)	Th 09
fire, the act of lighting a	Th 05	flamboyance	Th 05		
fire control (for guns) gear	Sh 01	flame(s)	Th 01	flow (stream)	Th 04
		Flamingo	My 07	flower garden	Pl 02
fire department	Or 09	flanks	Bd 08	flower grower	Oc 02
fire department	Pl 09	flash freezing	Th 08	flower growers	In 04
fire eater	Oc 01	flash of inspiration	Th 05	flowers	Th 02
fire engine	Th 09	flash of light	Th 05	fluctuation	Th 04
fire escape	Hs 12	flashback	Th 04	flue	Hs 03
fire opal	Ge 09	flashlight	Th 05	fluid flows	Bd 04
fire power	Sh 01	flask	Th 04	fluid retention	Bd 04
fire prevention services	In 06	flat (apartment)	Pl 04	fluids	Th 04

fluorescence	Th 04	food spill	Th 01	forest	Pl 02
fluorescent mineral	Ge 12	food stamps	Th 12	Forest Products	In 02
flush (discard)	Th 08	food storage	Th 06	forest ranger	Oc 06
flush (rich)	Th 02	food storage areas	Hs 06	forester	Oc 06
flying	Th 11	food wholesalers	In 04	Forestry Services	In 02
flying saucer	Th 09	fool (jester)	Oc 03	foretaste (advanced indication)	Th 09
flywheel	Th 10	foolhardiness	Th 01		
fo'c'sl	Sh 01	foolishness	Th 03	forethought (planning)	Th 10
foam	Th 12	foot diseases	Af 12	forever	Th 10
focal point	Th 05	footwear	Th 12	forfeiture	Th 08
focus	Ho 03	forage	Th 06	forge	Pl 06
focus (perspective)	Th 03	foray	Th 09	forger	Oc 12
focus, a central	Th 05	force (energy)	Th 05	forgery	Th 03
focus, your	Ps 05	force (significance)	Th 05	forgetfulness	Th 12
focus of things	Th 05	force (wrest)	Th 01	forging	Ge 06
fodder	Th 06	forces inclining to dissolution	Th 08	fork (eating utensil)	Th 06
foe	Oc 07			form	Ps 07
fog	Th 12	forcible control of people	Th 11	form (rules or procedures)	Th 10
foible	Th 11	forcing	Th 08		
fold	Th 11	fore deck	Sh 01	form (shape)	Th 01
folder (brochure)	Th 03	forearms	Bd 03	form, business	Mn 03
folder (storage envelope)	Th 06	foreboding	Th 08	formal dining room	Hs 10
folk culture	Mn 05	forecast	Th 09	formal living room	Hs 11
folklore	Th 09	forecaster	Oc 09	formal notice	Th 07
folklore, national	Mn 09	forecasting	Th 09	formal notification	Th 07
folks	Re 04	foreclosure	Th 08	formal occasion	Th 07
follow through	Th 06	forefather	Re 04	formality	Th 07
follower	Oc 11	forehead	Bd 01	formals	Th 07
folly	Th 03	foreign affairs	Mn 09	formation (arrangement)	Th 06
fondling	Th 05	foreign associate	Mn 09	formation (founding)	Th 05
fondness (liking)	Th 02	foreign commerce	Mn 09	formation, the act of	Th 05
food	Th 06	foreign country	Mn 09	formula	Th 06
food, chemistry of	Th 05	foreign country	Pl 09	formulation (mixture)	Th 11
food assimilation	Bd 06	foreign items	Mn 09	Fornax (furnace)	My 05
food chemist	Oc 05	foreign people	Mn 09	forsaking	Ps 12
food industry	Th 06	foreign policy, a nation's	Mn 07	fort	Pl 04
food markets	Pl 06			forthrightness	Ho 11
food preparation	Ho 06	foreign relations	Mn 09	forthrightness	Ps 11
food preparation	Th 06	foreign spies	Oc 12	fortifications	Th 04
food preparation area	Hs 06	foreign things	Th 09	fortitude	Ps 01
food preparer	Oc 06	foreign things, role of	Ps 09	fortress	Pl 04
food preservation	Th 06	foreign trade	Mn 09	fortuity	Th 05
food processing	In 06	Foreign Trade Services	In 09	fortune (destiny)	Th 05
food production (growing)	Mn 04	foreign travel	Ho 09	fortune (wealth)	Th 04
		foreign travel	Th 09	fortune, changes in	Th 08
food products	Th 06	foreigner	Oc 09	fortune teller	Oc 08
food retailers	In 04	foreman	Oc 10	forum (a radio program)	Th 03
food server	Oc 06	foreseeing the future	Th 12	forum (assembly)	Th 11
food service	Th 06	foresight	Th 09	forum (marketplace)	Pl 04

forum (public meeting place)	Pl 04	freehand drawings	Th 03	frugality	Th 10
forward motion	Th 01	freehand work	Th 06	fruit	Th 04
fossil	Th 10	freeing	Ho 12	fruitfulness	Th 02
foster child	Re 11	freeing	Ps 12	fruition	Th 05
foster relationships	Th 11	freemasonry	Th 08	frustrations	Ps 12
foul (infringement)	Th 07	freeway	Pl 03	frustrations, illness causing	Af 12
foul (penalty)	Th 07	freeze dried food	Th 06	fuel	Th 09
foul-up	Th 12	freezer	Th 08	fuel economy	Au 10
foundation	Hs 04	freezing things	Th 08	fuel injectors	Au 11
foundation	Ps 04	freight	Th 03	fuel lines	Au 04
foundation (base)	Th 10	frenzy	Th 08	fuel or oil filter	Au 06
foundation (founding)	Th 01	frequency (iteration)	Th 04	fuel pump	Au 03
founder	Oc 04	frequency (tone)	Th 11	fuel tank	Au 09
fountain	Th 04	fresh (new) thing	Th 01	fuel tank	Sh 09
fowl	An 06	fresh water supply	Sh 04	fugitive	Oc 07
fox	An 03	freshman (grade)	Th 01	fulcrum	Th 10
foyer	Hs 01	friction	Ho 11	fulfillment	Ps 05
fracture (break)	Th 08	friction	Th 11	full spectrum lighting	Th 05
fracture (separation)	Th 08	friend, close	Oc 07	fullness	Th 02
fragile item	Th 04	friend, response of a	Ps 11	fumigation	Th 12
fragment (piece)	Th 06	friend of a friend	Th 09	fun	Th 05
fragrance	Th 02	friend's health	Th 04	fun house	Pl 05
frame (mounting)	Th 04	friendliness	Ho 11	function (purpose)	Ps 10
frame (physique)	Th 01	friendliness	Ps 11	function (social)	Th 07
frame of mind (attitude)	Ps 01	friendliness	Th 11	functioning, inner ways of	Ps 04
framework (skeleton)	Th 10	friendly help	Th 11	fundamental indicator	Mn 10
franchise (ballot)	Th 11	friends	Ho 11	fundamental particles (physics)	Th 04
franchise (exclusive market)	Th 04	friends	Re 11	fundamentals (essentials)	Th 04
		friends (supporters)	Oc 11		
		friends of one's children	Re 03		
franchise (right)	Th 09	friends of the nation	Mn 11	fundraising	Th 09
franchisee	Oc 09	friendship	Ps 11	funeral	Th 08
franchiser	Oc 03	friendship	Th 11	funeral director	Oc 08
fraternal group	Th 11	frieze (decoration)	Th 02	funeral parlor	Pl 08
fraternal organization	Th 11	fright	Th 08	fungus	Th 12
fraternity	Pl 11	frigidity	Af 06	funk (depression)	Th 06
fraud	Th 03	frivolity	Th 03	fur	Th 10
fray (quarrel)	Th 01	frog	An 10	furlough	Th 05
freak (monster)	Th 12	frolic	Ps 05	furnace	Hs 05
free market	Mn 04	front bumper	Au 01	furnace	Th 05
free will	Ps 01	front door	Hs 01	furnishings	Hs 02
free-thinker	Oc 11	front grill	Au 01	furniture	Hs 02
freebie	Th 11	front line	Pl 01	furniture	Th 02
freedom	Ho 11	frontier	Pl 09	furniture, heavy	Th 02
freedom	Ps 11	frost	Th 08	furniture maker	Oc 02
freedom	Th 11	frostbite	Af 08	furniture rental	In 11
freedom, concept of	Th 11	frown	Bd 10	furniture/home furnishings	In 07
freedom, gaining of	Th 12	frozen food	Th 10		
freedom of action	Ps 01	frozen place	Pl 08		

243

furrow	Th 04	fuse box, the	Hs 11	future, the	Ho 02
fury	Th 07	fusion (uniting)	Th 11	future plans	Th 09
fuse	Th 04	fusion, nuclear	Th 11	futuristic programs	Th 11
fuse box	Pl 11	futility	Ps 04		

G

gad-fly	Oc 11	gap (interval)	Th 10	gaudiness	Th 05
gadget	Th 11	gap (opening)	Pl 09	gauge (evaluation)	Th 02
gaff	Th 12	gap (pass)	Pl 09	gauge (meter)	Th 06
Gaia	My 02	garage	Hs 06	gauntlet (challenge)	Th 01
gaiety	Th 05	garage	Pl 06	gauntlet (glove)	Th 03
gain (increase)	Th 09	garage workshop	Pl 06	gauze	Th 12
gain (winnings)	Th 05	garb	Th 06	gavel	Th 01
gain due to death	Th 08	garbage	Th 08	gaze	Th 01
gain from speculation	Mn 05	garbage can	Th 11	gazebo	Hs 05
gaining an office	Mn 10	garbage collector	Oc 08	gear (cog)	Th 06
gaining publicity	Th 09	garbage disposal	In 08	gear (material)	Th 06
gains through science	Th 02	garbage disposal	Th 08	gelatin	Th 11
gait (manner of walking)	Ps 01	garbage dump	Pl 08	Gemini (twins)	My 03
galaxy (stellar)	Th 11	garden	Pl 04	gems	Ho 02
gale (storm)	Th 07	garden (fertile area)	Th 04	gems	Th 02
gall bladder	Bd 06	garden, flower	Hs 02	gender of the fetus	Th 05
gall stone	Af 07	garden, vegetable	Hs 04	gene	Th 04
galleries, art	Pl 07	garden furniture	Th 05	genealogist	Oc 04
galley	Sh 06	gardener	Oc 04	genealogy	Th 04
gallows	Pl 08	gardening	Th 04	general	Oc 10
galoshes	Th 12	gardening services	In 02	general merchandise chains	In 04
gambit	Th 03	gargling	Th 03		
fambling	In 05	garland	Th 02	general public	Th 04
gambling	Ho 05	garment	Th 06	general trade	Mn 03
gambling	Mn 05	garnish	Th 05	general well-being	Ps 01
gambling	Th 05	garter	Th 10	generalist	Oc 04
gambling, illicit	Th 12	gas can	Th 04	generality	Th 04
gambling casino	Pl 05	gas products (compressed air)	In 10	generalization	Th 04
gambling equipment	Th 05			generation	Th 04
game preserve	Th 06	gas(es)	Th 03	generator	Au 11
game room	Hs 05	gases, pressurized	Th 11	generator	Sh 11
games	Th 05	gases in the blood	Bd 11	generosity	Ps 05
games of chance	Ho 05	gasket	Th 03	generosity	Th 05
games of chance	Th 05	gasoline	Th 09	genesis	Th 05
faming	In 05	gasoline station	Pl 09	genetics	Th 04
gangrene	Af 10	gate (entryway)	Pl 01	geniality	Th 05
gangster	Oc 08	gathering (assembly)	Th 11	genital love	Th 08
gangway	Pl 01	gathering experiences	Ps 09	genitals	Bd 08
gangway	Sh 01	gathering information	Ps 06	genius	Oc 10
gap (disparity)	Th 09	gathering of facts	Th 03	genre (grouping)	Th 06

gentility	Th 02	give-away (donation)	Th 11	goal (objective)	Th 10
gentleman	Oc 07	giving	Th 08	goal (score)	Th 10
gentleness	Th 02	giving love	Th 05	goals	Ho 10
gentry	Oc 10	glacier	Th 08	goals, national	Mn 11
genuineness	Th 09	gladiator	Oc 01	goat	An 10
geography of the country	Mn 04	gladness	Th 05	goblin	Th 08
		glamour	Th 05	god	Th 09
geologist	Oc 10	glance	Th 01	godchild	Re 11
geology	Th 10	glands	Bd 04	godfather	Re 09
geomancy	Th 09	glandular system (in general)	Bd 04	godmother	Re 03
geometry	Th 07			gods or goddesses	Oc 11
geopolitics	Mn 11	glare (disapproving look)	Th 07	going abroad	Th 09
germicides	Th 08	glare (reflection)	Th 07	goiter	Af 02
germination	Th 05	glass (clear)	Th 07	gold	Co 05
germs	Th 04	glass, colored or stained	Th 07	gold	Ge 05
gestation	Th 05	glass eye	Th 07	gold/silver mining	In 05
gesture (indication)	Th 01	glasses, drinking	Th 04	golden colors	Co 05
gesture (movement)	Th 03	glaucoma	Af 12	goldsmith	Oc 05
get-togethers with friends	Th 11	gleam (inkling)	Th 05	golf	Th 05
getting even	Ps 07	gleam (ray)	Th 05	golf course	Pl 05
getting high	Th 05	glee	Th 05	golf course design	In 09
geyser	Th 09	glibness	Th 03	golf course maintenance	In 05
ghetto	Pl 12	glimmer	Th 05	good (benefit)	Th 09
ghost (spirit)	Th 08	glimpse	Th 01	good (virtue)	Th 10
ghost town	Pl 12	glitter (luster)	Th 05	good fortune	Th 05
ghost writer	Oc 12	global travelers	Th 09	good life, the	Th 05
giant	Oc 10	gloom	Th 10	good luck	Th 05
gibberish	Th 12	glorification	Th 05	good taste	Th 07
gibe (taunt)	Th 03	glory (honor earned)	Th 10	good will	Th 10
giddiness (frivolity)	Th 05	glory (splendor)	Th 05	good-byes	Th 04
gift (legacy)	Th 08	glory (worship)	Th 05	goodness	Ps 02
gift (present)	Th 08	gloss (explanation)	Th 03	goods (merchandise)	Th 04
gift (talent)	Th 05	gloss (finish)	Th 05	goods (possessions)	Th 02
gift shop	Pl 08	glossary	Th 06	goods, demand for	Mn 04
gifts	Ho 08	glove compartment	Au 06	goods on a shelf	Th 06
gifts you give	Th 02	gloves	Th 03	goof-off	Oc 05
gifts you receive	Th 08	glow	Th 05	goose	An 06
giggles	Th 05	glucose	Th 02	gorge	Pl 08
gilt	Th 05	glue	Th 04	Gorgons (monsters)	My 08
gimmick	Th 12	glut (oversupply)	Th 09	goshenite	Ge 07
giraffe	An 10	glutton	Oc 02	gospel (biblical)	Th 09
girdle (corset)	Th 04	gluttony	Th 02	gospel (ultimate truth)	Th 09
girl	Oc 03	glyph	Th 09	gossip	Th 03
girl friend	Oc 05	gnat	An 01	gossiper	Oc 03
girth	Th 02	gnome	Oc 03	gouge (nick)	Th 04
gist	Th 02	go (ambition)	Th 05	gourd	Th 04
give (flexibility)	Th 03	go (attempt)	Th 01	gourmet	Oc 02
give and take relationships	Th 07	go-carts	Th 11	gout	Af 10
		goad (stimulus)	Th 11	governess	Oc 06

governing authority	Mn 10	graphology	Th 01	grip (holding place)	Th 03
government	Ho 10	grappling hook	Th 04	grip (suitcase)	Th 06
government, the	Mn 10	grasp (comprehension)	Ps 09	gripe (grievance)	Th 11
government agencies	Mn 10	grasp (embrace)	Th 04	grit (dirt)	Th 12
government building	Pl 12	grasp (scope or reach)	Th 04	grit (guts)	Th 01
government officials	Mn 10	grass	Th 02	grizzly bear	An 01
government representative	Oc 05	grate (covering)	Th 04	grocer	Oc 06
		grate (fireplace)	Th 05	grocery	In 04
government worker	Oc 06	gratefulness	Ps 05	grocery clerk	Oc 09
governmental authority	Mn 10	gratification	Ps 08	grocery stores	Pl 06
		gratification	Th 08	groin area	Bd 08
governmental interference	Mn 11	gratitude	Ho 02	groom (for animals)	Oc 09
		gratitude	Ps 02	groom (in a wedding)	Oc 07
governor	Au 10	gratitude	Th 02	groove (furrow)	Th 03
governor	Oc 10	gratuity	Th 08	groove (habit)	Th 04
gown	Th 06	grave (serious) matters	Th 10	gross (total)	Th 10
grace (holiness)	Th 09	grave, one's	Th 04	gross motor control	Bd 05
grace (mercy)	Th 12	grave digger	Oc 04	grossular	Ge 03
grace (skill)	Th 06	gravel	Th 10	grotto	Pl 08
grace (suppleness)	Th 03	graveyard	Pl 08	grouch	Oc 08
graciousness	Ps 07	gravitation	Th 07	ground, irregular	Pl 04
graduate	Oc 10	gravity (attraction)	Th 07	ground, the	Ho 04
graduation	Th 09	gravity (seriousness)	Th 10	ground, the	Th 04
graft (corruption)	Th 08	gray	Co 10	grounding	Th 10
graft (shoot)	Th 05	grease (bribe)	Th 08	groundwork (preparation)	Th 10
grain (seed)	Th 06	grease (lard)	Th 12		
grain (small particle)	Th 04	grease (lubricant)	Th 09	group (assemblage)	Th 11
grain elevator	Pl 06	great cattle	An 04	group (classification)	Th 06
grammar	Th 06	great grandchildren	Re 01	group, fraternal	Th 11
granary	Mn 06	great mansions or estates	Pl 05	group acting as an entity	Th 01
granary	Pl 06	great person	Oc 10	group activities	Th 11
grand losses	Th 08	greatness	Th 10	group connections	Th 11
grandchildren	Re 09	greed (selfishness)	Ps 04	group gatherings	Th 11
grandeur	Th 05	green	Co 07	group interests	Th 11
grandfather (maternal)	Re 01	green (common area)	Pl 04	group memory	Ho 11
grandfather (paternal)	Re 07	green eyeshade	Th 06	group memory	Th 11
grandiosity	Th 05	greenish blue	Co 02	grouping together	Th 11
grandmother (maternal)	Re 01	greetings	Th 01	groups	Ho 11
grandmother (paternal)	Re 07	grenade	Th 01	groups, use of	Ps 11
grandparent (in general)	Re 07	grief (misery)	Th 12	grove (thicket)	Pl 02
grandstand	Pl 05	grief, periods of	Th 12	growing	Th 04
granite	Ge 10	grievance (complaint)	Th 11	growth (progress)	Th 10
grant (allotment)	Th 02	grievance (injustice)	Th 07	growth (tumor)	Th 10
grant (bequest)	Th 08	Griffin	My 08	grudge	Th 08
graph	Th 06	grime (dirt)	Th 12	grumbling	Th 11
graphic artist	Oc 07	grinding	Th 11	Grus (crane)	My 06
graphic designers	In 07	grinding machine	Th 11	guarantee (pledge)	Th 08
graphite	Ge 10	grindstone	Th 11	guarantee (warranty)	Th 08
graphologist	Oc 01	grip (grasp)	Th 04	guard	Oc 08

guardian (legal custodian)	Re 10	guilt	Ps 06	gutter (bowling)	Th 03
guardian (protector)	Oc 10	guilty party	Oc 07	gutter (roadway)	Th 04
guess (estimate)	Th 09	guise (attire)	Th 06	gutter (roof)	Hs 03
guest (boarder)	Th 06	gulf (chasm)	Th 08	gymnasium	Pl 05
guest (visitor)	Th 03	gully (ditch)	Th 08	gynecologist	Oc 07
guidance	Ps 09	gun	Th 01	gynecology	Th 07
guidance	Th 09	gunpowder	Th 01	gyp (scam)	Th 03
guide (advisor)	Oc 11	gunshot	Th 01	gyp (swindler)	Oc 03
guide (instructions)	Th 03	gunshot wounds	Af 01	gypsum	Ge 02
guide (scout)	Oc 09	guru	Oc 10	gypsy	Oc 09
guidelines	Th 06	gust of wind	Th 03	gyrations	Th 03
guile	Ps 03	gusto	Th 05	gyroscope	Th 07
		guts (audacity)	Th 01		

H

haberdasher	Oc 01	halls (corridors)	Hs 03	handicraft work	Th 06
habit (dress)	Th 06	halls (corridors)	Pl 03	handicrafts	Th 06
habit (practice)	Th 04	hallucination	Th 12	handiwork	Th 06
habitat	Pl 04	hallucinogen	Th 12	handkerchief	Th 06
habitation	Th 04	hallway	Hs 03	handle (hold)	Th 04
habits, personal	Ps 01	hallway	Pl 03	handling (usage)	Th 04
hack (taxi)	Th 03	halo (aurora)	Th 05	handout (circular)	Th 03
hack (writer)	Oc 03	halo (magnificence)	Th 05	handout (dole)	Th 12
Hades	My 08	halt (cessation)	Th 10	hands	Bd 03
hades	Pl 08	halter (clothing)	Th 06	handshake (agreement rite)	Th 07
haggling	Th 03	halter (noose)	Th 08		
hail (frozen rain)	Th 08	halter (rope)	Th 01	handshake (greeting)	Th 01
hail (shout)	Th 01	ham radio	Th 11	handwriting	Th 01
hair	Bd 10	hamlet	Pl 04	handwriting expert	Oc 01
hair care services	In 07	hammer	Th 06	hang (droop)	Th 02
hair lip	Af 01	hammock	Th 02	hang (gist)	Th 03
hair on body	Bd 10	hamper (basket)	Th 06	hang glider	Th 09
hair on head	Bd 01	hamper, laundry	Hs 06	hang out	Pl 05
hair transplants	Bd 08	hamster	An 06	hang up	Th 12
hairbreadth	Th 01	hand fractures or breaks	Af 03	hanger (aircraft)	Pl 11
hairdo	Th 02	hand hold	Th 04	hanger (clothes)	Th 06
hairdresser	Oc 07	hand off	Th 12	hanging	Th 09
half (portion)	Th 04	hand-bill	Th 03	hangout	Pl 05
half-truth	Th 07	hand-me-down	Th 12	hangover	Th 12
half-wit	Oc 03	handbag	Th 02	hankering (longing)	Th 11
halftone (image)	Th 03	handbook	Th 03	happening (occurrence)	Th 01
halides (salts)	Ge 11	handcuffs	Th 10	happenstance	Th 07
halitosis	Af 04	handful (small number)	Th 04	happiness	Ps 05
hallmark (distinguishing trait)	Th 01	handgun	Th 01	happy hour	Th 05
		handicap (defect)	Th 12	harassment	Ps 08
hallmark (mark of origin)	Th 04	handicap (odds)	Th 09	harassment	Th 08

harbinger	Oc 01	head (climax)	Th 04	heart sac	Bd 05
harbor (haven)	Pl 12	head (first position)	Th 10	heart specialist	Oc 05
harbor (port)	Pl 04	head (in front)	Th 01	heartburn	Af 05
harboring (holding in)	Ps 04	head (leader)	Oc 10	hearth, the	Hs 05
hard back book	Th 03	head (source)	Th 01	heat (passion)	Th 05
hard core (diehard)	Oc 11	head (upper end)	Th 10	heat (warmth)	Th 05
hard hat	Th 04	head injury	Af 01	heat exchanger	Th 09
hard work	Th 06	head of an organization	Mn 10	heat exhaustion	Af 01
hardening	Th 01	head of government	Mn 10	heat rash	Af 01
hardness	Th 10	headache	Af 01	heated gases	Th 07
hardship	Th 10	headlights	Au 05	heathen (barbarian)	Oc 08
hardware	Th 06	healer	Oc 06	heating plant	Sh 05
hardware and Tools	In 06	healing	Ho 06	heating system, the	Hs 05
hardware dealer	Oc 04	healing	Mn 06	heaven (paradise)	Pl 10
hare	An 03	healing	Th 06	heaven (the sky)	Th 09
harem	Pl 04	healing after an	Th 09	heaviness	Th 10
harlequin	Oc 03	operation		heavy duty trucks	In 02
harlot	Oc 08	healing crisis	Th 08	heavy industry	Mn 11
harm (injury)	Th 08	healing measures	Th 06	heavy object	Th 02
harm (wickedness)	Th 08	health	Ps 01	hedgerow	Pl 02
harmonica	Th 02	health and fitness	In 01	height	Th 10
harmony	Ho 07	health (in general)	Bd 01	heights	Pl 10
harmony	Ps 07	health (in general)	Ho 01	heir	Oc 08
harness	Th 04	health (problems	Th 06	heir apparent	Oc 08
harp	Th 02	with illness)		heirloom	Th 04
harshness	Ps 01	health attitudes	Ps 06	helicopter	Th 11
harvest	Th 06	health care (diversified)	In 06	heliodor	Ge 07
harvester	Oc 06	health food	Th 06	Helios (sun)	My 05
haste	Th 01	health improvement	Th 06	helium	Th 11
hat	Th 01	health insurance	Th 08	hell	Pl 08
hatchet	Th 01	health maintenance	Th 06	helm	Sh 03
hatchling	An 05	health of friends	Th 04	helmet	Th 04
hate (detest)	Ps 08	health official	Oc 06	helpful biological insect	An 02
hate (disgust)	Ps 07	healthcare HMOs	In 06	help when in need	Th 12
haunches	Bd 07	healthcare information	In 08	helpless feelings	Ps 06
haunt	Pl 05	heap (accumulation)	Th 04	hematoma	Af 05
haven	Pl 12	hearing	Bd 01	hemisphere	Th 04
having	Th 02	hearing (conference)	Th 11	hemoglobin	Bd 11
havoc	Th 08	hearing aid	Th 10	hemorrhage	Af 01
hawk	An 08	hearing problem	Af 02	hemorrhoids	Af 08
hawser	Sh 04	hearsay (rumor)	Th 03	hen	An 04
hay	Th 06	hearse	Th 10	hepatitis	Af 07
hay fever	Af 06	heart (in general)	Bd 05	Hephaistos (the	My 06
haystack	Pl 06	heart afflictions	Af 04	wage earner)	
hazard (danger)	Th 01	heart condition, present	Th 05	Hera (the loyal friend)	My 04
hazards from	Th 08	heart disease	Af 04	heraldry	Th 04
natural phenomena		heart irregularities	Af 03	herbicide	Th 08
haze (mist)	Th 12	heart palpitations	Af 08	herbs (in general)	Th 02
head	Bd 01	heart problems	Af 04	Hercules (the warrior)	My 01

herd	Th 04	hierarchy (ranking)	Th 06	hobble	Th 10
herding	Th 04	hieroglyph	Th 03	hobby	Ho 05
here	Ho 01	high blood pressure	Af 01	hobby	Th 05
hereditary traits	Th 04	high court	Pl 09	hobby room	Hs 06
heredity	Th 04	high office	Pl 10	hobo	Oc 11
heresy	Th 08	high places	Pl 10	hock (debt)	Th 08
heretic	Oc 08	high society	Mn 05	hocus-pocus	Th 03
heritage	Th 04	high stakes	Th 01	hoe down	Th 05
Hermes (the swift traveler)	My 03	high tech	In 11	hog	An 04
		higher education	Ho 09	hoist	Sh 02
hermit	Oc 10	higher education	Th 09	hokum (evasion)	Th 12
hernia	Af 05	higher studies	Th 09	hold (delay)	Th 10
hero	Oc 05	higher-ups	Oc 10	hold (grasp)	Th 04
heroin	Th 12	highlands	Pl 09	hold (storage place)	Pl 06
heroine	Oc 05	highlights	Th 05	hold out	Oc 11
heron	An 06	highway	Pl 03	hold over (postponement)	Th 10
hesitancy	Ps 10	hiking	Th 09	hold up (robbery)	Th 07
hesitation	Th 10	hill	Pl 10	holding (property)	Th 04
Hestia (Vesta, the homemaker)	My 06	hindering factors	Th 10	holding (ruling of a court)	Th 04
		hindrance	Th 10	hole (cave)	Pl 04
heuristics	Th 03	hindsight	Ps 09	hole (flaw)	Th 12
hex	Th 12	hinge	Th 03	hole (golf)	Th 04
hi-fi	Th 02	hint	Th 09	hole (in a fix)	Th 12
hibernation	Th 12	hip displacia	Af 09	hole (opening)	Th 04
hiccups	Bd 06	hippie	Oc 11	holiday (vacation)	Th 05
hidden (lost) thing	Th 04	hippopotamus	An 11	hollowness	Th 01
hidden (secret) matters	Ho 12	hips	Bd 09	holocaust	Th 08
hidden (secret) matters	Th 12	hired hand	Oc 06	hologram	Th 11
hidden (secret) problem	Th 12	hireling	Oc 06	holy object	Th 09
hidden (secret) relationship	Th 12	hiring of employees	Mn 06	holy person	Oc 09
		hissing sounds	Th 08	home	Ho 04
hidden, sense of what is	Ps 12	histogram	Th 06	home	Pl 04
hidden affair	Th 12	historian	Oc 04	home	Th 04
hidden defect	Th 12	historical perspective	Mn 04	home, mobile	Th 06
hidden factors in experience	Th 12	history	Mn 04	home, quality of	Ps 04
		hit (bite)	Th 04	home appliances	In 06
hidden fear	Ps 12	hit (blow)	Th 01	hHome building	In 12
hidden ills	Mn 12	hit (contact)	Th 01	home environment	Th 04
hidden places	Pl 12	hit (request)	Th 03	home for the aged	Pl 12
hidden side of life	Ho 12	hit (winner)	Th 10	home front, the	Mn 01
hidden talents	Th 08	hit list	Th 06	home inspection	In 08
hidden treasure, regained	Th 04	hit upon (happen on)	Th 05	home life	Th 04
hidden vices	Th 12	hitch (enlistment)	Th 06	home maker	Oc 04
hiddenite	Ge 10	hitch (fasten)	Th 04	home of a neighbor	Th 06
hide (animal skin)	Th 10	hitch (knot)	Th 10	home of a sibling	Th 06
hideousness	Th 08	hitch (marriage)	Th 07	home port	Pl 04
hiding	Th 12	hitch (stoppage)	Th 10	home range	Pl 04
hiding place	Pl 12	hoarding	Th 04	Home Remodeling	In 08
hiding place of thieves	Th 04	hoax	Th 12	home repair at relatives	Th 11

home repair work	Th 09	horse racing	Th 09	houseboat	Th 04
home room	Pl 04	horse track	Pl 09	Household Appliances	In 06
home rule	Th 11	horse trainer	Oc 09	household chores	Th 06
home stretch	Pl 04	horsepower	Th 05	household furnishings	In 07
home team	Th 01	horticulture	Th 02	household help	Oc 06
homeless, the	Oc 12	hose (socks)	Th 11	household products	In 06
homeliness	Bd 08	hose (watering tool)	Th 03	housewares	In 06
homeopathy	Th 02	hoses	Au 03	housework	Th 06
homesickness	Af 04	hosiery	Th 11	housing	In 04
homespun goods	Th 06	hospice	Pl 12	housing	Mn 04
homespun virtues	Ps 04	hospital	Pl 12	housing	Th 04
homestead	Pl 04	hospital administrator	Oc 09	how others see you	Th 01
homestretch	Pl 04	hospital care	Th 12	how the marriage will end	Th 10
hometown	Pl 04	hospital care, national	Mn 12	hub (main place)	Pl 05
homework (piecework for pay)	Th 06	hospital management	In 04	huckster	Oc 03
		hospital records	Th 05	hue	Th 07
homework (school assignment)	Th 06	hospital stay	Th 12	hugs and kisses	Th 05
		hospitality	Ps 07	hull	Sh 10
homonym	Th 03	hospitalization	Ho 12	hull (husk)	Th 04
honesty	Th 09	hospitalization	Th 12	human nature	Ps 04
honey	Th 02	host	Oc 07	humanitarian	Oc 11
honey color	Co 05	hostage	Oc 07	humanitarian activities	Th 11
honeymoon	Th 07	hostess	Oc 07	humanitarian ideals	Th 11
honor (earned)	Th 10	hostility	Ps 07	humanitarianism	Th 11
honor (honesty)	Ps 10	hot air	Th 07	humanity (the masses)	Th 04
honor (privilege)	Th 10	hot things	Th 01	humanity, attitude toward	Ho 11
honor (respect given)	Th 10	hot tub	Th 05		
honor (unearned)	Th 05	hot water	Th 08	humanity, attitude towards	Ps 11
honorable mention	Th 05	hot water heater	Hs 04		
honoraria	Th 08	hotel	Mn 04	humid air	Th 04
hood (blinder)	Th 02	hotel	Pl 04	humidity	Th 04
hood (covering)	Th 04	hotel stay at a distance	Th 02	humiliation	Th 08
hood (crest)	Th 04	hotel worker	Oc 04	humility	Ps 06
hoodlum	Oc 07	hotel/motel Services	In 06	humming sounds	Th 02
hook	Th 10	hothouse	Pl 02	humor	Ps 05
hopelessness	Ps 06	hound	An 06	humor	Th 05
hopes	Ho 11	house	Ho 04	hunger	Th 04
hopes	Ps 11	house	Th 04	hunger after	Th 08
hopes	Th 11	house for sale	Th 04	hunter	Oc 09
horary astrology	Th 01	house hunting	Th 12	hunting	Th 09
horizontal direction	Th 07	house of detention	Th 12	hurricane	Th 11
hormones	Bd 04	house of parliament	Mn 11	hurt feelings	Af 04
horn	Au 01	house of representatives	Mn 11	husband	Re 07
horn (antler)	Th 01	house repair work	Th 09	husbandry	Oc 06
horologium (water clock)	My 10	house servant	Oc 06	husk	Th 04
horoscope	Th 11	house you live in or own	Pl 04	hussy	Oc 08
horrible thoughts	Th 01	house you plan to buy	Th 04	hustler	Oc 03
horror	Th 08	house you plan to move to	Th 07	hut	Pl 04
horse	An 09				

hyacinth	Ge 08	snake)		Hyperion	My 05
Hyades	My 12	hyena	An 12	hypersensitivity	Th 04
Hydra (water snake)	My 08	hygiene	Ho 06	hypnotism	Th 08
hydraulic machinery	Th 11	hygiene	Th 06	hypnotist	Oc 08
hydraulic system	Au 11	hygienic practices	Ps 06	hypochondriac	Oc 06
hydraulics	Th 11	hygienic practices	Th 06	hypodermics	Th 09
hydrocarbons	Th 09	hygienist	Oc 06	hypoglycemia	Af 06
hydroelectric power	Th 05	hymn	Th 10	hypothesis	Th 09
hydrogen	Th 05	hymnal	Th 09	hysteria	Af 08
Hydrus (little water	My 08	hyperactivity	Th 04		

I

ice	Th 08	illegal alien	Oc 04	imitation	Th 03
ice berg	Th 08	illegibility	Th 12	imitation (mimicry)	Th 03
ice flow	Th 08	illegitimacy	Th 11	imitation stone	Ge 12
icebreaker (comment)	Th 03	illegitimate children	Re 11	imitative behavior	Ps 03
icebreaker (vessel)	Sh 04	illiteracy	Th 02	immature person	Oc 02
idea (hint)	Th 03	illness	Ho 06	immaturity	Th 02
idea (mind picture)	Th 03	illness (in general)	Th 06	immediate future	Th 02
idea (suggestion)	Th 09	illness, acute	Th 06	immediate outcome	Th 07
ideal (hero)	Oc 10	illness, chronic	Th 12	of events	
ideal (objective)	Th 10	illness, coping with	Ps 12	immensity	Th 10
idealism	Ps 09	illness of aunts or uncles	Th 05	immersion (study)	Th 08
ideals	Ps 09	illness of father	Th 09	immersion (wetness)	Th 04
ideals	Th 09	illness of friend	Th 04	immigration	Th 09
ideals, national	Mn 10	illness of mother	Th 03	Immigration Services	In 09
identification	Ps 01	illness of partner	Th 12	immobility	Th 04
identification	Th 01	illness of pet	Th 11	immodesty	Th 11
identifying with	Ps 04	illogical solution	Th 12	immoral things	Th 08
identity	Ho 01	illogical solutions	Ho 12	immorality	Ps 08
identity	Ps 01	illumination	Th 07	immorality	Th 08
identity, the country's	Mn 01	(clarification)		immortality	Th 10
identity crisis	Th 01	illumination (lighting)	Th 05	immune system	Bd 04
ideology	Th 04	illusion	Th 12	immunity	Th 09
idiom	Th 03	illusionist	Oc 12	imp	Oc 03
idiosyncrasy (peculiarity)	Ps 01	illustration	Th 03	impact	Th 01
idiot	Oc 03	illustrator	Oc 03	impairment	Th 12
idleness	Th 02	image (idol)	Th 09	impartiality	Th 07
idol (hero)	Th 05	image (reflection)	Th 07	impasse	Th 07
idol (icon)	Th 09	image (replica)	Th 03	impatience	Ps 01
idolatry	Th 09	image (representation)	Th 03	impediment	Th 10
ignition system	Au 01	image of another, one's	Ps 07	impenetrable	Th 08
ignominy (humiliation)	Th 08	image you give out, the	Ps 01	imperfection (flaw)	Th 06
ignorance (illiteracy)	Th 02	imagination	Th 05	imperialism	Mn 05
ignorance (unfamiliarity)	Th 02	imaginative ability	Th 05	impersonal, sense of the	Ps 11
illegal acts	Th 08	imaging/photography	In 12	impersonal reactions	Ho 11

impersonation	Th 03	impurity	Th 08	income, tax return on	Th 08
impersonator	Oc 03	inability to fee complete	Ps 04	income from business or career	Th 11
impertinence	Th 03	inaccessibility	Th 09		
imperviousness	Th 08	inaccuracy	Th 09	income from others	Th 08
impetigo	Af 10	inaction	Th 02	income from real estate	Th 05
impetus	Th 01	inadequacy, feelings of	Ps 06	income property	Th 06
impiety	Th 03	inanity (emptiness)	Th 07	income supplement	Th 03
implement	Th 06	inappropriate behavior	Ps 07	income taxes	Th 08
implication	Th 03	inappropriate things	Th 08	incomparability	Th 11
impoliteness	Th 07	inarticulateness	Th 03	incompatibility	Th 09
import-export business	Mn 09	inattention	Th 11	incompetence	Ho 10
importance	Ho 10	inauguration	Th 01	incompetence	Ps 10
importance	Ps 10	inauspicious portent	Th 04	incompleteness	Th 09
important people	Th 10	inborn trait	Ps 04	incomprehensible, the	Th 09
importer, exporter	Oc 09	inbound direction	Th 05	incongruity	Th 08
imports	Mn 09	inbreeding	Th 04	inconsiderateness	Th 07
imposing limitations	Ps 12	incandescence	Th 05	inconsistency	Th 04
imposing one's will	Ps 05	incantation	Th 09	inconstancy	Th 04
imposition	Th 07	incapacity	Th 04	inconvenience	Th 10
impossibility	Th 10	incarceration	Th 12	increase	Th 09
impostor	Oc 03	incarnations	Th 04	incredibility	Th 09
impotence	Th 08	incendiary material	Th 01	increment (addition)	Th 05
impractical idea	Th 12	incense	Th 02	increment (enlargement)	Th 09
impregnation	Th 02	incentive	Th 11	increment (variation)	Th 04
impresario (promoter)	Oc 05	incentives received or given	Ps 11	incubator	Th 05
impression (effect)	Th 01			incurable illness	Th 12
impression (feeling)	Th 04	incest	Th 10	incursion (assault)	Th 08
impression (imprint)	Th 01	incident (event)	Th 01	incursion (invasion)	Th 08
impression (mark)	Th 01	incidental (minor item)	Th 04	indebtedness	Th 10
impression one makes	Ps 01	incineration	Th 01	indecency	Th 08
impressions from others	Th 07	incinerator	Pl 01	indecision	Ps 07
		incision	Th 08	indefiniteness	Th 07
impressions made on others	Th 01	inclemency (stormy)	Th 07	indelibility	Th 10
		inclinations	Ho 11	indemnity for damage suffered	Th 09
imprint (mark)	Th 01	inclinations	Ps 11		
imprisonment	Ho 12	incline	Th 10	indentation	Th 04
imprisonment	Th 12	including (containing)	Th 04	indentation (notch)	Th 04
improbability	Th 12	including (embracing)	Th 11	independence	Ps 11
impromptu action	Th 03	including (involving)	Th 07	independence	Th 11
improper action	Th 07	including others	Ps 07	index	Th 06
impropriety (incorrect action)	Th 07	including self	Ps 01	indication (marker)	Th 01
		inclusion (containment)	Ps 04	indication (signal)	Th 01
improvement	Th 10	incognito	Th 12	indicator	Th 01
improvisation	Ps 03	income	Ho 02	indicolite	Ge 11
impudence	Th 01	income	Th 02	indifference	Ps 11
impulse (sudden action)	Th 01	income, ability to add to	Th 02	indigestion	Af 04
impulse (urge)	Th 01	income, efforts to increase	Th 02	indignation	Th 08
impulsiveness	Th 01			indigo	Co 11
impunity	Th 12	income, source of	Th 02	indiscretion	Th 08

indispensability	Th 04	infinity	Th 09	initiative	Th 01
individuality	Ps 01	infirmary	Pl 12	injection	Th 08
individualization	Ps 04	infirmity	Af 06	injunction	Th 07
indivisibility	Th 04	inflammability	Th 02	injuries (in general)	Af 08
indoctrination	Th 01	inflammation	Af 05	injuries, the likelihood of	Ho 08
indolence	Th 02	inflation	Mn 09		
inducement	Th 11	inflation	Th 09	injury (harm)	Th 08
inductance	Th 12	inflexibility	Th 02	injury (self-inflicted)	Af 01
indulgence	Th 02	inflow	Th 01	injustice	Th 07
Indus (the indian)	My 09	influence (sway)	Th 10	inn	Pl 06
industrial equipment manufacturers	In 06	influence, a dominating	Th 10	inner development	Th 09
		influence, extent of	Ps 10	inner things	Th 04
industrial services	In 06	influential person	Th 10	inner unfolding	Ho 09
industrialist	Oc 10	influx	Th 01	inner unfolding	Ps 09
industriousness	Th 06	informal dining area	Hs 04	innkeeper	Oc 06
industry (business)	Th 10	informal notices	Th 11	innocence	Th 02
industry (zeal)	Th 09	informal notification	Th 09	innovation	Th 11
ineffectual actions	Th 12	informality	Th 09	innuendo	Th 09
ineligibility	Th 07	information	Th 03	inoculation	Th 01
ineptness	Th 12	information analyst	Oc 03	inquest	Th 08
inequality	Th 07	information booth	Pl 03	inquiry	Th 03
inequitable things	Th 07	information clerk	Oc 03	inquisition(s)	Th 08
inequity	Th 07	information processor	Oc 06	inquisitiveness	Ho 03
inertia	Th 02	information related questions	Ho 03	inquisitiveness	Th 03
inevitability	Ho 12			insanity	Af 12
inevitability	Th 12	information services	Or 06	insatiability	Th 08
inexperience	Th 03	information specialist	Oc 03	inscrutability	Th 12
inexplicable things	Th 08	informer	Oc 12	insect	An 08
infallibility	Ps 09	infrared	Co 01	insect bite	Af 01
infallibility	Th 09	infringement	Th 01	insecurity	Ps 04
infamy	Th 10	ingenuity	Th 11	insert	Th 03
infancy	Th 05	ingratitude	Th 01	insertion	Th 01
infantry	Th 06	ingredient	Th 04	insides (of anything)	Th 10
infants	Oc 05	inhabitant	Mn 04	insight	Th 09
infatuation	Th 05	inhabitant	Oc 04	insignia	Th 04
infection	Af 01	inhalation	Th 03	insignificance	Th 04
infectious substances	Th 01	inherent things	Th 04	insincerity	Th 08
inference	Th 03	inheritance	Ho 08	insinuation	Th 09
inferior	Oc 06	inheritance	Th 08	insistence	Ps 01
inferior things	Th 12	inheritance by descent	Th 04	insolubility	Th 10
inferiority, feelings of	Ps 06	inheritance from others	Th 08	insolvency	Th 08
inferiority complex	Ps 04	inherited money	Th 08	insomnia	Af 09
inferno	Th 01	inhibiting factors	Th 04	inspections	Th 06
infestation	Th 12	inhibitions	Ps 04	inspector	Oc 06
infidel	Oc 08	inhumanity	Th 08	inspiration	Th 09
infidelity	Th 08	iniquity	Th 07	instability	Ps 04
infinite, the	Ps 09	initiating (starting)	Th 01	instability	Sh 04
infinite, the	Th 09	initiation (rites)	Th 09	installation (induction)	Th 10
infinitesimal things	Th 04	initiation of projects	Th 01	installation (to set for use)	Th 06

installment	Th 04	insurance, unemployment	Mn 08	interloper	Oc 01
installment buying	Th 08			intermarriage	Th 07
installment plan buying	Th 08	insurance adjuster	Oc 08	intermediary	Oc 07
instant of time, an	Th 10	insurance agent	Oc 08	intermediate things	Th 07
instep	Bd 12	insurance broker	Oc 08	intermission	Th 10
instigator	Oc 01	insurance company	Mn 08	intern	Oc 06
instillation (imparting)	Th 05	insurance for fire or damage	Th 08	internal, that which is	Th 04
instinctive behavior	Ps 04			internal distributions systems	Mn 03
instincts	Ps 04	insurance matters	Ho 08		
institute	Pl 12	insurance policy	Th 08	internal opposition	Mn 07
institute of higher learning	Pl 09	insurance practices	Mn 08	internal revenue service, the	Mn 08
		insurance settlement	Th 08		
institution (establishment)	Pl 12	insurance worker	Oc 08	international disputes	Mn 07
		insurer	Oc 08	international friendships	Mn 11
institutionalization	Th 12	insurgence	Th 07	international orange	Co 03
institutions, attitudes toward	Ps 12	insurrection	Th 07	international relations	Mn 07
		intangible	Th 09	international trade	Mn 09
institutions, large public	Mn 12	integrating, ability to	Ps 12	interpersonal relationships	Th 07
		integration	Ps 10		
institutions of higher learning	Pl 09	integration (racial)	Th 11	interpretations	Th 09
		integrity	Ho 10	interpreter	Oc 09
instructing, ability for	Ps 05	integrity	Ps 10	interruption	Th 01
instruction	Th 05	intellect (common sense)	Th 10	interstate commerce	Mn 09
instruction books	Th 03	intellectual	Oc 03	interval	Th 10
instructions (directions)	Th 10	intellectual activity	Th 03	interviewer	Oc 03
instructions, a set of	Th 10	intellectual pursuits	Th 09	interviews	Th 03
instrument, gauge	Th 06	intelligence (intellect)	Ps 03	intestinal gas	Bd 06
instrument, legal	Th 07	intelligence (news)	Th 11	intestinal problems	Af 06
instrument, medical	Th 06	intemperance	Th 12	intestine	Bd 06
instrument, musical	Th 07	intense emotions	Ps 08	intimacy	Ps 08
instrument, tool	Th 06	intensification	Ho 08	intimate, that which is	Th 08
instrument, torture	Th 08	intensification	Ps 08	intolerance	Th 11
instrumentation	In 06	intensifying, needs for	Ps 08	intolerance of others	Ps 06
instrumentation	Au 06	intensity	Th 08	intoxicating substance	Th 12
instrumentation (devices)	Th 06	intentions	Ps 01	intoxication	Th 12
instrumentation (means)	Th 08	intentions	Th 01	intricate work	Th 06
insubordination	Th 07	interactions	Th 11	intrigue	Th 12
insufficiency	Th 10	interchange (junction)	Pl 03	intrinsic value	Th 02
insulation	Hs 04	intercourse	Th 08	introduction	Th 01
insulator, electrical	Th 02	interest rates	Mn 08	introspection	Ho 12
insulin	Bd 09	interests	Ps 01	introspection	Ps 12
insult	Th 01	interference	Th 07	introversion	Ps 04
insurance	Mn 08	interior, department of	Mn 04	introvert	Oc 04
insurance	Th 08	interior affairs	Mn 01	intruder	Oc 01
Insurance (diversified)	In 08	interior decorator	Oc 07	intrusion	Th 01
Insurance (health)	In 12	interior lamps	Au 11	intuition	Ps 09
Insurance (life)	In 08	interior part of the belly	Bd 08	intuition	Th 09
Insurance (property/casualty)	In 04	interior roominess	Au 04	inundation	Th 04
		interjections	Th 09	invader	Oc 08

invalid	Oc 12	investments, speculative	Th 05	irradiation	Th 05
invalidation	Th 10	invincibility	Ps 05	irrationality	Th 04
invasion	Th 08	invisibility	Th 12	irregularity (dishonesty)	Th 10
invention	Th 05	invitation	Th 07	irregularity (not conforming)	Th 11
inventor	Oc 11	invoice	Th 08		
inventor's workshop	Pl 11	involuntary actions	Th 04	irresponsibility	Ps 07
inventory	Mn 06	involuntary incarceration	Th 12	irrigation	Th 04
inversion (reversal)	Th 08	involuntary labor	Th 06	irritant	Th 01
investigation	Ho 08	involuntary labor ordered by law	Th 12	irritation	Th 01
investigation	Th 08			island	Th 04
investigative activities	Th 08	involvement (connecting with)	Ps 07	isolation	Th 12
investigator	Oc 08			itches	Af 10
investing	Th 02	involvement (entail)	Th 08	itemizing	Th 06
Investment (Banking)	In 05	involvement (take part in)	Th 07	items	Th 04
Investment (Brokerage)	In 05			items for practical comfort	Th 02
investment banker	Oc 02	IOU	Th 08		
investment(s)	Th 02	iridescence	Th 04	itinerancy	Th 09
investments, land	Th 04	iron	Ge 01	itinerant	Oc 09
investments, non-speculative	Ho 02	iron (eliminates wrinkles)	Th 01	itinerary	Th 06
		iron worker	Oc 01	IUD	Th 08
investments, non-speculative	Th 02	ironing board	Th 06	ivory	Ge 04
		irony	Th 08	Ixion (treachery)	My 09

J

jacinth	Ge 08	jester	Oc 03	have a job	
jack, the	Au 06	jests	Th 03	job sought if you have no job	Th 06
jack-knife	Th 01	Jesuit	Oc 09		
jacket (apparel)	Th 04	jet	Ge 06	job you work at	Th 06
jade	Ge 06	jet (airplane)	Th 11	jobbing	Th 06
jadite	Ge 06	Jewelry (Appraisal)	In 02	joblessness	Th 07
jail	Pl 12	jewelry (costume)	Th 03	jobs	Mn 10
jail	Th 12	jewelry (in general)	Th 02	jockey	Oc 09
jailer	Oc 12	Jewelry (Manufacture)	In 06	joining	Ho 11
jamboree	Th 05	Jewelry (Repair)	In 06	joining, willingness to	Ps 11
janitor	Oc 06	jewelry (sales)	In 10	joint	Bd 10
janitorial services	In 06	jewelry as adornment or vanity	Th 05	joint (dope)	Th 12
Janus	My 09			joint (linkage)	Th 03
jargon	Th 03	jewelry as wealth	Th 02	joint (tavern)	Pl 12
jargoon	Ge 08	jewels	Th 05	joint actions	Th 07
Jason (adventurer)	My 09	jingle (rhyme)	Th 03	joint activity	Th 07
jasper	Ge 09	jingle (telephone call)	Th 03	joint arrangements	Ho 07
jaundice	Af 07	jinx	Th 12	joint finances	Th 08
jealousy	Th 07	job, one's	Th 10	joint financing	Th 08
jeers	Th 03	job change	Th 09	joint problems	Af 10
jelly	Th 04	job opportunities	Th 06	joint savings	Th 08
jerky motions	Th 03	job sought if you	Th 11	joint undertakings	Th 07

joint ventures	Th 03	lawsuit		junk food	Th 11
jointly held property	Ho 08	judgment (discretion)	Ps 11	junk yard	Pl 08
joist	Hs 10	judgment (finding)	Th 04	Juno	My 04
joke	Th 03	judgment (opinion)	Th 09	Jupiter	My 09
joker	Oc 03	judicial decision	Th 04	jurisdiction	Th 10
journal	Th 03	judiciary, the	Mn 09	jurisprudence	Th 09
journalism	Th 03	judiciary, the	Th 09	jurist	Oc 09
journalist	Oc 03	judiciousness	Th 09	juror	Oc 09
journey, mother's	Th 12	juggler	Oc 03	jury	Th 09
journey, partner's	Th 03	juggling	Th 03	jury, deliberations of	Th 05
journey, sibling's	Th 11	juice	Th 04	jury as an executive body	Th 09
journey- father's	Th 06	juicy things	Th 04	jury as counseling body	Th 11
journeys, long	Mn 09	jumbles	Th 12	jury duty	Th 09
journeys, long	Th 09	jumping	Th 01	jury in a court of law	Th 09
journeys, short	Mn 03	junction (linkup)	Pl 03	jury member	Oc 09
journeys, short	Th 03	juncture (joining)	Th 03	justice	Ho 09
journeys by air	Th 11	juncture (moment)	Th 10	justice	Ps 09
journeys by water	Th 12	jungle	Pl 02	justice	Th 09
joust	Th 05	junior (grade)	Th 07	justice as practiced	Mn 09
joviality	Th 05	junior high school	Pl 03	justice of the peace	Th 09
joy	Th 05	junk	Th 08	justification	Th 08
jubilation	Th 05	junk bond	Th 08	juvenile	Oc 03
judge	Oc 09	junk collector	Oc 08	juvenile court	Th 09
judge's decision in a	Th 04	junk dealer	Oc 12	juvenile delinquency	Th 03

K

kaleidoscope	Th 03	keystone	Th 04	kink (cramp)	Af 10
kangaroo	An 09	keyword	Th 06	kink (twist)	Th 03
karma	Th 12	kicking	Th 01	kinship	Th 11
karmic responsibilities	Ps 12	kidnapper	Oc 12	kiss	Th 05
Kastor and Polydeukes	My 03	kidnapping	Ho 12	kitchen	Hs 06
keel	Sh 05	kidnapping	Th 12	kitchen	Pl 06
keenness	Th 03	kidney	Bd 07	kitchen appliance	Hs 06
keeper (custodian)	Oc 04	kidney disease	Af 07	kite	Th 05
keeping	Ps 04	kidney stone	Af 07	knee	Bd 10
keeping an inn	Th 05	kidney weakness	Af 07	knee injury	Af 10
keepsake	Th 04	killing	Th 08	kneecap	Bd 10
kennel	Pl 06	killjoy	Oc 10	kneeling	Th 06
kernel	Th 04	kiln	Th 05	knife	Th 01
kerosene	Th 09	kin	Re 03	knight	Oc 05
kettle	Th 04	kindling	Th 09	knitting	Th 06
key (for lock)	Th 01	kindness	Th 02	knocking	Th 01
key (information)	Th 09	kindred of the spouse	Th 09	knot	Th 04
key (solution hint)	Th 09	kinfolk	Re 03	knowledge, accumulating	Th 09
keyboard (input device)	Th 06	king	Oc 10	knowledge, searches for	Ps 09
keyboard (music)	Th 02	kingdom	Pl 04	known adversaries	Th 07

koala bear	An 07	kosher inspections	Th 06	kunzite	Ge 10
koan	Th 09	Kronos (saturn)	My 10		
kosher	Th 09	kundalini	Th 08		

L

lab	Pl 08	lady	Oc 02	lapse (discontinuance)	Th 08
lab technician	Oc 08	lagoon	Pl 04	lapse (slight error)	Th 12
label (brand name)	Th 01	lair	Pl 04	larceny	Th 07
label (descriptive phrase)	Th 01	lake	Pl 04	large animals	An 12
label (for commercial recordings)	Th 01	lamb	An 07	large animals	Ho 12
		lameness	Af 12	large institution	Th 12
label (name)	Th 01	lament	Th 12	large public meeting	Th 11
label (tag)	Th 01	lamp	Th 04	large thing	Th 12
labor (a cause of distress)	Th 10	lance	Th 01	large tree	Th 02
labor (duties)	Th 06	land	Ho 04	largess	Th 09
labor (effort expended)	Th 06	land	Mn 04	larvae	An 05
labor (giving birth)	Th 05	land	Th 04	larynx	Bd 02
labor (work)	Th 06	land developer	Oc 10	laser	Th 08
labor area	Pl 06	landed interests	Mn 04	lass	Oc 02
labor force, the	Mn 06	landed property	Pl 04	lassitude	Th 07
labor force, the	Th 06	landfill	Pl 08	last illness	Th 04
labor intensive task	Th 06	landlord	Oc 01	last will and testament	Th 08
labor leader	Oc 10	landmark	Th 10	lasting things	Th 10
labor organization	Th 06	landowner	Oc 04	latch	Th 04
labor trouble	Th 07	landscape (picture)	Th 07	lateness	Th 10
labor union	Mn 06	landscaper	Oc 07	latent things	Th 04
laboradorite	Ge 04	landscaping	Hs 07	later life	Th 04
laboratory	Pl 08	Landscaping Services	In 02	lateral side, the	Pl 05
laboratory apparatus	Th 06	lane (bowling)	Th 03	lather	Th 06
laborer	Oc 06	lane (narrow way)	Pl 03	latitude (geographic)	Th 10
laboring class	Mn 06	lane (ocean or air route)	Th 03	latitude (room)	Th 04
laboring under an illusion	Ps 12	lane (strip of road)	Th 03	lattice (framework)	Th 04
		language	Th 03	lattice (geometrical pattern)	Th 07
laborious effort	Th 06	languor	Ps 02		
laborious matters	Th 10	lap (clothing)	Th 06	laughter	Th 05
labyrinth	Pl 03	lap (course)	Th 03	launch	Sh 12
lace	Th 07	lap (little waves)	Th 04	launching	Th 01
laceration	Af 01	lap (one turn)	Th 03	laundry	Hs 06
Lacerta (lizard)	My 05	lap (overlap)	Th 05	laundry	Pl 06
lack	Ps 10	lap (panel)	Th 04	laundry	Sh 06
lack	Th 10	lap (polish)	Th 07	laundry	Th 06
lack of air circulation	Th 08	lap (take in food)	Th 04	laundry room	Pl 06
lacquer	Th 07	lap, one's	Bd 08	lava	Th 09
lad	Oc 03	lapidarian	Oc 07	lavatory	Pl 08
ladder	Sh 03	lapis lazuli	Ge 11	lavender	Co 12
ladder	Th 11	lapse (decline)	Th 08	lavish things	Th 05

law	Ho 09	learning, higher	Th 09	or ritual	
law	Mn 09	learning, the process of	Ps 05	legend	Th 09
law, the	Th 09	learning ability	Ps 03	legibility	Th 06
law enforcement	Mn 10	learning disability	Af 03	legislation	Ho 11
law profession, the	Th 09	lease	Th 04	legislation	Mn 11
lawbreaker	Oc 07	lease agreement	Th 07	legislation	Th 11
lawlessness	Th 07	lease document	Th 03	legislative activity	Mn 11
lawn	Hs 04	leash	Th 01	legislative body	Mn 11
lawn mower	Th 06	leasing	Th 04	legislative house	Mn 11
lawsuit	Th 07	leasing/rental services	In 11	legislative practice	Mn 11
lawsuit (open dispute)	Ho 07	leather article	Th 10	legislator	Oc 11
lawsuit, defendant in	Oc 07	leather worker	Oc 10	legitimacy	Th 09
lawsuit, result of	Th 04	leave (consent)	Th 07	legitimacy of children	Th 05
lawyer	Oc 09	leave (vacation)	Th 05	legs, lower part	Bd 11
lawyer in a court action, your	Oc 07	leaving (departing)	Th 09	legs, upper part	Bd 09
		lectern (platform)	Th 05	legs from knees to ankles	Bd 11
lawyer's office	Pl 06	lecture	Ho 09	leisure	Ps 05
laxative	Th 08	lecture	Th 09	leisure activities	Th 05
laxity	Th 07	lecture hall	Pl 09	leisure time	In 05
lay (lair)	Pl 04	lecturer (academic)	Oc 09	lemon	Co 06
lay (plan)	Th 10	lecturer (in general)	Oc 09	lender	Oc 02
lay (rest position)	Th 02	lecturing (correcting)	Th 10	lending	Th 02
lay (sexual act)	Th 08	leeway (room)	Th 04	lending agency	Mn 08
lay person	Oc 09	left-wing movement	Mn 11	lending institution	Pl 08
layer (stratum)	Th 06	leftovers	Th 04	length (measurement)	Th 06
layoff	Th 07	legacies from others	Th 08	length of life	Th 01
layout (arrangement)	Th 06	legacy	Ho 08	lengthening	Th 03
layout (expense)	Th 02	legacy	Th 08	leniency	Th 12
laziness	Th 02	legal, things which are	Th 09	lens	Th 04
lazybones	Oc 07	legal action	Ho 09	Leo (lion)	My 05
lead	Ge 10	legal action	Th 09	Leo Minor (little lion)	My 05
lead (clue)	Th 08	legal activities	Th 09	leopard	An 09
lead (front position)	Th 01	legal advice	Th 09	leprosy	Af 10
lead (leash)	Th 04	legal affairs	Th 09	Lepus (hare)	My 03
leader	Mn 10	legal agencies	Mn 09	lesion	Af 11
leader	Oc 10	legal claim	Th 09	less of anything	Th 08
leader of the opposition	Mn 04	legal contract	Th 07	let down (discouragement)	Th 12
leadership	Mn 11	legal department	Or 09		
leadership, the country's	Mn 11	legal dispute	Th 07	lethargy	Ps 07
leadership qualities	Ps 11	legal practice	Th 09	Leto (gentleness)	My 02
leaf (foliage)	Th 02	legal procedure or transaction	Th 09	letter carrier	Oc 03
leaf (page)	Th 03			letters (mail)	Ho 03
league (alliance)	Th 11	legal question	Th 09	letters (mail)	Th 03
leak (escape)	Th 12	legal sense	Ps 09	letters of the alphabet	Th 03
leak (loss)	Th 08	legal services	In 09	letting go	Ps 12
leak (urinating)	Bd 08	legalization	Th 09	leukemia	Af 08
leaning (bent)	Ps 03	legalization, the process of	Th 09	levee	Pl 04
learning	Ho 03			level (tool)	Th 07
learning (in general)	Th 03	legalizing by ceremony	Th 09	levelness	Th 07

lever (pry tool)	Th 06	light (illumination)	Th 05	linen (household)	Th 06
leverage (advantage)	Th 05	light (low weight)	Th 11	lingerie	Th 02
levitation	Th 09	light brown	Co 06	linguist	Oc 03
levity	Th 05	light bulb	Th 05	linguistic ability	Ps 03
lewdness	Th 08	light machining	In 06	liniment (ointment)	Th 06
liability	Mn 08	light ray	Th 05	lining	Th 04
liability (financial)	Th 08	lighter (boat)	Th 04	linkage	Au 03
liability to accidents	Th 09	lighter (cigarette)	Th 01	linkage (connection)	Th 03
liaison (affair)	Th 05	lighthouse	Pl 10	lion	An 05
liar	Oc 03	lighting	Hs 05	lips	Bd 01
libel	Th 07	lighting	Sh 05	liquidation (settlement)	Th 08
Liber	My 05	lighting (artificial)	Th 11	liquidity (financial)	Th 02
liberal	Oc 09	lighting (indirect)	Th 12	liquids (in general)	Th 04
liberal attitude	Th 09	lighting (natural)	Th 05	liquor	Th 12
liberal things	Th 09	lighting equipment	In 05	lisp	Af 01
liberalization	Th 09	lighting fixtures (decorative)	Th 07	list	Sh 10
liberation	Th 11			list (roll)	Th 06
liberator	Oc 11	lighting specialist	Oc 11	list making	Th 06
liberty	Ps 01	lightning	Th 01	listening	Th 01
liberty (familiarity)	Th 07	likability	Ps 05	listing	Th 06
liberty (freedom)	Th 11	likelihood	Th 11	listlessness	Th 02
libido	Th 05	likeness	Th 03	litany (prayer)	Th 09
Libra (scales)	My 07	likes or dislikes	Ps 08	literary ability	Th 03
librarian	Oc 03	liking (affinity)	Th 07	literary creative output	Th 05
library	Hs 09	limb	Bd 03	literary output	Th 08
library	Pl 03	limb, artificial	Bd 02	literary work	Th 03
library	Sh 09	lime	Co 07	literature	Th 03
lice	An 08	limelight	Th 05	literature, profound	Th 09
license (document)	Th 03	limerick	Th 03	litigation	Th 09
license (permission)	Th 08	limestone	Ge 07	litter (bed)	Th 02
licentiousness	Th 08	limit	Th 12	litter (newborn)	Th 05
lichen	Th 02	limitation	Th 12	litter (rubbish)	Th 12
liddicoatite	Ge 11	limitation, facing	Ps 12	litter (trash)	Th 12
lie	Th 03	limitations, self-imposed	Ho 12	live steam	Th 01
lien	Th 08	limiting condition	Th 12	livelihood	Ho 02
life	Ps 01	limousine	Th 03	livelihood Income)	Th 02
life	Th 01	limpness	Th 03	liver	Bd 09
life after death	Th 08	line (circuit)	Th 11	liver problems	Af 09
life guard	Oc 04	line (cord)	Th 04	liver system (in general)	Bd 09
life insurance	Th 08	line (in a play)	Th 03	livestock	An 04
life principles	Ps 04	line (lineage)	Th 04	living conditions in general	Mn 01
life support system	Th 04	line (mark)	Th 01		
life threatening actions	Ho 12	line (note)	Th 03	living room	Hs 05
life's circumstances	Ho 01	line (policy)	Th 06	living saint	Oc 09
life-style	Ps 04	line (queue)	Th 11	living space	Ho 04
life-style approach	Ps 04	line (transit route)	Th 03	living space	Pl 04
life-style orientation	Ps 04	line (wrinkle)	Th 04	lizard	An 05
lift (boost)	Th 09	lineage	Th 04	load (burden)	Th 10
ligament	Bd 10	linen (fine)	Th 07	load (capacity)	Th 06

loafer	Oc 02	loom	Th 06	lowering	Ho 08
loan	Ho 08	loop (circle)	Th 05	lowering	Ps 08
loan	Th 08	loose ends	Th 12	lowering, as in value	Th 08
loan company	Th 08	loose living	Th 05	lowlands	Pl 04
loan department	Or 08	looseness	Th 03	lowliness	Th 04
loathsome things	Th 08	loot (plunder)	Th 08	loyalty	Th 08
lobby	Hs 01	lopsided objects	Th 06	loyalty, showing	Ps 08
lobby	Or 01	lore	Th 03	loyalty to causes	Ps 11
lobby	Pl 01	loss (defeat)	Th 12	lubricant	Th 09
Lobbying	In 11	loss (deprivation)	Th 12	lubricating services	In 09
lobster	An 04	loss (destruction)	Th 08	lubrication	Th 09
local matters	Th 03	loss (financial)	Mn 08	luck	Ho 05
local neighborhood	Pl 03	loss (forfeiture)	Th 08	luck	Th 05
local travel	Th 03	loss (misplacing)	Th 04	lucky break	Th 05
locale (position)	Th 01	loss due to death	Th 08	luggage	Th 06
locality	Th 03	loss from speculation	Mn 05	lullaby	Th 02
location	Or 01	loss of public office	Mn 07	lumbar region	Bd 07
location (whereabouts)	Th 01	lost, being	Th 12	lumber	Th 02
location, another's	Pl 07	lost article	Th 04	luminosity	Th 05
location, changing	Th 01	lost item	Th 04	lump (a piece of)	Th 04
location, your	Pl 01	lost person	Oc 04	lump (knot)	Th 05
lock (at a canal)	Th 03	lost possession	Th 04	lunacy	Af 04
lock (security device)	Th 04	lot (fate)	Th 09	lunatic	Oc 04
locket	Th 02	lot (land)	Th 04	lunch	Th 04
lockout, management	Mn 11	lot (much)	Th 09	luncheon	Th 04
locomotion	Th 03	lottery	Th 05	lung problems	Af 03
locomotive	Th 05	loud person	Oc 01	lunge (rush)	Th 01
lodge	Pl 04	loud things	Th 01	lungs	Bd 03
lodge (fraternal)	Th 11	lounge	Pl 05	Lupus (wolf)	My 08
lodger	Oc 06	love	Ho 05	lure (bait)	Th 03
lodging	Th 04	love (beloved)	Oc 05	lust	Th 08
loft	Pl 12	love (fondness)	Th 05	lust after	Th 08
log (diary)	Th 03	love (friendliness)	Th 11	luster	Th 05
log (tree)	Th 02	love (passion)	Th 08	lustful love	Th 08
logic	Th 06	love (romance)	Th 05	luxuries (excesses)	Th 05
logo	Th 01	love, questions of	Th 05	luxurious things	Th 02
loins	Bd 07	love affair	Th 05	luxury (comfort)	Th 02
loitering	Th 07	love of freedom	Th 09	luxury (wealth)	Th 02
loneliness	Th 12	lover	Oc 05	lying	Th 03
long journey	Ho 09	low blood pressure	Af 09	lymphatic system	Bd 04
long journey	Th 09	low spot	Pl 04	lynching	Th 08
long term appreciation	Mn 02	lower, things which are	Th 04	lynx	An 06
long-range plans	Th 09	lower back	Bd 07	lynx (lynx)	My 12
longing (craving)	Th 08	lower back pain	Af 07	Lyra (lyre)	My 02
longitude (geographic)	Th 10	lower education	Th 03	lyricist	Oc 02
longshoreman	Oc 06	lower floors	Hs 04	lyrics (words)	Th 02
looking beyond	Ho 09	lower house of government	Mn 04		
looking beyond	Ps 09				
lookout	Oc 03	lower legislative house	Mn 04		

M

machination (scheme)	Th 03	main hall	Hs 05	manifestation (indication)	Ps 01
machine (labor saving)	Th 11	maintaining	Ps 04	manifold	Au 03
machine (political)	Mn 11	majesty (splendor)	Th 05	manifold (piping)	Th 03
machine tools	In 06	majority (the masses)	Th 04	manipulated, being	Ps 11
machinery	Th 11	make-over	Th 08	manipulated economies	Mn 09
machinery (construction/mining)	In 10	make-up	Th 02	manipulation	Ho 11
		make-up artist	Oc 02	manipulation	Ps 11
machinery (electrical)	In 11	making (producing)	Th 06	manipulation (adjustment)	Th 11
machinist	Oc 11	making love	Ps 08		
macho display	Ps 05	making something legal	Th 09	manipulation (influence)	Th 11
macrocosm	Th 09	malachite	Ge 02	manipulation (usage)	Th 01
madam (of brothel)	Oc 08	maladjustment	Ps 06	manipulator	Oc 11
madness (anger)	Th 01	malady	Af 06	mankind (in general)	Ho 04
magazine (armament storage)	Sh 01	malaise	Ps 06	mannerisms	Ps 01
		malcontent	Oc 11	manners	Th 07
magazine (periodical)	Th 03	male concerns	Ps 10	mansion	Pl 04
magazine article	Th 03	male disorders	Af 01	manslaughter	Th 08
magazine rack	Th 06	male relations	Re 07	manual (book)	Th 03
magenta	Co 08	male things	Th 01	manufactured goods	Mn 10
maggot (larva)	An 05	males	Oc 01	manufactured housing	In 04
magic (ceremonial)	Th 06	malevolence	Th 08	manufacturer	Oc 04
magic (mentalism)	Th 03	malformation	Th 12	manufacturing	Mn 06
magic (occult)	Th 08	malice	Th 08	manufacturing	Th 06
magic (slight of hand)	Th 03	malicious person	Oc 08	manuscript	Th 03
magician (occultist)	Oc 08	maliciousness	Ps 08	many (large number)	Th 11
magician (stage)	Oc 03	mall	Pl 04	map	Th 06
magistrate	Oc 09	mallet	Th 06	mar (scratch)	Th 01
magnanimity	Th 09	malnutrition	Af 06	marauder	Oc 08
magnesium	Ge 01	malpractice (negligence)	Th 12	marble	Ge 07
magnet	Th 11	mammal	An 04	march (hike)	Th 01
magnetism (attraction)	Ps 08	mammary glands	Bd 04	march (progress)	Th 10
magnetism (magnetic force)	Th 08	man (humankind)	Th 04	march (tune)	Th 02
		manacle (shackle)	Th 04	margin (edge)	Th 09
magnetite	Ge 06	management	Mn 10	margin (leeway)	Th 04
magnification	Th 09	management	Or 10	margin (narrowness)	Th 01
magnificence	Th 05	manager	Oc 10	marine contractors	In 04
magnitude (size)	Th 02	mandate (decree)	Th 03	mariner	Oc 04
maid	Oc 06	mandate (territory)	Mn 04	marital concerns	Th 07
maiden	Oc 02	maneuver	Th 03	marital happiness	Th 11
mail	Th 03	maneuverability	Ps 03	marital love	Th 07
mail box	Th 03	manger	Pl 04	maritime	In 04
mail carrier	Oc 03	mania	Af 04	mark (grade)	Th 06
mail room	Or 03	manicure	Th 03	mark (objective)	Th 10
maiming	Th 08	manicurist	Oc 03	mark (sign)	Th 01
main bathroom	Hs 06	manifest (list)	Th 06	mark (spot)	Th 09

261

marker	Th 01	mast	Sh 10	home	
market	Pl 04	master	Oc 10	matters regarding	Th 07
market leverage	Mn 05	master of ceremonies	Oc 05	strangers	
market maker	Oc 03	masterpiece	Th 05	matters taken for	Th 12
market price	Th 03	mastery	Ps 10	granted	
market research	Th 08	masturbation	Bd 08	mattress	Th 02
market statistics	Mn 03	match (contest)	Th 07	maturing, ability to	Ps 10
market value	Th 02	match (counterpart)	Th 07	maturity	Ho 10
marketer	Oc 09	match (light)	Th 01	maturity	Ps 10
marketing	Ho 09	match (prospective	Th 07	mausoleum	Pl 08
marketing	Or 09	partner)		mauve	Co 12
marketing	Ps 09	matchless	Th 11	maverick	Oc 11
marketing agent	Oc 09	(incomparable)		maximum, the	Th 09
marketplace, the	Mn 04	matchmaker	Oc 07	maya (illusion)	Th 12
marksman	Oc 09	mate	Sh 06	mayor	Oc 10
marksmanship	Th 09	mate, one's	Ho 07	mayoral appointees	Mn 03
maroon	Co 08	mate, one's	Re 07	maze	Th 03
marquee (tent)	Th 05	material (apparatus)	Th 06	me, sense of	Ps 01
marriage	Ho 07	material (cloth)	Th 06	meadow	Pl 04
marriage	Th 07	material (constituents)	Th 04	meal	Th 04
marriage, feelings about	Ps 07	material (possession)	Th 02	mean (average)	Th 04
marriage, happiness in	Ps 11	material (raw stuff)	Th 02	meandering	Th 03
marriage of child	Th 11	material (relevance)	Th 10	meaning (implication)	Th 03
marriage partner	Ho 07	material (repertoire)	Th 06	meaning (substance)	Th 02
marriage policies	Mn 07	material possessions	Th 02	meanness	Ps 01
marriage vows	Th 11	material resources	Th 02	means (funds)	Th 02
Mars	My 01	materialism	Th 02	means (method)	Th 10
marsh	Pl 04	materiality	Ps 02	measles	Af 01
marshal	Oc 06	materialization	Th 02	measurement	Th 10
marsupial	An 04	maternal instinct	Ps 04	measuring device	Th 10
marten	An 12	maternal kin	Re 10	meat	Th 04
martial arts	Th 01	mathematical ability	Ps 06	mechanic	Oc 11
martyr	Oc 12	mathematician	Oc 06	mechanical adjustments	Th 11
martyrdom	Th 12	mathematics	Th 06	mechanical advantage	Th 11
marvel (wonder)	Th 05	matinee	Th 05	mechanical engineer	Oc 06
mascot	An 04	matrimony	Th 07	mechanical linkages	Au 11
masculinity	Th 01	matrix (die)	Th 01	mechanical linkages	Th 11
mask (cover-up)	Th 12	matrix (embedding	Th 04	mechanism (internal	Th 06
mask (false face)	Th 12	material)		works)	
mason	Oc 10	matrix (math form)	Th 06	medal (decoration)	Th 05
masonry	Th 10	matrix (starter base)	Th 04	meddling	Th 07
masquerade	Th 12	matter (affair)	Th 07	media	Th 03
mass production	Th 11	matter (material)	Th 04	media analyst	Oc 06
mass transit	Th 03	matter (predicament)	Th 01	media personnel	Oc 03
massacre	Th 08	matter (textual material)	Th 03	median strip	Pl 03
massage	Th 06	matters depending	Ho 10	mediation	Th 07
massager	Oc 06	on others		mediator	Oc 07
masses, the	Th 04	matters of the heart	Ps 05	Medicaid	Th 12
masses of people	Th 04	matters outside of the	Ho 10	medical (supervisory care)	In 06

medical discovery	Th 08	memorandum	Th 03	Mercury	My 03
medical examiners	In 08	memorial	Th 10	mercury	Ge 03
medical products	In 08	memorization	Th 03	mercy	Th 12
medical services	In 06	memory	Ho 03	merit (substance)	Th 02
medical supplies	In 08	memory	Ps 03	merit (virtue)	Th 10
medical technician	Oc 08	memory, loss of	Th 12	merit, things without	Th 05
medical/nurses station	Or 12	memory jog	Th 03	meritorious work	Th 10
medication	Th 06	memory problems	Ps 03	mermaid	Oc 10
medicinal herb	Th 06	men	Oc 01	merriment	Th 05
medicine	Th 06	men, ages 25 to 35	Oc 01	merry making	Ps 05
medicine, socialized	Th 12	men, ages 35 to 45	Oc 05	mesa	Pl 10
medicine cabinet	Hs 06	men, young	Oc 03	mess	Sh 06
mediocrity	Th 04	men from the past	Oc 10	mess (clutter)	Th 12
meditation	Th 09	men's clothes	Th 06	mess deck	Sh 06
meditative desire	Ps 09	menace	Th 08	message	Ho 03
medium	Oc 08	mending (healing)	Th 06	message	Th 03
medium (environment)	Th 01	mending (patching)	Th 06	messenger	Oc 03
medium (means)	Th 10	mending (revising)	Th 08	messenger	Or 03
medium blue	Co 11	Mensa (table mountain)	My 10	messengers of the state	Mn 07
medley (assortment)	Th 11	menses	Bd 04	metabolism	Bd 05
Medusa	My 10	menstrual problems	Af 07	metal casting services	In 06
meekness	Ps 06	menstruation	Bd 04	metal craftsman	Oc 06
meeting (encounter)	Th 01	mental activity	Ps 03	mMetal fabricating	In 06
meeting (introduction)	Th 01	mental adaptation	Ps 03	metal worker	Oc 06
meeting hall	Th 11	mental attitudes	Ps 03	metallurgy	Th 06
meeting others	Ho 11	mental efforts	Ho 03	metals and mining	In 08
meeting room	Or 11	mental efforts	Ps 03	metals (in general)	Ge 01
meeting room	Pl 11	mental faculties	Bd 03	metamorphosis	Th 08
meetings, large gatherings	Th 11	mental health worker	Oc 06	metaphor	Th 09
		mental illness	Af 06	metaphysician	Oc 09
meetings, small gatherings	Th 07	mental instability	Ps 06	metaphysics	Th 09
		mental interests	Th 03	meteorology	Th 03
megalomania	Th 02	mental pursuits	Th 03	meter	Th 06
megaphone	Th 09	mental reservations	Ps 11	meter reader	Oc 06
melancholy	Ps 06	mental speculation	Ps 09	method (purpose)	Th 10
melee	Th 07	mental strain	Af 12	method (technique)	Th 06
melodrama	Th 05	mentality	Th 03	methodical task	Th 06
melody	Th 02	mention of something, the	Th 03	methodology	Th 10
melon	Th 04			methods of business	Mn 01
member	Oc 11	mentor	Oc 10	mezzanine (theater)	Th 04
member (appendage)	Th 03	menu	Th 06	mica	Ge 03
member of a support group	Oc 11	mercantilism	Mn 04	micro-organism	Th 04
		mercenary	Oc 06	microbe	Th 04
member of a wedding	Oc 10	merchandise	Th 04	microbiologist	Oc 04
membership	Ho 11	merchandiser	Oc 04	microcline	Ge 04
membership in clubs	Th 11	merchandising	Mn 04	microcosm	Th 04
membrane	Th 10	merchandising (small business)	In 04	microphone	Th 03
memoir	Th 04			microscope	Th 04
memorabilia	Th 04	merchant	Oc 04	Microscopium (microscope)	My 06

mid-afternoon	Th 08	minerals	Ge 10	mission (assignment)	Th 04
mid-day	Th 10	Minerva	My 06	mission (envoy)	Th 09
mid-morning	Th 11	mingling	Th 11	missionary	Oc 09
middle (center)	Th 05	miniature thing	Th 06	mist	Th 12
middle, the	Pl 05	minimum	Th 04	mistake (blunder)	Th 12
middle class, the	Mn 04	minister (clergy)	Oc 09	mistreatment	Th 08
middle management	Or 04	ministry, the	Th 09	mistress	Oc 08
middle position	Pl 07	mink	An 12	mistress	Re 08
middle position	Ps 07	minor	Oc 03	mistrust	Th 11
middle school	Pl 03	minor (unimportant)	Th 04	misunderstanding	Th 08
middleman	Oc 03	mint (makes money)	Mn 02	misuse	Th 08
midget	Oc 03	minute (moment)	Th 10	mittens	Th 04
midnight	Th 04	minutiae	Th 04	mix-up (mistake)	Th 12
midst	Th 05	miracle	Th 12	mixed signals	Th 07
midwife	Oc 05	mirage	Th 12	mixer (churn)	Th 11
might (power)	Th 01	mirror (reflection)	Th 07	mixer (dance)	Th 05
migraine headache	Af 09	mirror (vanity object)	Th 02	mixes, mixing	Th 11
migrant farm laborer	Oc 06	mirth	Th 05	mixing	Ho 11
migration	Th 09	misbehavior	Th 07	mixture (combination)	Th 11
mild things	Th 02	miscalculation	Th 12	mnemonic	Th 03
mildew	Th 12	miscarriage	Th 05	mnomosyne (memory)	My 03
milestone (epoch)	Th 01	miscellany	Th 04	moat	Pl 04
military (person in)	Oc 06	mischief	Th 03	mob (crowd)	Th 11
military forces	Mn 06	misconception	Th 03	mob (mafia)	Th 08
military regimen	Th 06	misconduct	Th 07	mob fury	Th 08
military service	Mn 06	misdeed	Th 08	mobile communications	In 03
military stores	Mn 06	misdemeanor	Th 07	mobile home	Pl 06
milk	Th 04	misdirection	Th 03	mobility	Th 03
Milky Way, the	My 04	miser	Oc 04	mobilization	Th 08
mill	Pl 11	misery	Th 12	mockery	Th 01
mill (grinder)	Th 11	misfortune	Ps 12	model	Oc 07
millennia	Th 10	misfortune, unexpected	Th 11	model (replica)	Th 03
millinery	Pl 01	misgivings	Ps 11	model building	Th 06
millionaire	Oc 10	mishap	Th 12	modeling agencies	In 07
millstone	Th 11	misinformation	Th 03	moderation	Th 02
mime	Oc 03	misjudgment	Ps 09	moderator	Oc 07
mimic	Oc 03	mislaid item	Ho 04	modern, things that are	Th 11
mimicry	Th 03	mislaid item	Th 04	modern gadget	Th 11
minaret	Pl 09	mislaying things	Th 04	modernization	Th 11
mind (in general)	Th 03	misnomer	Th 03	modesty	Ps 06
mindfulness	Th 07	misplaced item	Th 04	modification	Th 08
mindless destruction	Th 08	misrepresentation	Th 03	modify, ability to	Ps 06
mine	Pl 08	missile (projectile)	Th 01	modulation (tempering)	Th 07
mine (pit)	Mn 08	missile (rocket)	Th 01	moisture	Th 04
mine (tunnel)	Mn 08	missing item	Ho 04	mold (fungus)	Th 12
miner	Oc 08	missing item	Th 04	mold (ilk)	Th 03
mineral products	Th 10	missing link	Th 08	mold (shape)	Th 01
mineral spring	Pl 11	missing person	Oc 07	mold (the form itself)	Th 03
mineralogy	Ge 10	mission	Pl 09	molestation	Th 08

molester	Oc 08	monkey	An 03	mother	Re 04
molting	Th 08	Monoceros (unicorn)	My 07	mother love	Ps 05
moment of time	Th 10	monochrome	Th 10	mother's kin	Re 12
momentary thought	Th 03	monogamy	Th 10	mother's money	Th 05
momentum	Th 02	monograph	Th 03	mother-in-law	Re 09
monarch	Oc 10	monologue	Th 03	motherhood	Th 04
monastery	Pl 09	monopoly	Mn 08	mothering	Ps 04
monetary gain	Ho 02	monotony	Th 10	motif (theme)	Th 05
monetary partnerships	Mn 08	monster (demon)	Oc 12	motion (gesture)	Th 03
monetary standards	Mn 08	monster (deviant)	Th 12	motion (movement)	Th 01
money	Ho 02	monstrosity	Th 12	motion (proposal)	Th 07
money	Th 02	monument	Th 10	motion picture	Th 05
money, attitude toward	Ps 02	monument maker	Oc 10	motion picture industry	Th 05
money, paper based	Mn 03	moocher	Oc 03	motivation	Ps 05
money, recovery of lost	Th 04	mood	Ps 04	motivation	Th 05
money belonging to others	Th 08	moonstone	Ge 04	motivational trainers	In 05
		moor	Pl 04	motives	Ps 05
money by marriage	Th 08	moral (lesson)	Th 10	motor	Th 05
money for retirement	Th 08	moral credit	Th 10	motor, the	Au 05
money from career	Th 11	moral philosophy	Th 09	motor pool	Or 03
money from renter or tenant	Th 07	morale	Ps 05	motorcycle	Th 03
		morality (ethics)	Th 09	motorized equipment	Th 11
money laundering	Mn 09	morals	Ps 09	mound	Pl 09
money lender	Oc 02	morass	Th 04	mount (embankment)	Pl 04
money maker	Oc 02	moratorium	Th 10	mount (frame)	Th 04
money management services	In 02	morbid things	Th 08	mount (steed)	An 06
		morbidity	Th 08	mountain climber	Oc 10
money manipulation	Mn 12	morganite	Ge 07	mountain range	Pl 10
money market	Mn 02	morgue	Pl 08	mountains	Pl 10
money matters	Ho 02	morning	Th 12	mounting (climbing)	Th 10
money matters	Th 02	moron	Oc 12	mounting (climbs on)	Th 10
money of a deceased person	Th 08	morsel (nibble)	Th 04	mourner	Oc 12
		mortality	Th 08	mourning	Th 12
money of a parent	Th 05	mortality rates	Mn 08	mouse	An 08
money of others	Ho 08	mortality tables	Mn 06	mouth	Bd 01
money of others	Th 08	mortals	Oc 04	mouth ulcerations	Af 01
money of the business	Mn 11	mortar	Th 10	mouthpiece (on an instrument)	Th 01
money others owe you	Th 02	mortgage	Th 08		
money supply, a business's	Mn 11	mortgage brokers	In 08	mouthpiece (spokesperson)	Oc 03
		mortgage companies	Mn 08		
money supply, a country's	Mn 11	mortician	Oc 08	movable possessions	Th 02
		mortification	Th 10	move (as in chess)	Th 04
money supply, personal	Th 02	mortuary	Pl 08	move (change of location)	Th 03
money you owe others	Th 08	mosquito	An 08		
mongrel	An 09	moss	Th 04	move (movement)	Th 01
monitor (proctor)	Oc 08	mote (speck)	Th 04	movement (activity)	Th 01
monitor (sensor)	Th 02	motel	Pl 04	movement (crusade)	Th 11
monitor (TV type)	Th 03	mother	Ho 04	movement (motion)	Th 01
monk	Oc 09	mother	Oc 04	movement (restlessness)	Th 03

265

movement, facilitating	Th 03	munitions	Th 01	mutation	Th 08
mover	Oc 03	mural	Th 05	mute	Oc 10
movie film	Th 12	murder	Th 08	mute (noncommittal)	Th 10
movie house	Pl 05	murder victim(s)	Th 08	mute (silent)	Th 10
movie maker	Oc 05	murderer	Oc 08	mutilation	Th 08
movie making	In 12	murkiness	Th 12	mutiny	Th 07
movies	Th 05	murmur (soft sound)	Th 02	muttering	Th 03
movies, home	Th 04	Musca (fly)	My 12	mutual actions	Ps 07
moving (relocating)	Th 04	muscle system	Bd 01	muzzle (face)	Th 01
muck (sewage)	Th 08	muscles (in general)	Bd 01	muzzle of a gun	Th 01
mucous	Bd 12	muscular persons	Oc 02	my things or rights	Ho 01
mud	Th 10	muscular system (in general)	Bd 01	myocardial infarct	Af 05
muffler	Au 08			myopia	Af 04
mug (cup)	Th 04	muse (guiding spirit)	Oc 05	myself	Ho 01
mug (face)	Th 01	museum	Pl 04	myself	Ps 01
mule	An 02	museum/museum services	In 12	mysteries	Ho 08
multi-line insurance	In 08			mystery (puzzle)	Th 08
multi-media presentations	Th 03	mushroom	Th 12	mystery (sacred rite)	Th 09
		music	Th 02	mystery (unknown thing)	Th 12
multiplication (math)	Th 09	music, national	Mn 05	mystical things	Th 12
multitudes	Th 04	musical	Th 05	mysticism	Th 12
mumbling	Th 03	musical harmony	Th 07	myth (fantasy)	Th 09
mummy	Th 04	musical instrument	Th 02	myth (legend)	Th 09
mumps	Af 02	musician	Oc 02	mythical character	Oc 09
municipal government	Mn 11	musicians/orchestras	In 02	mythology	Th 09
municipality	Mn 04	muster (assembly)	Th 11		

N

nagging	Ps 06	nation's capitol	Mn 01	natural gas	Th 09
nail (finger)	Bd 01	nation's constitution	Mn 01	natural gas (diversified)	In 12
nail (tool)	Th 06	national affairs	Mn 10	natural gas (pipeline)	In 03
naivete	Ps 03	national approval, need for	Mn 10	natural gas distribution	In 03
nakedness	Bd 10			natural resources	Mn 04
name(s)	Th 01	national celebrities	Mn 10	natural settings	Pl 04
namesake	Th 03	national cemetery	Mn 08	natural touches	Th 04
nap	Th 02	national debt, the	Mn 08	natural wealth of country	Mn 08
napkin	Th 06	national glory	Mn 05		
narcissism	Th 05	national health policies	Mn 06	naturalist	Oc 04
Narcissus	My 05	national lifestyles	Mn 01	naturalization services	In 09
narcotic	Th 12	national pastimes	Mn 05	nature, mother	Oc 04
narration	Th 03	national policy	Mn 08	nature of land purchased	Th 04
narrator	Oc 03	national reputation	Mn 10	naturopathy	Th 06
narrow-mindedness	Th 10	national security, concerns of	Mn 04	nausea	Af 04
narrowness	Th 01			nautical things	Th 04
nastiness	Th 01	nationalism	Ps 04	naval architects	In 10
nation, the	Mn 01	natural beauty	Bd 02	navel	Bd 07

navigation	Th 11	nerves	Bd 03	newspapers	In 03
navigation desk	Sh 11	nervous aggravation	Ps 06	newspapers	Mn 03
navigational lights	Sh 11	nervous breakdowns	Ps 06	newspapers	Th 03
navigator	Oc 11	nervous disorders	Af 03	next lifetime	Th 09
navy	Co 10	nervous energy	Th 03	nibble	Th 04
navy	Mn 06	nervous habits	Ps 03	nicety (refinement)	Th 07
near neighborhood	Pl 03	nervous illnesses	Af 06	nicety (small detail)	Th 06
near relatives	Re 03	nervous system, the	Bd 03	niche in life	Th 04
nearsightedness	Af 04	nervous tension	Ps 06	nick (cut)	Th 01
nebulousness	Ho 12	nervous twitches	Ps 03	nickname	Th 09
nebulousness	Th 12	nervousness	Ps 03	nicotine	Th 12
necessary service	Th 06	nest	Th 04	niece	Re 07
necessity	Th 10	nesting instincts	Ps 04	niece or nephew	Re 01
necessity of life	Th 04	net (mesh)	Th 04	by marriage	
neck	Bd 02	netting (protection)	Th 04	night	Th 04
necklace	Th 02	network (interconnection)	Th 11	night on the town	Th 05
necktie	Th 06	networking	Th 11	night worker	Oc 04
nectar	Th 02	neuralgia	Af 01	nightclub performer	Oc 05
need (desire)	Ps 11	neuritis in arms or	Af 03	nightfall	Th 05
need for another	Ps 08	shoulders		nightgown	Th 02
needle	Th 09	neurologist	Oc 03	nightmare	Th 08
needlework	Th 06	neurosis	Af 12	nihilist	Oc 08
needs (in general)	Ps 04	neutering	Th 07	Niobe	My 04
needy, the	Oc 12	neutral stand	Ps 07	nip (sharp comment)	Th 03
negation	Th 10	neutrality	Th 07	nip (small portion)	Th 04
negative views	Ps 04	neutralization	Th 07	nipple	Bd 04
negatives (photographic)	Th 12	neutralizing	Th 07	nipple (artificial teat)	Th 04
negativity	Ps 06	neutron	Th 07	niter	Ge 09
neglect	Th 12	new, that which is	Th 11	nitrogen	Th 02
negligee	Th 06	new, the	Ho 11	nitroglycerine	Th 01
negligence	Ps 12	new acquaintance	Oc 11	no obligation offer	Th 07
negotiable assets	Ho 02	new age	Th 11	nobility	Oc 10
negotiable assets	Mn 02	new age gadget	Th 11	nobleman	Oc 10
negotiation	Mn 07	new beginning	Th 04	node (center or hub)	Pl 05
negotiation	Th 07	new idea	Ps 11	node (mass of substance)	Th 04
negotiator	Oc 07	new method	Th 11	node (on musical string)	Th 02
neighbor	Ho 03	new place of residence	Th 02	node (orbital)	Th 03
neighbor	Mn 03	new projects	Th 01	nodule	Th 04
neighbor	Oc 03	new surroundings	Pl 04	noise	Th 01
neighborhood	Ho 03	new technology	Mn 11	nomad	Oc 12
neighborhood	Pl 03	acceptance		nomenclature	Th 01
neighborhood politics	Mn 01	new venture	Ho 01	nomination	Th 11
neighboring country	Mn 03	new venture	Th 01	non-conformist	Oc 11
neighboring environment	Pl 03	newcomer	Oc 01	non-entity	Oc 12
neophyte	Oc 03	news	Th 03	non-participation	Ps 07
nephew	Re 07	news commentator	Oc 03	non-personal resources	Ho 08
nephrite	Ge 06	news personnel	Oc 03	non-personal resources	Th 08
Neptune	My 12	news rooms	Pl 03	non-violence, principle of	Ps 07
nerve sheath	Bd 06	newspaper worker	Oc 03	nonchalance	Ps 11

nonsense (foolery)	Th 03	nothing (obscurity)	Th 12	nucleus (of atom)	Th 05
noon	Th 10	nothingness	Th 08	nudist	Oc 05
noose	Th 08	notice (attention)	Th 01	nudity	Th 05
norm (average)	Th 04	notice (information)	Th 03	nugget (ore)	Th 10
Norma (level)	My 07	noticed, being	Ps 05	nugget (wisdom)	Th 03
north, the direction of	Th 04	noticing	Th 03	nuisance (blight)	Th 12
nose	Bd 02	notification	Th 01	nuisance (bother)	Th 01
nosebleed	Bd 02	notion (belief)	Th 09	numbers (in general)	Th 06
nostalgia	Th 04	notion (idea)	Th 03	numbness	Af 10
nostalgic item	Th 04	notoriety	Th 10	numismatics	Th 04
notability	Ps 05	nourishment	Th 04	nun	Oc 09
notaries	In 08	novel (book)	Th 03	nurse	Oc 06
notary	Oc 07	novelist	Oc 03	nursery	Hs 05
notation	Th 03	novelty (fad)	Th 04	nursing home	Pl 12
notch	Th 04	now	Th 01	nurturing	Ps 04
note (currency)	Th 02	nozzle	Th 10	nut meats (in general)	Th 04
note (importance)	Th 10	nuclear physics	Th 08	nutrition	Ho 06
note (memo)	Th 03	nuclear power generation	In 05	nutrition	Th 06
note keeping	Th 03	nuclear weapon	Th 08	nymph	My 12

O

oasis	Pl 04	oblivion	Th 08	occult, the	Th 08
oath (cursing)	Th 01	obnoxiousness	Th 01	occult ability	Ps 08
oath (solemn word)	Th 09	obscene thing	Th 08	occult experience	Th 08
obedience	Ps 06	obscenity	Th 08	occult matters	Ho 08
obesity	Bd 09	obscure thing	Th 12	occult matters	Th 08
obituary	Th 08	obscurity	Ps 12	occult religion	Th 04
object (anything perceived)	Th 01	observation	Th 03	occult society	Mn 12
		observation deck	Sh 03	occultist	Oc 08
object of affection	Th 05	observatory	Pl 03	occupancy	Th 04
object of state importance	Mn 03	observer	Oc 03	occupation (career)	Th 10
		observing powers	Ps 03	occupations involving unreality	Th 08
object of value	Th 02	obsession	Ho 08		
object taken for granted	Th 04	obsession	Ps 08	occupy (take up space)	Th 04
		obsidian	Ge 10	occupy time, things that	Th 04
objection	Th 07	obsolescence	Th 12	occurrence	Th 01
objectives	Ho 10	obstacle	Th 10	ocean	Pl 04
objectives	Ps 10	obstetrician	Oc 05	ocean depths	Pl 04
objectivity	Ho 11	obstetrics	Th 05	oceanographer	Oc 04
objectivity	Ps 11	obstinacy	Ps 02	oceans bordering the nation	Mn 04
obligation (pledge)	Th 08	obstruction	Th 10		
obligation, meeting an	Ps 08	obtrusiveness (interfering)	Ps 07	Octans (instrument)	My 06
obligingness	Th 06	obtuse angle	Th 09	octopus	An 03
obliqueness (slant)	Th 10	occasion (occurrence)	Th 01	odd skin disorder	Af 11
obliqueness (slyness)	Th 03	occlusions (blockages)	Af 10	odd-shaped thing	Th 03
obliteration	Th 08	occult, study of	Th 04	oddity (unusual)	Th 11

odds (chances)	Th 05	olivine	Ge 02	opinion (belief)	Th 09
odds and ends	Th 04	ombudsman	Oc 07	opinion (conjecture)	Th 09
odor	Th 02	omen	Th 08	opinion (feeling)	Th 04
odyssey	Th 09	omission	Th 09	opinionated person	Oc 09
offbeat thing	Th 11	omnipotence	Ps 05	opium	Th 12
offense (attack)	Th 01	omnivore	An 04	opossum	An 04
offense (outrage)	Th 08	one (you)	Ps 01	opponent	Ho 07
offensive (unpleasant) thing	Th 08	one of a kind item	Th 02	opponent	Oc 07
		one-liner	Th 03	opportunity (happenstance)	Th 05
offer (proposal)	Th 09	one-night stand	Th 05		
offering (gift)	Th 07	one-sidedness	Th 01	opportunity (self created)	Th 01
offering (sacrifice)	Th 12	one-upmanship	Th 05	opportunity (through others)	Th 07
office (employment)	Th 10	oneness	Ps 07		
office (status)	Th 10	onlooker	Oc 03	opposing view	Th 07
office (work place)	Mn 10	onrush	Th 01	opposite party	Mn 07
office (work place)	Pl 10	onset (beginning)	Th 01	opposites	Th 07
office building	Pl 10	onslaught (attack)	Th 08	opposition (planetary)	Th 04
office directors	Or 05	onus (burden of proof)	Th 07	opposition (rival)	Oc 07
office equipment and supplies	In 06	onus (stigma)	Th 12	opposition, behind the scenes	Mn 12
		onyx	Ge 09		
office holdings	Th 04	oomph (vitality)	Ps 05	opposition, sneaky or underhanded	Mn 12
office in the home	Hs 10	ooze (mud)	Th 10		
office of an agent	Mn 04	opacity	Th 07	oppression	Th 08
office of the partner	Mn 04	opal	Ge 09	optician	Oc 06
office space	Pl 10	opaque color	Co 07	optimism	Th 05
office where one works	Pl 06	open country	Pl 04	optimist	Oc 05
officers in authority	Mn 10	open enemy	Ho 07	optimization	Th 06
official	Oc 10	open enemy	Oc 07	optimum conditions	Th 09
official business	Mn 10	open farmland	Pl 04	option (alternative)	Th 07
offset (displacement)	Th 07	open secret	Th 11	option (claim)	Th 04
offshoot (sprout)	Th 05	open warfare	Th 07	option (freedom of choice)	Th 11
offspring (children)	Re 05	opener	Th 01		
offspring (ideas)	Th 05	opening (hole)	Th 04	options market	Mn 05
oil (lubricant)	Th 09	opening (initiation)	Th 01	optometrist	Oc 06
oil drilling	In 08	opening (vacancy)	Th 04	opulence (profusion)	Th 09
oil exploration	In 09	opening up	Ps 11	opulence (riches)	Th 02
oil field	Pl 09	openness	Ps 07	oracle	Oc 09
oil field services/ equipment	In 12	opera	Th 11	oral tradition	Th 04
		operation (action)	Th 01	orange	Co 03
oil pan	Au 09	operation (influence)	Th 10	orange-brown	Co 05
oil tank	Pl 09	operation (surgical)	Th 08	orangutan	An 03
oil well	Th 09	operations department	Or 07	oration (address)	Th 03
ointment	Th 02	operator (math)	Th 03	orator	Oc 03
old, that which is	Th 10	operator (of a fraud)	Oc 03	oratory	Th 03
old age	Th 04	operator (worker)	Oc 06	orbit	Th 06
old age problems	Af 10	Ophiuchus (serpent holder)	My 06	orchard	Pl 02
old people	Oc 10			orchard worker	Oc 02
old thing	Th 10	ophthalmology	Th 04	orchestra	Th 02
older person	Oc 10	opiate	Th 12	orchestra (theater)	Pl 07

orchestration (arrangement)	Th 06	orifice (opening)	Th 04	outcome of opposition (enmity)	Th 07
ordainment	Th 09	origin (ancestry)	Th 04	outcome of pleas	Th 07
ordeal (misery)	Th 12	origin (birth)	Th 01	outcome of the matter, final	Th 04
ordeal (trial)	Th 10	origin (source)	Th 04	outcry	Th 01
order (arrangement)	Th 06	originality	Ps 05	outer covering	Th 04
order (calm)	Th 02	origins of disturbances	Th 09	outfit (ensemble)	Th 06
order (command)	Th 10	Orion (the hunter)	My 09	outflow	Th 09
order (ministry)	Th 09	ornament	Th 02	outgrowth (shoot)	Th 05
order (religious rite)	Th 09	ornamentation	Th 02	outgrowth (the result of)	Th 10
order (society)	Th 11	ornate decoration	Hs 05	outhouse	Pl 08
order giver	Oc 01	ornate style	Th 05	outing	Th 05
order of magnitude	Th 06	ornery disposition, an	Ps 01	outlaw	Oc 07
orderliness	Th 10	ornithology	Th 06	outlawed person	Oc 07
orderly	Oc 06	orphan	Oc 12	outlay (expenditure)	Th 02
orders of the day	Th 06	Orpheus (musician and poet)	My 02	outlet (means of expression)	Ps 07
ordinance (rule)	Th 09	orthoclase	Ge 04	outlet (opening)	Th 07
ordinary, the	Ho 04	orthodox observance	Th 09	outlet (shopping place)	Pl 04
ordinary, the	Ps 04	orthodox religion	Th 09	outline (contour)	Th 01
ordinary business	Mn 04	orthodox rite	Th 09	outline (profile)	Th 03
ordination	Th 09	orthodoxy	Ps 10	outline (shape)	Th 01
ordnance	Th 01	Oscars	Th 10	outline (silhouette)	Th 03
ore	Ge 10	oscillate	Th 04	outline (synopsis)	Th 08
organ	Bd 04	ostentation	Th 05	outlook	Ps 01
organ (musical instrument)	Th 02	ostentatious behavior	Ps 05	outlook (possibility)	Th 09
organ (publication)	Th 03	osteopath	Oc 10	outpouring	Th 09
organ donor	Oc 12	osteoporosis	Af 09	output	Th 06
organism (institution)	Th 12	ostracism	Th 07	outrage	Ps 07
organism (living thing)	Th 04	ostrich	An 11	outside (out-of-doors)	Pl 05
organization	Ho 10	other, the	Th 07	outside chance	Th 01
organization	Ps 10	other party in a contest	Oc 07	outside influence	Th 09
organization	Th 10	other people (in general)	Oc 07	outsides (exterior)	Th 01
organization, the	Or 01	other persons	Ho 07	outskirts	Pl 09
organization's image, the	Or 01	other places	Pl 09	outward show	Ps 01
organized crime	Th 12	other side in an issue, the	Th 07	oval	Th 04
organized crime activities	Th 12	otter	An 05	ovaries	Bd 07
organized labor	Th 06	ouster	Mn 11	ovation (tribute)	Th 05
organizer	Oc 10	out buildings (utility)	Hs 06	oven	Pl 05
organizing ability	Th 10	out on bail	Th 12	oven	Th 05
orgasm	Bd 08	outbound direction	Th 11	over-tiredness	Ps 06
orgone	Th 11	outbreak (burst)	Th 01	overalls	Th 04
orgy	Th 05	outbuilding	Hs 04	overcoat	Th 06
orientation (familiarization)	Th 03	outburst	Th 01	overcoming adversity	Ps 10
orientation (sense of direction)	Th 07	outcast	Oc 12	overhaul	Th 06
		outcome (consequence)	Th 10	overindulgence	Ps 02
		outcome of anything, the	Ho 04	overmatched confrontation	Th 07
		outcome of contentions	Th 07		
		outcome of illness	Th 09		

overproduction	Th 09	overthrow	Mn 11	owner's cooperation	Or 07
overseas	Pl 09	overtone (hint)	Th 03	ownership	Th 02
overseer	Oc 10	overture (introduction)	Th 01	ownership, attitude about	Ps 02
overshoes	Th 12	overture (proposal)	Th 01	ox	An 02
oversight (care)	Th 04	overturning	Th 11	oxidation	Th 03
oversight (omission)	Th 09	overused things	Th 12	oxygen	Th 03
overstrain	Th 06	overweight condition	Af 09	oyster	An 04
oversupply	Th 09	owl	An 06		

P

pacification	Th 02	pajamas	Th 06	parade (ceremonial)	Th 09
pack (bundle)	Th 06	palace	Pl 05	parade (circus like)	Th 05
package (complete assemblage)	Th 10	palate	Bd 02	parade (procession)	Th 06
		paleontology	Th 04	parade (vaunting)	Th 05
package (parcel)	Th 03	palette	Th 09	paradigm (ideal)	Th 09
packaging	Th 02	pall bearer	Oc 08	paradise	Pl 09
packaging and container	In 04	palladium	Ge 09	paradox	Th 08
packer	Oc 06	pallor	Bd 01	parallelogram	Th 07
packet (mail)	Th 03	palm of hand	Bd 03	paralysis (incapacity)	Th 11
packing (stuffing)	Th 02	palmist	Oc 03	paralysis (loss of function)	Af 11
packing house	Pl 04	palpitations of heart	Bd 05		
pact (treaty)	Mn 07	pamphlet	Th 03	parameter (element)	Th 04
pad (bed)	Th 02	Pan	My 02	parameter (rule)	Th 06
pad (ink stamp)	Th 04	pan	Th 04	paramour	Oc 08
pad (on animal's foot)	Th 07	panacea	Th 12	paranoia	Af 08
pad (writing)	Th 03	pancreas	Bd 07	paraphernalia (furnishings)	Th 02
padding (cushioning)	Th 02	panda bear	An 07		
padding on the dashboard	Au 02	pandemonium	Th 08	parasite	An 12
		panel (piece)	Th 06	parasite	Oc 12
paddle (oar)	Th 01	panel discussion	Th 11	parasol	Th 04
paddle (used for hitting)	Th 01	panic	Th 08	parcel (lot)	Th 04
paddock	Pl 06	Panope (Allspy)	My 12	parcel (package)	Th 06
padlock	Th 04	panorama	Th 09	parcel (small piece)	Th 04
pagan	Oc 08	panther	An 12	parchment	Th 03
pageant	Th 05	pantograph	Th 03	pardon	Ho 12
pageantry	Th 05	pantomime	Th 03	pardon	Th 12
pail	Th 04	pantry	Hs 06	parent	Re 10
pain	Af 12	paper (document)	Th 03	parent, death of	Th 05
pain, causing	Th 01	paper (stationery)	Th 03	parent's money	Th 11
pain, chronic	Af 12	paper money	Mn 03	parent-in-law	Re 04
pain, having	Af 01	paper products	In 03	parentage (lineage)	Th 04
painkiller	Th 08	papers, one's	Th 03	parenthood	Th 10
paint	Th 07	par (evenness)	Th 07	parents (in general)	Ho 10
painter (artist)	Oc 07	parable	Th 09	parents, feeling towards	Ps 10
painter (house)	Oc 07	parabola	Th 04	parish (church district)	Pl 09
pairs	Th 03	parachute	Th 10	parish (congregation)	Th 04

parity (equivalence)	Th 07	party (recreational)	Th 05	patio	Pl 05
park (preserve)	Pl 02	party (social)	Th 07	patio door	Hs 05
park (recreational area)	Pl 05	party (surprise)	Th 11	patriarch	Oc 10
park ranger	Oc 05	party supplies	Th 05	patriot	Oc 04
parking area	Or 03	party to a contract	Mn 07	patriotism	Ps 04
parking lot	Pl 03	pass	Pl 03	patrolman	Oc 06
parking lot equipment	In 06	pass (overture)	Th 05	patron	Oc 09
parking lot management	In 10	pass (permit)	Th 09	patron of the arts	Oc 05
parks and preserves (gardens)	Pl 05	pass (toss)	Th 01	patronage	Th 09
		passage (death)	Th 08	pattern (form)	Th 03
parley (discussion)	Th 03	passage (opening)	Th 07	pattern (idea)	Th 03
parliament	Mn 11	passage (traveling)	Th 09	pattern maker	Oc 03
parlor	Hs 07	passage, rights of	Ps 08	patterning	Ps 04
parody (imitation)	Th 03	passageway	Sh 03	pauper	Oc 12
parole	Ho 12	passenger	Oc 03	pause	Th 10
parole	Th 12	passenger quarters	Sh 04	pavement	Th 10
parrot	An 03	passenger seat	Au 04	pavilion	Pl 07
parrot (mimic)	Th 03	passing grade	Th 10	Pavo (peacock)	My 05
parson	Oc 09	passion (emotion)	Ps 05	pawnbroker	Oc 08
part (lines in a play)	Th 05	passion (love)	Ps 05	pawned item	Th 12
part (organ)	Bd 08	passion (suffering)	Ps 12	pawnshop	Pl 08
part (piece)	Th 06	passive resistance	Ps 12	payee	Oc 08
part (share)	Th 06	passivity	Ps 04	payment	Th 02
participant	Oc 01	passport	Th 09	payment received	Th 02
participating	Ps 01	password	Th 08	peace	Th 07
participation (joining in)	Th 07	past, your	Th 12	peacemaker	Oc 07
participation (joint action)	Th 07	past life	Th 04	peacock	An 05
participation (sharing)	Th 07	past mistake	Th 12	peak	Pl 10
particle	Th 04	past moment	Th 12	peak experience	Ps 10
particular (fastidious)	Ps 08	past of the matter, the	Ho 12	pearl	Co 04
particularity	Ps 01	paste	Th 04	pearl	Ge 04
particulars (details)	Th 06	pastel	Th 07	peasant	Oc 04
parting	Th 09	pastime	Th 05	peat	Th 08
partisan	Oc 11	pastry	Th 02	pebble	Th 10
partition	Th 06	pasture	Pl 04	peculiarity	Ps 11
partner's money	Ho 08	patch (fix)	Th 06	pecuniary affairs	Th 02
partner's possessions	Th 08	patent	Th 10	pedal	Th 12
partner's relatives	Re 09	paternal kin	Re 12	pedigree	Th 10
partner's room	Pl 07	paternal role	Ps 10	Pegasus (winged horse)	My 11
partners	Ho 07	paternal uncle	Re 12	pelvis	Bd 08
partners	Oc 07	paternalism	Th 10	pen (animal)	Pl 04
partners	Or 07	path	Th 03	pen (corral)	Pl 04
partnership	Mn 07	pathfinder	Oc 01	pen (writing instrument)	Th 03
partnership arrangement	Ho 07	pathologist	Oc 08	penal colony	Pl 12
partnership finances	Th 08	pathology	Th 08	penalty	Th 08
parts hidden from view	Or 12	pathos	Th 05	penance	Th 12
parts underground	Hs 04	patience	Ps 10	pencil	Th 03
parts underground	Or 04	patient	Oc 06	pendulum	Th 04
party (political)	Mn 11	patio	Hs 05	penetration	Th 01

penis	Bd 08	permission	Ho 08	personal things	Th 02
penitentiary	Pl 12	permission (consent)	Ps 08	personal transformation	Th 09
pennant	Th 04	permit	Th 08	personal values	Ps 02
pension	Th 08	perpetrator	Oc 01	personal wealth	Th 02
pensioner	Oc 08	perpetuation	Th 10	personality	Ps 01
pensiveness	Ps 10	perpetuity	Th 10	personality test	Th 06
penury	Th 12	perplexity	Th 12	personhood	Ps 05
people (in general)	Th 04	persecution	Th 08	personification	Th 03
people, those who oppose the	Mn 07	persecutor	Oc 08	personnel, the	Mn 06
		Persephone	My 04	personnel, the	Or 04
people aged 60-70	Oc 10	Perseus (the hero)	My 05	persons aged 45-60	Th 09
people aged 70-85	Oc 11	perseverance	Ho 10	persons having power	Mn 10
people awareness	Ps 07	perseverance	Ps 10	persons in misery	Oc 12
people in power	Mn 10	persistence	Ho 10	persons of mature age	Th 10
people of high status	Mn 10	persistence	Ps 10	persons of middle age	Th 09
people one works with	Ho 06	person, a	Oc 01	persons of old age	Oc 10
people who give service(s)	Mn 06	person holding office	Mn 11	persons on relief	Oc 12
		person inquired about	Oc 07	persons with authority over you	Oc 10
peptic ulcer	Bd 06	person of rank	Oc 10		
perceiving	Ps 03	person stealing	Oc 07	perspective on one's life	Ps 01
perceiving ability for	Ps 03	personal affairs	Ps 01	perspiration	Bd 04
percentage (part of)	Th 06	personal ambassador	Oc 09	persuasion	Th 09
percentages (odds)	Th 05	personal appearance	Th 01	persuasive ability	Ps 09
perception	Th 03	personal belongings	Th 02	persuasiveness	Ho 09
perfection, meeting	Ps 06	personal computer	Th 06	persuasiveness	Th 09
perforation	Th 01	personal creativity	Th 05	pertinacity	Th 02
performance (acting)	Th 05	personal effort(s)	Th 06	perusal	Th 06
performance (attainment)	Ps 10	personal finances	Th 02	perverseness	Th 11
performance (exercise)	Th 06	personal importance	Ps 02	perversion	Ps 11
performance review	Th 06	personal inadequacies	Ps 06	perversity	Th 11
performer	Oc 05	personal independence	Ho 11	pervert	Oc 11
performing, ability for	Ps 05	personal interests	Ho 01	pessimism	Ps 06
perfume	Th 02	personal interests	Ps 01	pessimist	Oc 06
perfumer	Oc 02	personal involvements	Ho 01	pest (destructive insect)	An 08
pericardium	Bd 05	personal liberty	Ps 05	pest (destructive plant)	Th 01
peridot	Ge 02	personal life	Ps 04	pest (nuisance)	Oc 01
peril	Th 08	personal limitation(s)	Ho 12	pest (plague)	Th 08
period (ending)	Th 04	personal limitation(s)	Ps 12	pestilence	Th 08
period (interval)	Th 10	Personal Loans	In 08	pet	Ho 06
periodic condition	Bd 04	personal matters	Ho 04	pet (favored one)	Th 07
periodical	Th 03	personal matters	Ps 04	pet (small)	An 06
periphery	Th 09	personal outlook	Ps 01	pet as surrogate child	Ps 05
periscope	Th 09	personal possessions	Ho 02	petition	Th 11
perishing	Th 08	personal property	Th 02	petrified wood	Ge 10
peritonitis	Af 06	personal prowess	Ps 01	petroleum	Th 09
perjury	Ps 07	personal representatives	Oc 07	petroleum (integrated)	In 12
permanence	Ps 10	personal ruin	Ho 12	petroleum (producing)	In 12
permanent thing	Th 10	personal ruin	Th 12	petty thievery	Th 03
permeability	Th 12	personal space	Th 01	pewter	Ge 04

phallic symbol	Th 08	physical handicap	Af 12	pioneer	Oc 01
phantom (ghost)	Oc 08	physical sciences, the	Th 11	pious person	Oc 09
Pharmaceuticals	In 12	physical therapy	Th 06	pipe (conduit)	Th 03
pharmacist	Oc 06	physical you, the	Ps 01	pipe (smoker's)	Th 12
pharmacy	Pl 06	physician	Oc 06	pipe dream	Th 12
pharynx	Bd 02	physicist	Oc 10	pipeline companies	In 03
phase (facet)	Th 06	physiognomy	Th 01	piping	Sh 11
phase (stage)	Th 04	physique	Bd 01	pirate	Oc 12
phase of the tide	Th 04	piano	Th 02	Pisces (fishes)	My 12
pheasant	An 05	piano tuner	Oc 02	Pisces Austrinis (southern fish)	My 12
phenomena (incident)	Th 01	pick (choice)	Th 07		
phenomena (remarkable person)	Oc 05	pick of the lot (best)	Th 10	pistol	Th 01
		picket (protester)	Oc 11	piston	Au 05
phenomena (wonder of life)	Th 05	picket (sentinel)	Th 06	piston ring	Au 06
		picket (stake)	Th 02	pit (dimple)	Th 04
philanderer	Oc 05	picketing	Th 11	pit (hole)	Pl 08
philanthropic institution	Pl 09	pickpocket	Oc 03	pitcher	Oc 01
philanthropist	Oc 09	picnic	Th 05	pitchman	Oc 03
philanthropy	Ps 09	pictor (painter's easel)	My 07	pivot	Th 10
philanthropy	Th 09	picture (movie)	Th 05	pizza	Th 04
philia (love)	Th 11	picture (representation)	Th 03	place for pleasure	Pl 05
philosopher	Oc 09	picture window	Hs 07	place hidden or out of sight	Pl 12
philosophical institution	Mn 09	piece	Th 06		
philosophical society	Th 09	pier	Pl 04	place high up	Pl 09
philosophical thinking	Ps 09	piety	Ps 12	place in society	Ps 10
philosophy	Ho 09	pig	An 04	place near genitals	Bd 08
philosophy	Ps 09	pigeon	An 04	place near water or plumbing	Pl 04
philosophy	Th 09	pigment	Th 07		
phlegm	Bd 08	pigsty	Pl 06	place of amusement	Pl 05
phobia	Ps 04	piker	Oc 10	place of business	Mn 10
Phoenix (phoenix)	My 08	pile (heap)	Th 04	place of entertainment	Pl 05
phone call	Th 03	piles	Af 08	place of fun	Pl 05
phonograph	Th 02	pilfering	Th 03	place of removal	Pl 07
phonograph record	Th 02	pilgrim	Oc 09	place of residence	Pl 04
phosphorescence	Th 04	pilgrimage	Th 09	place of rest or abode	Pl 04
photograph	Th 12	pillar (support)	Th 10	place of worship	Pl 09
photographer	Oc 12	pillow	Th 02	place one currently occupies	Pl 04
photographic image	Th 12	pilot, airline	Oc 11		
photography	Th 12	pilot, ship	Oc 04	place setting (utensils)	Th 06
Photography/Imaging	In 12	pilot house	Sh 01	place where food is kept	Pl 06
physical abnormality	Af 01	pimple	Bd 01	place where money is kept	Pl 02
physical body	Bd 01	pin (brooch)	Th 02		
physical comfort	Ps 02	pin (straight)	Th 09	place where people gather	Pl 11
physical condition	Bd 04	pin-up photo	Th 07		
physical constitution	Bd 01	pinch (discomfort)	Th 12	place with clean air	Pl 07
physical control over body	Bd 11	pinch (small amount)	Th 04	place you are moving to	Pl 07
		pinch (squeeze)	Th 01	placidity	Ps 02
physical discomfort	Ps 06	pink	Co 03	plagiarism	Th 03
physical examination	Th 06	pinnacle	Th 10	plague	Th 08

plaid	Co 09	pleasurable pursuit	Ps 05	poison accumulation	Af 08
plainness	Th 10	pleasure	Ho 05	poisonous bite	Th 08
plains	Pl 04	pleasure	Ps 05	poker (card game)	Th 05
plaintiff, the	Ho 01	pleasure, things of	Th 05	poker (metal rod)	Th 01
plaintiff, the	Oc 01	pleat (fold)	Th 11	polar bear	An 01
plan (intention)	Th 10	plebeian	Oc 04	polar opposites	Th 07
plan (map)	Th 06	pledge (promise to pay)	Th 08	polarity	Th 07
plan (scheme)	Th 06	pledge (word of honor)	Th 09	police	Mn 06
plan for the future	Th 10	Pleiades, the	My 03	police (in general)	Oc 06
plane (aircraft)	Th 11	pleurisy	Af 03	police as authority	Mn 10
planet (body)	Th 11	pliers	Th 06	policing	Th 06
planning	Or 10	plight, current	Ps 01	policy	Mn 10
planning ahead	Ps 10	plot (conspiracy)	Th 12	polish (shininess)	Th 05
plant (flora)	Th 02	plot (story line)	Th 09	polish, social	Ps 07
plant (industrial)	Th 10	Plouton	My 08	politeness	Ps 02
plant (organic)	Th 02	plow	Th 04	political atmosphere	Mn 11
plant life	Th 02	plug (stopper)	Th 10	political awareness	Ho 11
planting	Th 04	plumber	Oc 04	political convention	Mn 11
plaque (honor)	Th 10	plumbing	Hs 04	political election	Mn 11
plasma (blood parts)	Bd 02	plumbing problem (leak)	Th 11	political force	Mn 11
plasma (charged particles)	Th 05	plume (feather)	Th 06	political machine	Mn 11
		plume of smoke	Th 08	political party in opposition	Mn 04
plaster	Th 07	plunder	Th 08		
plastic	Th 12	plundering	Th 08	political party in power	Mn10
plate (for eating)	Th 04	plunge (dive)	Th 09		
platform (policy)	Mn 10	plurality	Th 09	political party not in power	Mn 04
platform (rostrum)	Th 05	Pluto	My 08		
plating	Th 12	ply (layer)	Th 06	political party out of power	Mn 04
platinum	Ge 04	pneumatics	Th 11		
platonic love	Ps 11	pneumonia	Af 03	political preferment	Mn 11
platonic relationship	Th 11	poaching	Th 03	political propaganda	Mn 09
plaudit	Th 05	pocket	Th 06	political success	Mn 10
play (recreation)	Th 05	pocketbook	Th 02	politician	Oc 11
play (theatrical)	Th 05	pockmark	Th 04	politics	Ho 11
play area	Hs 05	pod (container)	Th 04	politics	Mn 11
play maker	Oc 01	podiatrist	Oc 12	politics	Ps 11
player	Oc 05	poet	Oc 12	poll, result of	Mn 02
playground	Pl 05	poetical phrasing	Th 03	poll taker	Oc 06
playhouse	Pl 05	poetry	Th 07	pollution	Mn 08
playing (having fun)	Th 05	point (item)	Th 03	pollution	Th 08
playing, fondness for	Ps 05	point (purpose)	Th 10	pollution, afflictions from	Af 08
playing cards	Th 05	point (tip)	Th 09		
playroom	Hs 05	point of view	Ho 03	Pollution Control	In 10
playwright	Oc 03	point of view	Th 03	pollution control device	Th 05
plea	Th 07	pointed object	Th 09	polygamy	Ps 03
pleading (cry for help)	Th 12	pointer	Th 03	pomp	Th 05
pleading (legal)	Th 07	poise	Ps 07	pond	Pl 04
pleasant time	Th 05	poise	Th 07	Pontos (sea)	My 04
pleasing others	Ps 02	poison	Th 08	pool of water	Pl 04

275

pool room	Pl 05	post office	Mn 03	practice (drill)	Th 06
poop deck	Sh 07	post office	Pl 03	practice (rehearsal)	Th 05
poor, the	Oc 12	postage	Th 02	pragmatism	Th 10
poorly paid occupation	Th 05	postage stamp	Th 02	prairie	Pl 04
pope	Oc 09	postal employee	Oc 03	praise	Ho 05
populace, the	Oc 04	postal system	Mn 03	praise	Ps 05
popular item	Th 04	poster	Th 03	prana	Th 05
popularity	Ho 05	posterior	Pl 07	prayer (plea)	Th 12
popularity	Ps 05	posterity	Th 10	prayer (worship)	Th 09
popularity of state	Mn 05	posthumous work	Th 10	preacher	Oc 09
population	Mn 01	posting an entry	Th 06	precariousness	Th 08
porcelain	Th 07	postmark	Th 01	precaution	Th 10
porch	Hs 05	postmortem	Th 08	precedence (importance)	Th 10
porcupine	An 09	postponement	Th 10	precedence (priority)	Th 10
pore	Bd 01	posture (attitude)	Ps 01	precedent	Th 10
pornography	Th 08	posture (attitude), another's	Ps07	precious possession	Th 02
porousness	Th 12			precious stone	Ge 02
port (home)	Pl 04	posture (bearing)	Bd 01	preciousness (likability)	Ps 05
port (non-home)	Pl 09	potassium	Ge 06	preciousness (value)	Th 02
port side	Sh 07	potency	Th 01	precipitation	Th 04
portable possession	Th 02	potential	Ps 05	precision	Ps 06
portent	Th 08	potential ability	Ho 05	precision	Th 06
porter	Oc 06	potential action	Th 02	precision instrument	In 06
portfolio	Th 04	potion	Th 12	preconception	Th 07
portion	Th 06	potpourri	Th 11	predator	An 08
pose (airs)	Th 07	pots and pans	Th 04	predecessor	Oc 04
pose (mannerism)	Ps 01	potter	Oc 07	predestination	Th 12
pose (posture)	Th 07	pottery	Th 06	predicament	Th 01
Poseidon	My 12	pouch	Th 04	predicting the future	Th 09
position (job)	Th 10	poultice	Th 06	prediction	Th 08
position (opinion)	Ps 09	poultry	An 06	preference	Ps 11
position (place)	Th 01	poultry farmer	Oc 06	preferment	Th 10
position (situation)	Th 01	poverty	Ps 12	pregnancy	Bd 05
position (status)	Oc 10	poverty, the fear of	Ps 02	pregnancy	Ho 05
position in society	Mn 07	powder (explosive)	Th 01	prejudice	Th 07
position of management	Th 10	powder (light snow)	Th 08	premier	Oc 10
positions of power or authority	Mn 10	powder (medicinal)	Th 06	premium	Th 08
		powder (particulates)	Oc 04	premonition	Th 08
positive view	Ps 05	power (authority)	Th 10	prep school	Pl 03
positiveness	Th 05	power (energy)	Th 05	preparation (mixture)	Th 11
possession	Th 02	power (strength)	Th 01	preparation (precaution)	Th 10
possession, fixed	Th 04	power, one's personal	Ps 05	preparation (training)	Th 06
possession, movable	Th 02	power assist systems	Au 11	preparation efforts	Th 10
possession, sibling's	Th 04	power generation	In 05	prerequisite	Th 04
possessiveness	Ps 08	power of attorney	Th 07	prerogative	Th 11
possibility	Th 09	power plant	Sh 05	presage	Th 08
post (marker)	Th 06	power struggle	Mn 10	prescription	Th 06
post (station)	Pl 04	powerful people	Oc 10	presence, one's	Ps 01
post (support)	Th 10	practical efforts	Ps 06	presence, takes a major	Th 04

presence of mind	Ps 03	primary education	Mn 03	procurement practices	Mn 04
present (gift)	Th 08	facilities		prodigy	Oc 10
present, the	Ho 01	prime minister	Mn 10	produce dealer	Oc 04
present, the	Th 01	prime minister	Oc 10	produce market	Pl 04
present circumstances	Ho 01	prince or princess	Mn 10	producer	Oc 04
present residence	Th 04	principal	Oc 05	producing	Ps 04
presentation, formal	Th 09	principles	Ps 10	product	Th 04
presentation, informal	Th 03	print shop	Pl 03	product information	Th 06
preservation	Th 04	printer	Oc 03	product recall	Th 11
preserve, game	Pl 09	printer (computer)	Th 03	production (introduction)	Th 01
preserved food	Th 06	Printing	In 03	production (making)	Th 06
president	Oc 10	printing	Th 03	production (show)	Th 05
presiding judge	Oc 09	prison	Mn 12	productivity	Ho 06
press (apparatus)	Th 10	prison	Pl 12	profanity	Th 08
press (of crowd)	Th 11	prisoner	Oc 12	profession	Ho 10
press (reporters)	Oc 03	prisoner-of-war	Mn 12	profession	Ps 10
pressure (atmospheric)	Th 11	privacy	Ho 04	profession	Th 10
pressure (compression)	Th 08	privacy	Ps 04	professional	Oc 10
pressure (distress)	Ps 01	private club	Pl 10	professional ability	Ps 10
pressure (force against force)	Th 07	private enemy	Oc 12	professional affairs	Ps 10
		private investigator	Oc 08	professional classes	Mn 10
pressure (urgency)	Th 01	private life	Ps 04	professional sports	In 05
pressure suit	Th 11	private matters	Ps 04	professional sports	Th 09
pressure vessel	Th 01	private parts	Bd 08	professional sports management	Th 06
prestige	Ho 10	private problems	Ps 12		
prestige	Ps 10	private scandal	Th 12	professional sports ownership	Th 10
presumption	Th 09	private study	Th 03		
pretense (trick)	Th 03	private thing	Th 04	professional standing	Ps 10
pretension	Ps 03	privilege	Th 09	professional work	Ps 10
pretext	Th 07	prize	Th 05	professionalism	Ps 10
prevention (forestalling)	Th 10	prize fight	Th 05	professor	Oc 09
prevention (stopping)	Th 10	probate	Th 08	proficiency	Th 06
preventive maintenance	Au 06	probation	Th 10	profile (outline)	Th 03
preventive medicine	Th 06	probe	Th 08	profit	Or 11
prey (hunted game)	Th 08	probing	Ho 08	profit (compensation)	Th 02
prey (victim)	Oc 12	probing	Ps 08	profit (gain)	Th 02
preying upon	Th 08	problem	Th 08	profit from a business	Mn 11
price	Th 02	problem, personal	Ps 04	profit from a corporation	Mn 11
price fixing	Mn 03	problems of others	Th 06		
price market will bear	Mn 10	procedure	Th 10	profit from a move	Mn 08
price of a house for sale	Mn 06	proceeds (profit)	Th 02	profit from a partnership	Mn 08
price of land	Mn 06	process	Th 10		
price quotation	Mn 03	procession	Th 05	profit from a publication	Mn 04
price stability	Mn 02	proclamation	Th 03		
price tag	Th 02	proclivity	Ps 04	profit sharing plan	Or 11
price war	Mn 04	procrastination	Ps 07	profiteer	Oc 05
prickly heat	Af 05	procreation	Th 05	profligacy	Th 09
pride	Ps 05	procurement interests	Mn 04	profound mental interests	Ps 09
priest	Oc 09	procurement policy	Mn 04		

profound study	Th 09	propeller	Sh 01	protection	Ps 04
profundity	Th 09	propensity	Ps 01	protection	Th 04
profusion (plenty)	Th 09	property (land)	Th 04	protectionism	Th 04
prognostication	Th 09	property (non-real estate)	Th 02	protectionist concerns	Mn 04
program (curriculum)	Th 05	property, movable	Th 02	protective custody	Th 12
program (description)	Th 06	property, personal	Th 04	protective instincts	Ps 04
program (list of instructions)	Th 06	property damage	Th 11	protective urges	Ps 04
		property dealer	Oc 12	protective wrapper	Th 04
program (performance)	Th 05	property in escrow	Th 08	protector	Oc 04
program (schedule)	Th 06	property jointly held	Th 08	protein	Th 05
progress	Th 10	property matters	Th 04	protest	Th 11
progressive person	Oc 11	property owner	Oc 04	protocol	Th 07
progressive thought	Ps 11	property related items	Ho 04	proton	Th 04
prohibited act	Th 12	property tax	Th 08	prototype	Th 03
prohibition (preventing)	Th 10	prophecy	Ho 09	protuberance	Th 05
project	Th 06	prophecy	Ps 09	proverb	Th 09
projectile	Th 01	prophecy	Th 09	provision (anticipation)	Th 09
projection	Ps 07	prophet	Oc 09	provision (requisite)	Th 10
projection (geometrical)	Th 03	prophetic dream	Th 09	provision (supply)	Th 06
projection (juts out)	Th 05	prophetic vision	Th 09	provocation (cause)	Th 01
projectionist	Oc 05	prophylactic	Th 04	prowess (bravery)	Ps 05
projector (movie)	Th 05	proportion (balance)	Th 07	prowess (skill)	Ps 06
projector (promoter)	Oc 09	proportion (quota)	Th 06	proxy	Th 07
promenade (ceremonial march)	Th 05	proportion (ratio)	Th 03	proxy fight	Th 05
		proposal (invitation)	Th 07	prudence	Ps 10
promenade (dance step)	Th 03	proposal (offer)	Th 09	prudery	Th 06
promenade (leisurely walk)	Th 05	proposal (plan)	Th 10	pseudonym	Th 12
		proposed place to remove to	Th 07	Psyche	My 07
Prometheus (thinker, humanist)	My 03			psychedelia	Th 12
		proposition	Th 09	psychedelic drug	Th 12
promiscuity	Th 05	proprietor	Oc 10	psychiatric treatment	Th 08
promise	Th 08	propriety	Ps 10	psychiatrist	Oc 08
promise made	Ps 08	propulsion	Th 01	psychic	Oc 08
promissory note	Th 02	prose	Th 03	psychic ability	Th 08
promoter	Oc 09	prosecution	Th 08	psychic experience	Th 08
promotion (advancement)	Th 10	prospect (client)	Oc 07	psychic fair	Th 12
		prospect (hope)	Th 11	psychic feeling	Ps 08
promotion (selling)	Th 09	prospect (outlook)	Th 09	psychic influence	Ps 12
promptness	Ps 10	prospect (view)	Th 09	psychic matters	Ho 08
prong	Th 09	prospective marriage	Th 07	psychic phenomena	Th 08
pronouncement	Th 09	prospector	Oc 09	psychism	Th 08
pronunciation	Ps 01	prospectus	Th 09	psychoanalysis	Th 08
proof	Th 08	prosperity	Ps 05	psychological counselor	Oc 08
proofreader	Oc 06	prostate gland	Bd 08	psychological health	Ho 12
propaganda	Th 09	prosthesis (artificial appendage)	Th 02	psychological problem	Ps 06
propagation (reproduction)	Th 08			psychologist	Oc 08
		prostitute	Oc 08	psychometry	Th 12
propagation (travel)	Th 09	prostitution	Mn 08	psychosis	Af 12
propellant	Th 01	prostitution	Th 08	psychotherapy	Th 08

puberty	Bd 03	publications	Mn 09	punishment of crime	Mn 12
public, attitudes of the	Mn 03	publications	Th 09	punk (novice)	Oc 03
public, being out in the	Ps 10	publications, ephemeral	Th 03	punk rocker	Oc 11
public, the (in general)	Mn 04	publications, non-ephemeral	Th 09	punster	Oc 03
public affairs, your	Ps 01			pupil	Oc 03
public attention	Mn 10	publications department	Or 09	pupil (eye)	Bd 03
public ceremony	Mn 06	publicity	Th 09	puppet (marionette)	Th 06
public convention	Mn 11	publicity, personal	Ps 09	puppet (pawn)	Th 06
public enemy	Ho 07	publicity director	Oc 09	Puppis (stern of the Argo)	My 12
public enemy	Mn 07	publicity received	Th 04		
public faith	Mn 09	publisher	Oc 09	purchase (advantage)	Th 11
public gathering	Mn 11	publishing	In 09	purchase (buying)	Th 04
public health	Mn 06	publishing	Th 09	purchaser	Oc 04
public health official	Oc 06	puff (exaggeration)	Th 09	purchasing	Or 04
public institution	Mn 12	puff (swelling)	Th 05	purchasing agent	Oc 04
public investment	Mn 02	puff (whiff)	Th 04	purgatory	Pl 08
public life	Ho 10	pugnacity	Th 01	purge	Th 08
public life	Ps 10	pull (attraction)	Th 07	purification	Th 08
public money	Mn 08	pull (extract)	Th 08	puritanism	Th 10
public office	Mn 11	pull (influence)	Th 10	purity	Th 06
public opinion	Mn 04	pulley	Th 09	purple	Co 12
public place, a	Pl 01	pulling (drags along)	Th 04	purpose	Ho 10
public recognition	Ps 10	pulp novel	Th 03	purpose	Ps 10
public relations	Mn 09	pulpit	Pl 09	purse (pocketbook)	Th 02
public sales	Mn 12	pulse	Bd 04	purse (prize)	Th 05
public school system	Mn 03	pump	Th 06	pursuit (chasing)	Th 01
public servant	Oc 06	pun	Th 03	pursuit, philosophical	Ps 09
public status	Ps 10	punctuality	Th 10	pus	Bd 08
public teaching	Th 05	punctuation mark	Th 06	push-over	Oc 07
public toilet	Pl 08	puncture (deflation)	Th 08	puzzle	Th 08
public trust	Mn 09	puncture (hole)	Th 01	pygmy (dwarf)	Oc 03
public utility	Mn 11	puncture wound	Af 01	pyramid	Th 10
public welfare	Mn 12	pungency	Th 09	pyrope	Ge 03
public works	Mn 06	punishment	Ho 12	Pyxis (compass)	My 11
public you face, the	Ps 07	punishment	Ps 12		
publications	Ho 09	punishment	Th 12		

Q

quack doctor	Oc 05	quality control	Or 12	quantity (greatness)	Th 09
quadruped	An 06	quality of land or houses	Th 08	quantity (sum)	Th 06
quagmire	Pl 04	quality of products	Or 05	quantum (amount)	Th 02
qualification (limit)	Th 10	quality of real estate	Th 08	quantum (form of energy)	Th 11
qualification (standard)	Th 10	qualms	Ps 04	quantum leap	Th 09
qualifier (modifier)	Th 03	quandary	Th 08	quantum mechanics	Th 09
quality	Th 05	quantifier (modifier)	Th 03	quarantine (isolation)	Th 12
quality, things without	Th 11	quantity (amount)	Th 02	quarrel	Th 07

quarrel with another	Mn 07	query	Th 03	quicksand	Th 04
quarry	Pl 08	quesited, one being asked about	Oc 07	quiet	Th 10
quarry (hunted prey)	Th 08			quilt	Th 02
quarterdeck	Sh 03	quest	Th 09	quintessence	Th 08
quartz	Ge 12	quest for knowledge	Th 09	quitting	Th 12
quartzite	Ge 12	question	Th 03	quivering (trembling)	Th 01
quasar	Th 11	questioner	Oc 03	quiz	Th 03
queen	Oc 05	questionnaire	Th 03	quota	Th 10
queer idea	Th 11	queue	Pl 11	quotation	Th 03
querent (questioner)	Ho 01	quibbling	Th 07		
querent (questioner)	Oc 01	quickness	Th 03		

R

rabbi	Oc 09	rafters	Hs 09	rank (pay class)	Th 07
rabbit	An 02	rag (cloth)	Th 12	rank (relative position)	Th 07
raccoon	An 07	rage (anger)	Th 07	rank (social class)	Th 07
race (nationality)	Th 04	rage (mania)	Th 04	ransom	Th 08
race (running)	Th 01	raider	Oc 08	rap (blame)	Th 07
race horse	An 09	railing	Sh 10	rap (knock)	Th 01
race track	Pl 09	railroad	Th 03	rape	Th 08
racer	Oc 01	railroad worker	Oc 03	rapids	Pl 04
racket (noise)	Th 01	railroads	In 03	rapist	Oc 08
racket (paddle)	Th 01	rain	Th 04	rapport (comradery)	Th 11
racketeer	Oc 08	rain forest	Pl 02	rapture	Th 09
rackets, the	Mn 08	rainbow	Th 07	rare wood	Th 02
radar	Sh 09	raincoat	Th 04	rarity (scarcity)	Th 10
radial symmetry	Th 05	raise (in salary)	Th 08	rascal	Oc 03
radiance	Th 05	rally (competitive try)	Th 07	rash	Af 01
radiation	Th 05	rally (meeting)	Pl 11	rash action	Th 01
radiator	Au 08	rally (summon or muster up)	Ps 08	rashness	Th 01
radiator (source of heat)	Th 05			rat	An 08
radical	Oc 11	ram	An 01	ratchet	Th 10
radical idea	Th 11	rampage	Th 08	rate	Th 08
radio	Au 03	rampart	Pl 04	ratification	Th 10
radio	Th 03	ramrod	Th 10	rating	Th 06
radio as communication	Th 03	ranch	Pl 04	ratio	Th 06
radio as entertainment	Th 05	rancher	Oc 04	ration	Th 04
radio broadcasting	Th 11	rancid item	Th 08	rationale	Th 04
radio equipment	Sh 03	rancor	Ps 01	rationalizing	Ps 07
radio or television acceptance	Mn 11	randomness	Th 07	rationing	Th 10
		range (domain)	Th 05	rattle (clatter)	Th 01
radio room	Sh 03	range (pasture)	Pl 04	rattle (toy)	Th 05
radio/TV	In 09	range (variety)	Th 03	rattle of death	Th 08
radiology	Th 09	range of mountains	Pl 10	ravaging (destroying)	Th 08
raffle	Th 05	ranger	Oc 06	raven	An 03
raft	Th 04	rank (ordering)	Th 06	ravine	Pl 08

raw material	Mn 04	rebuke	Th 07	recognizance	Th 08
ray (fish)	An 10	rebuttal	Th 07	recognize, refusal to	Th 12
ray (line of light)	Th 05	recall (call to return)	Th 08	recollection	Th 04
ray (protuberance)	Th 03	recall (of a product)	Th 11	(remembering)	
ray (radiance)	Th 05	recall (remember)	Th 03	recombination	Th 08
razor	Th 01	recall (remove by vote)	Th 11	recommendation	Th 10
razzing	Th 01	recall (retrieve	Th 03	(reference)	
re-examination	Th 08	information)		recommendation	Th 11
reaction (change)	Th 08	recall (revoke)	Th 08	(urging)	
reaction (response)	Th 01	recalling	Ps 03	recompense	Th 02
reader	Oc 03	recapitulation	Th 10	reconciliation	Th 07
readiness	Th 01	receipt (profit)	Th 02	reconnaissance (scrutiny)	Th 09
reading	Th 03	receipt (voucher)	Th 06	record (account)	Th 03
reading room	Hs 09	receiver (electrical)	Th 03	record (background)	Th 10
reading room	Pl 03	receiver (fence)	Oc 03	record (unbeaten mark)	Th 10
reading thoughts	Th 01	receivership	Th 07	record keeper	Oc 06
real estate	Ho 04	receiving love	Ps 07	record keeping	Th 06
real estate	Mn 04	receiving news	Th 03	record storage place	Pl 06
real estate	Or 04	receptacle (container)	Th 04	recorder	Oc 06
real estate agent	Oc 10	receptacle (receiver)	Th 07	recording medium	Th 03
real state Investment	In 04	reception (acquiring)	Th 04	records management	In 06
real estate transaction	Th 04	reception (greeting)	Th 01	recounting	Th 03
real property	Th 04	reception (party)	Th 07	recouping	Th 08
realism	Th 10	reception room	Hs 01	recover ability to	Ps 02
realist	Oc 10	receptionist	Oc 01	recovered wealth	Th 04
reality	Th 01	receptionist	Or 01	recovery (restoration)	Th 08
reality, search for	Ps 09	receptivity	Ps 04	recovery of debts	Th 08
realization of ambition	Th 10	recess (cavity)	Th 04	recreation	In 05
realm	Pl 04	recess (playtime)	Th 05	recreation	Ho 05
realtor	Oc 10	recession	Mn 10	recreation	Th 05
reaping (finding)	Ps 12	recipe	Th 04	recreation area	Mn 05
reaping (returning)	Ho 12	recipient	Oc 07	recreation area	Sh 05
rear (back part)	Pl 04	reciprocal acts received	Ps 12	recreation room	Hs 05
of anyplace		reciprocal agreement	Th 07	recreational sex	Th 05
reason (excuse)	Th 12	reciprocal arrangement	Th 07	recreational vehicles	In 07
reason (thinking)	Th 03	reciprocity	Ps 08	recrimination	Ps 01
reasoning ability	Ps 03	recital (concert)	Th 07	rectangle	Th 10
reasons, underlying	Ps 04	recital (discourse)	Th 03	rectification (adjusting)	Th 08
reassurance	Th 05	recitation	Th 03	rectification (setting	Th 12
rebate (abatement)	Th 08	recklessness	Th 01	right)	
rebate (diminish)	Th 10	reckoning (counting)	Th 06	rectitude	Th 10
rebel	Oc 11	reckoning (settling	Th 12	rector	Oc 09
rebellion	Th 11	accounts)		rectum	Bd 08
rebelliousness	Ps 11	recluse	Oc 12	recuperation	Th 08
rebirth (reincarnation)	Th 08	recognition (honor)	Th 10	recuperative powers	Bd 08
rebirthing	Th 08	recognition (met before)	Th 03	recycling	Th 08
rebound (recoil)	Th 08	recognition (noticing)	Th 03	red	Co 01
rebound (recovery)	Th 08	recognition, earning	Ho 10	red-orange	Co 02
rebuff	Th 07	recognition received	Ps 10	redecorating the home	Th 07

redemption	Ho 12	regimentation	Th 06	relativity	Th 04
redemption	Th 12	register (ledger)	Th 06	relaxant	Th 02
redistribution	Th 09	registered mail	Th 06	relaxation	Ho 02
redistribution of wealth	Mn 07	registrar	Oc 06	relaxation	Ps 02
redoing	Th 06	registration	Th 06	relaxing activities	Ps 05
redone work	Th 06	registry	Sh 04	relay (control device)	Th 08
redress (reparation)	Th 08	regression	Th 12	relay (teamwork)	Th 11
reduction (consolidation)	Th 10	regret	Ps 12	release (freedom)	Th 12
reduction (diminishing)	Th 08	regrets	Th 12	release, wanting to effect	Ps 12
redundancy	Th 03	regular, the	Th 10	release from tension	Th 02
reek (smell)	Th 02	regularity	Th 10	releasing	Th 12
reel (dance)	Th 02	regulation (control)	Th 08	relentlessness	Th 08
reel, fishing	Th 04	regulation (rule)	Th 10	relevance	Ps 10
referee	Oc 07	regulator	Oc 08	relevance (pertinence)	Th 10
reference (analogy)	Th 09	regurgitation	Bd 03	reliability	Th 10
reference (in relation to)	Th 03	rehabilitation	Ho 12	reliance	Ps 04
reference (source)	Th 03	rehearsal	Th 03	relic	Th 04
reference, indirect	Th 03	reimbursement	Th 08	relief (easement)	Th 02
referendum	Th 11	reincarnation	Th 08	relief (respite)	Th 12
referral	Th 03	reindeer	An 11	relief (welfare)	Th 12
refinement	Ps 07	reinforcement (assistance)	Th 08	relief agency	Pl 12
refinement	Th 07			relief work	Th 12
refinery	Pl 08	reinforcement (fresh addition)	Th 08	religion	Ho 09
reflection (memory)	Th 04			religion	Th 09
reflection (return of image)	Th 04	reinforcement (reward)	Th 08	religion, national	Mn 09
		reiteration	Th 03	religious affairs	Mn 09
reflectiveness	Ps 04	rejection (denial)	Th 07	religious education	Mn 09
reflector	Th 07	rejection, fear of	Ps 07	religious items	Th 09
reflex (inborn response)	Th 04	rejuvenation	Th 08	religious person	Oc 09
reflexes	Bd 01	relapse	Th 12	religious preferment	Th 09
reform school	Pl 12	relating (connecting)	Ps 07	religious pursuits	Ho 09
reformer	Oc 08	relating to other countries	Mn 07	religious sense	Ps 09
reforming activities	Ho 08			Religious Services	In 09
reforms	Th 08	relation (kin)	Th 03	religious views	Ps 09
refrain (in music or poem)	Th 03	relations of the quesited	Re 09	religious workers	Oc 09
		relations with educators	Mn 09	relinquish, ability to	Ps 12
refraining (abstaining)	Th 12	relations with elected officials	Or 11	relinquishing	Ps 12
refreshments	Th 02			relish (pleasure)	Th 05
refrigeration	Th 08	relations with family	Mn 04	relocating	Th 03
refrigerator	Hs 06	relations with leaders	Mn 10	relocation, place of	Pl 07
refuge	Pl 12	relations with other countries	Mn 07	relocation office	Or 03
refugee	Oc 12			reluctance	Th 08
refund	Th 02	relations with parents	Mn 04	relying on another	Ps 09
refusal	Th 07	relations with the public	Mn 07	remainder, the	Th 12
refuse (waste)	Th 12	relationships	Ho 07	remaindered items	Th 12
regalia	Th 05	relationships	Ps 07	remains	Th 04
regeneration	Th 08	relationships	Th 07	remake	Th 08
regime, the	Mn 01	relative	Re 03	remarks	Th 03
regiment	Th 06	relative of a parent	Re 12	remedy (cure)	Th 06

remedy (relief)	Th 12	repeal	Th 08	reputation	Ps 10
remembering	Th 03	repeating	Th 03	request (application)	Th 03
remembrance (memento)	Th 04	repellent	Th 08	request (demand)	Th 08
remembrance (memory)	Th 03	repentance	Ps 12	requirement (condition)	Th 07
reminder	Th 03	repercussion	Th 08	requirement (necessity)	Th 10
reminiscence	Th 09	repertoire	Th 06	requisition (formal demand)	Th 10
remission	Th 12	repertory	Th 06		
remnant	Th 12	repetition	Th 03	rerun	Th 03
remodeling	Th 06	replacement (restoration)	Th 08	resale	Th 08
remorse (regret)	Ps 12	replacement (substitute)	Th 03	resale value	Ho 10
remote consequences	Ho 12	replay	Th 03	rescue	Th 12
remote consequences	Th 12	replenishment (restocking)	Th 06	rescue mission	Pl 12
remote place	Pl 09			research	Th 08
remoteness	Th 09	replica	Th 03	research and development	Or 08
removal	Ho 08	replication (answer)	Th 03		
removing (extracting)	Th 08	replication (copy)	Th 03	research organization	Pl 08
removing the excess	Th 08	reply	Th 03	research project	Th 08
remuneration	Th 08	replying	Ps 03	research services	In 08
rendering	Th 08	report (account)	Th 03	researcher	Oc 08
rendezvous	Pl 11	report (detonation)	Th 01	researching new methods	Th 08
rendition	Th 03	report card	Th 02		
renegade	Oc 11	reporter	Oc 03	resemblance	Th 03
renewal	Th 08	repose	Th 02	resentment	Th 08
renewed or restored thing	Th 08	repository	Pl 06	resentment, harboring	Ps 08
		repossession	Th 08	reservation	Pl 04
renovation	Th 08	representation	Th 07	reservation (guarantee)	Th 08
renown	Th 10	representation of self	Ps 01	reserve (reticence)	Th 10
rent (fee)	Th 02	representative (business)	Oc 07	reserve (stockpile)	Th 06
rent (tear)	Th 08	representative (political)	Oc 11	reservoir	Pl 04
rental property	Pl 04	repression	Ps 08	reshape	Th 08
rental resided in, the	Pl 04	repression	Th 12	reshuffle	Th 11
rental/leasing services	In 11	reprieve	Ho 12	residence	Pl 04
renter	Oc 06	reprieve	Th 12	residence while abroad	Pl 11
renunciation	Th 12	reprimand	Th 07	resident	Oc 04
renunciation, ability for	Ps 12	reprint	Th 03	residuals	Th 12
reorganization	Th 08	reprisal	Th 08	residue	Th 12
reorganizer	Oc 08	reproach (blame)	Th 07	resignation (acceptance)	Ps 08
repair efforts	Ps 06	reprobate	Oc 12	resignation (quitting)	Th 10
repair person	Oc 06	reproduction (copying)	Th 03	resilience	Th 08
repair processes	Bd 05	reproduction (procreation)	Th 05	resin	Th 02
repair work	Th 06			resistance (opposition)	Th 07
repairer	Oc 06	reptile	An 08	resistance, electrical	Th 11
repairing	Th 06	republic, the	Mn 01	resolution (persistence)	Th 08
repairs	Th 06	republican	Oc 10	resolution (solving)	Th 10
repairs made	Au 06	repudiation	Th 12	resonance	Th 02
reparation	Th 08	repulsion	Th 07	resonance (orbital)	Th 07
repartee	Th 03	reputation	Ho 10	resort, pleasure	Pl 05
repast	Th 04	reputation	Mn 10	resort area	Pl 05
repayment	Th 08	reputation	Or 10	resource (leisure time)	Th 05

283

resource (natural wealth)	Mn 04	resurrection	Th 08	reversal	Th 08
resource (support)	Th 06	resuscitation	Th 08	reverses	Th 08
resourcefulness	Th 05	retail (apparel)	In 06	reversion	Ps 12
resources (funds)	Th 02	retail (department stores)	In 04	reverting	Th 08
respect (detail)	Th 06	retail (drugstore)	In 04	review (ceremonial inspection)	Th 06
respect (regard)	Th 10	retail (food chain)	In 04		
respect, demanding	Ps 08	retail (special lines)	In 04	review (critique)	Th 06
respectability	Th 10	retail building supply	In 07	review (journal)	Th 03
respects (greetings)	Th 03	retail stores	In 04	review (re-examine)	Th 08
respiration	Th 03	retainer	Oc 06	revision (change)	Th 08
respiratory problems	Af 03	retainer (fee)	Th 08	revival	Th 08
respiratory system, the	Bd 03	retaining	Ps 04	revocation	Th 08
respiratory therapist	Oc 03	retaliation	Th 08	revolt	Th 11
resplendence	Th 05	retardation	Th 12	revolution	Th 11
response (action)	Th 01	retelling	Th 03	revulsion	Th 08
response (reply)	Th 03	retention	Th 04	reward (appreciation)	Th 10
response to situations	Ps 04	reticence	Th 10	reward (prize)	Th 10
responsibility	Ho 10	reticulum (net)	My 04	rewards	Ho 10
responsibility (liability)	Th 10	retina	Bd 01	rhapsody	Th 02
responsibility, accepting	Ps 10	retired person	Oc 02	Rheia	My 03
responsiveness	Th 04	retirement	Ho 08	rheostat	Th 08
rest (relax)	Th 02	retirement	Th 08	rhetoric	Th 03
rest (remain motionless)	Th 02	retirement fund	Mn 08	rheumatism	Af 10
rest (remainder)	Th 12	retirement plan	Or 08	rhinoceros	An 12
rest (sleep)	Th 02	retort	Th 03	rhodolite	Ge 03
rest home	Pl 12	retraction	Th 08	rhyme	Th 03
rest room	Or 08	retreat	Pl 12	rhythm	Th 04
rest room	Pl 08	retreat (withdrawal)	Th 12	ribaldry	Th 03
restatement	Th 03	retribution	Ps 08	ribbon	Th 06
Restaurant	In 04	retrieval	Th 08	ribs	Bd 03
restaurant	Pl 06	retrofitting	Th 06	rich colors	Co 05
resting place, your final	Pl 04	retrogression	Th 12	rich people	Oc 05
restitution	Ho 08	retrospection	Th 08	riches	Th 02
restitution	Ps 08	return (election result)	Th 02	rickets	Af 10
restlessness	Ps 03	return (profit from investment	Th 02	ridding	Ps 08
restoration	Th 08			ridding	Th 08
restraint (control)	Ps 10	return (recurrence)	Th 04	riddle	Th 03
restraint (shackle)	Th 04	returning	Ps 12	ride	Au 05
restriction (limitation)	Th 10	returning (coming back)	Th 12	rider (addition)	Th 05
restrictions (rules)	Th 10	returns (restitution)	Th 08	ridge	Pl 10
restrictive conditions	Th 10	reunion	Th 11	ridicule	Th 03
restructuring a corporation	Mn 08	revelation	Th 09	rifle	Th 01
		revenge	Th 08	rigging	Sh 11
result (accomplishment)	Th 10	revenue	Mn 02	right (authority)	Th 10
result (consequence)	Th 10	revenue	Th 02	right and wrong (sense of)	Ps 09
result (outcome)	Th 04	reverberation	Th 01		
result of a lawsuit	Th 04	reverence (awe)	Th 09	right angle	Th 10
results orientation	Ps 11	reverence (honor)	Th 10	right-of-way	Th 07
resurgence	Th 08	reverie (daydream)	Th 12	right-wing movements	Mn 10

righteousness	Ps 09	role playing	Ps 05	program)	
righteousness	Th 09	roll (coast)	Th 02	routine (everyday things)	Th 04
rights, one's	Ps 01	roll (drumbeat)	Th 01	routine (skit)	Th 05
rigidity	Th 10	roll (food)	Th 06	routine, an entertainer's	Th 05
rigor	Th 06	roll (roster)	Th 06	routine activities	Ho 04
ring (group)	Th 11	roll (scroll)	Th 03	routine activities	Th 04
ring (jewelry)	Th 02	roll (tumble)	Th 10	routine movement or travel	Th 03
ringleader	Oc 10	roll of thunder	Th 01		
ringworm, skin	Af 10	roller coaster	Th 05	rover	Oc 03
rink	Pl 05	roller skates	Th 03	rowdiness	Th 01
riot	Th 08	romance	Ho 05	royal purple	Co 12
rip	Th 01	romance	Ps 05	royalty (commission)	Th 02
ripeness	Th 04	romance with commitment	Ps 07	royalty (nobility)	Oc 10
rising	Th 01			rubber	Th 03
risk (peril)	Th 01	romance without commitment	Ps 05	rubbish	Th 12
risk (speculation)	Th 05			rubble	Th 08
risk, taking on a	Ho 05	romantic feelings	Ps 05	rubellite	Ge 11
risks, national	Mn 05	romantic love	Ps 05	ruby	Ge 01
risky ventures	Th 05	romantic tragedy	Th 04	rudder	Sh 03
rite	Th 09	roof	Hs 10	rudeness	Ps 07
ritual	Th 09	roof garden	Pl 10	ruffian	Oc 08
rival	Oc 07	room (cubicle)	Pl 04	rug	Hs 07
rivalry	Th 07	room (margin)	Th 04	ruin, desires to	Ps 08
river	Mn 04	room (space)	Th 04	ruins	Pl 04
river	Pl 04	rooming house	Pl 04	rule (custom)	Th 04
river	Th 04	roost	Pl 04	rule (dominion)	Th 05
river barge	Th 03	rooster	An 01	rule (guide)	Th 01
rivet	Th 04	root (basic element)	Th 04	rule (measure)	Th 06
road	Mn 03	root (of plant)	Th 04	rule (regulation)	Th 10
road	Pl 03	root (origin)	Th 04	rule (reign)	Th 05
road grader	Th 01	rope	Th 04	ruler	Oc 05
roaring	Th 01	rosary	Th 09	ruler (measure)	Th 06
robber	Oc 07	rose	Co 03	rulership	Th 05
robbery	Th 07	rose colored glasses	Th 12	ruling (final decision)	Th 04
robe	Th 06	rose quartz	Ge 12	ruling classes	Mn 10
robot	Th 11	roster	Th 06	rumor	Th 03
rock	Th 10	rostrum (podium)	Th 05	runaway	Oc 07
rock climber	Oc 10	rot	Th 08	running	Th 01
rock concert	Th 05	rotation	Th 10	running lights	Sh 11
rock crystal	Ge 12	rotor	Th 10	rupture	Af 01
rock hound	Oc 10	rouge	Th 02	rupture (break)	Th 01
rocket	Th 11	rough spot	Th 01	ruse	Th 03
rocking chair	Th 04	rough-housing	Th 01	rust	Th 12
rocky ground	Pl 10	roughness (quality)	Th 01	rust prevention	Au 06
rodent	An 08	roughness of character	Ps 01	rust proofing	In 08
rodeo	Th 05	roulette	Th 05	rutilated stones	Ge 11
rogue	Oc 07	roulette wheel	Th 05		
role (expected behavior)	Ps 07	round object	Th 05		
role model	Oc 10	routine (computer	Th 06		

S

saber	Th 01	salute (greeting)	Th 01	saving (activity of)	Th 04
sabotage	Th 08	salute (honor)	Th 10	savings	Th 02
sachet	Th 02	salvage	Th 08	savings and loan	In 02
sacrament	Th 09	salvage brokers	In 08	savior	Oc 12
sacrifice	Ps 12	salve	Th 06	saw (tool)	Th 01
sacrifice	Th 12	samadhi	Th 09	saying	Th 09
saddle	Th 09	sameness	Th 10	scab	Th 04
sadism	Th 08	sample (specimen)	Th 03	scaffold	Th 10
sadist	Oc 08	sanatorium	Pl 12	scald	Af 01
sadness	Th 12	sanctuary	Pl 12	scale (musical)	Th 02
sado-masochism	Th 08	sand (common)	Ge 04	scale (weighing)	Th 07
safe (strongbox)	Th 02	sandals	Th 12	scale-back	Th 10
safe deposit box	Th 02	sandpaper	Th 11	scalp	Bd 01
safe haven	Pl 12	sandwich	Th 04	scalp infection	Af 01
safety	Th 04	sandy color	Co 05	scalpel	Th 01
safety cushion	Th 04	sandy place	Pl 04	scaly skin	Af 10
saffron	Co 09	sanidine	Ge 04	scandal	Th 12
sag	Th 02	sanitarium	Pl 12	scanner	Th 11
sagacity	Th 09	sanitary practices	Mn 06	scantiness	Th 10
sage	Oc 09	sanitary systems	Sh 08	scapegoat	Oc 12
Sagitta (arrow)	My 09	sanitation	Th 06	scar	Af 01
Sagittarius (archer)	My 09	sanitation worker	Oc 06	scarcity	Th 10
sail	Sh 05	sanity	Ps 03	scare	Th 08
sailing (departure)	Th 09	sap	Th 02	scarecrow	Th 08
sailing (recreational)	Th 05	sapling	Th 02	scarf	Th 02
sailor	Oc 04	sapphire	Ge 01	scarlet	Co 09
saint	Oc 09	sarcasm	Th 03	scattering	Th 11
salamander	An 10	sard	Ge 09	scavenger	An 08
salary	Ho 02	sardonyx	Ge 09	scenario (outline)	Th 06
salary	Th 02	Sasquatch	My 12	scene	Th 01
salary owed	Th 08	satan	Oc 08	scenery (backdrop)	Th 05
salary received	Th 02	satchel	Th 06	scenery (landscape)	Th 04
sales	Or 09	satellite (outpost)	Pl 09	scenery (vista)	Th 05
sales	Th 09	satellite (space)	Th 11	scepter	Th 05
sales person	Oc 09	satin	Th 07	schedule (agenda)	Th 06
sales promotion	Th 09	satire	Th 03	schedule (timetable)	Th 06
sales tax	Mn 08	satisfaction	Ps 02	schematic	Th 06
sales transaction	Th 03	satisfaction, receiving	Ps 02	scheme	Th 03
salesmanship	Ps 09	satisfaction, seeking	Ps 08	schemer	Oc 03
salivary glands	Bd 04	saturation (fullness)	Th 09	schism	Th 07
salon	Pl 07	saturation (permeation)	Th 04	scholar	Oc 09
salon	Sh 07	Saturn	My 10	school	Mn 03
saloon	Pl 05	Satyr	My 08	school	Pl 03
salt	Th 10	savage	Oc 08	school, elementary	Pl 03
salute (firecracker)	Th 01	savagery	Th 08	school, secondary	Pl 03

school child	Oc 03	script (cursive writing)	Th 03	seat (chair)	Th 02
school construction	In 10	script (manuscript)	Th 03	seat (membership)	Th 11
school equipment	In 10	scripture	Th 09	seat (residence)	Pl 04
school functions	Th 05	scrofula	Af 02	seat belt	Au 04
school master	Oc 05	scroll (for writing)	Th 03	seating room	Au 04
school room	Pl 03	scroll (ornamental)	Th 07	seats, the	Au 02
school teacher	Oc 05	scrotum	Bd 08	seaweed	Th 04
schooling	Ho 03	scrub brush	Th 06	secession	Mn 08
schooling	Th 03	scruples (anxiety)	Ps 06	secluded place	Pl 12
schoolmate	Oc 03	scruples (ethics)	Ps 09	seclusion (hiding place)	Pl 12
schooner	Th 04	scrutiny	Th 08	seclusion (solitude)	Th 12
schorl	Ge 11	scullery	Hs 06	second (helper)	Oc 06
sciatic nerve	Bd 09	sculptor	Oc 07	second (runner-up)	Oc 09
sciatica	Af 09	sculptor (sculptor)	My 07	second of time	Th 10
science	Th 08	sculpture	Th 07	secrecy	Th 12
science fiction	Th 04	scum	Th 08	secret	Th 12
science of astrology	Th 11	scurvy	Af 03	secret, keeping a	Ps 12
scientific equipment	Th 01	Scutum (shield)	My 04	secret, sibling's	Th 02
scientific societies	Th 06	scythe	Th 01	secret agent	Oc 12
scientific staff	Or 01	sea, the	Th 04	secret belief	Th 08
scientific work	Th 01	sea blue	Co 02	secret cabal	Mn 12
scientist	Oc 08	sea green	Co 02	secret dealings	Th 08
scissors	Th 01	sea gull	An 11	secret enemy	Ho 12
scolding	Th 07	sea voyage	Th 09	secret enemy	Mn 12
scope (extent)	Th 10	seal	An 05	secret enemy	Oc 12
scorching	Th 01	seal (mark)	Th 01	secret enmity	Ps 12
score (musical)	Th 02	seal (navy unit)	Oc 08	secret fear	Ps 04
score (nick)	Th 04	sealant	Th 10	secret organization	Mn 12
scorn	Th 07	seam (furrow)	Th 04	secret police force	Mn 12
scorpion	An 08	seam (joint)	Th 03	secret service	Mn 12
Scorpius (scorpion)	My 08	seam (layer)	Th 06	secret society	Mn 12
scouring	Th 11	seaman	Oc 04	secret sorrow	Ps 12
scout	Oc 09	seamstress	Oc 06	secret worry	Ps 12
scrap (junk)	Th 08	seance	Th 08	secretary	Oc 06
scrap dealer	Oc 12	seance room	Pl 08	secretions	Bd 08
scrap metal dealers	In 08	seaplane	Th 02	secretiveness	Ps 12
scrapbook	Th 04	seaport	Mn 04	secrets	Ho 12
scrape	Af 01	seaport	Pl 04	sect	Th 11
scraper	Th 01	search (hunt)	Th 09	section (area)	Pl 04
scraping	Th 01	search (investigation)	Th 08	section (branch)	Or 06
scratch	Th 01	search (probe)	Th 11	section (branch)	Th 06
scratching	Th 01	search (scrutiny)	Th 08	section (installment)	Th 04
scream	Th 01	search warrant	Th 08	section (specimen)	Th 03
screen (for hiding)	Th 04	searchlight	Th 05	sector (zone)	Th 04
screen (projection)	Th 12	seashore	Pl 04	securities	Mn 02
screening processes	Th 06	seasoning	Th 02	securities (bonds, etc.)	Th 02
screw (fastener)	Th 04	seasons, the	Th 04	securities brokerage	In 05
screw (propeller)	Th 01	seat (buttocks)	Bd 08	security	Ps 04
scribe	Oc 03	seat (center)	Th 05	security (defense)	Th 04

security (free from danger)	Th 04	self-indulgence	Ps 02	sensitization	Th 04
		self-injury	Ps 12	sensuality	Ps 08
security (pledge)	Th 08	self-integration	Ps 04	sensuous enjoyment	Ps 02
security blanket	Th 04	self-interest (things done in)	Ps 05	sentence (grammar)	Th 03
security force	Or 08			sentence (verdict)	Th 04
security guard	Oc 08	self-involvement	Ps 01	sentiment (feeling)	Ps 04
security needs	Ps 04	self-judgment	Ps 08	sentiment (opinion)	Th 04
security services	In 01	self-pity	Ho 12	sentry	Oc 06
security system providers	In 04	self-pity	Ps 12	separateness	Th 08
sedative	Th 12	self-possession	Ps 05	separateness (being apart)	Th 08
sediment	Th 10	self-preservation	Ps 01		
sedition	Th 07	self-projection(s)	Ps 07	separation (breaking apart)	Th 08
seduction	Th 08	self-restraint	Ps 10		
seed	Th 02	self-sacrifice	Ps 12	separation (division)	Th 06
seeing, sense of	Bd 01	self-transformation	Ps 08	separation (parting)	Th 09
seeing through anything	Ps 09	self-undoing	Ho 12	separation, undergoing	Th 07
seeking of admiration	Ps 05	self-undoing	Mn 12	separation anxiety	Ps 04
seer	Oc 09	self-undoing	Ps 12	separation in marriage	Th 07
segment (piece)	Th 06	self-wastage	Ps 12	septic system	Hs 08
segregation	Th 11	self-worth	Ps 02	sepulcher	Pl 08
seismology	Th 10	selfishness	Ps 07	sequel	Th 03
seizing	Ps 08	selfishness	Th 07	sequence (episode)	Th 03
seizure (attack)	Af 08	selfless deed	Th 12	sequence (succession)	Th 06
seizure (taking)	Th 08	selfless giving	Th 12	serenade	Th 02
selection	Th 06	selfless service	Th 12	serenity	Th 02
selectivity	Ps 06	seller	Oc 09	serf	Oc 06
Selene (moon)	My 04	seller (in an exchange)	Mn 07	serial	Th 03
self, pride in	Ps 05	selling	Th 09	series (progression)	Th 05
self, the	Ho 01	semantics	Th 03	serious people	Oc 10
self, the	Ps 01	semaphore	Th 03	seriousness	Th 10
self, the	Re 01	semen	Bd 08	sermon (lecture)	Th 09
self-analysis	Ps 08	semiconductor equipment	In 06	sermon (preaching)	Th 09
self-assertion	Ps 01	semiconductor manufacturers	In 11	Serpens (serpent)	My 08
self-centeredness	Ps 05			serpent	An 08
self-confidence	Ps 01	senate	Mn 11	servant	Oc 06
self-defeating behavior	Ps 12	senator	Oc 11	servants of the country	Mn 06
self-denial	Ho 12	senility	Af 10	service	Ho 06
self-denial	Ps 12	senior (grade)	Th 06	service	Ps 06
self-destruction	Ps 12	seniority	Th 10	service	Th 06
self-destructive processes	Ps 12	seniors (older people)	Oc 10	service (involuntary)	Th 12
self-development	Ps 10	sensationalism	Th 05	service, hidden	Th 12
self-discovery	Ps 01	sensations	Bd 02	service, military	Th 06
self-esteem sense of	Ps 02	sense of humor	Ps 05	service freely given	Th 06
self-expression	Ps 03	sense perceptions	Bd 02	service of repair person	Th 11
self-fulfillment	Ps 10	senses	Bd 02	service rendered or received	Th 06
self-hood	Ps 01	sensibility	Ps 07		
self-image	Ps 01	sensitive people	Oc 12	service repairman	Oc 06
self-importance	Ps 05	sensitivities, one's	Ps 04	service station	Pl 09
self-improvement	Ps 01	sensitivity to others	Ps 04	service to others	Th 06

serving	Th 06	shade (ghost)	Th 08	shift in attitudes, a	Ps 04
serving mankind	Mn 12	shadow (imitation)	Th 03	shift in location, a	Th 03
serving platter	Th 06	shadow (partial darkness)	Th 07	shift of values, a	Ps 04
servitude	Th 06	shadow nature	Ps 07	shifting positions	Ps 03
session (meeting)	Th 07	shaft	Sh 11	shiftlessness	Th 07
session (term)	Th 09	shaft (handle)	Th 03	shimmy (vibration)	Th 04
setting fires	Ps 08	shaft alley	Sh 10	shin splints	Af 11
settlement (finality)	Th 08	shakeout	Th 12	shingle (roofing)	Th 10
settlement, financial	Mn 08	shaking (quivering)	Th 01	shins	Bd 11
settlement of disputes	Mn 07	shallowness (lack of depth)	Ps 07	ship	Ho 04
settling	Hs 08			ship	Th 04
severance	Th 08	sham (hoax)	Th 12	ship at sea	Th 01
severity	Th 10	shambles (wreckage)	Th 08	ship's log	Sh 03
sewage	Th 08	shame	Ps 12	shipment	Th 03
sewer	Pl 08	shampoo	Th 06	shipper	Oc 04
sewer drain	Hs 08	shape (form)	Th 01	shipping	Th 04
sewing	Th 06	shape shifter	Th 12	shipping clerk	Oc 04
sewing machine	Th 11	shaping attitudes	Ps 11	shipwreck	Th 08
sewing room	Hs 06	shaping the future	Ho 11	shirt	Th 05
sex	Bd 08	share (portion)	Th 06	shivering	Bd 01
sex	Ho 08	share holders	Or 05	shock, electrical	Th 11
sex, orgasmic	Bd 08	shared assets	Th 08	shock, psychological	Ps 11
sex appeal	Ps 08	shared expenses	Th 08	shock absorbers	Au 07
sex object	Oc 08	shared resources	Mn 08	Shoe Manufacturers	In 12
sex organs, external	Bd 08	shared things or values	Ho 08	Shoe Repair	In 06
sex organs, internal	Bd 07	sharing	Ho 08	shoe repairer	Oc 12
Sextans (sextant)	My 06	sharing	Ps 08	shoe store	Pl 04
sextant	Th 06	sharing feelings	Ps 11	shoemaker	Oc 12
sexual activity	Th 05	sharp ache	Af 01	shoes	Th 12
sexual affairs	Th 08	sharp objects	Th 01	shooting(s)	Th 01
sexual deviant	Oc 06	sharpening stone	Th 10	shop	Pl 04
sexual disease	Af 08	sharpness	Th 01	shopkeeper	Oc 04
sexual energy	Ps 08	sharpness (alertness)	Ps 03	shoplifter	Oc 03
sexual harassment	Th 03	shawl	Th 04	shoplifting	Th 03
sexual intercourse	Bd 08	shears	Th 01	shopper	Oc 04
sexual merging	Ps 08	sheath (covering)	Th 04	shopping mall	Pl 04
sexual organs	Bd 08	sheath (knife case)	Th 04	shore (land)	Pl 04
sexual passion	Ps 08	sheep	An 06	shore (seacoast)	Pl 04
sexual perversion	Ps 11	shell	Ge 04	shore line (hawser)	Sh 04
sexual pleasure	Ps 05	shellfish	An 04	short changing	Th 03
sexual power	Ps 08	shelter	Pl 04	short distance travel	Ho 03
sexual release	Ps 08	shelving (for books)	Th 03	short selling	Mn 01
sexuality	Ho 08	shelving (for storage)	Hs 06	short trips	Ho 03
sexuality	Ps 08	shepherd	Oc 06	short trips	Th 03
sexuality	Th 08	sheriff	Oc 08	short trips of partner	Th 09
shabbiness	Th 12	shield	Th 04	shortage (deficit)	Th 10
shack	Pl 04	shift (displacement)	Th 08	shortage (lack)	Th 10
shackles	Th 04	shift (dodge)	Th 03	shortcoming (fault)	Th 06
shade (cool place)	Pl 10	shift (of work)	Th 06	shortcut	Th 03

shortening (abbreviating)	Th 03	sienna	Co 05	sinister actions	Th 12
shortening (fat)	Th 12	sieve	Th 12	sink	Hs 06
shorthand	Th 03	sigh	Th 12	sins of commission	Th 08
shortness (lack of height)	Th 03	sight	Th 01	sins of omission	Th 08
shorts (clothing)	Th 05	Sightseeing Services	In 09	sinus	Bd 01
shoulder blades	Bd 05	sign (hint)	Th 08	siphon	Th 06
shoulders	Bd 03	sign (message)	Th 03	siren	Oc 12
shoulders (of road)	Th 03	sign in	Th 01	siren	Th 01
shouting	Th 01	sign language	Th 03	sister	Re 03
shovel	Th 08	sign off	Th 09	sister-in-law	Re 09
show and tell	Th 01	sign on	Th 01	Sisyphos (betrayal)	My 12
show business	Th 05	signage	Th 03	sit-in	Th 07
showboat	Pl 05	signal	Th 03	sitcom	Th 05
shower	Hs 06	signal deck	Sh 03	site	Pl 04
shower (rain)	Th 04	signal equipment	Sh 03	sitting	Th 02
shower (rush of things)	Th 09	signatory	Oc 03	situation (job)	Th 06
shower stall	Hs 06	signature	Th 03	situation (location)	Th 01
showoff	Oc 05	significance	Ps 02	situation (plight)	Th 01
shrew	Oc 06	significance (importance)	Th 10	situation (status)	Th 01
shrewdness	Th 03	significance (meaning)	Th 01	size	Ho 02
shrimp	An 04	significant thing	Th 02	size	Th 02
shrine	Pl 09	significant vision	Th 09	skates (ice, roller, etc.)	Th 05
shrinkage (drawing back)	Th 12	signing a contract	Mn 03	skeletal system	Bd 10
shrinkage (shortening)	Th 08	signing of papers	Th 03	skeleton	Th 10
shroud	Th 08	silence	Th 10	skeleton in the closet	Th 12
shrubbery	Hs 02	silhouette	Th 03	skeptic	Oc 06
shunned objects / people	Th 12	silk	Th 02	skepticism	Th 06
shut-in	Oc 12	silo	Pl 06	sketch	Th 03
shut-out (big win)	Th 01	silt (fine dirt)	Th 10	skew (slant)	Th 03
shut-out (excluded)	Th 12	silt (obstruction)	Th 10	skewer	Th 01
shyness	Ps 03	silver	Co 04	ski tow	Th 03
shyster	Oc 03	silver	Ge 04	skid (support)	Th 10
siberite	Ge 11	silverplate	Ge 04	skid (wheel substitute)	Th 12
sibling	Ho 03	silversmith	Oc 04	skill (craft)	Th 06
sibling	Re 03	silverware	Th 04	skill (cunning)	Th 03
sibling rivalry	Ps 03	silvery gray	Co 04	skill (prowess)	Th 06
sick bay	Sh 06	silvery-blue	Co 04	skin	Bd 10
sick leave	Th 10	silvery-green	Co 04	skin	Sh 10
sick room	Hs 06	similarity	Ho 03	skin blemish	Bd 03
sick room	Pl 06	similarity	Th 03	skin condition	Bd 10
sickness	Ho 06	simplicity	Th 10	skin rash	Af 10
sickness	Th 06	simplification	Th 10	skin ulcer	Af 10
sickness, its quality or causes	Th 06	simulation	Th 03	skirmish	Th 07
		simulator	Th 03	skirt	Th 05
side trips on vacation	Th 07	sin	Ho 08	skit (performance)	Th 05
sides of the body	Bd 05	sin	Th 08	skull	Bd 01
sidestepping	Th 03	sincerity	Ps 10	skunk	An 08
sidewalk	Pl 03	singer	Oc 02	sky	Th 09
siege	Th 08	singularity	Th 08	sky blue	Co 11

Alpha Sort with Industries

skydiving	Th 05	slope (incline)	Th 10	snag (protuberance)	Th 05
skylight	Hs 05	sloppiness	Ps 12	snail	An 04
skyscraper	Pl 10	sloth	An 02	snake	An 08
slack (looseness)	Th 03	slouch (droop)	Th 12	snap (abrupt closing)	Th 01
slack (shortfall)	Th 08	slough	Pl 08	snap (as in football)	Th 01
slag	Th 08	slowing down	Ho 02	snap (weather change)	Th 12
slander	Ps 07	slowing down	Th 02	snapshot	Th 12
slang	Th 03	slowness	Th 02	snare (capture)	Th 07
slant (bias)	Th 09	sludge	Th 08	snare (difficulty)	Th 01
slant (diagonal)	Th 03	slug	An 04	snare (trap)	Th 04
slant (slope)	Th 10	slum	Pl 12	snarl (knot)	Th 03
slat	Th 04	slumber	Th 02	sneak	Oc 12
slate	Ge 10	slump (lapse)	Th 12	sneer	Th 03
slate gray	Co 10	slump (slouch)	Th 12	sneeze	Af 03
slaughter house	Pl 08	slyness	Th 03	snip (fragment)	Th 06
slave	Oc 06	small animals	An 06	snobbery	Th 07
slavery	Th 12	small animals	Ho 06	snootiness	Th 07
sleazy person	Oc 12	small boat	Th 04	snooze	Th 02
sled	Th 03	small intestine	Bd 06	snoring	Th 01
sleep	Th 02	small of the back	Bd 07	snow	Th 08
sleep, inability to	Th 06	small talk	Th 03	snub	Th 07
sleeping posture	Ps 04	smallness	Th 03	snugness (fits closely)	Th 04
sleeping posture	Th 02	smash (collision)	Th 01	soap	Th 06
sleepwalking	Th 01	smash (hit)	Th 10	sob story	Th 05
sleeve	Th 03	smear (slander)	Th 08	sobbing	Th 12
sleigh	Th 03	smear (stain)	Th 09	sobriety	Ps 10
slice (graft)	Th 05	smell: sense of	Bd 02	sociability	Ps 07
slicing (cutting)	Th 01	smelter	Th 05	social affair	Th 11
slide (chute)	Th 03	smile	Th 02	social alliance	Mn 11
slide (coast)	Th 02	smirk	Th 03	social call	Th 03
slide (photographic)	Th 12	smith	Oc 06	social change	Mn 09
slight of hand	Th 03	smoke house	Pl 06	social club	Or 11
slime	Th 08	smoke stack	Sh 12	social consciousness	Th 11
sling	Th 10	smoking (food preserving)	Th 06	social contact	Th 11
slip (berth)	Pl 04			social equal	Oc 07
slip (boat ramp)	Th 03	smoking (tobacco, etc.)	Th 12	social forces	Mn 11
slip (decline)	Ps 08	smoky quartz	Ge 12	social functions, formal	Th 07
slip (drop)	Th 10	smooth things	Th 02	social functions, informal	Th 11
slip (evasion)	Th 12	smoothness	Th 02	social gathering	Th 11
slip (fall)	Th 10	smothering (concealment)	Th 12	social graces	Th 07
slip (lapse)	Th 09			social group	Th 11
slip (pillowcase)	Th 06	smothering (inundate)	Th 02	social life	Th 11
slip (sideways movement)	Th 03	smothering (suffocation)	Th 08	social organization	Mn 11
		smuggling	Th 12	social place or standing	Th 10
slip (undergarment)	Th 02	smut	Th 08	social recognition	Th 10
slip of the tongue	Th 03	snack	Th 04	social security	Mn 08
slipperiness	Th 09	snag (delay)	Th 10	social security benefits	Mn 08
slipshod work	Th 12	snag (hazard)	Th 10	social sense	Ps 07
sliver	Th 01	snag (jagged tear)	Th 01	social skills	Ps 07

social status	Mn 10	son-in-law	Re 11	spaciousness	Th 04
social ties	Mn 11	sonata	Th 02	spade (shovel)	Th 08
social transformation	Th 07	song	Th 02	spar (rib)	Sh 10
social urges	Ps 07	song writer	Oc 02	spare (extra) item	Th 05
social worker	Oc 12	sonnet	Th 07	spare (reserve)	Th 04
socialism	Mn 11	soot	Th 12	spare tire	Au 06
socialized medicine	Mn 08	soothsayer	Oc 09	spark	Th 01
socializer	Oc 07	sophistication	Ps 07	spark of life	Th 05
socially inferior person	Oc 06	sophomore (grade)	Th 04	sparring partner	Oc 07
society (club)	Pl 11	sorcerer	Oc 08	sparseness	Th 10
society (social group)	Ho 11	sorcery	Th 08	spasm	Af 12
society (social group)	Mn 11	sore	Af 01	spastic effort	Ps 03
society (social group)	Th 11	sore eyes	Af 03	spatula	Th 01
society people	Oc 11	sore throat	Af 02	speaker	Oc 03
sociologist	Oc 11	sorority	Pl 11	speaker (hi-fi)	Th 02
sociology	Th 11	sorrow	Ho 12	speaking	Th 03
socks (stockings)	Th 11	sorrow	Ps 12	spear	Th 01
soda	Th 04	sorrow, public	Mn 03	special effects	Th 12
sofa	Th 02	sorrow- profound	Ps 12	special forces (army unit)	Oc 08
soft item	Th 02	sorrowful conditions	Ps 12	special offer	Th 09
softly curved object	Th 02	sorrows, secret	Th 12	specialist	Oc 06
softness	Th 02	sorting	Th 06	specialization	Th 06
soggy ground	Pl 04	soul (spiritual self)	Th 09	specialized education	Th 09
soil	Th 10	soul, feelings about	Ps 09	specialized services	In 06
soil ecologist	Oc 10	soul music	Th 02	specialty	Th 06
soil preparation	Th 02	soul research	Th 09	specialty printing	In 03
solace	Th 12	sound	Th 01	specification	Th 06
solar collector	Th 05	sound (body of water)	Pl 04	specimen (sample)	Th 03
solar panel	Th 05	sound (drift)	Th 03	speck	Th 04
solar panel installation	In 05	sound currency	Mn 05	spectacle (event)	Th 05
solar plexus	Bd 05	sound judgment	Ps 09	spectacles (eyeglasses)	Th 04
solarium	Pl 05	soundproofing	Th 08	spectacular things	Th 05
soldier	Oc 06	sourness	Th 10	spectator	Oc 03
solemnity	Th 10	south, the direction of	Th 10	spectrum	Th 07
solicitation	Th 09	souvenir	Th 05	speculation (gambling)	Ho 05
solid	Th 02	sovereignty (control)	Th 08	speculation (gambling)	Th 05
solidity	Th 02	spa	Pl 04	speculation (hypothesis)	Th 09
soliloquy	Th 10	space (interval)	Th 10	speculation (losses from)	Th 04
solitaire	Th 12	space (roominess)	Th 04	speculation (venture)	Mn 05
solitary person	Oc 12	space (seating)	Th 04	speculation, market	Mn 05
solitary pursuits	Ps 12	space (the heavens)	Pl 09	speculator	Oc 05
solitary things	Th 12	space, outer	Pl 09	speech (lecture)	Th 03
solitude	Th 12	space, the use of	Th 07	speech (talking)	Th 03
soloist	Oc 10	space exploration	Th 11	speech, the quality of	Ps 02
solution (explanation)	Th 03	space explorer	Oc 11	speech defect	Af 03
solution (mixture)	Th 11	Space Planning	In 07	speech pathologist	Oc 03
solution (resolution)	Th 10	space station	Th 11	speech problem	Af 03
somersault	Th 05	spacecraft	Th 11	speed	Th 01
son	Re 05	spaceship	Th 11	spell	Th 06

spending	Th 04	sponge	An 04	spread (ranch)	Pl 04
spending beyond means	Mn 12	sponsor	Oc 07	spread, bed	Th 04
spendthrift	Oc 02	spontaneity	Ps 05	spreader	Th 11
sperm	Bd 08	spontaneity	Th 05	sprig	Th 02
spessartine	Ge 03	spoof	Th 03	spring	Au 07
sphere	Th 09	spook	Oc 08	spring (elastic body)	Th 10
spice	Th 02	spool	Th 04	spring (leap)	Th 09
spider	An 08	spoon	Th 06	spring (water)	Pl 04
spigot	Th 03	spoor (track)	Th 01	spring season, the	Th 01
spike (briar)	Th 09	spore	Th 02	springboard	Th 01
spill	Th 08	sport (recreation)	Th 05	sprinkler system	Or 11
spin	Th 10	sport arena	Pl 05	sprite	Oc 03
spinal problem	Af 05	sporting event	Th 05	sprout	Th 02
spine (in general)	Bd 05	sports	In 05	spur (branch off)	Th 03
spinel	Ge 01	sports, competitive	Th 01	spur (climbing tool)	Th 04
spinster	Oc 10	sports, non-professional	Th 05	spur (cowboy's)	Th 01
spiral	Th 11	sports, organized	Th 09	spur (goad)	Th 11
spirit (ghost)	Th 08	sports, professional	Mn 09	spur (projection)	Th 03
spirit, your	Ps 01	sports, recreational	Th 05	spurt of activity, a	Th 01
spiritual attunement	Ps 09	sports, spontaneous	Th 05	spy	Mn 12
spiritual consciousness	Ps 09	sports car	Th 07	spy	Oc 12
spiritual emergence	Th 09	sports coat	Th 09	squabble	Th 07
spiritual feelings	Ps 09	sports team	Th 09	squadron	Th 06
spiritual matters	Ho 09	sportsman	Oc 09	squall	Th 04
spiritual matters	Th 09	sportsmanship	Ho 09	square (evenness)	Th 07
spiritual needs	Ps 09	sportsmanship	Ps 09	square (planetary)	Th 10
spiritual pain	Ps 08	spot (difficulty)	Th 10	square (rectangle)	Th 10
spiritual pursuits	Th 09	spot (disgrace)	Th 12	square (unsophisticated)	Oc 03
spiritual rebirth	Ps 08	spot (location)	Pl 04	square, town	Pl 04
spiritual richness	Ps 09	spot (stain)	Th 09	squeak (sound)	Th 01
spiritual sustenance	Th 09	spotlight	Th 05	squeegee	Th 01
spiritualism	Th 08	spotted colors	Co 09	squeeze (handclasp)	Th 01
spirituality	Ps 09	spotted patterns	Co 09	squeeze (hug)	Th 05
splatter	Th 01	spoumodine	Ge 10	squelch	Th 03
spleen	Bd 10	spouse	Re 07	squirrel	An 06
splendidness	Ps 05	spouse's health	Th 12	st. vitus dance	Af 03
splendor	Th 05	spouse's real estate	Th 10	stab (attempt)	Th 01
splice (knot)	Th 04	spouse's siblings	Re 09	stab (lunge)	Th 01
splicing (combining)	Th 11	spout	Th 03	stab (pang)	Th 12
splint	Th 10	sprain	Af 10	stab wound	Af 01
split (divergence)	Th 07	sprained ankle	Af 11	stability	Sh 07
split (division)	Th 06	sprained/broken toe	Af 12	stability (equilibrium)	Th 07
split (rift)	Th 07	sprawl	Th 03	stability (personal)	Ps 07
splitting up	Th 07	spray (water droplets)	Th 04	stability of emotions	Ps 10
spoilage	Th 08	spray gun	Th 11	stabilization	Th 07
spoiling	Ps 08	spread (commodity purchase)	Th 05	stabilizing influence	Th 10
spoils	Th 08			stable	Pl 09
spoken communication	Th 03	spread (expanse)	Th 09	stable owner	Oc 09
spokesperson	Oc 03	spread (food)	Th 04	stadium	Pl 05

293

staff (cane)	Th 10	state (ritual)	Th 06	step-sibling (mother's side)	Re 08
staff (crew)	Th 06	state, the	Mn 01		
staff (flagpole)	Th 04	state funeral	Mn 08	steps	Hs 03
stage, the	Pl 05	state legislature	Mn 11	stereo equipment	Th 02
staged burglary	Th 11	state of a ship at sea	Th 01	stereo music	Th 02
staged efforts	Th 05	state of a woman with child	Th 05	stereotype (preconception)	Th 04
stagnant air conditions	Th 08				
stagnation	Th 08	state of mind	Ps 01	sterilization (birth control)	Th 08
stain	Th 09	statement	Th 03		
stairs	Pl 03	statement of purpose	Th 12	sterilization (germ killing)	Th 08
stairway	Hs 03	stateroom	Sh 04		
stake (involvement)	Th 02	statesman	Oc 10	stern	Sh 07
stake (post)	Th 02	static (interference)	Th 07	steward	Oc 06
stake (wager)	Th 05	station (post)	Pl 04	stick	Th 02
stalemate	Th 07	station (social status)	Th 10	stickiness	Th 04
staleness	Th 08	station (transit stop)	Pl 03	stiffness (formality)	Th 10
stall (animal den)	Pl 09	station house	Pl 06	stiffness (rigidity)	Th 10
stall (delay)	Ho 10	stationary object	Th 10	stigma	Th 12
stall (delay)	Th 10	stationer	Oc 03	stillness	Th 02
stall (retail place)	Pl 04	stationers	Pl 03	stimulant (energizer)	Th 01
stamina	Th 05	statistician	Oc 06	stimulation	Ps 01
stammering	Th 03	statistics	Th 06	stimulus (activator)	Th 01
stamp (characteristic)	Th 01	statue	Th 07	stimulus (incentive)	Th 08
stamp (postage)	Th 03	stature	Bd 10	sting	Af 08
stamp (seal)	Th 04	stature (social class)	Ps 10	stinging insect	An 08
stampede	Th 08	status	Ps 10	stipend	Th 02
stamping (pounding)	Th 01	status symbol	Th 05	stipulation	Th 07
stamping (tramping)	Th 01	statute	Th 09	stirring things up	Th 11
stamping out (eliminating)	Th 08	staying informed	Ps 09	stitch (all of something)	Th 04
		steadfastness	Th 10	stitch (shred)	Th 04
stand (platform)	Th 10	stealing	Th 03	stitch (suture)	Th 06
stand (position)	Th 09	stealth	Th 12	stock (cattle)	Th 04
stand (retail outlet)	Pl 04	stealthiness	Ps 08	stock (inventory)	Th 02
stand (support)	Th 10	steam	Th 05	stock (ownership)	Th 05
standardization	Th 10	steam bath	Pl 05	stock certificate	Mn 05
standing (status)	Ps 10	steel	Th 01	stock exchange	Pl 05
standing before the world	Mn 10	steel (general)	In 01	stock market	Pl 05
		steel (integrated)	In 01	stock markets	Mn 05
standstill (deadlock)	Th 07	steel worker	Oc 01	stock option	Th 05
staple	Th 04	steep ground	Pl 10	stock pile	Th 04
starboard side	Sh 01	steerage	Pl 04	stock trading	Th 05
starch	Th 10	steering (navigation)	Th 03	stockade	Pl 04
stars, the	Th 11	steering system	Au 03	stockbroker	Oc 05
start of a cycle	Th 04	stench	Th 08	stockholder	Oc 05
starter system	Au 01	stencil	Th 03	stockholder	Or 05
starting	Th 01	stenographer	Oc 03	stockholder relations	Or 05
starts	Th 01	step child	Re 11	stockings	Th 11
starvation	Th 10	step-parent	Re 12	stoicism	Ps 10
state (frame of mind)	Ps 01	step-sibling (father's side)	Re 02	stolen article	Th 07

stomach	Bd 04	stranger	Oc 09	stubbornness	Ps 02
stomach ache	Af 04	strangulation	Th 03	(unbending)	
stomach cramp	Af 04	strata	Th 06	student (observer)	Oc 03
stone	Th 10	strategy	Ho 11	student (pupil)	Oc 03
stone (in general)	Ge 10	strategy	Th 11	students in a university	Th 09
stone sculpture	Ge 07	stratification	Th 06	studies	Th 03
stoneware	Th 04	straw	Th 06	studies, advanced	Th 09
stool (chair)	Th 04	strayed animals	Th 05	studio	Hs 05
stool (excrement)	Th 08	stream	Pl 04	studio	Pl 05
stool pigeon	Oc 03	street	Pl 03	studiousness	Th 03
stoop	Hs 01	street car	Th 03	study	Hs 09
stop (cessation)	Th 10	strength	Th 02	studying	Ps 03
stop (visit)	Th 03	stress	Af 06	stuff (gear)	Th 06
stop, transit	Th 03	stress	Ho 06	stuff (material)	Th 04
stopper	Th 10	stress	Ps 06	stuffiness	Th 12
storage	Th 06	stress	Th 06	stuffing	Th 04
storage facility	Mn 06	stretch (duration)	Th 10	stumbling	Th 02
store (retail outlet)	Sh 06	stretch (elasticity)	Th 03	stunt (trick)	Th 03
store (retail)	Pl 04	stretch (expanse)	Th 09	stuntperson	Oc 01
store designers	In 07	stretcher	Th 06	stupidity	Th 09
store display equipment	In 07	stretching exercises	Th 05	stupor	Th 02
store's inventory	Mn 06	strictness	Ps 10	stuttering	Af 03
stored crops or grains	Th 06	stricture	Th 10	style (fashion)	Th 07
stored products	Th 06	strife	Th 01	style (mannerism)	Th 01
stored wealth	Th 04	strike (labor)	Mn 06	style (type)	Th 06
storehouse	Pl 06	strikes, inception of	Mn 06	style of government	Mn 10
storehouse for dairy products	Pl 06	striking (hitting)	Ps 08	styling, the	Au 07
		string (cord)	Th 04	stylish clothes	Th 07
storekeeper	Oc 04	string (procession)	Th 06	sub sandwich	Th 04
storeroom	Hs 06	strip (airstrip)	Pl 11	sub-soil	Th 04
storeroom	Pl 06	strip (piece)	Th 04	subconscious attitudes	Ps 04
storing away	Th 06	stripe (pattern)	Th 07	subconscious mind	Th 04
storing food	Ps 06	stroke	Af 11	subculture	Th 02
storm	Th 07	stroke (blow)	Th 01	subdividing	Th 11
storm (incoming), forming	Th 07	stroke (caress)	Th 02	subdued colors	Co 06
		stroke (in writing)	Th 03	subject matter	Th 06
storm door	Hs 04	stroke (of luck)	Th 05	sublimation	Ps 12
storm window	Hs 04	stroke (tolling of chime)	Th 10	subliminal perceptions	Th 01
storms, the effect of	Th 04	stroll	Th 03	subluxation	Af 05
story line	Th 12	stronghold (fort)	Pl 04	submarine	Th 04
story teller	Oc 09	stronghold (refuge)	Pl 12	submerging	Th 04
story telling	Th 09	structure (building)	Pl 04	submission	Ps 06
stoutness	Th 02	structure (in general)	Hs 10	submission	Th 06
stove	Hs 05	structure (organization)	Th 10	submissiveness	Th 06
stove	Th 05	struggle	Th 12	subordinate	Oc 06
straight forward	Ps 09	stub (end)	Th 12	subordinate role	Th 06
straightness	Th 10	stub (receipt)	Th 06	subordination	Ps 06
strain	Th 06	stubbornness (persistency)	Ps 10	subpoena	Th 09
strange, the	Th 11			subscription (pledge)	Th 08

subscription to periodicals	Th 03	suit (of clothes)	Th 06	support (upkeep)	Th 02
		suit (plea)	Th 12	support, given or received	Ps 08
subservience	Th 06	suitability	Th 09		
subsidy	Th 02	suitable behavior	Ps 10	support group	Th 11
subsistence	Th 02	suitcase	Th 03	support members	Sh 10
subsistence levels	Th 02	sulphur	Ge 08	supporter (advocate)	Oc 11
substance (essence)	Th 02	summary	Th 10	suppression	Th 08
substance (matter)	Th 02	summation	Th 10	supremacy	Th 05
substance (merit)	Th 02	summer	Th 05	supreme authority	Mn 10
substance (possessions)	Th 02	summit	Pl 10	supreme court, the	Mn 09
substance (solidity)	Th 02	summons	Th 10	surcharge	Th 08
substantiation	Th 08	sump	Pl 04	sureness	Th 05
substitute (alternative)	Th 07	sump pump	Hs 04	surety	Th 02
substitute (replacement)	Th 03	sun	Th 05	surf	Th 04
subterfuge (trick)	Th 03	sun bathing	Th 05	surface (covering)	Th 04
subtlety	Th 12	sun roof	Au 09	surface (outer face)	Th 01
subtraction (math)	Th 08	sun room	Hs 05	surfing	Th 05
suburb	Pl 04	sun stroke	Af 05	surge	Th 01
subversion	Ps 12	sunburn	Af 05	surgeon	Oc 08
subversion	Th 12	sundial	Th 05	surgery	Ho 08
subversive	Mn 12	sunglasses	Th 04	surgery	Th 08
subway	Th 03	sunrise	Th 12	surgery, healing after	Th 09
success	Ho 10	sunset	Th 06	surgical supplies	Th 06
success	Th 10	sunshine	Th 05	surplus	Th 09
success in law	Th 09	sunstone	Ge 05	surprise	Th 11
success in politics	Th 11	superconscious mind	Ps 09	surrender (give up)	Th 12
success in religion	Th 09	superficiality	Th 03	surrendering	Ps 12
success in science	Th 09	superintendent	Oc 10	surrogate	Oc 07
successful ventures	Th 09	superior	Oc 10	surroundings	Pl 01
succession (assumption)	Th 08	superiority	Ps 05	surtax	Th 08
succession (series)	Th 04	superiority complex	Ps 05	surveillance	Th 03
succession rights	Mn 04	superiors	Ho 10	survey (a map)	Th 06
succumb	Th 08	superiors	Oc 10	survey (a poll)	Th 06
sucker	Oc 12	supernova	Th 09	surveyor	Oc 06
suction	Th 11	superstitions	Th 08	surveyors	In 10
sudden acts of God	Th 04	supervision	Th 10	survival	Ho 02
sudden break	Th 09	supplement (extension)	Th 09	survival, need for	Ps 02
sudden death	Th 07	supplement (rider)	Th 11	survivalist	Oc 02
sudden event	Th 11	supplemental income	Th 02	susceptibility	Ps 04
sudden happening	Th 11	suppleness	Th 03	suspect	Oc 07
suddenness	Ho 11	supplies (goods available)	Th 04	suspenders	Th 10
suffering	Th 12			suspense	Th 08
suffering, bearing	Ps 06	supplies for consumption	Mn 04	suspension (hanging)	Th 09
suffocation	Th 03			suspension (stoppage)	Th 10
sugar	Th 02	supply (market)	Th 09	suspension system	Au 07
suggestion (advice)	Th 09	support (back up)	Th 11	suspicion (hunch)	Th 11
suggestion (hint)	Th 09	support (boost)	Th 12	suspicion (mistrust)	Th 11
suicide	Th 12	support (brace)	Th 04	suspicion (reservation)	Th 11
suit (law suit)	Th 09	support (pillar)	Hs 04	sustained efforts	Ps 02

sustaining	Th 04	swimming pool	Hs 05	syncopation	Th 04
sustenance (economic)	Th 02	swimming pool	Pl 05	syndicate	Th 11
sustenance (food)	Th 06	swimming pool	Sh 05	syndrome	Th 06
suttee	Th 08	swindle	Th 03	synod	Th 09
swab (mop)	Th 06	swindler	Oc 03	synonym	Th 03
swallowing	Th 02	swine	An 04	synopsis	Th 08
swami	Oc 09	swing (on a playground)	Th 05	syntax	Th 10
swamp	Pl 04	swing (to and fro)	Th 04	synthesis	Ho 08
swan	An 07	switch (electrical)	Th 11	synthesis	Ps 08
swapping	Th 03	switchboard	Th 03	synthetic material	Th 12
sweat glands	Bd 08	sword	Th 01	synthetic stone	Ge 12
sweetheart	Oc 05	symbol (emblem)	Th 04	syrup	Th 02
sweetness (kindness)	Ps 02	symbol (mark)	Th 01	system (method)	Th 06
sweetness (taste)	Th 02	symmetry	Th 07	system (organization)	Th 10
sweets	Th 02	sympathy	Ps 04	systematic thinking	Th 06
swelling	Bd 05	symphony	Th 02	systems analyst	Oc 06
swelling (knot)	Th 05	symposium	Th 11	syzygy	Th 05
swimming	Th 05	symptom	Th 06		
swimming hole	Pl 05	synchronicity	Th 04		

T

tabernacle	Pl 09	take (catch)	Th 09	tangle (confusion)	Th 12
table (dining)	Th 06	take (proceeds)	Th 02	tangle (dispute)	Th 07
table (list)	Th 06	taking	Th 07	tank (military)	Th 01
tablecloth	Th 07	taking chances	Th 01	tank (storage)	Th 04
tablet (medicinal)	Th 06	tale (falsehood)	Th 03	tank, fish	Th 04
tablet (plaque)	Th 05	tale (hearsay)	Th 09	tank farm	Pl 04
tablet (writing paper)	Th 03	tale (story)	Th 09	tannery	Pl 12
taboo (ban)	Th 08	talent	Ps 05	tantalize, things which	Th 07
tabulation	Th 06	talent (musical, artistic, etc.)	Th 05	tantrum	Th 08
taciturnity	Th 10			tanzanite	Ge 07
tack (approach)	Th 06	talent agencies	In 07	tap (faucet)	Th 03
tack (nail)	Th 06	talisman (charm)	Th 08	tap water	Hs 04
tackle (equipment)	Th 06	talk	Th 03	tape recorder	Th 03
tackle (lift equipment)	Th 10	talker	Oc 03	tapestries	Th 07
tact	Ps 07	talking	Ps 03	tapeworm	An 08
tactic (maneuver)	Th 06	talking	Th 03	taproom	Pl 12
tactic (scheme)	Th 06	talking book	Th 03	tar	Th 08
tad (a little bit)	Th 04	tallness	Th 04	tar pit	Pl 08
tag (bill)	Th 02	tally	Th 06	tardiness	Th 07
tag (marker)	Th 01	talons	Th 03	target (butt)	Th 12
tag (name)	Th 01	tang (hint)	Th 09	target (objective)	Th 04
tail (end)	Th 12	tang (strong taste)	Th 01	tariff	Th 08
tailor	Oc 06	tangent (digression)	Th 03	tarnish	Th 12
taint (smear)	Th 08	tangent (trigonometric)	Th 03	tarot cards	Th 08
tainted thing	Th 08	tangible assets	Th 02	task (chore)	Th 06

taskmaster	Oc 10	technical indicator	Mn 06	teletype	Th 03
tasks involving adventure	Th 09	technical staff	Or 06	television	Th 05
tasks involving risk	Th 01	technicality	Th 06	television, educational	Th 03
tasks involving travel	Th 03	technician	Oc 06	television, for entertainment	Th 05
tassel	Th 05	technique	Ho 06		
taste	Bd 02	technique (procedure)	Th 06	television room	Hs 05
tasteless humor	Th 04	technique (skill)	Th 06	television technician	Oc 06
tastes, personal	Ps 01	technique (style)	Ps 06	teller, bank	Oc 02
tatters (rag)	Th 12	technology	Th 06	temerity	Ps 02
tattletale	Oc 03	tectonics	Th 10	temper (anger)	Th 01
tattoo	Th 08	teddy bear	An 04	temper (disposition)	Th 01
taunt (jeer)	Th 01	tediousness	Th 06	temperament	Ps 01
Taurus (bull)	My 02	tedium	Th 02	temperance (moderation)	Th 02
tavern	Pl 12	teenager	Oc 03	temperature	Th 05
tax audit	Th 08	teeth	Bd 10	temperature change	Th 11
tax collector	Oc 08	teeth, false	Th 03	tempest	Th 08
tax consultant	Oc 08	teetotaler	Oc 11	template	Th 06
tax records	Mn 01	telecommunication	Th 09	temple	Pl 09
taxation	Mn 08	telecommunication equipment	In 11	temporary plans	Th 04
taxes	Ho 08			temptation (enticement)	Th 12
taxes	Mn 08	telecommunication services	In 11	tenacity	Th 02
taxes	Th 08			tenant	Ho 06
taxi driver	Oc 03	telecommunications (domestic)	In 11	tenant	Oc 06
taxicab	Th 03			tenant (boarder)	Th 06
taxicabs	In 03	telecommunications (foreign)	In 07	tendency (inner inclinations)	Ps 04
taxidermist	Oc 06				
tea	Th 04	telecommunications (long distance)	In 07	tenderness	Ps 02
tea dance	Th 02			tendons	Bd 10
teacher	Mn 05	teleconferencing	Th 09	tenement	Pl 04
teacher	Oc 05	telecopier (facsimile)	Th 03	tenet	Th 09
teaching	In 05	telegram	Th 03	tenor (meaning)	Th 01
teaching	Th 05	telegraph	Th 03	tension (stress)	Af 06
team (gang)	Th 11	telegraph office	Pl 03	tension (stretching)	Th 01
team (pair)	Th 03	telekinesis	Th 09	tenure	Th 10
team (sports team)	Th 07	telemarketing	Th 05	term (span)	Th 10
team play	Th 07	telemetry	Th 09	term (standing)	Th 11
teammate	Oc 07	telepathy	Th 08	term (word)	Th 03
teamster	Oc 03	telephone	Hs 03	terminal	Pl 10
teamwork	Ps 07	telephone	Th 03	terminal, computer	Th 03
teamwork	Th 07	telephone call	Th 03	termination	Th 10
tear (rip)	Th 01	telephone directory	Th 06	terms (stipulations)	Th 08
tear drop	Bd 04	telephone number	Th 01	terrace	Pl 06
tear ducts	Bd 04	telephone system	Mn 03	terrain (ground)	Pl 04
tear gas	Th 12	telephone system	Or 03	territory	Th 04
tear sheet	Th 03	telephoto lens	Th 09	terror	Th 08
tearjerker	Th 04	teleportation	Th 09	terrorist	Oc 08
tears of pain	Th 01	teleprocessing	Th 09	terseness	Th 10
teasing (taunting)	Th 01	telescope	Th 09	test (exam)	Th 06
technical ability	Th 06	telescopium (telescope)	My 09	test (try)	Th 09

298   Alpha Sort with Industries

test case	Th 10	Thetis (shape changer)	My 12	those under detention	Oc 12
test pilot	Oc 11	thickening	Th 02	those who act strange	Oc 11
test-drive	Th 05	thicket	Pl 02	those who brings news	Oc 03
testament	Th 08	thief	Oc 07	those who cater to pleasure	Oc 05
testicle	Bd 08	thievery	Th 07		
testimonial	Th 05	thighs	Bd 09	those who deal with clothing	Oc 06
testimony (evidence)	Th 06	thimble	Th 06		
testimony (statement)	Th 03	thin clear objects	Th 03	those who entertain	Oc 05
tete-a-tete	Th 06	thin person	Oc 03	those who tend the sick	Oc 06
tether	Th 04	thing (object)	Th 04	those who waste	Oc 08
text (sermon)	Th 09	things dependent on chanc	Th 05	those who work with alcohol	Oc 12
text (text material)	Th 03				
text (theme)	Th 09	things dependent on something	Th 03	those who work with criminals	Oc 12
textbook	Th 03				
textile worker	Oc 06	things in the sky	Th 09	those who work with liquids	Oc 04
Textiles	In 06	things lost or stolen	Th 04		
textiles	Th 06	things of beauty	Th 02	those with wealth or influence	Oc 05
texture	Th 02	things that are noticed	Th 05		
Thamus (steersman)	My 03	things that engulf	Th 04	those with whom you consult	Ho 07
thank you	Th 07	things with sharp angles	Th 03		
thankfulness	Ps 07	things you begin	Th 01	those with whom you consult	Oc 07
thaw (melting)	Th 09	thinker	Oc 03		
theater	Mn 05	thinking	Ps 03	those you borrow money from	Oc 07
theater	Pl 05	thirst (desire)	Th 08		
theater	Th 05	thirst for water	Th 03	thought (idea)	Th 03
theatrical agent	Oc 05	thoracic region of chest	Bd 03	thoughtfulness	Ps 02
theatrical worker	Oc 05	thorax	Bd 04	thoughtlessness	Th 01
theatrics	Th 05	thorn (bane)	Th 12	thoughts	Th 03
theft	Th 07	thorn (sharp spine)	Th 09	threadbare item	Th 10
them	Ho 02	thoroughfare	Pl 03	threat (intimidation)	Th 08
theme (essay)	Th 03	thoroughness	Th 06	threat (menace)	Th 08
theme (motif)	Th 01	those at a distance	Oc 09	threshing	Th 06
Themis (justice)	My 09	those beneath the surface	Oc 04	threshold (beginning)	Th 01
theologian	Oc 09	those in a ceremony	Oc 09	threshold (end boundary)	Pl 09
theology	Th 09	those in artistic careers	Oc 05	threshold (gate)	Hs 01
theoretical research	Th 09	those in authority	Oc 10	threshold (point of action)	Th 01
theory (doctrine)	Th 09	those in confidential position	Oc 08		
theory (idea)	Th 09			threshold (sill)	Hs 04
therapeutic activity	Th 08	those in responsible positions	Oc 10	thrift (frugality)	Th 10
therapist	Oc 06			Thrift Institutions	In 02
therapy	Th 06	those in the armed forces	Oc 06	thriftiness	Th 10
there	Ho 07	those met in public	Oc 07	thrill (adventure)	Th 09
thermodynamics	Th 01	those of a different race	Oc 09	thrill (excitement)	Th 01
thermometer	Th 06	those of a different rearing	Oc 09	thriving conditions	Th 04
thermostat	Th 08			throat	Bd 02
thesaurus	Th 08	those on welfare	Oc 12	throat infection	Af 02
Theseus (hero)	My 05	those publicly noticed	Oc 10	throb	Th 04
thesis (conjecture)	Th 09	those residing in your house	Oc 04	throes (anguish)	Th 12
thesis (paper)	Th 03			throes (upheaval)	Th 08

throne	Th 05	tilt (contest)	Th 07	token (money substitute)	Th 04
throng (crowd)	Th 11	tilt (dispute)	Th 07	token (symbol)	Th 04
throttle	Au 01	tilt (slant)	Th 03	tolerance	Ps 07
through a glass darkly	Th 12	timber	Th 02	toleration	Th 07
through-put	Th 06	timbre	Th 02	tomb	Pl 08
throw (toss)	Th 01	time	Ho 10	tombstone	Th 08
throw (unseat)	Th 10	time (duration)	Th 10	tomorrow	Ho 02
throw-away item	Th 12	time (experience)	Th 10	tomorrow	Th 02
throwing missile	Th 09	time (tempo)	Th 10	tone (attitude)	Ps 01
thrust (assault)	Th 01	time to be alone	Th 12	tone (color)	Th 07
thrust (shove)	Th 01	timeliness	Th 10	tone (musical)	Th 02
thrust (stab)	Th 01	timidity	Ps 06	tongs	Th 04
thud (dull sound)	Th 02	timing (synchronicity)	Th 04	tongue	Bd 03
thug	Oc 07	tincture (dye)	Th 07	tongue (dialect)	Th 03
thumb	Bd 03	tincture (medicinal)	Th 06	tongue disease	Af 03
thump (thud)	Th 02	tingle (flutter)	Th 05	tongue of land	Pl 04
thunder	Th 01	tinsel (decoration)	Th 05	tongue of shoe	Th 12
thwarting	Th 08	tiny object (miniature)	Th 04	tonic (restorative)	Th 06
thymus gland	Bd 02	tip (gratuity)	Th 02	tonsillitis	Af 02
tic (twitch)	Th 03	tip (hint)	Th 09	tonsils	Bd 02
ticket (admission)	Th 03	tip (pointed end)	Th 09	tool (implement)	Th 06
ticket (ballot)	Th 11	tip (slant)	Th 03	tool (means)	Th 06
ticket (summons)	Th 08	tirade	Th 07	tool (pawn)	Oc 04
ticket (tag)	Th 01	tire	Au 12	tooth decay	Af 10
ticket counter	Pl 03	tire and rubber	In 12	toothache	Af 10
tickling	Th 01	tiredness	Th 02	toothbrush	Th 10
tidal force	Th 04	tissue paper	Th 12	toothpick	Th 10
tide	Th 04	tissues of the body	Bd 04	top (first place)	Th 10
tidings	Th 01	Titans	My 05	top (highest point)	Pl 10
tie (bond)	Th 03	title (crown)	Th 05	top (lid)	Th 06
tie (necktie)	Th 02	title (legal right)	Th 09	top billing	Th 10
tie (rope)	Th 04	title (name)	Th 01	top of anything, the	Pl 10
tie rod	Au 03	title (rank)	Th 10	topaz	Ge 05
tie score	Th 07	title search	Th 08	topic (text)	Th 03
tieback	Th 04	title to property	Th 08	topic (theme)	Th 01
tier (row)	Pl 06	TNT	Th 01	topical items	Th 04
ties of conjugality	Th 07	toast (commemoration)	Th 05	torch	Th 05
ties of consanguinity	Th 04	toasted bread	Th 08	torment	Ps 12
ties of friendship	Th 11	tobacco	In 12	tornado	Th 08
ties of legality	Th 07	tobacco	Th 12	torpedo	Th 01
ties with groups	Th 11	today	Ho 01	torrent	Th 04
tiff	Th 07	toe	Bd 12	torsion	Th 10
tiger	An 05	togs	Th 06	torsion bar	Au 07
tiger's eye	Ge 12	toil	Th 06	tortoise	An 04
tightness	Th 04	toilet	Hs 08	torture	Th 08
tightwad	Oc 10	toilet	Pl 08	torture chamber	Pl 08
tile	Th 07	toilet (flush)	Th 08	toss (cast)	Th 01
tillage of the earth	Th 04	toilet articles	Th 06	total (sum)	Th 04
tilt (bias)	Th 09	toiletries/cosmetics	In 07	totalitarian regimes	Mn 08

totem	Th 04	trademark	Th 01	transformer (electrical)	Th 11
Toucana (toucan)	My 01	trades, the	Mn 06	transfusion	Th 08
touch (contact)	Th 03	tradesman	Oc 06	transgression	Th 07
touch (deftness)	Th 03	trading (barter)	Th 03	transient	Oc 09
touch (texture)	Th 02	tradition (custom)	Th 04	transient activities	Th 04
touch (trace)	Th 04	tradition (legend)	Th 04	transit	Th 03
touch: sense of	Bd 02	traffic (dealings)	Th 03	transition	Th 08
toupee	Th 03	traffic (local)	Th 03	translation	Th 03
tour	Th 09	traffic (movement)	Th 03	translator	Oc 09
tour brokers/agents	In 09	traffic laws	Th 11	translucency	Th 12
tourism	Mn 09	traffic signal	Th 03	transmigration	Th 08
tourists, foreign	Th 09	tragedy (theatrics)	Th 05	transmission	Au 10
tourists, native	Th 03	tragedy, disaster	Th 08	transmitting	Th 03
tourmaline	Ge 11	tragedy, experiencing a	Th 08	transmutation	Th 08
tournament	Th 05	tragedy, playing out	Ps 05	transparency (film)	Th 12
tow (pulling)	Th 03	trail	Pl 03	transplant	Th 05
tow (tugboat)	Th 06	trail (track)	Th 01	transport	Th 03
towel	Th 06	trailer	Th 03	transportation	Th 03
tower	Pl 09	train (appendage)	Th 09	transportation	
tower (mainstay)	Th 10	train (retinue)	Th 06	(ambulances)	In 01
town	Pl 04	train (succession)	Th 06	transportation dept.	Or 03
town council	Mn 11	train, railway	Th 03	transportation	In 03
town hall	Pl 11	trainer	Oc 06	dispatching	
toxemia	Af 08	training	Ho 06	transportation	In 03
toxic condition	Af 08	training	Th 06	equipment	
toxic waste	Th 08	training (educational)	In 05	transportation	Th 03
toxicology services	In 08	training (health	In 01	equipment	
toy	Th 05	and fitness)		transportation hub	Mn 03
toys	In 05	training (sports)	In 05	transportation leasing	In 11
trace (hint)	Th 09	traitor	Oc 12	transportation systems	Mn 03
trace (sign)	Th 01	traits	Ps 01	transportation worker	Oc 03
track (course)	Th 03	trajectory	Th 06	transportation, distant	Th 09
track (mark)	Th 01	tramp	Oc 12	transvestite	Oc 07
track (rail)	Th 03	trance	Th 12	trap (ruse)	Th 03
track, race	Pl 05	tranquility	Th 02	trap (snare)	Th 04
tracker	Oc 09	trans-sexual	Oc 07	trapeze	Th 09
tract (pamphlet)	Th 03	transacting	Ps 03	trapper	Oc 09
traction (adhesive	Th 11	transaction	Th 03	trappings (dress)	Th 06
friction)		transcriber	Oc 03	trash	Th 08
tractor	Th 11	transcription	Th 03	trashcan	Th 08
trade (retail)	Th 03	transfer (a move)	Th 03	travails	Ps 12
trade (wholesale)	Th 04	transfer (iron-on design)	Th 03	travel	Th 03
trade, international	Mn 09	transfer (ticket)	Th 03	travel, alone	Ho 03
trade, local	Th 03	transferee	Oc 03	travel, desires for	Ps 09
trade embargo	Mn 07	transference	Ps 06	travel, distant	Mn 09
trade patterns	Mn 06	transferred, being	Th 03	travel, local	Th 03
trade union	Mn 12	transfiguration	Th 08	travel, long distance	Mn 09
trade within borders	Mn 03	transformation	Ho 08	travel, nearby	Th 03
trade-off	Th 03	transformation	Ps 08	travel, short distance	Th 03

travel agency	Pl 09	trial, legal	Th 07	trivial matter	Th 04
travel agent	Oc 09	trial lawyer	Oc 09	triviality	Th 03
travel agents	In 09	trial run	Th 06	trolley	Th 03
travel by air	Th 09	triangle	Th 03	troop (band)	Th 11
travel of children	Th 01	triangulation	Th 06	troops, military	Th 06
travel plans	Th 03	triangulum (triangle)	My 09	trophy	Th 05
travel services	In 09	tribal consciousness	Th 09	trotting	Th 03
travel to unfamiliar places	Ho 09	tribal customs	Mn 04	trouble (difficulty)	Th 12
		tribal groups	Mn 04	trough (channel)	Th 03
travel within the country	Mn 03	tribal loyalty	Th 10	trousers	Th 06
traveler	Oc 09	tribe (related strain of animals)	Th 04	truant	Oc 03
traveler, known to you	Th 03			truce	Mn 07
traveler, unknown	Th 09	tribe (social group)	Mn 04	truck	Th 03
travelers check	Th 02	tribe (taxonomic classification)	Th 06	truck driver	Oc 03
traveling light	Th 09			truck leasing	In 11
travesty (mockery)	Th 01	tribulation (bad luck)	Th 12	trucker	Oc 03
treachery	Ps 08	tribulation (unhappiness)	Th 12	trucking	In 03
tread (footfall)	Th 01	tribunal	Th 08	trudging	Th 03
treadle	Th 06	tribute (honor)	Th 05	truism (obvious truth)	Th 09
treadmill	Th 05	tribute (payment)	Th 08	trump card (final resource)	Th 08
treason	Mn 12	trick (clever act)	Th 03		
treasure	Mn 02	trick (joke)	Th 03	trunk	Au 12
treasure	Th 02	trick (knack)	Th 06	trunk (luggage)	Th 06
treasure, buried or hidden	Th 04	trick (ruse)	Th 03	trunk (torso)	Bd 05
		trickery	Ps 03	truss (band)	Th 04
treasurers office	Or 02	trident	Th 12	truss (beams)	Th 10
treasury, the	Mn 02	trifle (morsel)	Th 04	truss (medical)	Th 10
treasury, the	Or 02	trifle (trinket)	Th 05	trust	Ho 08
treasury, the	Pl 02	trifler	Oc 05	trust	Ps 08
treat (pick up the tab)	Th 09	trigonometry	Th 06	trust company	Pl 08
treat (that which pleases)	Th 05	trim (condition)	Th 08	trust funds	Th 08
treatise	Th 06	trim (cutting)	Th 01	trustfulness	Th 08
treatment (handling)	Th 04	trim (embellishment)	Th 05	truth	Ps 09
treatment (medical)	Th 06	trine (planetary)	Th 09	truth	Th 09
treaty	Mn 07	trinket	Th 05	try (endeavor)	Th 01
tree	Th 02	trip (err)	Th 09	try (trial)	Th 01
trembling (shaking)	Th 01	trip (stumble)	Th 10	try out (attempt)	Th 01
tremors	Th 10	trip, long or distant journey	Th 09	tryst	Th 05
tremors in body	Bd 11			tub	Th 04
trench	Pl 08	trip, short journey	Th 03	tube	Th 03
trend	Ho 11	trip along (skip)	Th 03	tuberculosis	Af 03
trend	Th 11	trip mechanism (release)	Th 12	tuck (gather)	Th 04
trendsetter	Oc 11	triplets	Th 11	tuft (as of hair)	Th 05
trespass (on a right)	Th 08	tripod	Th 10	tug (pull at)	Th 01
trespassing	Th 03	trips nearby	Th 03	tugboat	Th 06
trestle	Th 03	trips quick or short	Th 03	tuition	Th 03
trial (law)	Th 09	triteness	Th 07	tumor	Bd 04
trial (practice)	Th 03	triumph (success)	Th 10	tumult	Th 08
trial (trouble)	Th 12	trivia	Th 04	tune	Th 02

tunic	Th 06	turn on (arousal)	Th 01	twist (curl)	Th 03
tuning fork	Th 02	turn signal	Au 03	twist (surprise)	Th 11
tunnel	Pl 04	turnaround	Pl 08	twist (tangle)	Th 03
turbidity (unclear)	Th 12	turning, the act of	Th 10	twist of fate, a	Th 12
turbine	Th 11	turning point	Ps 08	twitching	Th 03
turbulence	Th 11	turntable	Th 10	type (class)	Th 06
turkey	An 06	turquoise	Co 04	type (specimen)	Th 04
turmoil, inner or psychic	Th 12	turquoise	Ge 11	typeface	Th 03
turn (bend)	Th 03	turtle	An 04	Typesetting	In 03
turn (chance)	Th 01	tutor	Oc 09	typewriter	Th 03
turn (curve)	Th 03	tuxedo	Th 07	Typhoon	My 11
turn (deed)	Th 01	tweezers	Th 04	typical things	Th 04
turn (shift)	Th 04	twilight	Th 06	typist	Oc 03
turn (shock)	Th 01	twine	Th 04	tyranny	Th 08
turn (spin)	Th 10	twinkle	Th 05	tyrant	Oc 08
turn (stroll)	Th 03	twins	Th 03	tyro (beginner)	Oc 03
turn off	Th 10	twist (approach)	Th 03		

U

U-haul trailer	Th 03	unconscious activity	Ps 09	(knowledge)	
ugliness	Th 08	unconscious mind	Ps 12	understanding	Ps 12
ulcers, stomach	Af 04	unconventional, the	Th 11	(sympathy)	
ulterior motive	Th 12	uncultured person	Oc 01	understudy	Oc 06
ultimate truths	Ps 09	under the earth,	Th 04	undertaker	Oc 08
ultimatum	Th 07	anything		undertaking (endeavor)	Th 01
ultra-violet	Co 12	under-rating	Th 06	undertaking a task	Th 01
ultramarine	Co 11	underclothes	Th 04	(doing it)	
umbilical cord	Bd 03	undercoating	Au 04	undertone (sense)	Th 04
umbrella	Th 04	undercover operator	Oc 12	undertow	Th 12
umpire	Oc 07	undercover work	Th 12	underwater object	Th 04
unadaptable thing	Th 08	undercurrent (mood)	Ps 04	underwear	Th 06
unanimity	Th 07	undercurrent (riptide)	Th 04	underworld, the	Pl 08
unauthorized action	Th 12	underdog	Oc 12	underworld character	Oc 12
unavailability	Th 10	undergarment	Th 04	undeserved reward	Th 09
unbonded relationship	Th 11	underground, the	Th 08	undesignated other	
unburdening	Ps 12	underground places	Pl 08	person	Oc 07
uncertainty (doubt)	Ps 04	underhandedness	Th 08	undesirable person	Oc 12
uncertainty (hesitancy)	Th 04	underling	Oc 06	undisclosed condition	Th 12
uncle, maternal	Re 06	undermining	Ps 11	undoing (reversal)	Th 12
uncle, paternal	Re 12	underneath, what is	Th 08	undoing (ruin)	Th 12
unclean, the	Th 06	undersea places	Pl 04	undulation	Th 04
uncles on the father's side	Re 12	underside	Pl 08	unearthing	Th 08
		understanding	Ps 09	uneasiness	Th 12
uncles on the mother's side	Re 06	understanding (agreement)	Th 07	unemployment	Th 12
				unemployment insurance	Th 07
uncommon, the	Th 11	understanding	Th 09	unequal relationships	Th 08

unexpected, the	Th 11	unluckiness	Th 12	urge (craving)	Th 08
unexpected obstacle	Th 12	unnamed item	Th 10	urge (drive)	Th 01
unexpected thing	Th 11	unorthodox, the	Th 11	urge (wish)	Th 11
unexplored area	Pl 09	unprecedented thing	Th 11	urge for security	Th 04
unfair thing	Th 08	unreality	Th 12	urge to adapt to others	Th 06
unfaithfulness	Th 07	unreasonableness	Th 08	urgency	Ps 01
unfamiliarity	Th 02	unrecognized potential	Th 04	urgings	Ps 04
unfinished item	Th 09	unrest	Th 11	urinary system	Bd 07
unforeseen event	Th 12	unruliness	Th 01	urinary tract	Bd 07
unfortunate	Oc 12	unruly mob	Th 12	urinary tract problems	Af 07
unfortunate activity	Th 12	unscrupulous person	Oc 12	urination	Bd 08
unfortunate circumstance	Th 12	unseating	Th 08	urine	Th 08
unhappiness	Th 12	unseemly thing	Th 08	urn	Th 04
unhealthy condition	Th 12	unsuccessful attempt	Th 08	Ursa Major (great bear)	My 01
unhinging	Th 08	unthinkable act	Th 08	Ursa Minor (smaller bear)	My 01
unicorn	An 07	untimely event	Th 12		
unidentifiable thing	Th 12	unusual, the	Th 11	us	Ho 01
unification (uniting)	Th 11	unusual method	Th 11	usage (practice)	Th 04
uniform (special clothing)	Th 11	unwanted delivery	Th 03	usage (treatment)	Th 04
uniformed worker	Oc 11	unwanted thing	Th 12	use (convenience)	Th 02
uniformity	Mn 04	unwanted things	Ho 12	use (utility)	Th 06
uniformity	Ps 04	unwilling conformity	Th 07	use (worth)	Th 02
unimportant matter	Th 04	up, the direction of	Th 09	used car salesman	Oc 12
uninvited guest	Oc 03	update	Th 03	used car/truck dealers	In 12
union (combination)	Th 11	upheaval	Th 08	useful things	Th 02
union (togetherness)	Th 11	upholstery	Th 02	useless things	Th 09
union, labor	Mn 11	upholstery, the	Au 02	usher	Oc 06
union leader	Oc 08	upper classes	Th 10	using others	Ps 07
union member	Oc 04	upper floors	Hs 09	usual, the	Th 04
union of two people	Th 07	upper house of government	Mn 10	usurer	Oc 08
unions, trade	Mn 06			usury	Th 08
unique, the	Th 11	upper legislative house	Mn 10	utensil	Th 06
unison, things done in	Th 07	upper levels	Pl 09	uterus	Bd 04
unit (part)	Th 04	uprising (rebellion)	Th 07	utility	Ps 02
unit (quantity)	Th 06	uproar	Th 11	utility (convenience)	Th 02
uniting	Th 11	uprooting	Th 08	utility (usefulness)	Th 06
unity (co-operation)	Ps 07	upset	Th 11	utility, public	Mn 12
unity (togetherness)	Th 11	upsetting condition	Th 11	utility closet	Hs 06
universal joint	Au 09	upshot (consequence)	Th 10	utility company	Mn 12
universality	Ho 09	uranium	Ge 08	utility shop	Or 06
universe, the	Th 10	Uranos (sky)	My 11	utilizing	Ps 02
university	Mn 09	urban development	Mn 04	uvarovite	Ge 03
university	Pl 09	urchin	Oc 03	uvite	Ge 11
unknown, that which is	Th 08	uremia	Af 07		
unknown adversary	Th 12	urethral structures	Bd 07		

V

vacancy (emptiness)	Th 01	variable	Th 04	ventriloquist	Oc 03
vacancy (opening)	Th 01	variance	Th 07	venture	Th 09
vacant property	Pl 01	variation (difference)	Th 03	venture capital	Mn 02
vacation	Ho 05	variation (discrepancy)	Th 07	Venus	My 07
vacation	Th 05	variation (type)	Th 11	veracity	Th 09
vacation resort	Pl 05	varicose veins	Af 11	veranda	Hs 05
vacillation	Ps 07	variety (assortment)	Th 11	verbiage	Th 09
vacuum (emptiness)	Th 08	variety (diversification)	Th 11	verbosity	Th 03
vacuum cleaner	Th 06	varnish	Th 07	verdict (judgment)	Th 04
vacuum producing equipment	In 08	vase	Th 07	verdict (jury's finding)	Th 12
		vastness	Th 09	verge (edge)	Th 03
vagabond	Oc 12	vault (dome)	Th 09	verification	Th 06
vagina	Bd 08	vault (safe)	Pl 02	vermin	An 08
vagrant	Oc 12	vaulted place	Pl 10	vernacular	Th 03
vagueness	Th 12	vegetable	Th 04	versatility	Ps 03
valedictorian	Oc 10	vegetarian	Oc 11	verse (rhyme)	Th 03
valentine	Th 07	vegetation	Th 02	version	Th 11
valet	Oc 06	vehemence	Th 08	vertebrae (in general)	Bd 05
validity (factual grounds)	Th 06	vehicle (means)	Th 03	vertical direction	Th 10
validity (truthfulness)	Th 09	vehicle (transportation)	Th 03	vertigo	Af 01
valise	Th 06	veil	Th 12	verve (liveliness)	Th 05
valley	Pl 04	vein (mood)	Ps 04	vespers	Th 09
valor	Th 01	vein (strata)	Th 06	vessel (container)	Th 04
valuable	Th 02	veins	Bd 02	vessel (ship)	Th 04
valuable thing	Th 02	Vela (sails of the Argo)	My 11	Vesta (the homemaker)	My 06
valuation	Th 02	velocity	Th 01	vestibule	Hs 01
value (expensive)	Th 02	velvet	Co 12	vestige (trace)	Th 04
value (ideal)	Ps 09	velvet	Th 02	vestment	Th 05
value (merit)	Ps 02	vending machine manufacturers	In 09	veteran	Oc 10
value retention	Au 02			veteran's group	Th 11
valuing	Ps 02	vending machine retailers	In 07	veterinarian, large animals	Oc 12
valve	Au 11	vendor	Oc 04		
valve	Th 11	veneer (facade)	Ps 05	veterinarian, small animals	Oc 06
valve lifter	Au 06	veneer (facing)	Th 01		
vampire	Oc 08	veneration	Th 09	veterinarians (large animal)	In 12
van (vehicle)	Th 03	venereal disease	Af 08		
vandal	Oc 08	vengeance	Ps 08	veterinarians (small animal)	In 06
vane	Th 03	venom	Th 08		
vanguard	Th 01	venous blood	Bd 02	veto (rejection)	Th 11
vanishing	Ps 12	vent (disclosure)	Th 03	vexation	Ps 08
vanity (dressing table)	Th 06	vent (exhaust)	Th 08	viability	Ps 01
vanity (make-up case)	Th 02	vent (opening)	Th 04	viaduct	Th 03
vanity (pride)	Ps 05	ventilation	Th 03	vial	Th 04
vantage point	Pl 09	ventilation system	Au 03	vibration (periodic oscillation)	Th 04
vapor (moisture)	Th 04	ventriloquism	Th 03		

vibration (quivering)	Th 11	violet	Co 12	vogue (fashion)	Th 04
vicarious experience	Th 11	virgin	Oc 06	voice (opinion)	Th 09
vicarious things	Th 12	virgin land	Pl 02	voice (speech)	Th 03
vice (corruption)	Th 08	virginity	Th 06	voice (tenor, baritone, etc.)	Th 02
vice (fault)	Th 06	Virgo (virgin)	My 06		
vice-president	Oc 04	virility	Th 05	voice organs	Bd 02
vicinity	Pl 03	virtue (moral strength)	Th 10	voice trainer	Oc 02
viciousness	Th 08	virtuoso	Oc 10	voices, hearing	Th 04
vicissitude (chance)	Th 04	virulence	Th 08	void (emptiness)	Th 01
vicissitude (mutability)	Th 03	virus	Th 06	Volans (flying fish)	My 11
victim	Oc 12	viscera	Th 06	volatility	Th 01
victim of a murder	Oc 08	viscosity	Th 02	volcano	Pl 08
victimization	Ps 12	visibility (clarity)	Th 09	volition	Ps 11
victor	Oc 10	visibility (view)	Th 09	volley (salvo)	Th 02
victor in battle	Th 07	visible event	Th 01	voltage	Th 11
victory (triumph)	Th 10	vision	Bd 04	voltage regulator	Au 08
Videoconferencing	In 03	vision (prophecy)	Th 09	volume (loudness)	Th 01
videotape	Th 03	vision (sight)	Th 04	volume (quantity)	Th 02
view (look)	Th 01	visionary	Oc 11	volume (size)	Th 02
view (opinion)	Th 09	visit (call)	Th 03	voluntary service	Th 06
view (vision)	Th 01	visiting	Ho 03	volunteer	Oc 06
view (vista)	Th 05	visiting	Th 03	volunteer labor	Th 06
viewer	Oc 03	visiting team	Th 07	volunteering	Ps 06
viewpoint	Th 03	visitor	Oc 03	vomiting	Af 04
vigilance (alertness)	Th 01	visitors	Ho 03	voodoo	Th 08
vigilance (caution)	Th 10	visits	Ho 03	voraciousness	Th 01
vigor (energy)	Th 01	vista	Th 09	vortex	Pl 11
vigor (enthusiasm)	Ps 05	visualization	Th 09	vote (ballot)	Th 11
village	Pl 04	vital issue	Th 01	vote (election)	Th 11
villain	Oc 07	vital records storage	In 08	voters in an election	Mn 04
vim (vigor)	Th 05	vitality	Th 05	voting	Mn 11
vindication (exoneration)	Th 12	vitalization	Th 08	voucher	Th 06
vindication (support)	Th 11	vitamin	Th 05	vow (promise)	Th 08
vindictiveness	Ps 08	vividness	Th 01	voyage	Th 09
vine	Th 02	vocabulary	Th 03	Vulcan	My 06
vineyard	Th 02	vocal cords	Bd 02	vulgarity	Th 08
vintage (era)	Th 10	vocalization	Th 03	vulnerability	Ps 04
vinyl tile	Th 06	vocation	Ho 10	Vulpecula (fox)	My 03
violation (breach)	Th 08	vocation	Th 10	vulture	An 08
violence	Th 01	vocational counselor	Oc 08	vulva	Bd 08
violent crime	Th 08	vociferousness	Th 01		

wager	Th 05	wagon	Th 03	wait (delay)	Th 10
wages	Mn 02	wail	Th 12	waiter	Oc 06
wages	Th 02	waist	Bd 05	waiting	Th 10

waiting room	Pl 02	waste (rubbish)	Th 12	wealth	Th 02
waitress	Oc 06	waste basket	Th 08	wealth, accumulating	Ho 04
waiver	Th 08	waste management	In 08	wealth, father's	Th 02
wake (backwash)	Th 08	waste management	Or 08	wealth, having	Th 02
wake (vigil)	Th 08	waste matter	Th 12	wealth, mother's	Th 08
walking	Th 01	wasteland	Pl 01	wealth, need for	Ps 04
wall (defense)	Th 04	wasting, needs for	Ps 08	weapon	Th 01
wall (partition)	Hs 10	wasting away	Th 08	weariness	Th 07
wall hanging	Th 07	wasting diseases	Af 08	weasel	An 03
wallet	Th 02	watch (clock)	Th 10	weather	Mn 03
walling in	Th 04	watch (look)	Th 03	weather	Th 03
wallpaper	Th 07	watch (surveillance)	Th 03	weather along the coast	Th 03
walrus	An 12	watchman	Oc 06	weather forecaster	Oc 03
waltz	Th 02	water	Th 04	weather forecasting	In 03
wanderer	Oc 09	water closet	Hs 08	weather instruments	Th 06
wandering	Th 09	water damage	Th 11	weaver	Oc 07
wanderlust	Th 09	water distribution	In 03	wedding	Th 07
want (a lack of money)	Th 12	water distribution	Mn 06	wedding announcement	Th 07
want (desire)	Th 11	system		wedding of a child	Th 07
want (need)	Th 11	water hose	Au 04	wedding of a friend	Th 05
wants	Ps 11	water imbalance	Af 11	wedding picture	Th 06
war	Mn 07	water on the knee	Af 10	wedge	Th 11
war	Th 07	water opal	Ge 09	weed	Th 01
war, the end of	Mn 10	water pipes	Hs 04	weevil	An 08
war of nerves	Ps 07	water pollution	Th 11	weight (bulk)	Th 02
ward	Oc 12	water pump	Au 04	weights and measures	Th 06
warden, game	Oc 12	water supply	Mn 04	weld	Th 04
warder	Oc 04	water tank	Hs 04	welder	Oc 06
wardrobe	Th 06	water tank	Sh 04	welding	In 06
wardroom	Sh 04	water tap	Th 03	welfare	Ho 12
warehouse	Pl 06	water utility	In 04	welfare	Th 12
wares	Th 04	watercourse	Th 06	welfare agency	Mn 12
warfare	Mn 07	waterfall	Th 01	welfare offices	Or 12
wariness (caution)	Th 08	waterfowl	Th 09	welfare recipient	Oc 12
warlike situation	Mn 07	waterfront area	Pl 04	welfare systems	Mn 12
warmest part of the house	Pl 05	watery place	Pl 04	welfare worker	Oc 12
warmth	Ps 05	wave (curl)	Th 02	well	Pl 04
warmth	Th 05	wave (gesture)	Th 03	well (hole)	Th 04
warning (alarm)	Th 01	wave (pulsation)	Th 04	well being, your overall	Ps 01
warning (sign)	Th 08	wave (rush)	Th 01	well head	Th 03
warrant (permit)	Th 08	wave (salutation)	Th 01	well wisher	Oc 11
warranty	Th 08	wave (swell of water)	Th 04	west, the direction of	Th 07
warrior	Oc 01	waving motion	Th 01	wetness	Th 04
warts	Af 10	wax	Th 09	whale	An 12
wash, the	Th 06	we	Ho 01	wharf	Pl 04
washcloth	Th 06	weakening	Th 06	wheat	Th 06
washing	Th 06	weakness	Af 05	wheedling	Th 03
washing machine	Th 11	weakness (in general)	Ps 06	wheel	Sh 03
wasp	An 08	wealth	Mn 02	wheel	Th 03

wheel and deal	Th 03	wile	Ps 03	wittiness	Th 03
wheel rim	Au 03	will	Ps 05	wizard	Oc 09
wheelbarrow	Th 03	will (legacy)	Th 08	wobble	Th 04
wheeler-dealer	Oc 03	will (legal document)	Ho 08	woes	Th 12
where books are kept	Pl 03	will of the people	Mn 08	wolf	An 10
where business is conducted	Pl 10	willful oversight	Th 07	wolverine	An 08
		willfulness	Ps 05	womb	Bd 04
where food is disbursed	Pl 06	willingness	Ps 07	womb	Th 04
where living things grow	Pl 04	willpower	Ps 05	women	Oc 04
where money is kept	Pl 02	wilting	Th 10	women, young	Oc 02
where partner spends time	Pl 07	wimp	Oc 12	women from the past	Oc 01
where you reside	Pl 04	win	Th 05	women's articles	Th 04
where you spend your time	Pl 01	winch	Sh 11	women's clothes	Th 04
whetstone	Th 11	wind	Th 03	women's liberation	Th 11
whim	Ps 04	wind burn	Af 01	wonder (a marvel)	Th 05
whine	Th 01	wind shear	Th 08	wonder (speculation)	Th 09
whining	Ps 07	wind sock	Th 03	wood (in general)	Th 02
whip	Th 08	windings	Th 03	wood pile	Th 02
whirling motion	Th 10	windlass	Sh 11	wood stove	Th 05
whirlpool	Th 10	windmill	Th 11	woodland	Pl 02
whirlwind	Th 10	window	Au 07	woodworker	Oc 02
whiskey	Th 12	window	Hs 07	woodworking	Th 06
whisper	Th 03	window	Th 07	wool	Th 06
whistle	Th 02	window (for re-entry)	Th 01	word	Th 03
whistling	Th 02	windpipe	Bd 02	work	Ho 06
white	Co 07	windshield	Au 07	work	Th 06
white magic	Th 06	windshield wiper	Au 07	work, willingness to	Ps 06
white opal	Ge 09	wine	Th 12	work area	Pl 06
white things	Th 07	winning	Ps 05	work behind the scenes	Th 12
white-gray	Co 04	winnings	Th 02	work commonly avoided	Th 12
whittling	Th 02	winter	Th 10	work done in solitude	Th 12
whoever has authority	Mn 10	wire	Th 04	work done quietly or alone	Th 12
wholeness	Ps 07	wisdom	Ho 09	work force	Th 06
wholesaler	Oc 04	wisdom	Ps 09	work gang	Th 06
wholesomeness	Th 09	wisdom gained	Th 10	work habits	Ps 06
wickedness	Th 08	wise person	Oc 09	work out	Th 05
wickerwork	Th 02	wisecracks	Th 03	work performance review	Th 06
widening	Th 09	wishes	Ho 11	work requiring wit or knowledge	Th 03
wider vision	Th 09	wishes	Ps 11		
widow, widower	Oc 12	wishes	Th 11	work room	Th 06
widowhood	Th 12	wishful thinking	Th 11	work schedule	Th 06
wife	Re 07	wit	Th 03	work with fire	Th 05
wig	Th 07	witch	Oc 06	work with heavy tools	Th 06
wild animal	An 12	witchcraft	Th 06	work with liquids	Th 04
wild dog	An 12	with-holding (anything)	Th 08	work with oil	Th 09
wild fowl	An 06	withdrawal	Ps 12	work with sharp instruments	Th 01
wild thing	Th 01	withdrawal (monetary)	Th 08		
wildcat	An 12	withdrawal into fantasy	Th 12	workers	Oc 06
wilderness	Pl 09	witness	Oc 03	workers at routine jobs	Oc 06

workers in all trades	Oc 06	worldly position	Mn 10	wrappings	Th 04
workers in stone	Oc 07	worldly possessions	Th 02	wrath	Ps 07
working capital	Mn 11	worldly success, power to get	Th 10	wreck	Th 12
working classes	Mn 06	worm	An 08	wreckage	Th 08
working conditions	Ho 06	worms in the body	Af 08	wrench (tool)	Th 06
working conditions	Mn 06	worry	Ps 06	wrinkle (crease)	Th 11
working environment	Mn 06	worry	Th 06	wrinkle (twist)	Th 08
workload	Th 10	worship (praise)	Th 05	wrinkles	Bd 11
workman's compensation	Mn 08	worship (reverence)	Th 09	wrist	Bd 03
		worship service	Th 09	writ	Th 10
workmanship	Th 06	worth, current	Th 02	writer	Oc 03
workshop	Hs 06	worth, future	Th 04	writer's block	Th 02
workshop	Pl 06	worth, self	Ps 02	writing skills	Th 03
world assemblies like UN	Mn 09	worthiness	Ps 02	writing(s)	Ho 03
world trade	Mn 09	worthless things	Th 11	writing(s)	Th 03
world view	Ps 09	worthlessness	Ps 06	written document	Th 03
world wide contacts	Th 09	wound	Af 01	written test	Th 06
world's fair	Mn 05	wrangler	Oc 06	wrong way movement	Th 12

X, Y

x-ray operator	Oc 09	yearbook	Th 04	yoke	Th 07
x-rays	Th 09	yearnings	Ps 11	you	Re 01
xerox copy	Th 03	yeast	Th 04	you, yourself	Ho 01
yacht	Th 05	yellow	Co 05	young, the	Oc 03
yacht brokers	In 12	yellow-green	Co 04	young children	Oc 03
YAG	Ge 12	yellow-orange	Co 05	young people (age 20 to 30)	Oc 02
yankee	Oc 11	yeoman	Oc 06		
yard	Pl 04	yesterday	Th 12	young people (under age 20)	Oc 03
yard, the	Hs 04	Yeti	My 12		
yard design and maintenance	In 02	yield (give up)	Th 12	younger brother	Re 03
		yield (rate of return)	Th 02	yourself	Ps 01
yard work	Th 05	yield (relinquish)	Th 12	youth	Oc 03
yardstick	Th 06	yoga (discipline)	Th 09	youth	Th 03
yawn	Th 12	yoga exercises	Th 05		
year	Th 06	yogi	Oc 09		

Z

zeal	Th 09	Zeus (the ruler)	My 09	zodiac	Th 11
zealot	Oc 11	zigzag	Th 03	zone (destination)	Th 09
zenith	Th 10	zinc	Ge 10	zone (region)	Th 04
zephyr	Th 03	zip code	Th 06	zoo	Pl 12
zero	Th 08	zipper	Th 04	zoo worker	Oc 06
zest	Th 01	zircon	Ge 08		

House Categories

Afflictions or Diseases

abortion spontaneous	5	bone disease	10	dandruff	10
abortion surgical	8	bone fracture	10	deafness	1
abrasion (scrape)	1	bowel disturbance	6	debility in general	7
abscess	8	bowel obstruction	6	deformity (disfigurement)	12
ache	1	brain injury	3	dehydration	3
acid body condition	1	breathing problems	3	delirium tremens	3
acid/alkaline balance	4	broken bone	10	diabetes	7
acne	1	bronchial infection	3	diarrhea	8
afflictions	12	bronchitis	3	dietary problems	6
ague	1	bruise	1	disease (in general)	6
AIDS	8	bullet wound	1	disease sexually transmitted	8
albumin in urine	7	bunion	12	disease caused by excess(es)	9
alkaline condition	7	burn	1	disfiguring illness	1
allergy	4	calcium balance	2	dislocated bones or joints	9
amnesia	12	callous	1	dizziness	1
anemia	7	cancer causing attitude	4	dropsy	4
aneurysm	5	cancerous growth	4	dull ache	10
angina	5	carbuncle	8	dysentery	6
apoplexy	9	caries dental	4	eczema	10
appendicitis	6	castration	8	edema	4
appetite abnormality	4	cataract	10	emotional problems	4
arm fractures or breaks	3	chills	10	encephalitis	1
arteriosclerosis	2	chronic ailment	12	enlarged heart	5
arthritis	10	chronic ill health	12	epidemic	8
asphyxiation	3	clumsiness	2	epilepsy	3
asthma	3	colds	6	exhaustion heat	1
astigmatism	4	colic	6	eyesight problems	4
atherosclerosis	4	colitis	6	facial injuries	1
athlete's foot	12	coma	12	fainting spell	5
atrophy	10	complaint (malady)	6	female disorders	7
bad breath	2	complexion problems	1	fever(s)	1
baldness	1	concussion	1	fit	3
bladder disorder	7	constipation	10	flatulence	6
bladder problem	7	consumption	12	foot diseases	12
blindness	1	continence	10	frigidity	6
blister	1	convulsions (spasms)	5	frostbite	8
bloating	5	corns	12	frustrations illness causing	12
blood loss of	10	cough	3	gall stone	7
blood clot	8	cramps	8	gangrene	10
blood disease	5	cramps in toes	7	glaucoma	12
blood impurities	10	crusty growth	4	goiter	2
boil	8	cut	1	gout	10
bone bruise	10	cyst	5	gunshot wounds	1

hair lip	1	lesion	11	puncture wound	1
halitosis	4	leukemia	8	rash	1
hand fractures or breaks	3	lisp	1	respiratory problems	3
hay fever	6	liver problems	9	rheumatism	10
head injury	1	low blood pressure	9	rickets	10
headache	1	lower back pain	7	ringworm skin	10
hearing problem	2	lunacy	4	rupture	1
heart afflictions	4	lung problems	3	scald	1
heart disease	4	malady	6	scalp infection	1
heart irregularities	3	male disorders	1	scaly skin	10
heart palpitations	8	malnutrition	6	scar	1
heart problems	4	mania	4	sciatica	9
heartburn	5	measles	1	scrape	1
heat exhaustion	1	menstrual problems	7	scrofula	2
heat rash	1	mental illness	6	scurvy	3
hematoma	5	mental strain	12	seizure (attack)	8
hemorrhage	1	migraine headache	9	senility	10
hemorrhoids	8	mouth ulcerations	1	sexual disease	8
hepatitis	7	mumps	2	sharp ache	1
hernia	5	myocardial infarct	5	shin splints	11
high blood pressure	1	myopia	4	skin rash	10
hip displacia	9	nausea	4	skin ulcer	10
homesickness	4	nearsightedness	4	sneeze	3
hurt feelings	4	nervous disorders	3	sore	1
hypoglycemia	6	nervous illnesses	6	sore eyes	3
hysteria	8	neuralgia	1	sore throat	2
impetigo	10	neuritis in arms or shoulders	3	spasm	12
indigestion	4	neurosis	12	speech defect	3
infection	1	numbness	10	speech problem	3
infirmity	6	occlusions (blockages)	10	spinal problem	5
inflammation	5	odd skin disorder	11	sprain	10
injuries (in general)	8	old age problems	10	sprained ankle	11
injury (self-inflicted)	1	osteoporosis	9	sprained/broken toe	12
insanity	12	overweight condition	9	st. vitus dance	3
insect bite	1	pain	12	stab wound	1
insomnia	9	pain chronic	12	sting	8
intestinal problems	6	pain having	1	stomach ache	4
itches	10	paralysis (loss of function)	11	stomach cramp	4
jaundice	7	paranoia	8	stress	6
joint problems	10	peritonitis	6	stroke	11
kidney disease	7	physical abnormality	1	stuttering	3
kidney stone	7	physical handicap	12	subluxation	5
kidney weakness	7	piles	8	sun stroke	5
kink (cramp)	10	pleurisy	3	sunburn	5
knee injury	10	pneumonia	3	tension (stress)	6
laceration	1	poison accumulation	8	throat infection	2
lameness	12	pollution afflictions from	8	tongue disease	3
learning disability	3	prickly heat	5	tonsillitis	2
leprosy	10	psychosis	12	tooth decay	10

toothache	10	varicose veins	11	water on the knee	10
toxemia	8	venereal disease	8	weakness	5
toxic condition	8	vertigo	1	wind burn	1
tuberculosis	3	vomiting	4	worms in the body	8
ulcers stomach	4	warts	10	wound	1
uremia	7	wasting diseases	8		
urinary tract problems	7	water imbalance	11		

Animals

alligator	10	crustacean	4	lice	8
amphibian	10	deer	6	lion	5
animal (creature)	1	destructive biological insects	8	livestock	4
animals large or wild	12	dog	6	lizard	5
animals small domesticated	6	dolphin	11	lobster	4
animals in zoos	12	dragon	8	lynx	6
anteater	1	drone (parasite)	8	maggot (larva)	5
ape	1	duck	6	mammal	4
armadillo	4	eagle	8	marsupial	4
badger	1	elephant	12	marten	12
barnacle	4	ferret	8	mascot	4
bat	6	fish	12	mink	12
bear	1	fleas	8	mongrel	9
bee	2	fowl	6	monkey	3
big game	12	fox	3	mosquito	8
birds (in general)	6	frog	10	mount (steed)	6
birds wild	12	giraffe	10	mouse	8
boar	1	gnat	1	mule	2
buck	6	goat	10	octopus	3
bull	2	goose	6	omnivore	4
burrowing animals	9	great cattle	4	opossum	4
burrowing reptiles	11	grizzly bear	1	orangutan	3
butterfly	7	hamster	6	ostrich	11
buzzard	8	hare	3	otter	5
camel	11	hatchling	5	owl	6
cat	6	hawk	8	ox	2
chameleon	3	hen	4	oyster	4
chicken	6	heron	6	panda bear	7
chimpanzee	1	hippopotamus	11	panther	12
clam	4	hog	4	parasite	12
cock	1	horse	9	parrot	3
condor	12	hound	6	peacock	5
constructive biological insect	2	hyena	12	pest (destructive insect)	8
cougar	12	insect	8	pet (small)	6
cow	4	kangaroo	9	pheasant	5
coyote	3	koala bear	7	pig	4
crab	4	lamb	7	pigeon	4
critter	1	large animals	12	polar bear	1
crocodile	10	larvae	5	porcupine	9
crow	3	leopard	9	poultry	6

predator	8	serpent	8	tortoise	4
quadruped	6	sheep	6	turkey	6
rabbit	2	shellfish	4	turtle	4
raccoon	7	shrimp	4	unicorn	7
race horse	9	skunk	8	vermin	8
ram	1	sloth	2	vulture	8
rat	8	slug	4	walrus	12
raven	3	small animals	6	wasp	8
ray (fish)	10	snail	4	weasel	3
reindeer	11	snake	8	weevil	8
reptile	8	spider	8	whale	12
rhinoceros	12	sponge	4	wild animal	12
rodent	8	squirrel	6	wild dog	12
rooster	1	stinging insect	8	wild fowl	6
salamander	10	swan	7	wildcat	12
scavenger	8	swine	4	wolf	10
scorpion	8	tapeworm	8	wolverine	8
sea gull	11	teddy bear	4	worm	8
seal	5	tiger	5		

Parts of an Automobile

air (in tires)	11	engines (in general)	5	jack the	6
alignment	7	exhaust	8	linkage	3
battery	11	exhaust header	11	manifold	3
body	1	exhaust pipe	8	mechanical linkages	11
body bolt	5	exhaust port	8	motor the	5
body ding	1	fan	3	muffler	8
body rust	12	fan belt	3	oil pan	9
carburetor	11	fender	3	padding on the dashboard	2
chassis	5	flat tire	12	passenger seat	4
clutch	10	front bumper	1	piston	5
combustion chamber	5	front grill	1	piston ring	6
connecting parts	3	fuel economy	10	power assist systems	11
convertible top	9	fuel injectors	11	preventive maintenance	6
coolant	10	fuel lines	4	radiator	8
demonstrator	9	fuel or oil filter	6	radio	3
dents and scratches	8	fuel pump	3	repairs made	6
distributor	3	fuel tank	9	ride	5
door	1	generator	11	rust prevention	6
drive shaft	10	glove compartment	6	seat belt	4
drive train	10	governor	10	seating room	4
driver's seat	1	headlights	5	seats the	2
electrical system the	11	horn	1	shock absorbers	7
electrical wiring	11	hoses	3	spare tire	6
emergency brake	10	hydraulic system	11	spring	7
emission control system	6	ignition system	1	starter system	1
engine block	5	instrumentation	6	steering system	3
engine fan	3	interior lamps	11	styling the	7
engine mount	5	interior roominess	4	sun roof	9

suspension system	7	undercoating	4	water hose	4
throttle	1	universal joint	9	water pump	4
tie rod	3	upholstery the	2	wheel rim	3
tire	12	value retention	2	window	7
torsion bar	7	valve	11	windshield	7
transmission	10	valve lifter	6	windshield wiper	7
trunk	12	ventilation system	3		
turn signal	3	voltage regulator	8		

Parts of Our Body or Body Functions

abdomen	6	brain	3	endocrine system	4
adenoids	2	breasts	4	esophagus	4
adipose tissues	9	breathing	3	excretion	8
adrenal gland	1	bronchi	3	excretory system	8
alignment	7	bronchial tubes	3	external sex organs	8
alimentary canal	4	buttocks	7	extremity (appendage)	3
ankle	11	calves (of legs)	11	eye color	1
anus	8	cartilage	10	eyes	1
appendage (subordinate body part)	3	cellular development	9	eyesight quality of	4
		chakra	5	face	1
appendage artificial	2	cheeks	2	fecal matter	8
arches of feet	12	chest	4	feet	12
armpits	3	chest region	4	fertility cycle	4
arms (limbs)	3	chewing	1	finger	3
arteries	1	chin	1	finger nail	3
artificial limb	2	circulatory system (blood)	5	fingerprint	3
autonomic nervous system	3	circulatory system (lungs)	3	flanks	8
back (in general)	5	climax (sexual)	8	flatus	6
back lower half	7	clitoris	8	flesh (tissue)	1
back small of the	7	co-ordination	3	fluid flows	4
beard	10	coagulation of blood	11	fluid retention	4
belching	6	colon	8	food assimilation	6
belly	5	complexion	1	forearms	3
bile	6	coordination	3	forehead	1
bladder	7	decapitation	1	frown	10
blood (in general)	11	defecation	8	gall bladder	6
blood cholesterol	2	dentures	3	gases in the blood	11
blood circulatory system	5	diaphragm	6	genitals	8
blood pressure	11	digestion	4	glands	4
blushing	1	digestive juices	4	glandular system (in general)	4
body care of the	6	digestive system	4	groin area	8
body one's	1	dimples	2	gross motor control	5
body fluids	4	ductless gland	4	hair	10
body hair	10	ducts tear	4	hair on body	10
body rhythms (biorhythms)	4	ears	2	hair on head	1
bone marrow	2	ejaculation	8	hair transplants	8
bones	10	elbow	10	hands	3
bowel movement	8	elimination system the	8	haunches	7
bowels	6	emotions	4	head	1

House Categories

health (in general)	1	natural beauty	2	respiratory system the	3
hearing	1	navel	7	retina	1
heart (in general)	5	neck	2	ribs	3
heart sac	5	nerve sheath	6	salivary glands	4
hemoglobin	11	nerves	3	scalp	1
hiccups	6	nervous system the	3	sciatic nerve	9
hips	9	nipple	4	scrotum	8
homeliness	8	nose	2	seat (buttocks)	8
hormones	4	nosebleed	2	secretions	8
immune system	4	obesity	9	seeing sense of	1
instep	12	organ	4	semen	8
insulin	9	orgasm	8	sensations	2
interior part of the belly	8	ovaries	7	sense perceptions	2
intestinal gas	6	palate	2	senses	2
intestine	6	pallor	1	sex	8
joint	10	palm of hand	3	sex orgasmic	8
kidney	7	palpitations of heart	5	sex organs external	8
knee	10	pancreas	7	sex organs internal	7
kneecap	10	part (organ)	8	sexual intercourse	8
lap one's	8	pelvis	8	sexual organs	8
larynx	2	penis	8	shins	11
leak (urinating)	8	peptic ulcer	6	shivering	1
legs lower part	11	pericardium	5	shoulder blades	5
legs upper part	9	periodic condition	4	shoulders	3
legs from knees to ankles	11	perspiration	4	sides of the body	5
ligament	10	pharynx	2	sinus	1
limb	3	phlegm	8	skeletal system	10
limb artificial	2	physical body	1	skin	10
lips	1	physical condition	4	skin blemish	3
liver	9	physical constitution	1	skin condition	10
liver system (in general)	9	physical control over body	11	skull	1
loins	7	physique	1	small intestine	6
lower back	7	pimple	1	small of the back	7
lumbar region	7	place near genitals	8	smell: sense of	2
lungs	3	plasma (blood parts)	2	solar plexus	5
lymphatic system	4	pore	1	sperm	8
mammary glands	4	posture (bearing)	1	spine (in general)	5
masturbation	8	pregnancy	5	spleen	10
menses	4	private parts	8	stature	10
menstruation	4	prostate gland	8	stomach	4
mental faculties	3	puberty	3	sweat glands	8
metabolism	5	pulse	4	swelling	5
mouth	1	pupil (eye)	3	taste	2
mucous	12	pus	8	tear drop	4
muscle system	1	rectum	8	tear ducts	4
muscles (in general)	1	recuperative powers	8	teeth	10
muscular system (in general)	1	reflexes	1	tendons	10
nail (finger)	1	regurgitation	3	testicle	8
nakedness	10	repair processes	5	thighs	9

thoracic region of chest	3	trunk (torso)	5	vertebrae (in general)	5
thorax	4	tumor	4	vision	4
throat	2	umbilical cord	3	vocal cords	2
thumb	3	urethral structures	7	voice organs	2
thymus gland	2	urinary system	7	vulva	8
tissues of the body	4	urinary tract	7	waist	5
toe	12	urination	8	windpipe	2
tongue	3	uterus	4	womb	4
tonsils	2	vagina	8	wrinkles	11
touch: sense of	2	veins	2	wrist	3
tremors in body	11	venous blood	2		

Colors

aqua	4	gray	10	royal purple	12
azure	2	green	7	saffron	9
beige	6	greenish blue	2	sandy color	5
black	10	honey color	5	scarlet	9
blue	2	indigo	11	sea blue	2
bright green	7	infrared	1	sea green	2
bright-yellow	5	international orange	3	sienna	5
brilliant blue	11	lavender	12	silver	4
brown	6	lemon	6	silvery gray	4
camouflage	6	light brown	6	silvery-blue	4
carmine	1	lime	7	silvery-green	4
checkered patterns	9	magenta	8	sky blue	11
clear	7	maroon	8	slate gray	10
colorless (clear)	7	mauve	12	spotted colors	9
cream	6	medium blue	11	spotted patterns	9
crimson	8	navy	10	subdued colors	6
dark black	8	opaque color	7	turquoise	4
dark blue	10	orange	3	ultra-violet	12
dark brown	8	orange-brown	5	ultramarine	11
dark red	8	pearl	4	velvet	12
dark shades	10	pink	3	violet	12
dull color	10	plaid	9	white	7
earth tones	6	purple	12	white-gray	4
electrical blue	11	red	1	yellow	5
fiery red	1	red-orange	2	yellow-green	4
gold	5	rich colors	5	yellow-orange	5
golden colors	5	rose	3		

Gems or Minerals

achroite	11	amber	5	azurite	2
agate	9	amethyst	12	bauxite	11
alabaster	7	andradite	3	beryl	7
alexandrite	8	antimony	10	black opal	9
almandine	3	aquamarine	7	bloodstone	9
aluminum	11	arsenic	8	borax	8
amazonite	4	asbestos	12	brass	5

bronze	6	iron	1	pyrope	3
buergerite	11	ivory	4	quartz	12
carbuncle	3	jacinth	8	quartzite	12
carnelian (cornelian)	9	jade	6	rhodolite	3
casting	6	jadite	6	rock crystal	12
cat's eye	9	jargoon	8	rose quartz	12
chalcedony	9	jasper	9	rubellite	11
chalk	4	jet	6	ruby	1
chert	9	kunzite	10	rutilated stones	11
chrome	6	laboradorite	4	sand (common)	4
chromite	6	lapis lazuli	11	sanidine	4
chrysoberyl	8	lead	10	sapphire	1
chrysocholla	2	liddicoatite	11	sard	9
chrysoprase	9	limestone	7	sardonyx	9
clay	10	magnesium	1	schorl	11
coal	10	magnetite	6	shell	4
copper	2	malachite	2	siberite	11
coral	4	marble	7	silver	4
corundum	1	mercury	3	silverplate	4
diamond	10	metals (in general)	1	slate	10
dioptase	2	mica	3	smoky quartz	12
dravite	11	microcline	4	spessartine	3
ebony	10	mineralogy	10	spinel	1
elbaite	11	minerals	10	spoumodine	10
emerald	7	moonstone	4	stone (in general)	10
feldspar	4	morganite	7	stone sculpture	7
fire opal	9	nephrite	6	sulphur	8
flint	9	niter	9	sunstone	5
fluorescent mineral	12	obsidian	10	synthetic stone	12
forging	6	olivine	2	tanzanite	7
gold	5	onyx	9	tiger's eye	12
goshenite	7	opal	9	topaz	5
granite	10	ore	10	tourmaline	11
graphite	10	orthoclase	4	turquoise	11
grossular	3	palladium	9	uranium	8
gypsum	2	pearl	4	uvarovite	3
halides (salts)	11	peridot	2	uvite	11
heliodor	7	petrified wood	10	water opal	9
hiddenite	10	pewter	4	white opal	9
hyacinth	8	platinum	4	YAG	12
imitation stone	12	potassium	6	zinc	10
indicolite	11	precious stone	2	zircon	8

Horary or Electional Ideas

ability	5	accomplishment	10	1	
abnormality	11	accumulation	4	adaptability	3
abstraction	9	achievement	10	advantage	2
acceptance	9	actions upon one's life	1	adventure	9
accidents the likelihood of	1	activities in one's own interest		advertising	9

advice	11	conviction for a crime	10	elimination	8
age	10	cooperation	7	employees	6
agreement	7	core (essence of anything)	5	end of the matter the	4
ambition	10	creative ability	5	entertainment	5
anger	1	credit	8	environment the	4
angles	3	crime	12	escape	12
appearance	1	criticism	6	evacuation	8
aptitude	5	danger (peril)	1	evaluation (valuing)	2
arbitration	7	dangerous activities	1	evolution	10
assistance	6	death	8	excellence	10
astrology	11	death in the family a	11	exception	11
atonement	12	decisions	4	exhaustion	8
authority persons in	10	dedication	6	exhibit	5
basics the	4	deity	9	exoneration	12
benefit things of	2	delusion	12	expansion of consciousness	9
body one's	1	denial (disavowal)	12	expectations	11
boss the	10	denial (refusal)	7	expelling	8
broadcasting	9	dependents (subordinates)	6	expenses	2
bureaucracy	6	depletion	8	experience	10
business matters	10	deportment	7	experimentation	9
business outcomes	10	descent	8	explanation	3
business potentials	10	desires	11	exploration	9
by-laws	3	desolate places	1	facts	6
capability	5	diet	6	faith	9
car	3	difficulty	1	family	4
career	10	dignity	10	family affairs	4
cause of death	8	dilemma	7	father	10
causes	11	diminishing	8	favor (gift)	8
change of location a	4	disability	12	fidelity	8
charity	12	disadvantages	12	finances	2
children	5	disagreement	7	financial affairs handling of	2
choices	11	disappointment	12	financial investing	2
circumventing	3	disapproval	7	financial loss	2
cleverness	3	disaster	8	financial matters	2
clothing	6	discontent	11	first person the (grammatical)	1
club (organization)	11	dispensing	11	fixed possessions	4
colds (illness)	6	dispersal	11	focus	3
communication(s)	3	disputes	7	food preparation	6
compassion	12	distribution	3	foreign travel	9
competition the	7	diversion (pastime)	5	forthrightness	11
compromise	7	divorce	7	freedom	11
concern for others	12	dowry	8	freeing	12
confidential matters	12	drugs	12	friction	11
confusion	12	duty	6	friendliness	11
conquest	8	ease	2	friends	11
conspiracy	12	eccentricity	11	future the	2
contracts	7	education	3	gambling	5
contractual agreement	7	effecting change	11	games of chance	5
control	8	elevation	10	gems	2

House Categories

gifts	8	law	9	new venture	1
goals	10	lawsuit (open dispute)	7	non-personal resources	8
government	10	learning	3	nutrition	6
gratitude	2	lecture	9	objectives	10
ground the	4	legacy	8	objectivity	11
group memory	11	legal action	9	obsession	8
groups	11	legislation	11	occult matters	8
harmony	7	letters (mail)	3	open enemy	7
healing	6	life threatening actions	12	opponent	7
health (in general)	1	life's circumstances	1	ordinary the	4
here	1	limitations self-imposed	12	organization	10
hidden (secret) matters	12	livelihood	2	other persons	7
hidden side of life	12	living space	4	outcome of anything the	4
higher education	9	loan	8	pardon	12
hobby	5	long journey	9	parents (in general)	10
home	4	looking beyond	9	parole	12
hopes	11	love	5	partner's money	8
hospitalization	12	lowering	8	partners	7
house	4	luck	5	partnership arrangement	7
humanity attitude toward	11	manipulation	11	past of the matter the	12
hygiene	6	mankind (in general)	4	people one works with	6
identity	1	marketing	9	permission	8
illness	6	marriage	7	perseverance	10
illogical solutions	12	marriage partner	7	persistence	10
impersonal reactions	11	mate one's	7	personal independence	11
importance	10	matters depending on others	10	personal interests	1
imprisonment	12	matters outside of the home	10	personal involvements	1
inclinations	11	maturity	10	personal limitation(s)	12
income	2	meeting others	11	personal matters	4
incompetence	10	membership	11	personal possessions	2
inevitability	12	memory	3	personal ruin	12
information related questions	3	mental efforts	3	persuasiveness	9
inheritance	8	message	3	pet	6
injuries the likelihood of	8	mislaid item	4	philosophy	9
inner unfolding	9	missing item	4	plaintiff the	1
inquisitiveness	3	mixing	11	pleasure	5
insurance matters	8	monetary gain	2	point of view	3
integrity	10	money	2	political awareness	11
intensification	8	money matters	2	politics	11
introspection	12	money of others	8	popularity	5
investigation	8	mother	4	potential ability	5
investments nonspeculative	2	my things or rights	1	praise	5
joining	11	myself	1	pregnancy	5
joint arrangements	7	mysteries	8	present the	1
jointly held property	8	nebulousness	12	present circumstances	1
justice	9	negotiable assets	2	prestige	10
kidnapping	12	neighbor	3	privacy	4
land	4	neighborhood	3	probing	8
large animals	12	new the	11	productivity	6

profession	10	schooling	3	survival	2
property related items	4	secret enemy	12	synthesis	8
prophecy	9	secrets	12	taxes	8
psychic matters	8	self the	1	technique	6
psychological health	12	self-denial	12	tenant	6
public enemy	7	self-pity	12	them	2
public life	10	self-undoing	12	there	7
publications	9	service	6	those with whom you consult	7
punishment	12	sex	8	time	10
purpose	10	sexuality	8	today	1
querent (questioner)	1	shaping the future	11	tomorrow	2
real estate	4	shared things or values	8	training	6
reaping (returning)	12	sharing	8	transformation	8
recognition earning	10	ship	4	travel alone	3
recreation	5	short distance travel	3	travel to unfamiliar places	9
redemption	12	short trips	3	trend	11
reforming activities	8	sibling	3	trust	8
rehabilitation	12	sickness	6	universality	9
relationships	7	similarity	3	unwanted things	12
relaxation	2	sin	8	us	1
religion	9	size	2	vacation	5
religious pursuits	9	slowing down	2	visiting	3
remote consequences	12	small animals	6	visitors	3
removal	8	society (social group)	11	visits	3
reprieve	12	sorrow	12	vocation	10
reputation	10	speculation (gambling)	5	we	1
resale value	10	spiritual matters	9	wealth accumulating	4
responsibility	10	sportsmanship	9	welfare	12
restitution	8	stall (delay)	10	will (legal document)	8
retirement	8	strategy	11	wisdom	9
rewards	10	stress	6	wishes	11
risk taking on a	5	success	10	work	6
romance	5	suddenness	11	working conditions	6
routine activities	4	superiors	10	writing(s)	3
salary	2	surgery	8	you yourself	1

Parts of a House

addition	4	bathroom	6	compost pile	8
alcove (recess)	6	bathtub	6	construction methods	2
areas behind walls	12	bedroom	2	corridors	3
art works of	7	boudoir	2	counter space	4
art studio	7	ceiling area	10	counter top	6
attic	9	ceilings	9	cupboard	6
back porch	5	cellar	4	curtains (drapery)	7
back yard	4	child's room	5	day room	9
balcony	9	chimney	3	deck	5
ballroom	5	clogged drain	8	decor	7
basement	4	closet	6	decorations	2
basic raw materials	2	coldest part of the house	10	den	5

design (shape)	1	hearth the	5	septic system	8
dining room	6	heating system the	5	settling	8
dishwasher	6	hobby room	6	sewer drain	8
door	1	hot water heater	4	sewing room	6
door rear or side	12	informal dining area	4	shelving (for storage)	6
doorway	1	insulation	4	shower	6
drainage of the land	12	joist	10	shower stall	6
drawing room	7	kitchen	6	shrubbery	2
dressing room(s)	7	kitchen appliance	6	sick room	6
driest part of the house	3	landscaping	7	sink	6
ductwork	3	laundry	6	skylight	5
eaves (roof)	9	lawn	4	stairway	3
electrical appliance	11	library	9	steps	3
electrical wiring	11	lighting	5	stoop	1
entrance	1	living room	5	storeroom	6
entryway	1	lobby	1	storm door	4
exhaust vent	8	lower floors	4	storm window	4
family room	4	main bathroom	6	stove	5
fire escape	12	main hall	5	structure (in general)	10
fireplace	5	medicine cabinet	6	studio	5
floor (level base of room)	10	nursery	5	study	9
floor (story)	4	office in the home	10	sump pump	4
flue	3	ornate decoration	5	sun room	5
food preparation area	6	out buildings (utility)	6	support (pillar)	4
food storage areas	6	outbuilding	4	swimming pool	5
formal dining room	10	pantry	6	tap water	4
formal living room	11	parlor	7	telephone	3
foundation	4	parts underground	4	television room	5
foyer	1	patio	5	threshold (gate)	1
front door	1	patio door	5	threshold (sill)	4
furnace	5	picture window	7	toilet	8
furnishings	2	play area	5	upper floors	9
furniture	2	playroom	5	utility closet	6
fuse box the	11	plumbing	4	veranda	5
game room	5	porch	5	vestibule	1
garage	6	rafters	9	wall (partition)	10
garden flower	2	reading room	9	water closet	8
garden vegetable	4	reception room	1	water pipes	4
gazebo	5	recreation room	5	water tank	4
gutter (roof)	3	refrigerator	6	window	7
halls (corridors)	3	roof	10	workshop	6
hallway	3	rug	7	yard, the	4
hamper laundry	6	scullery	6		

Mundane Ideas

advanced schooling	9	affairs of officials	10	air rights	9
advancement economic	11	agricultural interests	4	airport	11
advertising	9	agriculture	4	ally	7
advisor	11	air force	6	animals	6

aristocracy the	10	citizenship	4	consultant	11
army	6	city	4	consumable commodities	4
assets of the people	2	city council	11	consumer needs	4
asylum	12	city officials	10	consumerism	4
attitudes of the people	1	civic organization	11	consumption of goods	4
banking house	2	civil service	6	containment (prevention policy)	8
banking system the	2	civil unrest	7	contract negotiation	7
benefit package	8	civil violence	1	contractual relationship	7
birth rate	5	civil workers	6	cooperative arrangements	7
board of directors	11	civilian population	4	corporate assets	11
body of water	4	civilization	4	corporate position	1
bond (security)	2	clientele	4	corporation	10
boom (economic)	9	coalition	11	corporation law	6
borders of country	9	coast guard the	6	costs	2
boss the	10	coastline the nation's	4	council	11
bounty from the land	4	code of ethics	9	country the	1
bridge	3	collaboration	7	credit (allowance)	2
budget	8	collection agency	8	credit national	8
building	10	collective bargaining	11	credit standing	8
bureaucracy the	6	colonial offices	9	credit union	2
business	10	commander-in-chief	10	crisis economic	8
business affairs	10	commerce	3	crop raising	4
business assets	11	commercial trade	3	crops	4
business associate	7	commercialism	3	cultural life	4
business dealings abroad	9	committee of a fraternal group	11	currency	2
business finances	2	commodity (economic factor)	4	customs	8
business forms	3	commodity (product)	4	cutthroat competition	8
business income	11	communal possessions	12	dam	10
business obligation	5	communication systems	3	dealings with government	10
business partnerships	7	communications satellite	3	dealings with the public	7
business prosperity	11	communism	11	debt	8
business standing	10	community affairs	4	debt expansion	4
business success	10	community property	8	deficits	8
business world	10	community resources	5	demand for goods or services	10
buyer (in an exchange)	1	community standing	10	democracies	4
cable overseas	9	community's weather history	4	department heads	10
capitalism	2	competitive marketplace	7	department of defense	1
cash flow	2	competitor(s)	7	department of personnel	4
casualty (disaster)	8	concentration camp	12	department of state	7
celebrity national	5	conduct of business the	10	diplomat	9
censorship	7	confederation (alliance)	7	diplomatic corps	9
ceremony	9	confidential matters	12	disappointing earnings	1
ceremony official	9	confines (boundaries)	9	disputes	7
chairman of the board	10	conglomerate	11	domestic considerations	1
chamber of commerce	11	conspiracy	12	domestic employees	6
charge account	8	constitution	11	domestic interests	1
charity national	12	construction	10	durable goods	4
checks and balances (limits)	10	construction equipment	6	earning capacity	2
church	9	consulate	9		

House Categories

eating establishment	6	goals national	11	journeys long	9
economic outlook	6	goods demand for	4	journeys short	3
economy the	10	governing authority	10	judiciary the	9
educated classes the	9	government the	10	justice as practiced	9
educational matters	5	government agencies	10	labor force the	6
electorate the	4	government officials	10	labor union	6
electrical system	11	governmental authority	10	laboring class	6
employees	6	governmental interference	11	land	4
employers	10	granary	6	landed interests	4
enemies known	7	head of an organization	10	law	9
enemies open	7	head of government	10	law enforcement	10
enemies secret	12	healing	6	leader	10
environment the	4	heavy industry	11	leader of the opposition	4
epidemic	8	hidden ills	12	leadership	11
escrow account	8	high society	5	leadership the country's	11
espionage	12	hiring of employees	6	left-wing movement	11
establishment (business)	10	historical perspective	4	legal agencies	9
establishment (rulers) the	7	history	4	legislation	11
estate (assets of)	8	home front the	1	legislative activity	11
executive work	10	hospital care national	12	legislative body	11
exports	9	hotel	4	legislative house	11
factory	11	house of parliament	11	legislative practice	11
fair exchange	7	house of representatives	11	lending agency	8
fall from power	12	housing	4	liability	8
family	4	ideals national	10	living conditions in general	1
finances competitor's	2	identity the country's	1	lockout management	11
financial institution	2	imperialism	5	long term appreciation	2
folk culture	5	import-export business	9	loss (financial)	8
folklore national	9	imports	9	loss from speculation	5
food production (growing)	4	inflation	9	loss of public office	7
foreign affairs	9	inhabitant	4	lower house of government	4
foreign associate	9	institutions large public	12	lower legislative house	4
foreign commerce	9	insurance	8	machine (political)	11
foreign country	9	insurance unemployment	8	management	10
foreign items	9	insurance company	8	mandate (territory)	4
foreign people	9	insurance practices	8	manipulated economies	9
foreign policy a nation's	7	interest rates	8	manufactured goods	10
foreign relations	9	interior department of	4	manufacturing	6
foreign trade	9	interior affairs	1	market leverage	5
form business	3	internal distributions systems	3	market statistics	3
free market	4	internal opposition	7	marketplace the	4
friends of the nation	11	internal revenue service the	8	marriage policies	7
fundamental indicator	10	international disputes	7	mayoral appointees	3
gain from speculation	5	international friendships	11	mercantilism	4
gaining an office	10	international relations	7	merchandising	4
gambling	5	international trade	9	messengers of the state	7
general trade	3	interstate commerce	9	methods of business	1
geography of the country	4	inventory	6	middle class the	4
geopolitics	11	jobs	10	military forces	6

military service	6	oceans bordering the nation	4	population	1
military stores	6	office (work place)	10	position in society	7
mine (pit)	8	office of an agent	4	positions of power or authority	10
mine (tunnel)	8	office of the partner	4		
mint (makes money)	2	officers in authority	10	post office	3
monetary partnerships	8	official business	10	postal system	3
monetary standards	8	opposite party	7	power struggle	10
money paper based	3	opposition behind the scenes	12	price fixing	3
money laundering	9	opposition-underhanded or sneaky	12	price market will bear	10
money manipulation	12			price of a house for sale	6
money market	2	options market	5	price of land	6
money of the business	11	ordinary business	4	price quotation	3
money supply a business's	11	ouster	11	price stability	2
money supply a country's	11	overthrow	11	price war	4
monopoly	8	pact (treaty)	7	primary education facilities	3
mortality rates	8	paper money	3	prime minister	10
mortality tables	6	parliament	11	prince or princess	10
mortgage companies	8	partnership	7	prison	12
municipal government	11	party (political)	11	prisoner-of-war	12
municipality	4	party to a contract	7	procurement interests	4
music national	5	people those who oppose the	7	procurement policy	4
nation the	1	people in power	10	procurement practices	4
nation's capitol	1	people of high status	10	professional classes	10
nation's constitution	1	people who give service(s)	6	profit from a business	11
national affairs	10	person holding office	11	profit from a corporation	11
national approval need for	10	personnel the	6	profit from a move	8
national celebrities	10	persons having power	10	profit from a partnership	8
national cemetery	8	philosophical institution	9	profit from a publication	4
national debt the	8	place of business	10	prostitution	8
national glory	5	platform (policy)	10	protectionist concerns	4
national health policies	6	police	6	public attitudes of the	3
national lifestyles	1	police as authority	10	public the (in general)	4
national pastimes	5	policy	10	public attention	10
national policy	8	political atmosphere	11	public ceremony	6
national reputation	10	political convention	11	public convention	11
national security, concerns of	4	political election	11	public enemy	7
		political force	11	public faith	9
natural resources	4	political machine	11	public gathering	11
natural wealth of country	8	political party in opposition	4	public health	6
navy	6	political party in power	10	public institution	12
negotiable assets	2	political party not in power	4	public investment	2
negotiation	7	political party out of power	4	public money	8
neighbor	3	political preferment	11	public office	11
neighborhood politics	1	political propaganda	9	public opinion	4
neighboring country	3	political success	10	public relations	9
new technology acceptance	11	politics	11	public sales	12
newspapers	3	poll result of	2	public school system	3
object of state importance	3	pollution	8	public trust	9
occult society	12	popularity of state	5	public utility	11

House Categories

public welfare	12	servants of the country	6	tourism	9
public works	6	serving mankind	12	town council	11
publications	9	settlement financial	8	trade international	9
punishment of crime	12	settlement of disputes	7	trade embargo	7
quarrel with another	7	shared resources	8	trade patterns	6
rackets the	8	short selling	1	trade union	12
radio or television acceptance	11	signing a contract	3	trade within borders	3
raw material	4	social alliance	11	trades the	6
real estate	4	social change	9	transportation hub	3
recession	10	social forces	11	transportation systems	3
recreation area	5	social organization	11	travel distant	9
redistribution of wealth	7	social security	8	travel long distance	9
regime the	1	social security benefits	8	travel within the country	3
relating to other countries	7	social status	10	treason	12
relations with educators	9	social ties	11	treasure	2
relations with family	4	socialism	11	treasury the	2
relations with leaders	10	socialized medicine	8	treaty	7
relations with other countries	7	society (social group)	11	tribal customs	4
relations with parents	4	sorrow public	3	tribal groups	4
relations with the public	7	sound currency	5	tribe (social group)	4
religion national	9	speculation (venture)	5	truce	7
religious affairs	9	speculation market	5	uniformity	4
religious education	9	spending beyond means	12	union labor	11
republic the	1	sports professional	9	unions trade	6
reputation	10	spy	12	university	9
resource (natural wealth)	4	standing before the world	10	upper house of government	10
restructuring a corporation	8	state the	1	upper legislative house	10
retirement fund	8	state funeral	8	urban development	4
revenue	2	state legislature	11	utility public	12
right-wing movements	10	stock certificate	5	utility company	12
risks national	5	stock markets	5	venture capital	2
river	4	storage facility	6	voters in an election	4
road	3	store's inventory	6	voting	11
ruling classes	10	strike (labor)	6	wages	2
sales tax	8	strikes inception of	6	war	7
sanitary practices	6	style of government	10	war the end of	10
school	3	subversive	12	warfare	7
seaport	4	succession rights	4	warlike situation	7
secession	8	supplies for consumption	4	water distribution system	6
secret cabal	12	supreme authority	10	water supply	4
secret enemy	12	supreme court the	9	wealth	2
secret organization	12	tax records	1	weather	3
secret police force	12	taxation	8	welfare agency	12
secret service	12	taxes	8	welfare systems	12
secret society	12	teacher	5	whoever has authority	10
securities	2	technical indicator	6	will of the people	8
self-undoing	12	telephone system	3	working capital	11
seller (in an exchange)	7	theater	5	working classes	6
senate	11	totalitarian regimes	8	working conditions	6

working environment 6	world assemblies like the U.N. 9	world's fair 5
workman's compensation 8	world trade 9	worldly position 10

Mythical Figures or Constellation Names

Admetos (exaggerated promises) 5	crown) 5	Hydra (water snake) 8
Allspy (Panope) 12	Corona Borealis (northern crown) 5	Hydrus (little water snake) 8
Andromeda 12	Corvus (crow) 3	Hyperion 5
Antila (air pump) 11	Cottos (many headed monster) 12	Indus (the indian) 9
Antinous 3	Crateris (cup) 4	Ixion (treachery) 9
Aphrodite (the lover) 7	Cronos 10	Janus 9
Apollo (the healer) 5	Crux (southern cross) 10	Jason (adventurer) 9
Apollon 5	Cupid 5	Juno 4
Apus (bird of paradise) 5	Cyclops 12	Jupiter 9
Aquarius 11	Cygnus (swan) 7	Kastor and Polydeukes 3
Aquilla (eagle) 8	Delphinus (dolphin) 3	Kronos (saturn) 10
Ara (altar) 9	Demeter (the caregiver) 6	Lacerta (lizard) 5
Ares (the warrior) 1	Diana 4	Leo (lion) 5
Argus (the adventurers) 1	Dionysos (the escapist) 5	Leo Minor (little lion) 5
Aries 1	Dis Pater 8	Lepus (hare) 3
Artemis 4	Dorado (goldfish) 12	Leto (gentleness) 2
Athena (the counselor) 6	Draco (dragon) 8	Liber 5
Auriga (the charioteer) 3	Echo (the repeater) 12	Libra (scales) 7
Baccus 5	Eos (dawn) 12	Lupus (wolf) 8
Bootis (the herdsman) 9	Epimetheus (afterthought) 9	Lynx (lynx) 12
Cadmos (musician) 2	Equuleus (horse) 9	Lyra (lyre) 2
Caelum (chisel) 6	Erebos 4	Mars 1
Calm 2	Eridanus (river) 3	Medusa 10
Camelopardus (giraffe) 10	Eris (discord) 7	Mensa (table mountain) 10
Cancer (crab) 4	Eros 5	Mercury 3
Canes Major (large dog) 12	Eurydice (the unattainable) 11	Microscopium (microscope) 6
Canes Minor (small dog) 6	Faun 9	Milky Way the 4
Canes Venatici (hunting dogs) 8	Faunus 2	Minerva 6
Capricorn (sea goat) 10	Flamingo 7	Mnomosyne (memory) 3
Carina (keel of ship Argo) 4	Fornax (furnace) 5	Monoceros (unicorn) 7
Cassiopeia 10	Gaia 2	Musca (fly) 12
Castor and Pollux 3	Gemini (twins) 3	Narcissus 5
Centaur 9	Gorgons (monsters) 8	Neptune 12
Cepheus 7	Griffin 8	Niobe 4
Ceres 6	Grus (crane) 6	Norma (level) 7
Cetus (sea monster) 12	Hades 8	Nymph 12
Chamaeleon 3	Helios (sun) 5	Octans (instrument) 6
Chaos 4	Hephaistos (the wage earner) 6	Ophiuchus (serpent holder) 6
Chiron 8	Hera (the loyal friend) 4	Orion (the hunter) 9
Circinus (compass) 6	Hercules (the warrior) 1	Orpheus (musician & poet) 2
Columba (dove) 7	Hermes (the swift traveler) 3	Pan 2
Coma Berenices (Berenice's hair) 9	Hestia (Vesta the homemaker) 6	Panope (Allspy) 12
	Horologium (water clock) 10	Pavo (peacock) 5
Corona Australis (southn.	Hyades 12	Pegasus (winged horse) 11
		Persephone 4

Perseus (the hero)	5	Sagitta (arrow)	9	Titans	5
Phoenix (phoenix)	8	Sagittarius (archer)	9	Toucana (toucan)	1
Pictor (painter's easel)	7	Sasquatch	12	Triangulum (triangle)	9
Pisces (fishes)	12	Saturn	10	Typhoon	11
Pisces Austrinis (southern fish)	12	Satyr	8	Uranos (sky)	11
		Scorpius (scorpion)	8	Ursa Major (great bear)	1
Pleiades the	3	Sculptor (sculptor)	7	Ursa Minor (smaller bear)	1
Plouton	8	Scutum (shield)	4	Vela (sails of the Argo)	11
Pluto	8	Selene (moon)	4	Venus	7
Pontos (sea)	4	Serpens (serpent)	8	Vesta (the homemaker)	6
Poseidon	12	Sextans (sextant)	6	Virgo (virgin)	6
Prometheus (thinker, humanist)	3	Sisyphos (betrayal)	12	Volans (flying fish)	11
		Taurus (bull)	2	Vulcan	6
Psyche	7	Telescopium (telescope)	9	Vulpecula (fox)	3
Puppis (stern of the Argo)	12	Thamus (steersman)	3	Yeti	12
Pyxis (compass)	11	Themis (justice)	9	Zeus (the ruler)	9
Reticulum (net)	4	Theseus (hero)	5		
Rheia	3	Thetis (shape changer)	12		

Occupations or Person Types

Occupations or person types that end in "man," like seaman, statesman, con man, yeoman, draftsman, etc., are included. These occupation holders or person types may be of either sex. Language standards have forced the spelling used. These entries can be updated as accepted dictionary entries change.

academic	9	adversary	7	announcer	3
accessory (accomplice)	7	advertiser	9	anti-christ	8
accompanist	11	advisor	11	anti-hero	11
accomplice	11	advocate	11	apostle	11
account executive	10	affiliate	11	appraiser	7
accountant	6	agent	7	apprentice	6
acquaintance	11	aggressor	1	arbiter	7
acrobats	3	agitator	11	arbitrator	7
actor	5	agnostic	9	archaeologist	8
actress	5	agrarian	4	archer	9
ad writer	3	agricultural worker	4	architect	7
addict	12	aide (assistant)	6	archivist	4
adherents	11	airline host/hostess	6	aristocrat	10
adjuster (claims)	8	airline personnel	11	armament manufacturer	1
adjutant	6	alcoholic	12	art dealer	7
administrator	10	alderman	11	artillery man	1
adolescents	3	alien	9	artisan	6
adventurer	9	ally	7	artist	5
		alumnus	9	ascetic	12
		amateur	3	ass (fool)	3
		ambassador	9	assailant	7
		ambitious person	10	assassin	12
		ambulance driver	1	assayer	2
		amusement park worker	5	assessor	2
		analyst	8	assistant	6
		analytical scientist	8	astrologer	11
		anarchist	11	astronomer	10
		angel (backer)	6	athiest	8
		angler	4	athlete	5

attendant	6	bore	10	chancellor	11
attorney	9	boss the	10	channel (medium)	9
auctioneer	3	botanist	4	charity worker	12
auditor	6	bounty hunter	8	charlatan	12
author	3	boxer	5	cheater	3
authority (specialist)	10	boy	3	cheerleader	5
authority figure	10	boy friend	5	chemist	12
auto dealer	3	brethren	3	chief executive	10
auto manufacturer	11	brewer	12	children	5
aviator	11	bricklayer	10	chiropractor	6
baby sitter	8	bride	7	chiseler	3
backer	11	bridegroom	7	churchman	9
bad (evil) person	8	bridge builder	3	city manager	11
bail bondsman	8	bridge worker	3	civil engineer	10
bailiff	6	broadcaster	9	civil servant	6
baker	4	brokerage	3	civil service worker	6
bandit	7	brute	8	civilian	4
banished person	7	buddy	11	claimant	1
bank teller	2	budget manager	8	clandestine associate	12
banker	2	bug (hobbyist)	5	classmate	3
barbarian	9	builder	4	cleaner	6
barber	1	bully	1	clergy	9
bard	2	burglar	7	clerk	6
barker	3	bus boy	6	client (patron)	4
barmaid	12	bus driver	3	clinger	4
barrister	1	business partner	7	clock maker	10
bartender	12	busybody	3	clock repairer	6
beautician	7	butcher	1	clothier	6
bedfellow (ally)	7	butler	6	clothing designer	2
beggar	12	buyer	3	clown	3
believer	9	cabinet maker	6	co-worker	6
belly dancer	7	cad	8	coach	10
benefactor	9	cadet	6	coal miner	4
beneficiary	8	camper (occupies land)	4	cohort (companion)	11
bigot	8	canary (talker)	3	collaborator	7
bill collector	8	candidate	11	colleague	11
bimbo	12	cannibal	8	collector	4
biochemist	8	canvasser	3	college professor	9
biologist	2	caretaker	6	columnist	3
bishop	9	carny	5	comedian	5
bitch	7	carpenter	6	comic	5
blacksmith	6	cartoonist	3	commander	10
boarder	6	cashier	2	commentator	3
bomber	1	castaway	12	commissioner	10
book binder	3	catcher	4	commodity dealer	5
book seller	3	caterer	4	commuter	3
bookkeeper	6	cemetery worker	8	companion	11
bookworm	3	censor	8	competitor(s)	7
bootlegger	12	challenger in a contest	7	composer	2

House Categories

computer analyst	6	custodian	4	diamond cutter	10
computer operator	6	customer engineer	6	dictator	6
computer programmer	6	cynic	3	dietician	6
comrade	11	dairy farmer	4	digger	2
con artist	3	dairy worker	4	dignitary	10
con man	3	damsel	3	dilettante	7
concierge	3	dancer	2	diner	4
concubine	8	dandy	5	diplomat	9
conductor (orchestra)	10	darling (sweetheart)	5	director	1
conductor (vehicle)	3	data processor	6	disabled the	12
confectioner	2	date (escort)	7	disciple	11
confederate (ally)	7	day laborer	6	disciplinarian	8
confidante	11	dead the	8	dishonest person	7
confidential agents	12	deadbeat	3	dispatcher	3
connoisseur	2	dealer (cards)	5	displaced person	12
conqueror	10	dealer (negotiator)	3	dissident	11
conservative	10	dealer in future trends	11	distant people	9
conservator	4	dealer in liquids	4	distiller	8
consultant	11	dealer in ornaments	2	distributor	3
consumer	4	debater	3	diver	8
contestant	7	debtor	8	divinity (a god)	9
contract negotiator	7	debutante	7	doctor	6
contractor	6	deceiver	3	doer	6
convict	12	decorator	2	dolt (idiot)	3
cook	4	deed recorder	6	domestic	6
coordinator	3	deep sea diver	4	domestic (servant)	6
copy editor	6	defendant	7	donor	8
coroner	8	defender	1	doorman	1
correspondent	3	degenerate	12	dope (dummy)	3
cosmetician	2	deity	9	draftsman	6
counsel (lawyer)	9	delegate	11	drag (spoilsport)	10
counselor (advisor)	11	delivery personnel	3	dreamer	12
counterfeiter	3	democrat	4	dregs (riff-raff)	12
courier	3	demon	8	dressmaker	6
courtier	7	demonstrator (protester)	11	driller	10
coward	5	denizen	4	drip (jerk)	12
craftsman	6	dental hygienist	6	driver	3
crank	10	dental technician	6	drudge	6
credit manager	8	dentist	10	drug dealer	12
creditor	8	dependents (subordinates)	6	druggist	6
criminal	12	deportee	12	drunkard	12
criminologist	8	deputy	6	dry cleaner	6
cripple	12	derelict	12	duke	10
critic	6	designate	7	dummy	3
critical (necessary) worker	10	designer	7	dunce	3
crook	7	destroyer	8	dupe	3
crop grower	4	detective	8	dwarf	3
crusty people	4	devil the	8	dyer	12
culprit	7	devil's advocate	11	earl	10

eccentric	11	fanatic	9	funeral director	8
economist	10	farm hand	4	furniture maker	2
editor	9	farmer	4	gad-fly	11
educated classes the	9	favorite (front runner)	7	gangster	8
educational profession	5	favorite one	7	garbage collector	8
educator	5	fellow	11	gardener	4
elder	10	fellow club member	11	genealogist	4
electrician	11	fellow employee	6	general	10
electronic technician	6	fellow traveler	3	generalist	4
elite (select) the	7	felon	12	genius	10
embalmer	8	females	4	gentleman	7
embezzler	7	ferryman	3	gentry	10
emergency worker	6	fiance fiancee	7	geologist	10
emigrant	9	fiend	8	ghost writer	12
eminent people	10	fighter	1	giant	10
emissary	7	file clerk	6	girl	3
emperor empress	10	film actor	5	girl friend	5
employees	6	financial advisor	2	gladiator	1
employer	10	financier	2	glutton	2
enforcer	8	finder	11	gnome	3
engineer	10	fire eater	1	gods or goddesses	11
engraver	7	firebug	12	goldsmith	5
entertainer	5	fireman	9	goof-off	5
enthusiast	5	fisherman	4	gossiper	3
entrepreneur	5	flatterer	7	gourmet	2
envoy (representative)	7	flier	11	governess	6
epicure	2	florist	2	government representative	5
escaped convict	7	flower grower	2	government worker	6
escort	7	foe	7	governor	10
estate lawyer	8	follower	11	graduate	10
evaluator	2	food chemist	5	graphic artist	7
excavator	8	food preparer	6	graphologist	1
executioner	8	food server	6	grave digger	4
executive	10	fool (jester)	3	great person	10
executive business	10	forecaster	9	grocer	6
executive head	10	foreign spies	12	grocery clerk	9
exhibitor	5	foreigner	9	groom (for animals)	9
exile	12	foreman	10	groom (in a wedding)	7
expediter	3	forest ranger	6	grouch	8
expert	10	forester	6	guard	8
explorer	9	forger	12	guardian (protector)	10
exponent (advocate)	11	fortune teller	8	guide (advisor)	11
exposer	5	founder	4	guide (scout)	9
extra	5	franchisee	9	guilty party	7
extrovert	5	franchiser	3	guru	10
fair weather friend a	10	free-thinker	11	gynecologist	7
fairy	12	friend close	7	gyp (swindler)	3
faith healer	2	friends (supporters)	11	gypsy	9
famous person	10	fugitive	7	haberdasher	1

House Categories

hack (writer)	3	ideal (hero)	10	jockey	9
hairdresser	7	idiot	3	joker	3
half-wit	3	illegal alien	4	journalist	3
handwriting expert	1	illusionist	12	judge	9
harbinger	1	illustrator	3	juggler	3
hard core (diehard)	11	immature person	2	junk collector	8
hardware dealer	4	imp	3	junk dealer	12
harlequin	3	impersonator	3	jurist	9
harlot	8	importer exporter	9	juror	9
harvester	6	impostor	3	jury member	9
head (leader)	10	impresario (promoter)	5	juvenile	3
healer	6	industrialist	10	keeper (custodian)	4
health official	6	infants	5	kidnapper	12
heart specialist	5	inferior	6	killjoy	10
heathen (barbarian)	8	infidel	8	king	10
heir	8	information analyst	3	knight	5
heir apparent	8	information clerk	3	lab technician	8
heretic	8	information processor	6	labor leader	10
hermit	10	information specialist	3	laborer	6
hero	5	informer	12	lad	3
heroine	5	inhabitant	4	lady	2
higher-ups	10	innkeeper	6	land developer	10
hippie	11	inspector	6	landlord	1
hired hand	6	instigator	1	landowner	4
hireling	6	insurance adjuster	8	landscaper	7
historian	4	insurance agent	8	lapidarian	7
hobo	11	insurance broker	8	lass	2
hold out	11	insurance worker	8	lawbreaker	7
holy person	9	insurer	8	lawsuit defendant in	7
home maker	4	intellectual	3	lawyer	9
homeless the	12	interior decorator	7	lawyer in a court action, your	7
hoodlum	7	interloper	1	lay person	9
horse trainer	9	intermediary	7	lazybones	7
hospital administrator	9	intern	6	leader	10
host	7	interpreter	9	leather worker	10
hostage	7	interviewer	3	lecturer (academic)	9
hostess	7	introvert	4	lecturer (in general)	9
hotel worker	4	intruder	1	legislator	11
house servant	6	invader	8	lender	2
household help	6	invalid	12	letter carrier	3
huckster	3	inventor	11	liar	3
humanitarian	11	investigator	8	liberal	9
hunter	9	investment banker	2	liberator	11
husbandry	6	iron worker	1	librarian	3
hussy	8	itinerant	9	life guard	4
hustler	3	jailer	12	lighting specialist	11
hygienist	6	janitor	6	linguist	3
hypnotist	8	jester	3	living saint	9
hypochondriac	6	Jesuit	9	loafer	2

lodger	6	member of a support group	11	mountain climber	10
longshoreman	6	member of a wedding	10	mourner	12
lookout	3	men	1	mouthpiece (spokesperson)	3
lost person	4	men ages 25 to 35	1	mover	3
loud person	1	men ages 35 to 45	5	movie maker	5
love (beloved)	5	men young	3	murderer	8
lover	5	men from the past	10	muscular persons	2
lunatic	4	mental health worker	6	muse (guiding spirit)	5
lyricist	2	mentor	10	musician	2
machinist	11	mercenary	6	mute	10
madam (of brothel)	8	merchandiser	4	mythical character	9
magician (occultist)	8	merchant	4	narrator	3
magician (stage)	3	mermaid	10	naturalist	4
magistrate	9	messenger	3	nature mother	4
maid	6	metal craftsman	6	navigator	11
maiden	2	metal worker	6	needy the	12
mail carrier	3	metaphysician	9	negotiator	7
make-up artist	2	meter reader	6	neighbor	3
malcontent	11	microbiologist	4	neophyte	3
males	1	middleman	3	neurologist	3
malicious person	8	midget	3	new acquaintance	11
manager	10	midwife	5	newcomer	1
manicurist	3	migrant farm laborer	6	news commentator	3
manipulator	11	military (person in)	6	news personnel	3
manufacturer	4	millionaire	10	newspaper worker	3
marauder	8	mime	3	night worker	4
mariner	4	mimic	3	nightclub performer	5
market maker	3	miner	8	nihilist	8
marketer	9	minister (clergy)	9	nobility	10
marketing agent	9	minor	3	nobleman	10
marksman	9	miser	4	nomad	12
marshal	6	missing person	7	non-conformist	11
martyr	12	missionary	9	non-entity	12
mason	10	mistress	8	notary	7
massager	6	model	7	novelist	3
master	10	moderator	7	nudist	5
master of ceremonies	5	molester	8	nun	9
matchmaker	7	monarch	10	nurse	6
mathematician	6	money lender	2	observer	3
maverick	11	money maker	2	obstetrician	5
mayor	10	monitor (proctor)	8	occultist	8
mechanic	11	monk	9	oceanographer	4
mechanical engineer	6	monster (demon)	12	official	10
media analyst	6	monument maker	10	old people	10
media personnel	3	moocher	3	older person	10
mediator	7	moron	12	ombudsman	7
medical technician	8	mortals	4	onlooker	3
medium	8	mortician	8	open enemy	7
member	11	mother	4	operator (of a fraud)	3

House Categories

operator (worker)	6	peasant	4	plumber	4
opinionated person	9	pensioner	8	podiatrist	12
opponent	7	people aged 60-70	10	poet	12
opposition (rival)	7	people aged 70-85	11	police (in general)	6
optician	6	performer	5	politician	11
optimist	5	perfumer	2	poll taker	6
optometrist	6	perpetrator	1	poor the	12
oracle	9	persecutor	8	pope	9
orator	3	person a	1	populace the	4
orchard worker	2	person inquired about	7	porter	6
order giver	1	person of rank	10	position (status)	10
orderly	6	person stealing	7	postal employee	3
organ donor	12	personal ambassador	9	potter	7
organizer	10	personal representatives	7	poultry farmer	6
orphan	12	persons in misery	12	powder (particulates)	4
osteopath	10	persons of old age	10	powerful people	10
other party in a contest	7	persons on relief	12	preacher	9
other people (in general)	7	persons with authority over you	10	predecessor	4
outcast	12			premier	10
outlaw	7	pervert	11	president	10
outlawed person	7	pessimist	6	presiding judge	9
overseer	10	pest (nuisance)	1	press (reporters)	3
packer	6	phantom (ghost)	8	prey (victim)	12
pagan	8	pharmacist	6	priest	9
painter (artist)	7	phenomena (remarkable person)	5	prime minister	10
painter (house)	7			principal	5
pall bearer	8	philanderer	5	printer	3
palmist	3	philanthropist	9	prisoner	12
paramour	8	philosopher	9	private enemy	12
parasite	12	photographer	12	private investigator	8
park ranger	5	physician	6	prodigy	10
parson	9	physicist	10	produce dealer	4
participant	1	piano tuner	2	producer	4
partisan	11	picket (protester)	11	professional	10
partners	7	pickpocket	3	professor	9
passenger	3	piker	10	profiteer	5
pathfinder	1	pilgrim	9	progressive person	11
pathologist	8	pilot airline	11	projectionist	5
patient	6	pilot ship	4	projector (promoter)	9
patriarch	10	pioneer	1	promoter	9
patriot	4	pious person	9	proofreader	6
patrolman	6	pirate	12	property dealer	12
patron	9	pitcher	1	property owner	4
patron of the arts	5	pitchman	3	prophet	9
pattern maker	3	plaintiff the	1	proprietor	10
pauper	12	play maker	1	prospect (client)	7
pawnbroker	8	player	5	prospector	9
payee	8	playwright	3	prostitute	8
peacemaker	7	plebeian	4	protector	4

psychiatrist	8	religious person	9	scribe	3
psychic	8	religious workers	9	sculptor	7
psychological counselor	8	renegade	11	seal (navy unit)	8
psychologist	8	renter	6	seaman	4
public health official	6	reorganizer	8	seamstress	6
public servant	6	repair person	6	second (helper)	6
publicity director	9	repairer	6	second (runner-up)	9
publisher	9	reporter	3	secret agent	12
punk (novice)	3	representative (business)	7	secret enemy	12
punk rocker	11	representative (political)	11	secretary	6
punster	3	reprobate	12	security guard	8
pupil	3	republican	10	seer	9
purchaser	4	researcher	8	seller	9
purchasing agent	4	resident	4	senator	11
push-over	7	respiratory therapist	3	seniors (older people)	10
pygmy (dwarf)	3	retainer	6	sensitive people	12
quack doctor	5	retired person	2	sentry	6
queen	5	rich people	5	serf	6
querent (questioner)	1	ringleader	10	serious people	10
quesited one being asked about	7	rival	7	servant	6
		robber	7	service repairman	6
questioner	3	rock climber	10	sex object	8
rabbi	9	rock hound	10	sexual deviant	6
racer	1	rogue	7	shepherd	6
racketeer	8	role model	10	sheriff	8
radical	11	rover	3	shipper	4
raider	8	royalty (nobility)	10	shipping clerk	4
railroad worker	3	ruffian	8	shoe repairer	12
rancher	4	ruler	5	shoemaker	12
ranger	6	runaway	7	shopkeeper	4
rapist	8	sadist	8	shoplifter	3
rascal	3	sage	9	shopper	4
reader	3	sailor	4	showoff	5
real estate agent	10	saint	9	shrew	6
realist	10	sales person	9	shut-in	12
realtor	10	sanitation worker	6	shyster	3
rebel	11	satan	8	signatory	3
receiver (fence)	3	savage	8	silversmith	4
receptionist	1	savior	12	singer	2
recipient	7	scapegoat	12	siren	12
recluse	12	schemer	3	skeptic	6
record keeper	6	scholar	9	slave	6
recorder	6	school child	3	sleazy person	12
rector	9	school master	5	smith	6
referee	7	school teacher	5	sneak	12
reformer	8	schoolmate	3	social equal	7
refugee	12	scientist	8	social worker	12
registrar	6	scout	9	socializer	7
regulator	8	scrap dealer	12	socially inferior person	6

House Categories

society people	11	surrogate	7	those under detention	12
sociologist	11	surveyor	6	those who act strange	11
soil ecologist	10	survivalist	2	those who brings news	3
soldier	6	suspect	7	those who cater to pleasure	5
solitary person	12	swami	9	those who deal with clothing	6
soloist	10	sweetheart	5	those who entertain	5
song writer	2	swindler	3	those who tend the sick	6
soothsayer	9	systems analyst	6	those who waste	8
sorcerer	8	tailor	6	those who work with alcohol	12
space explorer	11	talker	3		
sparring partner	7	taskmaster	10	those who work with criminals	12
speaker	3	tattletale	3		
special forces (army unit)	8	tax collector	8	those who work with liquids	4
specialist	6	tax consultant	8	those with wealth or influence	5
spectator	3	taxi driver	3	those with whom you consult	7
speculator	5	taxidermist	6	those you borrow money from	7
speech pathologist	3	teacher	5	thug	7
spendthrift	2	teammate	7	tightwad	10
spinster	10	teamster	3	tool (pawn)	4
spokesperson	3	technician	6	tracker	9
sponsor	7	teenager	3	tradesman	6
spook	8	teetotaler	11	trainer	6
sportsman	9	television technician	6	traitor	12
sprite	3	teller bank	2	tramp	12
spy	12	tenant	6	trans-sexual	7
square (unsophisticated)	3	terrorist	8	transcriber	3
stable owner	9	test pilot	11	transferee	3
statesman	10	textile worker	6	transient	9
stationer	3	theatrical agent	5	translator	9
statistician	6	theatrical worker	5	transportation worker	3
steel worker	1	theologian	9	transvestite	7
stenographer	3	therapist	6	trapper	9
steward	6	thief	7	travel agent	9
stockbroker	5	thin person	3	traveler	9
stockholder	5	thinker	3	trendsetter	11
stool pigeon	3	those at a distance	9	trial lawyer	9
storekeeper	4	those beneath the surface	4	trifler	5
story teller	9	those in a ceremony	9	truant	3
stranger	9	those in artistic careers	5	truck driver	3
student (observer)	3	those in authority	10	trucker	3
student (pupil)	3	those in confidential position	8	tutor	9
stuntperson	1	those in responsible positions	10	typist	3
subordinate	6	those in the armed forces	6	tyrant	8
sucker	12	those met in public	7	tyro (beginner)	3
superintendent	10	those of a different race	9	umpire	7
superior	10	those of a different rearing	9	uncultured person	1
superiors	10	those on welfare	12	undercover operator	12
supporter (advocate)	11	those publicly noticed	10	underdog	12
surgeon	8	those residing in your house	4	underling	6

understudy	6	victim	12	widow, widower	12
undertaker	8	victim of a murder	8	wimp	12
underworld character	12	victor	10	wise person	9
undesignated other person	7	viewer	3	witch	6
undesirable person	12	villain	7	witness	3
unfortunate	12	virgin	6	wizard	9
uniformed worker	11	virtuoso	10	women	4
uninvited guest	3	visionary	11	women young	2
union leader	8	visitor	3	women from the past	1
union member	4	vocational counselor	8	woodworker	2
unscrupulous person	12	voice trainer	2	workers	6
urchin	3	volunteer	6	workers at routine jobs	6
used car salesman	12	waiter	6	workers in all trades	6
usher	6	waitress	6	workers in stone	7
usurer	8	wanderer	9	wrangler	6
vagabond	12	ward	12	writer	3
vagrant	12	warden game	12	x-ray operator	9
valedictorian	10	warder	4	yankee	11
valet	6	warrior	1	yeoman	6
vampire	8	watchman	6	yogi	9
vandal	8	weather forecaster	3	young the	3
vegetarian	11	weaver	7	young children	3
vendor	4	welder	6	young people (age 20 to 30)	2
ventriloquist	3	welfare recipient	12	young people (under age 20)	3
veteran	10	welfare worker	12	youth	3
veterinarian, large animals	12	well wisher	11	zealot	11
veterinarian, small animals	6	wheeler-dealer	3	zoo worker	6
vice-president	4	wholesaler	4		

Parts of an Organization

administrative services	10	construction	10	legal department	9
advertising department	9	consultant	11	loan department	8
agency (bureau)	6	credit department	8	lobby	1
allocation of assets	12	credit union	2	location	1
benefits for employees	2	customer satisfaction	5	mail room	3
board of directors	1	customer service	6	management	10
branch (division)	6	customers	4	marketing	9
budget office	8	data processing	6	medical/nurses station	12
cafeteria the	6	debt management	8	meeting room	11
cashier's office	2	department (division)	6	messenger	3
chairman of the board	10	dispatchers dept.	3	middle management	4
chief executive's office	5	driver's rooms	3	motor pool	3
clinic, the	6	electrical wiring	11	office directors	5
community relations office	3	emergency lighting	11	operations department	7
company the	1	energy costs	5	organization the	1
company benefits	12	engineering	10	organization's image the	1
company good will	12	executive board	1	owner's cooperation	7
competitor(s)	7	fire department	9	parking area	3
conference room	11	information services	6	partners	7

House Categories

parts hidden from view	12	relations with elected officials	11	sprinkler system	11
parts underground	4	relocation office	3	stockholder	5
personnel the	4	reputation	10	stockholder relations	5
planning	10	research and development	8	technical staff	6
profit	11	rest room	8	telephone system	3
profit sharing plan	11	retirement plan	8	transportation dept.	3
publications department	9	sales	9	treasurers office	2
purchasing	4	scientific staff	1	treasury the	2
quality control	12	section (branch)	6	utility shop	6
quality of products	5	security force	8	waste management	8
real estate	4	share holders	5	welfare offices	12
receptionist	1	social club	11		

Industry Categories

abrasives	1	automobile repair	6	claims adjusters	7
accounting services	6	automobile sales	9	cleaning services	6
acoustical materials	2	avionics	11	clerical services	6
advertising	9	bail bond services	12	coal (distribution)	3
aerospace/defense	6	bank holding companies	8	coal (mining)	8
agriculture (equipment)	10	bankruptcy services	8	coal (processing)	12
agriculture (growing)	4	banks (commercial)	2	commodity services	5
agriculture (harvesting)	6	banks (money center)	2	communication equipment manufacturers	4
air cargo	3	beauty supplies/equipment	7		
air purification	10	beverage (alcoholic)	12	computer and peripherals	11
air transport	11	beverage (soft drink)	12	computer software/services	11
aircraft manufacturing	7	blacksmithing	6	computer systems	6
alarm systems	1	boat/ship construction	10	conglomerate	12
alloy treating	6	bodyguards	1	construction equipment	10
alternate energies	11	broadcast media	3	containers (metal/plastic)	12
aluminum	11	broadcasting	9	containers (paper)	4
ammunition manufacture	1	building demolition	8	contractor's equipment	10
amusement equipment manufacturer	10	building designers	10	contractors (aerospace)	11
		building materials	10	contractors (defense)	6
animal control	12	business consulting	11	contractors (drainage)	3
animal handlers	6	business management	11	contractors (landscape)	2
animal health services	12	cable manufacturers	3	contractors (military)	6
animal husbandry services	6	cable tv	5	contractors (remodel)	8
apparel (designers)	6	capital goods	4	contractors (roofing)	10
apparel (manufacturers)	6	carpet manufacturers	6	contractors (sewer)	8
arbitration services	7	catalog services	4	contractors (siding)	7
art galleries/dealers	7	cement & aggregates	10	contractors (tile/stucco)	7
artists	7	cemetery management	8	copper	7
assembly and fabricating services	10	charter services	9	cosmetics	7
		chemical (basic)	12	credit agents	8
auto & truck	3	chemical (diversified)	12	currency exchanges	2
auto leasing/rental	11	chemical (specialty)	12	decorators	7
auto parts (after market)	8	church (design/construction)	10	dental services	6
auto parts (oem)	8	church (religious services)	9	designers	7
auto parts (replacement)	8	church (religious supplies)	9	diversified company	12

drain cleaning	8	golf course maintenance	5	machinery (construction/ mining)	10
driver's instruction	5	graphic designers	7		
drug abuse treatment	12	grocery	4	machinery (electrical)	11
drugs	12	hair care services	7	manufactured housing	4
dry cleaners	6	hardware & tools	6	marine contractors	4
electrical equipment	11	health & fitness	1	maritime	4
electrical power distribution	3	health care (diversified)	6	medical (supervisory care)	6
electrical switches	5	healthcare hmos	6	medical examiners	8
electrical utility	11	healthcare information	8	medical products	8
electronic games	3	heavy duty trucks	2	medical services	6
electronic instrumentation	6	high tech	11	medical supplies	8
electronics (defense)	6	home appliances	6	merchandising (small business)	4
electronics	11	home building	12		
energy	5	home inspection	8	metal casting services	6
energy conservation	10	home remodeling	8	metal fabricating	6
engineering and construction	10	hospital management	4	metals & mining	8
		hotel/motel services	6	mobile communications	3
engineers (consulting)	11	household appliances	6	modeling agencies	7
entertainment	5	household furnishings	7	money management services	2
environmental services	10	household products	6	mortgage brokers	8
equipment repair	6	housewares	6	motivational trainers	5
event management	5	housing	4	movie making	12
eye care (supplies)	6	imaging/photography	12	multi-line insurance	8
eye care (treatment)	6	immigration services	9	museum/museum services	12
financial (miscellaneous)	2	industrial equipment manufact'rs	6	musicians/orchestras	2
financial services	2			natural gas (diversified)	12
fire prevention services	6	industrial services	6	natural gas (pipeline)	3
firearms & ammunition	1	instrumentation	6	natural gas distribution	3
fireproofing services	10	insurance (diversified)	8	naturalization services	9
fish processing	12	insurance (health)	12	naval architects	10
fishing	12	insurance (life)	8	newspapers	3
florists	2	insurance (property/ casualty)	4	notaries	8
flower growers	4			nuclear power generation	5
food processing	6	investment (banking)	5	office equipment & supplies	6
food retailers	4	investment (brokerage)	5	oil drilling	8
food wholesalers	4	janitorial services	6	oil exploration	9
foreign trade services	9	jewelry (appraisal)	2	oil field services/equipment	12
forest products	2	jewelry (manufacture)	6	packaging & container	4
forestry services	2	jewelry (repair)	6	paper products	3
furniture rental	11	jewelry (sales)	10	parking lot equipment	6
furniture/home furnishings	7	landscaping services	2	parking lot management	10
gambling	5	leasing/rental services	11	personal loans	8
gaming	5	legal services	9	petroleum (integrated)	12
garbage disposal	8	leisure time	5	petroleum (producing)	12
gardening services	2	light machining	6	pharmaceuticals	12
gas products (compressed air)	10	lighting equipment	5	photography/imaging	12
general merchandise chains	4	lobbying	11	pipeline companies	3
gold/silver mining	5	lubricating services	9	pollution control	10
golf course design	9	machine tools	6	power generation	5

House Categories

precision instrument	6	shoe manufacturers	12	toxicology services	8
printing	3	shoe repair	6	toys	5
professional sports	5	sightseeing services	9	training (educational)	5
publishing	9	solar panel installation	5	training (health and fitness)	1
radio/tv	9	space planning	7	training (sports)	5
railroads	3	specialized services	6	transportation (ambulances)	1
real estate investment	4	specialty printing	3	transportation dispatching	3
records management	6	sports	5	transportation equipment	3
recreation	5	steel (general)	1	transportation leasing	11
recreational vehicles	7	steel (integrated)	1	travel agents	9
religious services	9	store designers	7	travel services	9
Rental/leasing services	11	store display equipment	7	truck leasing	11
Research services	8	surveyors	10	trucking	3
Restaurant	4	stlent agencies	7	typesetting	3
Retail (apparel)	6	taxicabs	3	used car/truck dealers	12
Retail (department stores)	4	teaching	5	vacuum producing equipment	8
Retail (drugstore)	4	telecommunication equipment	11	vending machine manufacturers	9
Retail (food chain)	4			vending machine retailers	7
Retail (special lines)	4	telecommunication services	11	veterinarians (large animal)	12
Retail building supply	7	telecommunications (domestic)	11	veterinarians (small animal)	6
Retail stores	4			videoconferencing	3
Rust proofing	8	telecommunications (foreign)	7	vital records storage	8
Salvage brokers	8			waste management	8
Savings and loan	2	telecommunications (long distance)	7	water distribution	3
School construction	10			water utility	4
School equipment	10	textiles	6	weather forecasting	3
Scrap metal dealers	8	thrift institutions	2	welding	6
Securities brokerage	5	tire and rubber	12	yacht brokers	12
Security services	1	tobacco	12	yard design and maintenance	2
Security system providers	4	toiletries/cosmetics	7		
Semiconductor equipment	6	tour brokers/agents	9		

Places

abandoned place	1	anchorage	4	arsenal	1
abbey	9	ancient dwelling	10	ashram	9
abode	4	annex	9	asylum	12
abyss (deep pit)	8	ante-chamber	1	atoll	4
academy	9	anterior place	1	attic	9
across the border	9	apiary	2	auditorium	5
advertising agency	9	aquarium	4	back (behind you)	7
after world	8	aqueduct	3	back country	9
airport	11	arbitration office	7	back stage	4
aisle	3	arcade	5	bakery	6
ale house	12	archaeological dig	8	balcony	9
alley	3	archive	4	ball room	7
alleyway	3	arena	5	bank (depository)	2
ammunition depot	1	arena of action in a contest	5	bank (river)	4
amphitheater	5	arid land	1	bar (law court)	9
amusement park	5	armory	1	bar (tavern)	12

barbershop	1	catacomb	4	courtroom	9
barn	4	cathedral	9	cove	4
barracks	6	cave	8	crag	10
barren ground	1	cavern	8	credit union	2
barren place	1	cellar	4	crematory	5
base of anything the	10	cemetery	8	crosswalk	3
basement	4	cesspool	8	crown (apex)	10
bath public	6	chapel	9	cul-de-sac	4
bath house	4	charitable institution	12	cultural center	4
bathroom	6	charity	12	curve (bend)	3
battlefield	7	church	9	dairy	4
bay	4	church yard	12	damp place	4
bayou	4	cinema	5	dance hall	2
beach	4	circus	5	dead end	12
beehive	2	cistern	4	deep the	8
birthplace	4	city	4	den (retreat)	12
blacksmith shop	6	city hall	11	den (shelter)	4
bluff	10	claim (mining)	4	department store	4
bog	4	clean room	6	depository	6
book shelf	3	clinic	6	depot	3
book store	3	clip joint	12	derrick	10
boot camp	6	closet	6	desert (wasteland)	1
booth (shelter)	4	club (organization)	11	desolate places	1
booth (stand)	4	club room	11	diggings (excavations)	4
borough	3	coliseum	5	dike (ditch)	3
botanical garden	2	college	9	diner	6
boutique	7	colony	9	dining room	6
breeding place	5	commodity exchange	5	dispensary	6
brewery	12	commodity market	5	disposal area	8
brick kiln	10	community (locale)	4	distant place	9
bridal chamber	7	compartment	6	distant shore	9
brook (stream)	4	concert hall	5	distillery	8
brothel	8	concession (franchise)	4	ditch	4
bunkhouse	4	concession stand	2	dock (wharf)	4
burial place	4	conference room	11	doctor's office	6
burrow	4	confessional	12	domain (estate)	4
business suite	10	construction site	10	domicile	4
butcher shop	1	continent (land mass)	4	drive-in	5
cabaret	5	convent	12	drug store	6
cafe	6	convention hall	11	dry cleaners	6
cafeteria	6	corral	4	dry dock	6
camp	4	correctional institution	12	dry wash	1
campground	4	corrections house of	12	dukedom	10
canal	3	council	11	dump (disposal area)	8
cannery	6	country foreign	9	dungeon	12
canteen (bar)	12	court of a king	5	dunghill	8
capitol building	11	court of justice	9	dwellings	4
casino	5	court of law	9	eatery	4
castle	4	courthouse	9	edge (border)	9

House Categories

embassy	9	garbage dump	8	home	4
employment agency	6	garden	4	home for the aged	12
emporium	4	gasoline station	9	home port	4
environs (local vicinity)	4	gate (entryway)	1	home range	4
estate	4	ghetto	12	home room	4
excavation	8	ghost town	12	home stretch	4
exchange (brokerage)	5	gift shop	8	homestead	4
exchange (e.g. money)	3	golf course	5	homestretch	4
exciting places	5	gorge	8	hometown	4
exclusive club	5	government building	12	horse track	9
exotic land	9	grain elevator	6	hospice	12
expanse	4	granary	6	hospital	12
expressway	3	grandstand	5	hotel	4
factory	11	graveyard	8	hothouse	2
falls (waterfall)	4	great mansions or estates	5	house you live in or own	4
farm	4	green (common area)	4	hub (main place)	5
farmland	2	grocery stores	6	hut	4
fatherland	4	grotto	8	incinerator	1
field (meadow)	4	ground irregular	4	infirmary	12
final resting place	4	grove (thicket)	2	information booth	3
fire department	9	gymnasium	5	inn	6
fish farm	3	habitat	4	institute	12
flat (apartment)	4	hades	8	institute of higher learning	9
florist shop	2	halls (corridors)	3	institution (establishment)	12
flower garden	2	hallway	3	institutions of higher learning	9
food markets	6	hamlet	4	interchange (junction)	3
foreign country	9	hang out	5	inventor's workshop	11
forest	2	hanger (aircraft)	11	jail	12
forge	6	hangout	5	joint (tavern)	12
fort	4	harbor (haven)	12	junction (linkup)	3
fortress	4	harbor (port)	4	jungle	2
forum (marketplace)	4	harem	4	junior high school	3
forum (public meeting place)	4	haunt	5	junk yard	8
fraternity	11	haven	12	kennel	6
freeway	3	haystack	6	kingdom	4
front line	1	heaven (paradise)	10	kitchen	6
frontier	9	hedgerow	2	lab	8
frozen place	8	heights	10	labor area	6
fun house	5	hell	8	laboratory	8
funeral parlor	8	hidden places	12	labyrinth	3
fuse box	11	hiding place	12	lagoon	4
galleries art	7	high court	9	lair	4
gallows	8	high office	10	lake	4
gambling casino	5	high places	10	landed property	4
gangway	1	highlands	9	landfill	8
gap (opening)	9	highway	3	lane (narrow way)	3
gap (pass)	9	hill	10	lateral side the	5
garage	6	hold (storage place)	6	laundry	6
garage workshop	6	hole (cave)	4	laundry room	6

lavatory	8	museum	4	penitentiary	12
lawyer's office	6	natural settings	4	pharmacy	6
lay (lair)	4	near neighborhood	3	philanthropic institution	9
lecture hall	9	neighborhood	3	pier	4
lending institution	8	neighboring environment	3	pigsty	6
levee	4	new surroundings	4	pit (hole)	8
library	3	news rooms	3	place for pleasure	5
lighthouse	10	node (center or hub)	5	place hidden or out of sight	12
living space	4	nursing home	12	place high up	9
lobby	1	oasis	4	place near water or plumbing	4
local neighborhood	3	observatory	3	place of amusement	5
location another's	7	ocean	4	place of entertainment	5
location your	1	ocean depths	4	place of fun	5
lodge	4	office (work place)	10	place of removal	7
loft	12	office building	10	place of residence	4
lounge	5	office space	10	place of rest or abode	4
low spot	4	office where one works	6	place of worship	9
lowlands	4	oil field	9	place one currently occupies	4
mall	4	oil tank	9	place where food is kept	6
manger	4	open country	4	place where money is kept	2
mansion	4	open farmland	4	place where people gather	11
market	4	orchard	2	place with clean air	7
marsh	4	orchestra (theater)	7	place you are moving to	7
mausoleum	8	other places	9	plains	4
meadow	4	outhouse	8	playground	5
median strip	3	outlet (shopping place)	4	playhouse	5
meeting room	11	outside (out-of-doors)	5	pond	4
mesa	10	outskirts	9	pool of water	4
middle, the	5	oven	5	pool room	5
middle position	7	overseas	9	port (home)	4
middle school	3	packing house	4	port (non-home)	9
mill	11	paddock	6	post (station)	4
millinery	1	palace	5	post office	3
minaret	9	paradise	9	posterior	7
mine	8	parish (church district)	9	prairie	4
mineral spring	11	park (preserve)	2	prep school	3
mission	9	park (recreational area)	5	preserve game	9
moat	4	parking lot	3	print shop	3
mobile home	6	parks and preserves (gardens)	5	prison	12
monastery	9	partner's room	7	private club	10
moor	4	pass	3	produce market	4
morgue	8	pasture	4	public place a	1
mortuary	8	patio	5	public toilet	8
motel	4	pavilion	7	pulpit	9
mound	9	pawnshop	8	purgatory	8
mount (embankment)	4	peak	10	quagmire	4
mountain range	10	pen (animal)	4	quarry	8
mountains	10	pen (corral)	4	queue	11
movie house	5	penal colony	12	race track	9

House Categories

rain forest	2	sanctuary	12	spring (water)	4
rally (meeting)	11	sandy place	4	square town	4
rampart	4	sanitarium	12	stable	9
ranch	4	satellite (outpost)	9	stadium	5
range (pasture)	4	school	3	stage the	5
range of mountains	10	school elementary	3	stairs	3
rapids	4	school secondary	3	stall (animal den)	9
ravine	8	school room	3	stall (retail place)	4
reading room	3	seance room	8	stand (retail outlet)	4
realm	4	seaport	4	station (post)	4
rear (back part) of anyplace	4	seashore	4	station (transit stop)	3
record storage place	6	seat (residence)	4	station house	6
refinery	8	secluded place	12	stationers	3
reform school	12	seclusion (hiding place)	12	steam bath	5
refuge	12	section (area)	4	steep ground	10
relief agency	12	sepulcher	8	steerage	4
relocation place of	7	service station	9	stock exchange	5
remote place	9	sewer	8	stock market	5
rendezvous	11	shack	4	stockade	4
rental property	4	shade (cool place)	10	store (retail)	4
rental resided in the	4	shelter	4	storehouse	6
repository	6	shoe store	4	storehouse for dairy products	6
rescue mission	12	shop	4	storeroom	6
research organization	8	shopping mall	4	stream	4
reservation	4	shore (land)	4	street	3
reservoir	4	shore (seacoast)	4	strip (airstrip)	11
residence	4	showboat	5	stronghold (fort)	4
residence while abroad	11	shrine	9	stronghold (refuge)	12
resort pleasure	5	sick room	6	structure (building)	4
resort area	5	sidewalk	3	studio	5
rest home	12	silo	6	suburb	4
rest room	8	site	4	summit	10
restaurant	6	skyscraper	10	sump	4
resting place your final	4	slaughter house	8	surroundings	1
retreat	12	slip (berth)	4	swamp	4
ridge	10	slough	8	swimming hole	5
rink	5	slum	12	swimming pool	5
river	4	smoke house	6	tabernacle	9
road	3	society (club)	11	tank farm	4
rocky ground	10	soggy ground	4	tannery	12
roof garden	10	solarium	5	taproom	12
room (cubicle)	4	sorority	11	tar pit	8
rooming house	4	sound (body of water)	4	tavern	12
roost	4	spa	4	telegraph office	3
ruins	4	space (the heavens)	9	temple	9
safe haven	12	space outer	9	tenement	4
salon	7	sport arena	5	terminal	10
saloon	5	spot (location)	4	terrace	6
sanatorium	12	spread (ranch)	4	terrain (ground)	4

theater	5	tunnel	4	warehouse	6
thicket	2	turnaround	8	warmest part of the house	5
thoroughfare	3	underground places	8	wasteland	1
threshold (end boundary)	9	undersea places	4	waterfront area	4
ticket counter	3	underside	8	watery place	4
tier (row)	6	underworld the	8	well	4
toilet	8	unexplored area	9	wharf	4
tomb	8	university	9	where books are kept	3
tongue of land	4	upper levels	9	where business is conducted	10
top (highest point)	10	vacant property	1	where food is disbursed	6
top of anything the	10	vacation resort	5	where living things grow	4
torture chamber	8	valley	4	where money is kept	2
tower	9	vantage point	9	where partner spends time	7
town	4	vault (safe)	2	where you reside	4
town hall	11	vaulted place	10	where you spend your time	1
track race	5	vicinity	3	wilderness	9
trail	3	village	4	woodland	2
travel agency	9	virgin land	2	work area	6
treasury the	2	volcano	8	workshop	6
trench	8	vortex	11	yard	4
trust company	8	waiting room	2	zoo	12

Psychological Qualities

abruptness	1	appearance	1	bootstraps (self-reliance)	5
abstaining (refraining)	12	apprehension (comprehension)	9	bossiness	10
abstract thought processes	9			bragging	5
abuse	8	aptitude	5	bravado	5
accomplishment (achievement)	10	arbitrariness	4	broader views adapting	9
		arrogance	5	busyness	6
accuracy	6	assertion of self	1	candidness	9
achievement	10	assertive attitude	1	capability (innate skill)	5
acquaintance (friendship)	11	assumption making processes	9	capacity (skill)	5
adaptability	3	assurance (confidence)	5	captivation	5
addiction (dependency)	4	attachment (caring)	7	caring	4
adequacy	2	attention focus of	1	causes attachment to	11
aesthetic sense	2	attention span	1	causes use of	11
affection warmth of	5	attitude (disposition)	1	central focus	5
agility (grace)	7	attraction (appeal)	7	changing one's mind	3
alertness	1	authority aura of	10	character	1
alienation	7	awareness of surroundings	1	character defects	12
allocated space	1	backwardness	4	characteristics	1
aloofness	11	badness	1	characteristics another's	7
alteration (internal)	8	balance	7	charity given	12
ambition	10	base your basis or start	4	charity received	12
amorality	8	bashfulness	6	charm	7
analogy	9	behavior	7	chastity	6
analysis self	8	belief structures	9	cheapness	10
anguish	12	belonging	11	cheating	3
anxiety	6	blahs the	11	cheer	5

childhood environment	4	
church affiliation	9	
civic-mindedness	11	
civil behavior	7	
civil disobedience	7	
claustrophobia	4	
cleanliness	6	
cleverness	3	
collapse (breakdown)	12	
color sense of	7	
coming unglued	12	
command of situation in	10	
common sense	10	
communication	3	
compassion	12	
compensation	5	
competence (ability)	5	
competition sense of	7	
complacency	2	
completeness	2	
completeness a lack of	1	
compliance	6	
complicating matters	3	
compromise	7	
compulsions	8	
concealment need for	4	
conceit	5	
concentration (mental focus)	8	
conceptualization	9	
concrete mind the	3	
condition physical	1	
conditioned response	4	
conduct in public	7	
confession (of guilt)	12	
confidence (self-assurance)	5	
confirmation (substantiation)	8	
confronting (anything)	1	
confronting obstacles	1	
confusion	12	
conscience	9	
consciousness	1	
consequences of one's actions	10	
considerateness	2	
contemplation	9	
contentment (satisfaction)	2	
control need for	8	
conversion (religious)	9	
conversion (transformation)	8	
convincing ability for	9	
conviviality	5	
cooperation	7	
cope ability to	4	
copying (mimicking)	3	
core identity	4	
correction need for giving	6	
court questions of law in	10	
craft (artifice)	3	
craft (skill)	6	
craft (trade)	6	
craftiness	3	
cravings	8	
creative talents	5	
creativity	5	
credibility	10	
credit reputation	5	
crime involvement with	12	
criticism	6	
culture attitude towards	4	
cunning	3	
curiosity	3	
cynicism	3	
death attitude towards	8	
deceiving sense of	3	
dedication	6	
defect of character	6	
defenses	4	
defensive qualities	4	
deity attitude towards	9	
delinquency	3	
delusion self	12	
demeanor	1	
denial (disavowal)	12	
dependence (reliance on others)	4	
dependency (addiction)	4	
dependency (needs for help)	4	
deportment	7	
depression	6	
deprivation	8	
depth of feelings	8	
deriving enjoyment	5	
desirability	2	
desire (craving)	11	
desires	11	
despair (hopelessness)	6	
despondency	6	
detachment ability for	11	
determination (tenacity)	10	
development of the mind	9	
deviousness	3	
devotion (dedication)	6	
devotion to a task	6	
dexterity	3	
dietary concerns	6	
diffidence (reserve)	6	
dignity	10	
diligence	10	
disappointment (let down)	8	
disciplined living or work	6	
discontent	11	
discouragement	6	
discovering of self	1	
discriminating sense	6	
dishonesty	7	
disillusionment	12	
disorientation	4	
disposition	1	
domination	5	
domination (supremacy)	8	
dramatics flair for	5	
drugs dependence upon	12	
duality	3	
duress	12	
duty	6	
earning power	2	
eating habits	4	
eccentricity	11	
ecstasy	9	
educational attitudes	3	
effecting change	11	
effeminacy	7	
efficiency	6	
ego	5	
elimination	8	
elocution	3	
eloquence	3	
embarrassment	10	
emergence	1	
emotional blocks	12	
emotional depletion	11	
emotional desires	11	
emotional expression	5	
emotional instability	7	
emotional isolation	4	
emotional needs	4	
emotional pain	4	
emotional security	4	

employers, attitude towards	6	freedom of action	1	hostility	7
emptiness feelings of	1	freeing	12	human nature	4
endurance	2	friend, response of a	11	humanity attitude towards	11
entanglement	2	friendliness	11	humility	6
equality	7	friendship	11	humor	5
equivalence	7	frolic	5	hygienic practices	6
escape	12	frustrations	12	idealism	9
escape ability to	12	fulfillment	5	ideals	9
essence (basic quality)	5	function (purpose)	10	identification	1
essential nature	4	functioning, inner ways of	4	identifying with	4
esteem (regard)	10	futility	4	identity	1
ethical responsibility	9	gait (manner of walking)	1	idiosyncrasy (peculiarity)	1
ethics	9	gathering experiences	9	illness coping with	12
excellence working for	6	gathering information	6	image of another one's	7
executive acumen	10	general well-being	1	image you give out the	1
expansion of consciousness	9	generosity	5	imitative behavior	3
expectations	11	getting even	7	immorality	8
experience(s) learned	10	goodness	2	impatience	1
experiencing	9	graciousness	7	impersonal sense of the	11
expression of emotion	5	grasp (comprehension)	9	importance	10
expressions of emotion	5	gratefulness	5	imposing limitations	12
expressiveness	5	gratification	8	imposing one's will	5
fair play	9	gratitude	2	impression one makes	1
faith	9	greed (selfishness)	4	improvisation	3
faith, giving up on	8	groups use of	11	inability to fee complete	4
fall (corruption)	8	guidance	9	inadequacy feelings of	6
fault-finding	6	guile	3	inappropriate behavior	7
fear (anxiety)	6	guilt	6	inborn trait	4
fear(s) inner	4	habits personal	1	incentives received or given	11
feelings	4	happiness	5	inclinations	11
fickleness	4	harassment	8	including others	7
fidelity	8	harboring (holding in)	4	including self	1
fights going to sleep	1	harmony	7	inclusion (containment)	4
financial needs	2	harshness	1	incompetence	10
finesse (tact)	7	hate (detest)	8	indecision	7
finesse (wile)	3	hate (disgust)	7	independence	11
fixation	8	health	1	indifference	11
flair	5	health attitudes	6	individuality	1
flattery	5	helpless feelings	6	individualization	4
focus your	5	hesitancy	10	infallibility	9
foreign things, role of	9	hidden sense of what is	12	inferiority feelings of	6
form	7	hidden fear	12	inferiority complex	4
forsaking	12	hindsight	9	infinite the	9
forthrightness	11	home quality of	4	influence extent of	10
fortitude	1	homespun virtues	4	inhibitions	4
foundation	4	honor (honesty)	10	inner unfolding	9
frame of mind (attitude)	1	hopelessness	6	insecurity	4
free will	1	hopes	11	insistence	1
freedom	11	hospitality	7	instability	4

House Categories

instinctive behavior	4	looking beyond	9	mood	4
instincts	4	lowering	8	morale	5
institutions attitudes toward	12	loyalty showing	8	morals	9
instructing ability for	5	loyalty to causes	11	mother love	5
integrating ability to	12	macho display	5	mothering	4
integration	10	magnetism (attraction)	8	motivation	5
integrity	10	maintaining	4	motives	5
intelligence (intellect)	3	making love	8	mutual actions	7
intense emotions	8	maladjustment	6	myself	1
intensification	8	malaise	6	nagging	6
intensifying needs for	8	male concerns	10	naivete	3
intentions	1	maliciousness	8	nationalism	4
interests	1	maneuverability	3	need (desire)	11
intimacy	8	manifestation (indication)	1	need for another	8
intolerance of others	6	manipulated being	11	needs (in general)	4
introspection	12	manipulation	11	negative views	4
introversion	4	mannerisms	1	negativity	6
intuition	9	marketing	9	negligence	12
invincibility	5	marriage feelings about	7	nervous aggravation	6
involvement (connecting with)	7	marriage happiness in	11	nervous breakdowns	6
		mastery	10	nervous habits	3
irresponsibility	7	materiality	2	nervous tension	6
joining willingness to	11	maternal instinct	4	nervous twitches	3
judgment (discretion)	11	mathematical ability	6	nervousness	3
justice	9	matters of the heart	5	nesting instincts	4
karmic responsibilities	12	maturing ability to	10	neutral stand	7
keeping	4	maturity	10	new idea	11
knowledge searches for	9	me sense of	1	non-participation	7
laboring under an illusion	12	meanness	1	non-violence, principle of	7
lack	10	meditative desire	9	nonchalance	11
languor	2	meekness	6	notability	5
leadership qualities	11	melancholy	6	noticed being	5
leaning (bent)	3	memory	3	nurturing	4
learning the process of	5	memory problems	3	obedience	6
learning ability	3	mental activity	3	objectives	10
legal sense	9	mental adaptation	3	objectivity	11
leisure	5	mental attitudes	3	obligation, meeting an	8
lethargy	7	mental efforts	3	obscurity	12
letting go	12	mental instability	6	observing powers	3
liberty	1	mental reservations	11	obsession	8
life	1	mental speculation	9	obstinacy	2
life principles	4	merry making	5	obtrusiveness (interfering)	7
life-style	4	middle position	7	occult ability	8
life-style approach	4	misfortune	12	omnipotence	5
life-style orientation	4	misgivings	11	one (you)	1
likability	5	misjudgment	9	oneness	7
likes or dislikes	8	modesty	6	oomph (vitality)	5
limitation facing	12	modify, ability to	6	opening up	11
linguistic ability	3	money, attitude toward	2	openness	7

ordinary the	4	personal matters	4	presence, one's	1
organization	10	personal outlook	1	presence of mind	3
originality	5	personal prowess	1	pressure (distress)	1
ornery disposition an	1	personal values	2	prestige	10
orthodoxy	10	personality	1	pretension	3
ostentatious behavior	5	personhood	5	pride	5
outlet (means of expression)	7	perspective on one's life	1	principles	10
outlook	1	persuasive ability	9	privacy	4
outrage	7	perversion	11	private life	4
outward show	1	pessimism	6	private matters	4
over-tiredness	6	pet as surrogate child	5	private problems	12
overcoming adversity	10	philanthropy	9	probing	8
overindulgence	2	philosophical thinking	9	problem, personal	4
ownership attitude about	2	philosophy	9	proclivity	4
parents feeling towards	10	phobia	4	procrastination	7
participating	1	physical comfort	2	producing	4
particular (fastidious)	8	physical discomfort	6	profession	10
particularity	1	physical you the	1	professional ability	10
passage rights of	8	piety	12	professional affairs	10
passion (emotion)	5	place in society	10	professional standing	10
passion (love)	5	placidity	2	professional work	10
passion (suffering)	12	planning ahead	10	professionalism	10
passive resistance	12	platonic love	11	profound mental interests	9
passivity	4	playing, fondness for	5	progressive thought	11
paternal role	10	pleasing others	2	projection	7
patience	10	pleasurable pursuit	5	promise made	8
patriotism	4	pleasure	5	promptness	10
patterning	4	plight, current	1	pronunciation	1
peak experience	10	poise	7	propensity	1
peculiarity	11	polish social	7	prophecy	9
pensiveness	10	politeness	2	propriety	10
people awareness	7	politics	11	prosperity	5
perceiving	3	polygamy	3	protection	4
perceiving ability for	3	popularity	5	protective instincts	4
perfection meeting	6	pose (mannerism)	1	protective urges	4
performance (attainment)	10	position (opinion)	9	prowess (bravery)	5
performing ability for	5	positive view	5	prowess (skill)	6
perjury	7	possessiveness	8	prudence	10
permanence	10	posture (attitude)	1	psychic feeling	8
permission (consent)	8	posture (attitude) another's	7	psychic influence	12
perseverance	10	potential	5	psychological problem	6
persistence	10	poverty	12	public being out in the	10
personal affairs	1	poverty the fear of	2	public affairs, your	1
personal importance	2	power one's personal	5	public life	10
personal inadequacies	6	practical efforts	6	public recognition	10
personal interests	1	praise	5	public status	10
personal liberty	5	preciousness (likability)	5	public you face, the	7
personal life	4	precision	6	publicity personal	9
personal limitation(s)	12	preference	11	punishment	12

purpose	10	restlessness	3	self-denial	12
pursuit, philosophical	9	restraint (control)	10	self-destruction	12
qualms	4	results orientation	11	self-destructive processes	12
rally (summon or muster up)	8	retaining	4	self-development	10
rancor	1	retribution	8	self-discovery	1
rationalizing	7	returning	12	self-esteem sense of	2
reality search for	9	reversion	12	self-expression	3
reaping (finding)	12	ridding	8	self-fulfillment	10
reasoning ability	3	right and wrong (sense of)	9	self-hood	1
reasons underlying	4	righteousness	9	self-image	1
rebelliousness	11	rights one's	1	self-importance	5
recalling	3	role (expected behavior)	7	self-improvement	1
receiving love	7	role playing	5	self-indulgence	2
receptivity	4	romance	5	self-injury	12
reciprocal acts received	12	romance with commitment	7	self-integration	4
reciprocity	8	romance without commitment	5	self-interest (things done in)	5
recognition received	10			self-involvement	1
recover ability to	2	romantic feelings	5	self-judgment	8
recrimination	1	romantic love	5	self-pity	12
refinement	7	roughness of character	1	self-possession	5
reflectiveness	4	rudeness	7	self-preservation	1
regret	12	ruin desires to	8	self-projection(s)	7
rejection, fear of	7	sacrifice	12	self-restraint	10
relating (connecting)	7	salesmanship	9	self-sacrifice	12
relationships	7	sanity	3	self-transformation	8
relaxation	2	satisfaction	2	self-undoing	12
relaxing activities	5	satisfaction receiving	2	self-wastage	12
release wanting to effect	12	satisfaction seeking	8	self-worth	2
relevance	10	scruples (anxiety)	6	selfishness	7
reliance	4	scruples (ethics)	9	sense of humor	5
religious sense	9	secret keeping a	12	sensibility	7
religious views	9	secret enmity	12	sensitivities, one's	4
relinquish ability to	12	secret fear	4	sensitivity to others	4
relinquishing	12	secret sorrow	12	sensuality	8
relying on another	9	secret worry	12	sensuous enjoyment	2
remorse (regret)	12	secretiveness	12	sentiment (feeling)	4
renunciation, ability for	12	security	4	separation anxiety	4
repair efforts	6	security needs	4	service	6
repentance	12	seeing through anything	9	setting fires	8
replying	3	seeking of admiration	5	sex appeal	8
representation of self	1	seizing	8	sexual energy	8
repression	8	selectivity	6	sexual merging	8
reputation	10	self pride in	5	sexual passion	8
resentment harboring	8	self the	1	sexual perversion	11
resignation (acceptance)	8	self-analysis	8	sexual pleasure	5
respect, demanding	8	self-assertion	1	sexual power	8
response to situations	4	self-centeredness	5	sexual release	8
responsibility, accepting	10	self-confidence	1	sexuality	8
restitution	8	self-defeating behavior	12	shadow nature	7

shallowness (lack of depth)	7	state of mind	1	torment	12
shame	12	stature (social class)	10	tragedy playing out	5
shaping attitudes	11	status	10	traits	1
sharing	8	staying informed	9	transacting	3
sharing feelings	11	stealthiness	8	transference	6
sharpness (alertness)	3	stimulation	1	transformation	8
shift in attitudes, a	4	stoicism	10	travails	12
shift of values, a	4	storing food	6	travel desires for	9
shifting positions	3	straight forward	9	treachery	8
shock psychological	11	stress	6	trickery	3
shyness	3	strictness	10	trust	8
sibling rivalry	3	striking (hitting)	8	truth	9
significance	2	stubbornness (persistency)	10	turning point	8
sincerity	10	stubbornness (unbending)	2	ultimate truths	9
slander	7	studying	3	unburdening	12
sleeping posture	4	subconscious attitudes	4	uncertainty (doubt)	4
slip (decline)	8	sublimation	12	unconscious activity	9
sloppiness	12	submission	6	unconscious mind	12
sobriety	10	subordination	6	undercurrent (mood)	4
sociability	7	subversion	12	undermining	11
social sense	7	suffering bearing	6	understanding	9
social skills	7	suitable behavior	10	understanding (sympathy)	12
social urges	7	superconscious mind	9	uniformity	4
solitary pursuits	12	superiority	5	unity (co-operation)	7
sophistication	7	superiority complex	5	urgency	1
sorrow	12	support given or received	8	urgings	4
sorrow, profound	12	surrendering	12	using others	7
sorrowful conditions	12	survival need for	2	utility	2
soul feelings about	9	susceptibility	4	utilizing	2
sound judgment	9	sustained efforts	2	vacillation	7
spastic effort	3	sweetness (kindness)	2	value (ideal)	9
speech the quality of	2	sympathy	4	value (merit)	2
spirit your	1	synthesis	8	valuing	2
spiritual attunement	9	tact	7	vanishing	12
spiritual consciousness	9	talent	5	vanity (pride)	5
spiritual feelings	9	talking	3	vein (mood)	4
spiritual needs	9	tastes personal	1	veneer (facade)	5
spiritual pain	8	teamwork	7	vengeance	8
spiritual rebirth	8	technique (style)	6	versatility	3
spiritual richness	9	temerity	2	vexation	8
spirituality	9	temperament	1	viability	1
splendidness	5	tendency (inner inclinations)	4	victimization	12
spoiling	8	tenderness	2	vigor (enthusiasm)	5
spontaneity	5	thankfulness	7	vindictiveness	8
sportsmanship	9	thinking	3	volition	11
stability (personal)	7	thoughtfulness	2	volunteering	6
stability of emotions	10	timidity	6	vulnerability	4
standing (status)	10	tolerance	7	wants	11
state (frame of mind)	1	tone (attitude)	1	war of nerves	7

House Categories

warmth	5	will	5	work habits	6
wasting needs for	8	willfulness	5	world view	9
weakness (in general)	6	willingness	7	worry	6
wealth need for	4	willpower	5	worth self	2
well being your overall	1	winning	5	worthiness	2
whim	4	wisdom	9	worthlessness	6
whining	7	wishes	11	wrath	7
wholeness	7	withdrawal	12	yearnings	11
wile	3	work willingness to	6	yourself	1

Family Members or Relations

adopted child	5	family member of immediate	4	near relatives	3
adopted sibling	3	family patriarch(s)	1	nephew	7
affairs of in-laws	9	famous relative	5	niece	7
ancestors	4	father	10	niece or nephew by marriage	1
anyone unrelated by blood	7	father's kin	6	offspring (children)	5
anyone who is a stranger	9	father-in-law	9	parent	10
aunt maternal	6	female relations	10	parent-in-law	4
aunt paternal	12	folks	4	partner's relatives	9
aunts from the father's side	12	forefather	4	paternal kin	12
black sheep	9	foster child	11	paternal uncle	12
brother	3	friends	11	relations of the quesited	9
brother or sister	3	friends of one's children	3	relative	3
brother or sister #1	3	godchild	11	relative of a parent	12
brother or sister #2	5	godfather	9	self, the	1
brother or sister #3	7	godmother	3	sibling	3
brother or sister #4	9	grandchildren	9	sister	3
brother or sister #5	11	grandfather (maternal)	1	sister-in-law	9
brother-in-law	9	grandfather (paternal)	7	son	5
child adopted	11	grandmother (maternal)	1	son-in-law	11
child another's	11	grandmother (paternal)	7	spouse	7
child biological	5	grandparent (in general)	7	spouse's siblings	9
child step	11	great grandchildren	1	step child	11
child first	5	guardian (legal custodian)	10	step-parent	12
child second	7	husband	7	step-sibling (father's side)	2
child third	9	illegitimate children	11	step-sibling (mother's side)	8
child fourth	11	kin	3	uncle maternal	6
child fifth	1	kinfolk	3	uncle paternal	12
close blood relative	3	male relations	7	uncles on the father's side	12
cousin maternal	10	mate one's	7	uncles on the mother's side	6
cousin paternal	4	maternal kin	10	wife	7
daughter	5	mistress	8	you	1
daughter-in-law	11	mother	4	younger brother	3
descendant	5	mother's kin	12	younger sister	3
distant relative	9	mother-in-law	9		

Parts of a Ship

anchor	4	armament(s)	1	auxiliary power	11
annunciator	3	auxiliary boat	12	auxiliary steerage	3

ballast	10	library	9	swimming pool	5
bilges	8	lighting	5	wardroom	4
boiler	5	list	10	water tank	4
bow	1	magazine (armament storage)	1	wheel	3
bridge	1			winch	11
bulkhead	10	mast	10	windlass	11
bunk	2	mate	6		
captain's cabin	4	mess	6		
cargo hold	6	mess deck	6		
chain locker	6	navigation desk	11		
chart house	6	navigational lights	11		
chart table	6	observation deck	3		
cofferdam	6	passageway	3		
combat information center	3	passenger quarters	4		
commissary	6	pilot house	1		
communication lines	3	piping	11		
communication quarters	3	poop deck	7		
compass	3	port side	7		
conn	1	power plant	5		
crew's quarters	4	propeller	1		
deck	10	quarterdeck	3		
dispensary	6	radar	9		
dry dock work	6	radio equipment	3		
emergency lighting	11	radio room	3		
engine	5	railing	10		
engine room	5	recreation area	5		
fantail	7	registry	4		
fender	4	rigging	11		
fire control (for guns) gear	1	rudder	3		
fire power	1	running lights	11		
fire suppression system	9	sail	5		
fo'c'sl	1	salon	7		
fore deck	1	sanitary systems	8		
fresh water supply	4	shaft	11		
fuel tank	9	shaft alley	10		
galley	6	ship's log	3		
gangway	1	shore line (hawser)	4		
generator	11	sick bay	6		
hawser	4	signal deck	3		
heating plant	5	signal equipment	3		
helm	3	skin	10		
hoist	2	smoke stack	12		
hull	10	spar (rib)	10		
icebreaker (vessel)	4	stability	7		
instability	4	starboard side	1		
keel	5	stateroom	4		
ladder	3	stern	7		
launch	12	store (retail outlet)	6		
laundry	6	support members	10		

House Categories

The Appendices

Appendix A

An Astrological House Formulary

This is an edited reprint of my (Michael P. Munkasey) article that appeared in the Winter 1988 *NCGR Journal*. Used with permission. Note: definitions of some of the technical terms used appear at the end of Appendix A.

Overview

Don't believe that the theory behind astrological house systems is unknowable. Like incantations from bearded gurus the mathematical reasoning that creates astrological houses appears esoteric. Once you realize that the mathematics of deriving house cusps is unremarkable, the mystery fades. Concentrate on the usage and meanings of the houses in your astrological practice, but learn something too about how the houses come together. This article is about that other side of houses: their technical descriptions and mathematical formulations. Early in my astrological studies I was given a wonderful chance to mathematically derive the various house systems. My curiosity compelled me to bring some order where I could find no reasonable or consistent information. There were few references on astrological house construction then, and I was driven to understand the thinking behind the various house systems.

This article is intended both to educate and provide specific information about calculating house cusps for the more popular house systems. Short written descriptions and formulae for all popular house systems and the seven personal sensitive points follow. The word descriptions of the house systems are brief, but each house system is rigidly and consistently described to allow you to calculate its house cusps. To quickly find success I recommend the use of a hand calculator or computer language with the trigonometric functions. Otherwise, only normal high school mathematics is required to calculate house cusps.

My History of Involvement

Contrary to the opinions of many who know me I was not well equipped psychologically to do this work. While I enjoyed arithmetic while in school, I did not have much formal learning in the type of mathematics needed for this study. I had to re-learn theories which I had either long ago conveniently forgotten, or had never formally learned. I started for all of the normal reasons. I wanted to understand why astrologers used different house systems; which house system was the mathematically best to use (a foolish pursuit it turns out); what the difference was among the various house systems; the role of houses and of space; what role houses have in astrology; how to find better ways to compute the various house cusps, etc. This last was particularly important because my work was being done in the era before personal computers or programmable calculators, and using logarithms to compute house cusps was a long and disagreeable task. So, necessity being the mother of invention, I forged into areas where others had not adequately left instructions for proceeding.

Months of effort later I had managed to find descriptions for 24 house systems in the astrological literature. Many astronomical drawings were made to show perspective from space on these houses systems. Doing this helped me find two general approaches for creating house systems: start with a point on the ecliptic and divide the ecliptic according to a systematic scheme. This gives fairly consistent houses. The Equal House System is one such example: the Ascendant (ASC) is the starting point and thirty degree increments are added to the ASC for each subsequent house cusp. This is an easy system to use, requires only a minimum of mathematics, and works anywhere there is an ecliptic visible. Having an ecliptic visible becomes an important consideration, especially in the far polar regions where distortions in space around the ecliptic are magnified, and an ecliptic may not be mathematically present on the eastern horizon. The second system requires using one of the other great circles of astronomy, dividing that in some defined manner, and then projecting that division onto the ecliptic. This creates projection house systems like Placidian and Regiomontanus. The Koch house system is a variation on the projection house system approach, and I classify by itself while terming its approach to the mathematics of houses 'intersection.'

What Houses Are

Houses are the divisions of space around an event. An event occurs. It may be a birth, it may be a mundane event, it may be a horary question, etc. It occurs and astrologers wish to erect a horoscope for that event. he next step is to locate the planets in the signs and houses. First we find the location of the planets using an ephemeris, and then we diagram them in their space using a selected house system. So, an event occurs, and now we must create a frame for picturing the planets within their space. Questions arise. How should we divide this space? What is our starting point for this division? How do we translate planets in a solar orbit into an earth framed reference? What about the parts of the sky we can not see—like those parts that are on the other side of the earth? How do we represent those 'hidden' spaces? Since space is rather 'plastic,' and if we can change our view of the event depending where in space we are viewing from, then what constant boundaries can we create for classifying the space around the event?

These questions have deep philosophical leanings and may be solved when an astronomical diagram of a horoscope is drawn. The diagrams can clarify what the houses look like, but they can not answer the question of which house system to use. (See Chapter 5 for some help with that.) One horoscope produced usually implies that one house system was chosen for dividing space. Another horoscope of the same event may use a completely different house system. But the nagging side issue question always remains: which house system is best to use?

There is no simple or direct answer to that question. However, I can give you two good thoughts on the subject: use that house system which divides space in such a way that the planets fall into houses which describe their function in the nature of the event; and, use that house system which gives cusps against which you can time events. That is, if the Moon function of this event is described well by a Moon in the eighth house, then the house system you choose should not place the Moon in the seventh or ninth, or some house other than the eighth house. Also, if subsequent events can not be timed to the house cusps derived mathematically and plotted on the horoscope, then choose some other house system. In general, I find that for natal events the Placidian system works well and fulfills these two guidelines. Why it works well I do not know. It may well be that the thought form created by a mass of astrologers using the Placidian system is all that lies behind its functioning. I can not explain why it works, but my practical side allows me to see that it does work well and consistently for natal events where it is used and applied. For events other than natal, other house systems seem to work better. Other house systems can also work well with natal events besides the Placidian. The question of which house system to use is more thoroughly addressed in Chapter 5.

Houses vs. the Personal Sensitive Points

One confusing issue concerns the difference between house cusps and the personal sensitive points. The primary difference between these in a horoscope is that houses show wedges or divisions of space while the personal sensitive points represent time. Looking at the space around an event it quickly becomes evident that many different astronomically defined frameworks for dividing space can be created. Four astronomical planes can help us mathematically divide space, the: ecliptic, equatorial, horizon, and lunar planes. Each of these planes contributes to the order of placing planets in space. Each of these planes divide space and time in ways that are astrologically meaningful. More importantly, though, the mathematical intersections of these planes gives us eight rigidly defined sets of places where peaks or points can gather energy and potential. Refer to these places as the personal sensitive points with the names: the ascendant (ASC), the MC (or Medium Coeli), the equatorial ascendant (EQA) [popularly, but incorrectly, called the east point], the vertex (VTX), the co-ascendant (CAS), the polar ascendant (PAS), the Aries point (ARI), and the Moon's node (NOD). (See also Chapter 1.)

Each of these points has a pair, and one part of the pair can not be thought of without also considering its companion: the ascendant has its descendant; the MC has its IC; etc. The pairings of the points are unchangeable—because one side exists by definition, so does the other. The points and their pair names are listed in Chapter 1. Further, each personal sensitive point is formed when some great astronomical circle from one of the four levels or planes mentioned above intersects the ecliptic. There are only eight ways this can be done, and there are only eight sets of personal sensitive points. Each is astrologically equal to the other in strength and function—but not all are equally well defined in popular astrological literature. Since the outer edge of a horoscope shows the ecliptic, then places where the ecliptic is astronomically intersected should be astrologically important.

The mathematical definitions for the personal sensitive points follow. They are not difficult to compute, requiring only the local sidereal time (LST) of an event, its early latitude, and a table of Ascendants and Midheavens, or the formulae and a full functioned calculator or computer. With just a little practice you can calculate the personal sensitive points (except the Moon's node) in less than two minutes. With the formulae tables are not needed. The definitions for these points may be addressed in other works.

Astronomical Considerations

In the astronomy defining an event, there are great circles which divide the sphere of space into logical parts. These great circles are called: meridian, horizon, prime vertical, celestial equator, polar axis circle, ecliptic, and horizon. The Moon's nodes are a special case, where the plane of the Moon's motion defines these where it cuts the ecliptic. All of the houses and sensitive points used in astrology are a result of these circles or mathematical derivatives from these circles where these circles or their derivatives cut the ecliptic. You may wish to use the notes and definitions at the end of this article for a reference.

House systems use the great circles of astronomy as starting points for their definitions and also for projection purposes. Having a good understanding of the astronomy of the horoscope does help in being able to visualize the construction of the individual house systems. The guides and definitions at the end of this article may help clarify these terms. Some house systems have more than one name. While I have searched diligently to compile a list of all house systems described in popular literature, I may have inadvertently overlooked some. I apologize in advance to those authors for my omission. Do not dwell too strongly on the word definitions which, admittedly, are short. It is the mathematics which really define the houses systems. I tried to show the mathematics clearly and consistently, but I may have inadvertently made some errors. I wish to thank Gary Duncan, Neil Michelsen, Rob Hand, Michael Erlewine, and George Noonan for their assistance with this effort when it was in its formative stages.

Definitions of the Individual House Systems

The Alcibitius Declination House System: (Sometimes spelled 'Alcabitius'). The diurnal arc of the Ascendant is tri-sected and projected by hour circles onto the ecliptic to form the house cusps.

The Alcibitius Semi-Arc House System: The diurnal arc of the Ascendant is tri-sected and projected by vertical circles onto the ecliptic to form the house cusps.

The Arcturan House System: The horizon circle is cut at thirty degree intervals starting at the east point of the horizon, and these points are projected onto the ecliptic using longitude circles.

The Campanus House System: The prime vertical is cut at thirty degree intervals starting at the east point of the horizon, and these points are projected onto the ecliptic using house circles.

The Classical House System: The diurnal arc of the Ascendant is tri-sected and projected by hour circles onto the ecliptic to form the house cusps, but five degrees is subtracted from the ASC to form the first house cusp. This slight correction to the Alcibitius Declination house system described above was used in antiquity to correct for observational effects due to atmospheric refraction close to the horizon.

The Earth House System: Zero degrees of Libra is taken as the first house cusp and each house cusp is thirty degrees farther along in the zodiac.

The Equal House System: The Ascendant is taken as the cusp of the first house and each house is thirty degrees further along in the zodiac. Note that in this house system the Midheaven is not necessarily the cusp of the tenth house.

The Horizontal House System: The horizon circle is cut at thirty degree intervals starting at the east point of the horizon, and these points are projected onto the ecliptic using vertical circles.

The Koch House System: The diurnal arc of the Ascendant is tri-sected and projected by Ascendant arcs onto the ecliptic to form the house cusps.

The Midheaven House System: The Midheaven (MC) is taken as the cusp of the tenth house and each house is thirty degrees further along in the zodiac. Note that in this house system the Ascendant (ASC) is not necessarily the cusp of the first house.

The Meridian House System: The celestial equator circle is cut at thirty degree intervals starting at the meridian (Midheaven), and these cut points are projected onto the ecliptic using hour circles. The Midheaven becomes the cusp of the tenth house, and the ascendant is not the cusp of any house.

The Moon House System: The Moon is taken as the tenth house cusp and each house cusp is thirty degrees farther along in the zodiac. Note that in this house system neither the ascendant nor the MC are necessarily house cusps.

The Morinus House System: The celestial equator circle is cut at thirty degree intervals starting at the Aries point, and these points are projected onto the ecliptic using longitude circles.

The Natural Graduation House System: A complicated mathematical variation of the Porphyry House System, as described on pp. 46-47 in *New Waite's Compendium* by Colin Evans.

The Natural Hours House System: The times of sunrise and sunset are noted for the location and date of the horoscope. The degrees of the Ascendant at sunrise and sunset give the degrees of the Ascendant and Descendant respectively. The hemispheres between the Ascendant and Descendant are divided into six sectors, each representing two 'hours' of time. These sectors also give the house cusps. Note that the Ascendant and Descendant are no longer tied together as a pair in this system, and the Midheaven may fall in any house.

The Octopos House System: The prime vertical is cut at forty-five degree intervals starting at the east point of the horizon, and these points are projected onto the ecliptic using house circles. This produces eight houses instead of twelve as by most other systems, and these are then numbered starting at the descendant and going counter-clockwise, so that the house placed at the seventh house is called the first house, and the house normally near the ninth house is the second house, etc. For those persons with a fear of the twelfth house, this is the one to use.

The Placidian House System: The celestial equator circle is cut at thirty degree intervals starting at the Aries point, and these points are projected onto the ecliptic using house circles. The original cusps are then recalculated in a complicated adjustment cycle which continues until no further cuspal movement is perceived. The house cusps are supposedly based on the time intervals of the rising degree, not its spatial divisions. It is mathematically very close to the Regiomontanus system which it is supposed to supplant.

The Porphyry House System: The arc between the Midheaven and the Ascendant is measured and trisected, with the ecliptic locations becoming the eleventh and twelfth houses. Then the arc between the Ascendant and IC is treated similarly for the cusps of the second and third houses. The Ascendant and Midheaven are the cusps of the first and tenth houses, and the other houses are opposite paired (e.g., the eighth cusp is opposite the second).

The Radiant House System: Same as the Horizontal House System.

Regiomontanus House System: The celestial equator circle is cut at thirty degree intervals starting at the Aries point, and these points are projected onto the ecliptic using house circles. This is similar to the Placidian house system, but without the complicated adjustment algorithm required by that method.

The Solar House System: The position of the Sun is taken as the first house cusp and each house cusp is thirty degrees farther along in the zodiac. Note that in this house system neither the Ascendant nor the Midheaven are necessarily house cusps. This system is commonly used when the Ascendant and Midheaen are not known.

The Sun House System: The Sun is taken as the fourth house cusp and each house cusp is thirty degrees farther along in the zodiac. Note that in this house system neither the Ascendant nor the Midheaven are necessarily house cusps.

The Topocentric House System: This is a very slight mathematical variation of the Placidian algorithm, which, supposedly, allows for a more accurate calculation of the intermediate house cusps in the polar regions.

The Whole Sign House System: Each house is the 30 degrees of a whole zodiacal sign, starting with the zodiacal sign of the Ascendant. If the Ascendant is (say) 14 Gemini, then the entire sign of Gemini, starting at zero Gemini, becomes the first house, the entire sign of Cancer becomes the second house, etc.

The Zariel House System: Identical to the Meridian House system, except in name.

Definition of Terms and Abbreviations

Body: A planet, a star, or some similar object which exists in space and time.

Celestial Equator: A great circle denoted by an extension of the Earth's equator infinitely projected into space. This is the circle along which the measurement of right ascension is made.

Celestial Sphere: That sphere which would be formed if one were to infinitely extend the 'sphere' of Earth outward into space.

Co-Equator: The mirror image of the Earth's equator. The equator mathematically associated with the co-latitude of a place on Earth.

Co-Latitude: The number obtained when the terrestrial latitude is subtracted from ninety degrees. For the city of Philadelphia, located at forty degrees north terrestrial latitude, the co-latitude, or angular distance of Philadelphia from the Earth's North Pole, is fifty degrees.

Co-Polar Axis Circle: The great circle formed when the mathematics used to derive the polar axis circle is mirrored from the Earth's poles, rather than from the Earth's equator.

Ecliptic: That great circle of the celestial sphere which the Sun traces, when seen from the Earth, in its yearly travels against the backdrop of the sky.

Ecliptic Plane or System: The mathematical plane which contains the Solar System, with the Sun as its center and its planets at the center of their motions. A sphere of space using the ecliptic as its equator.

Equatorial Plane: The mathematical plane represented by infinitely extending the Earth's equator into space.

Equatorial System: A sphere of space using the celestial equator as its main central circle or equator.

Great Circle: A circle contained within the celestial sphere which has as its center the center point of the celestial sphere.

Horizon: A great circle, for which there are four associated terms: Visible, Rational, Sensible, and Celestial. In the way that we use these terms, the Visible Horizon is our view of where the earth and the sky meet off in the distance from where we stand on or near the earth. The Celestial Horizon is the horizon we use mathematically as our starting point to calculate houses and sensitive points, and it is the visible horizon as if that horizon were starting at the center of the earth (as opposed to where we are located on or near the surface of the earth) and was extended infinitely into space.

Horizon Plane or System: The plane which contains the horizon. The same as the celestial horizon. A sphere of space, with the Celestial Horizon serving as its equator. See also: Horizon.

Hour Circle: A great circle which is perpendicular to the Celestial Equator and which passes through a particular body in space.

House Circle: A great circle that has as its poles the North and South points of the Horizon, and which is perpendicular to the Prime Vertical.

Local Sidereal Time: The time calculated for a horoscope when a time of event is added to the longitude correction, the time zone correction, the acceleration, the delta T correction, and the sidereal time from an ephemeris.

Longitude Circle: A great circle which starts at the pole of the ecliptic and travels around the Celestial Sphere perpendicular to the ecliptic. It is like a circle of longitude, but in the ecliptic system, as opposed to on a globe of the earth.

Meridian: A great circle of the Horizon system which passes through the Zenith, the nadir, and the North and South points of the horizon.

Nadir: The South Pole of the horizon system. Opposed to the Zenith.

Obliquity: The angle in space formed between the ecliptic and the celestial equator. Presently it is about twenty-three and a half degrees and decreasing slowly with time.

Perpendicular: Ninety degrees. Circles which meet at ninety degree angles.

Polar Axis Circle: A great circle which passes through the North and South Poles of the Earth and the East and West points of the horizon.

Pole: When describing three or four dimensional space (using time as a fourth dimension) a pole is a mathematical point that is ninety degrees everywhere from a circle. For instance, the earth's North or South Poles are ninety degrees from all points on the earth's equator.

Prime Vertical: A great circle which passes through the Zenith, the Nadir, and the East and West points of the horizon. It is ninety degrees from the meridian, and vice-versa.

Vertical Circle: A great circle which is perpendicular to the horizon and passes through the Zenith and the Nadir.

Zenith: The North Pole of the horizon system. The point in the horizon system which is over your head. Opposed to the nadir.

Zodiac: A small portion of the celestial sphere which is about eight degrees on either side of the ecliptic circle.

A Cross Reference of Terms used in Various Coordinate Systems

Earth System	*Equatorial Sys.*	*Ecliptic System*	*Horizon System*
North and South Poles	Celestial Poles	Ecliptic Poles	Zenith; Nadir
Equator	Celestial Equator	Ecliptic	Horizon
Latitude	Declination	Zodiacal Latitude	Altitude
Co-Latitude	Polar Distance	Polar Elevation	Zenith Distance
Parallels of Latitude, or Latitude Circles	Diurnal Circles	Latitude Circles	Altitude Circles
Meridians	Hour Circles	Longitude Circles	Vertical Circles
Longitude	Right Ascension	Zodiacal Longitude	Azimuth Angle
Greenwich Meridian	Hour Circle of Aries	Local Meridian	Prime Vertical

The Personal Sensitive Points

Personal Sensitive Point Name	*Its Opposite Side's Name*	*Formed by an Intersection of the Ecliptic and*	*Location side in the horoscope in general*
Ascendant	Descendant	Horizon	Left
MC	IC	Meridian	Up
Equatorial ASC	Equatorial DSC	Polar Axis	Left
Vertex	Anti-Vertex	Prime Vertical	Right
Co-Ascendant	Co-Descendant	Co-Equator	Left
Polar Ascendant	Polar Descendant	Co-Polar Axis	Right
The Aries Point	Libra Point	Equator	Zero Aries
Moon's North Node	South Node	Moon's Orbital Plane	As defined

House Keywords and More…

Appendix B

How to Calculate House Cusps

This reprint contains two slight modifications and corrections from the article that appeared in the Winter 1988 *NCGR Journal*. Used with permission.

Calculation Conventions

The following standard mathematical abbreviations are used in the explanations which follow:

e   represents the obliquity of the ecliptic

f   represents the terrestrial latitude

ASC   is the ascendant

MC   is the MC

RA   is the Right Ascension of a body

RAMC   is the Right Ascension of the MC, etc.

F, G, J, K, and L are working terms, unimportant astronomically

+. -, x (or, *), ÷, =   represent their normal arithmetic functions

SIN, COS, TAN, COT, etc. represent the trigonometric functions

For calculator purposes: COT = (1 ÷ TAN) and vice-versa, etc.

ARCSIN, ARCCOS, ARCTAN, etc. represent the trig inverses

H11, etc.   stands for the offset to compute the cusp of house eleven, etc.

C11, etc.   stands for the value of the cusp of house eleven, etc.

Standard computer notation parenthesis nesting conventions are used throughout the formulations. That is, three left parenthesis must be balanced by three right parenthesis. Calculations are always performed within the inner parenthesis first, and then outward to the outer parenthesis.

Persons attempting the mathematics herein should refer to reasonable reference books if they are unfamiliar with trigonometric procedures. The process of adjusting house cusp calculations for the correct trigonometric quadrant can be particularly tricky if not done with care.

House cusps that are over 360° or under 0o should be converted to lie between 0° and 360°. That is, if you compute a house cusp as being 372o then this should be changed to 12 Aries. Add 360o to any negative values or results. House cusps with values between 0° and 29.99° lie in Aries; between 30° and 59.99° in Taurus; between 60° and 89.99° degrees in Gemini, and so forth around the zodiac and through the signs.

Preliminary Calculations and the Personal Sensitive Points

1. The RAMC (the right ascension of the midheaven) is computed from Local Sidereal Time (LST) by converting time units to degree units. An example of this calculation follows:

    Given an LST of 12H 15M 00S, then first convert this to a decimal form of time, or 12.25 hours. 12.25 x 15 = 183.75o which is the RAMC.

Given an LST of 6H 27M 14S, then convert this to a decimal form of time, or 6.453889 hours. 6.453889 x 15 = 96.808333o.

2. MC = ARCTAN (TAN (RAMC) ÷ COS e)
3. ASC = ARCCOT (- ((TAN f x SIN e) + (SIN RAMC x COS e)) ÷ COS RAMC)
4. EQA = ARCCOT (- (TAN RAMC x COS e))
5. VTX = ARCCOT (- ((COT f x SIN e) - (SIN RAMC x COS e)) ÷ COS RAMC)
6. CAS = ARCCOT (- ((COT f x SIN e) + (SIN RAMC x COS e)) ÷ COS RAMC)
7. PAS = ARCCOT (((TAN f x SIN e) - (SIN RAMC x COS e)) ÷ COS RAMC)
8. ARI The Aries Point is always zero of Aries.
9. The declination of any point on the ecliptic can be calculated from:

    declination = ARCSIN (SIN (zodiacal longitude of point) x SIN e)

10. The obliquity of the ecliptic, for any date in modern times, is calculated by:

    e = 23° 27' 08.26" - 46.845" x T - .0059" x T^2 + .00181" x T^3

    where T is in fractions of a century from Jan 1, 1900

The Alcibitius Declination House System

1. Compute the RAMC, MC, and ASC in the normal manner.
2. Determine the number of zodiacal degrees between the ASC and MC:

    L = ASC - MC

3. Determine the Diurnal and Nocturnal Semi-arcs:

    D = ARCTAN (TAN L x COS e)
    P = 180o - D

4. Determine these intermediate working values:

    F = D ÷ 3   J = P ÷ 3
    G = F x 2   K = J x 2

5. Compute the house cusp intervals as follows:

    H11 = ARCTAN (TAN F ÷ COS e)
    H12 = ARCTAN (TAN G ÷ COS e)
    H2 = ARCTAN (TAN K ÷ COS e)
    H3 = ARCTAN (TAN J ÷ COS e)

6. Compute the individual house cusps as follows:

    C_{10} = MC C_4 = 180° + C_{10}
    C_{11} = MC + H_{11} C_5 = 180° + C_{11}
    C_{12} = MC + H_{12} C_6 = 180° + C_{12}
    C_1 = ASC C_7 = 180° + C_1
    C_2 = ASC + H_2 C_8 = 180° + C_2
    C_3 = ASC + H_3 C_9 = 180° + C_3

The Alcibitius Semi-arc House System

1. Compute the RAMC, MC, and ASC in the normal manner.
2. Determine the right ascension of the ASC (RASC):

    $RASC = ARCTAN\ (TAN\ (ASC)\ \times\ COS\ e\ )$

3. Compute the RAMC to RASC interval:

    $T = RASC - RAMC$ (Add 360° if negative)

4. Compute the trisections of the diurnal and nocturnal arcs:

    $D = T \div 3$

    $P = (T - 180°) \div 3$

5. Compute the RA of each of the house cusps:

    $RA_{11} = RAMC + D$

    $RA_{12} = RA_{11} + D$

    $RA_2 = RASC + P$

    $RA_3 = RA_2 + P$

6. Compute the house cusp intervals as follows:

    $H_{11} = ARCCOT\ (-((TAN\ f\ \times\ COS\ e) + (SIN\ RA11\ \times\ COS\ e)) \div COS\ RA_{11})$

    $H_{12} = ARCCOT\ (-((TAN\ f\ \times\ COS\ e) + (SIN\ RA12\ \times\ COS\ e)) \div COS\ RA_{12})$

    $H_2 = ARCCOT\ (-((TAN\ f\ \times\ COS\ e) + (SIN\ RA2\ \times\ COS\ e)) \div COS\ RA_2)$

    $H_3 = ARCCOT\ (-((TAN\ f\ \times\ COS\ e) + (SIN\ RA3\ \times\ COS\ e)) \div COS\ RA_3)$

7. Compute the individual house cusps as follows:

C10 =	MC	C_4 = 180° + C_{10}	
C11 =	MC + H_{11}	C_5 = 180° + C_{11}	
C12 =	MC + H_{12}	C_6 = 180° + C_{12}	
C1 =	ASC	C_7 = 180° + C_1	
C2 =	ASC + H_2	C_8 = 180° + C_2	
C3 =	ASC + H_3	C_9 = 180° + C_3	

The Arcturan House System

This house system works very well in polar areas, but gives erratic and unpredictable results in the tropical regions.

1. Compute the RAMC, MC, and ASC in the normal manner.
2. Determine the following constants for later usage:

    Compute the Decl. of the ASC: $D = ARCSIN\ (SIN\ ASC\ \times\ SIN\ e)$

    Oblique Ascension of the East Point: $J = RAMC + 90°$

    G, the angle between the ecliptic and the horizon:

    $G = ARCCOS\ ((SIN\ f\ \times\ COS\ e) + (COS\ f\ \times\ SIN\ e\ \times\ COS\ J))$

    K, the arc in degrees from the East Point to the ASC:

    $K = ARCSIN\ (SIN\ D \div COS\ f)$

House Keywords and More...

3. Determine the house cusp intervals:

$$H_{10} = K + 90° \quad H_1 = K + 0° \text{ (or, } 180°\text{)}$$
$$H_{11} = K + 60° \quad H_2 = K + 150°$$
$$H_{12} = K + 30° \quad H_3 = K + 120°$$

4. Determine the ecliptic to cusp angle:

$$R_{10} = \text{ARCTAN} (\text{COS } G \times \text{TAN } H_{10})$$
$$R_{11} = \text{ARCTAN} (\text{COS } G \times \text{TAN } H_{11})$$
$$R_{12} = \text{ARCTAN} (\text{COS } G \times \text{TAN } H_{12})$$
$$R_1 = \text{ARCTAN} (\text{COS } G \times \text{TAN } H_1)$$
$$R_2 = \text{ARCTAN} (\text{COS } G \times \text{TAN } H_2)$$
$$R_3 = \text{ARCTAN} (\text{COS } G \times \text{TAN } H_3)$$

5. Compute the individual house cusps as follows:

$$C_{10} = \text{ASC} - R_{10} \qquad C_4 = 180° + C_{10}$$
$$C_{11} = \text{ASC} - R_{11} \qquad C_5 = 180° + C_{11}$$
$$C_{12} = \text{ASC} - R_{12} \qquad C_6 = 180° + C_{12}$$
$$C_1 = \text{ASC} - R \qquad C_7 = 180° + C_1$$
$$C_2 = \text{ASC} - R_2 \qquad C_8 = 180° + C_2$$
$$C_3 = \text{ASC} - R_3 \qquad C_9 = 180° + C_3$$

The R value when added to the ASC may give you the opposite side house cusp as a result. Add 180° to your answer if this occurs.

The Campanus House System

1. Compute the RAMC, MC, and ASC in the normal manner

2. Determine the following house cusp intervals:

$$H_{11} = 30° \qquad H_2 = 120°$$
$$H_{12} = 60° \qquad H_3 = 150°$$

3. Compute an intermediate number:

$$J_{11} = \text{ARCCOT} (\text{COS } f \times \text{TAN H11}) \quad J_2 = \text{ARCCOT} (\text{COS } f \times \text{TAN } H_2)$$
$$J_{12} = \text{ARCCOT} (\text{COS } f \times \text{TAN H12}) \quad J_3 = \text{ARCCOT} (\text{COS } f \times \text{TAN } H_3)$$

4. Compute the Prime Vertical interval:

$$F_{11} = \text{RAMC} + 90° - J_{11} \quad F_2 = \text{RAMC} + 90° - J_2$$
$$F_{12} = \text{RAMC} + 90° - J_{12} \quad F_3 = \text{RAMC} + 90° - J_3$$

5. Compute the house cusp positions as follows:

$$P_{11} = \text{ARCSIN} (\text{SIN } H_{11} \times \text{SIN } f) \quad P_2 = \text{ARCSIN} (\text{SIN } H_2 \times \text{SIN } f)$$
$$P_{12} = \text{ARCSIN} (\text{SIN } H_{12} \times \text{SIN } f) \quad P_3 = \text{ARCSIN} (\text{SIN } H_3 \times \text{SIN } f)$$

6. Compute the associate angles as follows:

$$M_{11} = \text{ARCTAN}(\text{TAN } P_{11} \div \text{COS } F_{11}) \quad M_{12} = \text{ARCTAN}(\text{TAN } P_{12} \div \text{COS } F12)$$
$$M_2 = \text{ARCTAN}(\text{TAN } P_2 \div \text{COS } F_2) \quad M_3 = \text{ARCTAN}(\text{TAN } P_3 \div \text{COS } F_3)$$

7. Compute the ecliptic intervals:

$$R_{11} = \text{ARCTAN}((\text{TAN } F_{11} \times \text{COS } M_{11}) \div \text{COS}(M_{11} + e))$$
$$R_{12} = \text{ARCTAN}((\text{TAN } F_{12} \times \text{COS } M_{12}) \div \text{COS}(M_{12} + e))$$
$$R_2 = \text{ARCTAN}((\text{TAN } F_2 \times \text{COS } M2) \div \text{COS}(M_2 + e))$$
$$R_3 = \text{ARCTAN}((\text{TAN } F_3 \times \text{COS } M3) \div \text{COS}(M_3 + e))$$

8. Compute the individual house cusps as follows:

$$C_{10} = MC \quad\quad C_4 = 180° + C_{10}$$
$$C_{11} = MC + R11 \quad C_5 = 180° + C_{11}$$
$$C_{12} = MC + R12 \quad C_6 = 180° + C_{12}$$
$$C_1 = ASC \quad\quad C_7 = 180° + C1$$
$$C_2 = ASC + R_2 \quad C_8 = 180° + C2$$
$$C_3 = ASC + R_3 \quad C_9 = 180° + C3$$

The Classical House System

1. Compute the RAMC, MC, and ASC in the normal manner.
2. Determine the First Cusp Locus Longitude:

$$L_1 = ASC - 5°$$

3. Determine Right Ascension of the First Locus:

$$A_1 = RASC = \text{ARCTAN}(\text{TAN } L1 \times \text{COS } e)$$

4. Determine the local hour angle of the MC:

$$t = \text{ARCCOS}(-((\text{TAN } f \times \text{TAN } e) \times \text{SIN}(A_1)))$$

5. Tri-sect the hour angle arcs:

$$g = t \div 3$$
$$h = (180° - t) \div 3$$

6. Determine the right ascension of the tenth house cusp:

$$A_{10} = A_1 - t$$

7. Compute the house cusp positions as follows:

$$A_{11} = A_{10} + g$$
$$A_{12} = A_{11} + g$$
$$A_2 = A_1 + h$$
$$A_3 = A_2 + h$$

8. Compute the individual house cusps as follows:

$$C_{10} = \text{ARCTAN}(\text{TAN } A_{10} \div \text{COS } e) \quad C_4 = 180° + C_{10}$$
$$C_{11} = \text{ARCTAN}(\text{TAN } A_{11} \div \text{COS } e) \quad C_5 = 180° + C_{11}$$

$$C_{12} = \text{ARCTAN} (\text{TAN } A_{12} \div \text{COS } e) \quad C_6 = 180° + C_{12}$$
$$C_1 = \text{ARCTAN} (\text{TAN } A_1 \div \text{COS } e) \quad C_7 = 180° + C_1$$
$$C_2 = \text{ARCTAN} (\text{TAN } A_2 \div \text{COS } e) \quad C_8 = 180° + C_2$$
$$C_3 = \text{ARCTAN} (\text{TAN } A_3 \div \text{COS } e) \quad C_9 = 180° + C_3$$

The Horizontal House System

1. Compute the RAMC, MC, and ASC in the normal manner.
2. Compute the P point:

   $$P = \text{ARCTAN} (\text{TAN RAMC} \times \text{COS } e)$$

3. Compute the angle between the horizon and the ecliptic:

   $$G = \text{ARCSIN} ((\text{COS } f \times \text{SIN} (\text{RAMC} + 90°)) \div \text{SIN ASC})$$

4. Compute:

   $$J = \text{ASC} - P$$
   $$K = \text{ARCTAN} (\text{TAN } J \times \text{COS } G)$$

5. Assign the house cusp intervals:

   $H_{10} = 90°$ $H2 = 0°$
   $H_{11} = 60°$ $H2 = -30°$
   $H_{12} = 30°$ $H3 = -60°$

6. Compute an intermediate result:

   $M_{10} = H_{10} + K$ $M_1 = H_1 + K$
   $M_{11} = H_{11} + K$ $M_2 = H_2 + K$
   $M_{12} = H_{12} + K$ $M_3 = H_3 + K$

7. Compute the next intermediate result as follows:

   $R_{10} = \text{ARCTAN} (\text{TAN } M_{10} \div \text{COS } G)$
   $R_{11} = \text{ARCTAN} (\text{TAN } M_{11} \div \text{COS } G)$
   $R_{12} = \text{ARCTAN} (\text{TAN } M_{12} \div \text{COS } G)$
   $R_1 = \text{ARCTAN} (\text{TAN } M_1 \div \text{COS } G)$
   $R_2 = \text{ARCTAN} (\text{TAN } M_2 \div \text{COS } G)$
   $R_3 = \text{ARCTAN} (\text{TAN } M_3 \div \text{COS } G)$

8. Compute the individual house cusps as follows:

   $C_{10} = \text{ASC} - R_{10}$ $C_4 = 180° + C_{10}$
   $C_{11} = \text{ASC} - R_{11}$ $C_5 = 180° + C_{11}$
   $C_{12} = \text{ASC} - R_{12}$ $C_6 = 180° + C_{12}$
   $C_1 = \text{ASC} - R_1$ $C_7 = 180° + C_1$
   $C_2 = \text{ASC} - R_2$ $C_8 = 180° + C_2$
   $C_3 = \text{ASC} - R_3$ $C_9 = 180° + C_3$

The Koch House System

1. Compute the RAMC, MC, and ASC in the normal manner. Use the MC as the cusp of the tenth house.

2. Calculate the declination of the MC:

    $D = ARCSIN\ (SIN\ MC\ \times\ SIN\ e)$

3. Calculate the ascensional difference of the MC:

    $J = ARCSIN\ (TAN\ D\ \times\ TAN\ f)$

4. Calculate the oblique ascension of the MC:

    $OAMC = RAMC - J$

5. Calculate the general house cusp displacement interval:

    $DX = ((RAMC + 90°) - OAMC) \div 3)$

    (This should be a positive number; add 360° to any negative DX value.)

6. Compute the house cusp positions as follows:

    $H_{11} = (OAMC + DX - 90°)$
    $H_{12} = H_{11} + DX$
    $H_{1} = H_{12} + DX$
    $H_{2} = H_{1} + DX$
    $H_{3} = H_{2} + DX$

7. Calculate the individual house cusps:

    $C_{11} = ARCCOT\ (-((TAN\ f \times SIN\ e) + (SIN\ H_{11} \times COS\ e)) \div COS\ H_{11})$
    $C_{12} = ARCCOT\ (-((TAN\ f \times SIN\ e) + (SIN\ H_{12} \times COS\ e)) \div COS\ H_{12})$
    $C_{1} = ARCCOT\ (-((TAN\ f \times SIN\ e) + (SIN\ H_{1} \times COS\ e)) \div COS\ H_{1})$
    $C_{2} = ARCCOT\ (-((TAN\ f \times SIN\ e) + (SIN\ H_{2} \times COS\ e)) \div COS\ H_{2})$
    $C_{3} = ARCCOT\ (-((TAN\ f \times SIN\ e) + (SIN\ H_{3} \times COS\ e)) \div COS\ H_{3})$

8. Compute the individual house cusps as follows:

    $C_{10} = MC$ $C_{4} = 180° + C_{10}$
    $C_{11} = C_{11}$ $C_{5} = 180° + C_{11}$
    $C_{12} = C_{12}$ $C_{6} = 180° + C_{12}$
    $C_{1} = C1$ $C_{7} = 180° + C_{1}$
    $C_{2} = C2$ $C_{8} = 180° + C_{2}$
    $C_{3} = C3$ $C_{9} = 180° + C_{3}$

The Meridian House System

1. Compute the RAMC, MC, and ASC in the normal manner.
2. Determine the house cusp intervals:

   $H_{10} = 0°$ $H_1 = 90°$
   $H_{11} = 30°$ $H_2 = 120°$
   $H_{12} = 60°$ $H_3 = 150°$

3. Determine the ecliptic interval point for each cusp:

   $F_{10} = \text{RAMC} + H_{10}$
   $F_{11} = \text{RAMC} + H_{11}$
   $F_{12} = \text{RAMC} + H_{12}$
   $F_1 = \text{RAMC} + H_1$
   $F_2 = \text{RAMC} + H_2$
   $F_3 = \text{RAMC} + H_3$

4. Compute the house cusps:

   $C_{10} = \text{ARCTAN}\ (\text{TAN}\ F_{10} \div \text{COS}\ e)$
   $C_{11} = \text{ARCTAN}\ (\text{TAN}\ F_{11} \div \text{COS}\ e)$
   $C_{12} = \text{ARCTAN}\ (\text{TAN}\ F_{12} \div \text{COS}\ e)$
   $C_1 = \text{ARCTAN}\ (\text{TAN}\ F_1 \div \text{COS}\ e)$
   $C_2 = \text{ARCTAN}\ (\text{TAN}\ F_2 \div \text{COS}\ e)$
   $C_3 = \text{ARCTAN}\ (\text{TAN}\ F_3 \div \text{COS}\ e)$

5. Determine the individual house cusps as follows:

   $C_{10} = C_{10}\ C_4 = 180° + C_{10}$
   $C_{11} = C_{11}\ C_5 = 180° + C_{11}$
   $C_{12} = C_{12}\ C6 = 180° + C_{12}$
   $C_1 = C_1\ C7 = 180° + C_1$
   $C_2 = C_2\ C8 = 180° + C_2$
   $C_3 = C_3\ C9 = 180° + C_3$

The Morinus House System

1. Compute the RAMC, MC, and ASC in the normal manner.
2. Determine the house cusp intervals:

   $H_{10} = 0°$ $H_1 = 90°$
   $H_{11} = 30°$ $H_2 = 120°$
   $H_{12} = 60°$ $H_3 = 150°$

3. Determine the ecliptic interval point for each cusp:

$F_{10} = RAMC + H_{10}$

$F_{11} = RAMC + H_{11}$

$F_{12} = RAMC + H_{12}$

$F_{1} = RAMC + H_{1}$

$F_{2} = RAMC + H_{2}$

$F_{3} = RAMC + H_{3}$

4. Compute the house cusps:

$C_{10} = ARCTAN (TAN\ F_{10} \times COS\ e)$

$C_{11} = ARCTAN (TAN\ F_{11} \times COS\ e)$

$C_{12} = ARCTAN (TAN\ F_{12} \times COS\ e)$

$C_{1} = ARCTAN (TAN\ F_{1} \times COS\ e)$

$C_{2} = ARCTAN (TAN\ F2 \times COS\ e)$

$C_{3} = ARCTAN (TAN\ F_{3} \times COS\ e)$

5. Determine the individual house cusps as follows:

$C_{10} = C_{10}$ $C4 = 180° + C10$

$C_{11} = C_{11}$ $C5 = 180° + C11$

$C_{12} = C_{12}$ $C6 = 180° + C12$

$C_{1} = C_{1}$ $C7 = 180° + C1$

$C_{2} = C_{2}$ $C8 = 180° + C2$

$C_{3} = C_{3}$ $C9 = 180° + C3$

The Natural Hours House System

1. Compute the RAMC, MC, and ASC in the normal manner.

2. Determine the times of sunrise and sunset for the location of the chart. You can consult your local newspaper, tables in the "Nautical Almanac," or using a table of ascendants and MC's determine what clock time during the day the Sun's degree would be conjunct the ASC and the DSC. Finally, if you wish to calculate that information astronomically, you can also do that, but I am not providing those formulas or methods here because they can become too tricky, especially in polar latitudes where the Sun doesn't rise or set during every 24 hour period.

3. Suppose you determine that there are twelve hours and thirty-six minutes of daylight, and, thus eleven hours and twenty-four minutes of night for the day of the event at your event location. Then convert these hours and minutes to arcs of a circle as follows:

12H 36M = 12.6 Hrs $((12.6 \div 24) \times 360°) = 189°$ of daylight arc

$360 - 189 = 171°$ of night time arc

4. Compute the cuspal increments:

$D = 189° \div 6 = 31°\ 30'$ for the daylight increment

$N = 171° \div 6 = 28°\ 30'$ for the night time increment

5. Compute the house cusps:

$$C_{12} = ASC - D$$
$$C_{11} = C_{12} - D$$
$$C_{10} = C_{11} - D$$
$$C_{9} = C_{10} - D$$
$$C_{8} = C_{9} - D$$
$$C_{7} = C_{8} - D$$
$$C_{1} = ASC$$
$$C_{2} = ASC + N$$
$$C_{3} = C_{2} + N$$
$$C_{4} = C_{3} + N$$
$$C_{5} = C_{4} + N$$
$$C_{6} = C_{5} + N$$

The Placidian House System

1. Compute the RAMC, MC, and ASC in the usual manner. Use the MC as the cusp of the tenth house and the ASC as the cusp of the first house. This is a fast converging algorithm adapted from M. Vijayaraghavulu.

2. Determine the following house cusp intervals:

$$H_{11} = RAMC + 30° \qquad H_{2} = RAMC + 120°$$
$$H_{12} = RAMC + 60° \qquad H_{3} = RAMC + 150°$$

3. Set the Semi-arc ratios:

$$F_{11} = 1 \div 3 \qquad F_{2} = 2 \div 3$$
$$F_{12} = 2 \div 3 \qquad F_{3} = 1 \div 3$$

4. Compute the cuspal declinations:

$$D_{11} = ARCSIN\ (\ SIN\ e\ \ \times\ \ SIN\ H11\ ) \qquad D_{2} = ARCSIN\ (\ SIN\ e\ \ \times\ \ SIN\ H_{2}\ )$$
$$D_{12} = ARCSIN\ (\ SIN\ e\ \ \times\ \ SIN\ H12\ ) \qquad D_{3} = ARCSIN\ (\ SIN\ e\ \ \times\ \ SIN\ H_{3}\ )$$

5. Compute the first intermediate values:

$$A_{11} = F_{11} \times (\ ARCSIN\ (\ TAN\ f \times TAN\ D_{11}\ )\ )$$
$$A_{12} = F_{12} \times (\ ARCSIN\ (\ TAN\ f \times TAN\ D_{12}\ )\ )$$
$$A_{2} = F_{2} \times (\ ARCSIN\ (\ TAN\ f \times TAN\ D_{2}\ )\ )$$
$$A_{3} = F_{3} \times (\ ARCSIN\ (\ TAN\ f \times TAN\ D_{3}\ )\ )$$

6. Compute the house cusp positions as follows:

$$M_{11} = ARCTAN\ (\ SIN\ A_{11}\ \div\ (\ COS\ H_{11}\ \times\ TAN\ D_{11}\ )\ )$$
$$M_{12} = ARCTAN\ (\ SIN\ A_{12}\ \div\ (\ COS\ H_{12}\ \times\ TAN\ D_{12}\ )\ )$$
$$M_{2} = ARCTAN\ (\ SIN\ A_{2}\ \div\ (\ COS\ H_{2}\ \times\ TAN\ D_{2}\ )\ )$$
$$M_{3} = ARCTAN\ (\ SIN\ A_{3}\ \div\ (\ COS\ H_{3}\ \times\ TAN\ D_{3}\ )\ )$$

7. Compute the intermediate house cusps:

$$R_{11} = \text{ARCTAN}((\text{TAN } H_{11} \times \text{COS } M_{11}) \div \text{COS}(M_{11} + e))$$
$$R_{12} = \text{ARCTAN}((\text{TAN } H_{12} \times \text{COS } M_{12}) \div \text{COS}(M_{12} + e))$$
$$R_2 = \text{ARCTAN}((\text{TAN } H_2 \times \text{COS } M_2) \div \text{COS}(M_2 + e))$$
$$R_3 = \text{ARCTAN}((\text{TAN } H_3 \times \text{COS } M_3) \div \text{COS}(M_3 + e))$$

8. Substitute: $D_{11} = R_{11}$; $D_{12} = R_{12}$; $D_2 = R_2$; and $D_3 = R_3$. Then repeat steps 5 thru 8 again. Substitute the R's for the D's a third time and repeat steps 5 thru 8. The answer for R on the third try is the cusp you desire.

9. Compute the individual house cusps as follows:

$C_{11} = R_{11}$ $C_5 = 180° + C_{11}$
$C_{12} = R_{12}$ $C_6 = 180° + C_{12}$
$C_2 = R_2$ $C_8 = 180° + C_2$
$C_3 = R_3$ $C_9 = 180° + C_3$

The Regiomontanus House System

1. Compute the RAMC, MC, and ASC in the normal manner. Use the MC as the cusp of the tenth house and the ASC as the cusp of the first house.

2. Determine the following house cusp intervals:

$H_{11} = 30°$ $H_2 = 120°$
$H_{12} = 60°$ $H_3 = 150°$

3. Set the equatorial intervals:

$F_{11} = \text{RAMC} + H_{11}$ $F_2 = \text{RAMC} + H_2$
$F_{12} = \text{RAMC} + H_{12}$ $F_3 = \text{RAMC} + H_3$

4. Compute the house poles:

$P_{11} = \text{ARCTAN}(\text{TAN } f \times \text{SIN } H_{11})$ $P_2 = \text{ARCTAN}(\text{TAN } f \times \text{SIN } H_2)$
$P_{12} = \text{ARCTAN}(\text{TAN } f \times \text{SIN } H_{12})$ $P_3 = \text{ARCTAN}(\text{TAN } f \times \text{SIN } H_3)$

5. Compute the first intermediate values:

$M_{11} = \text{ARCTAN}(\text{TAN } P_{11} \div \text{COS } F_{11})$
$M_{12} = \text{ARCTAN}(\text{TAN } P_{12} \div \text{COS } F_{12})$
$M_2 = \text{ARCTAN}(\text{TAN } P_2 \div \text{COS } F_2)$
$M_3 = \text{ARCTAN}(\text{TAN } P_3 \div \text{COS } F_3)$

6. Compute the intermediate house cusps:

$$R_{11} = \text{ARCTAN}((\text{TAN } F_{11} \times \text{COS } M_{11}) \div \text{COS}(M_{11} + e))$$
$$R_{12} = \text{ARCTAN}((\text{TAN } F_{12} \times \text{COS } M_{12}) \div \text{COS}(M_{12} + e))$$
$$R_2 = \text{ARCTAN}((\text{TAN } F_2 \times \text{COS } M_2) \div \text{COS}(M_2 + e))$$
$$R_3 = \text{ARCTAN}((\text{TAN } F_3 \times \text{COS } M_3) \div \text{COS}(M_3 + e))$$

7. Compute the individual house cusps as follows:

C_{10} = MC $\quad$ C4 = 180° + C_{10}
C_{11} = R_{11} $\quad$ C5 = 180° + C_{11}
C_{12} = R_{12} $\quad$ C6 = 180° + C_{12}
C_1 = ASC $\quad$ C7 = 180° + C_1
C_2 = R_2 $\quad$ C_8 = 180° + C_2
C_3 = R_3 $\quad$ C_9 = 180° + C_3

The Topocentric House System

1. Compute the RAMC, MC, and ASC in the normal manner. Use the MC as the cusp of the tenth house and the ASC as the cusp of the first house.

2. Determine the following house cusp intervals:

H_{11} = RAMC + 30° $\quad$ H_2 = RAMC + 120°
H_{12} = RAMC + 60° $\quad$ H_3 = RAMC + 150°

3. Set the Semi-arc ratios:

P_{11} = ARCTAN (TAN f ÷ 3)
P_{12} = ARCTAN (2 × (TAN f ÷ 3))
P_2 = ARCTAN (2 × (TAN f ÷ 3))
P_3 = ARCTAN (TAN f ÷ 3)

4. Compute the intermediate angle M:

M_{11} = ARCTAN (TAN P_{11} ÷ COS H_{11}) $\quad$ M_2 = ARCTAN (TAN P_2 ÷ COS H_2)
M_{12} = ARCTAN (TAN P_{12} ÷ COS H_{12}) $\quad$ M_3 = ARCTAN (TAN P_3 ÷ COS H_3)

5. Compute the intermediate house cusps:

R_{11} = ARCTAN ((TAN H_{11} × COS M_{11}) ÷ COS (M_{11} + e))
R_{12} = ARCTAN ((TAN H_{12} × COS M_{12}) ÷ COS (M_{12} + e))
R_2 = ARCTAN ((TAN H_2 × COS M_2) ÷ COS (M_2 + e))
R_3 = ARCTAN ((TAN H_3 × COS M_3) ÷ COS (M_3 + e))

6. Compute the individual house cusps as follows:

C_{10} = MC $\quad$ C_4 = 180° + C_{10}
C_{11} = R_{11} $\quad$ C_5 = 180° + C_{11}
C_{12} = R_{12} $\quad$ C_6 = 180° + C_{12}
C_1 = ASC $\quad$ C_7 = 180° + C1
C_2 = R_2 $\quad$ C_8 = 180° + C2
C_3 = R_3 $\quad$ C_9 = 180° + C3

A variation of this system, devised by Alexander Marr of Germany to give 8 cusps instead of the 12 normally used, requires changing steps 2 and 3 above as follows:

Substitute: Ha = RAMC + 45° $\quad$ Hb = RAMC + 135°

Pa = Pb = ARCTAN (TAN f ÷ 2) & then recalculate

This gives a cusp with mid-point like qualities which Mr. Marr claims produces interesting correspondences. Investigation recommended.

Appendix C

Keywords Arranged by Significant Topic Headings

Quadrant Key Ideas

First Quadrant (Fourth, Fifth, and Sixth Houses)

Inception:
- The act of starting or beginning, acquiring the stimulation necessary to begin hard work
- Source, derivation, fountain, origin
- Root, well, wellspring
- Initial, beginning, incipient, introductory
- The nurturing or encouragement for what you want to do or plan to do
- The process of self-motivation, getting yourself in gear, inspiration

Origins:
- The initial thrust, the start, the results of your upbringing, the influences you allow your parents to have over you
- Your childhood, early childhood conditioning received
- Entry, the predisposition of your instincts
- Familial, the influences we gained from our home life
- The growth and development of your instinct mechanism
- The birth of your ideas

Preparations:
- Your entry into the working environment, how you will work for what you expect, preparations for living you make, involvement
- Developing, the influence your teachers have upon you
- The development of basic sympathies, developing likes and dislikes
- Stimulating experiences, experiences which help you grow
- The beginning of self-application, acquiring new skills
- Situations created when we seek love, or acceptance, how experiences affect us, working through pre-natal emotional responses
- Searching for love or acceptance, experiences with love, your behavior or conduct in trying to obtain love, emotional accentuation
- The gathering or storing of emotional resources
- Sensing, becoming a conduit for the feelings of others
- Feeling, feeling what has to be done

Regenerate:
- Regenerate, refresh, renew, revive, reinvigorate
- The start of a climb from a low point
- Causing something to be brought into existence again

Developing:
- Reactions to things which occur in your environment, learning to mature
- Learning to set up a base and then grow from that which you are setting up for yourself in life
- The means through which you develop a more secure base or foundation to work out of
- The development of good work and play habits
- Development of your self-image through family or play or work associations
- Development of the tools or materials of life which you need

Starting:
- Finding your potential
- Laying the foundation or framework
- The initial thrust, beginning
- The start, putting into action, introducing
- Originating, finding new ideas or courses of action
- The seeking out of information

Sustaining:
- Where you get your nourishment from
- Learning to provide nourishment for yourself, providing the support for your ideas and existence
- Determining what your personal needs and/or preferences are
- Consolidating, gathering, the gathering of resources
- Gathering support for your ideas from others
- Confirming where you can get help from others for the types of support you will need

Connecting:
- Development of the relationship(s) between the parts of your ideas or objectives
- Creating your own opportunities
- A more outward use of your talents to bring others along at the expense of yourself
- Providing for the communication of your ideas and thoughts

Second Quadrant (Seventh, Eighth, and Ninth Houses)

Growth:
- Learning to acquire and use what you must (people, things, etc.) to help you accomplish your goals
- Your ascent into consciousness, development of sufficient spiritual strength to sustain yourself
- Your efforts at conscious adaptation to living in the world
- Learning to grow from out of your base of consciousness
- Gradual and progressive change or development
- The process of development toward maturity, specialization
- Development, the formation of ideas previously expressed The process of working your ideas out
- Evolvement, advancing towards perfection, flowering, upgrowth
- Progress, moving onward with your ideas and schemes
- Unfolding, the assimilation of experience

Social Endeavors:
- Development of your sense of inter-social dependency, involvements in the world of others, formal encounters with others, seeking others out
- Determination of your role and/or function within society
- Your development as a social being
- Your usefulness to society
- Learning about the structure of society within which you live
- How you develop as a person who can be useful to society
- Acceptance of responsibility for helping society to progress
- The results of your social endeavors Your social realm

Dependency:
- Development of your interdependency needs with others
- Employment of resources obtained from others
- Learning to work with others
- The bonds of loyalty you build with others

Improving:
- Sharpening your skills, learning, re-doing
- Preparing yourself for action
- Learning to think in accordance with what others expect
- The combining of different processes and systems into and with your own interests
- Acquiring knowledge, gaining in understanding

Evolving:
- A movement toward a pattern which is part of a larger whole, development of your ideas and methods, evolution
- Unfolding, the making known of one's plans or purposes, disclosing, revealing what must be done, the opening up of paths for progress
- Meeting those who will help you in your work
- Making mistakes, learning from your mistakes
- Enlarging, the broadening of your work base, expansion of your plans and ideas to a larger scale
- Elaborate, the complication of simple ideas, statement of your objectives in a more detailed form, development of work plans in greater detail
- Development from a simple to a more complex form

Formatting
- The development of talent(s)

Supporting:
- The gathering of support from others for your work and your ideas
- Advertisement of your intentions, the gathering of support as a result of this advertisement
- Seeking of maintenance, the development of a backup plan
- Seeking support with your speeches, writings, or publishing before the educated masses
- Relating

Third Quadrant (Tenth, Eleventh, and Twelfth Houses)

Attainment:
- Gaining through your own efforts, seeing or recognizing what it is you must do to gain the recognition you seek
- Seeing your accomplishments, where you meet what you have been working towards
- Reaching, achieving, arriving or coming at that which you have been working toward, reaching out for your goal
- Your acceptance or receipt of the results of your endeavors
- What you have prepared for yourself, specialization
- The making or breaking of your reputation on what it is that you are working toward, the quality of your reputation in this regard
- Actualizing, making your goals realistic
- Accomplishing, your sense of having arrived
- Fruition, coming to fulfillment, realization
- Outer application, applying the ideas or goals that you have been working toward

Responsibility:
- Your acceptance of some responsibility for helping society to progress
- Extending yourself and your commitments, achieving a degree of dependability
- Becoming accountable for your actions, answerable
- Your sense of obligation towards your duties, development of rationality
- Development of the ability to distinguish right from wrong
- Assumption of one's duties or obligations

Endeavor:
- The efforts you put forth to grow in the world because of the talents or experiences you have or can offer
- The outward use of your talents to bring others along at the expense of yourself or others
- Attempts, trying, struggles, labor, loads
- Exertion, pains, toil

Using:
- Consolidating, bringing together all of the personal resources you have been developing
- The use of these resources, formation of your own efforts
- Creation of the means to press forward with your ideas
- Acquiring, getting, locating, finding
- The identity fully forming in social expression
- Efforts to bring the world into relationship with yourself

Accomplishment:
- Seeing what you have been working for come into being
- Happen, come off, be put into production, transpire
- The results of your actions as expressed within your environment the karmic results of your work
- The development of talent(s)
- Progression to a higher or more complex form
- Maturing, mellowing, ripening

Concession:
> Admission, the acknowledgement of the truth of what one has done
> Appeasement, reconciliation
> Capitulation, a giving in to change
> Indulgence, letting others have their way with your ideas or work
> Endorsement, acknowledgement of the spread of your work or ideas

Failure:
> The suggestion of failure if adequate preparation has not been made
> Having to face the possibility of failure, facing the possibility that you may not succeed in what it is that you are trying to accomplish
> A breakdown in operation or function
> Consequences for neglect or omission

Universalizing:
> Trying to see what good there is for all mankind
> Making your work good for all, the adaptation of your ideas and efforts to that which is good or useful to all

Finishing:
> Completing that which has to be done
> The total use of your talents or resources

Fourth Quadrant (First, Second, and Third Houses)

Adaptation:
> The natural outgrowth of self-based upon what has already transpired
> Your self-awareness in adapting to the ideas and goods of others
> Opportunities to develop the non-physical as well as the physical self
> Growth, the kind of growth that comes from the contemplation of what you can or have done with your life
> Development of the inner or spiritual side of self, life sustaining functions
> Development of the shadow side of your nature
> That which you must learn to add to your collective nature
> Materialistic concerns, how you are able to capitalize on what you have done
> The creation of defense mechanisms, personal reactions to what you have done
> Your natural abilities to meet the challenges of life
> An increase in personal flexibility, the internal way you deal with others
> Accommodation, the subordinating of something for personal growth of self
> Adjustment, a change in self to produce a better adaptation to one's new surroundings
> Conforming to the different sequences in one's environment

Style:
> Development of one's likes and dislikes, how one responds to their immediate environment because of their likes and dislikes
> Review of your method of operation
> Developing the power of your personality in communication with others
> Development of a personal manner of expression, specific execution, the personal way in which you do things

Recognition:
- Recognition of selfhood, learning to know and understand self better
- Awareness, determining the role of yourself in the world
- Acknowledgement of what has been accomplished
- Gratitude, appreciation
- Formal acknowledgement of one's attainment(s)
- Identification of self with a set of accomplishments

Reconsideration:
- Conscious or unconscious thinking about what it is that you must do or grow in life for
- Re-employing, reusing of wasted or unused force or energies
- To consider again, to review, to think over in the sense of trying to determine if something should be changed

Withdrawal:
- Move back, retire, retreat, remove oneself, removal of the work that you have done, a loss of recognition
- Go, leave, quit, depart
- To take out of existence, giving up on the use of
- Concerns with preservation of the self
- Concession, removal from use or consideration

Reflection:
- An expression or learning which comes from years of experience
- Contemplation, thinking it all over
- Study, weigh, meditate upon, thoughtful study
- Reflect upon, ponder, think about
- Summation, taking stock of yourself

Renewal:
- Replacement of that which has been misused or worn out, the introduction of new or fresh ideas
- Changing your outlook, a new outlook
- Restore, to be born again, making new again, causing to exist again, reestablishing what has been done before, reviving, resuming
- Reestablish, bringing it all back into use again
- Reforming, improving, bringing it back to the way it used to be, restoring to a former or original condition
- Learning things which you can add to your collective self

Orientation:
- Bringing self back into harmony with one's ultimate standards or principles
- Familiarization with the environment, adaptation of what one has done with the environment or surrounds that one finds themselves placed in
- Bringing one's work or ideas in harmony with the universal forces
- Self-Mastery

Dissemination:
> Telling others of the nature or usefulness of your ideas or efforts
> Communicating to others what has been done, your documentation
> Spreading knowledge that you have gained to others

Intuition:
> Development of an awareness of your surroundings
> The ability to meld together various sensory inputs into a cohesive and continuing fragment of consciousness

Hemisphere Key Ideas

Left Hemisphere

Free Will:
> The expression of your individual will
> An expression of your individual free will
> What you are able to build or do for yourself

Observing:
> Projection, projection of self into public situations
> Observing the actions of others and learning from these
> Developing a broad relatedness to others
> Learning how to read and use feedback from others for personal development
> Your thought and reaction patterns, the growth you go through because of what others do to you

Participation:
> Relating to others
> Gathering and interpreting feedback from others on your actions
> Alienation from the world or others in general

Action:
> Personal aggressiveness, the amount of self-control you have
> Assertive self-interests
> Activity, personal activity, being an action oriented person
> Initiates, induces self to begin efforts with self or others
> Starts, begins, orients self towards production
> Creates their own reality

Rethinking:
> Thinking again about the effect that you have on others
> Retreating within yourself to assess your impact on others or circumstances in general, withdrawal into the self for contemplation
> The energies which the self has to channel and mold
> How you are influenced by what others do to you
> Awakening, the dawning of light and consciousness

Self-Expression:
> Intensification within, the development of yourself as an individual
> Everything that is related to your concept of self
> Concern for self, ego emphasis, your forms of self-preservation
> Ego development, developing your free will
> Your psychological and mental interests, self-manifestation
> Your self-interests
> Your egocentric or individualistic traits
> The quality of personal security which you have
> Development of your personal potential, your efforts to stand as an individual

Right Hemisphere

Experiencing:
> Give and take, causing others to react in the ways which you desire, meeting or encountering others, reactions through others
> Seeking equivalent returns from others, returns
> Seeking the help or advice of others
> Encountering circumstances which involve your destiny or reason for being
> Interaction with others, getting others involved (or vice-versa), how you react to others and their demands
> Experiencing intensification of life outside of the self or without self-involvement
> Growing through experiences with others, gaining experience in life
> What life demands from you in terms of experience and interaction
> Confrontation with the needs of others, where you came into contact with the world's demands
> Reactions, reacting, reactive

External Events:
> Things which go on outside of the small environment which you normally confine yourself to, that which is happening
> Exchange, communications with others
> Your search for the fulfillment of your destiny within society
> Human society (in general), other people
> Societal structures built by man, the economic necessities of society
> Learning about the world, what the world offers you
> Duties you are given or accept towards society
> Ways in which you try to affect your world, results

Co-operation:
> Cooperating with others, objective unions with others, co-operating, learning to co-operate, resolves
> Coming together with others to share social experiences
> Forcing cooperation with others, relating to others
> A need to work through others, face to face encounters with others, your efforts to answer the needs of society
> Controlling one's responses to the experiences noted in order to gain more control and/or

responsibility for one's actions

The use of tact in achieving one's aims

The need for balance between personal feelings and attachments

Social requirements for partnerships which must be attended to by reason and cooperation

Reacting in a controlled and intentional manner

Alienation from self and your needs

Lower Hemisphere

Development:
- Personal concerns, those things which are of interest to you or your family, family focus, your sense of activity orientation
- Building your personal creativeness, increasing your productiveness
- Staying within your own needs, looking after your own needs first
- The preparations you make so you can go out into the world
- Development of your senses of personal honor and trust
- Helping others to develop
- Personal development directed toward self-realization and self-expression
- The process of unfolding to develop yourself, seeing your relationships with others primarily through how these can develop the self
- Learning to grow from what you are able to learn from life
- Deep and reflective reactions
- Efforts to bring yourself to a point where you can work with others, the process of existence, being, subjective thinking or acting

Integration:
- Building on skills and values which you have learned early in life, experiencing the self through activity, acting out and experiencing yourself
- Personal integration, recognition of how to bring together and use the inherent power which you have
- Taking what you have learned from your family environment and learning to apply this in your own life
- Preparing for relationships
- Yin factors which affect the formation of your character
- To actualize as fully as possible the potentials in you at birth
- Subconscious functioning
- The process of finding "self", your subjective consciousness of self
- Inner directed, contemplates

Common Sense:
- The building and guiding of your common sense, dealing with the ephemeral aspects of life
- The use of common sense to get you through life
- An accumulation of self-awareness What comes to you in the form of useful things or relationships
- Instinctive reactions, impulsive reactions, actions done in reflex
- Where you digest and ponder the impressions you receive about life

Privacy:
- Involvement in your own personal life and/or affairs, an inclination towards secretive actions
- Your subconscious needs for protection and security, where you look to find fulfillment of your needs for security and safety
- Withdrawal from the public view, secrecy, a tendency towards being withdrawn and remote
- Using your creations to contribute to your security
- Subjective feelings which protect and ensure your foundations for survival
- Having goals of sustenance
- Finding and keeping nourishment
- Personal resources
- Matriarchal concerns, motherly concerns, the rearing of children
- The symbolism of events which occur primarily at the psychological or unconscious level
- Self to self

Learning:
- Learning through the different areas of life which you must go through
- Development of your intelligence
- Learning to exert personal control over your actions
- Doing what you are told to do

Indirect:
- Learning and/or absorbing through the means other than conscious

Subjective:
- That which is subjective

Upper Hemisphere

Prominence:
- The limelight, being in the social limelight
- The natural sense of authority which you have
- Arriving at significant achievements, social prominence
- Getting recognition, being thrust into the limelight, public recognition
- Where you are most visible and vulnerable in the eye of the public, events which occur in the open, visible events
- Pinnacles
- Outer directed, acts directly

Exposure
- Externalization, encountering more objective situations
- Self-realization within your public experience
- Exposure of your self-development
- Yang factors which affect the development of your character
- Public exposure, learning how to come into contact with those who can help you
- Social and communal integration, recognizing the power you have within society
- Well defined roles, well defined objectives and/or alliances
- Finding your place within the organized processes of life, actions taken to find your way in society

    Use of your previously developed social skills
    How you use your personal honors
    Realizing the development of the exposure which comes from meeting and interacting with others
    The development of purposeful relationships
    Feedback

Self-Assuredness
    Building a sense of assurance about yourself, the self-esteem you can or are able to build
    Recognizing your position in the world
    Building a self-aware personality
    Career development, getting the right education
    Getting the right contacts
    Getting the right resources that you need
    Getting the right experiences
    Developing and/or using your leadership abilities, the manner in which you go about demanding your rights

Functioning:
    The process of functioning in the world, making what you want to do visible and noticed
    The increase of your ability to gather power among others
    Interacting

Perception
    What you see and perceive from life, imagined positions or postures
    How you analyze what life is and what it has to offer
    How you are able to seize upon the impressions you receive

Expressing:
    The expression of self and its needs to the world
    Experiencing, where you consciously experience life
    The theories of life you develop for yourself, sharing these theories with the world
    How you are or are not able to tie yourself to reality

Goal Setting and Seeking:
    Your drives for power or honor, drives for recognition
    Fulcrums, turning points
    Paternal concerns, development of the fathering side of your nature
    The plans you set for yourself, the activities you perform
    What you do to stand out from the world
    The courage you have to step before the world
    The results obtained from co-operation and/or sharing
    Participation in processes where more that self is concerned

Angular, Succedent and Cadent Key Ideas

Angular

Recognizing:
> Becoming aware of something or someone, having something made known to you, determination for action due to an outside cause
>
> Recognition, developing awareness, the recognition of action required
>
> Inspirations received which force future action or development
>
> Acknowledgment, admission of fact
>
> Focusing, concentrating your powers of attention to tasks
>
> Greeting, salutation
>
> A welcoming or introduction to situations which force you to mature

Announcement:
> Making the arrival of something known beforehand, anticipating the arrival of impressions before they are generally known to others
>
> Receiving impressions through the senses, the creation or exteriorization of meanings which are received inwardly
>
> Individualizing, feelings about that which is coming or may be
>
> Advertising, telling others what you want or expect

Developing:
> Development, going through stages or steps of growth, gradual growth or orientation in a specific direction
>
> The application of will, learning the circumstances in which will must be applied (as opposed to actually applying it)
>
> Strengthening your awareness and sense of direction in new areas, a gradual coming to know

Becoming:
> Being, making yourself and what it is that you want known
>
> Becoming, growing in a certain direction
>
> Coming into existence, adaptations made for forthcoming or anticipated circumstances, moving in some direction
>
> Making decisions quickly, the forcing of gut reactions

Activating:
> Initiating, the beginning of development, movement to action
>
> Generating, generative, the generation of energy
>
> The generation of circumstances which you can feed power from
>
> The setting of processes into motion
>
> Activate
>
> Having a greater scope for dynamic or personal action, circumstances which force one to exercise this type of activation

Motivation:
> The impulses and intentions which drive one to be or act in certain ways
>
> Working through others or circumstances to generate more self power
>
> How you acquire power

The application of forces of inducement or influence
Inducement, kicks, spurs, the goads that one receives to perform in a certain manner or way
Succedent

Structure:
- Building, constructing, organizing
- Setting up the structure for action
- Put together systematically
- The introduction of shape or substance to things or circumstances which need to be developed
- Determining the interrelationship of parts with the whole, arrangement, composition
- Organize, systematize, setting things into logical order

Consolidate:
- Merging, uniting, bring together, combining into a single whole
- Unify, integrate, join together systematically
- Make solid or compact, compress, condense
- Concentrate, fixate, focus, consolidate, collect, gather
- Bringing something into focus, making something more clearly defined
- Focalizes, focalization, identification and development of the starting points of anything

Stability:
- Adding steadiness, to make stable or firm, keep from changing or fluctuating
- Making firm or stable, adding or introducing stability
- Establishing firmly after something has been set in motion
- Firmness of character or purpose
- Fixity of purpose, the determination or setting of one's willpower in a way which does not make it easy to change or alter or adjust or adapt to new and hitherto unforeseen circumstances
- Not easily moved or thrown off balance, firm, steady
- Lasting, enduring, not likely to change or alter over time
- Capable of returning to equilibrium after having been displaced

Steadying:
- Firm, fixed, stable, that which does not shake or totter
- Relaxation, taking the time to get your ends accomplished
- Having a fixed regularity or constancy, an absence of deviation or fluctuation, without faltering
- Even, the absence of irregularity, uniform, has a sameness or likeness with others within a circumstance or place
- Equitable, having an inherent quality of evenness or regularity

Determination:
- Determined, resolved, having one's mind made up, not likely to change, resolute, unwavering
- Showing firmness of intention, showing determination, acting as if one knows how to have a particular action come out like it was intended
- Making a decision on something, knowing or realizing the effects which are desired, decidedness, firmness
- Having an intent or resolve, decided, set, settled Resistance to change, resistance to decomposition

Give a definite aim or direction to, providing the type of direction which puts an effort back onto the course for which it was originally intended

Dealing with the power made available to you

How you deal with power

The application of one's developed will power

Establish, make, show, prove out, demonstrate

Predestined, doomed to, fated, foreordained bias, disposed, inclined to, bound to, driven towards

Conclude:

Finding the means for doing and completing an action

Closing, completing, concluding, ending, resolving, finishing, halting, terminating, wrapping up

Get at, reach for, attain

Bring to a close, end, finish, arrange or settle, come to a conclusion about

Decide, infer from

Using:

Uses, utilized, put or bring into action or service, employ

Experiences which make form concrete, creating something for a definite purpose

Apply for a given or predetermined purpose

Adapt the impulses of, get to know, learn how to use

Developed, usable, put to use, find a use for

Consume, expend, exhaust

Become accustomed to, adapt to through or after many trials and usages

The inherent worth or utility of something

Cadent

Evaluation:

The evaluation of your actions, evaluating, appraisal of circumstances

Review, the process of determining why something has occurred in the manner in which it has, internal thought processes in this regard, personal ways of reviewing life's circumstances

Analysis, a separation of the whole into parts (or vice-versa)

Finding out what is at the core or bottom of something, determining why it works or reacts in the manner in which it does

Opportunities to learn new ways in order to avoid failure in the future

Gathering information from the sources which are available

Testing:

Testing knowledge acquired, testing ways of working through life

Examination, determining the value or worth of

Processes of evaluation and trial

The establishment of internal standards of performance or evaluation

Tests in life which you encounter which are designed to test the knowledge you have or the circumstances you are capable of reacting to, your responses to such tests or evaluations

Understanding:
- Gaining a clearer understanding of motives or circumstances
- Perceiving the meaning of, getting to know why, the processes of thorough understanding, realization
- Comprehension, mental grasping, gaining intelligence
- Refining, making more pure, bringing through
- Integration, ideas which become a part of self
- Fulfillment, finding what you need to proceed with life
- Appreciation, sensitive and discriminating perception of the value of something or some quality
- Compassionate endeavors

Reaction:
- Reaction to, reacts to, reacting to, reactant, tending to react, showing reaction, finding the direction in which you desire change
- React, reacting to that which is generated in the angular houses
- Responding (as to a stimulus), showing or demonstrating the effects that a stimulus or event has on one
- Movement back to a less developed state, showing less opportunity for free will, reverting to a more depressing condition
- Increased activity following depression
- Resultant, that which follows as a consequence of
- The combining of two or more forces to produce a single effect

Communicate:
- Communicates, communication of ideas and values
- Passes along, to make as common knowledge, to learn so well that you are able to give this type of advice to others
- Showing or learning the adaptability of ideas
- The process of exchanging information or signals
- Expansion, seeking new modes of expression

Distribute:
- How you distribute or allocate power, distribution, insuring that everyone gets something, sharing with others
- Disperse(s), distribute(s), spread(s) about, scatter(s) in all directions
- To classify and then divide or distribute, allot, give out in shares or proportions, making sure others get something
- Dispensing consciousness, opening others to new ideas
- The acquisition of skills to aid in expression
- Dispersive, dispel, sowing, the spreading of ideas
- Diffuse, spread out or disperse, being long winded or wordy, disperses

Modify:
- Change or alter, make modifications to, limit or change the meaning of, introduce a basic change in the nature of
- Transform, change the outward appearance of, change the inner or outer form or function of, convert, metamorphose, transfigure, transmute

- Synthesis, putting together a whole from the parts, the process of synthesizing one from the many pieces which are available
- The reconciliation of opposing or opposite forms of thought or existence
- Universalizing, the process of becoming aware of the impact of all things on particular objects within one's consciousness, becoming aware of how actions (no matter how trivial) do affect other realms of thoughts and existence, gaining in one's awareness of the functioning of the universe
- Mutable, tending toward frequent change, inconstant, mutating
- Extending earlier successes into new or different realms

Disintegrate:
- Disintegration, the process of separating into fragments so that the whole can be viewed piecemeal or later as a whole within itself, break up
- Cause to undergo a transformation
- Collapse, the withdrawal of support previously counted upon, failing, giving way, to fall or drop drastically in value or usefulness
- Perverse, deviating from that which is considered to be right or good, the realization that one has encountered an abnormal form
- Decay, the losing of strength or soundness, spoiling, decomposing
- Without stability, easily upset or unbalanced, unreliable, fickle

Harmonizing:
- Harmony, the re-establishment of a more pleasing or pleasant whole, introducing congruity within a system
- The emphasis is on working together
- Agreement in action or feeling
- The ability to get along with people
- Satisfaction, fulfilling the needs or wishes of others, make situations more contented
- The development of sympathetic or meaningful relationships
- Resilient, the ability to bounce or spring back, the recovering of strength or good humor

Appendix D

References

The keywords found in this book were gathered over a twenty-three year period from over 600 sources such as astrological articles, books, lectures, private discussions, personal letters, etc. Most of these sources provided less than ten words or ideas. However, references listed below proved more useful. The bulk (more than 95 percent) of the words in this book were created from the thesaurus and dictionary sources cited. My apologies for being unable to list all sources and persons involved in this comprehensive project. Grateful thanks to all those unmentioned people, living and dead, who find their ideas listed in this book. *The Rulership Book* was not used a word source for the material in this book, but it did provide significant inspiration and impetus for creating a more useable keyword product and format.

Family Word Finder, Reader's Digest Editors, The Reader's Digest Association, Inc., Pleasantville, NY

Horary Astrology, Anthony Louis, Llewellyn Publications, St. Paul, MN, 1991

House Keywords, Michael Munkasey, unpublished manuscript, 1978

The Rulership Book, Rex E. Bills, McCoy Publishing, Richmond, VA 1971

The Synonym Finder, J. I. Rodale, Rodale Press, Emmaus, PA, 1978

Webster's Ninth New Collegiate Dictionary, Merriam-Webster Inc, 1985

Other works from the same author:

Midpoints: Unleashing the Power of the Planets, Michael Munkasey Astro Communication Services, San Diego, CA, 1991

The Concept Dictionary; (presently unavailable)